THE HIDDEN WEALTH OF CITIES

THE HIDDEN WEALTH OF CITIES

Creating, Financing, and Managing Public Spaces

Jon Kher Kaw,
Hyunji Lee, and
Sameh Wahba, Editors

WORLD BANK GROUP

1 2 3 4 23 22 21 20

ISBN (paper): 978-1-4648-1449-5
ISBN (electronic): 978-1-4648-1493-8
DOI: 10.1596/978-1-4648-1449-5

Cover illustration: Ecosistema Urbano

Cover design: Jon Kher Kaw

Library of Congress Control Number: 2019953865

CONTENTS

Boxes

Figures

Maps

Photos

Tables

City Case Studies at a Glance

The case studies in this book build upon examples drawn from a number of cities from different global regions and from a mix of economies. They include concise mini cases and boxed references to comprehensive, detailed case studies, illustrated across the three parts of the book (map C.1).

- Case studies in Part I highlight specific aspects of public-space asset management or urban development in selected cities.
- Case studies in Part II examine the spatial qualities of urban spaces in selected cities.
- A series of in-depth case studies in Part III document the life-cycle processes of twenty public-space initiatives and projects across eight cities. These case studies are structured according to five phases: (a) context; (b) planning and design; (c) implementation; (d) management; and (e) impact evaluation.

MAP C.1 **Cities Referenced in Case Studies**

FOREWORD

The creation of this book started with a group of urban development professionals and practitioners wanting to share their experiences from cities around the world. They were fascinated with what they saw in the public realm of these cities—incredible crowding, litter, and an unruly mix of vehicles and people (photo F.1). But even in the densest and most unorganized cities in the world, they were able to find gems: public-space assets that worked surprisingly well, such as waterfronts that drew communities together, parks that were defined and managed, and dynamic and lively streets.

In the messiness that was the rest of the city, they saw vibrancy and opportunity. They asked, *"What if these cities better managed their public spaces? Could they transform the entire city?"*

This book also comes at a time of renewed global interest in the critical role public spaces play in shaping inclusive, resilient, and sustainable cities and communities for all.

The United Nations Sustainable Development Goal 11 (SDG 11) called for *"universal access to safe, inclusive and accessible, green and public spaces, in particular, for women and children, older persons and persons with disabilities"* by 2030. This target has also been integrated into the New Urban Agenda adopted in 2016 at the United Nations Conference on Housing and Sustainable Urban Development (Habitat III) and endorsed by the United Nations General Assembly.

It is in that spirit that the editors of this book crowdsourced and gathered stories of public-space initiatives and researched and documented global case studies to gain insights from experiences on the ground. They were particularly interested in the institutional dynamics and the actions that were taken throughout the public-space asset life cycle—how the spaces were created, designed, funded, and managed. Where city data were scarce, they

PHOTO F.1 **Aerial View of Bahadur Shah Park in Dhaka, Bangladesh**

Source: ©Fariduzzaman Zabir. Reproduced, with permission, from Fariduzzaman Zabir; further permission required for reuse.

developed spatial tools and technology to map cities and to provide insights into the spatial patterns and use of public spaces in dense cities.

Collectively, this book draws on the various threads of analytical work conducted through the World Bank's Urbanscapes Community of Practice platform. It frames the analysis and case studies into three components:

- *Part I* seeks to identify—through the lens of asset management—effective strategies to plan, fund, and manage government and privately owned public spaces. It explores the broad spectrum of ways to govern public spaces and how they can become financially sustainable assets.
- *Part II* focuses on the city scale, with analysis to characterize the patterns of distribution, quality, and use of public spaces in selected cities. Spatial analytical tools and city case studies were developed with the United Nations Human Settlements Programme's (UN-Habitat) Global Public Space Programme and with the European Space Agency (ESA) through the Earth Observation for Sustainable Development (EO4SD) program.
- *Part III* dives into the neighborhood scale with a series of case studies documenting the life-cycle processes for planning, implementing, and managing public spaces. The Centre for Liveable Cities (CLC) in Singapore and the Korean Research Institute for Human Settlements (KRIHS) contributed city-specific case studies to illustrate different models of funding, implementing, and managing public spaces. Other case studies were prepared by World Bank staff and consultants. The city cases were selected to demonstrate a broad range of innovative public-space initiatives.

I hope you will find the perspectives and analyses within this book insightful.

Laura Tuck
Vice President, Sustainable Development
The World Bank

ACKNOWLEDGMENTS

This book was authored by a team led by Jon Kher Kaw (senior urban development specialist, World Bank), Hyunji Lee (urban development consultant, World Bank), and Sameh Wahba (global director, Urban, Disaster Risk Management, Resilience and Land Global Practice), with contributions from the Centre for Liveable Cities, the Korean Research Institute for Human Settlements, and the United Nations Human Settlements Programme (UN-Habitat). Support activities were carried out by GISAT under the European Space Agency's Earth Observation for Sustainable Development (EO4SD) initiative's dedicated activity cluster on urban development, in partnership with the World Bank. Members of the World Bank team included Ming Zhang (practice manager, urban development and disaster risk management, for the Latin America and the Caribbean region); Peter D. Ellis (global lead for Sustainable City Infrastructure and Services); and urban development specialists Annie Gapihan, David Ryan Mason, and Jessica Schmidt. The team thanks the members of the World Bank's Urbanscapes Community of Practice for contributing inputs during this activity.

The team is grateful to the many direct contributors to the chapters, frameworks, analyses, and case studies, as follows:

- *Overview:* Jon Kher Kaw and Sameh Wahba (World Bank)
- *Chapter 1:* Jon Kher Kaw (World Bank)
- *Chapter 2:* Jon Kher Kaw, Olga Kaganova, and Hyunji Lee (World Bank)
- *Chapter 3:* Olga Kaganova and Jon Kher Kaw (World Bank)
- *Chapter 4:* Jon Kher Kaw (World Bank); Cecilia Anderson (senior manager, Global Public Space Programme, UN-Habitat); and Tomas Soukup (project manager, European Space Agency [ESA]/GISAT)

- *Chapter 5:* Jon Kher Kaw and Hyunji Lee (World Bank); and Tomas Soukup and Jan Kolomaznik (project and production manager) (ESA/GISAT)
- *Chapter 6:* Laura Petrella (leader, City Planning, Extension and Design Unit), Cecilia Anderson, José Chong (program management officer), Andrew Rudd (urban environment officer), and Joy Mutai (consultant) (all of UN-Habitat)
- *Chapter 7:* Dmitry Sivaev (urban specialist) and Wanli Fang (urban economist) (World Bank); and Joy Mutai (UN-Habitat)
- *Chapter 8:* Hyunji Lee and Jon Kher Kaw (World Bank)
- *Chapter 9, Beijing:* Zheng Jia (urban development specialist, World Bank); and Rong Jia (cofounder, Dashilar Regeneration Initiative and CitylinX Co. Ltd.)
- *Chapter 10, Colombo:* Nishanthi Marian Priyanka Perera (consultant, World Bank, and visiting academic, Open University of Sri Lanka), and Charmini Kodituwakku (environmental safeguard consultant, World Bank)
- *Chapter 11, Karachi:* Farhan Anwar (urban planning consultant, World Bank, and visiting faculty, Habib University, Karachi)
- *Chapter 12, Lima:* Sofía García Núñez (former World Bank consultant and current coordinator of urban pedagogy and technical cooperation, Municipality of San Borja, Lima)
- *Chapter 13, Brooklyn:* Vivian Liao, Manuel Mansylla, and Tucker Reed (principals, Totem)
- *Chapter 14, Seoul:* Seong Soo Kim (research fellow) and Kil Yong Lee, Jiyoung Lim, and Taehoon Ha (assistant research fellows) (Korean Research Institute for Human Settlements)
- *Chapter 15, Singapore:* Ken Lee (deputy director), Mina Zhan (senior assistant director), Elyssa Kaur Ludher (senior assistant director), and Thinesh Kumar Paramasilvam (manager) (Centre for Liveable Cities); and Viknesh Gnanasagaran (manager, National Parks Board)
- *Chapter 16, Tbilisi:* Irakli Zhvania (consultant, World Bank)

In addition, the team thanks the following advisers for their guidance in shaping the contents of this book: Catalina Marulanda (practice manager, urban development, for the South Asia Region); Olga Kaganova (lead asset management consultant); Stefano Negri (program manager, Strategic Initiatives Unit); and Barjor Mehta (lead urban specialist).

The following peer reviewers contributed valuable technical inputs to the book: Horacio Cristian Terraza (lead urban specialist); Alessandra Campanaro (senior urban specialist); Nancy Lozano Gracia (senior economist); Joanna Mclean Masic (senior urban specialist); Felipe Targa Rodriguez (senior urban transport specialist); Sangeeta Kumari (senior social development specialist); Gabriel Arrisueño Fajardo (senior urban specialist); Katherine Gail Davis (urban development specialist); Ishita Alam Abonee (urban development specialist); and Dmitry Sivaev (urban specialist). Luis Felipe Vera Benitez (consultant) from the Inter-American Development Bank provided external peer review.

This activity received generous funding support from the Korean Green Growth Trust Fund, a partnership between the World Bank Group and the Republic of Korea, established in 2011 to support client countries as they shift to a green development path. Both partners share a common goal to reduce poverty and promote shared economic prosperity in an environmentally responsible and socially inclusive way.

Editorial support was provided by Mary Anderson and Michael Alwan. Illustrations and graphics were provided by Belinda Tato and Jorge Toledo of Ecosistema Urbano. Kristyn Schrader-King (senior communications officer) and Andy Shuai Liu (communications specialist) provided publicity, social media, and dissemination support.

Special thanks go to the World Bank's formal publishing program, especially Patricia Katayama and Mary Fisk and her team, who skillfully guided the publication process.

ABOUT THE EDITORS

Jon Kher Kaw is a senior urban development specialist with the World Bank's Urban, Disaster Risk Management, Resilience and Land Global Practice. He also heads the Urbanscapes Community of Practice on urban planning, technology, and city innovation. Since 2013, he has led numerous city engagements, investment operations, and advisory and analytical work in the South Asia, Middle East and North Africa regions. He coauthored the city strategy report, "Transforming Karachi into a Livable and Competitive Megacity" (2018) and was the lead author for the spatial planning and connectivity chapter in the regional flagship publication, *Leveraging Urbanization in South Asia* (2016). Prior to joining the World Bank, he held various key positions at the Urban Redevelopment Authority, the national planning agency of Singapore, where he oversaw technical and policy work on urban planning and design, property and land markets, and urban resilience. He also undertook academic research and private sector work in Singapore and London. He holds a master's degree with a specialization in urbanization and real estate from Harvard University, and a master's degree in architecture from Columbia University. He received his bachelor's degree from the National University of Singapore.

Hyunji Lee is an urban specialist consultant at the World Bank based in Washington, DC, where she consults for various lending projects in Bangladesh and Nepal. She also leads global analytical work on urban development and public space management as part of the Urbanscapes Community of Practice. Before joining the World Bank, she worked at the United Nations in New York to convene international high-level forums, researched sustainable development topics, and contributed to the New Urban Agenda and Sustainable Development Goal (SDG) indicators. At the Organisation for Economic Co-operation and Development (OECD) in Paris, she contributed to policy reports on national urban policies and urban green growth strategies, as well as to the OECD regional indicator development. She holds a master's degree in public administration from the School of International and Public Affairs at Columbia University and a master's degree in civil engineering and urban planning from Seoul National University, with field planning experience in China, the Republic of Korea, and Vietnam.

Sameh Wahba is the global director for the World Bank's Urban, Disaster Risk Management, Resilience and Land Global Practice, in Washington, DC. This Global Practice—which also covers territorial development, geospatial, and results-based financing issues—has a portfolio of close to US$30 billion in commitments in investment projects, Program-for-Results financing, and development policy lending and employs about 450 staff members. He has more than 25 years of experience in urban planning, housing, land and slum upgrading, local economic development, municipal service delivery, and post-disaster resilient recovery. He has held numerous senior management and leadership positions at the World Bank, working extensively in the Africa, Latin America and the Caribbean, and Middle East and North Africa regions. He coauthored the World Bank's flagship publication, *Regenerating Urban Land: A Practitioner's Guide to Leveraging Private Investment* (2016), as well as the "Culture in City Reconstruction and Recovery" (2018) position paper published jointly with the United Nations Educational, Scientific and Cultural Organization (UNESCO). Before joining the World Bank in 2004, he worked at the Institute of Housing and Urban Development Studies in Rotterdam and at the Harvard Center for Urban Development Studies. He holds doctoral and master's degrees in urban planning from Harvard University.

ABBREVIATIONS

A&As	additions and alterations
ABC Waters	Active, Beautiful, Clean Waters (Singapore)
ADT	average daily traffic
AMI	area median income
APOPS	Advocates for Privately Owned Public Space
AUDA	Ahmedabad Urban Redevelopment Authority
BAM	Brooklyn Academy of Music
BCA	Building and Construction Authority (Singapore)
BDIC	Beijing Dashilar Investment Company
BID	business improvement district
BJDW	Beijing Design Week
BQE	Brooklyn-Queens Expressway
BRT	Bus Rapid Transit (Lima, Peru)
BTT	Brooklyn Tech Triangle
BWP	Beddagana Wetland Park (Colombo, Sri Lanka)
CBD	Central Business District (Singapore)
CBO	community-based organization
CCD	Coast Conservation Department (Sri Lanka)
CCTV	closed-circuit television
CEA	Central Environmental Authority (Sri Lanka)
CIBP	Crow Island Beach Park (Colombo, Sri Lanka)
CIBPMS	Crow Island Beach Park Management Society (Colombo, Sri Lanka)
CLC	Centre for Liveable Cities
CMC	Colombo Municipal Council
CMR	Colombo Metropolitan Region
CPCP	culture-place-client-product/program
DAP	Design Advisory Panel (Singapore)

DBAA	Downtown Brooklyn Arts Alliance
DBP	Downtown Brooklyn Partnership
DCP	Department of City Planning (New York City)
DGP	Development Guide Plan (Singapore)
DOT	Department of Transportation (New York City)
DUMBO	Down Under the Manhattan Bridge Overpass (Brooklyn, New York City)
DWC	Department of Wildlife Conservation (Sri Lanka)
EDR	Eduljee Dinshaw Road (Karachi, Pakistan)
EDRPT	Eduljee Dinshaw Road Project Trust (Karachi, Pakistan)
EIU	Economist Intelligence Unit
EMP	environmental management plan
EO4SD	Earth Observation for Sustainable Development
ESA	European Space Agency
FAR	floor area ratio
FAO	Food and Agriculture Organization of the United Nations
FOGSL	Field Ornithology Group of Sri Lanka
GCAC	Garden City Action Committee (Singapore)
GDP	gross domestic product
GHG	greenhouse gas
GiGL	Greenspace Information for Greater London
GIS	geolographic information system
GLFP	Gyeongui Line Forest Park (Seoul, Republic of Korea)
GLS	Government Land Sales (Singapore)
GST	Goods and Services Tax (Singapore)
HDB	Housing and Development Board (Singapore)
HDP	Healthier Dining Programme (Singapore)
HDB	Housing and Development Board (Singapore)
HRPT	Hudson River Park Trust
HVAC	heating, ventilating, and air conditioning
HVL5	high-volume low-speed
IAK	I AM KARACHI (Pakistan)
IBRD	International Bank for Reconstruction and Development
IFP	Independent Filmmaker Project
ISO	International Organization for Standardization
IT	information technology
KEPCO	Korea Electric Power Corporation
KRIHS	Korea Research Institute for Human Settlements
KRNA	Korea Rail Network Authority
LED	light-emitting diode
LIHTC	Low-Income Housing Tax Credit
LPC	Landmarks Preservation Commission (New York City)
LTA	Land Transport Authority (Singapore)
LUSH	Landscaping for Urban Spaces and High-Rises (Singapore)
LVC	land value capture
MCUDP	Metro Colombo Urban Development Project
MDUD	Ministry of Defense and Urban Development (Sri Lanka)
MIH	Mandatory Inclusionary Housing
MMDG	Mark Morris Dance Group (Brooklyn, New York City)

MoCADA	Museum of Contemporary African Diasporan Arts (Brooklyn, New York City)
MOLIT	Ministry of Land, Infrastructure and Transport (Korea, Rep.)
MOU	memorandum of understanding
MTA	Metropolitan Transit Authority (New York)
MTI	Ministry of Trade and Industry (Singapore)
MRT	Mass Rapid Transit (Singapore)
NEA	National Environment Agency (Singapore)
NGO	nongovernmental organization
NParks	National Parks Board (Singapore)
NPO	nonprofit organization
NUA	New Urban Agenda
NYU	New York University
O&M	operations and maintenance
OPU	Urban Planning Office (San Isidro Municipality, Lima)
ORDEC	Orchard Road Development Commission (Singapore)
ORBA	Orchard Road Business Association (Singapore)
PCCC	Pakistan Chowk Community Centre
PCI	Pakistan Chowk Initiative
PCN	Park Connector Network (Singapore)
$PM_{2.5}$	particulate matter of less than 2.5 micrometers
POPS	privately owned public spaces
PPP	public-private partnership
PPP	Pakistan People's Party
PUB	Public Utility Board (Singapore)
PUFFIN	Pedestrian User-Friendly Intelligent [crossings]
PV	photovoltaic
RIR	Round Island Route (Singapore)
RMB	renminbi
SAR	Special Administrative Region
SARS	severe acute respiratory syndrome
SDG	Sustainable Development Goal
SDI	Strategic Development Incentive (Singapore)
SGIS	Skyrise Greenery Incentive Scheme (Singapore)
SIAD	safety, inclusivity, accessibility, and distribution
SJKMC	Sri Jayawardenapura Kotte Municipal Council
SLLRDC	Sri Lanka Land Reclamation and Development Corporation
SLTDA	Sri Lanka Tourism Development Authority
SMG	Seoul Metropolitan Government
SOE	state-owned enterprise
SPV	special purpose visit
STB	Singapore Tourism Board
TFANA	Theatre for a New Audience (Brooklyn, New York City)
TIF	tax increment financing
TOD	transit-oriented development
TOR	terms of reference
UDA	Urban Development Authority (Sri Lanka)
UN	United Nations
UNDP	United Nations Development Programme

UNESCO	United Nations Educational, Scientific and Cultural Organization
UN-Habitat	United Nations Human Settlements Programme
UN-Women	United Nations Entity for Gender Equality and the Empowerment of Women
URA	Urban Redevelopment Authority (Singapore)
USAID	U.S. Agency for International Development
WG	working group
WHO	World Health Organization

OVERVIEW

Jon Kher Kaw and Sameh Wahba

URBANIZATION AND THE NEED FOR SPACE

Between 1960 and 2017, the world's urban population quadrupled from about 1 billion to more than 4 billion people. Today, some 55 percent of the world's population live in cities, and this figure is slated to increase to about two-thirds with the expected addition of another 2.5 billion people to urban areas by 2050. Close to 90 percent of this urbanization process will take place in Asia and Africa (UN DESA 2019).

Urbanization enables people to come together to benefit from economies of agglomeration through increased productivity due to economic density, accelerated innovation from knowledge spillovers, and greater mobility and access to jobs and services. However, it also puts immense pressure on land and natural resources, and the resulting urban environment is often riddled with undesirable outcomes—from housing shortages and unaffordability to poor basic services, increased pollution, and traffic congestion. The extent to which cities will continue to be sustainable as they grow will depend on how they manage the trade-offs between the benefits of urban agglomeration and the costs that an unplanned urbanization process creates.

In the public realm—the urban spaces between buildings such as streets and open space—the frictional forces of urbanization and their negative externalities manifest themselves in many forms, including neglected parks and open spaces that become collectors of trash and pollution, streets that divide communities without consideration for pedestrians, and vehicular traffic that dominates the use of public spaces. In the city of Dhaka, Bangladesh, for example—home to one of the world's densest urban populations at about 510 persons per hectare (UN DESA 2019)—traffic moves only slightly faster than a walking pace, at around 7 kilometers per hour (World Bank 2017a). In Nairobi, Kenya, average speeds of 14 kilometers per hour for informal, privately owned minibuses (matatus) imply that within a one-hour commute, riders can access only 20 percent of the jobs in the city (World Bank 2016). Poor-quality, uncomfortable, and unhealthy urban environments and public spaces have thus taken a toll on livability, resilience, and competitiveness in many of the world's densest cities. As a result, citizens who rely on public spaces to access jobs and services, enjoy open spaces and greenery, or earn their livelihoods—such as the street markets and vendors that form a sizable part of the informal economy (Skinner, Orleans Reed, and Harvey 2018)—are affected disproportionately.

Meanwhile, cities that have managed to deliver well-designed and maintained public-space assets fare better. Increasingly, the presence of high-quality public spaces and greenery has become a barometer of a city's quality of life, economic vibrancy, and innovation.[1] These cities put a priority on creating vibrant, accessible, and inclusive public spaces through careful planning and management, thereby enabling cities to attract talent and investments and to reap the rewards from them.

FUNCTIONAL CITIES, VIBRANT PLACES

"Public spaces," in the simplest terms, are the spaces between buildings and facilities that are open to the public, consisting broadly of three types of urban spaces: streets and pedestrian access; open and green spaces, including parks, plazas, waterbodies, and waterfronts; and public facilities like libraries, community centers, and municipal markets (UN-Habitat 2015). They range from informal street corners where people gather to prominent city plazas and landmarks. Global experience has shown how these varied types of public spaces can directly contribute to cities' functionalities, including social interactions, urban health, labor markets, and urban environment, to name a few.

Streets and Pedestrian Access

Streets are public spaces that range from narrow pedestrian alleys in historic cities to large boulevards such as La Rambla in Barcelona and the avenues of Beijing. The design of streets as public spaces necessitates significant improvements to enhance personal and traffic safety and to allow the underprivileged and users with special needs such as the disabled, elderly, women, and children to participate fully in public realm activities. Streets also provide critical spaces for intracity mobility and support livelihoods for the urban poor. The share of street vending as a percentage of total employment can vary from around 5 percent in many cities to 20 percent in some cities (UN-Habitat 2013).

Given that motorized vehicles are a big source of greenhouse gas (GHG) emissions,[2] cities that prioritize their streets for walkability and cycling over motor vehicles can tackle climate change by reducing carbon emissions. Copenhagen, for example, aspires to combat climate change by becoming carbon-neutral by 2025—a core strategy being the targeting of 75 percent of all trips to be on foot, by bike, or public transport (City of Copenhagen 2012).

Open and Green Spaces

Parks and greenery play a critical role in social interaction and recreation and provide safe routes for walking, physical activity, and other forms of nonmotorized transportation. The World Health Organization (WHO) estimates that physical inactivity, linked to poor walkability and lack of access to recreational areas, accounts for 3.3 percent of global deaths (WHO 2016). Greening public spaces in cities also help provide outdoor comfort for people and promote health and well-being by mitigating urban heat islands in hotter climates. A recent study of U.S. cities suggests that tree cover reduces heat-related mortality, morbidity, electricity consumption, and the need for cooling. Tree cover in urban areas in the United States saves US$5.3 billion to US$12.1 billion annually (McDonald et al. 2019).

Public Facilities

Public facilities and amenities such as libraries, community centers, and sports facilities not only serve as amenities for communities but also help create a sense of place and build social cohesion. Studies have indicated that people who live close to high-quality public spaces and amenities are more trusting of others, feel less socially isolated, and have more faith in the government (Cox and Streeter 2019).

At the city scale, the allocation and division of public and private urban spaces is considered one of the most important priorities, especially in rapidly expanding cities, because they help facilitate intracity mobility and regulate the functioning of land markets (Angel 2012). This reallocation of land for public spaces is often not feasible once development has set in and public spaces have not been safeguarded up front.

Public spaces can become effective *places* that have unique cultural and social identities, economic context, and histories to which communities attach meaning to. Many of the examples discussed in this book indicate that public spaces become successful when they are focused on local communities, urban life, and placemaking. Human-centered design and diverse activities in public space are what contribute to a sense of place, city vibrancy, inclusion, and safety with "eyes on the street" (Jacobs 1961) in addition to promoting social networking, the exchange of ideas, and innovation (Katz and Wagner 2014).

Further, the design and building of public spaces create value when those processes are place-based and incorporate a spirit and practice of cocreation with people and existing communities as the future users. In many successful places (as measured by their use and user satisfaction), a participatory approach and gradual enhancements have proven effective, over time, in transforming car-centric cities with poor public spaces into vibrant cities catering predominantly to diverse groups of people (Gehl 2011).

PUBLIC SPACES: LIABILITIES OR ASSETS?

In a city, a public space can be an asset or a liability. For example, a main street or a central park can either symbolize a city's vitality and character or embody its deterioration and sterility. From a municipal finance perspective, public spaces are often on the liability side of a city's balance sheet because of their operations and maintenance (O&M) costs, where most generate either no revenues at all or insufficient revenues to recoup costs.

It is not surprising that in many cities with limited budgets and revenue assignments, local governments tend to view public spaces as a liability without recognizing their benefits and the value they create. For instance, streets are expensive real estate, with cars consuming a surface area of 67 square meters per commuter when driving at average city speeds in the United States (Bertaud 2018). Yet few cities implement road pricing or adequately charge vehicle users for their exploitation of road space. The maintenance of public spaces in such cities is either deferred or kept at a bare minimum, such as fixing potholes, repairing sidewalks, or fixing the odd streetlight. In such cities, local governments struggle to ensure that public spaces are accessible, fit for purpose, and equitably distributed spatially to serve city neighborhoods. This ad hoc, piecemeal approach often creates a downward spiral, leading to a continuous drain on public resources.

However, as the case studies in Part III of the book demonstrate, this does not always have to be the case. If public spaces are well designed, well maintained, and responsive to diverse community needs, they can create economic benefits for the city by increasing land and property values in the surrounding area. To realize such returns, cities need fiscal instruments that enable them to capture a fair share of the increased land value—whether a property tax system based on up-to-date cadaster and property valuation databases or an asset management strategy to generate proceeds from the sale or lease of government-owned land and real estate. The resulting increase in municipal revenues can be reinvested in improved service delivery and further improvement of public spaces. Several examples show how public spaces enhance business sales, land and property values, and municipal revenues:

- *In Seoul,* the creative reuse of abandoned railway infrastructure land to create the *Gyeongui Line Forest Park* connecting several neighborhoods saw a doubling of adjacent local businesses, between 2015 and 2017, with average monthly sales per shop increasing by more than 150 percent. The increase in property values within a year of project completion was twice the average increase in other neighborhoods in Seoul (chapter 14).
- *In Beijing,* the restoration and adaptive reuse of historic buildings and a regeneration initiative on *Yangmeizhu Lane* led to a significant growth of

new culture- and design-driven businesses and commercial enterprises in the area. Reportedly, the total sales revenues grew from less than RMB 1 million (US$151,000) in 2012 to RMB 85 million (US$12.9 million) in 2018. Property values in the area more than doubled between 2012 and 2018 after the completion of the project (chapter 9).

- *In Tbilisi, Georgia,* the rental prices and property values along the rehabilitated and pedestrianized *Aghmashenebeli Avenue* doubled between 2015 and 2017, and consequently property tax revenues from commercial establishments adjacent to the rehabilitated street drastically increased (chapter 16).

With effective management, public spaces can be financially sustainable without dependence on public budgets. In New York City, the operation and maintenance of Bryant Park is fully sustained by revenues from park activities and contributions from the surrounding business improvement district, without any reliance on public funds (Murray 2010). Moreover, in climate-vulnerable cities, public spaces can also enhance urban resilience by reducing the negative effects and costs resulting from disasters such as flooding. For example, in Colombo, Sri Lanka, an economic analysis conducted for the Beddagana Wetland Park revealed that the total wetland benefits including flood protection are annually worth up to SL Rs 12 billion (US$66 million) to the Colombo Metropolitan Region (chapter 10).

The benefits of high-quality public spaces are not limited to enhanced land and asset values. They also improve city livability and competitiveness by improving public safety, citizen inclusion, and health outcomes while also attracting entrepreneurs and a talented workforce who value well-designed, managed, and vibrant public spaces, as in the following cases:

- *In Seoul,* the *Yonsei-Ro* transit mall project led to improved walkability and mobility in the area. One year after the project's completion, visitors to the adjacent areas increased by 28.9 percent, and pedestrians' satisfaction rate more than quadrupled. The project mitigated traffic congestion and reduced traffic accidents on the street by 54.5 percent (chapter 14).
- *In Singapore,* the *Park Connector Network (PCN)*—a network of pedestrian pathways and bicycle lanes along residual spaces of stormwater canals, roads, and viaducts connecting various neighborhoods and districts across the island state—saw an increase in the use of the PCN and its parks by 16 percent between 2014 and 2016 (chapter 15).
- *In Brooklyn,* between the initiation of the *Brooklyn Tech Triangle (BTT)* in 2012 and 2015, the number of innovation firms and employees increased by 22 percent and 45 percent, respectively. In fact, 45 percent of surveyed innovation firms in the BTT responded that they chose to be in Brooklyn because of the neighborhood character and amenities that Brooklyn offered (chapter 13).

Public spaces can be fertile platforms for addressing various city problems. When cities think beyond the typical uses of public-space assets, the resulting policy actions, targeted investments, innovative infrastructure, and design solutions can bring long-term city transformation. These transformed assets serve more than one function: they can be simultaneously areas of urban life and parts of the city infrastructure that improve city functioning and resilience beyond its immediate surroundings. In Medellín, Colombia, the innovative provision of public outdoor escalators, public libraries, and a "Metrocable"—a cable-propelled gondola lift system that brings residents of informal settlements in the Medellín River valley up the steep hills to commercial and employment districts—has improved movement and access to services within poor neighborhoods while also connecting those neighborhoods with the rest of the city. Through a process of inclusive "social urbanism," the city of Medellín has transformed from a "crime capital" to "the most innovative city in the world."[3]

Several trends will continue to change and reshape how public spaces are designed, managed, and used. Disruptive urban technology, for example, is poised to transform how some cities plan and manage urban services. The proliferation of remote sensing and earth observation has allowed many cities to monitor and measure urban expansion and land use (as examined in Part II, "Shaping the Public Realm: Data and Spatial Analysis"). On or near the ground, the use of drones, sensors, street imagery with object detection ability, mixed reality, 5G mobile technology, dockless bike-shares, and autonomous vehicles in some cities offers new opportunities for more efficient and innovative uses of public spaces. These trends also create new challenges in managing streets, open spaces, and air rights that necessitate adequate policies and regulations. Another trend is an increased focus on security. Public spaces—transit stations, stadiums, marketplaces, streets, and so on—have become increasingly targeted by terrorists, forcing governments to shape policies and plans to better secure public safety.

ATTRIBUTES OF SUCCESSFUL PUBLIC SPACES: A FRAMEWORK

The quality of public spaces influences how people, communities, and businesses interact in cities. Ideally, they can create value by enhancing social inclusion and diversity; generating productivity gains from urban agglomeration forces; and facilitating the exchange of goods, services, and knowledge spillovers. Conversely, poorly conceived public spaces can devalue places by dividing communities and exacerbating congestion forces that could hinder city livability and productivity.

Some of the factors that lead to poor-quality, *unsuccessful* public spaces are

- *Limited capacity of local governments* to plan, finance, implement, and maintain public spaces;
- *Poor and insensitive top-down design solutions,* resulting in urban forms that do not respond to community needs;
- *Poor O&M regimes,* resulting in deterioration of the public spaces and low service levels; and
- *Pressure on governments to turn over land* used as public space for other priorities or private developments, resulting in a loss of public space.

Successful public spaces, on the other hand, share many attributes—including being designed as human-centered places that are attractive, comfortable, accessible, walkable, enjoyable, and safe for all users, including the disabled and older persons. Such spaces create a sense of place, enhance the surrounding built environment, and connect a variety of neighborhoods. They are vibrant, full of people, support the local economy, and help to build inclusive communities. They accommodate multiple uses and are well managed and maintained throughout their life cycles. Often, these public spaces involve public and private collaboration during the process of their creation and management.

Globally, cities with livable urban environments take on a wide range of development pathways to implement and manage high-quality public spaces sustainably through a well-thought-out approach to the whole life cycle of every public space—from its planning, creation, implementation, and O&M to its replacement or rejuvenation. The scale may vary, from one that is space-specific (and based on the place's individual history) to systematic and strategic management of a network of public spaces. In either case, responsible entities and stakeholders should ask a set of critical questions:

- *Who* are the actors, and how are they involved?
- *What* public-space assets does a city own?
- *Which* implementation approaches should be taken?
- *How* can public spaces be funded?
- *How* can public spaces be managed sustainably?

Figure O.1 facilitates responses to these questions and serves as an initial checklist of items to consider. The sections below then discuss the foundations of this framework: the roles of the various actors and stakeholders as well as the processes involved, from strategic approaches to funding to management and governance.

ACTORS AND STAKEHOLDERS

Governments

The analysis of any city map reveals that the surface area occupied by streets forms roughly 20 percent of built-up areas globally, with a wide range between such cities as Dhaka and Dar es Salaam (less than 10 percent of built area) to cities such as Toronto and Singapore (around 30 percent of built area) (UN-Habitat 2013). When streets are added together with public facilities and open and green spaces, the resulting public spaces form an even larger percentage of the urbanized land in cities. This is significant compared with other categories of land use and is usually the second largest land use after housing.

Because public spaces are mostly municipally owned and managed, local governments can exert a substantial influence on cities' urban environment. Specifically, small improvements to public spaces could catalyze an important

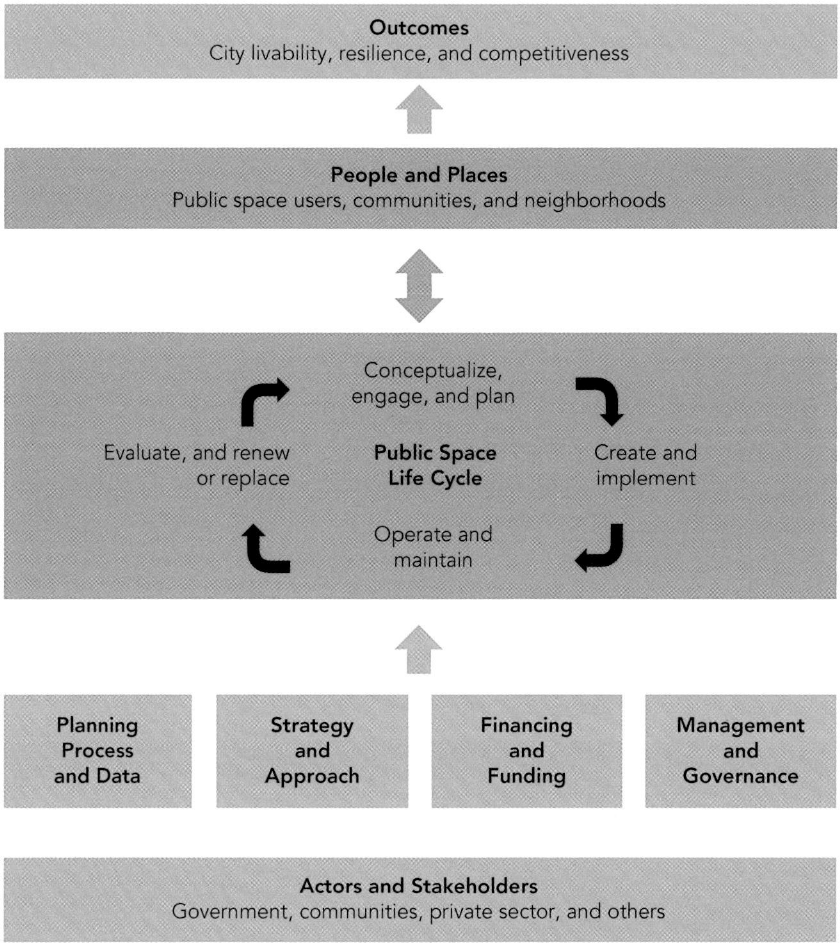

FIGURE O.1 **Framework for Conceptualizing and Managing Public-Space Assets**

process of urban transformation. However, the potential of these assets is often overlooked for several reasons: other pressing city priorities, budgetary constraints, the inertia of top-down planning traditions, and so on. To continue believing that local governments alone should be responsible for the planning and creation of public spaces for "public benefit" is simplistic and conflicts with a growing body of evidence that good public spaces are the results of multiactor collaboration.

Communities

Some of the most interesting public-space initiatives are a result of community mobilization from the ground up, combined with private funding. Even though these interventions tend to be among the smaller ones, they can be cost-effective, targeted investments enabled through placemaking and tactical-urbanism approaches that lead to big impacts on neighborhoods.[4] This point underscores another mechanism that local governments often fail to leverage—the very process of placemaking and of empowering local communities to play an active role in mobilizing and participating in the conception, design, implementation, and O&M of public places, which is as important as the physical outcome. This is especially true for cities where local governments are constrained in their ability to mobilize enough resources or capacity to support public-space initiatives.

In Karachi, Pakistan, for instance, several public-space projects were initiated by citizen groups and civil society with limited support from the government. A community-led initiative completed the Pakistan Chowk restoration project within a year to upgrade facilities and clean up the square. The Eduljee Dinshaw Road Project saw the pedestrianization of the street frontage of a historic building. This was led by a group of citizens who formed the Eduljee Dinshaw Road Project Trust (EDRPT), which raised funding from local stakeholders, including local businesses; the EDRPT also managed maintenance works at the site and its programming (chapter 11).

Private Sector

Partnerships with the private sector can play a big role and offer resources, innovative solutions, and efficient management to create and maintain well-run places that would not otherwise be possible in a context of limited resources and competing priorities, as these examples illustrate:

- *In Seoul,* the management of the *Gusandong Library* was outsourced and contracted by the local government to a private company that specializes in programming and managing library facilities (chapter 14).
- *In Brooklyn,* the *Down Under the Manhattan Bridge Overpass (DUMBO)* business improvement district (BID) collects special fees from businesses inside the BID to fund and maintain the public assets and services that benefit those businesses. It was responsible for the overall revitalization of the district, including public-space interventions (chapter 13).

In another clear trend, public spaces are becoming joint undertakings between government, the private sector, and the community, especially within territories where special land development or redevelopment projects are implemented—for example, through land readjustment, tax-increment financing (TIF), or transit-oriented development (TOD), as further discussed in the "Financing and Funding" section below. They are funded together with other infrastructure on their territories through land-based financing instruments on the basis that such projects increase land value, a part of which is captured and channeled to fund infrastructure and public spaces through land value capture (LVC). In Part III ("Sustaining the Public-Space Life Cycle: Lessons from Cities"), several case studies illustrate these relationships, including the following:

- *In Singapore,* modern-day *Orchard Road* was rejuvenated as part of continuous long-term public realm investments in line with city plans, involving both public and private participation (chapter 15). Streetscape enhancements, such as vibrancy and visual diversity, resulted from a combination of (a) urban design guidelines for private developments to invest in public spaces in return for density bonuses; (b) public sector funding of public infrastructure; and (c) long-term planning coordinated between multiple government agencies.

- *In Brooklyn*, the city government's investment in the *Brooklyn Cultural District* attracted over US$1 billion of private investment in the neighborhood, which covers the rejuvenation of public spaces (chapter 13).

Dynamics between Ownership, Management, and Use of Public Spaces

Historically, the term "public spaces" referred to spaces perceived as owned and used by the public, based on an understanding that there is a clear demarcation between public and private groups. This definition has evolved over the past several decades and expanded to reflect the more diverse roles that public spaces play in cities, underpinned by more complex property relations. For example, can a public space be "owned" privately but "used" by the public? Can a private space create "public benefit"?

A global scan of different types of public spaces reveals that the ownership and management of public spaces can be combined into three main groups:

- *Public* ownership and management
- *Private* ownership and management
- *Mixed* ownership and management—that is, either public ownership and private management or private ownership and public management.

In delivering public spaces, cities can go beyond the common scenario of public management and funding and rely on alternative means of creating and sustaining public-space assets. Private provision of public spaces (and, in many cases, of the necessary neighborhood services and amenities such as schools) by developers in large-scale developments is typical in many places, including in the Arab Republic of Egypt's new towns and Brazil's largest metropolitan agglomerations. The ownership of such public spaces is then transferred to municipalities, which then operate and maintain such spaces. Another variation is the privately owned, privately operated and maintained public spaces provided in New York City under incentive zoning schemes that gave developers additional development rights. What makes them public spaces is that they are nonexcludable—that is, de jure always accessible to the public.

No one model is the best, and, depending on the context, each approach has its own merits and pitfalls (figure O.2). For example, public spaces owned and managed by city governments often face challenges of insufficient funding to ensure adequate operations and free access for the public. At the other end of the spectrum, privately owned public spaces (POPS), while better managed in general, often fall prey to access restrictions. In general, public

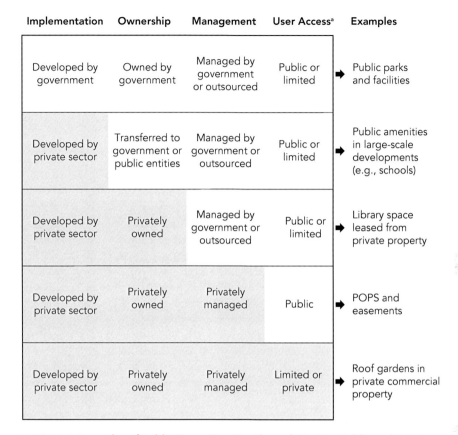

Implementation	Ownership	Management	User Access[a]	Examples
Developed by government	Owned by government	Managed by government or outsourced	Public or limited	➡ Public parks and facilities
Developed by private sector	Transferred to government or public entities	Managed by government or outsourced	Public or limited	➡ Public amenities in large-scale developments (e.g., schools)
Developed by private sector	Privately owned	Managed by government or outsourced	Public or limited	➡ Library space leased from private property
Developed by private sector	Privately owned	Privately managed	Public	➡ POPS and easements
Developed by private sector	Privately owned	Privately managed	Limited or private	➡ Roof gardens in private commercial property

FIGURE O.2 **Examples of Public Space Creation through Various Public and Private Arrangements**

Note: POPS = privately owned public spaces.
a. "Public" refers to spaces without fees or other access limitations. "Private" refers to spaces not accessible by the general public. "Limited" refers to spaces that limit access time or require an entrance fee or registration.

spaces are especially good arenas for cooperation between city governments, private sector partners, and citizens.

PLANNING PROCESS AND DATA

Uncovering "Hidden" Public-Space Assets

In many ways, public spaces are "hidden" assets or liabilities: local governments often do not know what they own, nor do they know the current and potential value of these assets or related liabilities. They are also unsure about how to manage underutilized public assets, and they often don't adopt optimal approaches to creating, preserving, and capturing value from high-quality public spaces.

Few cities have any spatial data on their public physical assets, whether from inventories or from land-use maps that consolidate all the public-space assets that local governments own and manage. (In fact, local governments typically lack such inventories for all publicly owned land and real estate.) And among cities that have inventory records, few assess the value of these assets. Despite the lack of an established, accepted set of comparable metrics to measure the qualities of public spaces and how users perceive and interact with them, there have been recent efforts to develop useful indicators to do so (chapter 4).

A detailed inventory with asset information on individual sites—such as the type, size, condition, and quality of these spaces; their ownership; their current management structure; and financial information such as O&M expenses and revenues—can be used to inform investment decisions, design choices, and management structure changes. Aggregating site-level and spatial characteristics (such as location, type, and size) at the neighborhood and city levels helps to identify gaps in service provision to communities. Such analysis (when layered over existing land uses, master plans, mobility patterns, population and census data, real estate metrics, urban heat island maps, and use patterns) can significantly enhance urban planning, design, and the prioritization of neighborhood improvements.

Although developing spatial databases and inventories and conducting analysis of public spaces can be costly and time-consuming in data-scarce environments, the proliferation of and access to new technology and open data sets have enabled many cities to discover quicker, cost-effective, and innovative ways for creating them. Even where data are limited, cities still can proceed to improve the management of selected public spaces—or to better plan new ones—within the framework depicted in figure O.1.

Toward an Evidence-Based Approach to Planning

Access to reliable data will be necessary for cities that intend to develop comprehensive, sustainable management plans and planning strategies through an evidence-based approach to policy making and planning. Part II of the book demonstrates and pilots several innovative ways of creating spatial data and indicators to measure public-space characteristics in selected cities. Satellite imagery, street-view images, surveys, and social data were used to analyze the patterns of how public spaces are distributed, designed, managed, and used by people.

Planning for Inclusive and Equitable Distribution of Public Spaces

In some of the largest and densest urban areas, existing public spaces are estimated to account for a relatively scarce but still sizable part of the urban footprint. A comprehensive land-use analysis and classification of public-space types using high-resolution satellite imagery in the megacities of Dhaka, Bangladesh; Karachi, Pakistan; and Lima, Peru, showed that public spaces make up about 14–27 percent of the cities' total built-up areas (chapter 5).[5] Up to two-thirds of these public spaces are composed of streets. This estimate does not account for large areas of vacant land and inaccessible green areas that could partly be developed into future public spaces. The land-use patterns are varied across these cities: public spaces are more equitably distributed or more diverse in type (such as waterfronts, parks, plazas, and other sports and recreational facilities that serve different functions) in some cities than in others.

Although there is no "right" level, distribution, or mix of public spaces that can be applied uniformly to all cities, these findings provide a starting point for developing several types of spatial strategies for shaping public-space programs and urban planning:

- *Rejuvenate existing public spaces and reclaim underutilized spaces innovatively.* Identify areas for urban rejuvenation or underutilized parcels for new public-space investments that had not been considered before, and reclaim them for another use. "Residual" spaces along infrastructure such as bridges, drains, and roads are valuable urban spaces that can potentially be repurposed into networks of walkable streets across the city for nonmotorized transportation, or create open spaces for the conduct of livelihoods or recreation. Explore opportunities for enhancing or reclaiming existing streets—the dominant form of public space—for efficient and safe pedestrian mobility and other active people-centric uses.
- *Create new public spaces.* Allocate new public land for public spaces up front in rapidly expanding city peripheries, or facilitate public-space development on vacant land and private development. Make natural assets such as urban forests and greenery available for recreation and enjoyment, and protect them from depleting to low levels. Rebuild public spaces in fragile and postconflict cities as part of their reconstruction efforts.
- *Provide for underserved neighborhoods.* Equitably plan for public spaces in underserved neighborhoods that require facilities such as community centers, libraries, public toilets, and health centers.
- *Connect public spaces.* Create clusters of different types of amenities such as libraries, community centers, sport facilities, and parks to provide neighborhood services, create a sense of place, and promote social inclusion. Connect neighborhoods through a network of public spaces by linking parks, pedestrian connections, and cycling lanes.

The options and approaches are varied, and Part III of the book provides numerous cases of how cities have managed to create, preserve, and reclaim more human-centered urban spaces.

Implementing High-Quality Design and Sustainable Management of Public Spaces

A survey of the ownership, management, and quality of public spaces in the cities of Nairobi, Kenya; Addis Ababa, Ethiopia; Wuhan, China; and Bamenda, Cameroon, suggests that governments are often the predominant owners of public spaces (chapter 6). Although a small fraction of these assets are privately owned, a sizable number of them relied on private, joint, or other models of management.

The survey also revealed that the public spaces, as with many other cities globally, often lacked maintenance or are characterized by poor design (such as inadequate access for people with specific needs, including people with disabilities, older persons, women, and children) and low levels of functioning utilities like street lighting. These findings highlight the need for cities to better meet related design and O&M requirements as well as to make adequate long-term management arrangements. Part I of this book digs deeper into some possible asset management models for public-space assets and an appropriate governance framework.

Responding to Communities and User Needs

A set of analytical work using social media, street image object recognition, and machine learning tools provides a rapid assessment of how public spaces relate to human use and activity (chapter 7). The analysis of Tbilisi, Georgia, and Wuhan, China, helped identify that a number of prominent public spaces were underused or "forgotten." People did not naturally gather in such urban spaces, either because of a lack of programming and place management or because the spaces' amenities and physical characteristics were not well-designed, lacked identity, or were not inviting.

In Beijing, China, indicators developed from street images to measure convenience, comfort, and other spatial characteristics linked with street vibrancy metrics offered new and innovative approaches for evidence-based city planning and zoning. These pilots demonstrate some emerging ways of monitoring and evaluating use patterns, pedestrian behavior, community preferences, and spatial characteristics that could be used to inform public-space programs, policies, and investments.

STRATEGY AND APPROACH

The planning and design process for public spaces can take several forms, each focused on a different combination of actors, scale, and required resources. This provides an extensive palette of options and approaches to realize public spaces. Depending on the city's context and challenges, an approach that worked in one city may not work for another, so cities need to choose how they want to embark on public-space initiatives along several lines: enhancement versus transformation; tactical urbanism versus comprehensive planning; and choices for integration and synergy with existing infrastructure, assets, and systems.

Enhancement versus Transformation

Enhancement

Enhancing or improving a public space is necessary when its quality has deteriorated but it is still vital to preserve its current use for a neighborhood. For instance, an abandoned beach area can be improved with better facilities and managed as a waterfront park, as with Crow Island Beach Park in Colombo (chapter 10). Upgrading streetscapes is another example of strengthening the role of streets in promoting mobility, accessibility, connectivity, and livelihoods (NACTO 2016a).

Transformation

On the other hand, a public space can be transformed and converted from another type of public space or other uses completely. The Plaza 31 project in Lima, for example, transformed an unused parking lot into a pocket square (figure O.3; also see chapter 12). A neighborhood's underused municipality-owned infrastructure and buildings can be repurposed to support other higher-value public-space uses, as illustrated by the Brooklyn Tech Triangle (chapter 13) and numerous "creative community spaces" around the world (World Bank 2017b).

Tactical Urbanism versus Comprehensive Planning

Tactical Urbanism

The approaches collectively known as tactical urbanism can offer visible and impactful outcomes at low cost where "simple physical alterations can improve the use of the city space noticeably" (Whyte 1980). By showing results fast, policy makers and practitioners build the confidence of communities that they can observe real change, and their opinions are reflected in the process. Interventions are usually simple and low-cost, and they do not require prominent public spaces or necessarily permanent alterations; examples include free mini-libraries, community gardens, art exhibitions, parklets, and so forth.[6]

However, tactical-urbanism approaches may have only a temporary impact unless they are supported by systematic, well-planned programming and ownership for managing the space. The Pakistan Chowk Initiative and the I AM KARACHI movements were started with temporary community action, such as exhibiting artworks on streets and cleaning squares. With the support and positive feedback from citizens, these initiatives evolved into more systematic arrangements, such as painting walls in deteriorated neighborhoods through international design competitions, upgrading facilities in a square in collaboration with a private design firm, developing sports programs for youth in existing sport facilities, and others (see chapter 11 on Karachi).

Comprehensive Planning

The comprehensive planning and design of a public space can help anchor and stimulate broader planning strategies that usually are part of a development vision or master plans, such as development focused on urban regeneration and TOD. This involves mid- to long-term implementation and is underpinned by robust planning and legislative frameworks. For instance, the Orchard Road and PCN developments in Singapore have evolved at both the neighborhood and city scales over a decade through the national planning authority (chapter 15). The pedestrianization of Yonsei-ro—a commercial street in Seoul and one of several TOD projects initiated across the city—required extensive traffic analysis and pilots led by the city and various

a. Calle 31, before its conversion to Plaza 31

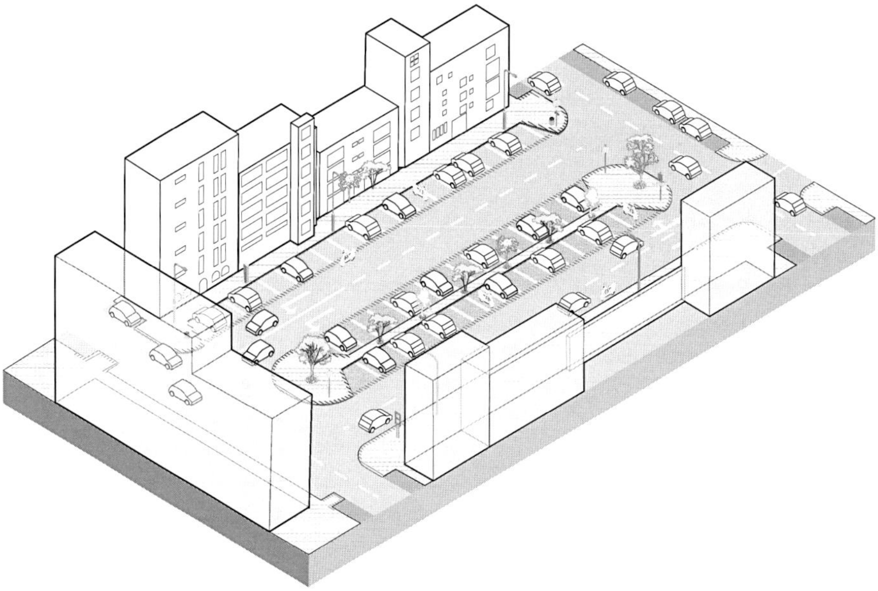

b. Completed Plaza 31 project

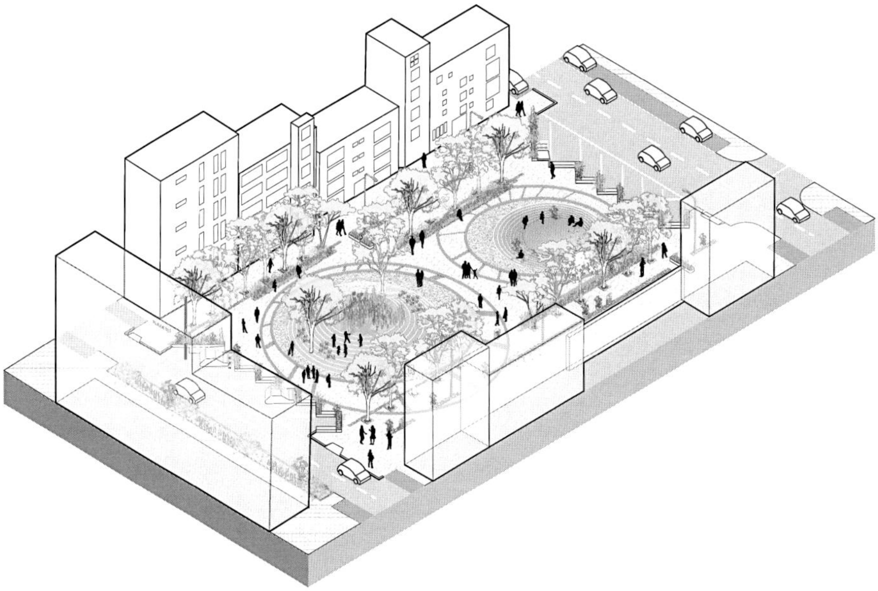

FIGURE O.3 **Transformation of Underused Parking Lots to Plaza 31, San Isidro District, Lima, Peru**

Source: ©World Bank. Further permission required for reuse.

government agencies to ensure an integrated approach to improved walkability on the street and enhanced traffic flows around the site (chapter 14).

Combination

These approaches are not mutually exclusive: a *comprehensive* development of an area can incorporate flexibility and involve communities from the onset or incorporate elements of *tactical urbanism* during its design process. Tactical-urbanism approaches can evolve from a groundswell of incremental improvements into a more comprehensive rejuvenation of an entire area. In Brooklyn, the Pearl Street Triangle—a pocket square transformed from a parking lot—was a successful pilot that enabled the city to scale up placemaking projects across Brooklyn neighborhoods (chapter 13).

These approaches also largely depend on various factors including timing, needs and priorities, and available resources. For example, tactical-urbanism approaches could be a solution for cities that lack financial resources for permanent public-space investments and could be used as an entry point to rejuvenate neighborhoods and cities. In other areas, the lack of resources doesn't need to be an obstacle to comprehensive regeneration: cities may fund comprehensive transformation of a declining neighborhood through own-source revenues generated from the proceeds of private activities in public spaces.

Integration, Synergy, and Reclamation

Integration with Green and Gray Infrastructure[7]

Resilient infrastructure creates placemaking benefits when designed in a way that enables people to enjoy the space. Green infrastructure—which uses nature-based solutions to manage stormwater—often has vast potential to integrate public-space elements. Conversely, public-space elements can be implemented in residual spaces alongside gray infrastructure such as conventional stormwater drains. Infrastructure that integrates public spaces not only helps build city resilience against floods but also adds value to the surrounding areas by improving access, connectivity, and aesthetics while adding public spaces for community activities (Browder et al. 2019).

Natural urban greenery such as mangroves and wetlands can double as ecological areas for enjoyment. In Colombo, Sri Lanka, for instance, the Beddagana Wetland Park (BWP) not only improved resilience by being a "sponge" to reduce the impact of flooding in the city but also capitalized on the area's rich biodiversity to offer citizens spaces for recreation (chapter 10). The park also serves an important function of raising environmental awareness within the community—specifically, on the importance of preserving biodiversity (figure O.4).

Synergy with Cultural Heritage, City Assets and Urban Systems

Cultural heritage assets, including historic buildings and landmarks, are often linked with public spaces. Investments in public spaces are a means to revitalize dilapidated historic areas, reclaim the use of urban spaces for cultural activities, and strengthen the cultural and historical identity of neighborhoods (UNESCO 2016). On a local scale, upgrading streets adjacent to

a. Before BWP project, 2009

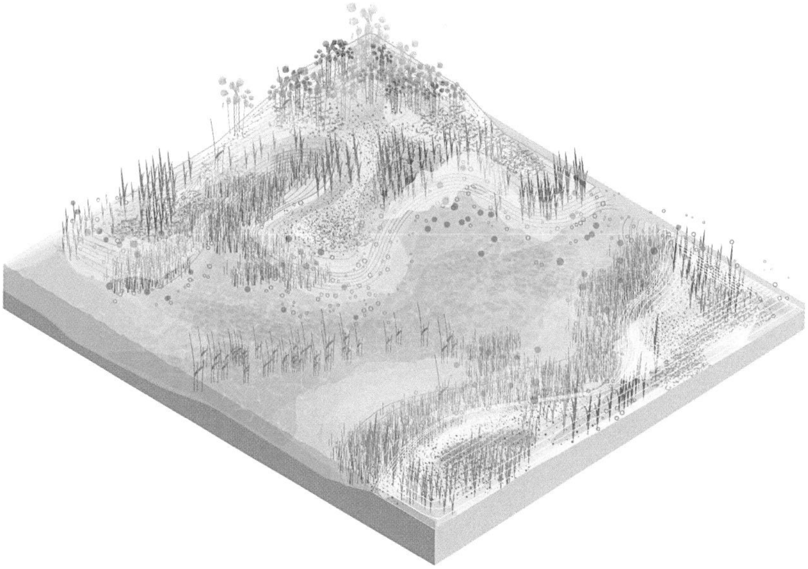

b. After BWP project, 2016

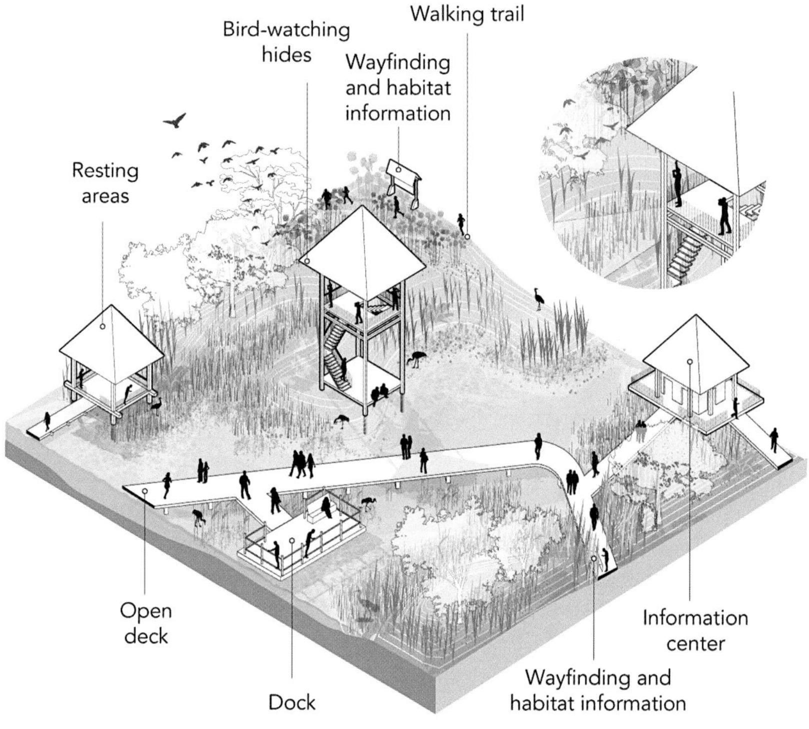

FIGURE O.4 **Landscapes Before and After Completion of BWP Project, Colombo, Sri Lanka**

Source: ©World Bank. Further permission required for reuse.
Note: BWP = Beddagana Wetland Park.

historic buildings improves accessibility to those buildings and attracts more tourists and visitors, as demonstrated in the Eduljee Dinshaw Road project in Karachi (chapter 11). On a more comprehensive scale, a collection of public spaces within historic neighborhoods can be revitalized under city-level heritage preservation programs, as in the Yangmeizhu Lane and Dashilar Pocket Spaces projects in Beijing (chapter 9).

In other places, public-space interventions are used to enhance cultural venues and rebrand neighborhoods. For example, Seoul's Gwanghwamun Square, once a car-oriented avenue with 16 lanes, has been rehabilitated as a cultural landmark (figure O.5) that connects people with adjacent attractions (including important cultural venues such as Sejong Center) and adjacent cultural heritage (including Gyeongbokgung, the main royal palace of Joseon Dynasty, built over 600 years ago). Also, to elevate the identity of the Brooklyn Cultural District, streetscapes, pocket parks, and cultural buildings were redesigned to connect the district's diverse cultural assets and to create a unique sense of place and animate the area through public art and performances (chapter 13).

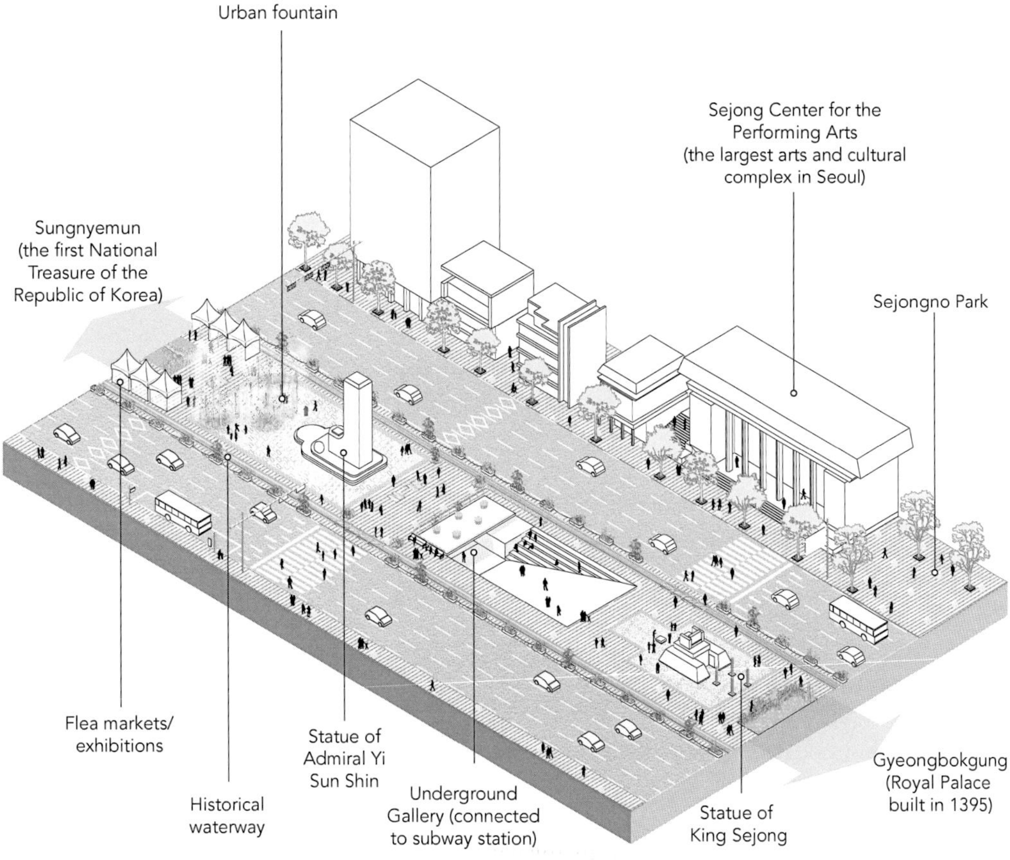

FIGURE O.5 **Rehabilitation of Gwanghwamun Square, Seoul, to Connect Cultural Attractions, 2018**

Source: ©World Bank. Further permission required for reuse.

Public spaces such as markets are an integral element of the functioning of urban food systems. In Singapore, public *hawker centers*—initially developed to accommodate unlicensed food vendors who ply their trade on Singapore's streets—have evolved into ubiquitous, inclusive, and community-centric spaces for selling clean, affordable, and culturally diverse foods across the city. Although early hawker centers were stand-alone, functional developments, the more recently built hawker centers incorporate universal design elements to meet the needs of older persons and people with disabilities, and food rating standards ensure food cleanliness and good public health. Some of them are co-located with a range of other community-centric amenities and facilities. The unique combination of food culture, public space, and community has evolved into a microcosm of Singapore's multicultural society (chapter 15).

Reclamation of Public Spaces for People

Streets make up most of the public land use in many cities. Transforming some streets from vehicular to pedestrian use allows for creating more human-centered spaces. This is not an easy task, because the trade-offs between allocating limited open space for cars and traffic versus people is often a difficult and politically fraught decision for local governments. Nonetheless, there has been an increasing trend to reclaim streets from cars in favor of pedestrians.

In Seoul, the removal of an elevated highway and the restoration of the Cheonggyecheon stream in downtown Seoul was lauded as a major success in urban renewal—creating a space with many environmental benefits. For example, the introduction of clean water and natural habitats to the city resulted in a cooling of the nearby areas by 3.6 degrees Celsius on average versus other parts of Seoul. The number of vehicles entering downtown Seoul has decreased by 2.3 percent, and the number of public transportation users has increased. This urban renewal project catalyzed revitalization throughout downtown Seoul, promoting the urban economy by making the businesses more profitable along the stream. The pedestrianization of these streets is also expected to reduce vehicle traffic by 21 percent.

Similarly, at the neighborhood scale, Aghmashenebeli Avenue in Tbilisi—previously one of the city's main roads dedicated to motorized traffic—has been pedestrianized as part of the New Tiflis project and repositioned as a popular destination for shops and restaurants (chapter 16).

FINANCING AND FUNDING

The expectations that public spaces should be funded by governments are common. However, financing from public budgets poses challenges because local governments usually suffer from chronic shortages of funds and have numerous other competing investment needs (such as water, sanitation, and so on) and therefore cannot fully fund large public-space investments. Creditworthy local governments can supplement their revenues by borrowing on the capital markets to supplement investment needs. The reality, however, is that creditworthy local governments in the developing world that can access capital markets are more the exception than the rule.

Capital Funding, O&M Funding, and Management

A common practical solution is to make capital investment in public spaces a joint undertaking, in one form or another, between government and either the private sector or the community. One option is the outsourcing of public-space development and management to private investors for a period long enough to recoup their capital expenses and turn a profit. However, to be feasible and successful, such public-private partnership (PPP) arrangements require both a robust regulatory framework (which is not always in place) and projects that have revenue generation potential. Alternatively, management contracts bring private expertise into the management and operation of public-space assets.

Philanthropy or community in-kind contributions are also important sources of capital funding or capital works in-kind. Philanthropy would not be common in low- and middle-income countries, but it does exist in some cities (see chapter 11 on Karachi).

Very often, local governments fail to consider future O&M arrangements when they plan and finance public spaces. Specifically, local governments do not plan who (which organization) will manage this new asset and do not estimate the impact of required O&M expenses on their operating budgets. This commonly leads to a lack of proper O&M after a public-space project has been implemented, causing a rapid deterioration of the asset.

Adequate budgeting for O&M is critical for sustainable operations, maintenance, and service delivery within public spaces. Like capital funding of public spaces, community organizations and private companies have roles to play: for example, partnering community organizations can help with effective fund-raising, while private operation of a public space often enables more innovative and intensive use for revenue generation, which helps cover the O&M costs. The latter approach can also defray or reduce O&M expenses from the public budget. Although the management and sources of O&M funding can take on many combinations, there are several common scenarios:

- *O&M performed by local governments* or subsidiary departments or companies and funded from the local budget
- *O&M outsourced to a community-based organiz*ation (CBO) and financed from the local budget or with an expectation of fund-raising by the CBO
- *O&M outsourced to a private company* through a management contract and paid from the local budget
- *O&M covered through a concession contract* wherein the management, operations, and maintenance of public spaces are outsourced to a private company, along with the right to generate revenues from the public space and an obligation to cover O&M costs.

Not all cities can take advantage of all four scenarios because outsourcing to private companies is more complex to launch than government-performed O&M and requires reasonably established systems of public procurement and well-established enforcement of written contracts in the public sector. Furthermore, PPPs would require specialized expertise and are expensive to launch. This may not be justifiable for the relatively small scale of capital investment associated with a single public space unless the process is established at scale citywide or as part of a larger infrastructure investment project.

Land-Based Financing and Planning Instruments

Securing rights-of-way for roads and streets or infrastructure networks and securing land for open spaces should ideally be carried out up front and ahead of development by governments, as part of an overall spatial and infrastructure planning approach. This approach may be feasible in expanding city areas where development has not fully set in or in greenfield developments where vacant public land is available. There will also be scenarios where public spaces such as roads need to be acquired from private owners in built-up areas.

Possible land acquisition instruments include voluntary purchases from private owners, public easements on private land, land swaps, and private land donations. However, the expropriation of urban land for certain types of public spaces (parks and open spaces, for example) is not a common practice and may turn out to be politically unacceptable. Moreover, the experiences in high-income countries indicate that expropriation is a costlier and slower process than other instruments. Depending on a country's regulatory regime, alternative financing and planning instruments have been used to assemble public land for public spaces or to create public spaces in private development.

Planning Tools

Exactions are in-kind contributions of public spaces by developers. For example, developers of large tracts of land may be required to build roads in (or leading to) their developments, then relinquish ownership of these roads to the local government. Impact fees are imposed on real estate developers by local governments as part of regular zoning and development or redevelopment approvals. They are one-time charges to extend public infrastructure to or for the project and can include items such as public spaces.

Incentive zoning such as density bonuses allows developers, voluntarily, to exceed the density limits permitted by standard zoning (such as floor area ratio or other bulk parameters) in exchange for delivering additional public space or amenities on their own sites. In New York, an incentive zoning system that granted 10 square feet of developable space over zoning limits for every square foot of public space in return for the provision of plazas and arcades and other public spaces (including through building setbacks) is responsible for many such public spaces in Manhattan (chapter 2).

The city of São Paulo, Brazil, has similar planning instruments, including (a) the parcel-level Outorga Onerosa (Onerous Grant) system whereby property owners receive density bonuses of up to 20 percent in return for payment to a fund that finances citywide infrastructure improvements; or (b) the area-based Urban Operations system, which auctions additional development rights from an up-zoning process and uses the proceeds for infrastructure improvement in the designated area.[8]

Despite some successes in creating more public spaces, there have been debates on whether these instruments artificially distort land markets and put a cost on building owners and users for a public benefit, as well on whether the resulting POPS are of good quality and remain accessible to the public.

Land-Based Financing Instruments and Land-Value Capture

When public spaces are created within territories that are implementing special land development or redevelopment projects, they are funded together with other infrastructure through land-based financing instruments. These instruments—such as land readjustment, TIF, and, in some cases, TOD—are based on the increased land value from such projects. A part of this increase is captured and channeled to fund infrastructure and public spaces through LVC.[9] These instruments require strong local institutions and a sound legislative and planning framework to be implemented effectively.

Land readjustment is a planning and financing instrument commonly used in East Asian countries such as Japan and the Republic of Korea. It has also been used in Germany to assemble privately owned land at the peri-urban fringe and in India to assemble rural land for urban development. The instrument is based on the concept of pooling privately owned land parcels within a demarcated area and reparceling them based on a master plan or detailed development plans, into a more efficient and rational layout that also allocates a certain amount of land for public infrastructure and services (such as roads and public spaces). Some land parcels are also reserved for auctioning on the market to recover costs. The government returns to each landowner a land parcel smaller than the original parcel, but it has a higher value because it is now on serviced urban land. This approach allows the government to avoid a massive up-front investment to acquire land. However, some challenges do exist, such as obtaining the consent of all existing landowners and the valuation of land.

TIF is a financing technique that U.S. municipalities have used to fund projects focused on urban regeneration. They do so by borrowing against the anticipated future increase in property tax revenues generated by the project to fund public infrastructure, including public spaces. This financing approach is possible when a municipal bond market exists and when a new development is of a sufficiently large scale, accompanied by a large enough increase in the value of surrounding real estate generated by the new project.

TOD revolves around the creation of compact, walkable, pedestrian-oriented, mixed-use communities centered around high-quality transit systems that attract people and businesses. In some TOD projects, local authorities set higher floor area ratios (FARs) surrounding these nodes to allow for densification and to generate revenue streams that they can capture to finance infrastructure and public spaces.

Opportunities and Risks of Public-Space Replacement

The disposition and rezoning of public spaces for other uses can be much more controversial than disposition of other public assets. This stems from the high value that some public groups and communities associate with parks and public spaces and an unwillingness to sacrifice them, even if for other legitimate and publicly supported purposes. Another peculiarity of parks is that the notion of disposition or replacement due to the end of useful life is less applicable to them than to other assets such as buildings or facilities. Parks and open spaces usually do not have a life cycle with a clear-cut end (like buildings have). Instead, they are subject to changes such as the gradual replacement of landscaping, street furniture, and lighting or the reconstruction of infrastructure (drainage and so on).

An increasing trend in cities is the integration of public spaces as part of infrastructure or as part of developments that preserve the function of open parks. At the same time, when old public places need reconstruction, this offers great opportunity for urban renewal and rejuvenation. Part III documents several cases of such transformation.

MANAGEMENT AND GOVERNANCE

An Asset Management Approach

Cities can do much better in the sustainable management of the entire life cycle of public spaces including design, implementation, and O&M. Part I of the book ("Planning, Funding, and Managing Public Spaces: An Asset Management Framework") explores a broad spectrum of ways to govern public spaces and make them financially sustainable assets. As noted earlier in the "Financing and Funding" section, the options to local governments' common practice of publicly financing and operating public spaces include entrusting O&M to community organizations or outsourcing it to a private company—as in Seoul, where the government contracted a firm that specializes in programming and managing library facilities to manage the Gusandong Library (chapter 14).

Cases of successful asset management of public spaces indicate that specific good governance elements must be built into the life cycle as a foundation for success: a sound regulatory environment, a cost-effective ownership structure, and sustainable management and oversight arrangements.

Regulatory Environment

A sound regulatory environment (such as policy instruments, laws and regulations, and contract enforcement) is a prerequisite to support the creation of viable public spaces, especially with PPPs or private operating models. For example, regulations governing impact fees and incentive zoning are critical to enable the delivery of public spaces as part of new development or revitalization projects. Specific laws and regulations will also be needed to govern contracts for the management of public spaces and determine the options and avenues available for creating, funding, and managing public-space initiatives.

Ownership Structure

Land ownership is an important determinant for the creation of public spaces. Public spaces can be created on land that the government already owns (including repurposing of old, government-owned infrastructure and facilities) or on land acquired from the private sector through voluntary instruments such as purchase at market value from private owners; land swaps; private land donations (as long as they are not coercive); land readjustment; or compulsory requirements such as expropriation, right of preemption, or public easements on private land.

Another channel, as described earlier, is the creation of POPS as a part of private land development wherein developers dedicate land for public spaces (and services) through development exactions. This instrument exists in cities in many regions around the world and is based on either (a) incentives for developers, such as the ability to exceed permitted land-use density in exchange for creating a public space; or (b) regulation requiring that public space be provided in conjunction with large land development.

Management and Oversight Arrangements

The responsibility for managing the public space, including O&M responsibilities, can be assigned to a range of actors including government agencies, the private sector, not-for-profit organizations, or community organizations. Such management arrangements, coupled with a corresponding oversight structure, can be deployed or modified depending on the context such as the available funding sources and the characteristics of the public-space interventions.

Institutional and Management Arrangements

A broad range of stakeholder coordination mechanisms are used to harmonize the joint efforts of public agencies, private owners, and communities. The forms these institutional arrangements take depend on the project's purpose, the roles of stakeholders, and the regulatory environment. They are often set up in the planning stages and deployed during the implementation stages. Some specific types of institutional arrangements include public initiatives (such as development corporations) or private initiatives (such as BIDS or trusts, including formal and informal structures), as illustrated in the case studies in Part III:

- *Steering committees.* Usually made up of high-level stakeholders or representatives, steering committees provide guidance on key issues. For instance, in Beijing, while the city government led the Dashilar regeneration program, the Dashilar Regeneration Steering Committee was created to coordinate across different government agencies (chapter 9). In the case of Yonsei-ro in Seoul, stakeholders organized a steering committee to implement the project, consisting of a mix of city government officials, Seodaemun-gu (district office) representatives, relevant agencies such as the Seoul Metropolitan Police, the Korea Electric Power Corporation, residents, merchants, and civic groups, as well as Yonsei University and Hyundai Department Store. The committee's work was grouped into three main sections: transportation, design and construction, and visitor services (chapter 14).

- *Development corporations.* The state-owned enterprise Beijing Dashilar Investment Company (BDIC) is the implementing entity of the Dashilar project in Beijing. The corporation organized a partnership platform (Dashilar Platform) to attract private and technical resources and link the city government and private sector (chapter 9). One of the BDIC's main objectives was to attract private sector investments and participation by seeding the funding of selected assets.
- *Business improvement districts.* A typical BID is a defined area within which a special fee is imposed and collected from businesses inside the BID to fund or maintain specific assets and services benefiting all businesses within the BID territory. In Brooklyn, the DUMBO BID was responsible for the overall revitalization of the district, including public-space interventions such as the DUMBO archway improvement (chapter 13). In the case of the Brooklyn Cultural District, the Downtown Brooklyn Partnership proposed to expand the footprint of an existing BID (Metro Tech BID) and to operate the Cultural District as its subdistrict. It was approved by the New York City Council in 2016, and it covers the implementation and maintenance of nine cultural venues within the Cultural District area.
- *MOUs and other public or private arrangements.* Other arrangements include memorandums of understanding (MOUs) and other types of arrangements between government entities and the private sector. To bypass the need to pay an "occupation fee" before developing the Gyeongui Line Forest Park in Seoul, the city government signed an MOU with the state-owned agency that owns the site (the Korea Rail Network Authority [KRNA]) that obtained permission to use the site free of charge for 50 years in exchange for authorizing the KRNA's development projects near the Gyeongui Railway in the city (chapter 14). In the case of Las Begonias, Lima, the Municipality of San Isidro worked with a private real estate company that had a stake in the area to implement the project. The planning studies were funded by the private company, while the municipality funded the execution of the project (chapter 12).

STRATEGIES FOR UNLOCKING THE VALUE OF PUBLIC-SPACE ASSETS

The case studies of this book reveal many strategies for creating great public spaces for people, addressing three broad areas of focus (table O.1):

- *Stakeholders and partnerships:* Creation of public spaces for communities and their well-being in ways that ensure the inclusive engagement of different groups of actors and users
- *Policies, planning, and design:* Equitable and inclusive spatial distribution, quantity, and design quality that enhance access to public spaces across the city
- *Management, governance, and finance:* Sustainable financial and organizational arrangements for creating and managing public-space assets during their life cycles.

TABLE O.1 **Strategies and Recommendations for Unlocking the Potential of Urban Public-Space Assets**

Strategies	Recommendations	Key References (Part/Chapter)
Stakeholders and partnerships		
Seek champions and build coalitions	• Identify local leaders within the government, community, and private sector	I/3 and III/8
	• Empower and build ownership with the community, and engage stakeholders	III/8 (most cases)
	• Seek private partners for innovation and resources	I/3; III/9 (Beijing), 12 (Lima), 13 (Brooklyn), and 15 (Singapore)
Coordinate across stakeholders	• Define a shared vision, purpose and the roles of stakeholders	I/2
	• Adopt suitable stakeholder coordination mechanisms and feedback channels	III/8 (most cases)
Adopt appropriate planning, design, and placemaking approaches	• Explore suitable planning and design approaches in the short and long terms, based on needs and envisaged outcomes	III/8
	• Build in participatory and cocreation approaches with stakeholders	III/8, 9 (Beijing), 11 (Karachi), 12 (Lima), and 13 (Brooklyn)
Manage unintended outcomes	• Develop practical approaches for managing stakeholder friction during a project's life cycle, and instances of nimbyism	III/12 (Lima) and 14 (Seoul)
	• Adopt equitable and inclusive measures to address potential displacement, resettlement, and mitigate the effects of gentrification	III/9 (Beijing), 10 (Colombo), and 13 (Brooklyn)
Policies, planning, and design		
Create for people, and build sense of place	• Connect neighborhoods with a mix of public spaces, focusing on spatially underserved areas	II/4, 5; III/13 (Brooklyn), 14 (Seoul), and 15 (Singapore)
	• Preserve valuable public spaces from urbanization pressures and make existing public spaces accessible	II/5, III/10 (Colombo), 12 (Lima), 14 (Seoul), and 16 (Tbilisi)
	• Design human-centered public spaces to address safety, inclusion, outdoor comfort, and access for all	II/6 and III/8 (most cases)
	• Promote urban health through the active use of public spaces	III/10 (Colombo), 11 (Karachi), and 15 (Singapore)

(table continues next page)

TABLE O.1 **Strategies and Recommendations for Unlocking the Potential of Urban Public-Space Assets *(Continued)***

Strategies	Recommendations	Key References (Part/Chapter)
Leverage policy instruments and work with land and real estate markets	• Review and apply effective planning and land-use policy and/or regulatory instruments available to the city for creating and managing public spaces and POPS	I/3, III/13 (Brooklyn), 14 (Seoul), and 15 (Singapore)
	• Deliver public spaces through land-based financing, as part of a broader development approach (such as TOD)	I/3 and III/15 (Singapore)
Adopt an evidence-based decision-making process	• Take stock of public-space asset inventories, adopt tools to measure spatial characteristics and user activity patterns at the city level	II/4, 5 (Dhaka, Karachi, Lima, Bamako, Fallujah, and Ramadi), 6 (Nairobi, Addis Ababa, Wuhan, and Bamenda), 7 (Tbilisi and Wuhan)
	• Prioritize public-space programs and investments using data-informed spatial planning strategies, local knowledge, and align with broader areas' development plans	II/4 and III/8 (most cases)
	• Actively evaluate and monitor the impact and outcomes of public-space interventions, and reiterate solutions	II/6 (Nairobi, Addis Ababa, Wuhan, and Bamenda), 7 (Tbilisi, Wuhan, and Beijing); III/8
Integrate with resilient city infrastructure	• Protect natural urban greenery, biodiversity, and ecological assets (including urban forests and wetlands); and integrate public spaces into green and gray infrastructure	III/10 (Colombo); 15 (Singapore)
	• Green the city, by protecting mature trees, and through initiatives such as tree-planting programs and community gardening	III/8 (most cases)
	• Adopt sustainable development principles such as green buildings and resource efficiency, starting their implementation with public facilities	I/3
Seek synergies with other city assets and urban systems	• Leverage public art, tangible and intangible cultural heritage, and historic areas for urban rejuvenation	III/9 (Beijing), 11 (Karachi), 13 (Brooklyn), and 16 (Tbilisi)
	• Enhance urban food systems with public spaces (markets and hawker centers, urban agriculture) for food security and urban health	III/12 (Lima) and 15 (Singapore)

(table continues next page)

TABLE O.1 **Strategies and Recommendations for Unlocking the Potential of Urban Public-Space Assets *(Continued)***

Strategies	Recommendations	Key References (Part/Chapter)
Reclaim streets for pedestrians	• Prioritize, and design complete streets for safe mobility and non-motorized transportation	III/8 (most cases)
	• Reclaim and reconfigure street and parking spaces for human-centered activities through permanent or temporary interventions	III/8 (most cases)
Creatively repurpose existing, old, or vacant public infrastructure	• Identify potential public spaces, and creatively transform infrastructure into usable public spaces	III/13 (Brooklyn) and 14 (Seoul)
	• Seek innovative business models and feasible design ideas from the private sector and communities through appropriate platforms	I/3 and III/8
Management, governance, and finance		
Plan and design for flexibility and resource efficiencies	• Deploy innovative design solutions or placemaking interventions that optimize limited operations and maintenance (O&M) resources	I/3
	• Consider developing public-space asset management policies to improve resource (energy, water, and other) efficiencies	I/3
	• Activate and design public spaces to accommodate multiple functions, more intensive uses, and other spontaneous activities	II/5, 6 (Nairobi, Addis Ababa, Wuhan, and Bamenda); and III/8 (most cases)
Adopt a public-space life-cycle management framework	• Adopt a comprehensive asset management framework and oversight to ensure financial and organizational sustainability of public spaces throughout their life cycles	I/3
	• Build institutional capacity to manage new public spaces that may require new expertise	I/3
Seek feasible financing and funding models	• Ensure that the capital planning needed for public spaces is built into the city's overall capital investment planning	I/3 and III/8
	• Adopt sustainable and efficient organizational and O&M funding models through partnerships between government entities, communities, and the private sector	I/3 and III/8
	• Leverage appropriate financing, development, and land value capture models compatible with the regulatory environment and management instruments	I/3 and III/8

(table continues next page)

TABLE O.1 **Strategies and Recommendations for Unlocking the Potential of Urban Public-Space Assets *(Continued)***

Strategies	Recommendations	Key References (Part/Chapter)
Factor in long-term costs and risks in decision-making	• Factor in costs avoided from disasters and poor health (such as flooding and urban heat islands) mitigated by the preservation of open spaces, greenery and wetlands, and waterbodies in urban areas	III/10 (Colombo)
	• Address the risks of the disposition of public spaces that hold high value with community groups (such as historic public spaces) into other uses	I/3 and III/16 (Tbilisi)
Anticipate opportunities and challenges arising from future trends and disruptive technology	• Leverage innovative and appropriate technological approaches to manage and monitor public spaces	II/4, 5 (Dhaka, Karachi, and Lima), 7 (Tbilisi, Wuhan, and Beijing)
	• Anticipate how technology and user trends will change how public spaces are used and calibrate policies accordingly	II/4

Note: POPS = privately owned public spaces. TOD = transit-oriented development.

To unlock the value of public spaces, cities must adopt effective strategies across their life cycles within specific contexts to plan, design, develop, deliver, and maintain these assets—always prioritizing their value to *people* by making them accessible, inclusive, and attractive to diverse individuals and communities.

Only then can public spaces—whether on the streets, within infrastructure spaces and public facilities, or in open and green areas—yield returns on investment far exceeding the monetary costs. Global cases proved that high-quality public spaces help cities enhance livability, resilience, and competitiveness by strengthening social cohesion and urban health; protecting urban greenery; and attracting further investment, entrepreneurship, and talent.

NOTES

1. The United Nations Human Settlements Programme's (UN-Habitat) City Prosperity Initiative (CPI) includes the quantity and quality of public spaces as key dimensions of its Quality of Life Index (http://cpi.unhabitat.org/). The Economist Intelligence Unit's (EIU) Global Liveability Report (EIU 2017) and Mercer's Quality of Living survey (Mercer 2018) also evaluate cities on quality-of-life criteria including an assessment of road networks, public transport networks, and recreational facilities.
2. Transportation accounted for the largest portion (28 percent), by sector, of total U.S. GHG emissions in 2016 (EPA 2018). Within the sector, light-duty vehicles (including passenger cars and light-duty trucks) were the largest category (with 60 percent of GHG emissions), while medium- and heavy-duty trucks made up the second largest category (with 23 percent of emissions).
3. Medellín, Colombia, was named "City of the Year"—the world's most innovative city—in a 2013 competition organized by the Urban Land Institute (Riggs et al. 2013). It also received the 2014 Lee Kuan Yew World City Prize Special Mention and was named the 2016 Prize

Laureate for its approach to small, high-impact urban developments that targeted the city's social inequity and economic inequality (URA 2016).

4. "Placemaking" refers to a multifaceted, holistic approach to the planning, design, and management of public spaces. It capitalizes on a local community's assets, inspiration, and potential to create public spaces that promote people's health, happiness, and well-being ("What Is Placemaking?" Project for Public Spaces, 2018, https://www.pps.org/article/what-is-placemaking). "Tactical urbanism" is an implementation and design tactic that offers visible and impactful outcomes at low cost by showing results fast. Through this approach, policy makers and practitioners build stakeholder ownership, and user opinions are reflected in the process. Interventions are usually simple, which can evolve over time into more permanent public-space interventions. Examples include free mini libraries, guerrilla gardening, art exhibitions, and parklets.
5. This figure uses a stricter criterion than other estimations of streets and public spaces: it excludes major infrastructure such as highways and motorways because they are unlikely to form public spaces for people.
6. "Parklets" refers to curbside parking spaces that have been converted and reclaimed into vibrant community spaces such as seating, greenery, or even bicycle racks along neighborhood retail streets or commercial areas. These initiatives are often a result of partnerships between the city and local businesses, residents, or neighborhood associations (NACTO 2016b).
7. "Green infrastructure" refers to nature-based solutions to manage stormwater, and "gray infrastructure" refers to conventional engineered infrastructure such as drains, pipes, and water treatment systems for stormwater management ("What Is Green Infrastructure?" United States Environmental Protection Agency: https://www.epa.gov/green-infrastructure/what-green-infrastructure).
8. For more information, see "Costly Grant: Understand the Onerous Grant of Right to Build," Municipal Secretariat of Urban Development, City of São Paulo, August 31, 2009: https://www.prefeitura.sp.gov.br/cidade/secretarias/urbanismo/urbanismo/index.php?p=1393.
9. LVC, also known as "value sharing," is a policy approach that enables communities to recover and reinvest land value increases that result from public investment and other government actions (Germán and Bernstein 2018).

REFERENCES

Angel, Shlomo. 2012. *Planet of Cities*. Cambridge, MA: Lincoln Institute of Land Policy.

Bertaud, Alain. 2018. *Order without Design: How Markets Shape Cities*. Cambridge, MA: MIT Press.

Browder, Greg, Suzanne Ozment, Irene Rehberger Bescos, Todd Gartner, and Glenn-Marie Lange. 2019. *Integrating Green and Gray: Creating Next Generation Infrastructure*. Washington, DC: World Resources Institute and World Bank.

City of Copenhagen. 2012. "CPH 2025 Climate Plan." Political framework and public action document, Technical and Environmental Administration, City of Copenhagen.

Cox, Daniel A., and Ryan Streeter. 2019. "The Importance of Place: Neighborhood Amenities as a Source of Social Connection and Trust." Research report, American Enterprise Institute, Washington, DC.

EIU (Economist Intelligence Unit). 2017. "Global Liveability Report 2017." Annual urban quality-of-life ranking report, EIU, London.

EPA (United States Environmental Protection Agency). 2018. "Fast Facts: U.S. Transportation Sector Greenhouse Gas Emissions 1990–2016." Report No. EPA-420-F-18-013, Office of Transportation and Air Quality, EPA, Washington, DC.

Gehl, Jan. 2011. *Life Between Buildings: Using Public Space*. Rev. ed. Washington, DC: Island Press.

Germán, Lourdes, and Allison Ehrich Bernstein. 2018. "Land Value Capture: Tools to Finance Our Urban Future." Policy brief, Lincoln Institute of Land Policy, Cambridge, MA.

Jacobs, Jane. 1961. *The Death and Life of Great American Cities*. New York: Random House.

Katz, Bruce, and Julie Wagner. 2014. "The Rise of Innovation Districts: A New Geography of Innovation in America." Report for the Metropolitan Policy Program, The Brookings Institution, Washington, DC.

McDonald, Robert I., Timm Kroeger, Ping Zhang, and Perrine Hamel. 2019. "The Value of US Urban Tree Cover for Reducing Heat-Related Health Impacts and Electricity Consumption." *Ecosystems* (2019), 1–14. https://doi.org/10.1007/s10021-019-00395-5.

Mercer. 2018. "Vienna Tops Mercer's 20th Quality of Living Ranking." Press release, March 20. https://www.mercer.com/newsroom/2018-quality-of-living-survey.html.

Murray, Michael. 2010. "Private Management of Public Spaces: Nonprofit Organizations and Urban Parks." *Harvard Environmental Law Review* 34 (1): 179–255.

NACTO (National Association of City Transportation Officials). 2016a. *Global Street Design Guide*. New York: Island Press.

———. 2016b. "Parklets." In *Global Street Design Guide*. New York: Island Press.

Riggs, Trisha, Michael Mehaffy, Bendix Anderson, and Leslie Braunstein. 2013. "Which Cities Are the Most Innovative?" *UrbanLand*, March 1. https://urbanland.uli.org/economy-markets-trends/which-cities-are-worlds-most-innovative-winner/.

Skinner, Caroline, Sarah Orleans Reed, and Jenna Harvey. 2018. *Supporting Informal Livelihoods in Public Space: A Toolkit for Local Authorities*. Manchester, U.K.: Women in Informal Employment: Globalizing and Organizing (WIEGO); Brussels: Cities Alliance.

UN DESA (United Nations Department of Economic and Social Affairs). 2019. *World Urbanization Prospects: The 2018 Revision*. New York: United Nations.

UNESCO (United Nations Educational, Scientific and Cultural Organization). 2016. *Culture: Urban Future; Global Report on Culture for Sustainable Urban Development*. Paris: UNESCO.

UN-Habitat (United Nations Human Settlements Programme). 2013. *Streets as Public Spaces and Drivers of Urban Prosperity*. Nairobi: UN-Habitat.

———. 2015. *Global Public Space Toolkit: From Global Principles to Local Policies and Practice*. Nairobi, Kenya: United Nations Human Settlements Programme (UN-Habitat).

URA (Urban Redevelopment Authority). 2016. "2016 Prize Laureate: Medellín." Jury citation of the Lee Kuan Yew World City Prize, URA and Centre for Liveable Cities, Singapore. https://www.leekuanyewworldcityprize.com.sg/laureates/laureates/2016/medellin.

WHO (World Health Organization). 2016. "Urban Green Spaces and Health: A Review of Evidence." European Environment and Health Process Report, WHO Regional Office for Europe, Copenhagen.

Whyte, William H. 1980. *The Social Life of Small Urban Spaces*. New York: Project for Public Spaces.

World Bank. 2016. "Republic of Kenya: Kenya Urbanization Review." Report No. AUS8099, World Bank, Washington, DC.

———. 2017a. "A Modern Dhaka Is Key to Bangladesh's Upper-Middle Income Country Vision." Press release, July 19.

———. 2017b. "Creative Community Spaces: Spaces that Are Transforming Cities into Information Hubs." Working paper no. 117300, World Bank, Washington, DC.

———. 2017c. "The High Toll of Traffic Injuries: Unacceptable and Preventable—The Macro-Economic and Welfare Benefits of Reducing Road Traffic Injuries in Low- & Middle-Income Countries." Study report, World Bank, Washington, DC.

———. 2018. "Dar es Salaam Metropolitan Development Project: BRT Phase 1 Corridor Development Strategy." 7 vols. Working paper no. 135866, produced for the President's Office of Regional Administration and Local Government, Dar es Salaam, Tanzania.

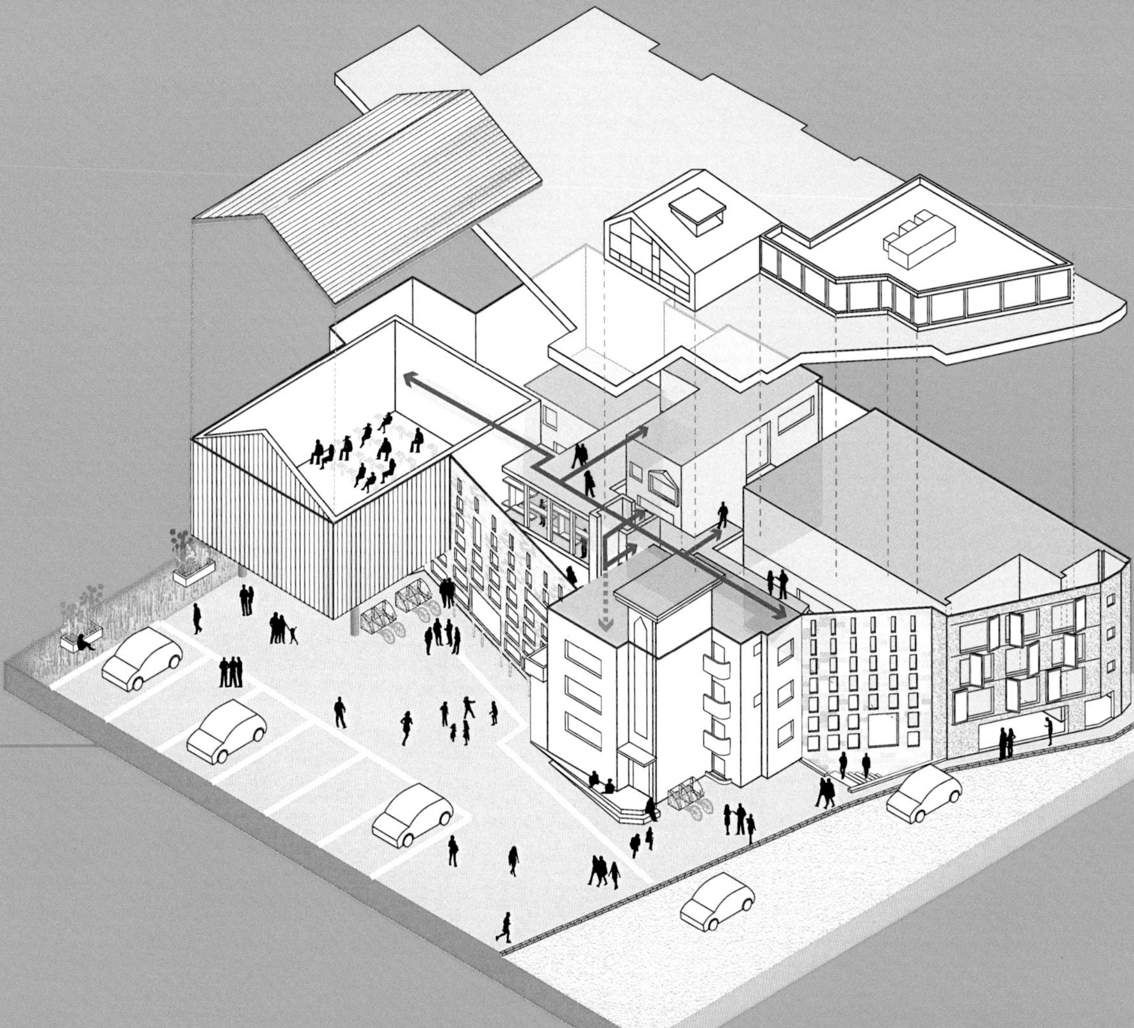

PART I

PLANNING, FUNDING, AND MANAGING PUBLIC SPACES

An Asset Management Framework

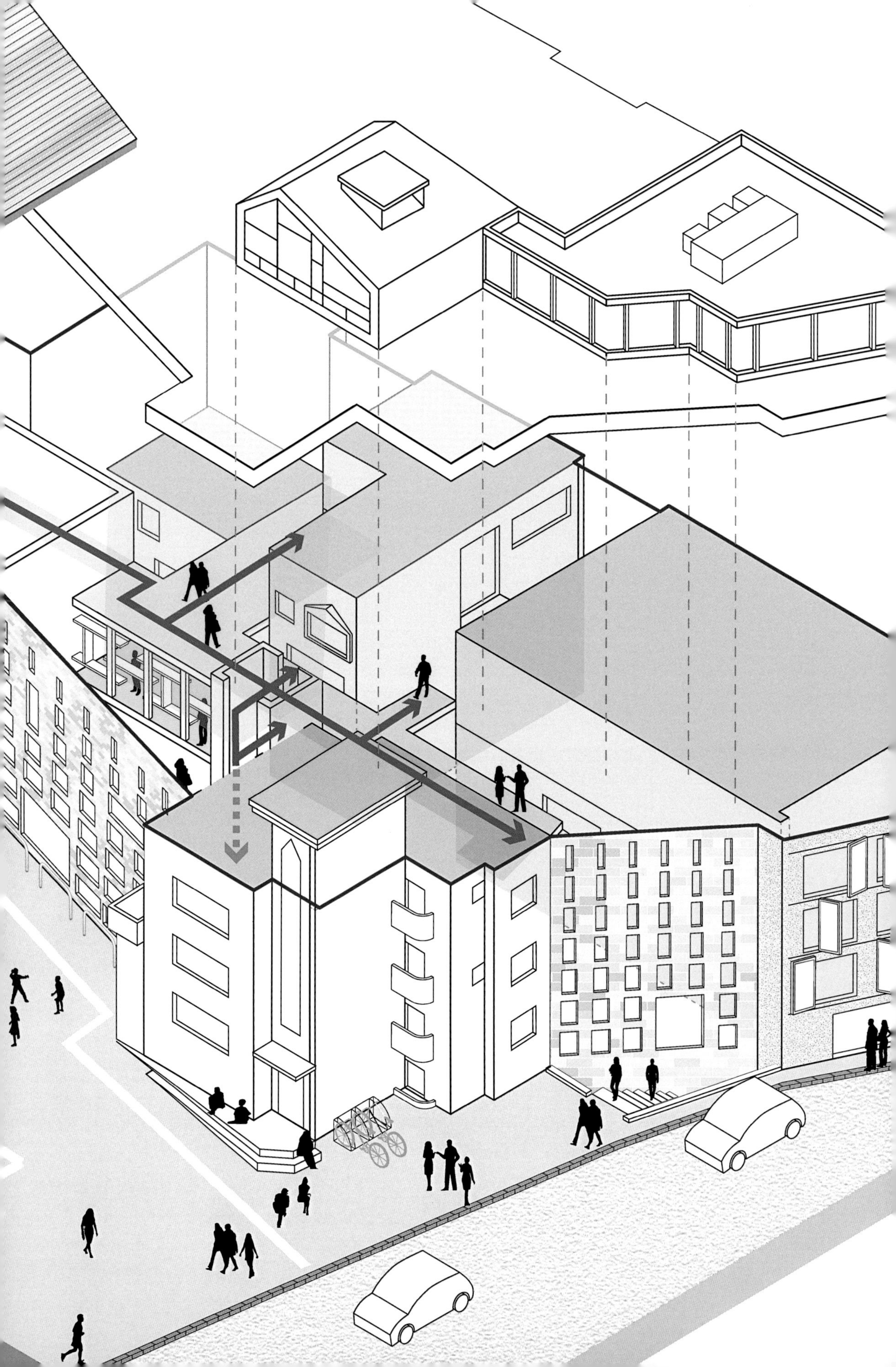

CHAPTER 1

THE IMPORTANCE OF INVESTING IN PUBLIC SPACES

Jon Kher Kaw

INTRODUCTION

There is a growing international recognition that good public spaces are important for urban dwellers and their quality of life. This chapter reviews the main reasons why this new focus on public spaces emerged and how the focus relates to the present challenges of urban growth management—and of municipal financial management in particular.

Chapter 2 briefly explores the notions of public spaces and related debates, including discussions of "publicness." Most importantly, it introduces the subject of private sector and other nongovernmental participation in the delivery and management of public spaces—a matter central to many current debates. In particular, the chapter reviews privately owned public spaces (POPS) and the varying viewpoints on this instrument.

Chapter 3 presents a framework for considering public spaces from an asset management viewpoint. Then, it provides guidelines for applying this framework when planning and implementing a public space for it to be sustainable, both financially and organizationally.

THE GLOBAL AGENDA FOR PUBLIC SPACES

The provision of adequate, accessible, and inclusive public spaces in urban areas is now a global agenda. The New Urban Agenda (NUA) of the United

Nations Human Settlements Programme (UN-Habitat) and the United Nations (UN) 2030 Agenda for Sustainable Development emphasize the need for public spaces to be open, inclusive, and accessible to all, regardless of gender, race, ethnicity, age, or socioeconomic level (UN 2015; UN-Habitat 2017). UN Sustainable Development Goal (SDG) 11 explicitly highlights the importance of public spaces for all, and a specific indicator has been assigned to monitor achievements.[1] The NUA repeatedly refers to high-quality public space as a key driver of urban sustainability.

Moreover, diverse organizations have started piloting the role of urban planning and public spaces in cities. For instance, the United Nations Entity for Gender Equality and the Empowerment of Women (UN-Women) launched the "Safe Cities and Safe Public Spaces" report, which monitors the enhancement of public-space designs with better lighting and closed-circuit televisions (CCTVs) to prevent and respond to sexual violence against women (UN-Women 2017). Others on board include the Food and Agriculture Organization of the United Nations (FAO) on sustainable forestry and the World Health Organization (WHO) on green spaces and health (WHO 2016). The World Bank has also committed to bringing best practices for public spaces into its operational activities.

A recent paradigm shift—from a focus on growth to a focus on quality of life—has occurred in many cities and urban areas looking to transform themselves to remain competitive. While the world's urban population has dramatically increased,[2] many cities are constrained by livability. The pressure on land resources and urban space is becoming acute globally, especially in Asia and Latin America.[3]

A closer look at cities in South Asia reveals polarization and stark spatial segregation in the distribution and provision of public services, often recognized as among the root causes of crime and degraded livability (Ellis and Roberts 2016). This unbalanced distribution of urban public-space assets has raised questions about how the physical environment should be organized and managed to achieve inclusive green growth, whereby everyone—including the most marginalized—have access to basic services and opportunity for better livelihoods. Danish architect and urban designer Jan Gehl advocates that "density, which represents quantity, must be combined with quality in the form of good city space" (Gehl 2010).

EMERGING ISSUES AND CHALLENGES FOR CITIES

Managing public spaces is a challenge for cities. Rapid urban development is often associated with the shrinking of public spaces, urban greenery, and bodies of water. Even when city governments recognize the importance of public spaces, it is difficult for them—especially in low- and many middle-income countries—to secure public spaces and funding for them, given the many competing development priorities. In some cases, cities' efforts to improve public spaces do not even produce desirable results, because their design and maintenance plans do not reflect the needs and preferences of the intended users.

In many cases, governments are faced with difficult trade-offs: In light of increasing traffic congestion, how do cities safeguard places for people and businesses? How do cities address encroachments of vendors in public spaces? The choices and trade-offs between integrating livelihood activities in public spaces and displacing communities are not easy ones. Even in the more successful cases—when public spaces are recognized as creating long-term value for users or nearby property owners—managing such spaces is typically an organizational and financial liability for local governments.

Given the costs and benefits, are public spaces liabilities or assets for local governments? The land for current or potential public spaces is usually owned by local and central governments. However, *how much* of this type of land is held by governments is usually unknown, mostly because many governments lack good inventories of their land.[4] Anecdotal evidence and estimates using open-source data and land-use maps derived from earth observation and remote sensing indicate that landholdings for current or potential public spaces are considerable, including "leftover" spaces from infrastructure, underused vacant land, government-owned buildings, or open and green areas at municipal or ministry sites that are fenced off from the public. Further, the public value of those spaces is even higher if they are considered not only on their own merits but also as elements of a network of connected urban spaces.

Finally, many examples indicate (as in the chapters of Part III) that creative reuse of underutilized infrastructure and industrial properties can be a source of new public spaces. For example, city-initiated and city-supported redevelopment of old private industrial and warehouse properties along waterfronts can convert or adapt those properties for new public or commercial uses.

THE EVOLVING ROLE OF PUBLIC SPACES IN CITIES

Public spaces play a critical role in ensuring the diversity of a city and in facilitating inclusiveness of communities across socioeconomic, ethnic, and cultural divides. They are especially important to residents of poorer neighborhoods. Public spaces in these areas can serve as

- Pathways for public transport, water supply, electricity, drainage, and street lighting
- Venues for informal trade and commerce such as hawking and street vending
- Centers of religious and cultural exchange, recreation, and social interaction
- Extended sites of various household activities.

Public spaces that are flexible enough to accommodate different uses tend to allow for more spontaneous and varying activities, as opposed to more-formal places with clearly defined land uses or service facilities like community centers.

Many people in cities of the low- and middle-income world, particularly the poor, depend heavily on access to public spaces for their healthy daily activities as well as for sociocultural and political events and job creation.[5] Good quality of such public spaces, therefore, needs to be considered as a critical part of poverty reduction and inclusive green growth strategies—just as important as other infrastructure development, such as transport, water supply, and sanitation. To successfully link public spaces with residents, the government must involve them in a participatory, cocreative process of designing and implementing urban public spaces.

Moreover, public spaces are potential testing grounds for innovative solutions. The advent of technology offers numerous opportunities to improve the use of public spaces and to foster cooperation between government and the public. One example is the growing use of geographic information system (GIS)-linked maps that allow people to either find information about public spaces or contribute to their maintenance. The United Kingdom's adoption of the Digital Economy Bill in 2017 and subsequent release of more than 30,000 nonpersonal data sets in machine-readable formats—free and accessible for all to use or build upon—led to the emergence of more than 400 different apps, including ones that help people find the closest public toilet or report problems with public-space infrastructure.[6]

Innovative approaches to the revitalization of underused or deteriorated public spaces can be "early wins" that can deliver highly visible improvements to daily life. Other avenues that cities can take to design public spaces include adoption of technology, green building design, and integration with green infrastructure, which has the potential not only to realize operational cost savings in the long term but also to increase urban resilience and reduce overall carbon footprints.

These innovative approaches can also show political commitment to longer-term planning processes such as urban regeneration or transit-oriented development at a neighborhood or city level. For instance, in Medellín, Colombia, the city successfully and dramatically enhanced the urban environment in slums through the creation of public spaces, accompanied by the innovative use of outdoor escalators and cable cars to provide mobility for residents. The city was able to transform its reputation from being one of the most violent cities in the world to one of the most innovative cities globally. In Colombo, Sri Lanka, an abandoned wetland area was recreated into an ecological park with improved accessibility, environmental integration and flood resilience, an example of how public space, natural assets, and city infrastructure can come together in a single space (see the discussion of Beddagana Wetland Park in chapter 10). Other innovative examples include creatively repurposing underutilized urban infrastructure, implementing "smart" and responsive public spaces utilizing disruptive technology, and reclaiming street spaces through placemaking approaches for active and vibrant uses—all of which can improve the social, economic, and environmental conditions of residents' daily lives (WHO 2016).

To achieve these outcomes, cities must adopt effective strategies across their public-space life cycle to plan, engage, design, develop, implement, maintain, evaluate, and renew these assets—to create sustainable and high-quality spaces that prioritize their value for people and communities.

NOTES

1. SDG 11, on "Sustainable Cities and Communities," calls for "[Making] cities and human settlements inclusive, safe, resilient and sustainable." Target 11.7 is "By 2030, provide universal access to safe, inclusive and accessible green and public spaces, in particular for women and children, older persons and persons with disabilities." For more information, see the UN SDG Knowledge Platform (website): https://sustainabledevelopment.un.org/sdg11.
2. The world's urban population quadrupled, from 1.02 billion to 4.13 billion, between 1960 and 2017 (UN DESA 2018).
3. The population density (persons per square kilometer) in Africa, Asia, Canada and the United States, the European Union, and Latin America and the Caribbean are 4,200; 8,200; 3,100; 3,900; and 4,500, respectively (EIU 2017).
4. Part II ("Shaping the Public Realm: Data and Spatial Analysis") presents new quantitative analysis that provides insights on such holdings.
5. The share of street vendors in urban employment is substantial (with a higher share of women than men in the sector) in low- and middle-income countries. For instance, street vendors make up 14 percent, 11.3 percent, 9.2 percent, and 24 percent of urban informal jobs in Ghana; Hanoi, Vietnam; Lima, Peru; and Lomé, Togo, respectively (Skinner, Orleans Reed, and Harvey 2018).
6. See The Great British Public Toilet Map at https://www.toiletmap.org.uk/; and the FixMyStreet app at https://www.fixmystreet.com/.

REFERENCES

EIU (Economist Intelligence Unit). 2017. "Global Liveability Report 2017." Annual urban quality-of-life ranking report, EIU, London.

Ellis, Peter, and Mark Roberts. 2016. *Leveraging Urbanization in South Asia: Managing Spatial Transformation for Prosperity and Livability*. Washington, DC: World Bank.

Gehl, Jan. 2010. *Cities for People*. Washington, DC: Island Press.

Skinner, Caroline, Sarah Orleans Reed, and Jenna Harvey. 2018. *Supporting Informal Livelihoods in Public Space: A Toolkit for Local Authorities*. Manchester, UK: Women in Informal Employment: Globalizing and Organizing (WIEGO); Brussels: Cities Alliance.

UN (United Nations). 2015. "Transforming Our World: The 2030 Agenda for Sustainable Development." Resolution A/RES/70/1, adopted October 21, 2015, by the UN General Assembly, New York.

UN DESA (United Nations Department of Economic and Social Affairs). 2018. *World Urbanization Prospects: The 2018 Revision*. New York: UN DESA.

UN-Habitat (United Nations Human Settlements Programme). 2017. *New Urban Agenda*. Adopted October 20, 2016, at the United Nations Conference on Housing and Sustainable Urban Development (Habitat III). Quito, Ecuador: United Nations.

UN-Women (United Nations Entity for Gender Equality and the Empowerment of Women). 2017. "Safe Cities and Safe Public Spaces: Global Results Report." Report on the UN-Women Global Flagship Program Initiative "Safe Cities and Safe Public Spaces," UN-Women, New York.

WHO (World Health Organization). 2016. "Urban Green Spaces and Health: A Review of Evidence." European Environment and Health Process Report, WHO Regional Office for Europe, Copenhagen.

World Bank. 2019. "World Bank Helps Improve Livability of Four Localities in Dhaka City." Press release, March 29 (accessed June 15, 2019), https://www.worldbank.org/en/news/press-release/2019/03/29/world-bank-helps-improve-livability-of-four-localities-in-dhaka-city.

CHAPTER 2

DEFINING PUBLIC SPACES

Jon Kher Kaw, Olga Kaganova, and Hyunji Lee

FRAMING PUBLIC SPACES AND "PUBLICNESS": OWNERS, MANAGERS, AND USERS

The definition of "public spaces" has evolved over the past several decades. Historically, the term referred to spaces perceived as owned and used by the public, based on an understanding of a clear line between public and private groups (Mitchell 2003). Later, the notion expanded, reflecting the more diverse role that public spaces play in cities, underpinned by more-complex property relations. For example, can a public space be "owned" privately but "used" by the public? Can a private space create "public benefit"?

Given the importance of well-designed and managed public spaces in cities today, various efforts have sought to reach an international consensus on the definition of public spaces. In 2012, the Charter of Public Space referred to public spaces as "all places publicly owned or of public use, accessible and enjoyable by all for free and without a profit motive," which puts a focus on both public ownership and public use (UN-Habitat 2015).[1] More recently, in 2015, United Nations (UN) Sustainable Development Goal (SDG) 11, Target 11.7, stated that public space is "the built-up area of cities that is open space for public use for all" (UN 2015).

This chapter and the next complement the above notions by casting a spotlight on the issues associated with a category of public spaces that are not strictly publicly owned or freely accessed. These chapters offer an asset management framework to better plan, fund, and manage public spaces sustainably while providing public benefit. The discussion draws upon global experience showing that access to many public spaces is not free and that for-profit businesses such as street retailers, along with nongovernment nonprofit organizations, are at the heart of many public spaces.

To better understand how public spaces work in complex urban contexts, it is useful to consider the "publicness" of public spaces according to stakeholder groups. Academic research shows that "publicness" can be viewed as a combination of ownership, management, and users (De Magalhães and Trigo 2016; Németh and Schmidt 2011), as detailed below.

Who Owns and Operates Public Spaces?

Ownership and management of public spaces can be combined into three main groups: (a) public ownership and management, (b) private ownership and management, and (c) mixed ownership and management—the latter referring to either public ownership and private management or private ownership and public management (Murray 2010).

Public ownership and management. Public spaces are owned and managed by governments at different levels including the national, regional, and municipal levels. One example is a public square in front of a city hall that is owned and managed by a municipality. Organizationally, this "public" category is relatively simple, given that government is responsible for this type of public space throughout its life cycle and transfer-related costs are negligible. This model, while the most common, does not necessarily mean that it is the most sustainable organizationally and financially, especially when a municipality lacks fiscal and technical capacity. In many low- and middle-income countries, municipalities have very limited budgets and therefore underinvest in managing their assets, including public spaces. A lack of technical capacity in asset management also is a common problem. Many urban local governments in South Asia, for instance, suffer from unclear institutional roles and limited functional and revenue assignments.

In dense urban areas, accessible and well-managed public spaces would make a significant difference in the quality of life. However, overlapping functions and poor coordination among various agencies prevent local governments from effectively delivering municipal services such as local road maintenance, street lighting, public spaces, solid waste management, and community services (World Bank 2018). Municipal and city development functions are also highly fragmented, leading to a lack of coordinated planning and integration at the city level.

Private ownership and management. The second category—privately owned (and managed) public spaces (POPS)—plays a role in many cities. A standard form of POPS is based on special land-use *incentive zoning*. It allows real estate developers, *voluntarily*, to exceed the densities permitted by zoning rules in exchange for creating and managing public spaces. Such spaces can take the form of public plazas, arcades, small parks, atriums, and ground floors of high-rise buildings on their own privately owned sites (Kayden 2000). The benefit to developers is that the financial value of the extra density is greater than the cost of providing the public space. The benefit to the city and its residents is that they obtain new public spaces without using public land or budgetary funding. This instrument is only financially viable in high-density (high-rise or skyscraper) areas. It has been used in Germany, Japan, the Republic of Korea, Singapore, and the United States (box 2.1).

However, POPS have also been the subject of intense debates and critique. A long-standing critique, recently reinforced by urbanist Alain Bertaud, is that the very idea of POPS results from artificial restrictions on land-use density imposed by zoning (Bertaud 2019). Bertaud argues that POPS have dual costs to society: First, the entire urban population incurs various costs from zoning limitations on land-use density (longer commuting distances between homes and jobs, higher housing and office prices, and so on). Second, tenants and owners of properties with POPS pay for the operations and maintenance (O&M) expenses of these presumably "free" public spaces.

Another critique emphasizes that the use of POPS by the public is governed by restrictions drawn up by landowners that are not publicized and are usually enforced by private security companies. As a result, unless landowners volunteer the information on use restrictions (which they typically do not), members of the public have no way of knowing what regulations they are bound to or whether the activities they enjoy as a legal right in other public areas—such as taking photos, holding a political protest, or even simply sitting down on the grass—are permitted, or whether certain activities will cause security guards to make them leave. In Seoul, for example, of the 1,587 POPS across the city, 17 percent were reportedly limiting public access by illegally installing fences, hosting private facilities, and advertising. In 2016, the Land, Infrastructure and Transport Committee of the Republic of Korea's National Assembly criticized this practice as hampering walkability in the city, especially in dense areas where POPS play a critical role in providing resting areas for citizens (Kim 2016). In London, in response to the *Guardian* investigation on POPS (Garrett 2017; *Guardian* 2017; Vasagar 2012), Mayor Sadiq Khan has vowed to publish new guidelines on how these spaces—which include some of the city's most prominent squares and plazas—are governed. The previous administration already negotiated that one of the largest of such spaces, in the new development around Kings Cross, would be transferred to the government.

Some special cases of the application of POPS are worth mentioning. For example, POPS in Singapore are a special case in two regards: First, POPS are highly regulated by the guidelines on urban design, as a tool to regulate the quality of public spaces within private development such as Orchard Road in Singapore (see chapter 15). Second, POPS are *mandatory* for all new commercial development sites and for redevelopment projects in the newly identified Park and Waterbodies Plan areas (URA 2017a). However, the Singapore government's ability to make POPS mandatory is predicated on public ownership of land: although the government of Singapore uses the term "POPS," in fact these public spaces are part of the development conditions imposed on private developers when the government leases land for long-term. Making POPS mandatory for development in countries with private ownership of land (such as Japan or the United States) will be challenging and may not be legally feasible.

Finally, the introduction of POPS will typically face certain challenges. First, they require a special regulation (that is, incentive zoning). Second, this instrument has only been tested, thus far, in high-income countries, and its

BOX 2.1 EXPERIENCES WITH POPS IN NEW YORK CITY

Privately owned public spaces (POPS) emerged in New York City in 1961, when a new zoning resolution, called incentive zoning, was introduced. It allowed developers to exceed the densities permitted by zoning rules in exchange for creating and managing public spaces on their own private developments. For example, for each square meter of a public space created, a developer could build 10 square meters of extra floor space in a building (but not more than 20 percent above the base maximum). The bonus incentive could be applied to other bulk characteristics as well (such as setbacks and height). As a result, 503 POPS (plazas, pedestrian passages, public atriums, small gardens, and so on) were created between 1961 and 2000, adding more than 33 hectares of public spaces to the city. To date, there are more than 530 POPS.

Research has found that although the incentive zoning produced an impressive *quantity* of public spaces, it failed to yield similarly impressive *quality* (41 percent were deemed to be of marginal quality). Further, a significant number of owners illegally privatized their public spaces, partly or fully, by encroaching on the public space with private cafés and restaurants. Owners of POPS can be fined (up to US$4,000) for deviations from the requirements, but a special audit

(box continues next page)

transferability remains to be seen. Finally, POPS have certain prerequisites: (a) a well-functioning private real estate market; (b) base zoning that is transparent and binding for both the government and developers (meaning that if the zoning is approved, development does not require extra development permits); and (c) base zoning that is responsive to signals from the real estate market (meaning zoning provides parameters of land uses that allow landowners to realize a sufficient profit).

In addition to POPS, there are privately owned and used buildings, sometimes called "quasi-public" spaces, that stimulate urban activities such as shopping and dining. For example, restaurants and cafés on the street level are recognized as important to successful public spaces, even if they are run for profit. Private buildings can contribute to enhancing public spaces through urban design (integration of accessible spaces within the public realm, or public art) and greening (such as vertical gardens).

It should also be noted that the incentive zoning deployed to stimulate POPS falls under the definition of land-based financing (Peterson 2008). In this case, government uses its power to regulate land use to increase the land's market value in exchange for a POPS perceived as a public benefit.

Mixed (public and private) ownership and management. The third category refers to publicly owned but privately managed spaces.[2] This category has a wide

BOX 2.1 **EXPERIENCES WITH POPS IN NEW YORK CITY *(Continued)***

in 2017 showed that the two New York City departments responsible for oversight—the Department of Buildings (DOB) and Department of Planning—have not conducted adequate POPS monitoring. In particular, the DOB did not even have a completed, current database of POPS or a monitoring policy.

Notably, public advocates stepped in. Advocates for Privately Owned Public Space (APOPS) was founded in 2002 to invigorate the stewardship of POPS.[a] APOPS led the development of a complete inventory and created an interactive electronic map of POPS that are open to the public.[b] This map became a reference point for an effort in London to map public spaces, led by *The Guardian* newspaper in partnership with Greenspace Information for Greater London (GiGL).[c]

Sources: City of New York 2017; Grabar 2012; Kayden 2000.

a. For more information, see "Organizations," Privately Owned Public Space in New York City, on the APOPS website: https://apops.mas.org/about/organizations/.

b. See the "Find a POPS" map, Privately Owned Public Space in New York City, on the APOPS website: https://apops.mas.org/find-a-pops/.

c. See the map of London's privately owned public spaces, created by The Guardian and GiGL (Guardian 2017): https://www.theguardian.com/cities/2017/jul/24/pseudo-public-space-explore-data-what-missing.

variety of forms, including something as simple as a municipality outsourcing street cleaning and maintenance of street greenery to a private contractor. An advanced and relatively rare form is a long-term public-private partnership for operating a public space. For instance, Bryant Park in Manhattan is managed jointly by two nonprofit organizations, to which the city government granted the exclusive right to operate and manage the park and programs held there (Murray 2010). It is estimated that about half of the parks in New York City have private groups involved in some management capacity.

Various driving forces are behind the trend to outsource management of public spaces: First, urban planning practitioners acknowledge that budget constraints are pushing municipalities to transfer management to the private sector, either to reduce costs through competition among contractors or to recover the costs by generating revenues both on-site and off-site. Second, there is apparently a growing interest from stakeholders such as nongovernmental organizations (NGOs) and the real estate industry in engaging in the public-space management process. NGOs want to better represent local needs, while real estate developers are interested in sharing the potential benefits from increased property values related to better-managed public spaces (Martin 2017). In low- and medium-income countries, there are also pilots to train youth groups as voluntary participants specialized in managing public spaces (UN-Habitat 2015).[3]

Who Uses Public Spaces (and When and How)

Understanding the users of public spaces is important to enhance the spaces' accessibility and inclusiveness. Users can be categorized into three groups: public, public with limited access, and private. The first category, the public, denotes all users who can access the public space without conditions such as fees or authorizations; that is, the spaces are "open to all." Given that public users consist of various groups, however, carefully designed public spaces are critical to ensure their "publicness" for many different types of users. In other words, it is important to avoid situations where users can physically "access" the space but cannot "use" it (for example, when a park has no benches). More generally, a well-designed park should attract and accommodate different groups for different purposes such as walking, gathering, picnicking, resting, and just passing through.

The second group of public-space users is the limited-access public group, which applies to spaces that have time limitations on access or require registration, authorization, or a fee to access them. For example, some university

BOX 2.2 CREATING OPEN AND GREEN SPACES IN DENSE URBAN ENVIRONMENTS

Urban Ventilation in Hong Kong SAR (Special Administrative Region), China

The 2002 severe acute respiratory syndrome (SARS) outbreak in China focused global attention on the issue of poor air quality in major cities. The government of Hong Kong SAR, China, responded by developing an air ventilation assessment framework for new development plans to ensure that the massing of new developments is specifically designed to enhance air ventilation at the street level and avoid stagnant pockets of contaminated air (Government of Hong Kong SAR 2018).

Vertical Greenery in Singapore

The Landscaping for Urban Spaces and High-Rises (LUSH) program in Singapore is a government-led incentive scheme (floor area exemptions and bonus floor areas) to encourage private sector development to inject more greenery into the city and replace the greenery taken away when a building is developed or redeveloped. Under the scheme (as further discussed in chapter 15), vertical greenery or green roofs should be well-designed, lushly landscaped, and integrated with the overall building form and design (photo B2.2.1). In assessing such features, the planning authority administering the scheme will assess whether they are externalized such that they are visible to the building users and the public (URA 2017b).

(box continues next page)

libraries have different access rules for their students and the general public. In many cases, a community center in a city hall can be accessed only after registration. Public museums or botanic gardens often have entrance fees. Also falling under this category are public spaces dedicated to use-specific groups. For example, some cities provide designated spaces and programs for women in public buildings such as clubs, community spaces, or recreational activities.

The last category of public-space users denotes those with access to spaces that are mostly privately used as well as owned and managed by private owners. Here, "private" users are people who regularly pay for the benefits of the spaces, such as residents of an apartment building with a private garden or registered members of private golf courses. These spaces do not cater to the general public and do not replace a city's accessible public spaces, but they still offer some benefits to the city as a whole. The city takes advantage of "borrowed scenery" of those private green spaces, which adds to the overall greenery of the city, mitigates heat islands, or enhances urban ventilation. (See box 2.2 for examples of policies that created open and green spaces in

BOX 2.2 **CREATING OPEN AND GREEN SPACES IN DENSE URBAN ENVIRONMENTS *(Continued)***

PHOTO B2.2.1 **Lush Landscaping on a Rooftop of a High-Rise Building on Orchard Road, Singapore**

Source: ©Ken Lee. Further permission required for reuse.
Note: LUSH = Landscaping for Urban Spaces and High-Rises.

dense urban environments.) Notably, some researchers have found that private greenery, such as a private garden of a detached house, improves the livability of surrounding communities, including benefits to mental health and satisfaction (WHO 2016).

It can help to visualize the classification of public spaces according to their degree of "publicness" as defined by the ownership, management, and user groups discussed earlier (figure 2.1).

However, it is important to acknowledge that discussions of public spaces from a "publicness" viewpoint—even using the above three-pronged framework of analysis (ownership, management, and users)—is insufficient when the planning and sustainability of public spaces is under consideration. Other critical dimensions include sources of capital and O&M funding, along with overall governance and oversight. The complete framework is discussed in chapter 3.

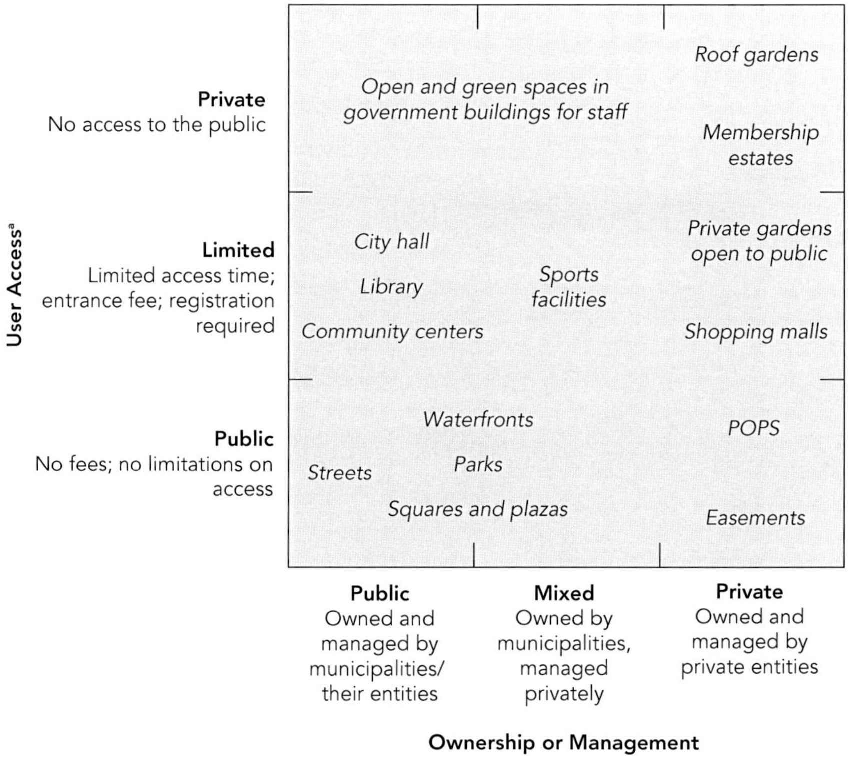

FIGURE 2.1 **Examples of Public Spaces by Ownership, Management, and User Group**

Note: POPS = privately owned public spaces.
a. "Public" refers to spaces without fees or other access limitations. "Limited" refers to spaces that limit access time or require an entrance fee or registration. "Private" refers to spaces not accessible by the general public.

PHYSICAL PUBLIC-SPACE ASSETS: STREETS, OPEN AND GREEN AREAS, AND PUBLIC FACILITIES

Public spaces comprise different physical types: horizontal spaces like roads and pedestrian networks; open green spaces such as squares and parks; and public buildings such as public libraries (UN-Habitat 2015). Each type serves different, often multiple, purposes such as recreational, educational, and commercial activities, as follows:

- *Streets.* Streets are recognized as a key element of connecting and activating urban life. This category includes neighborhood streets, sidewalks, and bicycle paths. Streets provide intracity mobility and support livelihoods and social cohesion in surrounding neighborhoods by accommodating various users such as pedestrians, public transport, vehicle drivers, and street vendors (Gehl 2011; UN-Habitat 2013).
- *Open and green spaces.* "Open green space" is often used as a proxy for public space because it is easy to identify by its physical characteristics, and it is the most visible space for city dwellers. There are different sizes of parks and squares, gardens, and waterfronts. People are walking, running, resting, interacting with others, and enjoying greenery in these spaces. They benefit cities by mitigating densities and improving urban resilience.
- *Public facilities.* Some public facilities are public spaces, given their contribution to facilitating social interaction and civic engagements and providing services to neighborhoods and communities. Such public buildings can include public libraries, community centers, sport facilities, and markets.[4]

These three types can be further disaggregated into more detailed categories of public spaces, and having the detailed classification can be important in developing targeted policies and managing public spaces more efficiently. However, detailed classification of public spaces is surprisingly rare, especially in low-income and some medium-income countries.[5]

NOTES

1. The Charter of Public Space was adopted at the 6th World Urban Forum in Rome in 2012. For details, see UN-Habitat's "World Urban Forum" web page: https://unhabitat.org/wuf.
2. In principle, there is a reverse case as well—when privately owned public spaces are operated by government entities (for example, certain private streets)—but it is rare and not considered here.
3. One of the shortcomings of this voluntary approach is its limited sustainability in the long run. As experienced in the United Kingdom during the 2010s against a backdrop of local budget cuts, the use of volunteers may not guarantee certain amounts or periods of work, and they lack technical expertise as well (Brant 2012).
4. Other public facilities, such as schools, kindergartens, and hospitals, are not "public spaces" in the sense implied in this publication.
5. See chapter 4 for a discussion on innovative ways to acquire data on public spaces for spatial analysis.

REFERENCES

Bertaud, Alain. 2019. *Order without Design: How Markets Shape Cities*. Cambridge, MA: MIT Press.

Brant, Paul. 2012. "Big Society? Legal Wrangles Turn Voluntarism into Big Headache." *The Guardian*, February 6 (accessed October 15, 2018), https://www.theguardian.com/local-government-network/2012/feb/06/big-society-legal-wrangles-voluntarism.

City of New York. 2017. "Audit Report on the City's Oversight over Privately Owned Public Spaces." Audit No. SR16-102A, April 18. Office of the Comptroller, City of New York.

De Magalhães, Claudio, and Sonia Freire Trigo. 2016. "Contracting Out Publicness: The Private Management of the Urban Public Realm and its Implications." *Progress in Planning* 115: 1–28.

Garrett, Bradley L. 2017. "These Squares Are Our Squares: Be Angry about the Privatisation of Public Space." *The Guardian*, July 25 (accessed April 10, 2019), https://www.theguardian.com/cities/2017/jul/25/squares-angry-privatisation-public-space.

Gehl, Jan. 2011. *Life Between Buildings: Using Public Space*. Washington, DC: Island Press.

Government of Hong Kong SAR (Special Administrative Region), China. 2018. "Hong Kong Planning Standards and Guidelines." Technical manual, Planning Department, Government of Hong Kong SAR, China.

Grabar, Henry. 2012. "A Matchmaker for New York's Privately-Owned Public Spaces." *CityLab* (newsletter), October 23 (accessed October 30, 2018), https://www.citylab.com/design/2012/10/matchmaker-new-yorks-privately-owned-public-spaces/3646/.

Guardian. 2017. "Revealed: The Insidious Creep of Pseudo-Public Space in London." *The Guardian*, July 24 (accessed April 10, 2019), https://www.theguardian.com/cities/2017/jul/24/revealed-pseudo-public-space-pops-london-investigation-map.

Kayden, Jerold S. 2000. *Privately Owned Public Space: The New York City Experience*. New York: John Wiley & Sons.

Kim, Gwang-nyeon. 2016. "Severely Privatized Use of Privately Owned Public Spaces in Seoul." *Gukto-Ilbo*, October 11 (accessed May 30, 2018), http://www.ikld.kr/news/articleView.html?idxno=62887.

Martin, David. 2017. "Why Private Investment In Public Space Is the New Normal." *Forbes*, July 30 (accessed October 15, 2018), https://www.forbes.com/sites/dmartin/2017/03/30/why-private-investment-in-public-spaces-is-the-new-normal/.

Mitchell, Don. 2003. *The Right to the City: Social Justice and the Fight for Public Space*. New York: The Guilford Press.

Murray, Michael. 2010. "Private Management of Public Spaces: Nonprofit Organizations and Urban Parks." *Harvard Environmental Law Review* 34 (1): 179–255.

Németh, Jeremy, and Stephen Schmidt. 2011. "The Privatization of Public Space: Modeling and Measuring Publicness." *Environment and Planning B: Planning and Design* 38 (1): 5–23. https://doi.org/10.1068/b36057.

Peterson. George E. 2008. "Unlocking Land Values to Finance Urban Infrastructure: Land-Based Financing Options for Cities." *Gridlines* Note No. 40, World Bank, Washington, DC.

UN (United Nations). 2015. "Transforming Our World: The 2030 Agenda for Sustainable Development." Resolution A/RES/70/1, adopted October 21, 2015, by the UN General Assembly, New York.

UN-Habitat (United Nations Human Settlements Programme). 2013. *Streets as Public Spaces and Drivers of Urban Prosperity*. Nairobi: UN-Habitat.

———. 2015. *Global Public Space Toolkit: From Global Principles to Local Policies and Practice*. Nairobi: UN-Habitat.

URA (Urban Redevelopment Authority). 2017a. "Design Guidelines and Good Practice Guide for Privately Owned Public Spaces (POPS)." Circular to Professional Institutes, Circular No. URA/PB/2017/02-PCUDG, URA, Singapore.

———. 2017b. "Updates to the Landscaping for Urban Spaces and High-Rises (LUSH) Programme: LUSH 3.0." Circular to Professional Institutes, Circular No. URA/PB/2017/06-DCG, URA, Singapore.

Vasagar, Jeevan. 2012. "Privately Owned Public Space: Where Are They and Who Owns Them?" *The Guardian Datablog*, June 11 (accessed April 10, 2019), https://www.theguardian.com/news/datablog/2012/jun/11/privately-owned-public-space-map.

WHO (World Health Organization). 2016. "Urban Green Spaces and Health: A Review of Evidence." European Environment and Health Process Report, WHO Regional Office for Europe, Copenhagen.

World Bank. 2018. *Transforming Karachi into a Livable and Competitive Megacity: A City Diagnostic and Transformation Strategy*. Directions in Development Series. Washington, DC: World Bank.

CHAPTER 3

AN ASSET MANAGEMENT APPROACH TO PLANNING, FUNDING, AND MANAGING PUBLIC SPACES

Olga Kaganova and Jon Kher Kaw

INTRODUCTION

Asset management of municipal physical assets (land, buildings, and infrastructure) can be understood as a process of making and implementing decisions about acquiring or developing these assets and then operating, maintaining, refurbishing, and eventually replacing them cost-effectively. The ultimate objective is to provide the best possible service to local citizens and contribute toward other goals established by the government (Kaganova and Kopanyi 2014).

Public spaces always include at least some physical assets, such as public-use buildings, streets, roads, and open spaces. This definition implies that those involved in planning and establishing public spaces must also consider them, from the outset of the process, from an asset management viewpoint. An asset management approach immediately brings up two important considerations. First, the planning and creation of a public space should include a plan for future operations and maintenance (O&M); in asset management, this principle is known as *life-cycle management.* Although this principle has been recognized for more than 50 years in asset management, the link between creating a public space and maintaining it only came into focus relatively recently. Second, when a public space is created, operated, and maintained with funding from a municipal budget, planning for the space should be properly linked to the municipal budgeting process.

The asset management approach has significant, practical benefits. First, it provides tools for planning and implementing long-lasting, sustainable (financially and organizationally) public spaces. For example, the history of current thriving public spaces such as Central Park, Bryant Park, and the High Line in New York City demonstrates how a park's sustainability can be made possible by the organizational and management arrangements, including funding sources for operations that were carefully considered and established at the time a park was revitalized or created. This contrasts with non–asset management practices, whereby public spaces are created without realistic (or any) stipulations on who will manage these places or on the sources of O&M funding. Second, applying life-cycle costing (a key element of the asset management approach) can minimize the overall expenses from public budgets without sacrificing the quality of public spaces—in some cases, even improving those spaces (as discussed in box 3.4).

This chapter starts with a summary of the asset management approach and then presents the overall framework for considering public spaces from an asset management viewpoint. It concludes with step-by-step guidance on applying this framework to the practical planning, creation, and management of public spaces. The guidance first addresses the case where a government entity is the owner and administrator of a land site or building that is slated for development into a new or improved public space, then considers privately owned public spaces (POPS), which, as covered in chapter 2, are a distinct—and apparently growing—approach to delivering public spaces.

Launching a public-space project is a complex, multifaceted process that requires multiple interactions between the involved parties and often multiple iterations of some steps within the process. The entire process combines multiple activities, some within the realm of asset management, some outside of it. While this guide mentions most of the critical elements of the process, it mainly focuses on the elements directly related to asset management. The guide also addresses principal issues of managing public spaces and comments on the difficult issue of disposing of public spaces.

A FRAMEWORK FOR PLACING PUBLIC SPACES WITHIN AN ASSET MANAGEMENT CONTEXT

An Asset Management Approach and Good Practices

The key elements of a common asset management framework are depicted in figure 3.1. In particular, the figure identifies elements of the broader context in which AM takes place; lists the key components of good asset management practices; and shows the four main stages of an asset's life cycle, from planning to disposal.

This approach is fully applicable to all public-space assets. The city of Adelaide, Australia, illustrates one type of strategic plan for managing urban parks and open spaces (box 3.1). This case also conveys an important lesson: a strategic asset management plan might not cover all assets at once (for example, not all park trees are included in the current Adelaide plan).

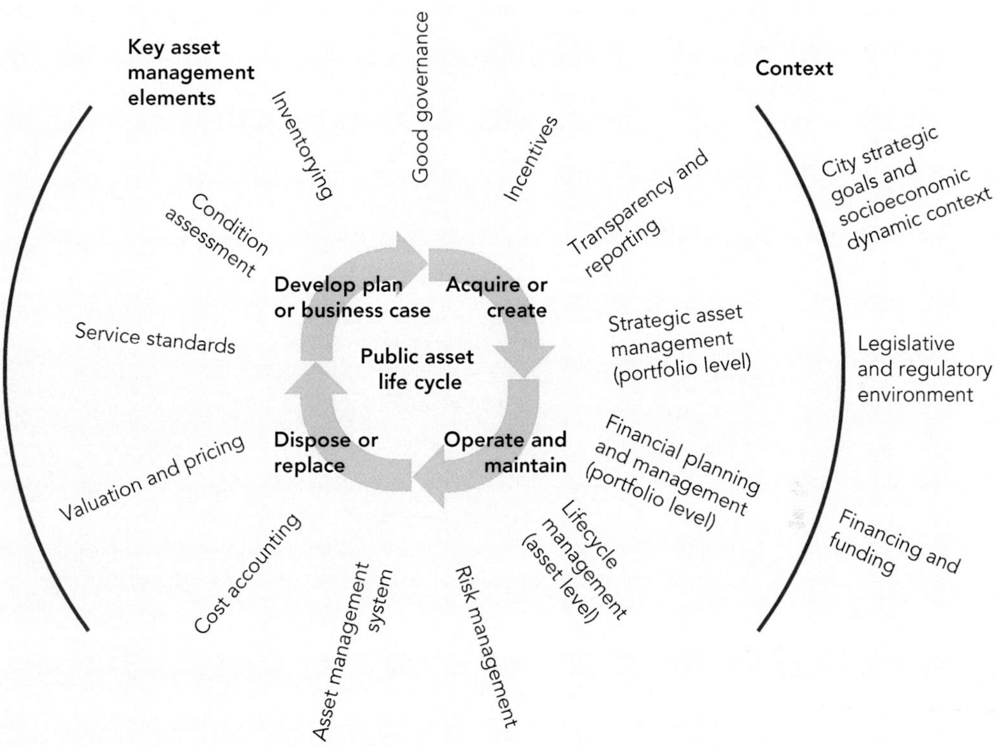

FIGURE 3.1 **Key Elements and Context of an Asset Management Framework**

Source: ©World Bank. Further permission required for reuse.
Note: The figure reflects international good practices aligned with ISO 55000, the International Organization for Standardization (ISO) standard, "Asset Management—Overview, Principles, and Terminology."

How Public-Space Asset Management Differs from Other Public Assets

However, asset management of public spaces—and their life-cycle management in particular—has some specifics, complexities, and unknowns that differ from asset management of other public assets. First, the possession of thorough asset information on public spaces (such as inventory data by asset type, condition, and spatial distribution) would aid in the prioritization of new public-space creation as well as in their management. However, detailed spatial inventories of public spaces are rare, especially in low-and medium-income countries (chapter 4 discusses the importance of data, indicators, and evidence-based planning).

Much has to be done by governments to improve data and information on public space assets—in particular, making sure that the data and information satisfy the varying needs of multiple stakeholders. In some cases, advocacy groups and nonprofit organizations can help collate some of the information needed for public-place users. For example, the nonprofit Hong Kong Public Space Initiative maintains a searchable and publicly accessible spatial inventory of government-managed, privately owned public spaces in Hong Kong. The inventory specifies the name, type of public space, and the responsible management entity.[1]

BOX 3.1 ADELAIDE, AUSTRALIA: PARK LANDS AND OPEN SPACE ASSET MANAGEMENT PLAN, 2016–20

Inventory, Condition, and Valuation of Assets

Adelaide's park lands and open space network comprises 5,728 street trees and approximately 200,000 park trees. (However, only 20,232 park trees are included in this asset management plan and valued for it.) Other assets include irrigation systems (200 hectares), turf, garden beds, major medians, pocket parks, and ornamental lakes and water features (not included in this version of the plan). The plan does not include playgrounds, barbecues, furniture, paths, and lighting.

These infrastructure assets have an estimated replacement value of $A 44.17 million. The dominant condition rating of the assets is average. The plan notes that horticultural assets do not depreciate in the normal sense because they appreciate before they depreciate.

Costs and Funding

The projected outlays necessary to provide the services covered by the asset management plan include operations, maintenance, renewal, and upgrade of existing assets. Over the 10-year planning period, this cost amounts to $A 12.81 million on average per year.

Estimated available funding, based on the city's 2014–15 Long Term Financial Plan (LTFP), was $A 10.34 million on average per year, or 81 percent of the cost to provide the service, with a funding shortfall of $A 2.47 million on average per year. The City Council committed to resolve this issue and fully fund asset management, which was to be reflected in the next revision of the asset management plan.

Risk Management

The major risks associated with providing the service but being unable to complete all identified activities and projects include the following: not meeting community expectations for services; reduction in asset condition and service levels (requiring excessive

(box continues next page)

However, this information alone is not sufficient for managers of public places who need various technical and financial data (such as size; condition of trees, drainage, pavement, and the like; past and current O&M expenses; and so on). Toward this goal, technology is changing the ease of collecting data on public spaces. The World Bank has worked with the European Space Agency (ESA) on piloting a rule-based identification system for public spaces through a combination of satellite imagery, open spatial data such as OpenStreetMap, and GIS (geographic information system) analysis of physical characteristics using six criteria: distance to roads, proximity to

BOX 3.1 **ADELAIDE, AUSTRALIA: PARK LANDS AND OPEN SPACE ASSET MANAGEMENT PLAN, 2016–20 *(Continued)***

investment in later years); increased service standards generated by the Adelaide Design Manual but not fully known and currently unfunded; and structural tree failure.

The asset management plan stipulates that these risks will be managed within available funding by (a) reviewing the asset management plan upon balancing the LTFP with service levels; (b) conducting condition inspections; (c) undertaking pilot projects incorporating Adelaide Design Manual materials to assess cost impacts; and (d) prioritizing resources.

Next Steps

Results from the asset management plan should include

- Better alignment of the plan with the City Council's Strategic Plan 2016–20;
- Identification of opportunities to coordinate infrastructure renewals with enhancement projects (such as greening and smart initiatives);
- Understanding of the increased capital and maintenance costs of extending greening to new areas of the city as part of this plan;
- Review and improvement of available asset-related data; and
- Advancement of asset management systems and balancing of available funding against service levels.

The asset management plan further discusses such issues as why a funding shortfall happened in the city's Park Lands and Open Space network; which options asset managers have; and what would happen if the shortfall is not managed.

Source: City of Adelaide 2017.

water, compactness, land-cover pattern, location, and size.[2] More-detailed methodologies and their application in five city case studies are described in Part II, "Shaping the Public Realm: Data and Spatial Analysis."

A second way in which asset management of public spaces differs from asset management of other public assets is that common metrics to measure the quality of public spaces are not yet well established, although they would provide useful guidance for public-space designers and managers. Visitor satisfaction surveys are one possible instrument to measure quality. Another measure, developed by the United Nations Human Settlements Programme

(UN-Habitat), consists of a set of indicators to capture how public spaces perform in terms of safety, accessibility, inclusiveness, and distribution (see chapter 6). One particular auxiliary instrument that may help design public places to better fit citizens' needs is the Public Life Data Protocol, which the Gehl Institute developed in collaboration with the City of Copenhagen and the City and County of San Francisco (Gehl Institute 2017). This protocol is a data specification that measures what people do in public spaces and adds to the understanding of public life in public spaces.

Third, there is the issue of acquiring land for public spaces if the government lacks its own land for them. In this case, the land should be acquired from private owners, which brings up the potentially contentious issue of acquisition methods. In particular, obtaining land through involuntary transactions, using the government's power of eminent domain (expropriation), is usually politically unpopular and often leads to court appeals over the amount of compensation or how the government uses the expropriated land. Typically, "public uses" that have historically been associated with expropriation include roads, government buildings, and public infrastructure facilities. Expropriating urban land for public parks is less common, and the precedents for this are limited. It therefore remains unknown how acceptable this might be politically.

BOX 3.2 LAND-BASED FINANCING ASSOCIATED WITH CREATION OF PUBLIC SPACES

Land Readjustment

Land readjustment is a financing approach commonly used in East Asian countries, such as Japan and the Republic of Korea. It has also been used in Germany to assemble privately owned land at the peri-urban fringe, and in India to assemble rural land for urban development. Within a demarcated area, privately owned land parcels are pooled together, and land is replanned and reparceled, which includes allocating a certain amount of land for public infrastructure and services (such as roads and public spaces) and also reserving some parcels for auctioning on the market to recover costs (figure B3.2.1). After the plan and trunk[a] infrastructure are developed, the government returns to each landowner a land parcel proportional to its original parcel but smaller (for instance, 50–60 percent of the original land parcel). The returned land parcel is of a higher value because it is now on serviced urban land.

A key benefit from land readjustment is that the government does not require a massive up-front investment to acquire land from the owners. Land readjustment instruments, however, require strong local institutions and a sound legislative framework to be implemented effectively. Another key challenge is obtaining the consent of all existing landowners to join the land readjustment scheme. Land readjustment also involves valuation of the land, on which it may be difficult to reach a consensus between the government and the landowners.

(box continues next page)

In this regard, urban planners must be conscious about land ownership when they create various spatial plans (master plans, detailed development plans, and so on). In particular, they need to know which land is government-owned and available, to the extent feasible and justified, for public facilities including public spaces. Moreover, it would be critical for urban planners to estimate public costs associated with implementation of their plans, and these estimates must include the cost of land assembly when such is required. Requirements of this kind exist in some countries, such as Poland.

Notably, for areas slated for large new private development or substantial redevelopment, several types of instruments can be used to secure land for public spaces: (a) developers' exactions; (b) land readjustment schemes (which aim to make land suitable for development and generate revenues for local infrastructure); and (c) instruments such as tax-increment financing (TIF) and transit-oriented development (TOD). The applicability of these instruments to the creation of public-space assets is described in box 3.2. Another instrument for delivering public spaces without government-owned land is POPS, as discussed in chapter 2.

Moreover, there are enormous opportunities for creating vibrant public-spaces by repurposing old public infrastructure. Some cities have

BOX 3.2 LAND-BASED FINANCING ASSOCIATED WITH CREATION OF PUBLIC SPACES *(Continued)*

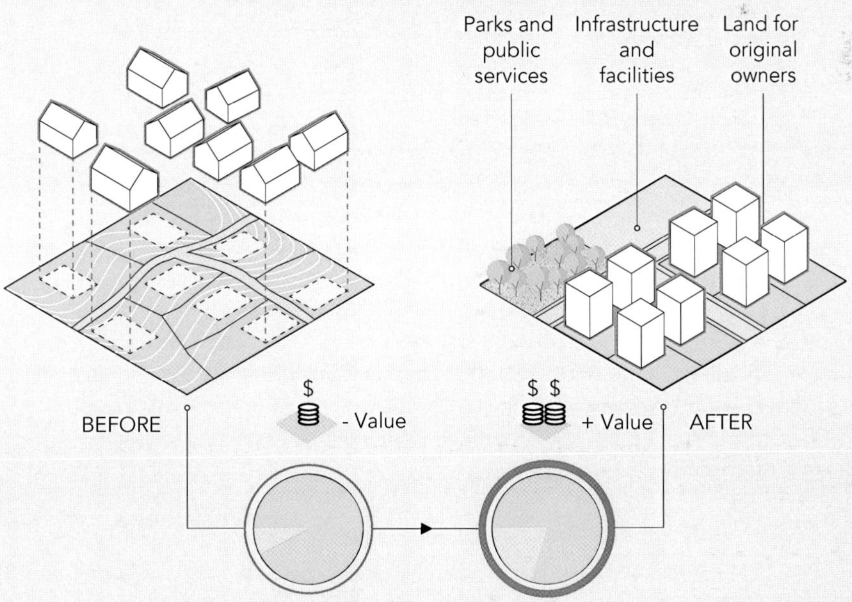

FIGURE B3.2.1 **Model of Land Readjustment for Public Spaces and Infrastructure**

Source: ©World Bank. Further permission required for reuse.

a. Trunk infrastructure typically refers to infrastructure that serves several developments in an area—for example, arterial roads that connect different destinations within a city.

(box continues next page)

BOX 3.2 LAND-BASED FINANCING ASSOCIATED WITH CREATION OF PUBLIC SPACES *(Continued)*

Tax-Increment Financing

Tax-increment financing (TIF) is a financing technique that U.S. municipalities have used to fund projects focused on urban regeneration. It is designed to exploit the rise in market value of real estate and associated increase in tax receipts that accompanies successful urban redevelopment, allowing local governments to invest in public infrastructure and other improvements up front. They do so by borrowing against the anticipated future increase in property tax revenues generated by the project. This financing approach is possible when a municipal bond market exists, when a new development is of a sufficiently large scale, and when its completion is expected to result in a large enough increase in the value of surrounding real estate that the resulting incremental property tax revenues generated by the newly developed properties can support a bond issuance.

TIF bonds have been used to fund basic services upgrades, environmental remediation, and the construction of public spaces such as parks and roads, which not only provide required infrastructure services but also are critical in creating real estate value. This instrument can be potentially applicable only in countries with developed municipal bond markets and well-established ad valorem property taxation.

Transit-Oriented Development

Transit-oriented development (TOD) revolves around the creation of compact, walkable, pedestrian-oriented, mixed-use communities centered around high-quality transit systems. TOD approaches generate synergies between public investment in infrastructure and the ensuing private investment in commercial development at and around transportation nodes. In TOD projects, urban planners and local authorities usually set higher floor-area ratios (FARs) surrounding these nodes to allow for densification and to generate revenue streams that they can capture to finance infrastructure and public spaces. Such an approach has an impact on both land values and compactness.

(box continues next page)

created innovative platforms to do so, such as open calls for ideas or design competitions. For example, the City of Paris, led by the mayor, has launched a "Reinventing Paris" competition to invite designers to come up with sustainable public uses for a list of subterranean and disinvested infrastructure sites owned by the city or its transit authority, such as tunnels, garages, parking lots, and substations. Pro-pedestrian, pro-bike policies have notably

BOX 3.2 LAND-BASED FINANCING ASSOCIATED WITH CREATION OF PUBLIC SPACES *(Continued)*

Example: Transforming the Commercial Center of Ahmedabad, India

Ahmedabad's central business district (CBD) is set to change with an ambitious local area plan drafted by the Ahmedabad Urban Redevelopment Authority (AUDA). Today, the CBD is a fragmented stretch of mostly small-scale buildings. The current FAR in some areas is a mere 1.0, and the area is often choked with traffic, impeding pedestrian movement. Highly restrictive building bylaws have led to the scattering of new commercial and residential buildings across the city (figure B3.2.2a).

The plan proposes to transform the CBD by leveraging its connectivity to a proposed Metrorail system and its location along the waterfront by allowing the FAR to increase from 1.8 to 5.4 and quadrupling the population from 85,000 to 357,000 in the long run. The increase in density is also envisaged as accompanied by a doubling of the street network coverage and green cover (figure B3.2.2b). The plan is designed to work with, rather than against, market forces to realize public objectives.

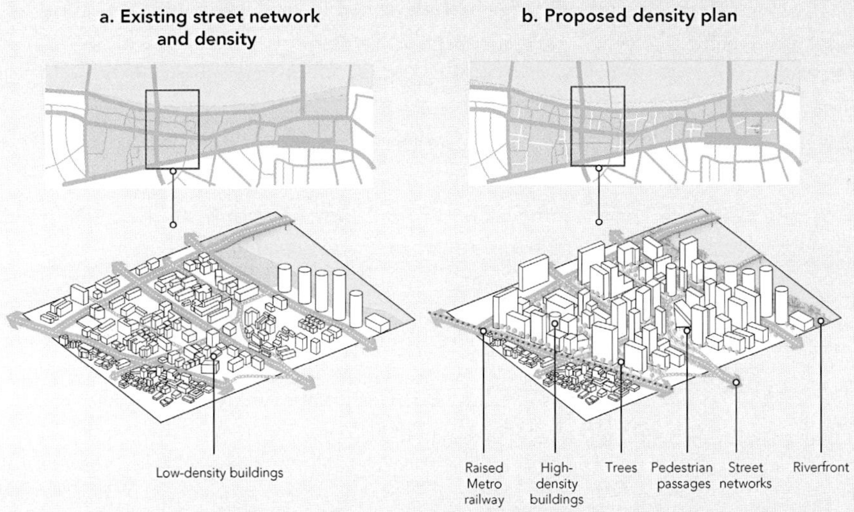

FIGURE B3.2.2 **Planning for the Central Business District, Ahmedabad, India**

Source: ©World Bank. Further permission required for reuse.

increased the number of such spaces through pedestrianization of the Seine quays, closure of some tunnels, and a steady phaseout of access for more heavily polluting cars, which made parking less of a priority.[3]

Similarly, Singapore's national planning agency and land authority have teamed up to launch a public call for innovative, bold, and sensitive proposals to test new uses and ideas for selected state-owned properties and land. These sites include historic shophouse units (a building typology comprising living and business uses), stand-alone buildings, utility infrastructure, and open spaces. This call for proposals targets business owners, architects, designers, and developers to reimagine how to regenerate these assets into vibrant places with new interim uses. The proposals must consider the design and implementation, operation, and maintenance of the sites for the duration of their tenure (URA 2019).

Last but not least, the disposition and rezoning of common public spaces for other uses can be much more controversial than disposition of other public assets. This stems from the high value that some public groups and communities associate with parks and public spaces, and an unwillingness to sacrifice them, even if for other legitimate and publicly supported purposes. This challenge is illustrated by the controversies over parks in Stuttgart, Germany (box 3.3), and Tbilisi, Georgia (see chapter 16). Another peculiarity of parks is that the notion of disposition or replacement due to the end of useful life is less applicable to them than to other assets such as buildings or facilities. Parks usually do not have a clear-cut end of life cycle (like buildings have); instead, parks are subject to changes such as the gradual replacement of trees or the reconstruction of infrastructure (drainage and so on).

An increasing trend in cities is the integration of public spaces as part of infrastructure or as part of developments where the function of open parks is preserved. At the same time, when old public places need reconstruction, this offers great opportunity for urban renewal and rejuvenation. Part III ("Sustaining the Public-Space Life Cycle: Lessons from Cities") documents several cases of such transformation.

A Detailed Framework for Applying the Asset Management Approach to Public Spaces

Cases of successful asset management of public spaces indicate that although the life-cycle approach and elements of good asset management (shown

BOX 3.3 STUTTGART 21, GERMANY: CONTROVERSY OVER A PUBLIC PARK

A park in Stuttgart, along with parts of a historic railway station building, were slotted for demolition and redevelopment into commercial mixed-use real estate, as a way to defray some of the cost of modernizing segments of the old railway system and building a high-speed track and tunnel for the high-speed Magistrale for Europe (Paris–Vienna). In the mid-2000s, the project, named Stuttgart 21, went through all of the proper public consultations and was approved. However, in 2008 when the government scheduled the demolition, regular protests and demonstrations began.

Throughout the escalating confrontation, the Stuttgart government and the state government of Baden-Württemberg maintained that the law was on their side, because the project had been properly discussed and approved, and they claimed that the rule of law should

(box continues next page)

earlier in figure 3.1) constitute an intrinsically useful framework, specific good-governance elements must be built into the life cycle as a foundation for success. In particular, good governance includes six key elements that must be considered when any public space is planned, created, and operated according to its life cycle (table 3.1):

- *Regulatory provisions*
- *Ownership*, including the institutional arrangements for creating or acquiring public space assets
- *Sources of capital investment*
- *Management arrangements*—that is, assignment of responsibility for managing the public space, including O&M responsibilities
- *Source(s) of O&M funding*
- *Oversight arrangements*

The second column of table 3.1 presents potential instruments and entities related to each element.

As table 3.1 indicates, each key governance element can be implemented, in principle, through several channels. Such channels, in turn, can either be mutually exclusive or may coexist. For example, ownership typically involves only a single option: either government or a private entity owns the capital assets that host a public space. In contrast, O&M funding is often assembled from several sources (for example, a government budget, fees from services on a public-space site, and labor of local residents). When all six elements of governance are combined, there is a plethora of possible combinations of instruments to use—and this reflects the diversity of how public spaces are governed in reality. Some common combinations are detailed later in this chapter.

BOX 3.3 STUTTGART 21, GERMANY: CONTROVERSY OVER A PUBLIC PARK *(Continued)*

prevail even for unpopular projects. On the eve of the demolition, about 100 people were injured in a public protest.

At least partly because of this confrontation and controversy, the ruling party lost to the Green Party in the next municipal elections, and in the state elections a member of the Greens became a premier for the first time in history. However, the statewide referendum in 2011 upheld the majority support for the Stuttgart 21 project, and the demolition and construction proceeded as planned. This case highlights the political risks associated with repurposing a public space.

Sources: Hustwit 2011; Kaganova 2012.

TABLE 3.1 **Elements of Good Governance during the Public-Space Life Cycle**

Governance element	Instruments or entities involved
Stage 1: Conceptualizing, engaging, and planning	
Required regulatory instruments	• Policies (implicit or explicit, in writing) • Government laws, resolutions, and the like • Contracts (leases, concessions, other PPP contracts, management contracts, O&M contracts, and so on) • Informal agreements
Stage 2: Implementing and creating	
Ownership of assets and implementation arrangements for acquisition or creation	• Public: Government department • Public: Government nonprofit corporation • Private: For-profit company • Private: Not-for-profit organization
Source of funding for capital expenses	• Government (usually municipal) • Private company • Private donations • International donor
Stage 3: Operations and maintenance (O&M)	
Organizational arrangements for O&M	• Public: Government department • Public: Government nonprofit corporation • Public: Government for-profit company • Private: For-profit company (managing its own public spaces or under a contract with government as owner) • Private: Not-for-profit organization (including charitable organizations) • Private: Informally organized community group
Source of funding for O&M	• Owner budget • Private donations • Fees for services on a public-space site • Earmarked revenues from off-site sources (for example, a fee imposed on business owners in a business improvement district or a cross-subsidy from revenues generated by commercial properties controlled by a PS manager) • Crowdsourcing (for temporary public spaces) • In-kind contributions (such as labor) by PS users and volunteers
Oversight and accountability mechanisms[a]	• Government department (including an audit entity) • Private not-for-profit organization • Citizens and citizens' groups • The media • Reporting

Sources: Authors building on City of New York 2017; De Magalhães and Trigo 2016; Grabar 2012; Guardian 2017; and Kayden 2000.
Note: The last life-cycle stage, disposal, is not included because such events are rare. PPP = public-private partnership. PS = public-space.
a. Oversight should take place during both Stage 2 and Stage 3.

From an implementation viewpoint, it is important to recognize the local limitations on which options can be realistically deployed in a particular country or city. For example, in cities with serious budget constraints, funding O&M expenses for public spaces solely from the local budget would be problematic. Or, if a culture of philanthropy is not yet vibrant in a particular country, it might be unrealistic to expect that private donations will fund or cofund capital or O&M expenses. Similarly, management arrangements that rely on a sophisticated contract between a local government and a nongovernment manager of a public space can fail in a country or city that lacks a history of observing and enforcing contracts. To put it more generally, a critical issue is the *transferability* of specific public-space policies and instruments from one country or city to another.

How should one proceed in applying the above framework? What are useful considerations in choosing instruments from the multiple options that the framework presents (table 3.1)? A good start is familiarizing oneself with the local policy and regulatory background for public spaces, including past experiences. It is also important to realize that in the complex reality of municipal governance, it is impossible to isolate asset management issues from many other policy issues, such as the relevant forms of public participation in the planning process or the state of the municipal budget. Therefore, launching a successful public space that is sustainable (organizationally and financially) is a complex task that is interlinked with many other processes. The subsections below outline the key elements of the process of planning and launching a public space.

As mentioned in chapter 2 and in table 3.1, there are two distinctly different "channels" for delivering public spaces, both within the above framework: The first, more traditional way is for public spaces to be located on government-owned land and properties. The other is for public spaces to be located on private land or property, hence being POPS. These "channels" complement one other, and the introduction of POPS does not replace traditional public spaces. Indeed, POPS typically are voluntary for real estate developers to create, and they are usually only financially viable as part of high-density commercial properties (for example, skyscrapers). Meanwhile, public spaces are needed throughout the entire city, and it remains the government's responsibility to ensure that they are delivered.

Introduction of POPS, along with other forms of private participation in public spaces, reflects (a) a pragmatic recognition that governments lack sufficient financial resources, and (b) a deeper paradigm shift about the roles of various actors in urban societies. In this case, the shift is from governments being solely responsible for providing and maintaining public spaces to broader approaches that make communities and the private sector active contributors as well.

Linkage to Planning Tools and Development Policies

As table 3.1 indicates, governance of public spaces is based on underlying policies, explicit or implicit. "Policy" can be defined as a statement of a current or intended practice, with the implication that this practice is regular. Local government policies on public spaces typically adhere to two main forms: (a) the policies themselves, which often do not specify who (that is, the public or private sector) will deliver public spaces; and (b) mandatory regulatory instruments, usually targeted at private sector stakeholders in public spaces. For example, the policy could take the form of a mayor's or governor's written declaration, or it could simply be an executive program (supplemented by an action plan and funding for implementation), as in these examples:

- *Former London Mayor Boris Johnson* issued "A Manifesto for Public Space: London's Great Outdoors," securing compliance through administrative channels and budget allocations (Johnson 2009).
- *Paris Mayor Anne Hidalgo* launched a campaign and allocated some funding to reclaim seven popular squares in Paris for pedestrians (UCLG 2016).
- *Former Jakarta Governor Basuki "Ahok" Tjahaja Purnama* launched a campaign to create child-friendly public spaces in high-density districts. By February 2017, 188 such places had been inaugurated, with 123 built by a private contractor (using US$11.4 million from the city's 2016 budget) and another 65 delivered by private companies as a part of their corporate social responsibility schemes (Anya 2017).

Mandatory (that is, legally binding) regulatory instruments related to public spaces always reflect a specific policy, even if this policy was not formally articulated before issuing the regulation. Examples of regulatory instruments that express implicit public policies related to creating or managing public spaces include exactions or impact fees, incentive zoning, and case-specific local laws.

Exactions or impact fees. Exactions are in-kind contributions of public spaces (streets and so on) by developers. Thus, developers of large tracts of land may be required to build roads in (or leading up to) their developments, and then they must relinquish ownership of these roads (and the land they are on) to the local government. Developers of single parcels are often required to dedicate a certain percentage of their parcels to open public spaces; in Montgomery County, Maryland (United States), for example, the required percentage is 5 percent.

Impact fees, also called "development fees," are imposed on real estate developers by local governments as part of regular zoning and development or redevelopment approvals (Walters 2012). They are one-time charges to extend public infrastructure to or for the project and can include items such as public spaces. For example, Regatta Park (in the Coconut Grove neighborhood of Miami, Florida) was built by earmarking a portion of such development fees (Martin 2017). These instruments are widely used across the globe (for example, in the Balkan States, Colombia, the Russian Federation, Saudi Arabia, the United States, and other countries). Notably, however, research reveals that these fees drive up the price of housing and other real estate (Walters 2012).

Incentive zoning. Incentive zoning allows developers, voluntarily, to exceed the density limits permitted by standard zoning (such as floor area ratio or other bulk parameters) in exchange for delivering additional public space or amenities on their own sites. This instrument is not without controversies (for example, accusations, in some jurisdictions, of a lack of transparency), but it has been broadly used in various cities in several countries (WBUR 2017), including Chicago, San Francisco, and Montgomery Country (Maryland), in the United States; Toronto and Vancouver in Canada; Stuttgart, Germany; Tokyo, Japan; and Seoul, Republic of Korea.

Special case-specific local laws. For example, the Hudson River Park Act, a New York State law issued in 1998, established the four-mile-long Hudson River Park in New York City and its accompanying requirements. The park was established in conjunction with the Hudson River Park Trust (HRPT), a public benefit corporation that created a partnership between the city and the state, which was charged with the park's design, construction, and operation. The HRPT operates on the premise of financial self-sufficiency, supporting the staff as well as the O&M of the park through income generated within the park area by rents from commercial tenants, fees on concession revenues, grants, and donations. Donations are generated through the Hudson River Park Friends, an independent nonprofit organization designated as a fundraising partner of the HRPT. Capital funding has historically come primarily from the state and New York City as well as federal budget appropriations.

In low- and middle-income countries, policies on public spaces found in the literature are either highly controversial—such as attempts to regulate street vendors in Bangkok, Thailand (Batréau and Bonnet 2016)—or simply consist of high-level declarations on how such policies should connect with other urban issues such as social policies, governance and participation, the natural environment, and so on (UCLG 2016).

APPLYING THE ASSET MANAGEMENT FRAMEWORK TO PUBLICLY OWNED PUBLIC SPACES

Stage 1: Conceptualization, Engagement, and Planning

Stage 1 starts with preliminary research on the policy and regulatory environment and on experiences with public spaces in the city. Is there a formal policy on public spaces? If not, is there a political will or interest in the subject? What is the legal and regulatory environment for public spaces and the particular instruments that might be potentially deployed? For example, is there a law on business improvement districts (BIDs)?[4] Are the necessary regulations in place to use POPS? What methods are currently used to enforce service or lease contracts between local governments and private companies?

Further, if there were past attempts to create and maintain public spaces in the city, what are the lessons learned? This investigation will inform decision makers about instruments that have worked in the past and help them avoid any mistakes made in those cases.

In general, this exercise will help to clarify which public-space instruments and approaches can be realistically launched within the available timeline and resources, and which ones may need to be postponed. For example, if there is no BID law, are there resources and time to pursue its development and passage through legislative channels, along with the needed bylaws? Similarly, if zoning rules for incentivizing POPS do not exist, are the time and resources available to (a) conduct research on how relevant and feasible POPS would be for the city, and (b) assess what would be required to establish this instrument within the country's land-use planning system—including moving the necessary reforms through the relevant legislative and regulatory authorities?

Finally, where a citywide inventory of public spaces does not yet exist, the conceptualization and planning of particular public spaces may proceed on an ad hoc basis while the inventory records are being designed and populated. However, siting decisions need to be aligned with existing or to-be-modified spatial development plans, which ideally would cover a citywide network of public spaces. (For an example—Singapore's Park Connector Network—see chapter 15.) Siting plans for public spaces can be made with active public engagement, through participatory planning. Locations for smaller public spaces can be identified through citizens' initiatives that rely on the knowledge of local communities.

Further activities can be split into several steps.

Step 1: Identify and Conceptualize Potential Public Spaces

Scoping is required in the initial stages of identifying and conceptualizing potential public spaces. One would consider at least five groups of questions here:

- *What are the potential locations (sites or buildings)?* How do these potential public spaces relate to area development plans, if any, and what are the future development plans for the area? As already discussed and further demonstrated in Part II ("Shaping the Public Realm: Data and Spatial Analysis"), familiarity with formal spatial development plans is useful here.
- *What are the problems or issues that these locations or properties present?* Are these issues localized (such as traffic congestion), or do they relate to the broader city (for example, drainage and solid waste management)?
- *How would potential public spaces address or ease these problems or issues?*
- *What are the key physical elements of each that need to be built or renovated—and then operated and maintained?*
- *Who are the key beneficiaries and stakeholders?* Note that beneficiaries and stakeholders are not the same. Beneficiaries are natural persons (people) and legal entities (such as businesses) that will gain directly from public-space implementation (for example, through convenience, safety, pleasure, extra profit, and so on). Stakeholders include those who believe they may lose something if the public space is implemented; they also include remote, indirect beneficiaries, such as a government department whose role would change as a result of the public-space implementation.

Preliminarily discussing ideas with potential stakeholders is recommended—for example, with heads of neighborhood organizations or businesses that could be potential providers of services. For example, if considering the improvement of conditions and amenities in an existing public park by outsourcing its management to a private operator, it would be prudent to float this idea within potentially affected neighborhoods and with companies that provide similar services elsewhere. A full-scale public and private sector engagement can come in later stages.

Detailed examples of the issues surrounding the conceptualization of public spaces are also presented in the city case studies in Part III of this publication. Each case study documents the city and neighborhood context and highlights the challenges and opportunities in each project.

Step 2: Secure Administrative and Political Support

Identifying government counterparts or agencies must be treated as a crucial task.[5] Cooperation of the immediate land or building administrator would be required, such as the department of transportation in the case of a street. In addition, support from the higher echelons of local government is needed. Typically, these might include a mayor or deputy mayor in charge of the sector (for example, culture or transportation) and the city council, depending on the local administration and politics.

When seeking the cooperation of relevant government counterparts, four main lines of argument can help obtain such support:

- *Convincing analysis of a well-known problem or issue* that this public space would address and ease (including whether public space also performs an infrastructure purpose such as flood mitigation and the like)
- *Reference to a formal government policy* on public spaces, if one exists (or at least to high-level political support of the concept of public spaces)
- *Outlining other benefits*, for example, establishment of a good working relationship between the city or department and a donor entity
- *Ensuring coordination* across different government agencies managing different sections of the public space (for example, drains, parks, and streets) that are typically siloed. Better coordination and integration of these separately owned and managed spaces can potentially result in better-designed public spaces while also minimizing land consumption and reducing costs (box 3.4).

Step 3: Engage Citizens and Suggest Service Levels

The purpose of citizen engagement is to assemble a representative view of what citizens value in this public asset as well their concerns. At the minimum, surveys may be used to rate the current quality of O&M of the space. They also should identify citizens' priorities for the use of the asset. Results of the survey should later be used to finalize the concept of the public space. For example, if free features or amenities (for example, a playground) were listed as the top priority in the survey, it is advisable to include them in the public space. The survey is also an important instrument to test interest in potential fee-based services.

Various complementary instruments for soliciting public participation can be used as well. There are several approaches to citizen engagement and participatory planning:

- *Government-led exhibitions or public information* to inform and solicit feedback from stakeholders
- *Collaborative use of charrettes or citizen dialogue* to help cocreate public spaces
- *Community- or government-led tactical urbanism and placemaking approaches* that rely on reiterative interventions to shape public spaces, an important result of which is an initial outline of services and their levels.

BOX 3.4 ENHANCING ASSET MANAGEMENT EFFICIENCY THROUGH SUSTAINABLE DEVELOPMENT

Green infrastructure such as rooftop solar panels, green roofs, bioswales, permeable pavement, water harvesting, and other stormwater management practices can produce long-term savings or, in some cases, revenue streams that can create value for cities and neighborhoods.

Savings and Returns on Investment

Public-space assets can realize cost savings by using energy-efficient building practices. For example, green roofs and natural ventilation keep buildings cooler in tropical climates and reduce the need for air conditioning, leading to annual cost savings. These savings could then be used for the operations and maintenance (O&M) of these assets.

Projects with these features need to consider potential up-front costs and the payback period before savings can be realized. Notably, the adoption of some technologies is advancing at a pace where solutions such as rooftop photovoltaics (PV) are reaching or have reached grid parity, so that some countries can realize operational savings immediately.[a] In high-income economies, power purchase agreements provide investors with rights to the revenue produced by the solar system in public facilities.

In general, some green infrastructure can return the up-front investment over time in the form of an ongoing revenue stream. This revenue can supplement funding for public-space maintenance over the long term.

Dhaka, Bangladesh: Co-Locating Services and Greening Community Centers

Initiated by the mayor of Dhaka South, the Dhaka South City Corporation plans to provide improved services to neighborhood communities through better use of community centers scattered around the city. Today, the

(box continues next page)

Step 4: Forecast Expected Costs, Both Capital and Annual O&M

Cost estimations should be done for each potential public space. At this stage, these are only rough initial estimates, but they are needed to make informed decisions about which potential funders might be able to cover costs. The capital costs should be estimated by an experienced municipal infrastructure engineer, based on the parameters suggested under Step 1. For existing elements that require restoration, the cost will depend on a condition assessment.

BOX 3.4 ENHANCING ASSET MANAGEMENT EFFICIENCY THROUGH SUSTAINABLE DEVELOPMENT *(Continued)*

community centers are typically single-use structures that function as wedding halls (figure B3.4.1, panel a). Under the World Bank-supported Dhaka City Neighborhood Upgrading Project, the city plans to redevelop selected community centers into multistory, multiuse public facilities that can accommodate a variety of functions such as public toilets, sports facilities, classrooms, and health centers (figure B3.4.1, panel b).

The co-location of services will maximize the use of these buildings in a city with limited land. There are plans to also integrate the use of green building approaches and improve resource efficiency through use of renewable energy (for example, solar panels) and rainwater harvesting (figure B3.4.1, panel c).

a. Existing single-use community centers | **b. Proposed multiple-use centers with facilities** | **c. Public facilities integrated with green building solutions**

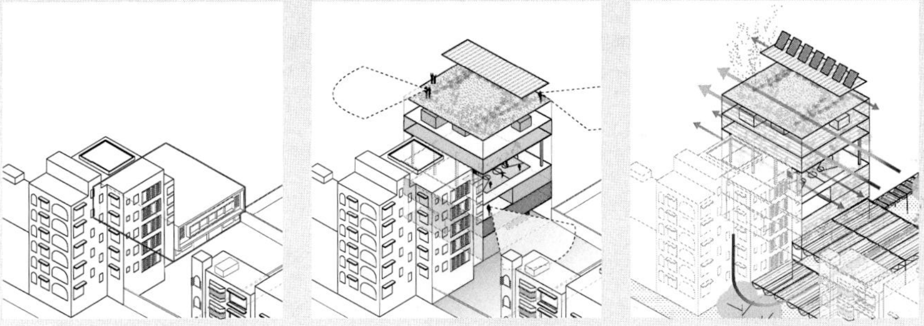

FIGURE B3.4.1 **Proposed Redevelopment of Community Centers in Dhaka, Bangladesh**

Source: ©World Bank. Further permission required for reuse.

a. "Grid parity" refers to a point when an alternative energy source, such as solar energy, can generate power at less than or equal to the price of power from the grid. The term is most commonly used when discussing renewable energy sources, notably solar power and wind power.

At this preplanning stage, annual O&M can be estimated as a simple percentage of the capital cost, using, for example, suggestions from table 3.2. As the table indicates, there are substantial variations in O&M costs, depending on the characteristics of an asset (for example, whether there is heating and air conditioning in a building) and external factors such as climate and topography. Table 3.2 covers traditional public assets and excludes the O&M costs for additional improvements that the private sector could make to generate revenues. For example, if rides are added to park facilities, they will add both capital and O&M costs.

TABLE 3.2 **Initial Estimated O&M Cost for Public Assets, by Type**
Percentage of capital cost

Type	Component	Variables	O&M cost
Public buildings	Structural components, including the roof system and façade	Materials, quality, climate	1.0–1.5
	Electrical	Installed mechanical equipment	0.5–1.0
	Heating, ventilating, and air conditioning (HVAC)	Climate	3–7
	Landscaping, parking	Area, climate, use	0.5–2.0
Parks, recreation, and open space	Baseball or softball fields	Climate, intensity of use, cost of water	5–15
	Soccer fields	Quality, climate, intensity of use	10–15
	Tennis courts	Materials, quality	3–6
	Basketball courts	Materials, quality	2–5
	Swimming pool (outdoor)	Materials, climate, safety standards	15–25
	General park facilities	Assumes an open, actively landscaped parkland with an irrigation system, lighting, trash cans, benches, picnic tables, stationary barbecue units, bike rack, restrooms, drinking fountains, and playground equipment	15–35
Roads and streets	Gravel roadway	Topography, geology, climate, vehicle type, average daily traffic (ADT)	5–10
	Asphalt roadway	Topography, geology, climate, vehicle type, ADT	2–8
	City streets (hard-surfaced)	Topography, geology, climate, vehicle type, ADT	5–10

Source: Windolph 2013.
Note: O&M = operations and maintenance.

Stage 2: Implementing Public Spaces and Funding Capital Expenses

Acquisition or Creation

The public places considered in this section are created on either land that the government already owns (including repurposing of old, government-owned infrastructure and facilities) or land acquired from the private sector. Possible land acquisition instruments include voluntary purchases from private owners; public easements on private land; land swaps; private land donations; dedication of land by developers or owners through developer exactions, land readjustment, and so on as a part of private land development; and expropriation. However, as already discussed, the expropriation of urban land for parks is not a standard action and may turn out to be politically unacceptable. Moreover, the experiences in high-income countries indicate that expropriation is a costlier and slower process than other instruments.

Which particular instrument(s) can be used for land acquisition depends, first of all, on a country's specific regulatory regime. Obviously, using available government-owned land is the simplest solution.

Institutional Arrangements

Determining the appropriate institutional structures is key to the successful delivery of public-space projects. Depending on the projects' need, scale, and complexity, institutional arrangements can take various forms with different levels of authority, accountability, and responsibility. They can range from formal organizational structure to informal committees and can be led by public agencies or the private sector. When implementing public-space projects, institutional coordination should be considered (a) between government agencies, and (b) across governmental agencies, communities, and private stakeholders. These arrangements are implemented either citywide or at the project level.

Government interagency coordination. Even within a single project, the same public space is often managed by several separate government departments that have very different mandates, usually resulting in less-than-optimal design solutions and management arrangements. In contrast, when government departments come together to plan, fund, design, and manage public spaces, they open possibilities of creating more innovative solutions and of better managing public spaces as an integrated space. For example, the conversion of a stormwater concrete canal separating a park and housing estate into a contiguous public space while retaining its flood mitigation function in Singapore required the water and parks agencies to work across demarcated zones to reinvent the public spaces. Streets are also great opportunities for government agencies to come together, work across silos, and rethink how streets can be better designed and managed as complete streets (box 3.5).

At the city level, urban planning should be integrated into interagency coordination to ensure that public spaces are equitably distributed and provided for. Even a master plan that stipulates the creation of public spaces across the city will not alone guarantee that these public spaces are implemented unless institutional capacities and implementation mechanisms are also in place.

Partnership with communities and private stakeholders. Public agencies can have a wide variety of partnerships with nonprofit groups. Nonprofits can help and act as catalysts to initiate and raise funds for public-space projects on a volunteer basis. Engagement of nonprofit groups at the stage when a public space is created often evolves into their participation later as well, during the O&M stage (PPS 2001).

The institutional arrangements between government, community, and private stakeholders will also largely depend on the needs for and purposes of these arrangements, ranging from less formal "steering committees" (comprising public and civil-society representatives to shape the public-space implementation) to legally sophisticated development corporations or BIDs (responsible for investing and creating public spaces as part of area development). Case-study examples of these structures can be found in chapter 8.

Funding Sources

As identified earlier in table 3.1, four potential funding sources are commonly used internationally: government, private companies, private donations, and international donors.

BOX 3.5 TYPICAL DIVISION OF STREET SPACE MANAGEMENT AMONG GOVERNMENT AGENCIES

In general, streets consist of different sections, including vehicle lanes, parking lanes, sidewalks, linear plazas, and street market areas. They are often planned and managed by different public agencies and institutions (figure B3.5.1)—building façades and overflow areas by a planning authority; linear green areas by a park department; vehicle lanes by transport authority and police; sidewalks and street facilities by the public works department; and hygiene conditions of shops by a health department. It should be noted that this is not an exhaustive list of relevant stakeholders, but only an illustrative example. The real-world cases are documented in more detail in Part III ("Sustaining the Public-Space Life Cycle: Lessons from Cities"), including Yonsei-ro in Seoul, Republic of Korea (chapter 14); Las Begonias in Lima, Peru (chapter 12); and Orchard Road in Singapore (chapter 15).

To facilitate optimal use of streets as integrated space, all relevant agencies and departments need to collaborate throughout the life cycle of street assets (NACTO 2016).

(box continues next page)

Government. This would be the easiest source from a legal or regulatory viewpoint, but in reality, municipal governments cannot always cover the entire cost for a couple of reasons. First, municipal governments usually suffer from chronic shortages of capital funding in general. In this regard, the cost of the suggested public space needs to be considered within the process of the city's capital investment planning instead of being promoted separately. A critical question is where this public space stands on the city's priority list of needed capital investments. For example, if a city receives about 2,000 requests for capital funding annually from its departments and typically has been able to satisfy only about 200 each year, the chances for the public space to be funded will depend on its relative cost and how high it is on the priority list. To prepare their case, public-place promoters may want to obtain data from the city on the following:

- How many capital investment projects have been requested, annually, in the past fiscal years?
- How many were budgeted for?
- What was the total capital investment planned or budgeted for those fiscal years? (This is to estimate an average amount per budgeted project for comparison with an estimated cost of the proposed public-space project.)

BOX 3.5 TYPICAL DIVISION OF STREET SPACE MANAGEMENT AMONG GOVERNMENT AGENCIES *(Continued)*

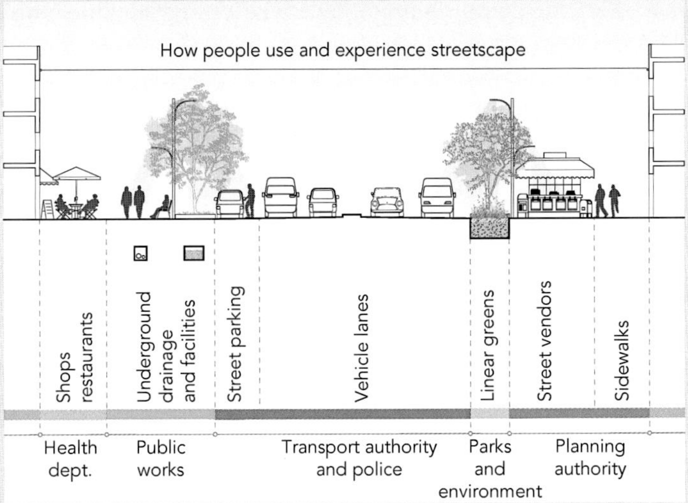

FIGURE B3.5.1 **How People Use and Experience Streetscapes and How Streets Are Managed by Institutional Jurisdictions**

Source: ©World Bank. Further permission required for reuse.

Second, governments are less likely to be sole funders given the clear trend of public spaces becoming joint undertakings between government, the private sector, and the community. The bottom line is that in many cases one may—and should—expect the local government to contribute, but its share may be minor (say, 10 percent of the total capital expenses). In particular, when public spaces are created within territories where special land development or redevelopment projects are implemented (for example, land readjustment, TIF, or TOD), they are funded together with other infrastructure on this territory, through land-based financing instruments. Such instruments are based on the fact that such projects result in an increased land value, and a part of this increase is captured and channeled to fund infrastructure and public spaces through land value capture (LVC) (as discussed earlier in box 3.2).[6]

Private companies. One possibility can be the outsourcing of public-space management to a private company long enough for an investor or operator to recoup capital expenses and turn a profit. This option combines capital investment and O&M of a public space into one arrangement and is, in fact, one of the more typical forms of public-private partnerships (PPPs).

Private donations. Private donations typically take two forms: philanthropy or community in-kind contributions. Philanthropy would not be as common in low- and middle-income countries, but it does exist (see chapter 11 on Eduljee

Dinshaw Road in Karachi). However, with some creativity (for example, exchanging the donation for a "naming right"), this source may be worth considering. Legally, accepting such donations should not be a challenge, because in most countries local governments may accept gifts of money or property.

A community's (that is, the beneficiaries') in-kind contributions usually take the form of labor but also may include materials or loans of machinery. As noted earlier, the "community" of beneficiaries may include both individuals and businesses.

International donors. Donor funding can be an option for some cities. Moreover, there may be more than one donor organization willing to contribute to capital investment in public spaces; therefore, it may be useful to explore multiple avenues. If this option is deployed, an important asset management question is who will *own* the asset or improvements created with the donors' funding—and this applies to any donor's investment in local infrastructure, not only in public spaces. It is assumed that the owner will be the local government. In practice, however, once a conveyance document is signed between the donor and the city and the groundbreaking ceremony is complete, no one typically monitors whether municipal ownership formally takes place. Moreover, in some countries, mayors and municipal accountants are reluctant to place the asset on the municipal balance sheet, because by law they would be personally liable for this added value, which can be substantial compared with other, mainly depreciated, capital assets on the municipal balance sheet.

After considering options for funding capital expenses, one would have some preliminary ideas about which sources can be assembled along with government and private counterparts. Funding may come from a combination of two or three sources—for example, 80 percent from an international donor, 10 percent from the local government (monetary), and 10 percent (in-kind) from the beneficiaries. Or funding may be 100 percent from the private sector, with attractive conditions to recoup the cost and make a profit. However, these ideas would need to be discussed with stakeholders (as further discussed below).

Stage 3: Managing and Funding O&M of Public-Space Projects

These two governance elements—who will manage a public space and how O&M will be funded—should be considered together because they are closely connected. Most importantly, private management of a public space often results in more inventive, intensive use of the public space for revenue generation, with a part of these revenues covering O&M costs.

The management and sources of O&M funding can take on many combinations (table 3.3). Four "base" scenarios are the most common:

- *Scenario 1:* O&M is performed by a local government, funded by a local budget.
- *Scenario 2:* O&M and related fund-raising are entrusted to a community organization.
- *Scenario 3:* O&M is outsourced to a private company that is paid for its services from the local budget.
- *Scenario 4:* Management (including O&M) is outsourced to a private company, along with the right to generate revenues from the public space and an obligation to cover O&M costs.

TABLE 3.3 **Scenarios for Managing and Funding O&M of Government-Owned Public Spaces**

Scenario 1: Local government (or its entity) operates and maintains PS, funded by local budget		**Scenario 2: O&M is entrusted to a community organization, as is raising funding for O&M**		**Scenario 3: O&M is outsourced to a private company that is paid for its services from the local budget**		**Scenario 4: Management (including O&M) is outsourced to a private company, along with the right to generate revenues from the PS and an obligation to cover O&M costs**	
Pros	**Cons**	**Pros**	**Cons**	**Pros**	**Cons**	**Pros**	**Cons**
Traditional: no innovative actions needed	• High risk of PS's declining condition if budget is insufficient—a common case • As a rule, no innovative, diversified or intensified, and demand-driven uses can be expected • No benchmarks for controlling O&M costs	Reduces organizational and financial burden on local government	• High risk of PS's declining condition if the community loses interest or ability to operate and maintain PS • No mechanisms to enforce community compliance	• Expected higher quality of O&M • Expected lower cost, due to competition • Possibility to accumulate data on O&M cost • Adds private sector jobs	• High risk of PS's declining condition if budget is insufficient—a common case • Requires noncorrupt procurement and good-quality contracts • Requires contract monitoring and enforcement	• Expected higher quality of O&M • Removes financial burden on local government • Diversifies services provided at PS • Adds jobs in the private sector	• May require new local bylaws • Requires noncorrupt procurement and good-quality contracts • Requires contract monitoring and enforcement
Example: Specialized public-use buildings, such as a library or museum		*Example:* Small neighborhood gardens		*Example:* Street cleaning and beautification		*Examples:* Public parks; repurposed public-use buildings (for example, a renovated former church converted into a multiuse or time-sharing property)	
Note: May generate small revenues from on-site vendors		*Note:* Not suitable for assets whose operations require technical expertise and skills (for example, a librarian for a library or a plumber for a swimming pool)		Note: It can be useful to keep competitive pressure on service providers by outsourcing to two or three different contractors, each working on different set of public spaces.		*Note:* Often includes initial capital investment by the operator, thus becoming a PPP. May combine government and public use of property through time-sharing.	

Source: World Bank.
Note: O&M = operations and maintenance. PPP = public-private partnership. PS = public space.

Table 3.3 presents the pros and cons for each scenario, along with examples. In general, Scenarios 3 and 4 (related to outsourcing O&M or management of a public space to the private operator) are more complex to launch and monitor, but they promise better returns in terms of the quality and diversity of services, as well as lower or no O&M expenses from the public budget. In addition, outsourcing O&M to the private sector under Scenario 3 helps determine the true cost of these services and sets some benchmarks for municipal governments.[7] Hybrids of the base scenarios are also possible. For example, in a combination of Scenarios 1 and 2, the local government and the community can share O&M expenses.

However, Scenarios 3 and 4 require reasonably established systems of public procurement as well as well-established use and enforcement of written contracts in the public sector. Moreover, preparations under Scenario 4, as for any PPP, are expensive and require specialized expertise. Given the relatively small scale of capital investment associated with a single public space, this up-front cost is often not justifiable—unless the process can be standardized and a specialized entity established to launch such public spaces citywide or for several cities, thus reducing the initial cost.

There is no standardized method to determine which scenario to pursue, given that many factors can contribute to decision making, including, to a large extent, the political climate of the day. Nevertheless, each scenario that appears to have potential can be subjected to "reality checks" to further inform decision making by stakeholders and eventually zero in on the most promising scenario. In particular, the due diligence and prefeasibility studies discussed below for each scenario can help rule out some options that are still under consideration.

In addition, table 3.4 shows typical tools used for various sources of O&M funding.

Scenario 1: Local Government Operates and Maintains Public Space, Funded by Local Budget

A key issue for this scenario is the affordability of the O&M expenses for the municipality. One must first estimate what percentage of the city government's annual operating budget these expenses would consume and then objectively assess how realistic it is to expect consistent allocation of the required O&M funding for this public space.

To illustrate: assume that the estimated O&M expenses for one public space would constitute 10 percent of the municipal operating budget,[8] which still must pay for staff salaries and O&M of hundreds of other municipal assets. In this case, the share of this public space's O&M is disproportionally high compared with other needs and cannot realistically expect to be consistently funded.

Scenario 2: O&M Is Entrusted to a Community Organization, as is Raising Funding for O&M

As table 3.3 indicates, this scenario has substantial limitations: (a) it is not suitable for facilities whose operation requires professional expertise, and (b) agreements with community groups about O&M are often not legally enforceable. However, for small public spaces, such as a 50-square-meter public garden at a corner of a residential block, this may be the best option.

Cases of this model for prominent public spaces have been presented in cities, including Karachi (see chapter 11).

Scenario 3: O&M Outsourced to Private Company that Is Paid for Services from the Local Budget

This model is widely and successfully used in many middle- and high-income countries with market economies. A main issue for this scenario is the same as for Scenario 1: affordability of the O&M expenses for the municipality if its operating budget is under stress. Therefore, due diligence should honestly assess whether the municipal budget will be able to meet its contractual obligations. This scenario may, however, need to be modified to use additional funding from other sources.

For instance, in Seoul, the Eunpyeong Library Village Cooperative, a private company that specializes in programming and managing library facilities, was contracted by the local government to manage the Gusandong Library. The cooperative not only manages facilities at the library but also conducts research on library-related policies and organizes relevant events (see chapter 14).

Scenario 4: Management (Including O&M) Outsourced to Private Company, Along with Rights to Generate Revenues from the Public Space and Obligation to Cover O&M Costs

This scenario requires a financial prefeasibility study and a legal feasibility study. On the financial side, one needs to develop, even if preliminarily, a convincing business case to illustrate to stakeholders and potential bidders that the public space will make sufficient profit after returning the operator's initial capital investment and paying recurrent O&M expenses for the entire public space (including the parts that do not generate revenues) (box 3.6).

TABLE 3.4 **Common Tools for Funding O&M of Public Spaces**

O&M funding source	Funding tools
Local operating budget	• Revenue sources varying by country, main sources including property taxes, income or profit taxes, taxes on goods, and so on
Private donations	• Private individuals' and companies' philanthropic donations
On-site fees	• Entry fees • Parking fees • Revenues from services (cafés, kiosks, ice skating, sideshows, and so on) • Event fees: music festivals, exhibitions, movie festivals
Earmarked revenues from off-site sources	• Corporate sponsorships: sponsored event, advertising, "naming rights," exclusive product placement • Districts established to fund public spaces: special service district, business improvement district • Cross-subsidies from off-site revenues of a private operator • Park dedication fee
Crowdsourcing	• Community association's pooling of funds from residents
In-kind contributions	• Voluntary works, donations of facilities (for example, chairs)

Note: O&M = operations and maintenance.

BOX 3.6 OUTSOURCING PLANNING AND MANAGEMENT OF PUBLIC TOILETS TO A PRIVATE START-UP IN DHAKA, BANGLADESH

Dhaka, Bangladesh, is a megacity of almost 20 million people with 5.5 million people commuting daily on the streets. However, there are only 57 public-toilet facilities across the entire city, which is equivalent to one public toilet for every 350 thousand people. While clean and accessible public toilets are critical facilities that benefit public-space users, such as pedestrians, shoppers, and street vendors, they remain a neglected amenity in this densely populated city.

The lack of public toilets is further exacerbated by poor operation and maintenance of the existing facilities, mainly owing to a lack of adequate budget and technical expertise within the city government. Out of 57 public toilets, only 5 are in good condition, 42 are partially operational, and 10 are nonoperational. Moreover, 74 percent of the existing operational toilets do not have separate spaces for women, which severely affects women's health. It is common knowledge in Dhaka that most women in public spaces avoid or delay using toilets, which often leads to related health issues, such as urinary tract infections (UTIs). According to a survey by Bhumijo, a local social enterprise start-up established in 2016, 79 percent of women in Dhaka experienced UTIs.

To address this issue in a sustainable manner, Bhumijo researched and developed various viable business models to upgrade existing, underutilized public toilets.[a] A suitable O&M model for each toilet project was developed based on a comprehensive assessment of its location, user age group, gender preferences, and a future user projection. It was also found that the traditional sociocultural context has created an environment where the needs for specially designed public toilets for women and/or people with disabilities has been almost neglected. Based on this understanding, Bhumijo piloted several public toilet upgrades and operations in 2017. As of September 2019, it operated six public toilets, and an additional six are in the pipeline across Dhaka and other secondary cities in Bangladesh. The pilots were encouraging and saw the daily average number of women users increase from 35 before the projects in 2017 to about 245 in 2019.

One of the Bhumijo's pilot projects was to upgrade and operate a women-only toilet at the Nur Mansion Market, also known as *Gawsia*, a popular shopping destination for women in Dhaka. Even though there was a great demand for women-only toilets for shoppers and vendors, it was challenging to persuade skeptical stakeholders of this need. After extensive discussions with the stakeholders, Bhumijo introduced two innovative solutions that benefited not only women users but also for

(box continues next page)

BOX 3.6 OUTSOURCING PLANNING AND MANAGEMENT OF PUBLIC TOILETS TO A PRIVATE START-UP IN DHAKA, BANGLADESH *(Continued)*

the market at large: the provision of specialized design components for women, such as menstrual hygiene amenities, kids-friendly facilities, and the sense of safety; and a new revenue model for this facility (photo B3.6.1). Bhumijo adopted a user fee of Tk 10 for individual shoppers, which was twice the rate in other public toilets, and offered a monthly discounted subscription fee of Tk 100 for shops that usually have three to four women vendors who needed access to toilets regularly.

As a result, the annual average number of users dramatically increased from 1,500 women in 2017, before the project, to 50,000 in 2019. Further, the toilet also catered to other user groups, annually serving an average of 5,400 children, including 1,500 diaper changes. The successful approach is being scaled up to other locations. The pilot also showed promising results in terms of its financial sustainability. The capital expense for renovating one toilet facility of 220 square feet averaged Tk 500,000. Monthly O&M costs and fee revenues were about Tk 11,200 and Tk 14,800, respectively. Further cost efficiencies and other revenue streams are being explored by Bhumijo.

Even though it is common for city governments to outsource the O&M of toilet facilities to external operators, it should be noted that public toilets in Dhaka are not well maintained despite being heavily subsidized. According to Bhumijo, inadequate oversight mechanisms and lack of quality control are to be blamed. In addition to applying a feasible O&M model, credible supervision and a monitoring system are also important elements in the long run.

a. Before the project (2017) **b. After the project (2019)**

PHOTO B3.6.1 **Before and after: The Women-Only Toilet Project at the Nur Mansion Market in Dhaka, Bangladesh**

Source: Shafi et al. 2011.
a. See Bhumijo's website for further details (website), accessed September 10, 2019: https://bhumijobd.wixsite.com/bhumijo.

Conducting a detailed feasibility study can be time-consuming and relatively expensive, but it will instill confidence in policy makers, stakeholders, and bidders that outsourcing the management of the public space is well justified. Even with a rough prefeasibility study, assumptions will need to be realistic.

Often, a contentious technical and ideological issue in shaping such outsourcing is the profit assumption. Indeed, how much of a profit for a private operator should be assumed in the feasibility study? Profit requirements from the private sector side reflect not only market risks but also substantial additional risks of working with governments as clients. Besides, other characteristics of the project are critical in this regard: duration of the contract, the time required to recoup the initial capital investment, and so on. Therefore, it is recommended that when conducting the feasibility or prefeasibility study, assumptions should not be made based on either academic considerations or a government's (low) profit assumption. Instead, interviews should be conducted with potential private operators to obtain and use their input,

BOX 3.7 BALYKCHY, KYRGYZ REPUBLIC: A COUNTRY'S FIRST COMPETITIVE OUTSOURCING OF MUNICIPAL PARK MANAGEMENT

A 16-hectare park on Lake Issyk-Kul in Balykchy, the Kyrgyz Republic, had a 500-meter lake beach and several recreational facilities, including rides, summer eateries, a disco club, and a guarded parking lot. Despite substantial recent public investment, the park was in poor condition and quickly deteriorating, mainly because of the poor service by the company managing the park and a four-year absence of investment in the park's infrastructure. The company had no incentives to perform its management functions or maintain the municipal assets. In fact, the entity was siphoning cash revenues from the park while complaining that operating the park was not profitable and required cross-subsidies from other, more profitable activities and from the municipal budget. Key local officials—the head of the city's property management department and the city council chairperson—were willing to try to change the situation and participate in a pilot project of placing the park under private management, with technical assistance offered by the Urban Institute and sponsored by the U.S. Agency for International Development (USAID).

The project was prepared and launched in 2004 by a joint working group (WG) that included eight representatives of the city and four experts from the Urban Institute's offices in Bishkek, the Kyrgyz Republic, and Washington, DC. The WG was supported by additional specialized technical expertise from local Kyrgyz Republic engineers, business expertise from the Kyrgyz Republic operators of private amusement

(box continues next page)

including an understanding of how they estimate risks and required profits. This is important because profit assumptions below the real expectations in the private sector can have a negative chain effect later in the process (for example, no qualified and responsible bidders, failure of a winner soon after contract signing, and so on).

On the legal side, even if all national or provincial laws and bylaws are in place, a detailed list must be prepared of documents needed to launch the outsourcing project, including an estimate of how long the whole preparation and launch would take. When the process is rigorous and applies international good practices, the legal side may become a substantial element, especially if this is the first experience of its kind in the country. For example, the first PPP to outsource management of a municipal park in the Kyrgyz Republic (with some capital investment by the operator) took 11 calendar months and required the development of 20 substantial documents, including 9 legal and procurement documents (box 3.7).

BOX 3.7 BALYKCHY, KYRGYZ REPUBLIC: A COUNTRY'S FIRST COMPETITIVE OUTSOURCING OF MUNICIPAL PARK MANAGEMENT *(Continued)*

parks, and procurement and performance management expertise from U.S.-based advisers.

The entire preparatory process, including key documents such as a request for proposals and rules for proposal evaluation, drew substantially upon British and Canadian manuals on public-private partnerships (PPPs). A total of 20 technical and legal documents were prepared or obtained. The nine legal documents included, among others, (a) a city resolution on placing the park under private management; (b) a property title; (c) a "Park Passport" consisting of an inventory of the park's assets, a map, and zoning specifications on permitted land uses; (d) a city regulation on concession competition procedures, including rules for proposal evaluation and winner selection; and (e) a draft concession agreement. The technical documents included expert assessments of park landscaping and plants and the condition of engineering infrastructure and rides; chemical and sanitary analysis of drinking water; results of a detailed feasibility study; results of a survey of citizens' satisfaction and expectations about park improvements and services; and others.

The preparation process, on the Urban Institute side, took about 300 person-days (80 by a project director and an international asset management expert and 220 by local professionals, including a lawyer, engineers, a financial analyst, a public relations expert, and others).

Source: Kaganova, Naruzbaeva, and Undeland 2012.

Stage 4: Developing Oversight and Accountability Mechanisms

As table 3.1 indicated earlier, oversight can be either formal (for example, by government auditing authorities) or less formal (such as through citizen participation and nongovernmental organizations [NGOs]). Citizen participation tools seem to be suitable in most cases. However, in the case of formal contractual relations regarding a public space, the government body that issued the contract (for example, under Scenarios 3 or 4) has an obligation to control and enforce compliance by the contractor.

Which oversight instruments to deploy depends on many factors: resources available, potential synergies with other projects, proliferation of technology in the society, and others. In addition, there should be a reasonable proportion between (a) the capital and O&M costs of a public space, and (b) the cost of oversight. In other words, it does not make sense to apply expensive oversight techniques to low-cost public spaces. Further, proliferation of technology will continue to make new instruments possible. At this stage, for the conceptual design of a public space, one or two potential instruments could be short-listed and a final approach decided upon only when the public space reaches an advanced implementation stage.

Strategies for Successful Launch of a Public-Space Asset Management Plan

Developing the Conceptual Design with Beneficiaries and Stakeholders

An informed selection of a preferred scenario should be made from the variety of base and hybrid scenarios (following the above guidelines and any other considerations), and beneficiaries and stakeholders should be consulted on the preferred option. The conceptual design should include a clear conceptual summary of the suggested public space that includes all six elements of governance (from table 3.1) and designates the responsible parties for various tasks, suggested funding sources, and estimated costs. In particular, the future obligations of beneficiaries and other stakeholders need to be clearly spelled out and discussed. It can also be useful to mention at stakeholder meetings which other scenarios were considered and why the preferred one was selected.

The purpose of this step is twofold:

- To gauge whether support for the suggested scenario is sufficient to move to implementation; if so, it is recommended to sign a memorandum of understanding with key stakeholders that reflects expected mutual obligations and agreement to start implementation
- To collect and record feedback, for fine-tuning the conceptual design.

Launching the Selected Scenario

This is a multicomponent process, including several important asset management elements (the first three of which require a qualified municipal infrastructure engineer):

- *Conduct engineering studies,* with sufficient detail to design the public space and to estimate both capital and O&M costs

- *Decide which technological or engineering solutions for capital improvements would minimize future O&M expenses*, and estimate the capital costs
- *Develop an O&M plan for at least five years, and estimate the cost*—for each year listing each maintenance activity and its required frequency, cost, who is responsible for conducting it, and who covers its cost[9]
- *Present the total costing and O&M plan to stakeholders, and sign an agreement* with them about who is responsible for various items. For example, for a hybrid of Scenarios 1 and 2 with mixed capital funding, this agreement may say the following:
    - The donor will cover the 80 percent of the capital funding, the municipal government will cover 10 percent, and the community will cover 10 percent (in kind, by labor); and
    - The municipality and community will share the O&M costs according to the O&M plan.

Notice that in most cases, such an agreement will not be legally enforceable, but it will make mutual commitments explicitly acknowledged.

For scenarios with private participation, the above elements are not sufficient, and a party responsible for public-space implementation needs to develop a procurement procedure, a request for proposals (including terms of reference [TOR]) for bidders, and a draft contract. And, eventually, the responsible party must conduct the procurement, which ideally would include the possibility for bidders to reflect on the draft TOR and contract. However, further details regarding procurement or contracts are beyond the scope of these guidelines.

It should be emphasized here that implementation of a public space does not end with the completion of capital construction or a ribbon-cutting ceremony; it continues into the O&M period, dealing in particular with periodic assessments of the public space's condition, beneficiaries' satisfaction, and compliance of responsible parties regarding their O&M obligations.

Note to Stakeholder

Creating and operating a public space may require substantial efforts, some beyond the influence of some of the stakeholders. However, a set of questions underlies the asset management approach that all stakeholders—from urban planners to community organizers to owners of nearby homes and businesses—should ask and seek answers to:

- Do we have the power to do what we intend to do?
- Who owns what here?
- Who provides funding for capital investment?
- Who is responsible for operating and maintaining the public space?
- Where does funding for O&M come from?
- Who has the authority and voice to monitor how things are going at the public space?

APPLYING THE ASSET MANAGEMENT PLAN TO PRIVATELY OWNED PUBLIC SPACES (POPS)

Chapter 2 introduced POPS and discussed the prerequisites for the success of this instrument—prerequisites perhaps taken for granted in cities where POPS have been used but that might not be in place in other countries:[10]

- *A well-functioning private real estate market*
- *Base zoning that is transparent and binding* for both the government and developers (meaning that if the zoning is approved, development does not require extra development permits)
- *Base zoning that is responsive to signals from the real estate market* (meaning that zoning provides parameters of land uses that allow landowners to realize a sufficient profit).

How to introduce this instrument depends, quite substantially, on whether it applies to truly *privately owned land* or to private development on *government-owned land*. In the latter case, government may simply add requirements about a public space on a site to other mandatory conditions under which it releases the land site for private development under a long-term lease[11]—(a) assuming that development still would be profitable for potential investors or developers; and (b) keeping in mind that the public-space requirement may reduce the amount that bidders would be willing to pay for the land (that is, competition between immediate public financial interests and a desire to create a public space should be foreseen).

The introduction of the POPS mechanism on privately owned land would require several substantial steps during the initial planning, conceptualizing, and engagement stages.

Step 1: Assess Required Regulatory Changes

In particular, can the needed changes to zoning regulations and rules be made at the city level, or will they require engagement of the state or central government? The answer will affect the time and effort needed to legislate the instrument.

In practice, if the higher echelons of government must be involved, most probably some law will need to be modified (which should be clarified as a part of the assessment). If this is the case, the task then enters the realm of structural reform of urban planning—perhaps beyond the scope of the project. If, however, the POPS instrument can be introduced at the city level, one would likely continue the exploration.

Step 2: Assess Private Sector Interest

Would real estate developers be interested? If not, why not, and what needs to be done to generate interest? This assessment should be performed through extensive one-on-one or collective consultations with developers of commercial real estate. Their interest is a prerequisite for any further action. A more systematic approach can then be conducted to determine which instruments (stand-alone projects, development incentives, or land-based financing with urban design requirements) would be most appropriately used to create or regenerate public spaces.

Also, there may be a need to conduct due diligence on what expenses and obligations developers can bear and to calibrate incentives or find win-win arrangements. There is a need to determine how developers view the role of public spaces in their development: are they a liability, or are they an asset that drives commercial activity and creates real estate value for the surrounding developments?

Step 3: Secure High-Level Support, Both Political and within the Urban Planning Hierarchy

For a POPS instrument, it is critical to gain firm support not only from the political leadership of the city but also from the top urban planning officials. In many countries, the head of the urban planning authority in a city is a key power player, and without that individual's support, changes in zoning rules would rarely take place even if a mayor and city council are interested.

Step 4: Spearhead Joint Public-Private Development of the POPS Conceptual Design

The ideal way to spur joint government and private sector development would be to establish a temporary task force of key urban planning officials; established real estate developers (nominated, for example, by the local chamber of commerce); and a member of the city council. There is a need to facilitate and technically guide their elaborations toward agreement on several predefined central questions: for example, which areas in the city and types of real estate should be subject to the incentive zoning; what the main quantitative parameters of the incentive should be; what kind of oversight and enforcement instruments should be stipulated; and so on. The result of the elaborations should form the basis of the POPS conceptual design.

After the conceptual design is confirmed with city's policy makers and the public, it should be codified into the incentive zoning regulation though standard legislative channels and enacted. If the previous steps were done properly, further implementation would proceed through individual developers using this instrument. However, both formal (stipulated in the zoning regulation) and public oversight will be needed regarding developers' compliance with POPS requirements; without such oversight, developers may tend to underperform (for example, limit public access to what is supposed to be a public space).

Step 5: Develop Accountability and Oversight Mechanisms

As demonstrated in chapter 2, government agencies and the public use various accountability and oversight mechanisms for POPs. The specifics depend largely on the regulatory environment for POPs and the traditions of public engagement. Moreover, this area of public management is actively evolving through experiments around the world.

What is important to establish from the start, however—when POPs are envisioned—is (a) a clear stipulation of some feasible and realistic accountability and oversight mechanism, and (b) encouragement of further public oversight initiatives according to evolving public perception of what is important for stakeholders.

CONCLUSIONS: WHAT CAN BE LEARNED?

Public spaces on government-owned land represent a complex case of government asset management—in some senses, more complex than other public assets—because of the explicit public engagement and multiplicity of expectations by various beneficiaries and other stakeholders.

Internationally, there is a broad spectrum of ways to govern public spaces. However, whether public spaces can be established, on a large scale, in low- and many middle-income countries as organizationally and financially sustainable assets remains in doubt. Indeed, on one hand, the scenarios implying that the local government and community would defray the capital and O&M costs face a huge challenge because these costs are not affordable for either municipal governments or households. In particular, municipal funding—both capital and operating—is usually dramatically insufficient to meet many of the current, urgent demands on municipal budgets. On the other hand, the successful public-space governance models that include private sector delivery or management require well-developed systems of procurement and effective contract enforcement, and they are often characterized by forms of public participation (such as philanthropy) more common in wealthy countries. In addition, models of this type are, for all practical purposes, PPPs and therefore expensive to prepare and launch according to good practices, which may limit their practicality for scaling up from pilot tests.

Meanwhile, POPS—whereby real estate developers participate voluntarily and deliver public spaces on their private sites in exchange for permission to exceed the maximum land-use parameters allowed by base zoning—can be a promising instrument in cities that have the necessary institutional, legislative, regulatory, and urban planning frameworks in place. Indeed, POPS convert the government's power to regulate land uses into material public benefits, without using either public land or public funding. However, introduction of the needed incentive zoning requires a special regulation, which can be difficult to enact at the city level, given that in many countries urban planning is still centralized, in one way or another, and generally tends to resist reform. In addition, POPS are not a substitute for public spaces on public land.

Then, what are the ways forward?

Lessons at the Local or Project Level

- The conceptual design of each public space, however imperfect or challenged in terms of organization and financial sustainability, should spell out all six governance elements: (a) which regulatory documents will be required, (b) who will own the assets, (c) who will fund capital investment, (d) who will manage the public space (including O&M), (e) from which sources will the O&M expenses be covered, and (f) how oversight will be organized.

- Each public space needs to have its capital costs assessed and a five-year O&M plan developed with estimated costs.
- It can be useful to sign a joint contract among responsible parties, even if it is not legally enforceable.
- Given that engaging the private sector in managing public spaces on public land is critical, especially when the public-space assets could generate revenues, consider deviations from international good practices. For example, minimize the complexity of the procurement process for selecting an operator.
- Find local champions, both inside and outside government, and help them to internalize "ownership" of the process.
- Regarding POPS in low- or middle-income countries, it would be useful to identify countries where the required incentive zoning can be introduced at the city level, without central government involvement, and to conduct assisted pilot projects in a number of cities there.
- Secure professional capacity in a preparation team.
- Consider designs that optimize limited O&M resources, such as (a) co-locating and consolidating services in the same public building (for example, community centers that have flexible spaces and include other facilities like health centers, police posts, sports facilities, and public toilets); and (b) incorporating green infrastructure principles that could reduce O&M costs, such as naturally ventilated buildings or the use of solar photovoltaics (PVs) for street lights (as illustrated in box 3.4).

Lessons on a Broader Policy Level

- Make sure that the capital planning needed for public spaces is integrated into the city's overall capital investment planning—and is not trying to override other priority needs (such as potable water, sanitation, traffic management, solid waste management, and so on).
- Consider incorporating good public-space designs within high-priority resilient infrastructure investments such as flood mitigation and streets. In some cases, this may require innovative design solutions combining infrastructure and public spaces, which may imply additional capital costs but have the advantage of being more appealing to and better supported by local communities. In other cases, these public spaces are marginal additions to infrastructure (for example, ensuring that proper sidewalks are part of a complete street design or adding pedestrian paths along drainage infrastructure).
- Understand how O&M expenses related to public spaces would affect the local operating budget, and promote budgetary reform when feasible.
- Consider the feasibility of and opportunities for building an "incentive zoning module" into a national law on land-use planning (in countries where the central government determines, to a certain extent, how each city's zoning is defined).

- Identify and strengthen critical areas of institutional coordination among government entities or units from the planning, design, and O&M viewpoints (for example, between a municipal transportation department responsible for design of local roads and intersections and the traffic police, which is responsible for the O&M of these intersections when they are built).
- Consider developing public-space asset management policies to improve resource efficiencies (in energy, water, and so on) using technology, such as light-emitting diode (LED) street lights and solar PVs, in publicly owned and managed public-space assets. However, the financial feasibility of such systems needs to be understood up front. For example, how much larger would the up-front capital investment costs be, and how many years would it take to recoup this extra cost through annual savings on O&M costs?
- Consider policies to improve the use of public-space assets. For example, intensify the use of spaces in public facilities, such as by leasing vacant spaces in public buildings for complementary uses (perhaps as cafés, or as a bookstore in a library facility). Alternatively, dispose of public-space assets that do not perform well or do not serve their intended functions.

NOTES

1. See the Hong Kong Public Space Directory, Hong Kong Public Space Initiative (website), accessed June 18, 2019: http://database.hkpsi.org.
2. For details on the World Bank's work with the ESA on the identification system for public spaces, see the Earth Observation for Sustainable Development (EO4SD) Urban Development project (EO4SD-Urban) website: http://www.eo4sd-urban.info/.
3. "Reinventing Paris II: The Subterranean Secrets of Paris." City of Paris (website), accessed June 18, 2019: http://www.reinventer.paris/.
4. Establishing a BID requires a legal instrument to enforce participation of all businesses within the BID area (if the legally defined majority voted to participate).
5. This step, and the whole process, is assumed to be spearheaded by some "organizer." Any of the stakeholders may play this role: a municipal official or department, a community group, a donor-sponsored project, and so on.
6. Describing these instruments, on which there is an extended literature, goes beyond the scope of this book.
7. Knowing and benchmarking O&M costs is not a public-place-related task, but it is a required element of good asset management, which currently is lacking in most local governments.
8. This example is based on a real case.
9. Annual O&M costs can be uneven over time, because some maintenance is only needed after three to five years of operation. For details, see Kaganova (2011).
10. As discussed in chapter 2, this instrument has been used, so far, mostly in high-income countries.
11. For a discussion of such an arrangement, see the case of Singapore, chapter 15.

REFERENCES

Anya, Agnes. 2017. "Jakarta Now Has 188 Child-Friendly Public Spaces." *Jakarta Post,* February 14 (accessed April 10, 2019), http://www.thejakartapost.com/news/2017/02/14/jakarta-now-has-188-child-friendly-public-spaces.html.

Batréau, Quentin, and Francois Bonnet. 2016. "Managed Informality: Regulating Street Vendors in Bangkok." *City & Community* 15 (1): 29–43.

City of Adelaide. 2017. "Park Lands and Open Space: Asset Management Plan." Planning document, City of Adelaide, Australia.

City of New York. 2017. "Audit Report on the City's Oversight over Privately Owned Public Spaces." Audit No. SR16-102A, April 18. Office of the Comptroller, City of New York.

De Magalhães, Claudio, and Sonia Freire Trigo. 2016. "Contracting Out Publicness: The Private Management of the Urban Public Realm and its Implications." *Progress in Planning* 115: 1–28.

Gehl Institute. 2017. "The Open Public Life Data Protocol." Version: Beta / September 27, 2017. Protocol for collection and storage of data about people in public space, Gehl Institute, New York.

Grabar, Henry. 2012. "A Matchmaker for New York's Privately-Owned Public Spaces." *CityLab* (newsletter), October 23 (accessed October 30, 2018), https://www.citylab.com/design/2012/10/matchmaker-new-yorks-privately-owned-public-spaces/3646/.

Guardian. 2017. "Revealed: The Insidious Creep of Pseudo-Public Space in London." *The Guardian*, July 24 (accessed April 10, 2019), https://www.theguardian.com/cities/2017/jul/24/revealed-pseudo-public-space-pops-london-investigation-map.

Hustwit, Gary. 2011. *Urbanized*. Documentary film produced and directed by Gary Hustwit. New York: Swiss Dots Ltd.

Johnson, Boris. 2009. "A Manifesto for Public Space: London's Great Outdoors." Statement of principles and initiatives to revitalize public spaces, Mayor of London (accessed April 10, 2019), https://www.london.gov.uk/sites/default/files/londons_great_outdoors_-_mayors_manifesto.pdf.

Kaganova, Olga. 2011. "Guidebook on Capital Investment Planning for Local Governments." Urban Development Series, Knowledge Papers No. 13, World Bank, Washington, DC.

———. 2012. "Government-Owned Land and Other Immovable Property: Policy and Regulatory Framework." IDG Asset Management Toolkit No. 4, Urban Institute Center on International Development and Governance (IDG), Washington, DC.

Kaganova, Olga, and Mihaly Kopanyi. 2014. "Managing Local Assets." In *Municipal Finances: A Handbook for Local Governments*, edited by Catherine Farvacque-Vitkovic and Mihaly Kopanyi, 275–324. Washington, DC: World Bank.

Kaganova, Olga, Ulara Naruzbaeva, and Charlie Undeland. 2012. "Case Study Involving Private Investment and Management to Improve Public Property: A Concession to Manage a Municipal Park and Beach in Balykchy, Kyrgyzstan." IDG Asset Management Toolkit No. 3, Urban Institute Center on International Development and Governance (IDG), Washington, DC.

Kayden, Jerold S. 2000. *Privately Owned Public Space: The New York City Experience*. New York: John Wiley & Sons.

Martin, David. 2017. "Why Private Investment in Public Space Is the New Normal." *Forbes*, July 30 (accessed October 15, 2018), https://www.forbes.com/sites/dmartin/2017/03/30/why-private-investment-in-public-spaces-is-the-new-normal/.

NACTO (National Association of City Transportation Officials). 2016. *Global Street Design Guide*. New York: Island Press.

PPS (Project for Public Spaces). 2001. *Public Parks, Private Partners*. New York: PPS.

Shafi, Salma A., Abu Mehedi Imam, Aftab Opel, and Khairul Islam. 2011. *Making public toilets work: an assessment of public toilets in Dhaka City*. Dhaka: WaterAid.

UCLG (United Cities and Local Governments). 2016. "UCLG Public Space Policy Framework by and for Local Governments." Policy framework document, UCLG, Barcelona (accessed April 10, 2019), https://www.uclg.org/sites/default/files/public_space_policy_framework.pdf.

URA (Urban Redevelopment Authority). 2019. "Reinventing Spaces into Vibrant Places." Press release, May 14, URA, Singapore (accessed May 19, 2019), https://www.ura.gov.sg/Corporate/Media-Room/Media-Releases/pr19-22.

Walters, Laurence. 2012. "Are Property-Related Taxes Effective Value Capture Instruments?" In *Value Capture and Land Policies: Proceedings of the 2011 Land Policy Conference*, edited by Gregory Ingram and Yu-Hung Hong, 187–214. Cambridge, MA: Lincoln Institute of Land Policies.

WBUR. 2017. "How Privatization Impacts Public Spaces And Infrastructure." Jeremy Hobson interview of Jerold Kayden and Eduardo Engel, *Here & Now*, produced by National Public Radio (NPR) and WBUR, Boston, May 11, 10:51 (accessed April 10, 2019), https://www.wbur.org/hereandnow/2017/05/11/privately-owned-public-space.

Windolph, Gary. 2013. "Municipal Asset Management: Estimating Operation and Maintenance Costs for Municipal Infrastructure." Technical Briefings Series (unpublished), National Opinion Research Center (NORC) at the University of Chicago.

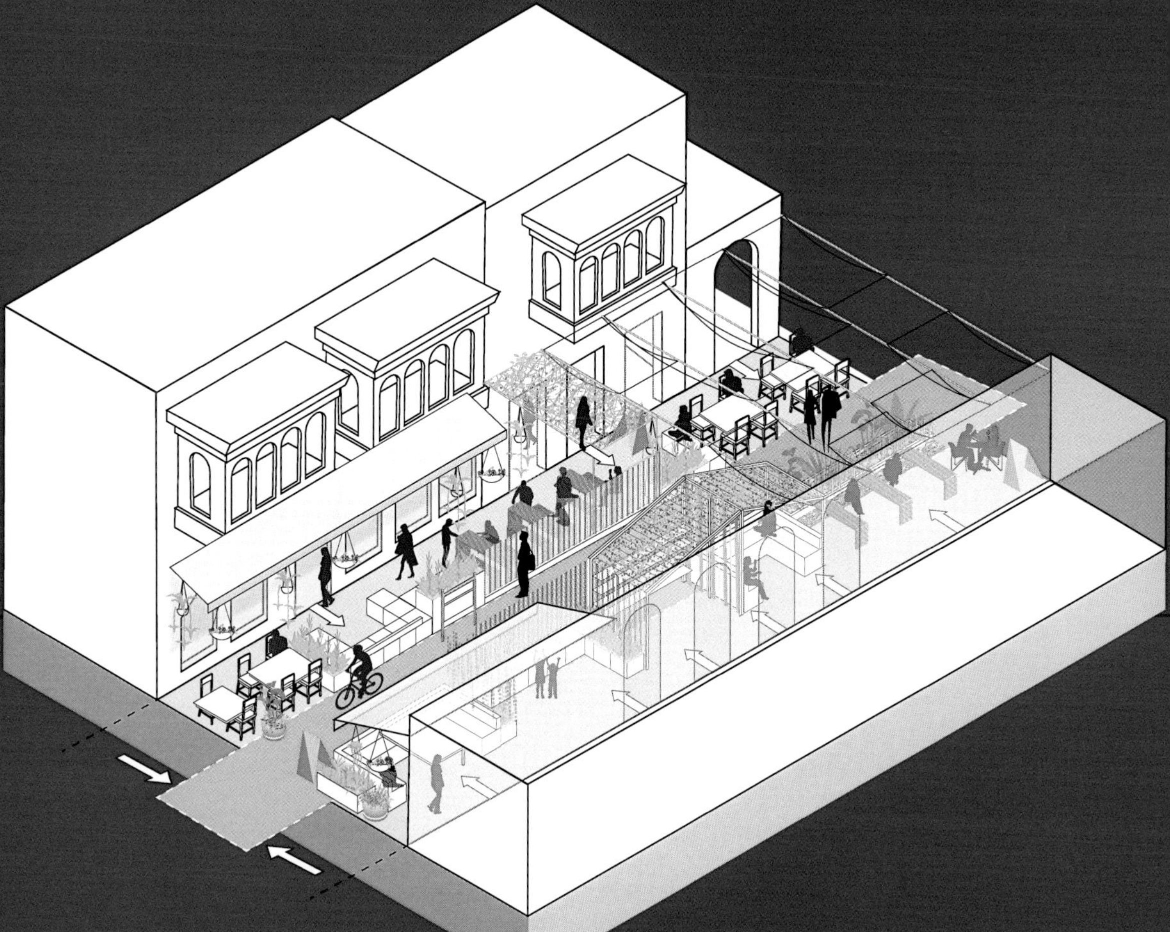

PART II

SHAPING THE PUBLIC REALM

Data and Spatial Analytics

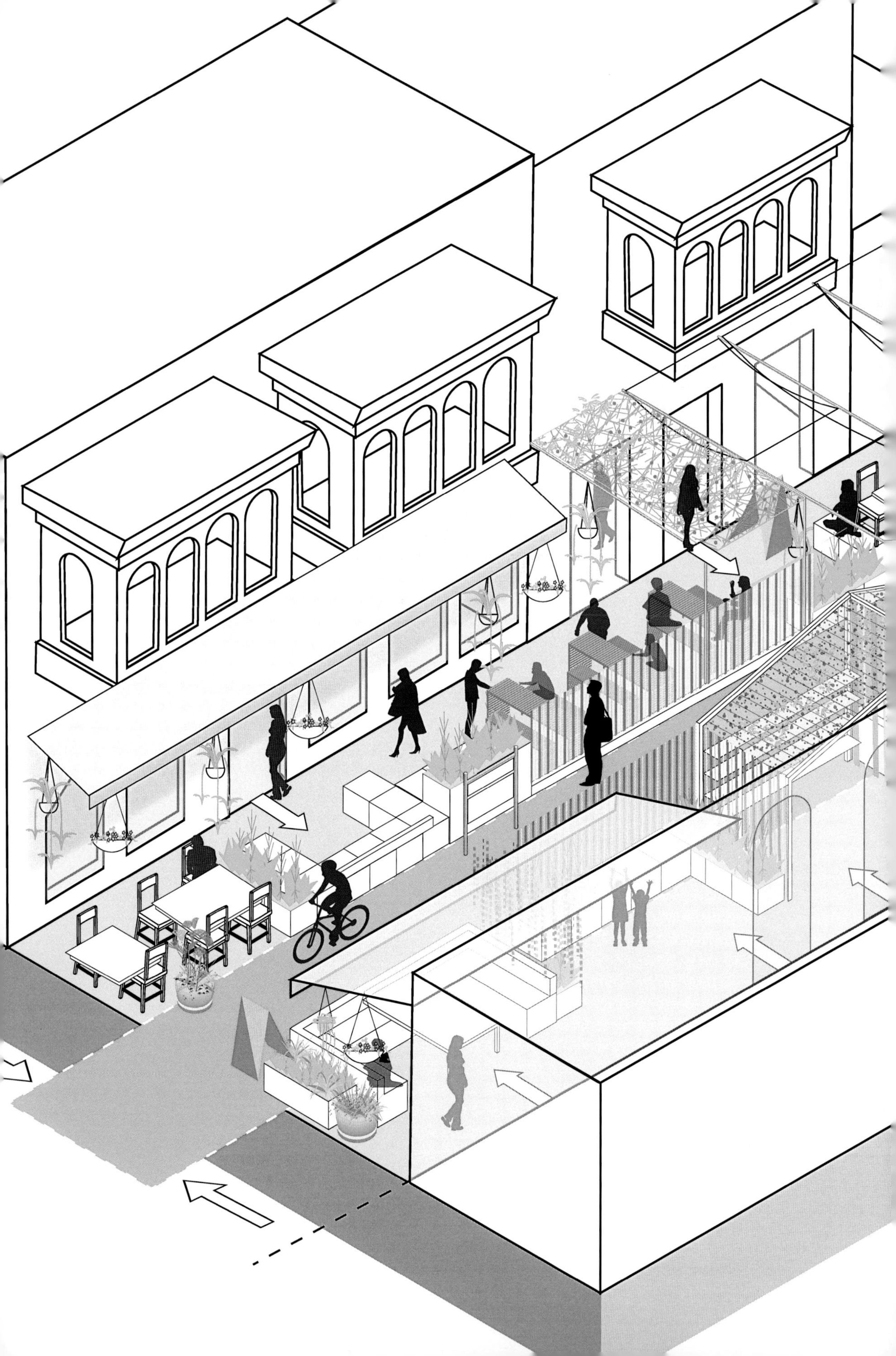

CHAPTER 4

EVIDENCE-BASED PLANNING AND DESIGN

Jon Kher Kaw, Cecilia Anderson, and Tomas Soukup

PUBLIC SPACES AS CITYWIDE NETWORKS

Public spaces are the most beneficial when they function as an interconnected network that spans the whole city and caters to the needs of communities—a result that requires a systematic approach to planning, the stakeholder engagement process, design, and management policies. However, in many cities, inadequate legal frameworks, coupled with poor planning policy and weak political will, have resulted in ad hoc urban development, grabbing of public land, the capture of benefit by private actors, and conflict between communities and government over the use of public space.

Accelerated urbanization puts pressure on the preservation and creation of meaningful public spaces and places, particularly at urban peripheries where growth is typically fastest.[1] This pattern portends a significantly worsened distribution of public space along with a reduction in its overall connectivity and programmatic diversity. Unfortunately, this aggregated reduction is often obscured by disproportionate attention to individual iconic public spaces. Understanding and improving the state of public spaces—in both its quantitative and qualitative aspects—is most holistically monitored and effectively counteracted at the citywide scale. To formulate strategies for successful planning, design, and management of citywide public-space networks in the long term, cities must first know where they stand: Are existing public spaces equitably distributed to serve neighborhoods adequately? Are they of good quality and well maintained? How are communities using and interacting with these spaces?

With these questions in mind, the following subsections describe three categories of spatial data and analysis that would be crucial in helping cities make informed decisions by benchmarking performance and providing insights into the development of comprehensive public-space strategies.

Asset Inventories

A reliable data inventory of public-space assets will be necessary for cities desiring to develop comprehensive and sustainable management plans and planning strategies through an evidence-based approach. A detailed inventory with asset information of individual sites—such as the type, condition, and quality of these spaces; their ownership; their management structure; and financial information such as expenses and revenues from operations and maintenance (O&M)—can be used to inform investment decisions, design choices, and management structure. One example can be the cost-benefit and trade-offs between repurposing existing deteriorated public spaces and creating new ones.

However, detailed spatial inventories—classification of public spaces and their spatial locations—are still lacking, especially in many low- and medium-income countries. It is often costly and time consuming for a city to dispatch staff to survey the entire city. And data collection protocols that are critical to control data quality and make inventories replicable have been almost nonexistent.

Spatial Patterns, Land Use, Urban Form, and Climatic Data

Aggregating site-level and spatial characteristics (such as location, type, and size) at the neighborhood and city levels helps to identify gaps in service provision to communities. Such analysis, when layered over urban extent (see more discussion about urban extent in appendix A), existing land uses, master plans, census data, real estate metrics, and traffic analysis can serve as a starting point for urban planning and the prioritization of neighborhood improvements. It contributes to well-planned, citywide public-space strategies whose policy priorities and actions reflect on-the-ground conditions. The use of high-resolution satellite imagery and land-use cover pattern recognition has gained momentum in generating land-use composition and changes in data-scarce cities. Other essential layers are urban heat island maps that could help identify areas of heat stress and to simulate outdoor comfort for interventions in public spaces (box 4.1). Flood maps are also useful in identifying potential public-space areas for integration with flood infrastructure and the implementation of water-sensitive urban designs.

Cities globally have used citywide public-space assessments to inform and initiate public-space programs as part of comprehensive master plans (see the Addis Ababa, Ethiopia, and Nairobi, Kenya, case studies in chapter 6). However, even if a master plan stipulates public spaces across the city, it does not alone guarantee that these public spaces will be implemented unless institutional capacities and implementation mechanisms are in place. For example, a recent study of seven secondary cities in Tanzania (Huang et al. 2018) using remote sensing, open-source data, and geographic information system (GIS) analysis showed that less than half of the case cities' populations have adequate access to health facilities, schools, and urban parks (within 1 kilometer or a 20-minute walk). The study also found that master plans were largely ineffective in guiding land use—having poor implementation mechanisms and exhibiting poor alignment of spatial plans with budgeting and investing decisions driven by a siloed approach to service delivery.

User Activity Data

Public spaces are effective only if they are inclusive and used by communities for their well-being. The physical and spatial attributes of public-space assets must be coupled with metrics and methods of understanding how people behave and use these spaces to be meaningful in evaluating how "successfully" they are being used by people. Such evaluation also underscores the continued need for placemaking and place-led approaches that use local community knowledge to shape public spaces through participatory processes and cocreation.

Although there are many ways to collect this information through studies, surveys, and observation, an accepted set of comparable metrics to measure the use of public spaces that factor in cultural nuances and context is not well established. Recent efforts to do so include the Public Life Data Protocol developed by the Gehl Institute in collaboration with the Municipality of Copenhagen and the City of San Francisco (Gehl Institute 2017). The Public Life Data Protocol is an open-data specification that measures what people do in public spaces and attempts to make public-life data sets compatible, scalable, and comparable across research institutions, government agencies, cities, and regions. Social data from digital sources—such as online reviews of places, event check-ins, and social media—is also enabling quicker and more cost-effective means to map and analyze public-space uses.

INNOVATIONS IN MEASURING THE PUBLIC REALM

The proliferation of crowdsourced, open-source geospatial data and easy access to earth observation tools are rapidly changing how cities monitor land-use patterns, even for entire cities that typically do not have good land-use or planning data. In the future, disruptive civic tech and GovTech;[2] street-level image object detection systems; sensors embedded in everyday objects in the public realm of smart districts; artificial intelligence; and machine learning will drive how cities monitor and manage public spaces. More dynamic city planning; better parking and traffic management, public safety, and information; smarter public-space operations and maintenance; and civic engagement are all areas in which technology can make an impact.

Connecting different technological standards and sharing data beyond silos will be a big challenge. In today's parlance, where the success of a place is measured by how "Instagrammable" it is, innovative new tools have also started to mine nontraditional data sources like social media and street imagery to analyze the characteristics of public spaces and places and how they are being used by people.

BOX 4.1 USING URBAN HEAT MAPS TO BETTER DESIGN PUBLIC SPACES IN HODONIN, CZECH REPUBLIC

Urban areas exhibit a significant increase in thermal discomfort compared with rural regions both during the night and the day. This is mainly due to increased radiative exposure, lower wind speeds, and higher air temperatures. In particular, extreme heat waves within cities heavily impact sensitive population groups such as children and older people. Moreover, global climate projections consistently point toward an increase of the frequency, duration, and intensity of heat waves (Meehl and Tebaldi 2004; Diffenbaugh and Giorgi 2012). Recent research has also shown that climate change may lead to a tenfold increase in the expected number of heat wave days within cities by the end of the century (Lauwaet et al. 2015).

In this context, urban heat island assessments using high-resolution satellite imagery help cities to better understand and mitigate potential thermal discomfort associated with changes in land cover and vegetation. Such assessments were used, for example, in the planned rehabilitation of the historic Masaryk Square in the city of Hodonin, Czech Republic. The proposed planting of trees and installation of facilities for users initially faced opposition from private stakeholders where shopowners in the surrounding areas preferred to secure more parking spaces for visitors to the square.

To provide the city government with scientific evidence relating to this project, two geospatial research organizations, GISAT and VITO, conducted simulations of the impacts of various design scenarios on heat stress levels. One-meter-resolution thermal comfort maps of the square were created, using the urban climate model called UrbClim (De Ridder, Lauwaet, and Maiheu 2015) (figure B4.1.1).[a] A set of input layers included land cover, floor plans and heights of buildings, and distribution of trees.

The results of the assessment clearly showed that the lack of urban vegetation would result in increasing heat stress levels of the site. The comparison across five design scenarios enabled the city government to successfully persuade stakeholders to accept a more human-centered design scenario that offers various types of trees, shadows, and resting areas for people.

(box continues next page)

The advent of autonomous vehicles, drones, food and grocery delivery, and augmented reality—as well as the trend toward a sharing economy in general (such as ride-hailing platforms, dockless bike sharing, and coliving and coworking spaces) and other forms of urban tech[3] focused on disrupting

BOX 4.1 USING URBAN HEAT MAPS TO BETTER DESIGN PUBLIC SPACES IN HODONIN, CZECH REPUBLIC *(Continued)*

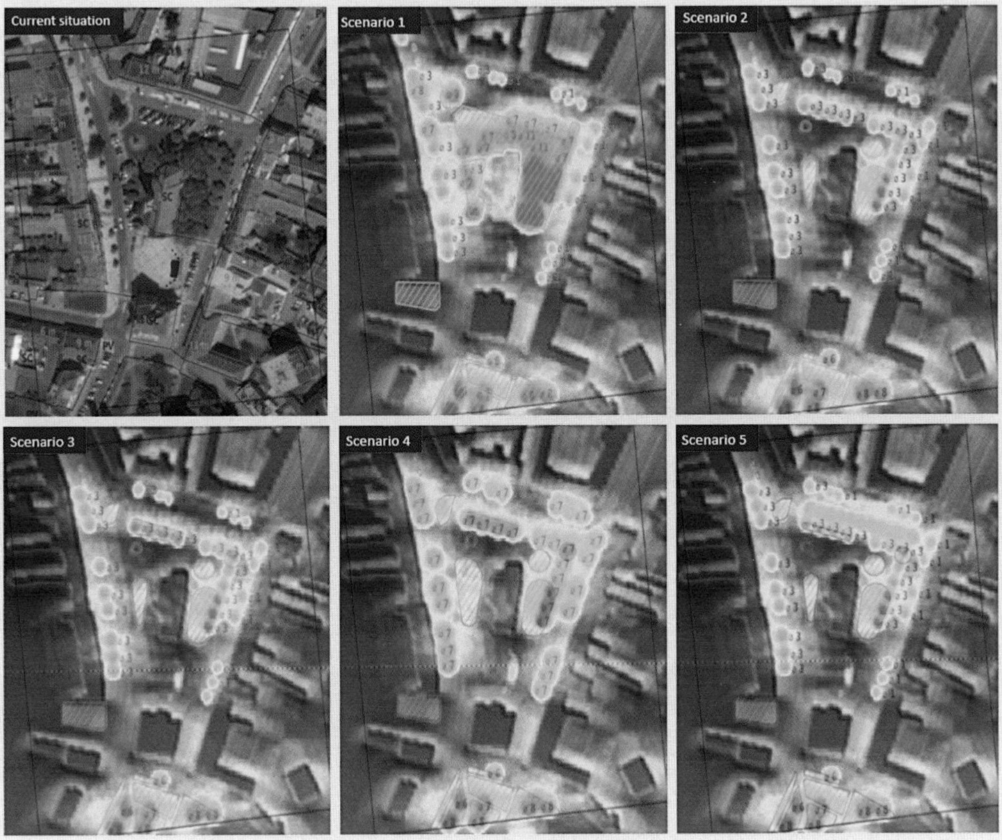

FIGURE B4.1.1 **Various Scenarios of Square Designs and Urban Heat Maps in Masaryk Square, Hodonin, Czech Republic**

Source: ©GISAT and VITO. Reproduced with permission from GISAT and VITO; further permission required for reuse.
Note: The dark orange color indicates the highest level of heat stress, while the green color indicates the lowest heat stress levels.
a. This study was conducted as a part of the H2020 project Climate-fit.City (website), accessed August 15, 2019: www.climate-fit.city

urban systems—will also change how residents and businesses use the public realm. Public spaces may need to accommodate new uses, offering vast potential for public benefit but also new challenges in their management (box 4.2).

BOX 4.2 **INTELLIGENT NEIGHBORHOODS**

A set of urban technology (urban tech) applications for streets provides a glimpse into how streetscapes might change in the future. Figure B4.2.1 illustrates some of the global examples of experiments on the ground:

- *Reconfigurable streets for different needs.* In Toronto, the development plan of the Toronto Waterfront led by Sidewalk Labs, an urban innovation company, is leveraging technology and modular, reconfigurable construction to prototype "dynamic streets." These modular pavements are embedded with lights to help direct vehicle and pedestrian traffic as well as to designate bike lanes or hazard zones, depending on traffic needs (Stinson 2018). For instance, a street for vehicles by day can be reconfigured to other uses at different times: pedestrian uses by night, a performance stage during weekends, and expanded sidewalks for food and beverage outlets during events.
- *Smart street lighting with sensors.* In Brooklyn, the nonprofit Downtown Brooklyn Partnership, which supports local development, collaborated with an urban data-measurement start-up called Numina to learn how to support the city's effort to stop illegal driving on car-free streets. Numina used light-pole-mounted cameras to detect not only illegal driving but also various other objects in streetscapes, such as pedestrians, cyclists, buses, trash bags, and more (Anzilotti 2019).
- *Smart traffic lights for safer pedestrian crossings.* In New Zealand, Pedestrian User-Friendly Intelligent (PUFFIN) crossings have been applied in many cities with intelligent sensors that detect and adjust crossing times. They make streets safer for the elderly and other groups with diverse needs (FLIR 2016).
- *Smart parking solutions and bike stations.* In Bad Hersfeld, Germany, an integrated intelligent parking management solution with sensors was developed to give drivers information—helping to direct traffic to vacant parking lots, reduce emissions, increase parking efficiency, and identify problematic parking areas (Hohenacker 2018).
- *Smart furniture.* In Australia, the Smart Social Spaces Project has been launched by the Georges River Council and University of New South Wales, in collaboration with manufacturer Street Furniture Australia. This project plans to install smart furniture in popular plazas and parks to understand which facilities are being used and to keep tracking the conditions of those facilities. The project also enables experimental research on how furniture design affects uses (Street Furniture Australia 2018).
- *Crowdsourced repairs.* In Boston, the city developed a mobile app called Smart Bump that gathers data about streets using resident drivers' smartphone data from built-in sensors. This crowdsourced data helped the city not only to fix street problems, like potholes

(box continues next page)

BOX 4.2 INTELLIGENT NEIGHBORHOODS *(Continued)*

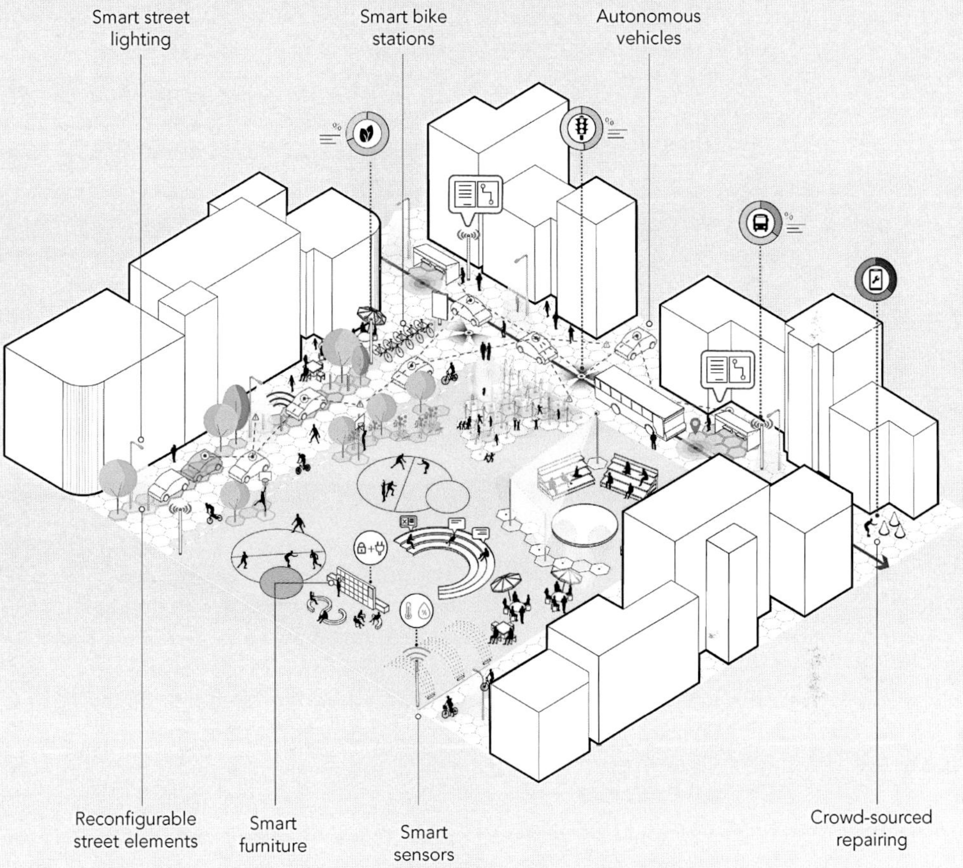

FIGURE B4.2.1 **Applications of Urban Tech to Street Design and Management**

Source: ©World Bank. Further permission required for reuse.

and sunk manhole covers, but also to plan long-term public facilities maintenance plans.[a]

These innovations aim to enhance the use of streets and improve street management. These pilots are likely to be part of a growing trend of many future initiatives to apply and adapt to urban infrastructure. These opportunities will also bring new challenges, especially to cities that are not able to develop robust policies to regulate and facilitate the use of technology in public spaces.

a. "Street Bump," New Urban Mechanics, City of Boston (website), last updated July 1, 2019: https://www.boston.gov/departments/new-urban-mechanics/street-bump.

COMPARATIVE ANALYSIS AND CASE STUDIES

The next three chapters of Part II present three types of spatial analysis with accompanying city case studies. The analyses apply methods and metrics that are consistent across cities and are focused on assessing different quantitative and qualitative aspects of public spaces in cities, as follows:

- *Chapter 5, "Analyzing Spatial Patterns of Public Spaces in Cities through Remote Sensing":* The analysis uses a combination of remote sensing using satellite imagery, semiautomated land-cover pattern recognition techniques and open spatial data to identify and classify public space types, and to map how they are distributed and connected spatially across cities. The analysis focused on three megacities with populations of 10 million or more—Dhaka, Bangladesh; Karachi, Pakistan; and Lima, Peru—where manual data collection had been particularly challenging.
- *Chapter 6, "Assessing the Quality and Use of Public Spaces":* The comparative analysis uses a set of metrics to document the ownership and management structure of public spaces, and measure how public spaces perform in terms of safety, accessibility, inclusiveness, and distribution in four selected cities: Nairobi, Kenya; Addis Ababa, Ethiopia; Wuhan, China; and Bamenda, Cameroon.
- *Chapter 7, "Mapping User Activity Using Social Media and Big Data":* The analysis demonstrates the use of technology and nontraditional tools and methods—street image object recognition using machine learning models, social media, and big data—to map spatial qualities of public spaces and user activity in three cities: Tbilisi, Georgia; Wuhan, China; and Beijing, China.

KEY TAKEAWAYS

The analysis of 12 cities in chapters 5, 6, and 7 utilizing spatial analytics and data provides a starting point for developing public-space programs and urban planning strategies:

- *Sizing and taking stock of existing and potential public spaces.* In dense megacities such as Dhaka, Karachi, and Lima, existing public spaces account for a scarce but sizable part of city land—at least 14–27 percent of the total built-up areas, of which about two-thirds are taken by streets. This estimate excludes major infrastructure such as highways and motorways, vacant areas, and disconnected parcels of land that are unlikely to function as public spaces for people. Having inventories and spatial databases of the types, distribution, quality, and service levels of public spaces are useful indicators for monitoring the performance of public spaces in cities, and for identifying gaps and highlighting opportunities for asset enhancement. For example, by assessing the quality of public space assets portfolios, local governments can more accurately budget the overall resources needed for O&M and prioritize capital investments in advance. Planners can also measure the amount of green spaces over time and monitor how much natural assets are preserved.

- *Distributing equitably*. The total area of public spaces alone are not good indicators of urban livability. The cities of Dhaka and Lima possess about 10 percent of nonstreet public spaces such as parks and sport and leisure facilities, twice the area compared to Karachi's (about 5 percent). However, despite the much larger areas dedicated to nonstreet public spaces in Dhaka and Lima, they reach about three-quarters of people living within a 5-minute walking distance (equivalent to 400 meters). Karachi's nonstreet public spaces, on the other hand, reach an estimated 95 percent of the population, meaning that almost all residents have at least one public space, such as a neighborhood park or a public facility, in close proximity within their neighborhood. This underscores the need for planners and local governments to monitor that public spaces are equitably provided in underprivileged neighborhoods that might need them—whether they are parks, markets, or community centers.
- *Diversifying types*. The composition of public-space typologies across cities can vary significantly. For instance, despite a similar variety of nonstreet public spaces, Dhaka's public spaces are dominated by waterfronts, because of the presence of rivers, and neighborhood parks, while Lima's urban landscape is more dominant in smaller pocket parks that are scattered across the city. Cities often take advantage of their topographical opportunities in the creation of open spaces, as well as the consideration that each typology of public space generally serves a different primary function—streets for mobility; open spaces for social interactions; and public facilities, such as libraries, markets, and health centers, for civic engagements. The composition of public spaces can evolve over time, depending on the stages of development of the city and its vision and needs. For example, the Superblock initiative in Barcelona, Spain, seeks to free up 60 percent of streets currently dedicated to motorized traffic in favor of open spaces for pedestrians (see chapter 5, box 5.1). Many cities around the world are also freeing up roads and highways along waterbodies for waterfront areas that are accessible to people.
- *Creating new public spaces*. In urban areas that have vacant land, there are opportunities for extending more public spaces to underserved areas. Interestingly, despite being some of the densest urban areas in the world, cities like Dhaka and Karachi have large areas of vacant and open land—around 15–21 percent of total built-up areas. These areas could be transformed as new public spaces, either on government-owned land or incorporated as part of private urban developments (land-based financing and planning instruments are discussed in chapter 3). Cities also can take differentiated approaches in public-space provision according to a neighborhood's characteristics—be it safeguarding new land for public spaces on city peripheries or reclaiming centrally located ones from one type of use to another (e.g., pedestrianization of streets). In the postconflict cities of Fallujah and Ramadi, the total area dedicated to public spaces is particularly low at 10 percent, of which virtually all are streets. Incorporating and allocating land up front for other types of public spaces, such as open spaces, markets, and other public facilities, as part of the reconstruction efforts, could be opportunities for those cities.

- *Connecting isolated public spaces.* A closely knit cluster of public spaces can be more valuable than a series of isolated standalone public spaces. Concentrations of different types of amenities such as libraries, community centers, sport facilities, and parks not only provide services to communities and neighborhoods, but also promote a sense of place and social cohesion. An analysis of how public spaces are connected in the case studies presented in chapter 5 shows large variations between cities—for instance, a sizable 25 percent of public spaces in Dhaka are isolated—and public spaces are highly concentrated within central areas and not equitably provided in some outlying neighborhoods. In Karachi and Lima, almost all public spaces have at least one or two other public spaces nearby. Some cities have also been able to implement creative solutions to connect neighborhoods through a network of public spaces by linking parks through pedestrian connections and cycling lanes using residual spaces alongside infrastructure such as roads and drains. Case studies in this book include the Brooklyn Strand in New York (chapter 13) and the Park Connector Network in Singapore (chapter 15).
- *Implementing effective ownership and management arrangements.* A survey of the ownership and management of existing public spaces in the case cities indicate that, not surprisingly, local and national governments predominantly own these public spaces (chapter 6). While a small fraction of these assets are privately owned (14–25 percent of public spaces[4]), in terms of management, the study observed that a much larger fraction of these assets (38–53 percent of public spaces[5]) rely on private, joint, or other arrangements. This suggests that the outsourcing of public space management to private or nongovernment organizations is not uncommon in the case cities; however, further analysis of the institutional and regulatory frameworks would be needed to understand the efficacy of such arrangements. Possible models for asset management governance are discussed in greater detail in chapter 3.
- *Designing and maintaining spaces.* The analysis in chapter 6 also reveals that the quality and management of these public spaces are often poor with ample opportunities to improve basic design requirements and O&M strategies. Design-related issues include poor accessibility for groups and people with specific needs—people with disabilities, older people, young adults, women, and children. Almost none of the public spaces surveyed had proper wheelchair access. Other issues include the need to better manage O&M of public-space facilities. In Addis Ababa, Ethiopia, and Bamenda, Cameroon, for example, only 25 percent and 10 percent of street lighting was working, respectively. The low levels of functioning utilities within public spaces could point to severe inadequacies in resources and/or management, which could lead to other undesired outcomes such as poor safety.
- *Planning and programming places to respond to use patterns.* A critical finding from the analysis of Tbilisi, Georgia, and Wuhan, China, suggests that public spaces can better relate to how people use them. In some cases, prominent public spaces were underutilized and devoid of human activity. Such spaces were not urban places where people naturally gather,

because they lacked programming or human-centered design components (chapter 7). Local governments can also look toward intensifying public spaces for more than one function or service. In the case studies of Addis Ababa, Ethiopia; Wuhan, China; and Bamenda, Cameroon, half of all public spaces surveyed were monofunctional (chapter 6) with opportunities to adopt better programming and placemaking initiatives. An understanding of how people use and perceive these public spaces can inform the creation of a successful public space during the planning and design process.

NOTES

1. Data on public spaces on city peripheries come from the "Atlas of Urban Expansion," an online mapped data set developed by the Lincoln Institute of Land Policy, Cambridge, MA: http://www.atlasofurbanexpansion.org/.
2. Civic tech refers to information technology that focuses on enhancing the relationship between people and governments by informing, engaging, and connecting citizens with their governments. It is used to improve service delivery as well as decision making on infrastructure investments. GovTech includes information technology that enhances the internal operational efficiencies of governments as a whole and between their agencies.
3. Urban tech refers to a set of innovations using technology focused on city systems such as urban mobility, living, and working.
4. Based on surveyed public spaces with known ownership status.
5. Based on surveyed public spaces with known management status.

REFERENCES

Anzilotti, Eillie. 2019. "How Smart City Tech Is Helping to Keep Cars from Illegally Driving on This Car-Free Street." *FastCompany,* June 3 (accessed June 15, 2019), https://www.fastcompany.com/90316266/how-smart-city-tech-is-helping-to-keep-cars-from-illegally-driving-on-this-car-free-street.

De Ridder, Koen, Dirk Lauwaet, and Bino Maiheu. 2015. "UrbClim—A Fast Urban Boundary Layer Climate Model." *Urban Climate* 12: 21–48.

Diffenbaugh, Noah S. and Filippo Giorgi. 2012. "Climate change hotspots in the $CMIP_5$ global climate model ensemble." Climate Change 114: 813–822.

FLIR (FLIR Systems Inc.). 2016. "Traffic Video Detection and Monitoring: Discover a Wide Variety of Applications." Promotional booklet, FLIR Systems Inc., Wilsonville, OR.

Gehl Institute. 2017. "The Open Public Life Data Protocol." Version: Beta / September 27, 2017. Protocol for collection and storage of data about people in public space, Gehl Institute, New York.

Hohenacker, Thomas. 2018. "A Parking Solution for Smart Cities." *Meeting of the Minds* (blog), September 27 (accessed June 15, 2019), https://meetingoftheminds.org/a-parking-solution-for-smart-cities-28397.

Huang, Chyi-Yun, Ally Namangaya, MaryGrace M. Lugakingira, and Isabel D. Cantada. 2018. "Translating Plans to Development: Impact and Effectiveness of Urban Planning in Tanzania Secondary Cities." Report No. 136362, World Bank, Washington, DC.

Lauwaet, Dirk, Hans Hooyberghs, Bino Maiheu, Wouter Lefebvre, Guy Driesen, Stijin Van Looy, and Koen De Ridder. 2015. "Detailed urban heat island projections for cities worldwide: dynamical downscaling $CMIP_5$ global climate models." *Climate* 3 (2): 391–415.

Meehl, Gerald A. and Claudia Tebaldi. 2004. "More intense, more frequent and longer lasting heat waves in the 21st century." *Science* 305 (5686): 994–997.

Stinson, Liz. 2018. "Futuristic Road Concept Is Made of Reconfigurable Parts that Light Up." *Curbed* (blog), August 6 (accessed April 30, 2019), https://www.curbed.com/2018/8/6/17654122/carlo-ratti-sidewalk-labs-dynamic-street.

Street Furniture Australia. 2018. "Smart Furniture Project Launches with Goerges River Council." *StreetChat* (blog), March 14 (accessed April 30, 2019), http://streetfurniture.com/au/smart-furniture-project-launches-georges-river-council/.

CHAPTER 5

ANALYZING SPATIAL PATTERNS OF PUBLIC SPACES IN CITIES THROUGH REMOTE SENSING

Jon Kher Kaw, Hyunji Lee, Tomas Soukup, and Jan Kolomaznik

OVERVIEW

This chapter analyzes the types and network characteristics of public spaces identified from remote sensing in selected cities. This pilot analysis relies solely on the use of spatial remote sensing tools (that is, semiautomated pattern recognition using very high-resolution satellite imagery) and open data to:

- Identify the different typologies of public spaces and the proportion of area they occupy based on land-use patterns;
- Map the spatial distribution of these public spaces; and
- Shed light on the current spatial distribution and potential in providing adequate public spaces for their residents.

The analysis—prepared within the European Space Agency (ESA) Earth Observation for Sustainable Development (EO4SD)-Urban project[1]—demonstrates the current potential of remote techniques to effectively support identification, quantification, and characterization of public spaces on a citywide scale.

TABLE 5.1 **Public-Space Types and Key Characteristics Identified in Spatial Pattern Analysis through Remote Sensing**

Public-space type and subtype		Key characteristics
Open and green area (OGA)	Pocket square, neighborhood square, city square,[a] suburban square	Apparent squares or plazas or large crossings with visible "public" function
	Pocket park, neighborhood park, city park, linear green	Horticultural management is visible or very likely from land cover composition
	Waterfront	Beaches, parks alongside water bodies, berthing, and boardwalks
	Cemetery	Cemetery land-use pattern
	Other potential areas	Inaccessible OGAs, unsorted green areas (residual), fragmented or vacant parcels, and forest or dense tree areas
Street		Roads surrounded predominantly by urban residential and nonresidential structures (excluding capacity roads, highways, overpasses, underpasses, and road links)
Facility	Open markets	Large streets with concentrations of stalls
	Sport and leisure facilities[b]	Green sport areas including buildings and associated land (for example, stadiums and sport fields), playgrounds, amusement parks, golf courses, and so on

Source: World Bank.
a. Pocket, neighborhood, and city squares are categorized based on size: pocket (less than 1 hectare), neighborhood (less than 2 hectares), and city-size squares (larger than 2 hectares). The same thresholds are applied to parks.
b. Sport and leisure facilities cover both privately and publicly owned or used spaces. Other facilities such as libraries, universities, and schools have also been identified based on OpenStreetMap data (https://www.openstreetmap.org/) but are not included as the share of land in this analysis. For further details, see appendix B of this volume.

Public spaces in this chapter refer to open and green areas (OGAs), streets, and facilities such as open-sky markets and sport facilities that are identifiable through remote sensing (table 5.1). Spaces that possess spatial characteristics or land-use patterns that could be developed into public spaces, but that are not used or vacant, were also identified.[2] For example, "leftover" green spaces along stormwater drains may not have been intended for public use but could potentially be repurposed to provide better access for neighborhood residents.

To identify these public spaces in cities, the following main criteria were considered in the spatial assessment and classification of public-space typology: land-use patterns, proximity to access roads, adjacency to features such as water bodies, location, shape, and size. The methodology for this research is explained in appendix B of this volume. Site-level land ownership, access, and quality were not assessed in this chapter but will be discussed in chapter 6. Other policy issues related to the implementation of individual public-space projects are discussed in the city case studies of Part III (chapters 8–16).

The cities selected for this analysis are some of the world's largest and densest cities. Dense urban environments often face pressures from increased

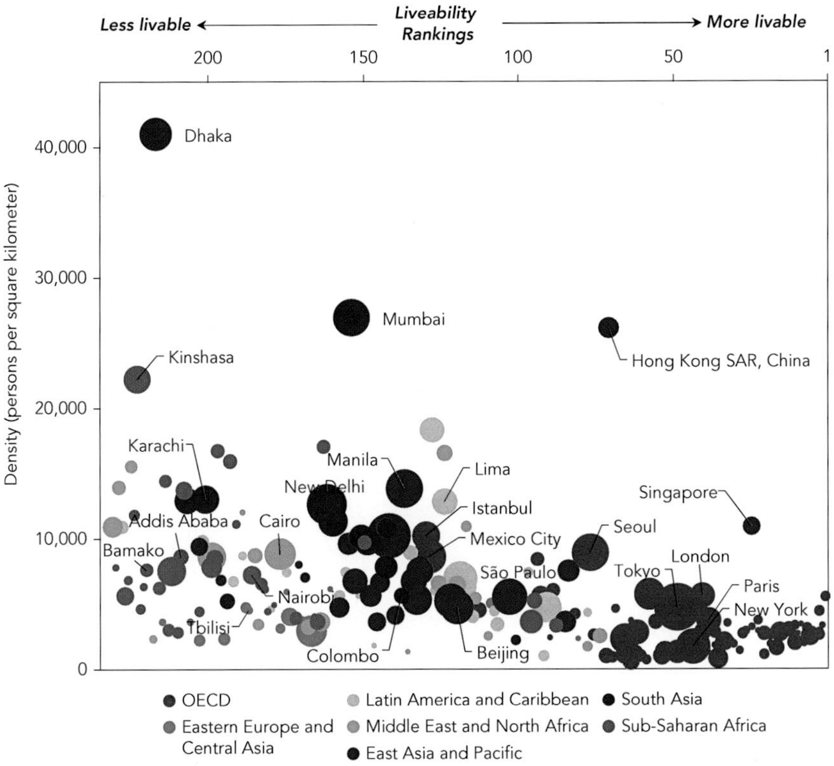

FIGURE 5.1 **Cities' Quality of Living Rankings in Relation to Population Density, 2019**

Source: World Bank, based on 2019 Mercer Quality of Living Rankings (https://mobilityexchange.mercer.com/Insights/quality-of-living-rankings) and Demographia 2019 population density data (http://www.demographia.com/db-intlua-cover.htm).

Note: The Mercer Livability Index ranking ranges from 1 (most livable) to 231 (least livable). Bubble size is proportional to total population of the city. OECD = Organisation for Economic Co-operation and Development.

demands on land for different types of land uses. Existing public spaces are often susceptible to development pressures and real estate interests. They are also vulnerable to potential transformation into other, nonpedestrian uses such as parking lots and to encroachment by nonpermitted uses (UN-Habitat 2013). Two cities—Dhaka, Bangladesh, and Karachi, Pakistan—were selected as case studies because they represent two large, densely populated megacities in South Asia that are ranked low on livability measures and are accompanied by weak planning and enforcement capacity (figure 5.1). Lima, Peru, is a densely populated Latin American megacity facing similar challenges, although it exhibits medium levels of livability.[3] The spatial analysis in this chapter also covers other medium and small cities in Africa and the Middle East as comparators: Bamako, Mali,[4] and Fallujah and Ramadi in Iraq. Both Fallujah and Ramadi are postconflict cities that had a large part of their urban areas destroyed.

SPATIAL ASSESSMENT

Typology and Share of Public Spaces

Different types of public spaces serve different functions: some serve neighborhoods and local communities (such as small neighborhood parks), while others are destinations for larger city populations (such as larger city parks, plazas, and waterfronts). Other areas provide physical spaces for livelihoods (markets and streets) or recreation (parks, playgrounds, and stadiums). Streets, linear parks, and waterfronts help connect different neighborhoods and districts within the city. Cities can thus benefit from a good mix of different types of public spaces.

The spatial distribution of differentially sized public spaces also matters. Two cities can have a similar share of total public spaces, but those spaces could vary in function and characteristics, even within the same type of public space. For example, City A may have one big, centrally located park that accounts for most of the total public-space area, while City B's public space might consist of small pocket and neighborhood parks distributed across the city. In City A, residents enjoy a large green open space that offers more services (such as events, botanic gardens, and so on) as a key citywide destination, but it would be less accessible for residents who live farther away. On the other hand, City B's residents can better access small resting and gathering areas in their neighborhoods and communities.

The composition of public-space typologies across selected cities can vary significantly. For example, in the comparative analysis, Dhaka appears to possess a more diverse and distinct mix of public spaces than Karachi, where street areas and unclassifiable small parcels predominate. This difference is also shown in Dhaka's and Karachi's relative diversity indexes, which are 0.83 and 0.62, respectively.[5] In Dhaka, a large proportion of public spaces exhibit characteristics that resemble neighborhood parks, sport and leisure facilities, and waterfront areas, which are less represented in Karachi. In Lima, pocket-size public spaces account for a relatively large share (2.9 percent of total built-up area), compared with less than 1 percent in the other cities. This implies that public spaces in Lima tend to be more scattered.[6] In Fallujah and Ramadi, parks appear almost nonexistent and composed mainly of streets—a likely result of the destruction from the recent conflict in these cities. These various compositions resulted in the cities' different levels of diversity of public spaces.

In general, streets occupy about two-thirds of the total area of public spaces (figure 5.2). Within the study area, Lima had significantly more street spaces (about twice the number) than Dhaka and Karachi. The share of street space is an important indicator as a proxy for mobility and prosperity (UN-Habitat 2013). Furthermore, understanding how the street areas are composed and function is a critical first step in reclaiming streets for people (box 5.1) and to promote walkability and accessibility (NACTO 2016; Targa et al. 2019).

Large tracts of spaces that could be potential public spaces were observed in the case cities. In Dhaka and Karachi, around 15–21 percent of total built-up areas were identified as "other potential spaces"—areas that had the potential but were not being classified in the analysis or were vacant. This suggests the opportunity for the creation of new public spaces, whether through public investments or integrated as part of private development.

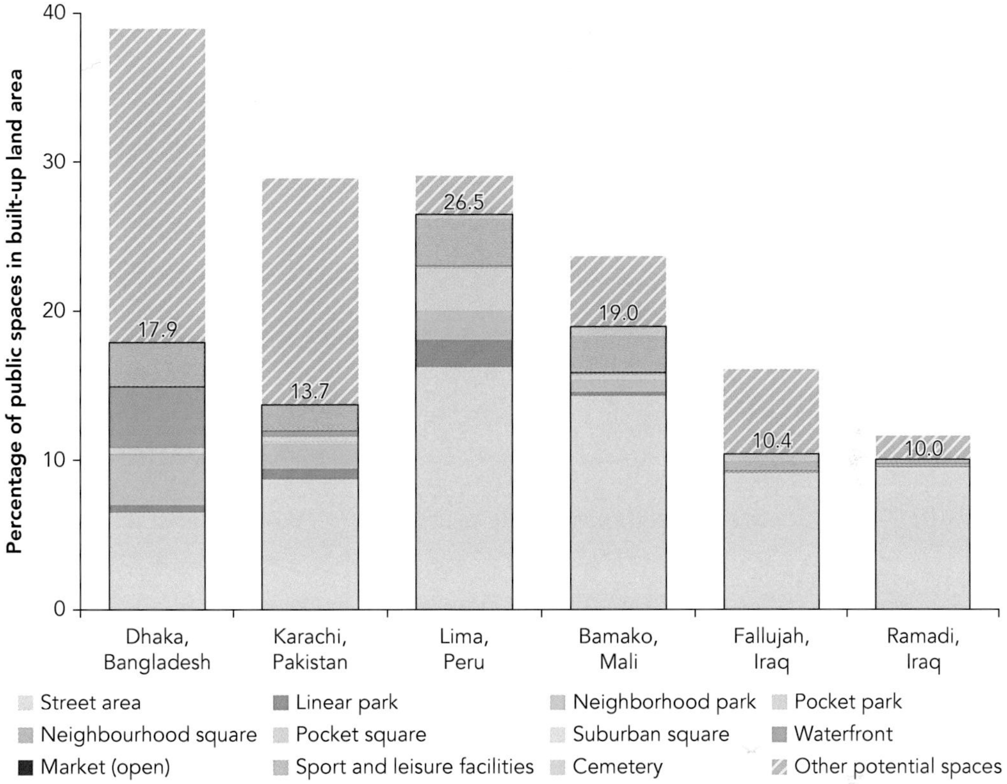

FIGURE 5.2 **Proportion of Public Spaces in Selected Cities, by Type, Identified from Remote Sensing, 2018**

Source: World Bank, based on EO4SD-Urban data, http://www.eo4sd-urban.info/.
Note: "Other potential spaces" include vacant areas, residual green areas, forest and dense trees, and inaccessible areas. This list of public-space types is not exhaustive. For detailed definitions of each category, see appendix B. EO4SD = Earth Observation for Sustainable Development, a joint project between the World Bank and the European Space Agency.

Coverage of Public Spaces

Despite the lack of high-quality public spaces in many cities, a spatial analysis of some of the world's densest megacities shows that the coverage of public spaces is not insignificant. Even the densest cities and least livable cities can achieve good distribution of public spaces. For example, in Karachi, 95 percent of people live within 400 meters of public spaces (about a five-minute walk), compared with 74 percent in Dhaka and 75 percent in Lima, even though the total share of public spaces in Karachi is lower than in Dhaka and Lima.[7]

Not surprisingly, public spaces are mostly concentrated within urban core areas. The coverage of public spaces (excluding streets) within a five-minute walking distance (400 meters)[8] accounts for 70–90 percent within the city center, but it rapidly declines in neighborhoods farther from city centers (figure 5.3). Lima exhibits a more gradual decline in public-space coverage farther from the city center.

BOX 5.1 BARCELONA, SPAIN: CONVERTING NEIGHBORHOOD STREET GRIDS TO "SUPERBLOCKS" AND SCALING UP TO CITY LEVEL

As part of Barcelona's urban mobility plan in 2015, Superblocks[a] is an approach to urban mobility that seeks to create pedestrian porosity, encourage nonmotorized transport (NMT), and reclaim public spaces in the city. The Barcelona government defines the superblocks model as a way of organizing the city by reversing the distribution of public space between vehicles and people—and giving priority to pedestrians—to improve environmental conditions and people's quality of life.

Each superblock refers to a grid of nine city blocks where most traffic flow is redirected to the perimeter roads and vehicular restrictions applied within internal streets (figure B5.1.1). Some of the restrictions within a superblock include the following:

- Only residents and those serving local business within the superblock can access the interior streets by vehicle.
- The speed limit is 10 kilometers per hour.
- All interior streets are one-way.
- Curbside parking is replaced by underground parking.

The superblocks initiative seeks to (a) improve the habitability of public spaces, (b) move toward more sustainable mobility, (c) increase and improve urban greenery and biodiversity, and (d) promote public participation and joint responsibility. The initiative hopes to free up 60 percent of streets currently dedicated to motorized traffic and to reduce vehicle traffic by 21 percent within two years (Bausells 2016).

The city plans to implement 500 superblocks in the city, accounting for almost 70 percent of the total streets to mixed land use. Some of the plan's pilot projects were implemented in several neighborhoods, including the

(box continues next page)

Cities' overall green coverage is also scarce and decreasing as a proportion of the built-up areas over time.[9] For example, between 2006 and 2017, the share of green areas out of the built-up areas has declined by 4.4 percent and 1.41 percent in Dhaka and Karachi, respectively. Moreover, the green area per capita in dense cities tends to be low—for example, 4.8 square meters per capita in Dhaka.

Connectivity of Public Spaces

"Connectivity" refers to how public spaces are connected to each other as part of a network. A neighborhood served by a concentration of different

BOX 5.1 BARCELONA, SPAIN: CONVERTING NEIGHBORHOOD STREET GRIDS TO "SUPERBLOCKS" AND SCALING UP TO CITY LEVEL *(Continued)*

Poblenou neighborhood and around the Sant Antoni market. With lessons learned from these pilots, the superblock plan is to be scaled up across the city (Roberts 2019).

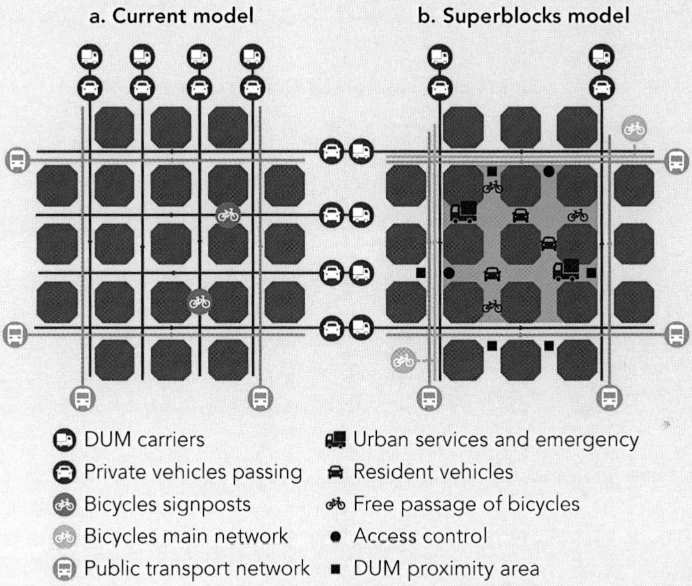

FIGURE B5.1.1 **Barcelona's Superblocks Model for Urban Mobility in Public Spaces**

Source: World Bank based on Bausells 2016. ©World Bank. Further permission required for reuse.
Note: DUM = distribució urbana de mercaderies (urban merchandise distribution) for the loading and unloading of goods.
a. "Superblocks" here is different from the "superblock" typology referred to in other parts of the world (like in China), which are long city blocks consisting of high-rise residential buildings and surrounded by large arterials, stretching many lanes across, that are not walkable.

types of public spaces and amenities such as libraries, community centers, sport facilities, and community parks can contribute to the creation of a sense of place and build neighborliness and social cohesion, as evidenced by a study of U.S. cities (Cox and Streeter 2019). The number of public spaces within 400 meters from another public space is used as a proxy to indicate the concentration and connectedness of public spaces accessible by walking.

In Dhaka, almost 25 percent of total public spaces are isolated (no others are within 400 meters), while in Karachi most (65 percent) of the public spaces have at least one or two public spaces nearby (figure 5.4). At the same time, Dhaka has some areas where public spaces are highly concentrated

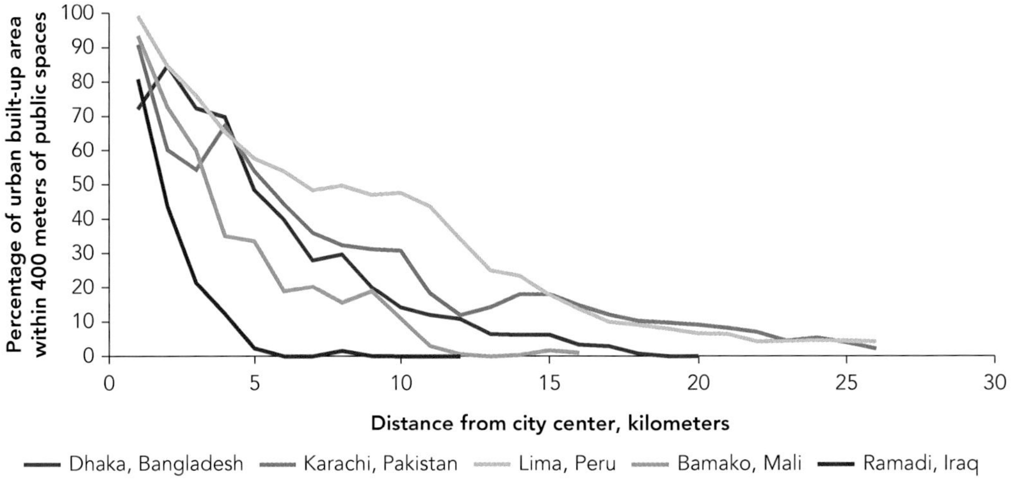

FIGURE 5.3 **Share of Urban Built-Up Areas Near Public Spaces, by Distance from City Center, in Selected Cities, 2017**

Source: World Bank, based on 2019 EO4SD-Urban data, http://www.eo4sd-urban.info/.
Note: "Near" refers to a distance of 400 meters or less. The definition and locations of city centers are explained in each case study later this chapter, and the public spaces included in this analysis are parks, waterfronts, squares, and markets, excluding streets. EO4SD = Earth Observation for Sustainable Development, a project of the European Space Agency. Because of data availability, Lima and Bamako refers to data from 2018.

(more than six within a 400-meter buffer), whereas Karachi has almost none. In Lima, almost all (96 percent) of the public spaces are well connected and located within walking distances from each other. Unlike in Dhaka and Karachi, Lima's public spaces are primarily pocket-scale, suggesting that the public spaces in Lima are mostly small but equally distributed across the city.

The connectivity of streets is also a proxy for urbanity (that is, highly urbanized areas have denser street grids) and is associated with better walkability. The density of street intersections is used as a measure of mobility and safety on streets, given that wider roads with fewer intersections are associated with more pedestrian fatalities (Salat and Ollivier 2017; UN-Habitat 2013).

Using the benchmark of 100 intersections per square kilometer in city core areas as a proxy for good connectivity and access to services (UN-Habitat 2013), some areas within cities fall short of this benchmark, but with considerable variation across neighborhoods (figure 5.5). For example, in Karachi, while about 17 percent of the city's core area (within 10 kilometers of the city center) exceeds 100 intersections per square kilometer, a sizable amount of land (about 30 percent) has 25 or fewer intersections per square kilometer. Notably, some of the significant valley points in figure 5.5—such as the 10–15 kilometer area of Bamako and the 4–6 kilometer area of Karachi—are observed mainly because of the locations of massive infrastructure such as airport sites.

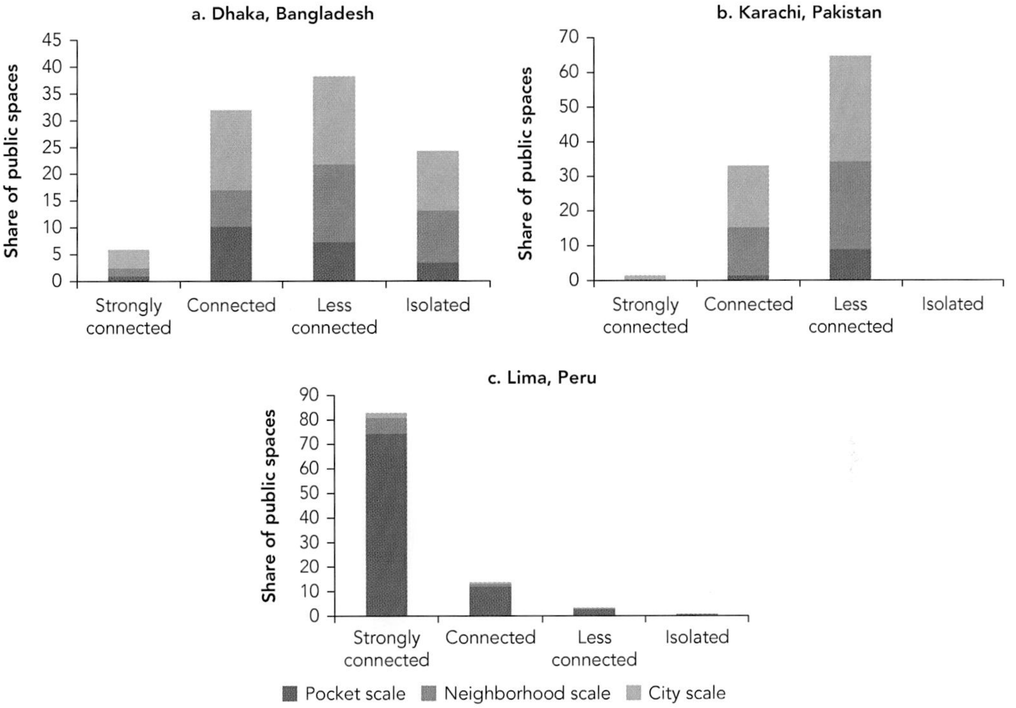

FIGURE 5.4 **Connectivity of Public Spaces in Selected Cities, 2017**

Source: World Bank, based on 2019 EO4SD-Urban data, http://www.eo4sd-urban.info/.
Note: "Strongly connected" means six to eight public spaces are within 400 meters of a public space. "Connected" means three to five public spaces are within 400 meters. "Less connected" means only one to two public spaces are within 400 meters. "Isolated" means that no public spaces are within 400 meters. Pocket, neighborhood, and city scales refer to the following: pocket (less than 1 hectare), neighborhood (less than 2 hectares), and city scale (larger than 2 hectares). EO4SD = Earth Observation for Sustainable Development, a project of the European Space Agency.

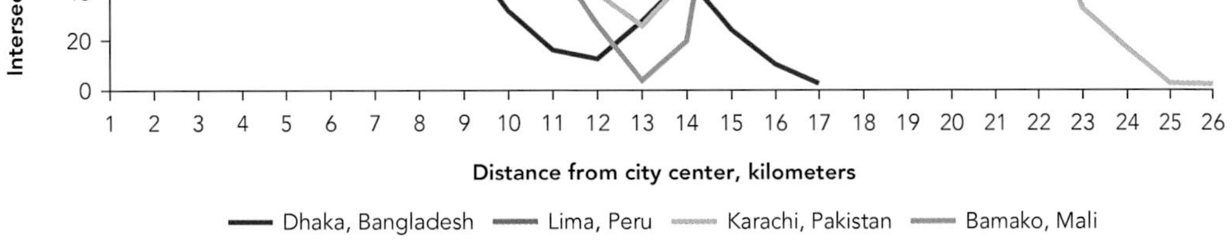

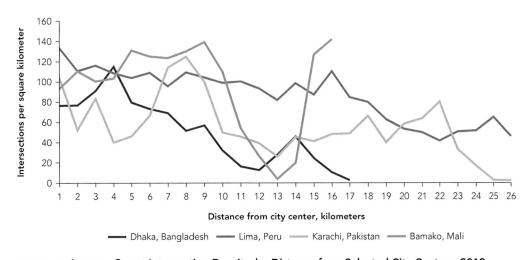

FIGURE 5.5 **Average Street Intersection Density, by Distance from Selected City Centers, 2019**

Source: World Bank, based on 2019 EO4SD-Urban data, http://www.eo4sd-urban.info/.
Note: The total area is defined by administrative boundaries of the cities. EO4SD = Earth Observation for Sustainable Development, a project of the European Space Agency.

CASE STUDIES: DHAKA, KARACHI, AND LIMA

Dhaka, Bangladesh

The Dhaka Metropolitan Area is the political and economic hub of Bangladesh. In recent decades, Dhaka has grown rapidly: its population increased to 18 million in 2015, 10 times the population of 40 years ago. This growth has contributed to Dhaka having one of the densest populations, with 440 persons per hectare (UN DESA 2018). Its urban footprint has expanded by 26 percent between 2006 and 2017 (map 5.1, panel a).

Despite its rapid urban growth, Dhaka is ranked as one of the least livable cities in the world (EIU 2017), mainly because its growth has not been accompanied by adequate public services. For instance, road networks are insufficient to support walking and traffic. The share of street areas out of total built-up areas is only 6.5 percent, which is lower than in other case cities.[10] Significant gaps in the provision of roads also exist between the central and eastern parts of Dhaka (map 5.1, panel b). Moreover, green areas in Dhaka have declined by 4.4 percent as a proportion of total built-up areas between 2006 and 2017, and its green space per capita is limited as 4.8 square meters in 2017.[11]

Public spaces in Dhaka are distributed along the north-south direction, where a main railway and highway of Dhaka are located, and they are heavily

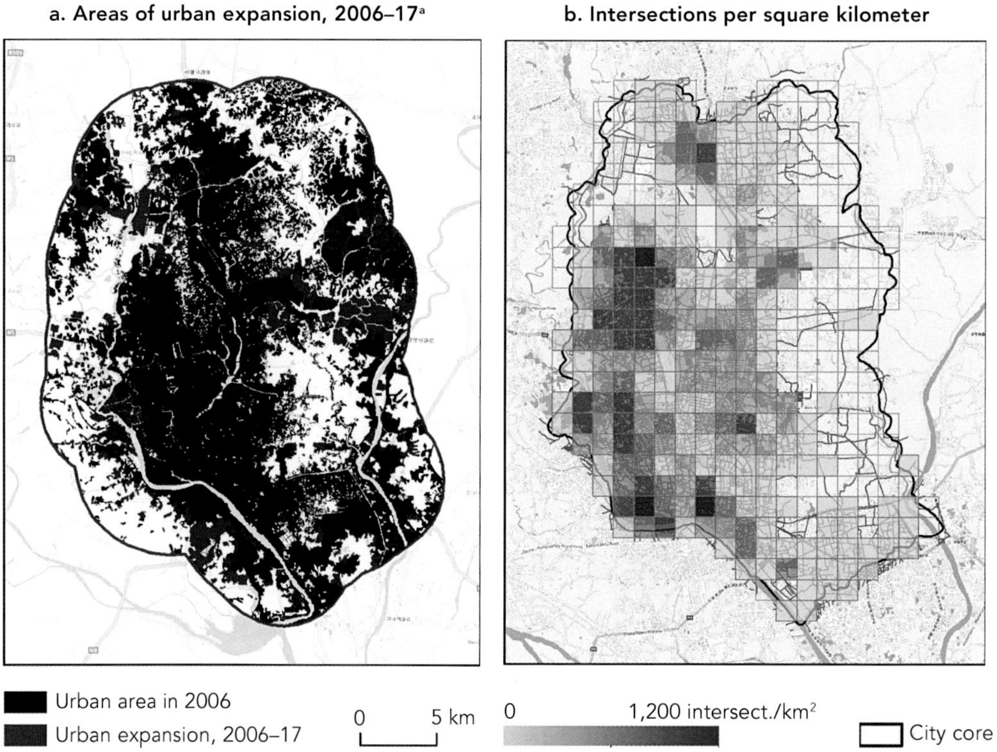

MAP 5.1 **Spatial Distribution of Urban Growth and Transport Network in Dhaka, Bangladesh**

Source: 2019 EO4SD-Urban data, http://www.eo4sd-urban.info/. ©World Bank. Further permission required for reuse.
Note: EO4SD = Earth Observation for Sustainable Development, a project of the European Space Agency.
a. In panel b, "urban" areas refer to built-up (impervious) areas detected from high-resolution satellite imageries.

concentrated in the central and western parts of the city. Many public spaces in eastern Dhaka, however, are isolated from road networks (map 5.2, panel a) as well as public-space networks (map 5.2, panel b). This disparity lowered the city's overall level of accessibility to public spaces; the share of people who live within 400 meters of OGA in Dhaka is 74 percent, which is relatively lower than in Karachi (95 percent).

Benefiting from the city's rich natural assets such as the presence of rivers and high vegetation areas, Dhaka is endowed with a variety of different types of public spaces, ranging from waterfronts to city parks. Map 5.3 illustrates the distribution of different types of public spaces across the city, where neighborhood park and leisure facilities are the dominant types. Large land areas in the northern part of the city include leisure facilities in military areas and a national zoo. Although Dhaka seemingly has access to a large variety of public spaces, these areas are often poorly managed. For instance, many waterfronts are fenced and filled with trash, while they are informally being used by people as public spaces. Of the total built-up area, 21 percent is identified as "other OGA" that can be better used as proper public spaces.[12] The public-space classification in this analysis was found to be about 85 percent accurate, based on ground-truth verification (for details, see appendix B).

a. Distance from public space to nearest road **b. Distance between closest public spaces**[a]

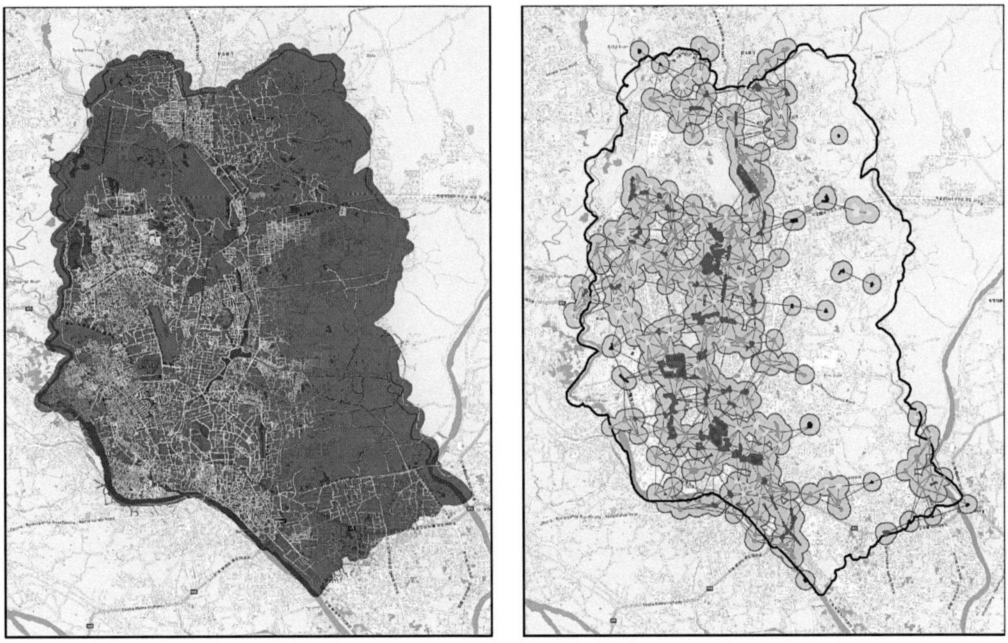

City core
0 6,500 m

Distance (Euclidean) to neighboring park
400 meter catchment area
0 m 1,000 m 2,000 m
0 5 km

MAP 5.2 **Connectivity of Public Spaces in Dhaka, Bangladesh, 2019**

Source: 2019 EO4SD-Urban data http://www.eo4sd-urban.info/. ©World Bank. Further permission required for reuse.

Note: EO4SD = Earth Observation for Sustainable Development, a project of the European Space Agency.

a. In panel b, distances are calculated based on Euclidian (straight-line) measurement.

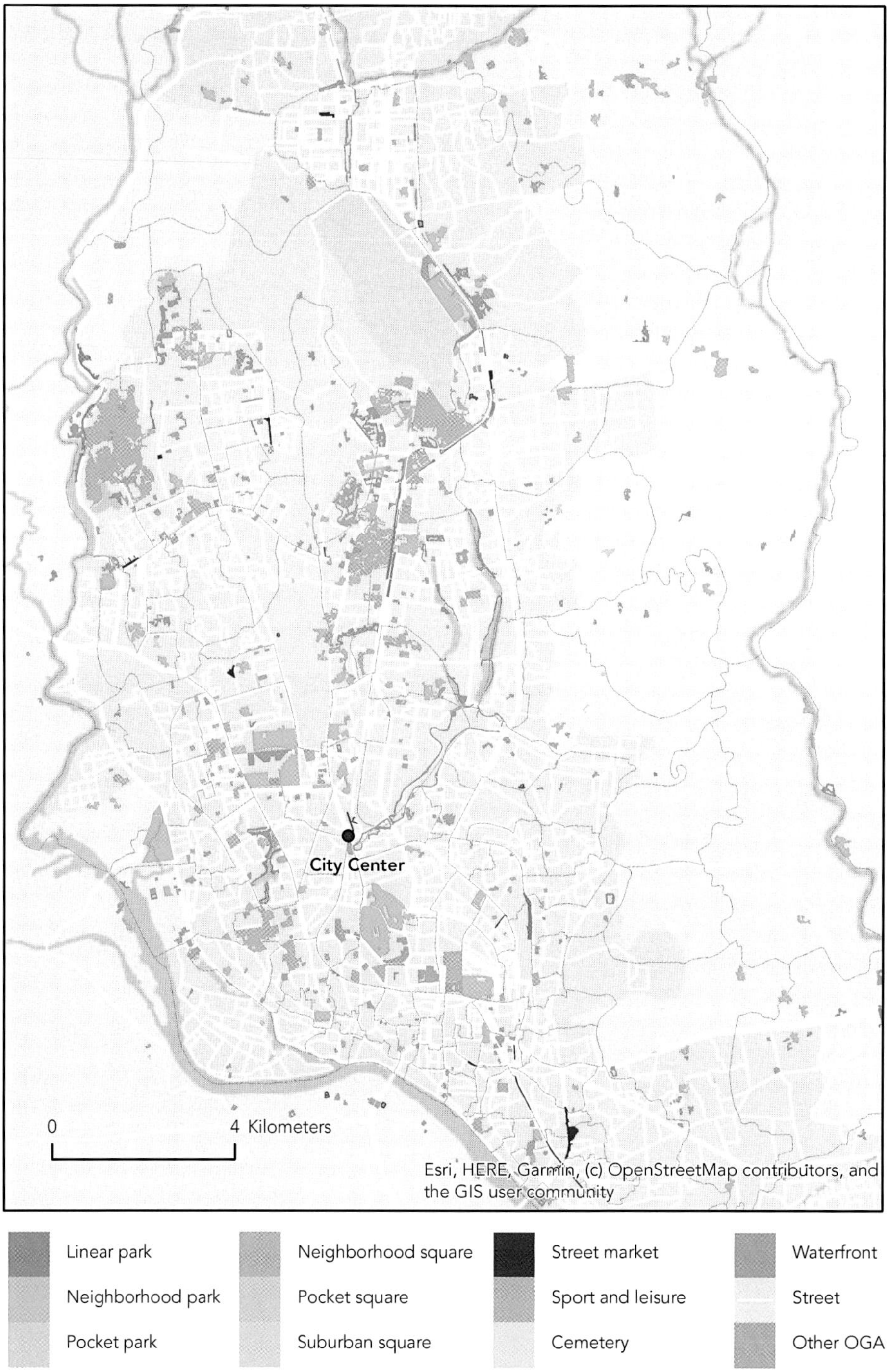

MAP 5.3 **Public-Space Distribution, by Type, in Dhaka, Bangladesh, 2019**

Source: World Bank, based on 2019 EO4SD-Urban data, http://www.eo4sd-urban.info/. ©World Bank. Further permission required for reuse.

Note: EO4SD = Earth Observation for Sustainable Development, a project of the European Space Agency. OGA = open and green area. The city center point in Dhaka was defined on the Karwan Bazar circle (23°45′ N, 90°23′36″ E).

Karachi, Pakistan

Karachi is the center of the economic and demographic growth of Pakistan. In 2012, the city contributed at least 11.4 percent to the national gross domestic product (GDP), and it reduced poverty by 14 percent between 2005 and 2015. The city's population grew from 10 million in 1998 to 16 million in 2017, primarily through immigration.[13] The urban extent also grew by 8 percent from 2005 to 2017, consisting of 13.4 square kilometers in the core city and 211.8 square kilometers in the larger urban zone (map 5.4, panel a).

However, the city's urban environment and infrastructure provision have not kept pace with its growth. Green areas have decreased by 4 percent, whereas the urban extent in the core city has expanded by 8 percent between 2005 and 2017. The average number of street intersections per square kilometer is 71.7—which is lower than the United Nations Human Settlements Programme's (UN-Habitat) benchmark of 100 intersections per square kilometer (map 5.4, panel b)—and the average road length per square kilometer is 13.21. Informal settlements are also pervasive in the central part of Karachi.

Karachi appears to have an equally accessible and connected public-space network. The share of public spaces out of total built-up areas is 14 percent; the share of street areas is 8.7 percent. Even though the share is relatively lower than in Dhaka and Lima, almost 95 percent of people live within 400 meters of OGAs. Public spaces in Karachi appear to be highly connected to each other (map 5.5).

A closer examination of public-space typology shows a considerable number of unclassifiable public spaces and a relative lack of city and neighborhood parks in the city. In map 5.6, areas that are identified as "other OGA" are mostly vacant land or construction sites that haven't been used for a long time. Moreover, despite being a highly residential city, many residential neighborhoods in Karachi have almost no green areas that can provide environmental and social benefits for people. To further interpret these results, additional direct observation is required.

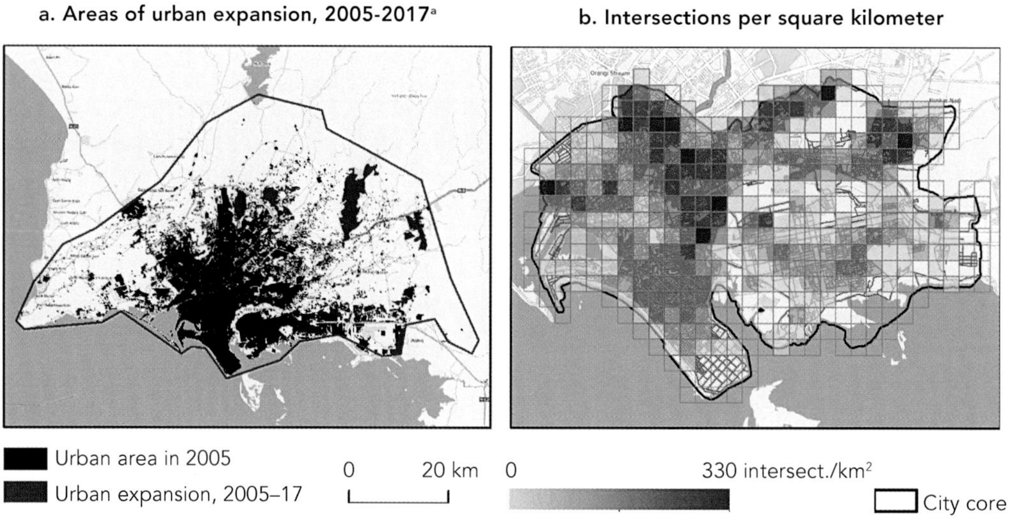

MAP 5.4 **Spatial Distribution of Urban Growth and Road Networks in Karachi, Pakistan**

Source: 2019 EO4SD-Urban data http://www.eo4sd-urban.info/. ©World Bank. Further permission required for reuse.
Note: EO4SD = Earth Observation for Sustainable Development, a project of the European Space Agency.
a. In panel a, "urban" areas refer to built-up (impervious) areas detected from high-resolution satellite images.

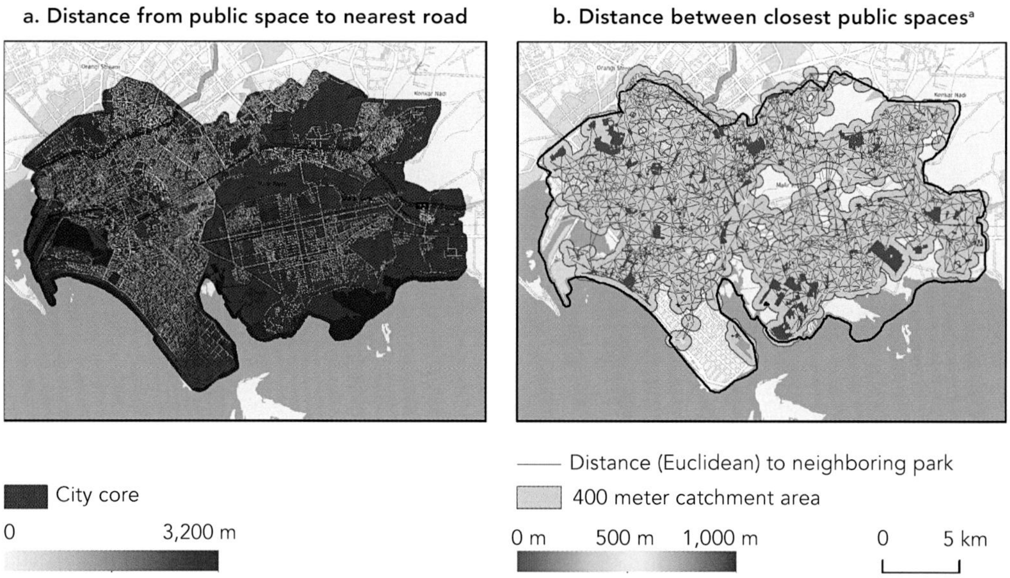

MAP 5.5 **Connectivity of Public Spaces across Karachi, Pakistan, 2019**

Source: 2019 EO4SD-Urban data, http://www.eo4sd-urban.info/. ©World Bank. Further permission required for reuse.
Note: EO4SD = Earth Observation for Sustainable Development, a project of the European Space Agency.
a. In panel b, distances are calculated based on Euclidian (straight-line) measurement.

MAP 5.6 **Public-Space Distribution, by Type, in Karachi, Pakistan, 2019**

Source: World Bank, based on 2019 EO4SD-Urban data, http://www.eo4sd-urban.info/. ©World Bank. Further permission required for reuse.
Note: EO4SD = Earth Observation for Sustainable Development, a project of the European Space Agency. OGA = open and green area. The city center was defined on the western end of the I.I. Chundrigar Road (24°50′57″ N, 66°59′52″E).

Lima, Peru

Lima is a megacity of 10 million people that covers 1,500 square miles, concentrates 32 percent of the country's population, and accounts for 45 percent of national GDP (Berube et al. 2015). Since the mid-1950s, Lima started to experience an unprecedented stream of immigration, and after 2000, it has experienced leapfrog development, mainly in the northern part of the city (map 5.7). These unplanned developments have been associated with public service disparities between neighborhoods and pervasive informal settlements mostly in the foothills on the peripheries of Lima.

Public spaces are relatively well distributed across the study area, excluding some mountain areas. The average number of street intersections per square kilometer is 154, which is considered high based on UN-Habitat's benchmark of 100 per square kilometer (map 5.8).[14] The public spaces are also accessible from streets (map 5.9, panel a) and are well connected to one another as a network (map 5.9, panel b). Most people (75 percent) live within 400 meters of OGAs, which is similar to Dhaka (74 percent) but lower than Karachi (95 percent).

Even though Lima's public spaces seem to be well connected as a network, they lack city-scale public spaces and are physically inaccessible in many cases. The share of public spaces out of total built-up areas is 26.5 percent, including 16.2 percent of the street areas. Among all types of public spaces, pocket-size public spaces (smaller than 1 hectare) are predominant, at almost 90 percent (map 5.10). The insufficiency of larger public

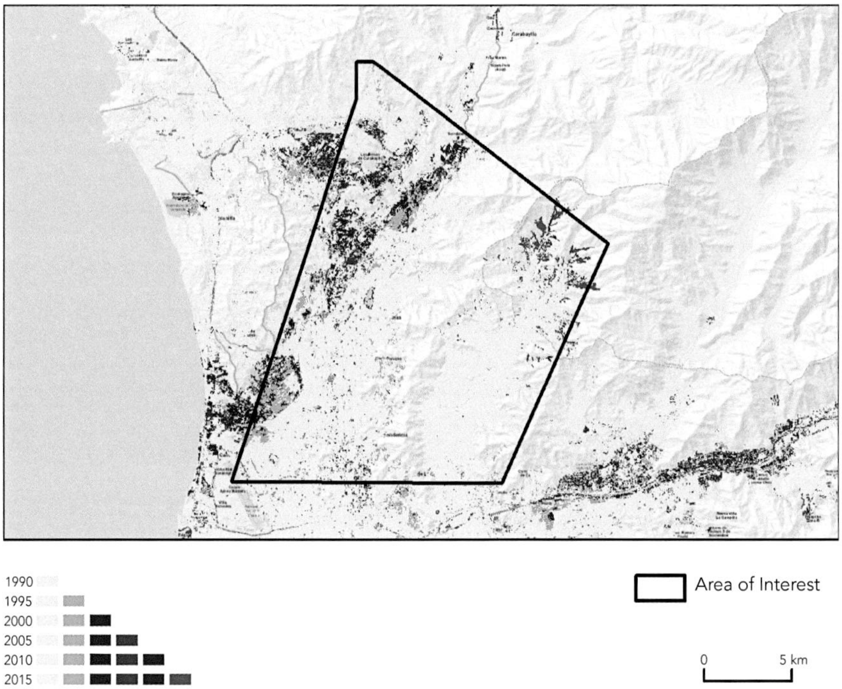

MAP 5.7 **Extent of Settlement Development in Study Area of Lima, Peru, 1990–2015**

Source: World Bank, based on 2019 EO4SD-Urban data, http://www.eo4sd-urban.info/. ©World Bank. Further permission required for reuse.

Note: EO4SD = Earth Observation for Sustainable Development, a project of the European Space Agency.

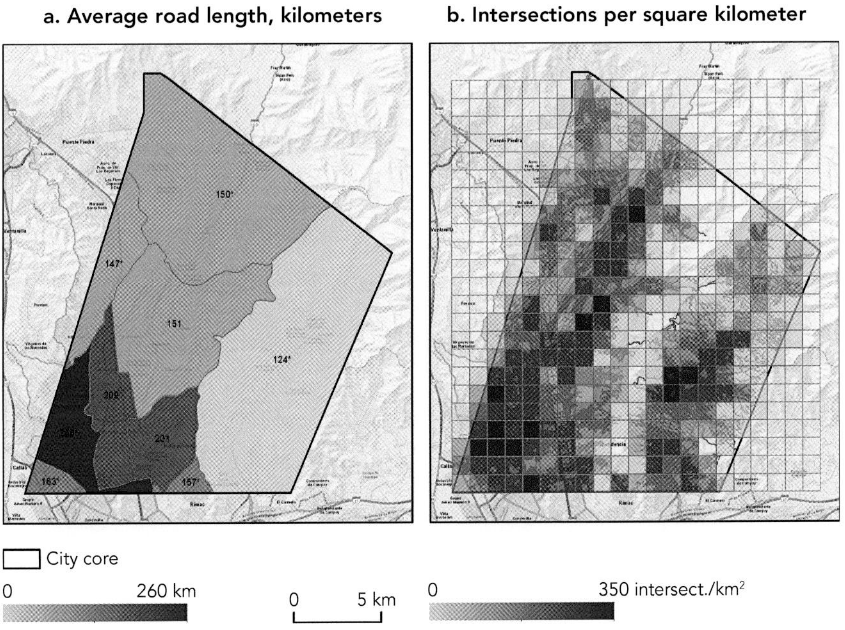

MAP 5.8 **Road Networks in Lima, Peru, 2019**

Source: World Bank, based on 2019 EO4SD-Urban data, http://www.eo4sd-urban.info/. ©World Bank. Further permission required for reuse.
Note: EO4SD = Earth Observation for Sustainable Development, a project of the European Space Agency.

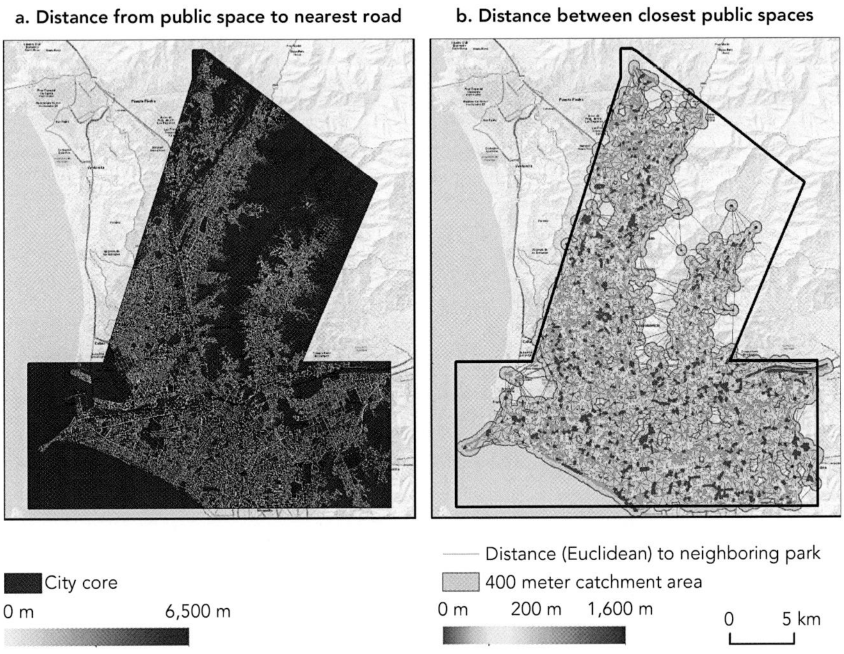

MAP 5.9 **Connectivity of Public Spaces across Lima, Peru, 2019**

Source: World Bank, based on 2019 EO4SD-Urban data, http://www.eo4sd-urban.info/. ©World Bank. Further permission required for reuse.
Note: Distances are calculated based on Euclidian (straight-line) measurement. EO4SD = Earth Observation for Sustainable Development, a project of the European Space Agency.

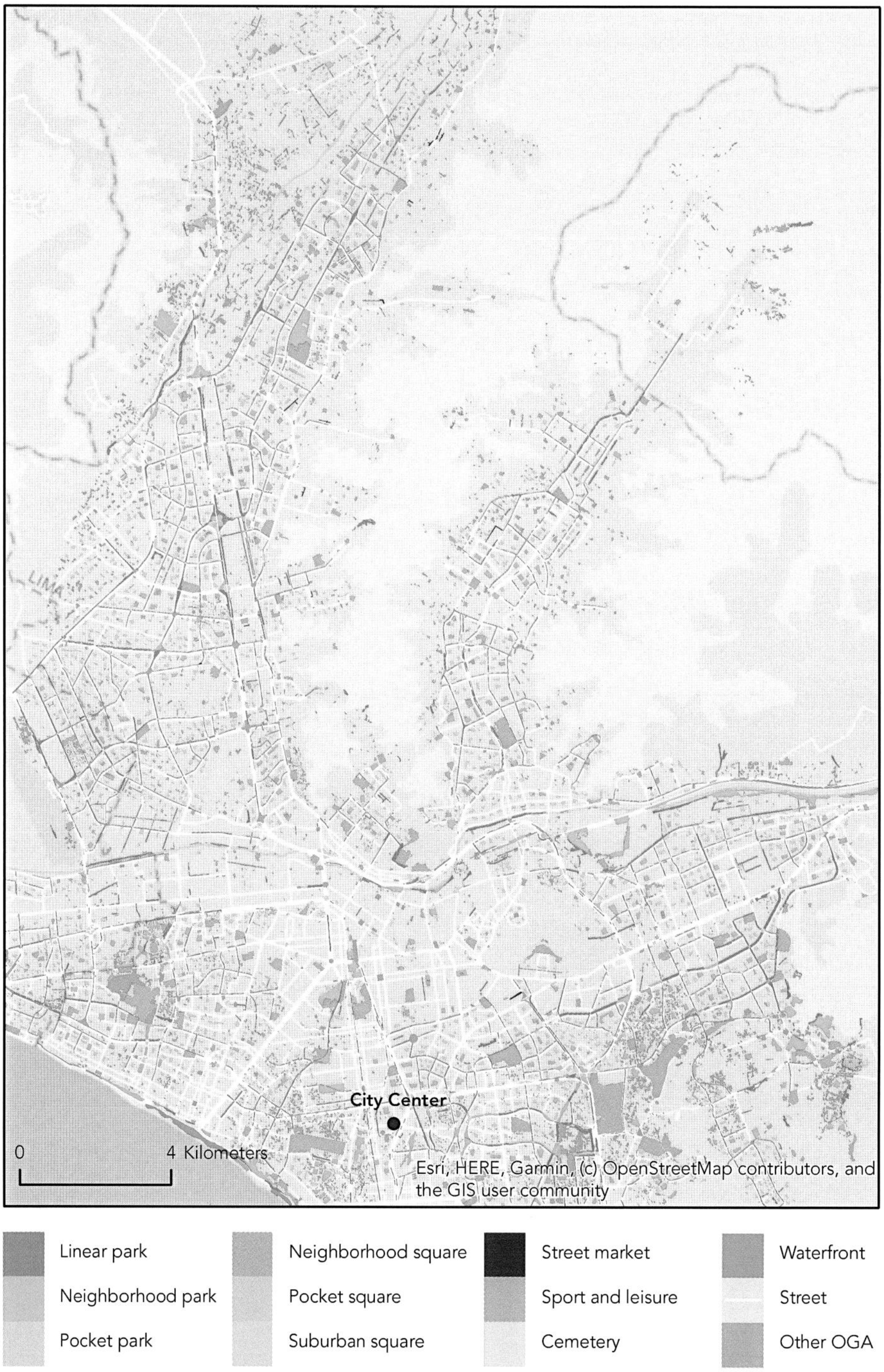

MAP 5.10 **Public-Space Distribution, by Type, in Lima, Peru, 2019**

Source: World Bank, based on 2019 EO4SD-Urban data, http://www.eo4sd-urban.info/. ©World Bank. Further permission required for reuse.

Note: EO4SD = Earth Observation for Sustainable Development, a project of the European Space Agency. OGA = open and green area. The Lima city center was defined based on the location of a central square near Lima's town hall (12°38′19″ N, 7°59′48″ W) in the main financial district, San Isidro.

spaces and landmarks could limit the diversity of places suited for different activities. Also, importantly, public spaces in Lima tend to be fenced and used privately, which hampered active use of public space by people (see more in the Lima case study, chapter 12). This emphasizes the importance of a comprehensive set of assessments—not only on quantity but also on the quality and use of public spaces—to have a balanced picture of the city (see chapter 6).

NOTES

1. Since 2008, the ESA has worked closely with the international financial institutions (IFIs) and their client states to harness the benefits of earth observation (EO) in their operations and resources management. In this context, EO4SD is an ESA initiative that aims to increase the uptake of EO-based information in the IFIs' regional and global programs by means of a systematic user-driven approach. The EO4SD-Urban consortium represented by GISAT has developed a methodology supporting open-spaces identification, quantification, and characterization in collaboration with the World Bank Urbanscapes Group. For more information, see the EO4SD website: http://www.eo4sd-urban.info/.
2. The split between existing public spaces and "leftover" spaces identified through this analysis needs to be further investigated through ground truthing—that is, on-site collection of information.
3. Lima has a population of 11,355,000 and a density of 12,700 persons per square kilometer based on data derived from the 2018 Demographia data (http://www.demographia.com/). It was ranked 80 out of 140 in the Economist Intelligence Unit (EIU) 2017 Global Livability Index (EIU 2017).
4. Bamako has a population of 3,455,000 and a density of 8,300 persons per square kilometer based on the 2018 Demographia data (http://www.demographia.com/).
5. The diversity index (DI) here is calculated using the inverse normalized Herfindahl Index formula:

$$1-\left(\frac{\left(\sum_{i=1}^{N} ps_i^2\right)-\frac{1}{N}}{1-\frac{1}{N}}\right),$$

   where ps_i is the share of public-space type i in a city, and N is the number of types of public spaces. The DI ranges from 0-1. A DI of 0 means that public spaces are composed of just one type of public space. The DIs of various cities are as follows: Dhaka (0.82), Karachi (0.62), Lima (0.65), Bamako (0.46), Fallujah (0.24), and Ramadi (0.10).
6. This finding is also supported by a qualitative study on public spaces in Lima (chapter 12).
7. This analysis excluded street areas and considered only the share of selected open and green spaces and public facilities.
8. For further discussion of proximity to public spaces, see appendix B.
9. "Green coverage" refers to green patches detected from high-resolution satellite imagery, regardless of their accessibility and quality, to measure overall greenness of cities.
10. Street-area data from 2019 EO4SD-Urban: http://www.eo4sd-urban.info/.
11. Green-area data from 2019 EO4SD-Urban: http://www.eo4sd-urban.info/.
12. Even if these areas are not owned by governments, there are policy tools for municipalities to better manage those spaces for the general public. For more detailed discussions of these tools, see chapters 2 and 3.
13. GDP, poverty, and reduction data from World Bank Open Data: https://data.worldank.org.
14. The results of this analysis need to be carefully interpreted because the study area was limited to the partial city (excluding the southern area) owing to Lima's extremely large size.

REFERENCES

Bausells, Marta. 2016. "Superblocks to the Rescue: Barcelona's Plan to Give Streets Back to Residents." *The Guardian*. May 17 (accessed June 30, 2019), https://www.theguardian.com/cities/2016/may/17/superblocks-rescue-barcelona-spain-plan-give-streets-back-residents.

Berube, Alan, Jesus Leal Trujillo, Tao Ran, and Joseph Parilla. 2015. "Global Metro Monitor 2014: An Uncertain Recovery." Report of the Metropolitan Policy Program, The Brookings Institution, Washington, DC.

Cox, Daniel A., and Ryan Streeter. 2019. "The Importance of Place: Neighborhood Amenities as a Source of Social Connection and Trust." Report, American Enterprise Institute, Washington, DC.

EIU (Economist Intelligence Unit). 2017. "Global Liveability Report 2017." Annual Urban Quality-of-Life Ranking Report, EIU, London.

NACTO (National Association of City Transportation Officials). 2016. *Global Street Design Guide*. New York: Island Press.

Roberts, David. 2019. "Barcelona Is Pushing Out Cars and Putting In Superblocks. Here Are the 2 Biggest Challenges Ahead." *Vox*, April 10 (accessed June 30, 2019), https://www.vox.com/energy-and-environment/2019/4/10/18273895/traffic-barcelona-superblocks-gentrification.

Salat, Serge, and Gerald Ollivier. 2017. "Transforming the Urban Space through Transit-Oriented Development: The 3V Approach." Working Paper No. 113822, World Bank, Washington, DC.

Targa, Felipe, William Moose, Nicolás Estupiñán, and Carlos Mojica. 2019. "Urban Mobility, Health and Public Spaces: Reshaping Urban Landscapes." Urban 20 (U20) White Paper, Development Bank of Latin America, Inter-American Development Bank, and World Bank, Buenos Aires.

UN DESA (United Nations Department of Economic and Social Affairs). 2018. *World Urbanization Prospects: The 2018 Revision*. New York: UN DESA.

UN-Habitat (United Nations Human Settlements Programme). 2013. *Streets as Public Spaces and Drivers of Urban Prosperity*. Nairobi: UN-Habitat.

CHAPTER 6

ASSESSING THE QUALITY AND USE OF PUBLIC SPACES

Laura Petrella, Cecilia Anderson, José Chong, Andrew Rudd, and Joy Mutai

OVERVIEW

This chapter discusses the quality, use, and management of public spaces through four illustrative city case studies—Nairobi, Kenya; Addis Ababa, Ethiopia; Wuhan, China; and Bamenda, Cameroon—using the United Nations Human Settlements Programme's (UN-Habitat) framework focused on two dimensions:

- *A citywide public-space inventory* and a quantitative mapping focused on (a) typology of public spaces, and (b) ownership and management (UN-Habitat 2018)
- *A citywide scan* on public-space performance focused on an assessment of four main dimensions: safety, inclusivity, accessibility, and distribution (SIAD). The relative performance of public spaces in each case study was assessed using the SIAD framework, which scores each dimension on a scale of 0 percent (worst) to 100 percent (best). Each dimension comprises numerous citywide and site-specific indicators (methodologies for which are detailed in appendix C).

PUBLIC-SPACE INVENTORY

Types of Public Spaces

A citywide public-space inventory classifies and assesses the quality of public spaces—consisting of open public spaces, public facilities, and streets[1]—based on various criteria, such as functions or use, size, type of activity, and ownership and management actors (UN-Habitat 2015) (table 6.1). (Further details on data collection protocol can be found in appendix C.) These criteria also serve as a basis for the evaluation of the public spaces' performance, which will be discussed later in this chapter.

Ownership and Management

Among the various aspects of public spaces, the ownership and management structures deserve special attention in this section, because establishing a sustainable ownership and management plan for a city at the earliest stage of individual public-space interventions would be critical for the city's overall capital investment planning. An assessment of the current institutional arrangements for existing public spaces reveals that open public spaces are largely owned and managed by local governments (figure 6.1).

From most to least local government involvement, the government of Addis Ababa owns 71 percent and actively manages and maintains 39 percent of the city's public spaces; the private sector owns 13 percent; and the ownership status is unclear for 6 percent. In Wuhan, the local government owns 70 percent of the public spaces and manages 52 percent. Similarly, in Nairobi, a total of 50 percent and 43 percent of the open public spaces are owned and managed by the local government, respectively. Finally, Bamenda differs from other cities in having the most national government ownership (24 percent) and management (23 percent).

TABLE 6.1 **Types of Public Spaces and Key Evaluation Criteria**

Category	Function or use	Type of activity[a]	Users	Availability of amenities	Ownership and management actors
Open public spaces	Parks, playgrounds, squares, plazas, gardens, riparian areas, waterfronts	• Monofunctional • Multifunctional • Plurifunctional • Multifunctional and plurifunctional	• Children • Women • Youth • Older persons • People with disabilities	• Street lighting • Benches • Garbage bins • Toilet facilities • Signage and so on	• National government • Local government (county or city level) • Private • Others
Public facilities	Community centers, markets, and civic centers				
Streets	Alleyways, streets, passageways				

Source: Original prepared for this publication.
a. Activity type can be further disaggregated by specific activities, such as socializing, play-related, and art-related activities.

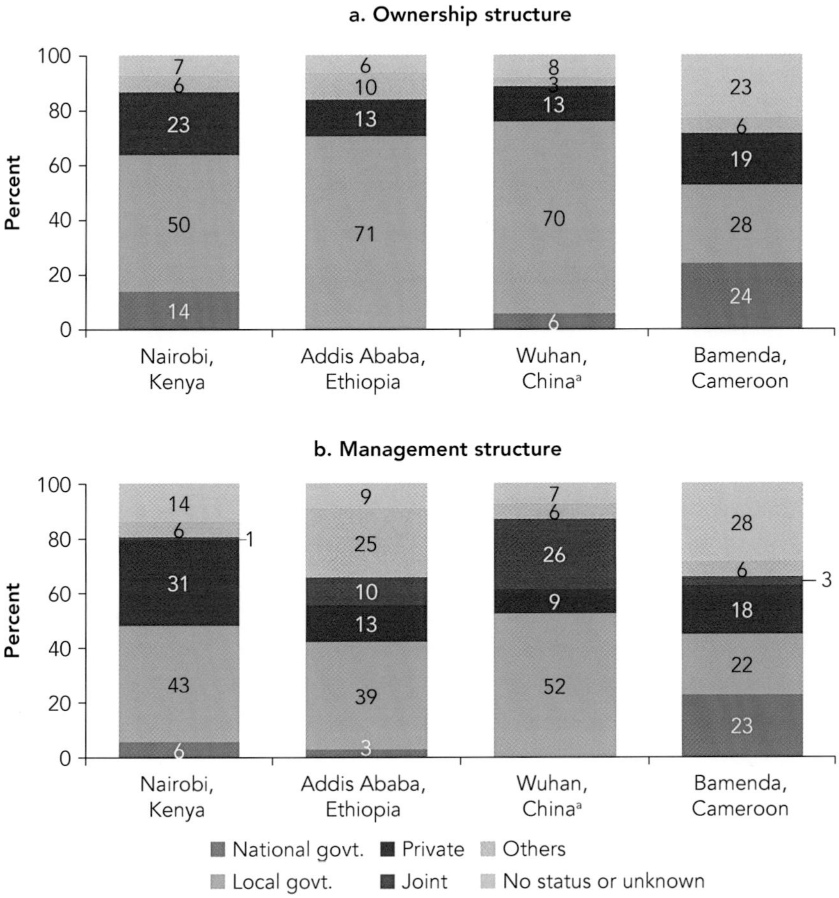

FIGURE 6.1 **Distribution of Ownership and Management Structure of Open Public Spaces in Four Case Cities**

Source: World Bank, based on United Nations Human Settlements (UN-Habitat) internal data.
Note: "Local government" refers to county or city government. "Private" includes private firms, corporations, associations, and so on. "Joint" management refers to the public spaces that are managed by both government and nongovernment entities. "Others" includes community organizations, nongovernmental organizations (NGOs), international organizations, and the like.
a. Jianghan District within the city of Wuhan.

PUBLIC-SPACE PERFORMANCE

SIAD public-space performance assessments were conducted for the cities of Nairobi, Addis Ababa, Wuhan, and Bamenda based on a selected 18 indicators around the four dimensions.[2] Overall, Nairobi and Addis Ababa were assessed to have relatively lower overall quality of public spaces, scoring 37.5 percent and 41.2 percent on the SIAD comparative index. Wuhan and Bamenda performed better, at 50.9 percent and 56.8 percent, respectively, which are mainly attributed to their high scores in safety (84.5 percent) and accessibility (59.7 percent), respectively. Each city's comparative index score as well as the score on each of the four dimensions can be depicted in a radar diagram (figure 6.2).

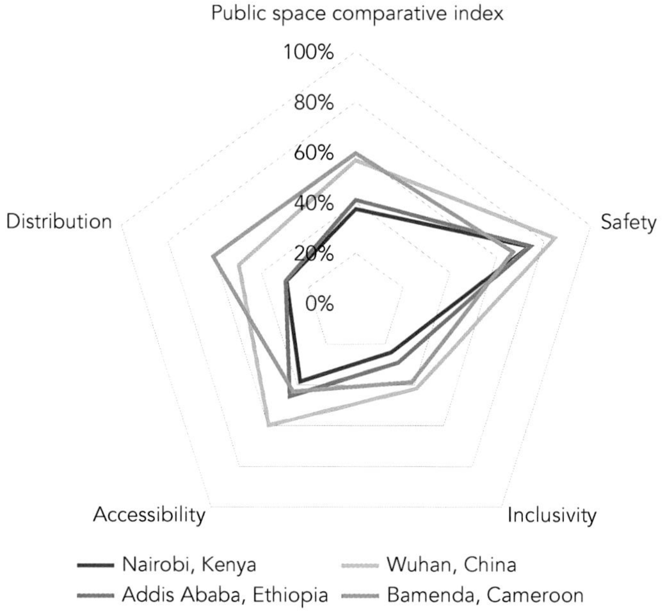

FIGURE 6.2 **Radar Diagram of Public-Space Comparative Index Scores in Four Case Cities**

Source: World Bank, based on United Nations Human Settlements Programme (UN-Habitat) internal data.

Safety

Safety is a significant factor in influencing the use of public spaces.[3] The perception of insecurity or fear of crime is just as much a deterrent in the use of public space as actual incidents of crime and violence. Fear of crime, and crime itself, especially deter women and girls from using public spaces. A global study showed that about 60 percent of women reported feeling unsafe in public spaces (WICI 2010).

There are various ways to measure the safety of public spaces. Safety for women is one of the most persuasive proxies because it is highly correlated with safety for all. For example, in Jianghan District of Wuhan, China—where more than half of the open public spaces were perceived as very safe during the day—women were well represented. The presence of multifunctional activities is also an important factor in safety because it increases "eyes on the street" (Jacobs 1961; UN-Women 2017). In this assessment, safety of open public spaces is measured by the following indicators: the absence of crime; the absence of antisocial behavior; the absence of accidents near or within public spaces; and the presence of working streetlights.

The lack of street lighting limits the use of public spaces after sunset, especially for women and girls. In Dhaka, Bangladesh, 28 percent of women who use public spaces tend to return home after dusk and are reluctant to send their girls to public spaces after dark (ActionAid 2015). According to the assessment, the presence of working streetlights was correlated with

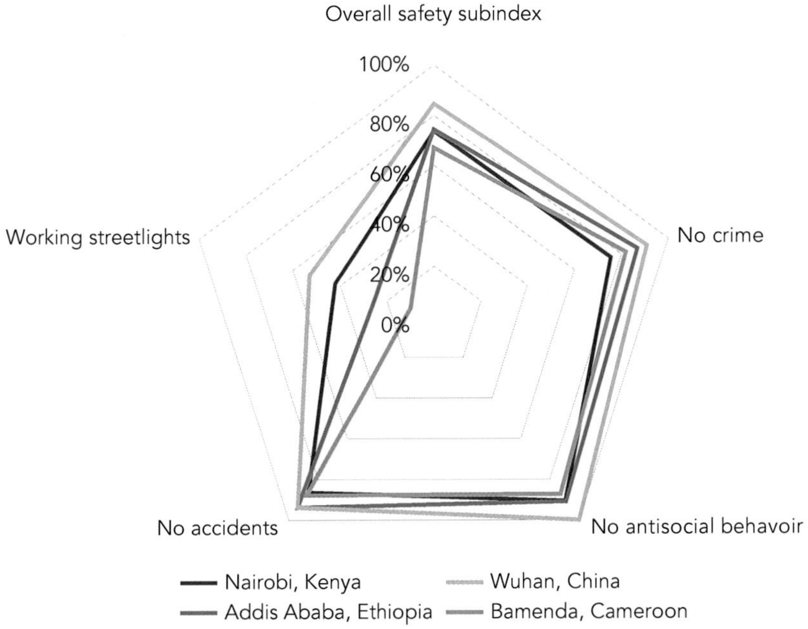

FIGURE 6.3 **Radar Diagram Comparing the Safety of Public Spaces in Four Case Cities**

Source: World Bank, based on United Nations Human Settlements Programme (UN-Habitat) internal data.
Note: "Safety" is one of four subindexes of an overall "Public Space Comparative Index."

perception of safety. Wuhan, which has the highest percentage of working streetlights, stands out as the only one of the four case cities that had not experienced any antisocial behavior in open public spaces.[4] This, coupled with a low incidence of traffic accidents, positively affects Jianghan District's overall ranking, with a safety subindex score of 84.5 percent. Bamenda ranks the lowest, with a safety subindex score of 66.9 percent. Nairobi and Addis Ababa scored 73.7 percent and 74.2 percent, respectively (figure 6.3).

Inclusivity

Fully inclusive public space simultaneously promotes growth and equity by enabling and empowering everyone—regardless of their economic means, gender, race, ethnicity, or religion—to fully enjoy the social, economic, and political opportunities of a city. Four key criteria were applied to assess a public space's inclusivity: (a) presence of diverse activities; (b) amenities for use; (c) noise levels; and (d) user-friendliness for children, youth, older persons, and persons with disabilities.

Presence of diverse activities. The diversity of activities indicates how responsive a space is to different users and purposes. In this study, an underused public space that has just one type of activity all the time is defined as "monofunctional," while a more vibrant public space is either

(a) a "plurifunctional" space that has different types of activities at the same time, or (b) a "multifunctional" space that has different types of activities at different times. This assessment showed that almost half of open public spaces tend to be monofunctional. From the highest to the lowest, monofunctional public space in Addis Ababa accounted for 66 percent, whereas this figure was 58 percent in Nairobi, 49 percent in Bamenda, and 28 percent in Nairobi (figure 6.4).

Amenities for use. The presence of amenities determines the attractiveness of a space and the opportunities for people to linger there. This indicator assesses the presence of open public-space facilities such as seating furniture, lighting fixtures, garbage bins, water dispensers, cycle parking, and signage. Although these facilities are important in promoting people's use and extending the duration of stay in public spaces, they are lacking in most of the public spaces in the four case cities. In Nairobi, only 8 percent of the total open public spaces have the listed facilities, whereas this figure was 18 percent in Addis Ababa, 20 percent in Bamenda, and 35 percent in Wuhan.

Noise levels. The overall environment of surrounding areas—such as noise levels, odors, and garbage disposal on the ground—affects the "quality of stay" in a public space. Where there is a loud, irritating sound or a bad odor, people will not linger, and the use of the space tends to decrease. This study assessed the share of open public spaces with sound (noise levels) below 70 decibels as a representative indicator in this regard. The result showed that public spaces in the case cities were mostly quiet, given that on average 89 percent of the public spaces had sound levels below 70 decibels. The lowest figure was 74 percent in Nairobi.

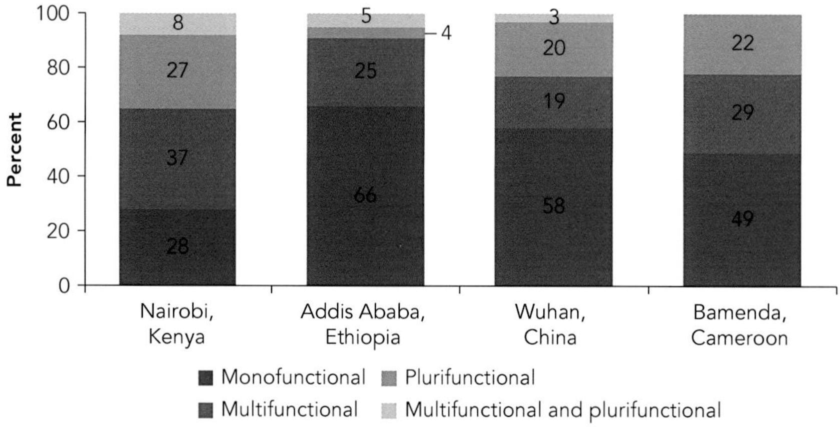

FIGURE 6.4 **Intensity of Activities in Public Spaces in Four Case Cities**

Source: World Bank, based on United Nations Human Settlements Programme (UN-Habitat) internal data.
Note: "Monofunctional" public spaces are used for only one type of activity; "multifunctional" are those used for different types of activities at different times; and "plurifunctional" are those used for different types of activities at the same time. Multifunctional and plurifunctional public spaces are the most actively used and tend to be safe.

User-friendliness. The presence of user-friendly facilities for diverse user groups such as women, children, older persons, and persons with disabilities is essential to accommodate their different needs. Out of all user groups, this assessment identified that persons with disabilities were significantly disadvantaged in the provision of special facilities for them, which resulted in a small representation of them in public spaces. For instance, the share of open public spaces where persons with disabilities were present in Nairobi and Wuhan was only 3 percent and 6 percent, respectively.

Public spaces that had amenities for persons with disabilities such as wheelchair access, texture change for the blind, and signs for the blind were also very few. For example, in Nairobi the share of open public spaces with facilities for persons with disabilities was 0.5 percent, and in Bamenda it was 5 percent. This attests to the poor integration of the needs and desires of the elderly and persons with disabilities in these cities' open public spaces and the activities therein.

The overall inclusivity scores for Wuhan's Jianghan District (41.6 percent) and Bamenda (38.4 percent) were relatively higher than for Addis Ababa (28.8 percent) and Nairobi (24 percent). Nairobi did not fare well, given its few public spaces that are user-friendly for persons with disabilities and the elderly. It also had a low percentage of public spaces with amenities for use and comfort (8 percent) (figure 6.5).

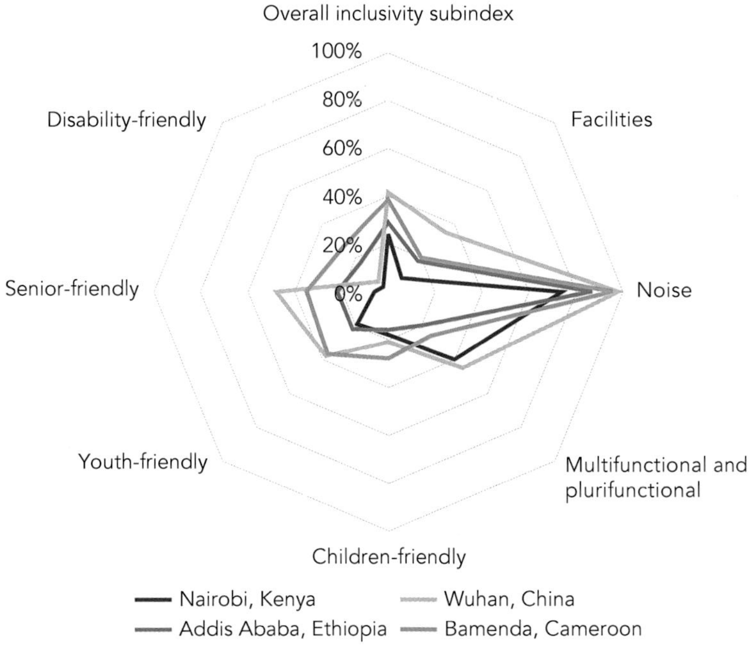

FIGURE 6.5 **Radar Diagram Comparing the Inclusivity of Public Spaces in Four Case Cities**

Source: World Bank, based on United Nations Human Settlements Programme (UN-Habitat) internal data.
Note: "Inclusivity" is one of four subindexes of an overall "Public Space Comparative Index."

Accessibility

Access to public space and connectivity is important because it fosters social cohesion, allowing the built environment to be connected to streets and open public spaces and providing people with areas of respite. In this assessment, accessibility measures the ease by which spaces (a) can be accessed with no restrictions, (b) have wheelchair access, and (c) can be reached via walkable sidewalks.

Access without restrictions. The access levels were first categorized according to restrictions, such as the entrance fee charged and the duration of use. Public spaces have "unrestricted access" if they allow users to enter and leave the space without a required fee or restricted duration of stay. Public spaces with "controlled access" might not require an entrance fee but might be accessible only at certain times of day, while "limited access" public spaces require an entrance fee. The "restricted access" public spaces are open only to specific designated groups, such as members of a religious group or a club.

The distribution of the access types of public spaces can vary between cities. In Addis Ababa, for example, 64 percent of public spaces have unrestricted access, while in Wuhan, unrestricted access is much higher, at 87 percent (figure 6.6). The access types are not strongly associated with the ownership types but rather tend to be determined by the purposes of the public spaces (as discussed in chapter 2). In Nairobi, for instance, 25 percent of open public spaces had "restricted access," and only 26 percent of those were privately owned. On the other hand, an average of 49 percent of government-owned public spaces in the four case cities are open to all, with "unrestricted access."

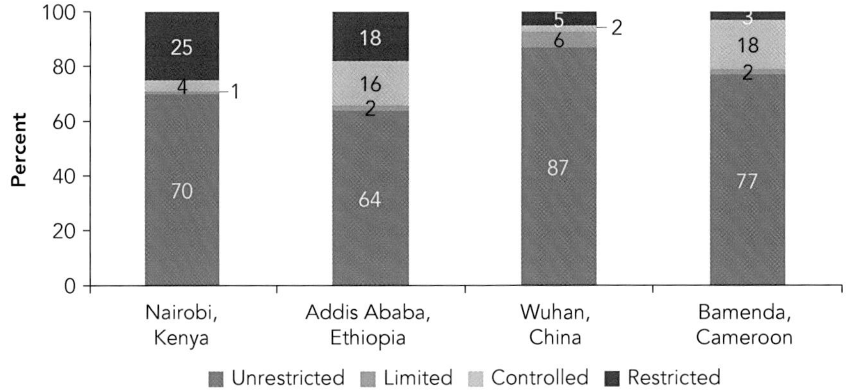

FIGURE 6.6 **Distribution of Public-Space Access, by Type, in Four Case Cities**

Source: World Bank, based on United Nations Human Settlements Programme (UN-Habitat) internal data.
Note: "Unrestricted" access means the absence of required fees or any restriction on duration of stay. "Limited" access requires an entrance fee. "Controlled" access might not require an entrance fee but might be accessible only at certain times. "Restricted" access means the spaces were open only to specific designated groups.

Wheelchair access and walkable streets. Physical accessibility of public spaces is also determined by whether they have proper entrances and access facilities, such as wheelchair access and connectivity to walkable streets. Importantly, on average, only 5 percent of open public spaces have wheelchair access, with the lowest share being 0.5 percent in Nairobi. This low score on wheelchair access was partially complemented by reasonable presence of proper pedestrian lanes connected to open public spaces. In all case cities, at least half of the open public spaces have pedestrian lanes.

On accessibility, Nairobi scored the lowest (38.2 percent) because it had the greatest lack of public spaces with wheelchair access. Wuhan scored the highest (59.7 percent), and this was attributed to the number of public spaces with unrestricted access for all. The main barrier to accessibility across all four cities was the lack of wheelchair access (figure 6.7).

Distribution

The spatial distribution of public space is determined by four indicators: per capita public space, share of built-up area that is open public space, green space per capita, and the share of land within walking distance to

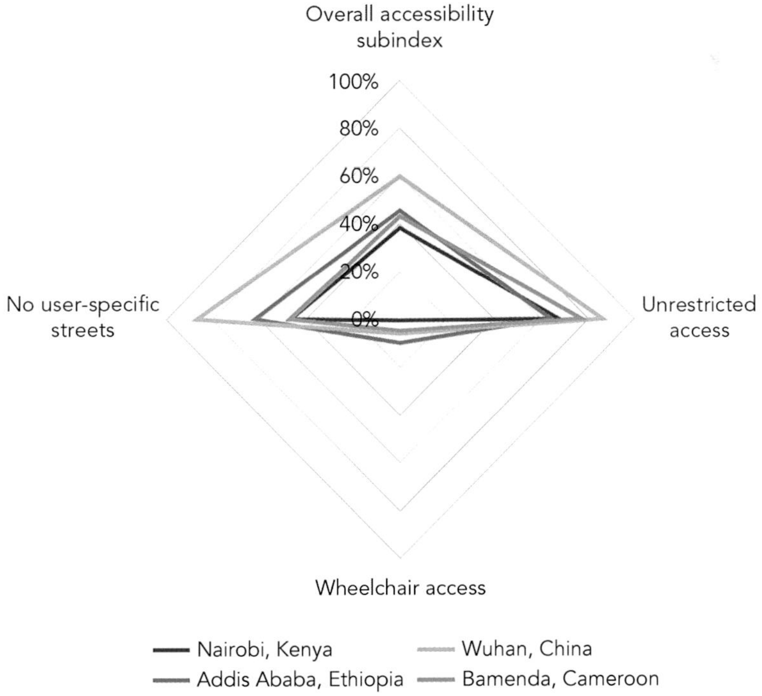

FIGURE 6.7 **Radar Diagram Comparing the Accessibility of Public Spaces in Four Case Cities**

Source: World Bank, based on United Nations Human Settlements Programme (UN-Habitat) internal data.
Note: "Accessibility" is one of four subindexes of an overall "Public Space Comparative Index."

public space.[5] The assessment revealed that each of the four cities has allocated 10–30 percent of land to streets and open public spaces and may require a deeper understanding of whether these spaces are adequately distributed to serve communities.

In addition, the share of green spaces is assessed separately, considering the importance of green networks for livability and climate resilience. A result of citywide assessments in Wuhan showed that the presence of green spaces is strongly correlated with cooling surface temperature (map 6.1). UN-Habitat projects that both the per capita public space and the share of land allocated to public spaces is expected to fall in the cities experiencing rapid urban growth unless strong legislation and policies to protect and create public spaces are adopted.[6] Another important indicator to assess the distribution of public space is the share of land within walking distance (400 meters, or a five-minute walk) to public space.[7]

The results from the analysis shows that spatial distribution in Bamenda was the highest, having a score of 60.8 percent, while Nairobi had the lowest score, 29.3 percent (figure 6.8). Nairobi's low score is attributed mainly to the low share of land that is public space, coupled with its very low per capita public space.

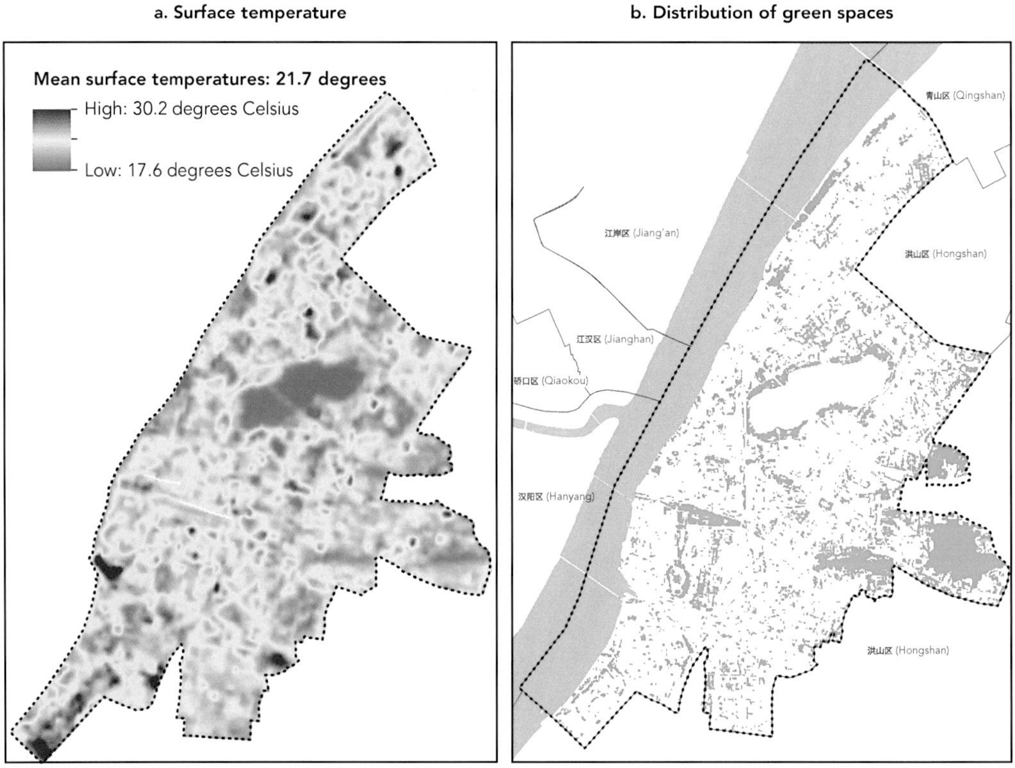

MAP 6.1 **Relationship between Green Spaces and Surface Temperature in Wuchang District, Wuhan, China, 2018**

Source: ©United Nations Human Settlements Programme (UN-Habitat). Reproduced, with permission, of UN-Habitat; further permission required for reuse.

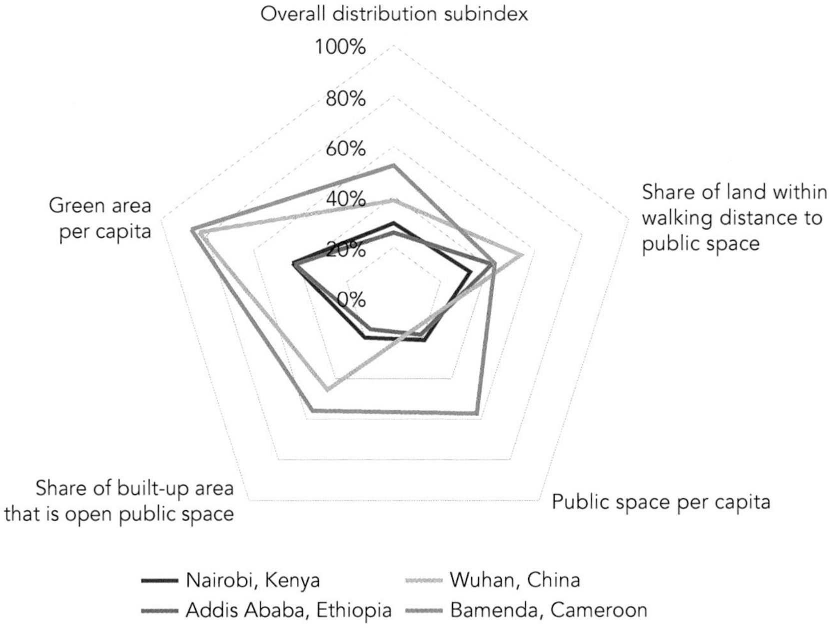

FIGURE 6.8 **Radar Diagram Comparing the Spatial Distribution of Public Space in Four Case Cities**

Source: World Bank, based on United Nations Human Settlements Programme (UN-Habitat) internal data.
Note: "Distribution" is one of four subindexes of an overall "Public Space Comparative Index."

CASE STUDIES: NAIROBI, ADDIS ABABA, WUHAN, AND BAMENDA

Nairobi, Kenya

The Nairobi metropolitan area has a population of about 4.5 million, which is projected to grow to 7 million by 2030 (UN DESA 2018). This large and growing population is one of the main forces behind the city's overwhelming challenges. Poor basic infrastructure and inappropriate city planning have triggered the city's dramatic spatial growth and increases in land values and in informal settlements, which has had major impacts on the city's environmental and economic sustainability.

In 2014, the governor envisioned a city where all residents would be within walking distance of a public space and therefore launched a program to upgrade 60 public spaces across the city. The main objective was to improve accessibility by enhancing a network of good-quality public spaces. However, the per capita open public space decreased from 9.44 square meters in 2009 to 7.43 square meters in 2016. A UN-Habitat analysis projects a further decrease to 4.3 square meters by 2030 based on current trends if no action is taken to protect the open spaces that exist or create new ones (UN-Habitat 2016).

In this context, the assessment provided the city with an inventory of more than 1,500 public spaces, including identification of the ownership and management of public spaces as well as the spatial gaps in the city's provision of public spaces and those that needed to be prioritized for upgrading.[8] The assessment set the pace to ensure that public space is an integral part of the city's normative programs, of implementation of the Nairobi Integrated

Urban Development Master Plan (NIUPLAN), and of any other future development road maps in Nairobi.

The assessment showed that Nairobi had a total area of 27.1 square kilometers dedicated to open public spaces, which accounted for 4.5 percent of the city's total area (map 6.2). There was also disparity in public-space distribution across the city, with most of the open public spaces and street connectivity within the city's central area. As a result, 51.2 percent of the total land area lacked public spaces, mainly on the city periphery. The land area in which residents were within a five-minute walk to an open public space accounted for only 32.6 percent of the area of Nairobi, and the number of public spaces that required the most improvement accounted for 29.8 percent of all open public spaces.

The distribution of open public spaces in Nairobi City County reinforces the social and economic inequalities regarding access. An estimated 4.5 percent of total land area is used as an open public space. However, Mathare Subcounty, a low-income neighborhood north of the city center, has only 1.23 square meters per capita of open public space, compared with 9.2 square meters per capita in Westlands Subcounty, a high-income area west of Mathare. Moreover, the assessment shows that most of the open public spaces in the low-income neighborhoods are of low quality relative to those in predominantly affluent subcounties.

Out of the mapped, assessed, and documented open public spaces in Nairobi, 49 percent are under the custodianship of the government—43 percent being managed by the Nairobi County government and 6 percent by the national

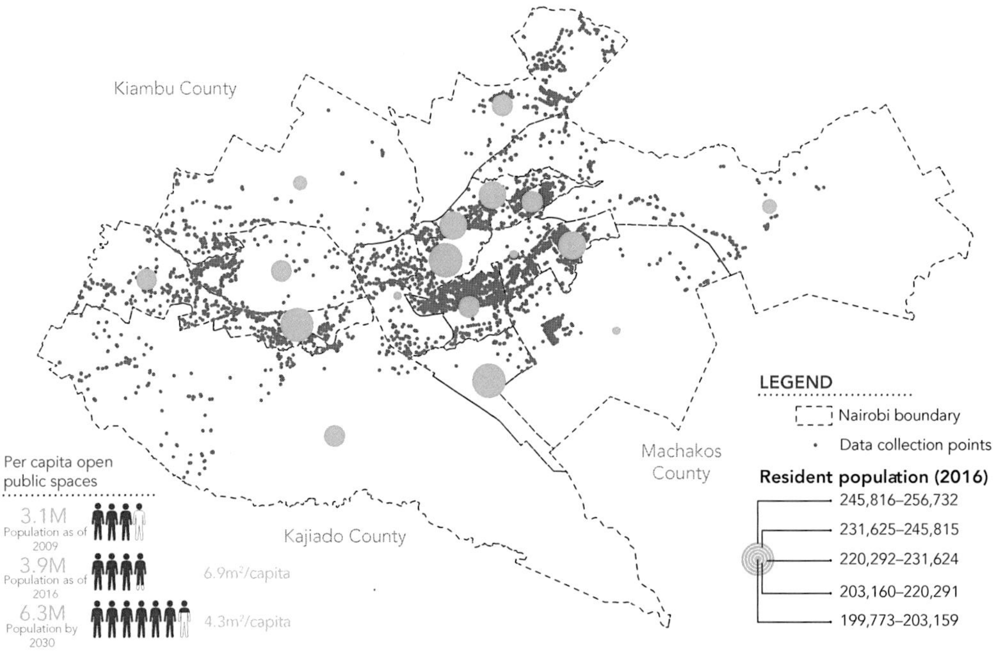

MAP 6.2 **Summary of Public-Space Spatial Assessment in Nairobi, Kenya, 2016**

Source: ©United Nations Human Settlements Programme (UN-Habitat). Reproduced, with permission, from UN-Habitat; further permission required for reuse.

Note: The dotted lines within the Nairobi boundary indicate subcounty divisions.

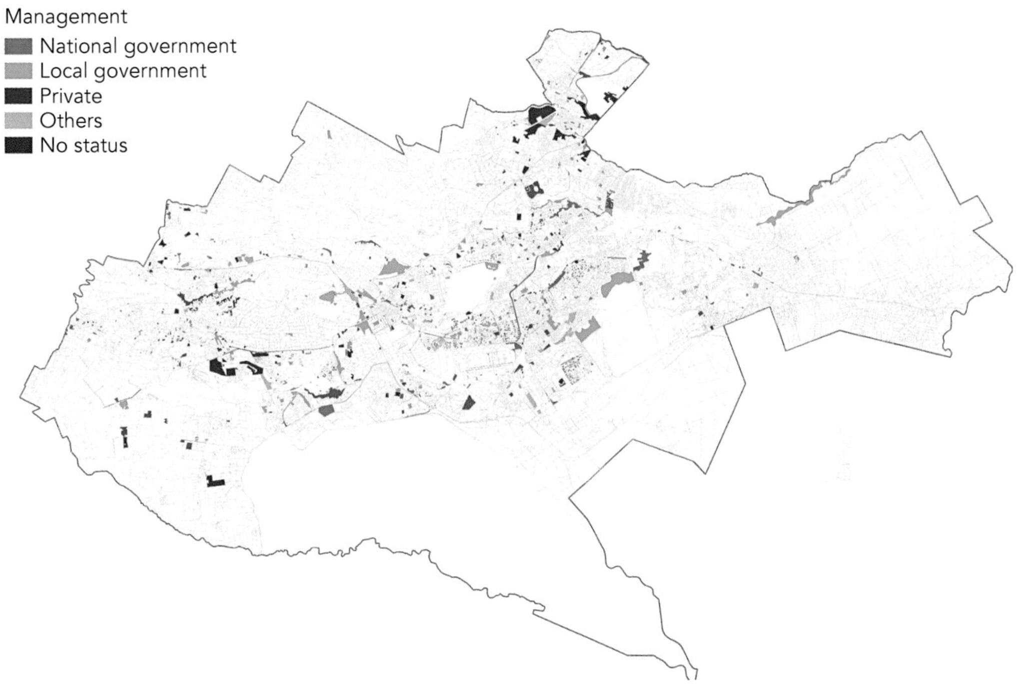

MAP 6.3 **Spatial Distribution of Public Spaces, by Management Type, in Nairobi, Kenya, 2016**

Source: World Bank, based on United Nations Human Settlements Programme (UN-Habitat) internal data.
Note: "Others" includes community organizations, nongovernmental organizations (NGOs), international organizations, and the like.

government (map 6.3). Another 31 percent are under the custodianship of the private sector, consisting largely of undeveloped land being enjoyed by the public. It is unclear if these public spaces would remain once they have been developed. Of the remaining public spaces, 14 percent lack any form of management or custodianship attributed to them, increasing their vulnerability to misappropriation. Finally, of the 6 percent under various types of nonstate groups, only 1 percent are being jointly managed.

Addis Ababa, Ethiopia

The city of Addis Ababa has a population of 3.4 million and is characterized by open markets, agricultural lands, and low-density settlement. The city is expanding spatially and is among the 15 fastest-growing urban settlements in Africa.[9] The city administration has taken steps and made significant investments toward improving basic service delivery. Despite the progress, there is still a gap between demand and supply of good-quality public spaces, clean water, and efficient public transport. Addis Ababa is rich in culture, heritage, and natural beauty, but it also grapples with an increasing population, growing congestion, and unprecedented levels of construction because of urban development.

The citywide inventory and assessment of public space has been instrumental in mobilizing partners and communities in realizing the value and quality of their own public spaces. This assessment has provided a basis for the implementation of the Addis Ababa Integrated Development Plan (2014–2038) focusing on developing, revitalizing, and upgrading public spaces (UN-Habitat 2017).

For the assessment, UN-Habitat and Addis Ababa's Beautification, Parks and Cemetery Development and Administration Authority collected data to assess the SIAD of public space across the city (1,372 public spaces, covering 478.5 square kilometers). The assessment found that the open public spaces covered an area of 16.52 square kilometers, accounting for 3.5 percent of the city's urban footprint. The per capita open public space was 2.8 square meters, and if the city of Addis Ababa does not create more public spaces for its growing population, this is projected to decrease to 2.1 square meters by 2030 (UN-Habitat 2017).

The public spaces in the city need more safe facilities (especially for nighttime use) and social programming. Although nearly half of the open public spaces were perceived as very safe during the day (map 6.4), this number drops to 31 percent at night, mainly because of inadequate lighting and lack of seating facilities. About half of all open public spaces have had incidents of crime and violence in the past 12 months, which partially explains why these spaces were perceived as unsafe. This perception is important because it affects the use of

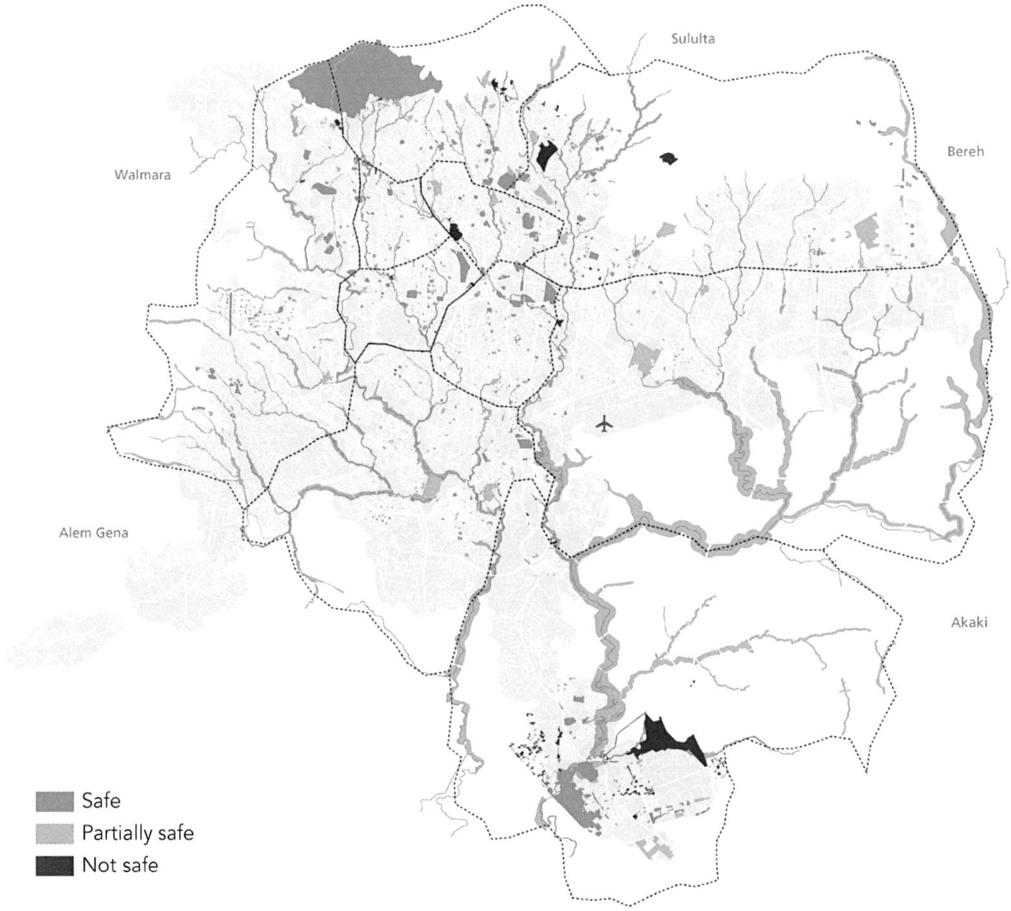

MAP 6.4 **Perception of Daytime Safety in Addis Ababa, Ethiopia, 2017**

Source: UN-Habitat 2017. ©United Nations Human Settlements Programme (UN-Habitat). Reproduced, with permission, from UN-Habitat; further permission required for reuse.

Note: The dotted lines illustrate boundaries of districts of Addis Ababa. The surrounding labels, such as Akaki and Alem Gena, are neighboring cities.

public spaces. Most (63 percent) of the unsafe open public spaces during the day were monofunctional spaces, being used for only one type of activity.

As in other cities, public spaces for people with disabilities were significantly limited. Among all user groups, the least use of public space was among people with disabilities, who accounted for only 17 percent of public-space users at the time of the survey.

Wuhan, China

Wuhan is the provincial capital of Hubei Province and the most populous and largest industrial city in the province and central China. Its population in 2015 was 10.6 million, which is projected to reach approximately 11.2 million by 2030. It is also predicted to become China's third largest city economy by 2025 and the world's 15th largest metropolis by 2030 (UN-Habitat 2018). The city's growth potential is mainly attributed to its unique geographical characteristics. At the intersection of the Yangtze River and its largest tributary, the Han River, Wuhan has historically worked as a multimodal transport hub that links to China's nine central provinces via railway, road, and waterway. The city also has rich natural assets, such as many lakes and parks. However, the city's growth has also posed social and environmental challenges such as air and water pollution. These problems have negatively affected overall quality of life in the city (UN-Habitat 2018).

In the case of Wuhan, two representative districts were studied differently. Each had a different entry point: Wuchang District's was on heritage, and Jianghan District's was on protection of public space. Although citywide public-space inventories were developed for both districts, the SIAD results were standardized and based on Wuhan's Jianghan District.

Jianghan District

Jianghan is one of the 13 districts in Wuhan, China. It is situated at the confluence of the Yangtze and Han Rivers and covers a land area of about 28.3 square kilometers. According to the 2015 Population and Housing Census, the district has a resident population of more than 680,000 resulting in a population density of 24,290 persons per square kilometer. The population is projected to reach 735,313 by 2030 (UN DESA 2018).

The total open public spaces in Jianghan District cover 1.6 square kilometers (map 6.5), and the per capita open public space based on 2015 population is 2.3 square meters. Air pollution, which harms the residents' health, is also a problem: the annual average particulate matter of less than 2.5 micrometers ($PM_{2.5}$) is 52.5 micrograms per cubic meter, which is five times higher than the World Health Organization (WHO) recommended limit of 10 micrograms per cubic meter.[10]

The inclusivity and accessibility of public spaces in Jianghan District are relatively higher than in other case cities. The assessment found that 54.4 percent (15.4 square kilometers) of the area of Jianghan is within 400 meters (a five-minute walk) from open public spaces.[11] However, only 6 percent of all open public spaces were used by persons with disabilities during the survey, possibly because of the low number of public spaces with wheelchair access infrastructure in good condition. Of all the open public spaces, 76 percent had separate pedestrian lanes, but only 10 percent of these were in good condition. Notably, public spaces that were perceived as very comfortable had a good representation

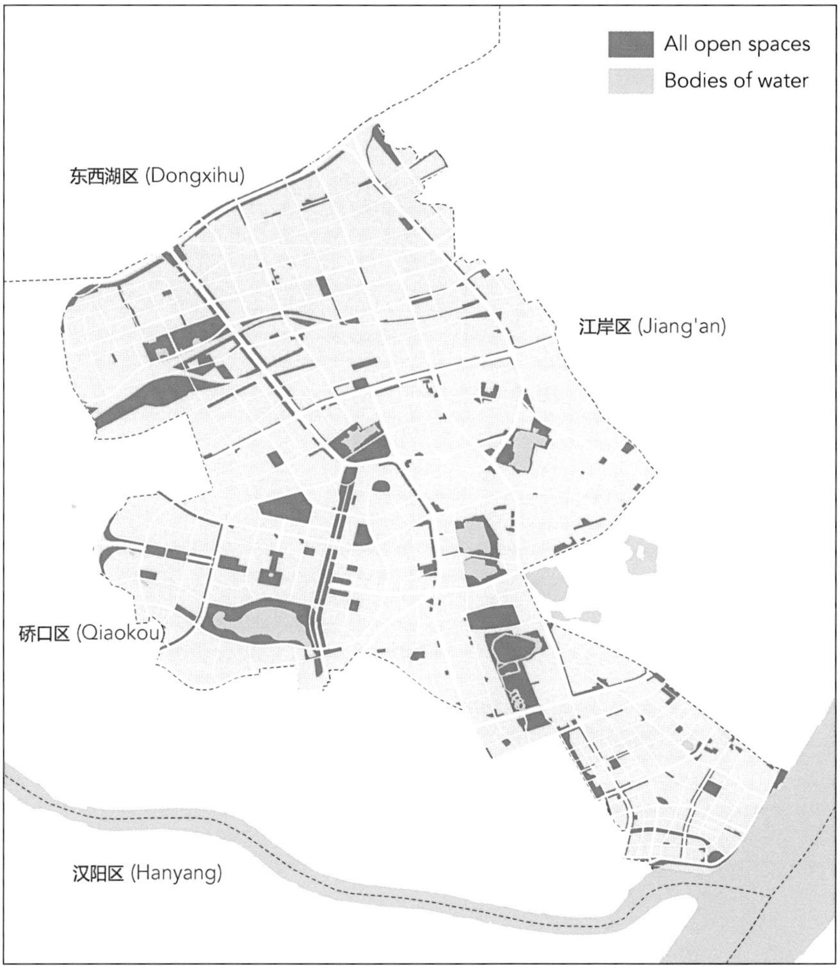

MAP 6.5 **Open Public Spaces in Jianghan District, Wuhan, China, 2017**

Source: UN-Habitat 2018. ©United Nations Human Settlements Programme (UN-Habitat). Reproduced, with permission, from UN-Habitat; further permission required for reuse.
Note: Dotted lines indicate the Jianghan District boundary. Labels outside the boundary indicate surrounding districts.

of users from all age groups as well as both genders. A gender survey showed that 59 percent of the open public spaces were perceived as very safe during the day, and in those spaces, women were well represented among the users.

The overall assessment results provided a case for Jianghan District to prepare annual action plans that identified key stakeholders working on public space and incorporated public-space rehabilitation projects in their work plans and municipal budgets. This will ensure that public spaces in Jianghan are functional, and through better design and management, these spaces will have high-quality characteristics.

Wuchang District

Wuchang is the oldest of the three former districts of Wuhan. According to the 2017 population and housing census projections, the district had a resident population of 1,037,441 and a population density of 9,627 persons per square kilometer. It has the largest area and the largest population of the city's seven central urban areas. The Wuchang historical area is rich in historical and cultural resources: it has 2 national-class relic units, 23 province-class relic units, and 23 historic buildings.

However, the district has lost its historic and aesthetic value, with an evident lack of open public spaces for recreation. The districtwide public-space assessment of the heritage district revealed a fragmented network of open public space, with only 28.6 percent of the total area being within five minutes' walking distance to an open public space. Moreover, the share of open public spaces accounts for only 4.8 percent of the total area of Wuchang, which results in a low per capita open public space of 3.1 square meters. The overall safety assessment of open public spaces revealed that 28 percent were perceived as safe (map 6.6). In all, the results of the assessment formed a basis for Wuchang District's strategy to maintain, reconstruct, and renew the

MAP 6.6 **Perceived Safety of Public Spaces in Wuchang District, Wuhan, China, 2017**

Source: World Bank, based on United Nations Human Settlements Programme (UN-Habitat) internal data.

heritage areas as well as to formulate and enforce laws to protect these areas. In addition to the districtwide public-space assessment indicators, open public spaces were categorized according to their priority for upgrading.

Bamenda, Cameroon

Bamenda is Cameroon's third largest city and the capital of its Northwest Region. The population as of 2016 was 500,000, but according to the city's latest master plan, the city is expected to be home to about 2.1 million inhabitants by 2026. The city is well known for its marketplaces, which are the basis of the economy and job creation. Bamenda is also Africa's most polluted city: $PM_{2.5}$ is measured at 132 micrograms per cubic meter, which is 13.2 times the WHO-recommended level.[12] The ambiguity of the city's land tenure system, high population growth, and uncontrolled spatial expansion are main contributors to its population's high vulnerability to flooding and growing urban poverty.

UN-Habitat collaborated with the Bamenda City Council to conduct a citywide inventory and assessment of all open public spaces within the city's built-up area and included a unique focus on municipal markets as an important public-space asset. The assessment showed that even though Bamenda has only 7 percent of its urban land dedicated to open public space, these spaces are well distributed, with a very high 7.8 square meters of open public space per capita (map 6.7). Government entities largely owned (53 percent) and managed (47 percent) the open public spaces. Most of the open public

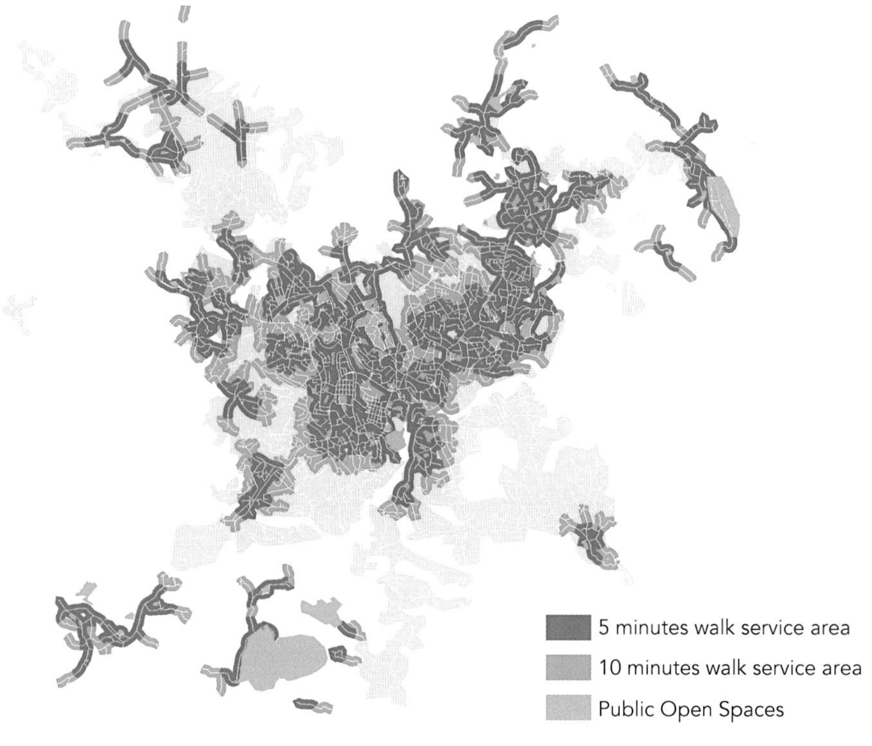

MAP 6.7 **Service Areas, by Walking Distance, of Public Spaces in Bamenda, Cameroon, 2016**

Source: ©United Nations Human Settlements Programme (UN-Habitat). Reproduced, with permission, from UN-Habitat; further permission required for reuse.

MAP 6.8 **Accessibility Levels of Public Spaces in Bamenda, Cameroon, 2016**

Source: ©United Nations Human Settlements Programme (UN-Habitat). Reproduced, with permission, from UN-Habitat; further permission required for reuse.
Note: "Unrestricted" access means the absence of required fees or any restriction on duration of stay. "Controlled access" might not require an entrance fee but might be accessible only at certain times. "Restricted access" means the spaces were open only to specific designated groups. "Limited access" requires an entrance fee.

spaces (77 percent) have unrestricted access, and these were mainly community yards and playgrounds (map 6.8).

The survey results highlighted issues such as the importance of markets and open public spaces; the gaps in their distribution, quality, inclusivity, safety, and accessibility; and the ways they can be used to promote sustainability and form the basis of market and open-public-space policy. This participatory process established key recommendations to meet the current challenges faced by the city's markets. It also informed the way forward for their renovation and modernization to meet citizens' needs and social changes. A citywide open-public-space strategy has been drafted based on the results of the assessment, with two pilot projects being launched and currently being implemented (Bamenda City Council 2018).

NOTES

1. "Open public spaces," "public facilities," and "streets" are three broad types of public spaces as defined by UN-Habitat's *Global Public Space Toolkit* (UN-Habitat 2015). Although the

definition of "open public spaces" mostly overlaps with that of "open and green areas" as used in chapter 5, "open public spaces" in chapter 6 is a term that highlights the ownership perspective of a public space.

2. These 18 indicators were selected out of 129 indicators prepared for UN-Habitat's citywide assessments. They were carefully selected to reduce redundancy and ensure validity and accuracy after intensive discussions with global stakeholders.
3. Sustainable Development Goal (SDG) Target 11.7 calls for the following: "By 2030, provide universal access to safe, inclusive and accessible green and public spaces, in particular for women and children, older persons and persons with disabilities." The target's Indicator 11.7.2 measures safety by the "proportion of persons [who were a] victim of physical or sexual harassment, by sex, age, disability status and place of occurrence, in the previous 12 months" ("Sustainable Development Goal 11," UN Sustainable Development Goals Knowledge Platform [accessed June 23, 2019]: https://sustainabledevelopment.un.org/sdg11).
4. Wuhan is represented by two districts: Jianghan and Wuchang. Although districtwide public-space inventories were developed for both districts, the SIAD results were standardized and based on Wuhan's Jianghan District.
5. Because of lack of data availability, land allocated for public facilities is not included in this analysis.
6. It is important to note that these assessments were based on the current state of the cities' population and the spatial growth.
7. Outside the city core area and in the broader metropolitan area, a public space is accessible if it can be reached within 1,000 meters (a 10-minute walk). For this analysis, the benchmark of 400 meters is used. In general, the distance considers barriers to access the space such as highways or rivers. However, in cases where data are not available, all streets are assumed to be walkable and without barriers to access public spaces.
8. As part of the analysis, a total of 75 data collectors, 83 ward administrators, 97 community people, 52 students, and 15 subcounty administrators supported the data gathering effort.
9. "15 Biggest Cities in Africa," World Facts, WorldAtlas (website): https://www.worldatlas.com/articles/15-biggest-cities-in-africa.html.
10. $PM_{2.5}$ data are from the WHO Global Health Observatory (GHO) database: https://www.who.int/gho/en/.
11. The walking-distance assessment assumes that all streets are walkable with no barriers such as rivers and highways.
12. $PM_{2.5}$ data are from the WHO Global Health Observatory (GHO) database: https://www.who.int/gho/en/.

REFERENCES

ActionAid. 2015. "Women and the City III: A Summary of Baseline Data on Women's Experience of Violence in Seven Countries." Report of the Safe Cities for Women Programme, ActionAid International Secretariat, Johannesburg.

Bamenda City Council. 2018. "Bamenda Great Public Open Spaces: A City-Wide Public Spaces and Markets Strategy." Unpublished report, Bamenda City Council, Bamenda, Cameroon.

Jacobs, Jane. 1961. *The Death and Life of Great American Cities.* New York: Random House.

UN DESA (United Nations Department of Economic and Social Affairs). 2018. *World Urbanization Prospects: The 2018 Revision.* New York: UN DESA.

UN-Habitat (United Nations Human Settlements Programme). 2015. *Global Public Space Toolkit: From Global Principles to Local Policies and Practice.* Nairobi, Kenya: UN-Habitat.

———. 2016. "Nairobi Community-Led, City-Wide Open Public Space: Inventory and Assessment." Unpublished assessment report, United Nations Human Settlements Programme (UN-Habitat), Nairobi.

———. 2017. "Addis Ababa, Ethiopia: City-Wide Public Space Assessment." Unpublished assessment report, United Nations Human Settlements Programme (UN-Habitat), Nairobi.

———. 2018. "Jianghan District, Wuhan, China: The First Assessment of Public Spaces in a Dense Urban Area." Unpublished assessment report, United Nations Human Settlements Programme (UN-Habitat), Nairobi.

UN-Women (United Nations Entity for Gender Equality and the Empowerment of Women). 2017. "Safe Cities and Safe Public Spaces: Global Results Report." Report on the UN-Women Global Flagship Program Initiative, Safe Cities and Safe Public Spaces, UN-Women, New York.

WICI (Women in Cities International). 2010. *Learning from Women to Create Gender Inclusive Cities: Baseline Findings from the Gender Inclusive Cities Programme.* Montréal: WICI.

CHAPTER 7

MAPPING USER ACTIVITY USING SOCIAL MEDIA AND BIG DATA

Dmitry Sivaev, Wanli Fang, and Joy Mutai

OVERVIEW

The following case studies demonstrate some emerging ways of using data analytics to measure public-space quality and to assess use patterns. The case studies all rely on several alternative data sources, such as (a) social data, (b) open-source and big data, and (c) street-view imagery. These methods offer the possibilities of scaling up data collection in urban areas, and they make the planning, monitoring, and management of public spaces more systematic, efficient, and cost-effective.

CASE STUDIES: TBILISI, WUHAN, AND BEIJING

Tbilisi, Georgia

In Tbilisi, one of the newly elected administration's policy priorities in 2017 was to improve quality of life, including by enhancing the quality and accessibility of the city's parks and other recreational amenities. Moreover, developing and marketing Tbilisi as a green city was the mayor's vision and one of the main pillars of the city's recently prepared master plan. The World Bank discussed with the Tbilisi city government how it could help analyze the city's public-space assets and identify opportunities to upgrade them.

As part of a comprehensive assessment of diverse aspects of Tbilisi's public spaces, the World Bank analyzed social media and smartphone georeferenced data from 2017 to 2018 to spatially map the temporal patterns of park use. These analyses complemented traditional data sources such as on-site quality surveys. Map 7.1 overlays park locations with heat maps of where social media posts were made.

The analysis confirmed that parks vary greatly in their use intensity. The parks closer to the city center are generally used most intensely, while those farther away tend to be "forgotten" by users. A closer look at individual parks shows that the territories of some popular parks were unevenly used; social media activity was concentrated in areas that represent only a small portion of the park, which may suggest that space is not well designed and maintained to invite more even use (like in the case of Mziuri Park, map 7.2).

Semantic analysis showed that, overall, parks lack a strong identity and are rarely mentioned in social media posts, which indicates that the population is not well informed about the park assets that the city has to offer. Programming of parks also appears to be ineffective, given that social media activity in the parks doesn't increase substantially during major events in the parks. This suggests that there is room for better use of the parks through rebranding, reprogramming, and physical

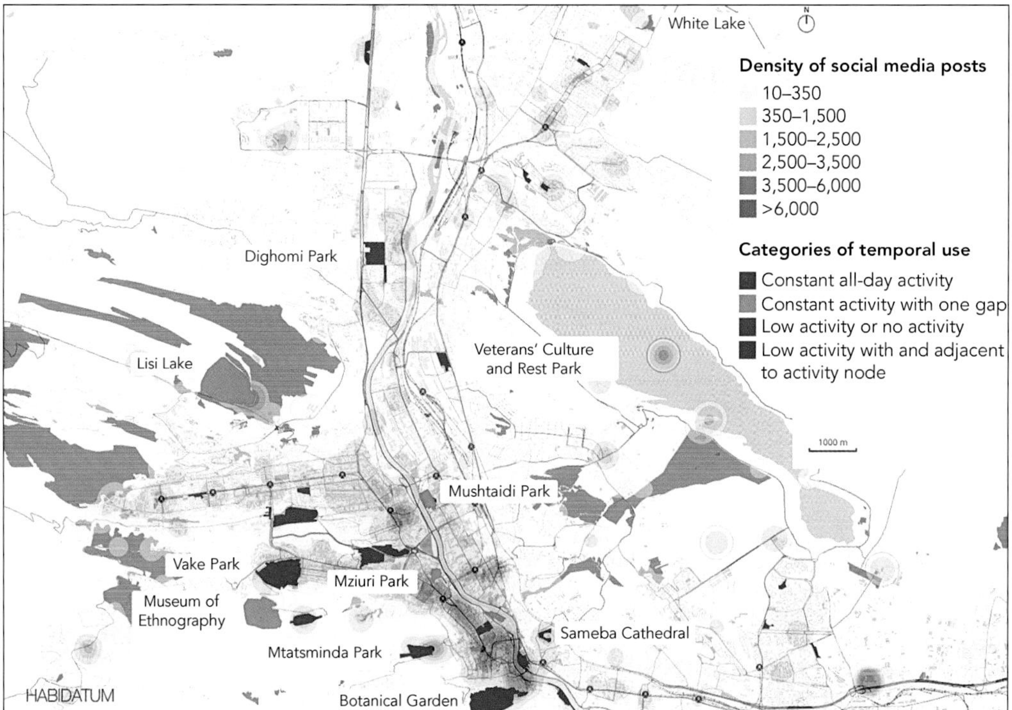

MAP 7.1 **Density of Social Media Posts in City Parks, Tbilisi, Georgia, 2018**

Source: ©World Bank. Further permission required for reuse.

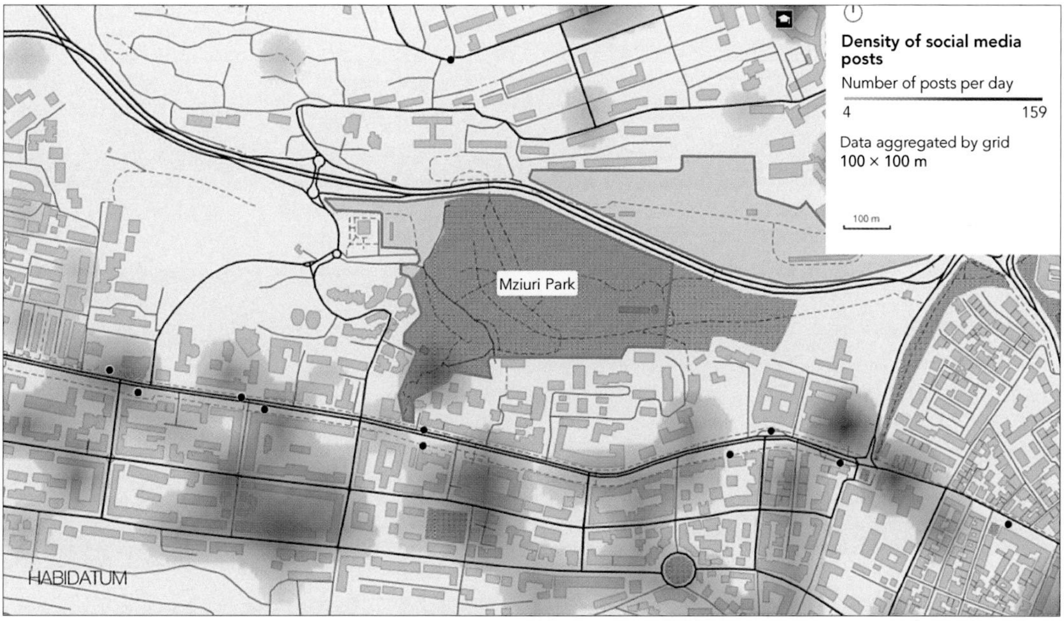

MAP 7.2 **Density of Social Media Posts at the Neighborhood Level, Mziuri Park, Tbilisi, Georgia, 2018**

Source: ©World Bank. Further permission required for reuse.

rehabilitation of the city's parks, reflecting local needs identified from the analyses.

Wuhan, China

In Wuhan, the United Nations Human Settlements Programme (UN-Habitat) used open-source big data of pedestrians and traffic activities to complement districtwide public-space assessment results. It developed thermogram maps of pedestrian and traffic activities on several days, at different times of day, during April–May 2017 by using the Baidu Maps platform (UN-Habitat 2018). The thermogram maps were overlaid with public spaces to understand activity patterns associated with different types of public spaces (map 7.3).

The analysis found that public spaces with the most users had a high number of adjacent pedestrian and traffic activities. The actively used spaces are also well equipped with physical facilities (such as lighting, benches, toilets, and water taps) that were in good working condition. Accessibility to these spaces was also good, and they were perceived as being very safe. However, most of these spaces were perceived as relatively less comfortable because of the presence of noise and garbage disposal in their environs. The spaces were mainly used for social activities such as sitting, resting, and chatting. The user experiences in these spaces can be further improved if more organized activities, such as exhibitions and performances, are present in the area.

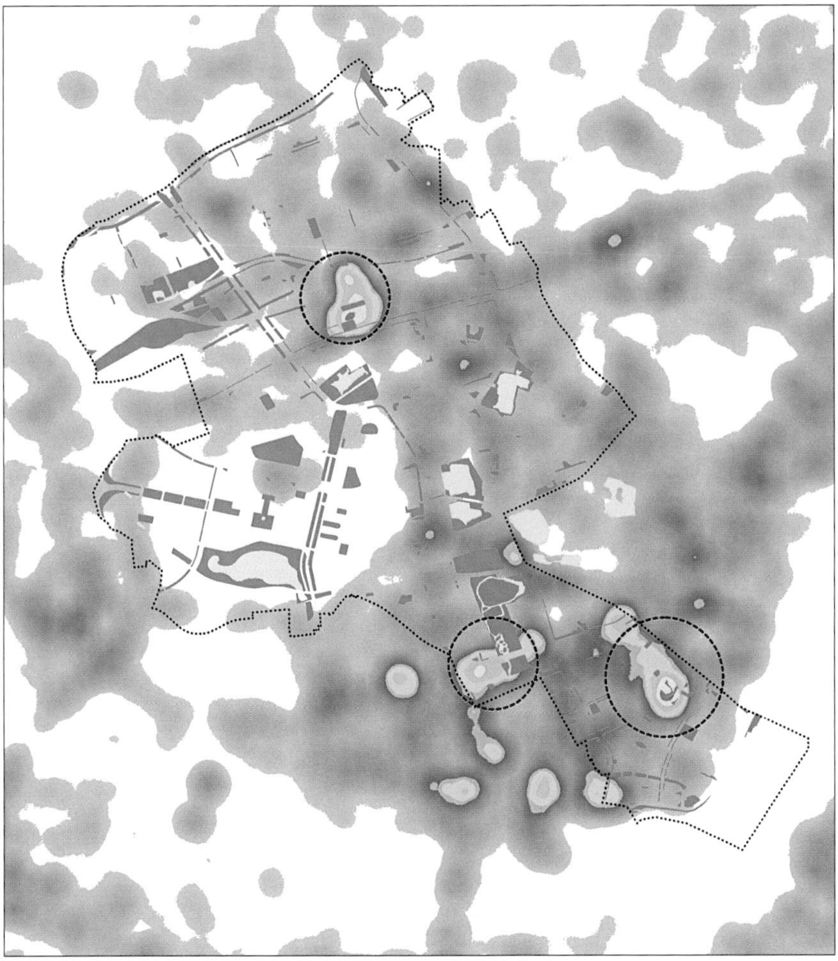

MAP 7.3 **Areas of High Pedestrian Activity in Public Spaces in Wuhan, China, 2017**

Source: UN-Habitat 2018. ©UN-Habitat. Further permission required for reuse.

Beijing, China

In Beijing, the World Bank evaluated the streetscapes within a 10-minute walking distance from 201 metro stations (Fang, Liu, and Zhou 2019). This ongoing exercise used more than 2 million street-view images collected by map service providers (such as Gaode, Tencent, and Baidu Maps) and image object recognition technology powered by machine learning models to extract key elements and features of the built environment from the map data.

The assessment provides overall scores of physical environments across the study area, based on selected indicators around four dimensions: convenience, comfort, vibrancy, and other spatial characteristics. Among the diverse methodologies applied, the machine learning model was used for the comfort and vibrancy assessments. For instance, street facilities and users were detected through pattern recognition methodology to analyze subindicators of the comfort level: sky openness, greenness, safety, and aesthetics. Street vendors were also detected as a subindicator to assess street vibrancy (photo 7.1).

The aggregated scores for the selected indicators revealed how streetscapes of 201 metro station areas performed differently. For example, the Guomao Station streetscape outperformed the Olympic Center Station streetscape in all aspects (figure 7.1), such as having more pedestrian facilities like sidewalks and benches and better access to public transport. The area

PHOTO 7.1 **Detection of Street Vendors through Pattern Recognition Methodology in Beijing, China**

Source: ©World Bank. Further permission required for reuse.
Note: Photos taken and processed by data scientists at CitoryTech. Photos on the left show street vendors. In the images on the right, red color indicates a high density of street vendors detected by object recognition technology powered by machine learning models.

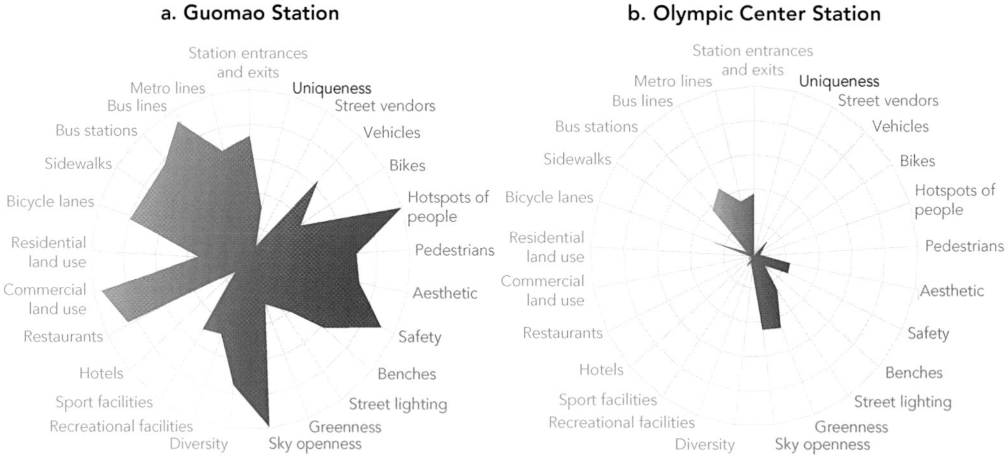

FIGURE 7.1 **Radar Diagrams of Overall Physical Conditions of Metro Station Areas, Beijing, China**

Source: Fang, Liu, and Zhou 2019.
Note: Blue letters designate subindicators of convenience; green letters, comfort; and pink letters, vibrancy. The scale shown in the diagram is on a 0–100 scale (lowest to highest) through standardizing the subindicators based on the minimum and maximum scores.

around Guomao Station also scored higher on aesthetics and safety and drew more pedestrian activity. The results can be further complemented by other data sources to better support evidence-based city planning and zoning. This methodology can be replicated in other cities and at different times to monitor the change over time.

REFERENCES

Fang, Wanli, Liu Liu, and Jianhao Zhou. 2019. "Assessing Physical Environment of TOD Communities around Metro Stations using Street View Photos and Machine Learning Models." Unpublished working paper, World Bank, Washington, DC.

UN-Habitat (United Nations Human Settlements Programme). 2018. "Jianghan District, Wuhan, China: The First Assessment of Public Spaces in a Dense Urban Area." Unpublished paper, UN-Habitat, Nairobi.

PART III

SUSTAINING THE PUBLIC-SPACE LIFE CYCLE

Lessons from Cities

CHAPTER 8

FRAMING THE PUBLIC-SPACE CASE STUDIES

Hyunji Lee and Jon Kher Kaw

OVERVIEW

There are often many obstacles surrounding the creation of successful places throughout a public-space project life cycle: poor and insensitive design solutions that do not respond to community needs; poor operations and maintenance regimes; and poor capacity of municipalities to plan, finance, and implement these public spaces. Globally, cities with livable urban environments and vibrant, inclusive public realms take on a wide range of development pathways in their creation, implementation, and management, which underscores the importance of a well-thought-out approach.

To illustrate these challenges and opportunities, 20 public-space project cases across eight cities were selected across different global regions and across a different mix of economies: Beijing, China; Colombo, Sri Lanka; Karachi, Pakistan; Lima, Peru; Brooklyn, New York City; Seoul, Republic of Korea; Singapore; and Tbilisi, Georgia. The selection also includes a mix of different types of public spaces in core city areas, including streets, waterfronts, different hierarchies of parks and squares, and public buildings such as a library and a food market.

All case studies presented in Part III are organized to cover these five phases:

Phase 1: Context
Phase 2: Planning and design
Phase 3: Implementation

Phase 4: Management
Phase 5: Impact evaluation

Table 8.1 lists the case studies, and figure 8.1 depicts the broad approach taken by the case studies.

The case studies convey how cities addressed the issues of planning, implementing, and managing public spaces in practice. Not all lessons and principles from these case studies can be universally applied to all places and regions, because contexts differ. However, the common threads are discussed in this chapter.

TABLE 8.1 **City and Public-Space Profile**

Intervention	Type	City[a]	Country	Region[b]
Yangmeizhu Lane	Street and heritage	Beijing	China	East Asia and Pacific
Dashilar Pocket Spaces	Pocket square and heritage			
Beddagana Wetland Park (BWP)	City park	Colombo	Sri Lanka	South Asia
Crow Island Beach Park (CIBP)	Waterfront			
Eduljee Dinshaw Road (EDR)	Street and heritage	Karachi	Pakistan	South Asia
Pakistan Chowk	Pocket square			
I AM KARACHI (IAK) Walls of Peace and sport facilities	Street and sport facilities			
Plaza 31	Neighborhood square	Lima	Peru	Latin America and the Caribbean
Las Begonias	Street			
Parque Ecológico	Neighborhood park			
Brooklyn Cultural District	Arts facility and streetscape	Brooklyn, New York City	United States	North America
Down Under the Manhattan Bridge Overpass (DUMBO)	Waterfront			
Gyeongui Line Forest Park (GLFP)	Linear park	Seoul	Korea, Rep.	East Asia and Pacific
Yonsei-ro	Street			
Gusandong Library	Public facility			
Park Connector Network (PCN)	Linear parks network	Singapore	Singapore	East Asia and Pacific
Orchard Road	Street			
Hawker Centers	Market typology			
Vake Park	Historical park	Tbilisi	Georgia	Europe and Central Asia
New Tiflis	Street			

a. Cities are listed in alphabetical order.
b. Regions are according to World Bank classifications.

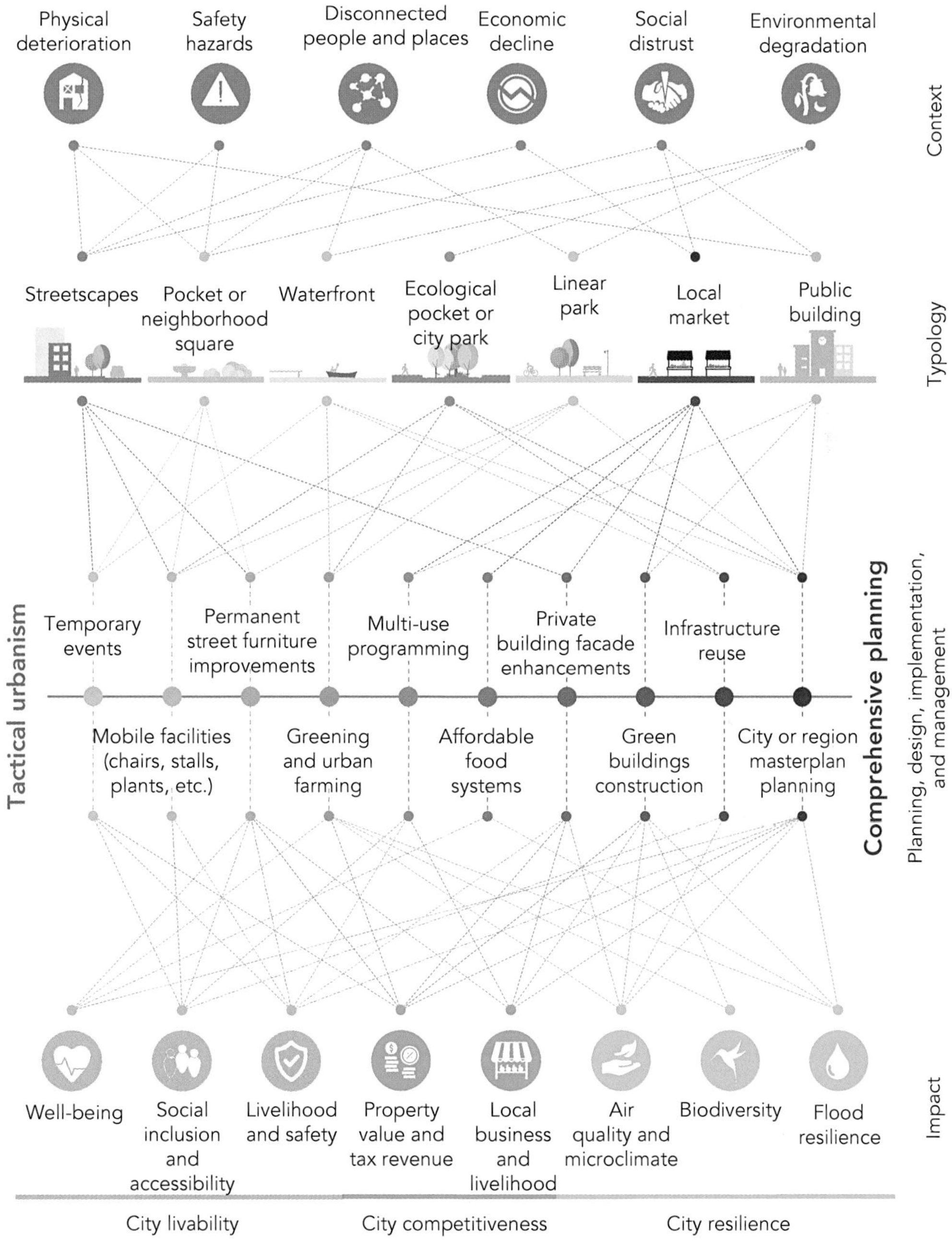

FIGURE 8.1 **Phases of Public-Space Enhancement Projects, by Type**

Source: ©World Bank. Further permission required for reuse.

PHASE 1: CONTEXT

In each case study, the Context section documents the issues and challenges related to the selected public spaces (including their surroundings and communities) prior to their intervention (table 8.2). Where relevant, it discusses the city's or neighborhood's economic and social demographic profile and citizens' priorities and needs that influenced the approach to public-space interventions. For example, a low-income neighborhood within a flood-prone city might prioritize the transformation of abandoned impermeable concrete areas to ecological parks to improve drainage and flood resilience, whereas a booming neighborhood in a growing city could face citizen demands to protect its greenery and open spaces against development pressures.

Challenges and Opportunities

Creating and managing high-quality public spaces as an integral part of urban infrastructure requires a contextual understanding of the challenges and opportunities that face each city and its neighborhoods. Some of the challenges are localized, while others affect the broader city. For example, Colombo, Karachi, and Lima sought ways to overcome real or perceived safety threats that caused people to avoid public spaces. Social cohesion in Lima was strained because of fragmented and fenced public spaces and gated communities.

Other cities, like Seoul and Singapore, sought policy solutions to improve economic growth and city competitiveness globally through public-realm investments. Many cities have "locked-in," dense urban settings, and this has often pushed governments, citizens, and other stakeholders to creatively maximize available assets (including outdated infrastructure such as abandoned land parcels, old railways, and deteriorated public spaces) to transform them into attractive areas with new uses that serve residents and visitors.

Community- or Government-Initiated Interventions

Public-space-related interventions can be initiated by one or several different actors: communities, governments, or other stakeholders. Community-initiated projects are often established informally and in many cases scaled up in cooperation with other entities, whereas government-initiated ones tend to rely on top-down approaches that are part of city strategies and visions.

In Seoul and Singapore, public spaces are generally planned as part of comprehensive master plans or regional development strategies. In Brooklyn (chapter 13), public spaces—including DUMBO (for Down Under the Manhattan Bridge Overpass) and the Brooklyn Strand—were re-created in line with the city's Tech Triangle Strategic Plan and in cooperation with diverse stakeholders such as a local development corporation, the Downtown Brooklyn Partnership. In Beijing (chapter 9), the government sought new approaches in regenerating public spaces in historic neighborhoods by creating a multistakeholder platform and a state-owned company (Beijing Dashilar Investment Company [BDIC]). In these cases, well-established

TABLE 8.2 **Dynamics Related to Public Spaces, by Case Study**

Public-space intervention		Challenges						Initiator	
Type	Name	Economic decline	Social distrust	Environmental degradation	Physical deterioration	Safety hazards	Disconnection of people and spaces	Community	Government
Streetscape	Yonsei-ro, Seoul	•			•		•		•
	Orchard Road, Singapore						•		•
	Eduljee Dinshaw Road, Karachi		•		•	•	•	•	
	Walls of Peace, Karachi		•		•	•		•	
	Las Begonias, Lima		•		•	•	•		•
	New Tiflis, Tbilisi	•			•				•
	Brooklyn Cultural District, Brooklyn	•			•		•		•
	Yangmeizhu Lane, Beijing				•		•		•
Linear park	Gyeongui Line Forest Park, Seoul			•	•		•		•
	Park Connector Network, Singapore						•		•
Market	Hawker Centers, Singapore				•		•		•
Pocket or neighborhood square	Pakistan Chowk, Karachi		•		•	•	•	•	
	Plaza 31, Lima		•		•	•	•	•	•
	Dashilar Pocket Spaces, Beijing				•				•
Waterfront	Crow Island Beach Park, Colombo			•		•	•	•	
	DUMBO (Down Under the Manhattan Bridge Overpass), Brooklyn	•			•		•	•	•
Public building	Gusandong Library, Seoul						•	•	
	I AM KARACHI Sports Facility						•	•	
Ecological park	Beddagana Wetland Park, Colombo			•	•		•		•
	Parque Ecológico, Lima			•	•	•	•		•
Historical park	Vake Park Preservation, Tbilisi						•	•	

planning systems and regimes are important enablers of creating and managing public spaces.

When local governments cannot meet the demand for public spaces, communities sometimes take the lead, as in these cases:

- *In Seoul,* Gusandong Library was initiated as a community-driven project in a low-income neighborhood that lacked public services. Acting upon the community's request for a public library, the municipality purchased old residential buildings and remodeled them to create a new library while preserving the original neighborhood character (chapter 14).
- *In Karachi,* multiple public-space projects were initiated by citizen groups with limited support from the government. Nongovernmental organizations (NGOs) were formed to tackle prevailing issues, such as unsafe public spaces and disconnected communities, through behavior change (chapter 11).
- *In Tbilisi,* a citizen-organized movement helped protect a part of the historical Vake Park from being used for private development (chapter 16).

PHASE 2: PLANNING AND DESIGN

The second phase examined in the case studies focuses on the planning and design of public spaces. In addition to site-specific or project-level considerations such as accessibility, usability, comfort, safety, and authenticity, this section also describes how public-space planning and design approaches responded to neighborhood and city needs as part of an integrated network or system across a city (table 8.3). Finally, it also illustrates how participatory approaches were carried out.

Planning and Design Approach

The planning and design process can take any of several forms, described below.

Enhancement. Rehabilitating deteriorated facilities, renewing the design, and enhancing place management are some ways to reactivate an existing public space. For instance, an abandoned beach area can be improved through design features and better management, into a waterfront park, as exemplified by the Crow Island Beach Park in Colombo (chapter 10). Upgrading streetscapes is another example of strengthening the role of streets in promoting mobility, accessibility, connectivity, and livelihoods (NACTO 2016). The streetscape upgrading projects presented in this report include Yangmeizhu Lane in Beijing, Yonsei-ro in Seoul, Orchard Road in Singapore, Las Begonias in Lima, and Eduljee Dinshaw Road in Karachi.

Transformation. A public space can be transformed into another type of public space that a neighborhood or city lacked, or converted into spaces to serve other uses—as in Lima, where the Plaza 31 project transformed an unused parking lot into a pocket square (chapter 12). In Brookyln, New York, and other innovation districts around the world, underused municipality-owned buildings and infrastructure were repurposed into open spaces

TABLE 8.3 **Design and Planning Approaches in the Selected Cases**

Public-space intervention		Planning approach							
Type	Name	Tactical improvement	Tactical transformation	Comprehensive improvement	Comprehensive transformation	Participatory planning	Integration with resilient infrastructure	Synergy with cultural heritage	Reclamation of streets[a]
Streetscape	Yonsei-ro, Seoul			•		•			•
	Orchard Road, Singapore			•		•			•
	Eduljee Dinshaw Road, Karachi			•		•		•	•
	Walls of Peace, Karachi	•				•			
	Las Begonias, Lima		•	•		•			
	New Tiflis, Tbilisi			•				•	•
	Brooklyn Cultural District, Brooklyn			•		•		•	
	Yangmeizhu Lane, Beijing			•		•		•	•
Linear park	Gyeongui Line Forest Park, Seoul				•	•	•		
	Park Connector Network, Singapore				•		•		
Market	Hawker Centers, Singapore				•			•	
Pocket or neighborhood square	Pakistan Chowk, Karachi	•				•		•	
	Plaza 31, Lima		•			•			•
	Dashilar Pocket Spaces, Beijing	•				•		•	
Waterfront	Crow Island Beach Park, Colombo	•		•		•	•		
	DUMBO (Down Under the Manhattan Bridge Overpass), Brooklyn		•		•	•	•		
Public building	Gusandong Library, Seoul				•	•		•	
	I AM KARACHI Sports Facility	•				•			
Ecological park	Beddagana Wetland Park, Colombo				•	•	•		
	Parque Ecológico, Lima		•		•	•	•		
Historical park	Vake Park Preservation, Tbilisi					•			

a. Both permanent pedestrianization and temporary street closures for activities.

or creative community spaces for entrepreneurs and the creative industry (World Bank 2017).[1]

Tactical urbanism. The approaches collectively known as tactical urbanism can offer visible and impactful outcomes at low cost where "simple physical alterations can improve the use of the city space noticeably" (Whyte 1980). By showing results fast, policy makers and practitioners build confidence that they can observe real changes, and their opinions are reflected in the process. Interventions are usually simple, and examples include free mini libraries, guerrilla gardening, art exhibitions, parklets, and so forth.[2]

However, tactical-urbanism approaches may only have a temporary impact unless there is systematic, well-planned programming and ownership for managing the space. The Pakistan Chowk Initiative and the I AM KARACHI (IAK) movements were started with temporary initiatives, such as exhibiting art works on streets and cleaning squares (chapter 11). After receiving positive feedback from citizens, these initiatives evolved to include more systematic actions, such as painting walls in deteriorated neighborhoods through international design competitions, upgrading facilities in a square in collaboration with a private design firm, developing sports programs for youth in existing sport facilities, and others.

Comprehensive planning. The comprehensive planning and design of a public space are often created as part of broader planning strategies, such as development focused on urban regeneration and transit-oriented development (TOD), which involve mid- to long-term implementation and are underpinned by robust planning systems. For instance, the Orchard Road and Park Connector Network (PCN) developments in Singapore have evolved at both the neighborhood and city scale over a decade through the national planning authority (chapter 15). The pedestrianization of Yonsei-ro—a commercial street in Seoul and one of several TOD projects initiated across the city—required extensive traffic analysis and pilots led by the city and various government agencies to ensure that an integrated approach to improved walkability on the street enhanced traffic flows around the site (chapter 14).

The approach taken largely depends on various factors, including timing, needs and priorities, support, and available resources. For example, tactical-urbanism approaches (as further discussed below) could be an option for cities that lack financial resources for permanent public-space investments and could be used as an entry point to rejuvenate neighborhoods and cities. In other areas, own-source revenue from growing private investments might allow cities to invest in comprehensive transformation of a declining neighborhood, including public spaces (table 8.4).

Participatory Planning and Placemaking

Participatory planning takes on many forms. The most basic level of citizen participation is by means of public information or citizen consultations where policy or design solutions are presented through exhibitions, public hearings, or workshops where stakeholders are heard and decisions can be influenced. Other, more engaged forms of citizen participation include empowering citizens to participate and lead in the planning or design processes. For example,

TABLE 8.4 **Planning and Design Approaches of the Selected Cases**

Objective	Tactical urbanism	Comprehensive planning
Enhancement: Improvement or restoration of existing spaces and/or temporary measures	• Temporary social programs (such as exhibitions or performances in a square) • Street furniture restoration and improvements (installing benches, street lighting, and so forth)	• Renovation of buildings or open spaces (for example, renovating an old library) • Streetscape improvements
Transformation: Repositioning or introduction of new uses	• Change of the use of spaces (for example, parklets) • Change of the use of buildings (for example, using a historical cathedral as a community center)	• Creation of new parks or gardens in built-up areas • Creation of new public buildings or open spaces in underused or private areas • Upgrading whole neighborhoods (for example, from old manufacturing plants to innovation incubators and services)

community leaders or representatives work closely with local authorities to identify gaps and make recommendations.

Sometimes, the involvement of citizens extends beyond planning and design into the implementation and management phases. In Karachi, after the Pakistan Chowk Initiative (PCI) was established to rehabilitate Pakistan Chowk square into a more inviting gathering space, local communities recognized the importance of having community-building activities (called Muhalla Sazi) and sustaining neighborhood vibrancy. During implementation, the PCI complemented the outdoor space with a new community center nearby—the Pakistan Chowk Community Centre (PCCC)—to further accommodate diverse cultural activities for communities (chapter 11).

Placemaking is a collaborative process that leverages communities to collectively reimagine and reinvent public spaces (PPS 2016). Its approach for doing so lies in engaging communities as urban designers and architects to cocreate public spaces using local knowledge. This process can build trust, a sense of belonging, and community ownership. For instance, Gyeongui Line Forest Park (GLFP) in Seoul was largely designed by communities themselves (chapter 14). The project's lead designer left the project site plan flexible to let people decide how they wanted to walk around and interact with others. Communities were satisfied with the park's final form and layout and were motivated to maintain the park even after the project has been implemented. The design process complemented early placemaking efforts, such as programming social events, as temporary actions to promote vibrancy.

Festivals, pop-ups, and other street-life events have also grown to be part of public-space projects. In Singapore, for example, Orchard Road is closed to traffic on selected occasions and converted into public spaces for events. In Lima, San Isidro municipality launched a placemaking initiative, called +Ciudad, a deliberate effort to engage citizens in revitalizing abandoned public spaces, because there was a fear that inviting people to public spaces would threaten safety in the neighborhoods (chapter 12). The municipality organized activities—from public hearings and campaigns, to more than 200 events, including concerts and magicians' shows for kids—as part of this effort.

Participatory budgeting can be an important aspect of facilitating place-making. For example, the Gusandong Library project in Seoul initially faced funding problems, but the city government introduced a system that allowed citizens to participate in the budgeting process (chapter 14). The process secured about US$1.9 million from the city government as well as additional funding from central and local governments.

BOX 8.1 SINGAPORE AND BANGKOK: INTEGRATING RESILIENT INFRASTRUCTURE WITH PUBLIC SPACES

Bishan-Ang Mo Kio Park, Singapore

The US$56 million park project is part of Singapore's Active, Beautiful, Clean Waters (ABC Waters) Program[a] to enhance the drainage infrastructure while allowing people to enjoy the water and greenery. The project transformed a concrete canal separating a public housing estate and a regional park into a naturalized, 3-kilometer meandering floodplain. The project also sought to increase the capacity of the river channel through bioengineering to prevent the nearby roads from flooding during heavy rainstorms and to provide a more natural area for wildlife and residents to enjoy.

The project was innovative in several ways. Technically, this was a design solution that required extensive research and testing of new technologies to ensure that the park would function well as a floodplain. Instead of concrete channels, a variety of plants and bedding materials were used to stabilize the riverbanks, slow down water flows, and remove coarse pollutants. Public education was also integral to the project's design to raise awareness about the importance of climate adaptation and water management. The project's implementation also took sustainable construction approaches entailing efforts to reduce tree cutting and reuse concrete from the old canal, and timber from trees in poor condition were used as construction materials for the river embankment or as park furnishings.

Institutional coordination was necessary. The Public Utilities Board (PUB) and the National Parks Board (NParks) are the two main government agencies in charge of the project. The water agency, PUB, was concerned with the need for an efficient stormwater conveyance channel, while NParks was focused on creating a quality recreational environment. This clear demarcation of roles was also reflected in how the park and canal were maintained before the renovation of the park: the park area was under NParks, while the concreate canal and the drainage reserve were PUB's responsibility (figure B8.1.1). The project required both agencies to coordinate in the project's technical design and subsequent management phases.

(box continues next page)

Integration with Resilient Infrastructure

Resilient infrastructure creates placemaking benefits when designed in a way that allows people to enjoy the space. Green infrastructure, such as nature-based solutions for mitigating stormwater, can incorporate public space elements, or public spaces can be implemented within gray infrastructure, such as along conventional drains. Infrastructure that integrates public spaces not only helps build city resilience (for example, from floods) but also adds value to the surrounding areas by improving access, connectivity, and aesthetics. Examples of such projects include Chulalongkorn University Centenary Park in Bangkok and the Bishan-Ang Mo Kio Park in Singapore (box 8.1).

BOX 8.1 SINGAPORE AND BANGKOK: INTEGRATING RESILIENT INFRASTRUCTURE WITH PUBLIC SPACES *(Continued)*

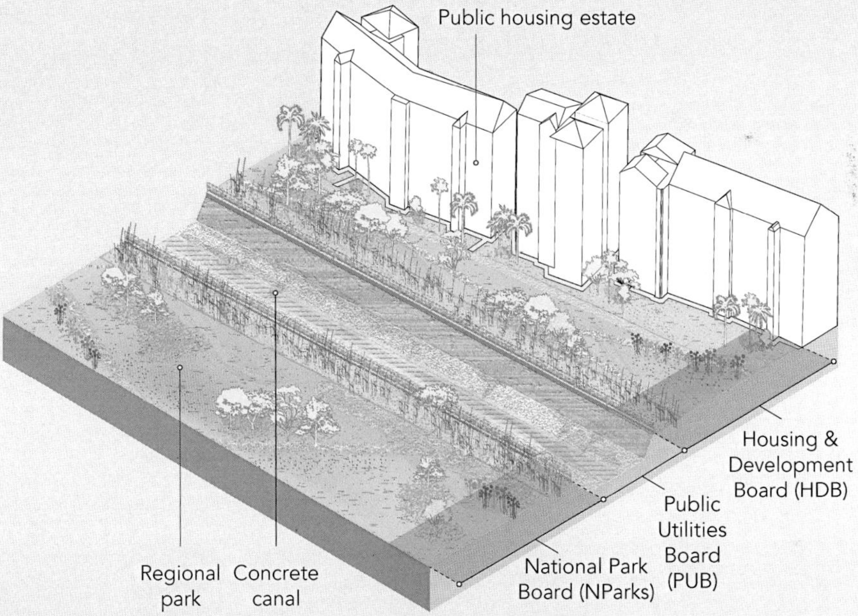

FIGURE B8.1.1 **Institutional Division before Renovation of Bishan-Ang Mo Kio Park, Singapore**

Source: ©World Bank. Further permission required for reuse.

Apart from being a public space that is now connected with the adjacent housing estate, the park provides more areas for recreational outdoor activities and a more appealing area for businesses like cafés and restaurants (figure B8.1.2, panel a). Biodiversity has reportedly increased by 30 percent in the park, with sightings of otters, egrets, and other wildlife (figure B8.1.2, panel b).[b]

(box continues next page)

BOX 8.1 SINGAPORE AND BANGKOK: INTEGRATING RESILIENT INFRASTRUCTURE WITH PUBLIC SPACES *(Continued)*

a. Recreational space

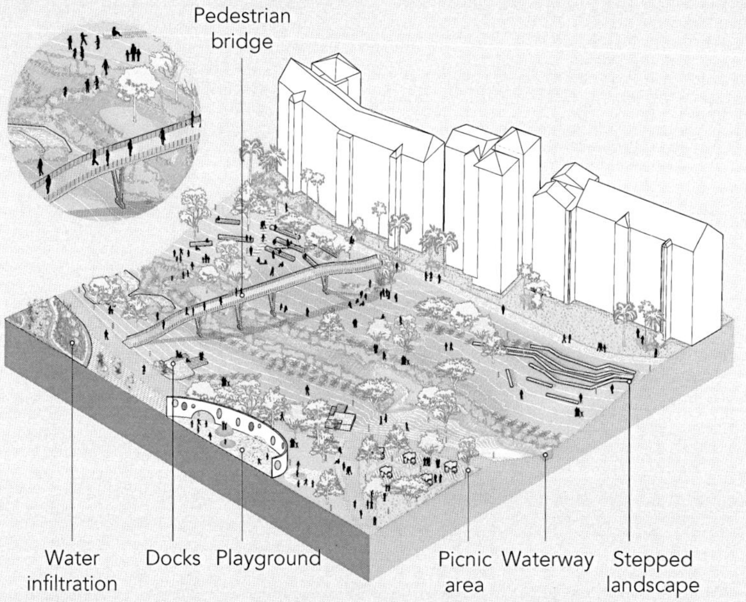

b. Biodiverse ecosystem and floodplain

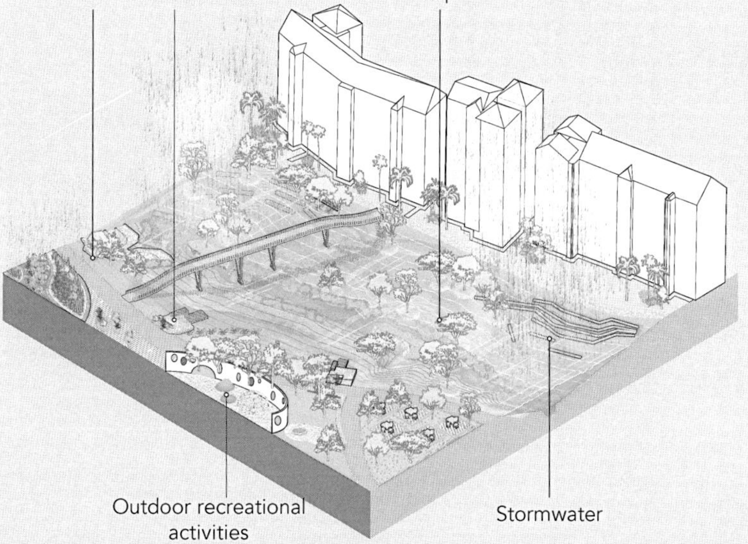

FIGURE B8.1.2 **Functions of Bishan-Ang Mo Kio Park, Singapore**

Source: ©World Bank. Further permission required for reuse.

(box continues next page)

BOX 8.1 SINGAPORE AND BANGKOK: INTEGRATING RESILIENT INFRASTRUCTURE WITH PUBLIC SPACES *(Continued)*

Chulalongkorn University Centenary Park, Bangkok

As part of an extensive water management plan developed for Bangkok, an antiflooding project—the Chulalongkorn University Centenary Park—was developed as an 11-acre green space that can hold up to 1 million gallons of rainwater. The raised green roof allows for rainwater runoff through sloped rain gardens with native plants and an artificial wetland before draining into a large retention pond below the park. During extreme storms, the retention pond can nearly double in size by expanding onto the park's main lawn.

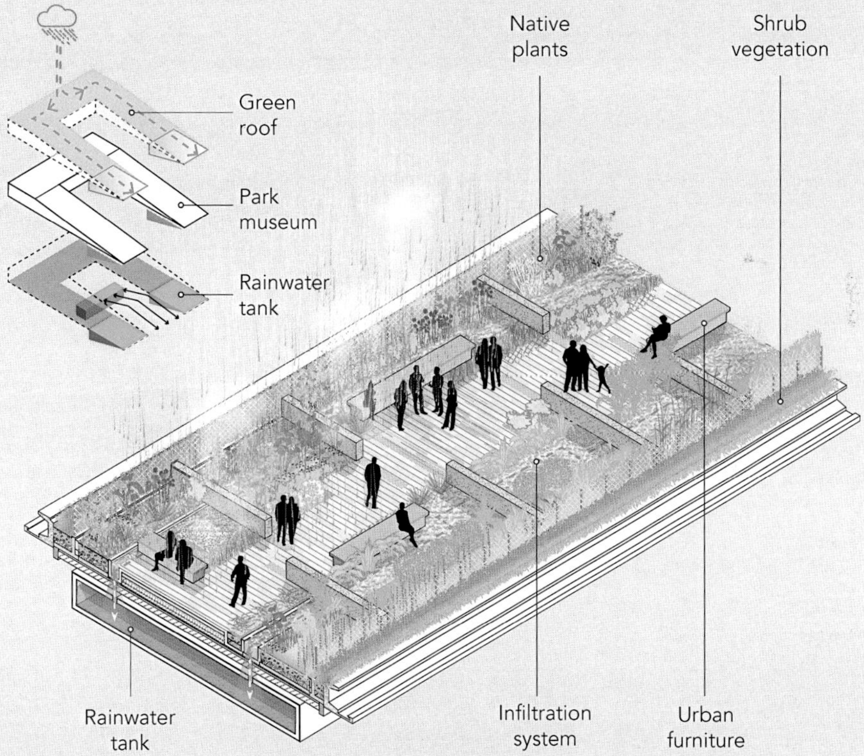

FIGURE B8.1.3 **Features of Chulalongkorn University Centenary Park, Bangkok**

Source: ©World Bank. Further permission required for reuse.

a. The ABC Waters Program is a government-led, long-term strategic initiative to enhance Singapore's bodies of water. For more information, see the ABC Waters Program website of Singapore's Public Utilities Board (PUB): https://www.pub.gov.sg/abcwaters.

b. "Singapore: Bio-Engineering Works at Bishan-Ang Mo Kio Park to Prevent Urban Flooding," case study, C40 Cities website: https://www.c40cities.org/case_studies/singapore-bio-engineering-works-at-bishan-ang-mo-kio-park-to-prevent-urban-flooding.

Although the two cited examples in Singapore and Bangkok demanded up-front investments for more sophisticated bioengineering and design solutions, there are simpler ways to reuse infrastructure as public spaces. Residual or "leftover" spaces created by infrastructure such as overpasses, bridges, and drainage reserves can sometimes be used as public spaces. In Singapore, the PCN uses the spaces within the roads and drainage reserves to create a network of cycling and walking routes across the city (figure 8.2). In Brooklyn, the Manhattan Bridge Archway—which used to be a deteriorated, abandoned space under the bridge separating the north and south sides of DUMBO—now provides a passage to Brooklyn Bridge Park and has become a popular venue for cultural events (chapter 13).

Natural urban greenery such as mangroves and wetlands can also double as ecological areas for enjoyment and as city educational assets. In Colombo, for instance, the Beddagana Wetland Park (BWP) not only improved resilience by being a "sponge" to reduce the impact of flooding in the city but also capitalized on the area's rich biodiversity to offer citizens spaces for recreation and education (chapter 10).

Repurposing abandoned industrial or infrastructure sites into public spaces can be opportunities for neighborhood regeneration and transformation.

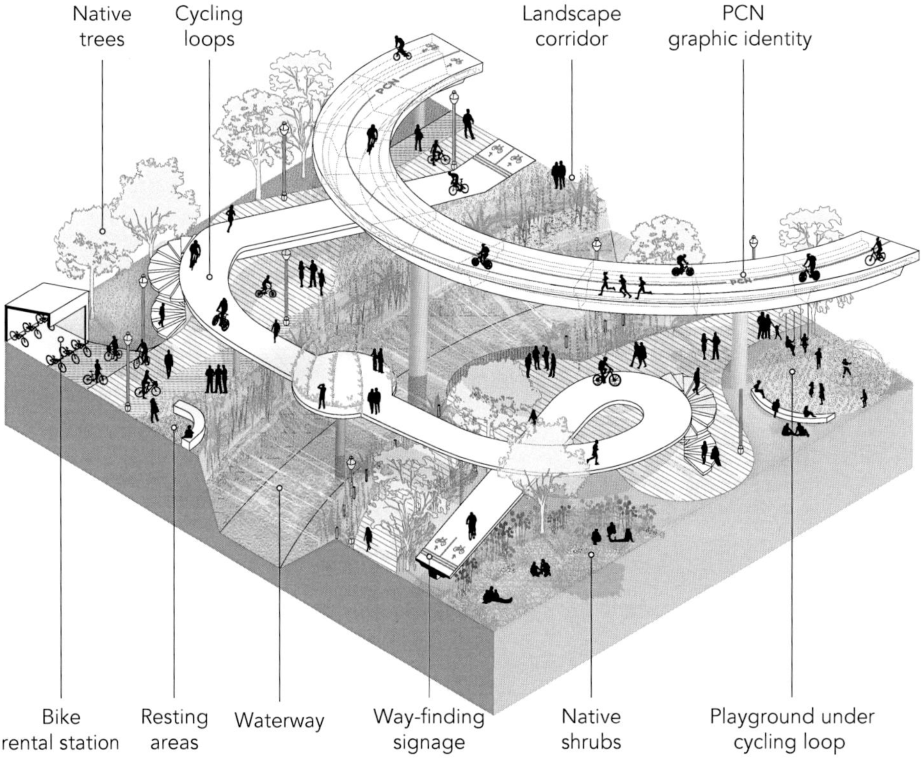

FIGURE 8.2 **The Park Connector Network (PCN), Singapore: Incorporating Public Spaces alongside Infrastructure**

Source: ©World Bank. Further permission required for reuse.

In Seoul, the GLFP was once an abandoned railway but has been converted into one of the city's most popular linear parks, connecting seven different neighborhoods. Similarly, in Lima, the Parque Ecológico site was historically used by the municipality as storage spaces, for machinery repair operations, and as municipal offices—uses that interrupted access along the park's 9-kilometer coastline. This area has been freed up for uses such as urban farming, local markets, and spaces for respite.

A key challenge for the integration of green infrastructure and public space is the need for institutional integration, coordination, and capacity, given that the responsibilities for the design and maintenance of drainage, roads, and parks span several ministries and agencies that may lack the specialized expertise in creating and maintaining green infrastructure.

Leveraging Cultural Assets: Historical Buildings and Parks, and Cultural Venues

Cultural and heritage buildings or landmarks are city assets that many public spaces are centered around. Investments in public spaces are a means to revitalize dilapidated historical assets and reclaim the use of urban spaces for cultural activities and strengthen the cultural and historical identity of neighborhoods (UNESCO 2016).

On a local scale, upgrading streets adjacent to historic buildings improves accessibility to those buildings and attracts more people, as demonstrated in the Eduljee Dinshaw Road (EDR) project in Karachi (chapter 11). A historical monument in a pocket square, such as Karachi's Pakistan Chowk, can be better appreciated by cleaning up the square and installing more facilities for communities. In Tbilisi, historical building facades along Aghmashenebeli avenue were preserved (figure 8.3) as part of the New Tiflis project. This preservation not only protected the cultural heritage of the neighborhood, but it also enhanced the street character and identity (chapter 16).

On a more comprehensive scale, a collection of public spaces within historic neighborhoods can be revitalized under a city-level heritage preservation program, such as the Yangmeizhu Lane and Dashilar Pocket Spaces in Beijing (chapter 9). Sometimes, when historical assets are at risk because of private development—as shown through the Vake Park case study in Tbilisi (chapter 16)—citizens collectively move to demonstrate the historic space's value and secure such areas as publicly accessible spaces.

In other places, public-space interventions are used to promote cultural venues and rebrand neighborhoods. For example, to elevate the identity of the Brooklyn Cultural District, streetscapes, pocket parks, and cultural buildings were redesigned to stitch together the district's diverse cultural

FIGURE 8.3 **Preserved Historical Building Facades of Aghmashenebeli Avenue in Tbilisi, Georgia**

Source: ©World Bank. Further permission required for reuse.

assets, create a unique sense of place, and animate the area through public art and performances (chapter 13). Although the idea of rebranding a cultural district in Brooklyn dates back to the 1970s, the area lacked a cohesive identity and struggled to attract private investments. Recently, however, the district upgraded street designs and pocket parks that had been abandoned, and in so doing, made them physical connectors to cultural venues such as the Brooklyn Academy of Music, the Museum of Contemporary African Diasporan Arts, and famous theaters.

Human-Centered Design Components

Although different types of public spaces necessitate different design approaches, this subsection extracts some of the common features from the case studies that are in line with the human-centered urban design principles used in many successful public-space strategies.[3]

Improving the accessibility, inclusivity, and openness of public spaces is one of the many priorities in public-space design. Removing physical barriers to existing public spaces may sound simple, but in reality it requires some challenging steps, such as changing negative public perceptions of public spaces and securing pedestrian safety. For example, in Lima, although local residents initially strongly opposed the idea of removing fences and walls surrounding squares and streets, the local government persuaded them to do so, benefiting the broader area (chapter 12). The GLFP, in Seoul, demolished soundproof walls and barriers along the boundary of the site provided unencumbered access to people (figure 8.4) and used differentiated pavement materials to guide vehicles and pedestrians safely (chapter 14).

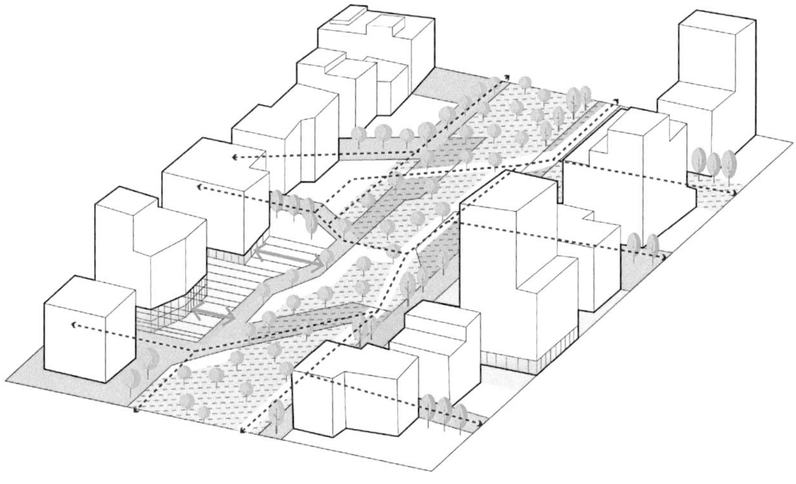

FIGURE 8.4 **Gyeongui Line Forest Park in Seoul: Well Connected to Urban Environments**

Source: ©World Bank. Further permission required for reuse.
Note: The red dotted lines indicate the porous walking paths for pedestrians, which were unavailable when the site was disconnected by soundproof walls and barriers.

Other approaches to making public spaces open and connected involve establishing paths and connecting points with the surrounding urban fabric, through urban design and planning policies. Along Orchard Road in Singapore, the use of through-block easements within private buildings not only provide direct access from Orchard Road to Mass Rapid Transit stations but also feature a host of uses that lend them a street-like character (chapter 15).

Activities that attract and support diversity and social mixing are key elements of successful public spaces (Gehl Institute 2016). According to the New York-based Project for Public Spaces, the "Power of 10+" concept, where places thrive when public-space users have a range of reasons to be there, is applicable to cities and neighborhoods (PPS 2016).[4] The BWP in Colombo uses different zones to cater to differentiated activities, including bird lookout points, walkways, canals, and ponds (chapter 10). Similarly, the GLFP in Seoul has thematic zones, such as open-sky libraries, ecological waterways, and squares for different types of events (chapter 14). These intentional design nuances are often critical in successfully attracting different groups of people to a public space.

Weather protection and outdoor comfort also make a public space walkable and enjoyable (Gehl 2010). In Lima, a satisfaction survey for the Plaza 31 project showed that users desired more shade and trees so that they could spend more time in the plaza (chapter 12). As such, planters, large trees, and shade and other elements that improve outdoor urban comfort are common and valued elements of all public spaces, especially in cities with hotter climates (figure 8.5).

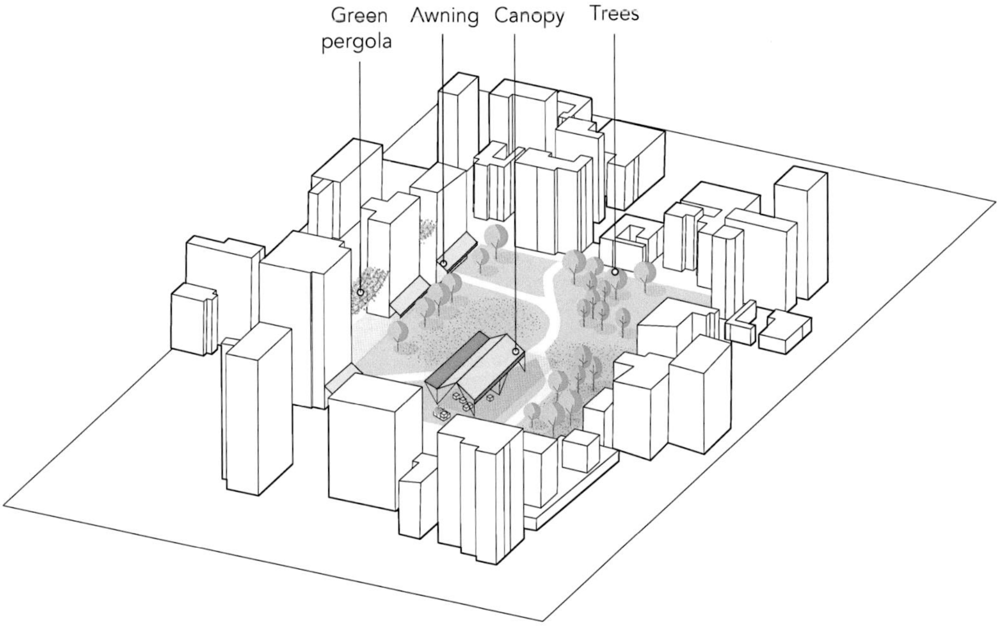

FIGURE 8.5 **Public Space Features to Protect People from Extremely Hot Weather**

Source: ©World Bank. Further permission required for reuse.

Reclaiming Streets for Pedestrians

To unlock the full potential of streets as public spaces, many cities have shifted their street design paradigms from automobile-oriented ones characterized by wide roads and large areas dedicated to parking lots, to more inclusive and balanced ones accommodating diverse users such as pedestrians, street vendors, and cyclists (Targa et al. 2019). For instance, the San Isidro District in Lima piloted this approach on a commercial street, Las Begonias (chapter 12). Recognizing that the street privileged vehicles with three wide lanes and many underused parking lots (figure 8.6, panel a), the local government transformed this street to a high-quality public space that catered to people and activities. Accompanying the physical intervention, the local government launched a placemaking campaign, "14 m^2 of Life." For two weeks, it demonstrated how 14 square meters (the normative size of a parking lot) can be better used for a variety of activities, such as art performances, urban farming, yoga classes, and exhibitions. The government also designed and installed temporary grass benches and potted plants in the spaces liberated from cars (figure 8.6, panel b). This intermediate intervention enabled the municipality to build strong citizen support and to successfully execute the permanent installation of wider sidewalks, trees, bike parking stations, and benches (figure 8.6, panel c).

PHASE 3: IMPLEMENTATION

The on-the-ground implementation of public-space interventions is the third phase covered in the case studies, which can be roughly categorized by implementation period:

- *Short-term:* Rapid interventions, taking roughly a couple of years, or less
- *Medium-term:* Interventions during a phased process that could take up to around five years
- *Long-term*: More-comprehensive interventions that can span more than five years.

Implementation of public-space projects are accompanied by different regulatory, funding, and management instruments and mechanisms (table 8.5). For instance, low-cost, tactical-urbanism types of projects that are nonpermanent can be implemented within a year, often led by a single entity such as a municipality or an NGO. On the other hand, reshaping streetscapes and building façades could require sophisticated planning and regulatory systems that engage different groups of stakeholders (such as property owners) and can take longer. Each case study also documents and discusses the funding sources and implementation actors, when that information is available.

Time Frame, Funding, and Leading Stakeholder

The case studies present a range of implementation approaches to public spaces. Community-led projects are associated with smaller, short-term projects that were funded by private investments or philanthropically.

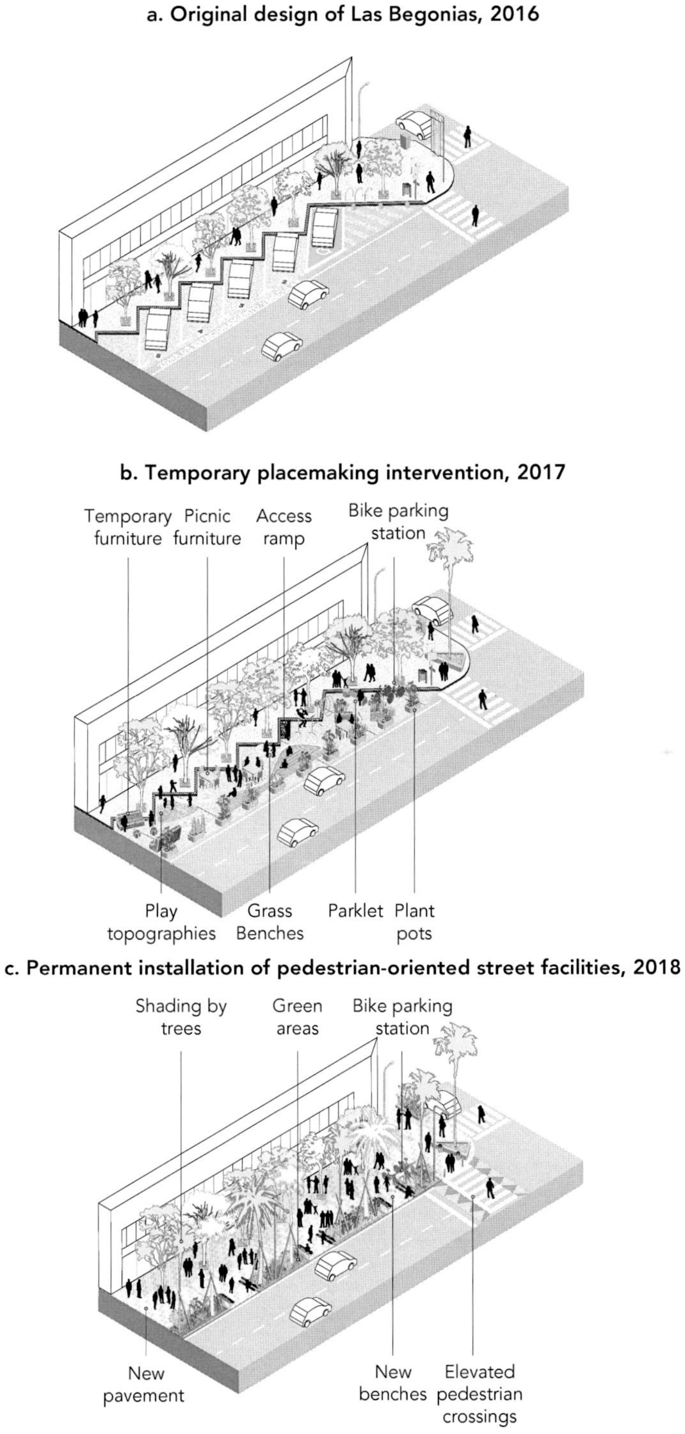

FIGURE 8.6 **Shift from Car-Oriented to Human-Centered Street Design in Las Begonias, Lima**

Source: ©World Bank. Further permission required for reuse.

TABLE 8.5 **Implementation Components of the Selected Cases**

Public-space intervention		Time frame[a]			Funding source				Lead stakeholder	
Type	Name	Short-term	Medium-term	Long-term	Public budget	Philanthropic	Private investment	International donor	Government	Private or NPO
Streetscape	Yonsei-ro, Seoul		•		•				•	
	Orchard Road, Singapore		•	•	•		•		•	
	Eduljee Dinshaw Road, Karachi	•				•	•			•
	Walls of Peace, Karachi	•				•				•
	Las Begonias, Lima	•	•		•				•	
	New Tiflis, Tbilisi		•		•				•	
	Brooklyn Cultural District, Brooklyn		•		•		•			•
	Yangmeizhu Lane, Beijing		•		•				•	
Linear park	Gyeongui Line Forest Park, Seoul		•		•				•	
	Park Connector Network, Singapore		•	•	•				•	
Market	Hawker Centers, Singapore		•	•	•				•	
Pocket or neighborhood square	Pakistan Chowk, Karachi	•				•				•
	Plaza 31, Lima	•	•		•				•	
	Dashilar Pocket Spaces, Beijing	•			•				•	
Waterfront	Crow Island Beach Park, Colombo	•	•		•			•	•	
	DUMBO (Down Under the Manhattan Bridge Overpass), Brooklyn		•	•	•		•			•
Public building	Gusandong Library, Seoul		•		•				•	
	I AM KARACHI Sports Facility	•				•				•
Ecological park	Beddagana Wetland Park, Colombo		•					•	•	
	Parque Ecológico, Lima		•	•	•				•	
Historical park	Vake Park Preservation, Tbilisi		•			•				•

Note: NPO = nonprofit organization.
a. Short term = up to about two years. Medium term = up to about five years. Long term = exceeding five years.

For instance, the EDR project in Karachi (chapter 11) took about a year to complete at a cost of US$500,000, led by a group of citizens who formed the Eduljee Dinshaw Road Project Trust. Similarly, the PCI completed the Pakistan Chowk restoration project within a year at a cost of US$8,000 to upgrade facilities and clean up the square. In Colombo, residents formed the Crow Island Beach Park Management Society to start cleaning, planting, and installing coastal defense structures with support from the city government's Coast Conservation Department (chapter 10). This led to a medium-term project with the assistance of the local government and international support.

Several case studies exhibit medium-term public-space interventions that were led by governments and publicly funded. In Seoul, for example, the GLFP consists of six zones across different neighborhoods, which were implemented in three phases from 2011 to 2016 (chapter 14). A critical challenge for the city government was coordinating and negotiating the lease of the land with a state-owned railway agency as well as engaging stakeholders.

Other case studies point to long-term public realm investments that were part of city plans, involving both public and private participation. For example, the case study on modern-day Orchard Road in Singapore (chapter 15) illustrates how the project was realized from a combination of urban design incentives, public sector funding of public infrastructure, and long-term planning that was coordinated between multiple government agencies.

Institutional Arrangements

A broad range of stakeholder coordination mechanisms are used to coordinate the joint efforts of public agencies, private owners, and communities. The forms these institutional arrangements take depend on the project's purpose, the roles of stakeholders, and the regulatory environment. They are often set up in the planning stages and deployed during the implementation stages (Amirtahmasebi et al. 2016). The institutional arrangements used in the case studies include the several specific types discussed below.

Steering committees. Usually made up of high-level stakeholders or representatives, steering committees provide guidance on key issues. For instance, in Beijing, while the city government led the Dashilar program, the Dashilar Regeneration Steering Committee was created to coordinate different government agencies (chapter 9). In the case of Yonsei-ro, in Seoul, stakeholders organized a steering committee to implement the project, consisting of a mix of city government officials, Seodaemun-gu (district office) representatives, relevant agencies such as the Seoul Metropolitan Police, the Korea Electric Power Corporation, residents, merchants, and civic groups, as well as Yonsei University and Hyundai Department Store (chapter 14). The committee's work was grouped into three main pillars: transportation, design and construction, and visitor services.

Development corporations. The state-owned BDIC is the implementation entity of the Dashilar Project in Beijing (chapter 9). The corporation organized a partnership platform (Dashilar Platform) to attract private and technical resources and bridge the city government and private sectors. One of the BDIC's main objectives was to attract private sector investments and participation by seeding the funding of selected assets.

Business improvement districts (BIDs). A BID is a defined area within which funding streams typically drawn from businesses located inside the BID are used to fund or maintain projects within the defined area. In Brooklyn, the DUMBO Improvement District was responsible for the overall revitalization of the district, including public-space interventions such as reopening the Manhattan Bridge Archway (chapter 13).[5] In the case of the Brooklyn Cultural District, the Downtown Brooklyn Partnership proposed to expand the footprint of an existing BID (the Metro Tech BID) and to manage the Cultural District as its subdistrict. It was approved by the New York City Council in 2016, and it covers the implementation and maintenance of public spaces surrounding nine cultural venues within the Cultural District area.

MOUs and other private arrangements. Other arrangements include memorandums of understanding (MOUs) and other types of private arrangements. For the GLFP in Seoul, the city government signed an MOU with the state-owned agency that owns the site—the Korea Rail Network Authority (KRNA)—to obtain the KRNA's permission to use the site free of charge for 50 years in exchange for authorizing the KRNA's development projects near the Gyeongui Railway in the city (chapter 14). In the case of Las Begonias, Lima, the municipality of San Isidro worked with a private real estate company that had a stake in the area to carry out and fund the planning studies needed for the project (chapter 12).

PHASE 4: MANAGEMENT

The fourth phase of public-space interventions covered in the case studies focuses on the actors responsible for the management of public spaces and on how operations and maintenance (O&M) are funded (table 8.6).

Management Structure Type and O&M Funding Source

In most case studies, management and funding were provided by the public sector. Sustaining public spaces in good condition in such a scenario requires adequate budgeting and political will to maintain them as well as a functioning organizational structure. The BWP in Colombo (run by a management committee under local government) had to overcome severe operating challenges, including insufficient on-site revenues to meet the O&M costs (chapter 10). Yonsei-ro in Seoul represents a case where several local government units—including construction, community revitalization, and facility management—manage public space in coordination, each with a specific role: The community revitalization unit takes the lead on engaging street vendors who are major stakeholders of the street (chapter 14). The facility management unit takes charge of street cleaning and maintenance and monitors the legal use of street facilities, including tracking illegal dumping or other misuse.

Other case studies point to public spaces managed by communities and nonprofit groups. In Karachi, for example, a trust of concerned citizens was formed, called the Eduljee Dinshaw Road Project Trust, and they manage maintenance works at the site and programming (chapter 11). They also raised funding from local stakeholders, including local businesses. In general, although such approaches can help promote greater community bonding and social cohesion, they may require additional technical expertise for maintenance, along with the need for future funding, which is not guaranteed.

Other arrangements from the case studies include outsourcing management to specialized private companies or nonprofit groups that rely on public funding. In Seoul, for instance, a nonprofit organization (NPO)—the Friends of GLFP (mainly consisting of local experts, volunteers, and residents)—was formed in 2015 to manage the park and resolve conflicts between residents

TABLE 8.6 **Operations and Maintenance Components of the Selected Cases**

Public-space intervention		Actor			O&M funding source					
Type	Name	Government	Community	Private or NPO	Public budget	Philanthropy or crowdsourcing	On-site fees and revenues	Earmarked off-site revenues	In-kind contributions	Management structure type[a]
Streetscape	Yonsei-ro, Seoul	•			•					❶
	Orchard Road, Singapore	•			•			•		①
	Eduljee Dinshaw Road, Karachi		•			•				❷
	Walls of Peace, Karachi			•		•				❹
	Las Begonias, Lima	•		•	•					①
	New Tiflis, Tbilisi	•		•	•					❸
	Brooklyn Cultural District, Brooklyn			•				•		❹
	Yangmeizhu Lane, Beijing	•		•	•			•	•	①
Linear park	Gyeongui Line Forest Park, Seoul	•		•	•		•		•	①
	Park Connector Network, Singapore	•			•					❶
Market	Hawker Centers, Singapore	•			•					❶
Pocket or neighborhood square	Pakistan Chowk, Karachi			•		•				❹
	Plaza 31, Lima	•			•					❶
	Dashilar Pocket Spaces, Beijing	•	•	•	•			•	•	①
Waterfront	Crow Island Beach Park, Colombo	•			•		•		•	①
	DUMBO (Down Under the Manhattan Bridge Overpass), Brooklyn			•		•	•	•		❹
Public building	Gusandong Library, Seoul			•	•					❸
	I AM KARACHI Sports Facility			•		•				❹
Ecological park	Beddagana Wetland Park, Colombo	•			•		•			①
	Parque Ecológico, Lima	•			•					❶
Historical park	Vake Park Preservation, Tbilisi[b]		•		•	•				②

Note: NPO = nonprofit organization. O&M = operations and maintenance.

a. ❶ = public sector management and funding. ❷ = community management and funding. ❸ = private company or NPO managed with public funding. ❹ = private company or NPO with rights to generate revenues and cover O&M costs. ① ② = hybrid. If hybrid, scenario is combined with other management structure types. Details of this classification are discussed in Part I, chapter 3.

b. Vake Park is an existing historic park generally managed by the Tbilisi city government, but in this report, the case study focuses on how the community has protected part of the park from private construction of a hotel building by managing and programming the park themselves.

and visitors (chapter 14). The NPO's operating costs and facilities are covered by the local municipal budget, together with capacity-building support from the city. The Eunpyeong Library Village Cooperative, a private company that specializes in programming and managing library facilities, was contracted by the government to manage the Gusandong Library for a three-year term. These types of arrangements often require strong contract enforcement and procurement or legal frameworks to ensure good management of public spaces.

Managing Differences between Stakeholder Groups

A major task of management is mediating tensions between various stakeholder groups during the management phase of the public space. For example, after the GLFP in Seoul was successfully launched, it became popular with young people. Residents living near the park raised privacy, noise, and litter concerns. To address these concerns, the designated NPO organized a public campaign and an exhibition at the site to encourage visitors to keep the noise down (chapter 14).

The Las Begonias area in Lima faced similar issues: residents were strongly against the plans to upgrade the street, because some of them preferred parking lots to public spaces, while others were afraid of attracting unfamiliar visitors to their neighborhood. The San Isidro municipality managed to overcome the not-in-my-backyard (Nimby) characterization and instead, welcome the vibrancy resulting from active public spaces (chapter 12).

PHASE 5: IMPACT EVALUATION

The fifth and final phase examined in the case studies evaluates the impacts of the public-space enhancement on communities and cities. Successful public-space interventions often lead to positive outcomes such as improved public health (physical and mental), social interaction, and safety (table 8.7). Successful public-space projects also contribute to neighborhood rejuvenation, increased foot traffic for businesses, visitorship, and enhanced property value. In addition, walkable streets can improve mobility, access to jobs, and the overall connectivity and attractiveness of a neighborhood, as observed in the Brooklyn case (chapter 13). Moreover, green areas improve air quality, the microclimate, and resilience to flooding by increasing permeable areas. Not all impacts are always positive; the negative impacts of public-space interventions can include issues related to gentrification and resettlement. In some of the case studies, these unintended consequences are acknowledged, recognized, and proactively addressed.

Social Impacts

Improved inclusion, safety, health, and well-being are some of the observed outcomes from the case studies, as these examples illustrate:

- *In Karachi,* the IAK movement's renovation of 14 sports facilities for youth in underserved neighborhoods has benefited more than 5,000 people, including 1,500 girls. In addition, Pakistan Chowk saw increased use after its rehabilitation. It was reported that 65 events conducted by the PCCC

TABLE 8.7 **Multisectoral Positive Impacts of Public-Space Enhancement Projects**

Public-space intervention		Social impact			Environmental impact			Economic impact		
Type	Name	Vibrancy and safety	Health and well-being	Social inclusion	Air quality and/or microclimate	Retention and flood resilience	Biodiversity	Property value and tax revenue	Local businesses	Innovative job creation
Streetscape	Yonsei-ro, Seoul	•	•	•				O	•	
	Orchard Road, Singapore	•			•			•	•	•
	Eduljee Dinshaw Road, Karachi	•	•	•						
	Walls of Peace, Karachi	•	•	•						•
	Las Begonias, Lima	•		•	O			O	O	
	New Tiflis, Tbilisi	•						•	•	
	Brooklyn Cultural District, Brooklyn	•		•				•	•	•
	Yangmeizhu Lane, Beijing	•	•	•	O			O	•	•
Linear park	Gyeongui Line Forest Park, Seoul	•	•	•	•	O	O	O	•	
	Park Connector Network (PCN), Singapore	•	•	•	•	•	•			
Market	Hawker Centers, Singapore	•	•	•					•	
Pocket or neighborhood square	Pakistan Chowk, Karachi	•		•					O	
	Plaza 31, Lima	•		•	O				O	
	Dashilar Pocket Spaces, Beijing	•	•	•	O	O	O			
Waterfront	Crow Island Beach Park, Colombo	•	•	•	•	O	O		•	
	DUMBO (Down Under the Manhattan Bridge Overpass), Brooklyn	•	O	•				•	•	•
Public building	Gusandong Library, Seoul	•	•	•				O		
	I AM KARACHI, Sports Facility		•	•						
Ecological park	Beddagana Wetland Park, Colombo		•	•	O	•	•			
	Parque Ecológico, Lima		O	O	O	O	O			
Historical park	Vake Park preservation, Tbilisi			•						

Note: "•" refers to benefits that are quantified or raised in the respective case studies, while "O" refers to anticipated long-term impacts.

within an eight-month period attracted audiences averaging 120 people from different backgrounds (chapter 11).

- *In Lima,* Plaza 31 sits on the border of wealthy and underserved neighborhoods. It now serves both neighborhoods, and the injection of diverse cultural programs in public spaces helped bridge socioeconomic and intergenerational divides (chapter 12).

- *In Colombo,* the Crow Island Beach had a reputation for being a hotspot for antisocial behavior, but after its rehabilitation into a waterfront park, it attracted more than 2,000 visitors each weekend from both local communities and elsewhere. Safety measures, such as the presence of security officers and police posts, along with improvements to the physical designs of the park made the area a popular destination for citizens (chapter 10).
- *In Brookyn,* the Archway of the Manhattan Bridge—previously used as a storage area and a wall separating the north and south sides of DUMBO (figure 8.7, panel a)—was reopened in 2008 as an anchor point in the neighborhood for a wide variety of events, including sporting events, concerts, and markets (figure 8.7, panel b). These included more than 90 public events that attracted approximately 30,000 visitors in 2018. The intervention also led to a 200 percent increase in nighttime and weekend foot traffic between 2007 and 2017 (chapter 13).

Encouraging healthy living and having people be physically active outdoors are some of the anticipated outcomes of better-designed, more-accessible parks. In Singapore, for example, visitors to the PCN and its parks increased by 16 percent between 2014 and 2016 (chapter 15).

Environmental Impacts

Urban green and ecological spaces can contribute to city resilience. They help mitigate heat island effects and improve air quality in urban areas. After the construction of the GLFP in Seoul (chapter 14), the surface

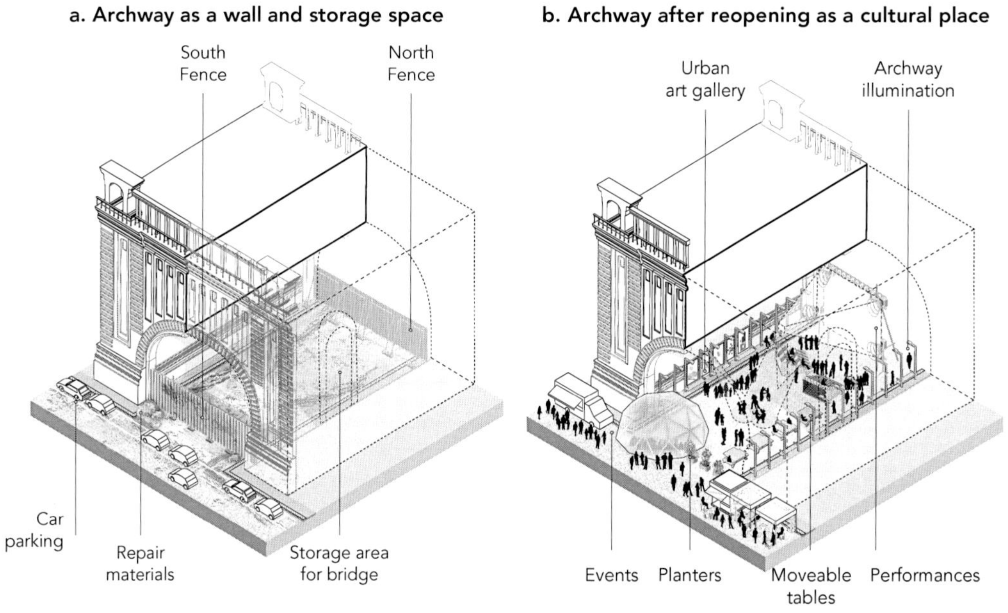

FIGURE 8.7 **Archway of the Manhattan Bridge, Brooklyn, before and after 2008 Reopening**

Source: ©World Bank. Further permission required for reuse.

temperatures dropped in the park and surrounding areas (Kim, Yi, and Lee 2019). In Colombo (chapter 10), the Crow Island Beach Park suffered from air pollution because of heavy traffic in the surrounding areas, and the poor air quality was partially mitigated by planting trees and lawn along the beach park. Greening can also make a big difference in small spaces, such as those in Beijing's Dashilar Pocket Spaces (chapter 9).

Ecological spaces in cities also strengthen resilience by helping to improve drainage, mitigate flooding, and enhance biodiversity. For instance, an economic analysis conducted for the BWP in Colombo revealed that the total wetland benefits including flood protection and carbon storage are annually worth SL Rs 10–12 billion (approximately US$80 million) to the Colombo Metropolitan Region (chapter 10). The BWP also preserved more than 200 species of the wetland ecosystem. In Singapore, the PCN project intentionally planted fast-growing native trees and shrubs to attract and protect biodiversity along the PCN as well as to connect natural reserves and patches of forest to make a conducive environment for both park users and wildlife (chapter 15).

Economic Impacts

Public spaces can create economic benefits for a city by increasing land and property values in the surrounding areas. To realize such returns, cities need fiscal instruments to enable them to capture a fair share of the increased land value, whether a property tax system based on up-to-date cadaster and property valuation databases or an asset management strategy to generate proceeds from the sale or lease of government-owned land and real estate. The resulting increase in municipal revenues can be reinvested into improved service delivery and public spaces. Examples of how public spaces enhance business sales, land and property values, and municipal revenues include:

- *In Seoul,* property values along the GLFP area increased by 6.7 percent within a year of project completion—twice the average increase of other neighborhoods in Seoul. The number of local businesses adjacent to the GLFP also increased by 101 percent between 2015 and 2017, with average monthly sales per shop increasing by 151 percent (chapter 14).
- *In Singapore,* 76 percent of all international tourists visited Orchard Road in 2003, spending more than S$340 million (chapter 15).
- *In Beijing,* the average asset value on Yangmeizhu Lane more than doubled since before the regeneration and placemaking project (chapter 9). Total sales revenues were less than RMB 1 million (US$151,000) before regeneration in 2012; by 2018, they had significantly increased, to RMB 110 million (US$16.7 million).
- *In Tbilisi,* the rental prices and property values on Aghmashenebli Avenue doubled between 2015 and 2017, and consequently property taxes from commercial companies adjacent to the rehabilitated street drastically increased (chapter 16).

Efforts to regenerate urban public spaces can also spur neighborhood transformation, which in turn encourages the development of districts focused on innovation and entrepreneurship.

- *In Beijing*, the Dashilar Pocket Spaces and Yangmeizhu Lane projects catered to new types of enterprises that are culture-driven or design-oriented, using design to attract broad interests beyond the conventional retail and restaurant networks and inspiring diverse partners to potentially set up businesses in the area (chapter 9). Since 2012, 80 new culture-driven businesses—such as publishing companies, bookstores, art galleries, design studios, boutique shops, and craft workshops—came into the area, which also benefited more than 100 previously established local businesses. Both new and old businesses coexist and have gradually strengthened the cultural identity of Dashilar and attracted more people.
- *In Brooklyn*, the number of innovation firms and employees had increased by 22 percent and 45 percent, respectively, from 2012 (when the BTT was initiated) to 2015 (chapter 13). In fact, 45 percent of surveyed innovation firms in the BTT responded that they chose to be in Brooklyn because of the neighborhood character and amenities that Brooklyn offered.

Gentrification can be a consequence of urban rejuvenation: as property values increase in a neighborhood, a decline in affordable housing and services could displace residents, resulting in a loss of social capital from the neighborhood. It is noteworthy that the complex nature of gentrification can be viewed through different lenses. For example, some scholars have framed this as a result of a market economy instead of as solely a social consequence (Amirtahmasebi et al. 2016).

Although this book does not discuss gentrification in great detail, the case studies provide some examples of different efforts to address the unintended consequences of urban rejuvenation, including the following:

- *In Beijing,* an inclusive and participatory process was set from the outset to achieve a consensus among communities (chapter 9). A pioneering participatory regeneration program launched in 2017—the "Re-Up Dashilar—Livable Yangmeizhu" initiative—directly targeted this issue through pension programs, eldercare facilities, community activities, a community development seed-funding program, and others.
- *In Colombo,* the Crow Island Beach Park project compensated previous users such as informal vendors and farmers with alternatives such as leases for newly created kiosks or resettlement packages (chapter 10).
- *In the Brooklyn Cultural District,* the Culture Forward initiative was launched to maximize opportunities for low-income artists by providing affordable housing and capacity-building programs (chapter 13).

CONCLUSION: LESSONS FROM CASE STUDIES

The case studies show clearly that shaping activities and investments in the public realm will invariably involve a multitude of actors, and coordination among these actors, across different stages of the project implementation cycle. Local community and private sector engagement during the life cycle of creating, funding, and managing public spaces is a critical element that will determine the success and sustainability of these interventions. This process, if conducted well, can help public-space interventions better address community needs and build ownership and pride among citizens, which motivates citizens to proactively take charge of public spaces as "owners." The process also strengthens social networks by involving a diverse set of stakeholders.

The selected case studies in this volume show that municipalities often own a significant portion of public spaces (see chapter 6) and will continue to play key roles in the planning, implementation, and management of these city spaces. Among these cases, more than half of the public-space interventions were initiated, implemented, and managed in some part by local governments. In some cases, *local governments* initiated and invested in urban development pilots that later attracted private participation and investments. When *communities* took the lead in creating public-space projects (with limited public support), local governments were engaged more actively later to sustain these efforts in the longer term. In many cases, strong political leadership, agency coordination, and capacity for urban planning were needed to ensure that cities have well-designed, well-managed urban environments that support a high quality of life.

There is no one way to create great places. As the case studies demonstrate, there are numerous pathways and opportunities to shape, reimagine, and manage public spaces. A key element is to recognize the strengths of different physical assets—whether by leveraging cultural and historically significant assets (heritage buildings, historical parks, and cultural places) to create accessible places to enjoy, by integrating natural greenery (urban wetlands and forests) that add to city resilience, or by using a combination of the above. In neighborhoods where physical public-space assets are seemingly absent, repurposing old infrastructure such as canals and railways into accessible and inclusive places or simply adapting underused or leftover spaces as gathering spaces are some examples of how public spaces can be creatively used. Often the success of these places is also determined by how public spaces that have a mix of ownership types—for example, a streetscape comprising private buildings along a public street or private street vendors on public lands—are managed.

NOTES

1. Creative community spaces enable innovation by creating a physical convening point for a community of entrepreneurs and start-ups. They anchor entrepreneurial communities and influence the urban economic and physical landscape (World Bank 2017). Also see the BTT website: http://brooklyntriangle.com.
2. See examples of tactical urbanism interventions on the Spontaneous Interventions online archive: http://www.spontaneousinterventions.org.
3. Local governments, such as Washington, DC, and Victoria, Australia, have published and adopted detailed design guidelines for public spaces (DDOT 2019; Victoria State Government 2016). Other notable institutions that have developed public-space strategies extensively include the Project for Public Spaces (PPS 2016), the United Nations Human Settlements Programme (UN-Habitat 2014), and Gehl Institute (Gehl Institute 2016).

4. "Power of 10+" refers to the idea that cities need more than 10 attractive destinations, each of which should have 10 different types of places within it, such as a café, a children's play area, a place to sit, a place to meet friends, and so on (PPS 2016).
5. Notably, because none of these squares in DUMBO was classified as a park zone, they were ineligible for financial support from the city government. The Department of Transportation, which does own the land, had no mechanism or resources to maintain these spaces.

REFERENCES

Amirtahmasebi, Rana, Mariana Orloff, Sameh Wahba, and Andrew Altman. 2016. *Regenerating Urban Land: A Practitioner's Guide to Leveraging Private Investment*. Urban Development Series. Washington, DC: World Bank.

DDOT (District Department of Transportation). 2019. "Public Realm Design Manual: A Summary of District of Columbia Regulations and Specifications for the Design of Public Space Elements. Version 2.1." Guidance manual, Government of the District of Columbia, Washington, DC.

Gehl, Jan. 2010. *Cities for People*. Washington, DC: Island Press.

Gehl Institute. 2016. "The Public Life Diversity Toolkit 2.0." Methodology of the Public Space/Public Life project, Gehl Institute, New York.

Kim, Kijung, Changhyo Yi, and Seungil Lee. 2019. "Impact of Urban Characteristics on Cooling Energy Consumption before and after Construction of an Urban Park: The Case of Gyeongui Line Forest in Seoul." *Energy and Buildings* 191: 42–51.

NACTO (National Association of City Transportation Officials). 2016. *Global Street Design Guide*. New York: Island Press.

PPS (Project for Public Spaces). 2016. "Placemaking: What if We Built Our Cities around Places?" Booklet, PPS, New York.

Targa, Felipe, William Moose, Nicolás Estupiñán, and Carlos Mojica. 2019. "Urban Mobility, Health and Public Spaces: Reshaping Urban Landscapes." Urban 20 (U20) White Paper, Development Bank of Latin America, Inter-American Development Bank, and World Bank, Buenos Aires.

UNESCO (United Nations Educational, Scientific and Cultural Organization). 2016. *Culture: Urban Future; Global Report on Culture for Sustainable Urban Development*. Paris: UNESCO.

UN-Habitat (United Nations Human Settlements Programme). 2014. *Global Public Space Toolkit: From Global Principles to Local Policies and Practice*. Nairobi: UN-Habitat.

Victoria State Government. 2016. "Public Spaces Principles." In "Public Spaces," chapter 3 of "Urban Design Guidelines for Victoria." Online guidance document (accessed April 10, 2019), http://www.urban-design-guidelines.planning.vic.gov.au/guidelines/public-spaces.

Whyte, William H. 1980. *The Social Life of Small Urban Spaces*. New York: Project for Public Spaces.

World Bank. 2017. "Creative Community Spaces: Spaces that Are Transforming Cities into Innovation Hubs." Working Paper No. 17300, World Bank, Washington, DC.

CHAPTER 9

BEIJING, CHINA: REGENERATING TRADITIONAL PUBLIC SPACES IN THE HISTORIC CITY CORE

Zheng Jia and Rong Jia

KEY TAKEAWAYS

- In contrast with the previous large-scale, top-down urban redevelopment model widely practiced in China, the Beijing municipal government sought incremental, inclusive approaches to neighborhood regeneration efforts in the Yangmeizhu Lane and pocket spaces projects in Dashilar, a historic neighborhood in the center of the city.
- The Dashilar regeneration program aimed not only to address the constraints of *hutongs* (traditional lanes) but also to innovatively create green and cultural spaces that preserve the authentic hutong culture. By catering to culture-driven businesses such as art galleries, design studios, and boutique shops, the regeneration projects also benefited previously established local businesses. New and old businesses coexist and have strengthened the cultural identity of Dashilar, which attracted more people and increased total revenues tremendously.

- The cocreation approach of involving various stakeholders allowed the projects to better address community needs while also building ownership and pride among residents, which strengthened social networks. Private sector engagement helped to create multifunctional spaces that spurred economic opportunities for surrounding businesses.

CITY DYNAMICS

Context and Background

Beijing is the capital of China and one of the largest cities in the world. The city's development in recent decades has reflected China's rapid urbanization, massive rural-to-urban migration, and swift economic growth. The population of Beijing grew from 8.7 million in 1978 to 21.7 million in 2017, and the city's gross regional domestic product (GRDP) per capita grew from RMB 1,300 (US$797) to RMB 129,000 (US$19,095) during the same period.[1] Within a total land area of 16,808 square kilometers administrated by the metropolitan government, the urban built-up areas of Beijing expanded from 239 square kilometers in 1980 to 1,401 square kilometers in 2017.[2] Beijing has a high concentration of government agencies and universities; a rich ecosystem for research, technology, education, art, entertainment, and culture; and strong service and finance sectors—all of which constantly attract talent and job seekers from all over the country.

Beijing's city form has been shaped by its history as an imperial capital and its rapid urban development during the 20th century. Based on ancient principles for the design of capital cities dating back to the fifth century BC, the Old City of Beijing was planned and built as the capital of the Ming Dynasty about 600 years ago.[3] The capital was a symmetric, walled city centered around the imperial palace and with a long and prominent south–north axis—elements that still define much of the urban structure seen today.

In the 1950s and 1960s, the planning and development of Beijing, as capital of the new People's Republic of China, were heavily influenced by city planners and engineers from the Soviet Union. This phase of development featured the Forbidden City and Tiananmen Square as the city center, along with wide roads; monumental buildings and squares; and large, gated blocks for public institutions and factories (Bian 2016). Since 1978, when China opened its economy, the city has rapidly expanded and redeveloped. This growth includes a large increase in urban built-up areas, four ring-road expressways as the city's transport arteries, newly constructed and widened roads that define a large-scale grid and large city blocks, mid- and high-rise residential compounds, commercial skyscrapers and mixed-use complexes, iconic public buildings, and an extensive transit system (Chen 2004; Gaubatz 2008).

The coexistence of the old and new is a constant theme in Beijing. Three thousand years of urbanized history and as the capital of six different Chinese dynasties has imprinted Beijing with a rich and unique level of cultural heritage.[4] Beijing has seven United Nations Educational, Scientific and Cultural Organization (UNESCO) World Heritage Sites and 126 national-level cultural heritage sites, the highest concentration of any city in China.[5] The systematic, spatial design of the Old City of Beijing represented the pinnacle of China's imperial city planning, distinguished by a hierarchical ordering of society through space, advanced urban water systems, and ritual and religious spaces, as well as royal architecture and gardening. Inside Beijing's walled city were more than 2,000 hutongs connecting the countless enclosed and inward-looking *siheyuan* (courtyard-style residences) that formed the basic units of the Old City fabric (Wang, Mao, and Dang 2007).

However, over the past 100 years, despite conservation of some key cultural heritage sites, Beijing's extensive city wall was demolished, and the holistic system of traditional spaces and architecture in the historic city core have gradually been divided by the large grid of arterial roadways and replaced by modern buildings. Many hutongs thus have become fragmented and dilapidated. Moreover, widespread subdivision of the traditional courtyard houses after the revolutionary appropriation of private assets in the 1950s, along with a deterioration of infrastructure, has led to substandard living conditions, low rents, and concentration of lower-income households in the traditional neighborhoods of the Old City of Beijing.

China's recent high-level policies have increasingly emphasized sustainable and inclusive urbanization, and these goals have directed Beijing's latest master plan. The government of China has committed itself to meeting the UN Sustainable Development Goals (SDGs) and has adopted a set of core principles contained in the UN's New Urban Agenda[6] through China's National New-Type Urbanization Plan (2014–20) and the 13th Five-Year Plan (2016–20) (*Xinhua News* 2014). The government's subsequent sectoral policies on urban planning, development, and management—led by the National Development and Reform Commission and the Ministry of Housing and Urban-Rural Development—further detailed how to implement such guiding principles (CPC Central Committee and State Council 2016; MoHURD 2017).[7] In response to tendencies toward rapid city sprawl, the recent policies highlighted regeneration of built-up areas instead of greenfield expansion as the main paradigm of urbanization in the next phase.

The latest Beijing Municipal Master Plan (2016–35) aims to develop the capital as "a livable city" and the country's "political, cultural, global, and innovative center."[8] It also highlighted balancing conservation and regeneration of historic neighborhoods. Along with the increasing recognition of the value of cultural heritage nationwide, Beijing's new master plan identified the abundant historical and cultural assets in Beijing as the city's "gold business card" and elevated conservation of cultural heritage to its highest policy priority since the 1950s (PGBM 2017). To conserve the historic city core, the master plan aims to strictly conserve the south–north axis and key visual corridors in the Old City, employing cross-agency and multistakeholder coordination, designs for adaptive reuse, innovative financing models, and improved administrative procedures.

Public Spaces in Beijing

Before 1911, public spaces in Beijing emerged naturally from commercial clusters around transport nodes, marketplaces, and temples. During the Qing Dynasty (1644–1912),[9] spaces in Beijing were generally walled, closed, and exclusive—reflecting the supreme control of royal power. However, public spaces naturally and spontaneously emerged as commercial clusters around city gates, transport nodes, marketplaces, and temples, all of which influenced the commercial areas and surrounding spaces in modern periods up to today (Bian 2016).

During 1911–49, modern public buildings and spaces were established in Beijing, and the old royal compounds became open to the public. This period was after the 1911 Revolution, which overthrew the imperial dynasty and established the Republic of China. The Capital Municipal Bureau, established in 1917, led multisectoral service delivery and urban development functions, including the opening of the formerly walled royal city to the citizens and improved transport. Select royal temples, ritual spaces, and gardens that had been "forbidden" during the imperial dynasties were transformed into city parks and opened to the public. The earliest modern universities, hospitals, banks, office buildings, and shopping centers in Beijing were also established during this period (Lin 2013).

Since 1949, when the People's Republic of China was established, creation and improvement of public spaces in Beijing have evolved through multiple stages. From 1949 to 1978, modern public spaces were established in Beijing, featuring large, monumental squares, wide roads, and symbolic public buildings that represented the socialist ideology and the nation's political center. The royal palace as well as additional royal gardens and temples were opened to the public. Urban parks were created from patches of wasteland (Lin 2013).

From 1978 to today, when China opened up its economy, the improvement of public spaces became important on the agenda for urban development, and therefore public spaces increased in number and typology, driven by both the public and private sectors. The number of parks open to the public in the central city increased from approximately 10 royal spaces in the 1940s to 140 in 2017. The green-space coverage ratio in urban built-up areas in Beijing grew from 20.1 percent in 1980 to 48.2 percent in 2017, and the per capita green space in Beijing increased from 5.1 square meters to 16.2 square meters during the same period (BLGB 2019; PGBM 2017). Urban greenery has also become more sophisticated and aesthetically attractive. The main achievements since 2010 include creating widespread recreational parks and green corridors, improving green spaces in residential areas and traditional neighborhoods, enhancing landscape design, and generating pocket parks on underused land in urban areas (BLGB 2019).

The latest master plan for Beijing highlighted green and public spaces. The plan laid out a comprehensive greenery system across the city through a series of green belts, corridors, parks, and small green spaces. In line with the human-centered National New-Type Urbanization Plan, the master plan emphasized the quantity as well as the quality of public spaces that are accessible, beautiful, convenient, comfortable, usable, green, and culturally distinguishable. The plan also set goals for residents' accessibility to public spaces to be within a 500-meter walking distance from their homes and encouraged community participation and community surveys in public-space improvement projects. A series of programs followed the master plan, such as the Second Ring Road Green Corridor Program, and the Pilot Program for Innovative Public Place-Making (Beijing DRC 2017; PGBM 2017).

A number of challenges remain despite the significant improvements in public spaces. First, myriad government agencies and entities are involved in delivering and managing public spaces, including the Municipal Planning Commission, Landscape and Greening Bureau, Construction Commission, Traffic Management Bureau, Water Bureau, Environment and Sanitation Center, and so forth. However, these agencies lack strong coordination, which often leads to uncoordinated facilities and infrastructure and suboptimal conflicts with public spaces.

Second, planning, design, and implementation processes lack clear regulations for synergy and quality. The planning agencies' permitting procedures focus on regulatory parameters such as land use, scale, green-space ratio, and others—and not on human-scale considerations. The Beijing Landscape and Greening Bureau focuses on designated green spaces but lacks permitting authority over public spaces affiliated with construction projects.[10]

Third, between the high-level city control plans[11] and the detailed architectural or engineering designs, a key stage of urban design is missing—the opportunity to synergistically enhance the quality of urban public spaces through careful, place-based urban design (Lian, Li, and Yin 2016). Notably, however, the latest national policies and programs aim to address these issues.

DASHILAR REGENERATION MODEL AND YANGMEIZHU LANE

Phase 1: Context

The centrally located area around Qianmen Gate, Dashilar, and Xianyukou was an important gateway, transport hub, and commercial and cultural center of the Beijing Old City. The Qianmen, or Zhengyang, Gate is 1.4 kilometers south of the Forbidden City and 900 meters south of Tiananmen Square, and this south-central gate was the largest among the nine gates of the inner Old City of Beijing during the Ming and Qing Dynasties. For about 500 years, merchants from all over the country used to enter the capital city through the Qianmen Gate. Thus, the neighborhoods outside Qianmen Gate, including the Dashilar and Xianyukou Districts, became one of the most bustling commercial districts in the Old City of Beijing. Because of Qianmen Gate's central location, the first train station of Beijing was also constructed here in 1901. Later, a tram was operated along the wide Qianmen Avenue as part of the public transport in the early 20th century.

The greater historic area of Qianmen Gate, Dashilar, and Xianyukou was redeveloped through different models. Regeneration of this area started in 2004–06 with the widening and upgrading of Meishi Road and Qianmen East Road to divert traffic and solve severe congestion problems. Around the same time, the redevelopment of Qianmen Avenue and Xianyukou District was launched, followed by massive relocation of residents and businesses as well as the demolition of many buildings that were not classified as cultural heritage sites. These areas were rebuilt as low-rise commercial streets and zones, using both traditional and modern styles. The redeveloped Qianmen Avenue was opened to the public in 2008 before the Beijing Olympic Games, and the Xianyukou historic district, featuring a "food street" and rebuilt low-rise commercial blocks, was reopened in 2011. Unfortunately, business in the redeveloped streets has not been successful, mainly because of the mismatch between high rents after the large-scale resettlement and reconstruction and a low willingness to pay among customers, who are mainly tourists from all over the country passing on their way to or from the Forbidden City and Tiananmen Square.[12]

With lessons learned from the previous model, the Government of Beijing Municipality selected the regeneration of the Dashilar area west to Qianmen Avenue—a pilot for incremental, innovative regeneration in 2009—as an alternative approach for regenerating historic neighborhoods. The Dashilar historic and cultural district, southwest of the Qianmen Gate, is one of the largest remaining historic neighborhoods in Beijing. Designated as a historic and cultural district by the Beijing Municipal Master Plan, Dashilar covers an area of 126 hectares with approximately 25,000 households. Dashilar was one of the most important commercial and cultural centers of Beijing during the Ming and Qing Dynasties—home to famous shopping streets, the earliest banks, guildhalls, a concentration of renowned brands, teahouses, and restaurants. The area was also popular for its art, culture, and entertainment, featuring traditional operas, bookstores, publishers, handicrafts, textiles, and the first cinema in Beijing (Zhang 2008).

Over the decades in Dashilar, the old street patterns have remained nearly intact, and the traditional architecture has been partially preserved. The remaining 116 hutongs in Dashilar organically formed outside the inner city and were later organized during the Yuan, Ming, and Qing Dynasties. Approximately 85 percent of the buildings built during the Ming and Qing Dynasties and the Republic of China period fully or partially remain in Dashilar (map 9.1).

Today, most of the buildings in Dashilar are dense and low-rise, often having been incrementally expanded or rebuilt from the traditional courtyard houses. The area is mainly residential, with pockets of public buildings as well as commercial and cultural areas. Heritage buildings are concentrated along the Dashilar shopping street and dotted throughout the entire district, including temples, mosques, renowned shops, guildhalls, Chinese opera houses, famous residences, old restaurants, bookstores, teahouses, bathhouses, movie theaters, and others.[13]

Phase 2: Planning and Design

Dashilar Regeneration Model

Three main objectives were set for the regeneration of historic Dashilar: (a) improving local quality of life, (b) conserving historical and cultural heritage, and (c) revitalizing socioeconomic development. These objectives target multidimensional benefits, based on diagnostics of the area that recognized the complexity, diversity, richness of heritage, and multisectoral challenges accumulated over more than 100 years.

As a pilot urban regeneration project in Beijing, Dashilar explored an incremental, organic, and participatory regeneration approach in revitalizing traditional spaces. This pilot approach is called the "Dashilar regeneration model" among local governments, urban planning and governance professionals, and academicians. At the planning and policy levels, holistic, multidimensional planning as well as coordinated, multistakeholder mechanisms were established. Dashilar was one of the first historic neighborhoods in China to be identified and planned as an interconnected spatial, socioeconomic,

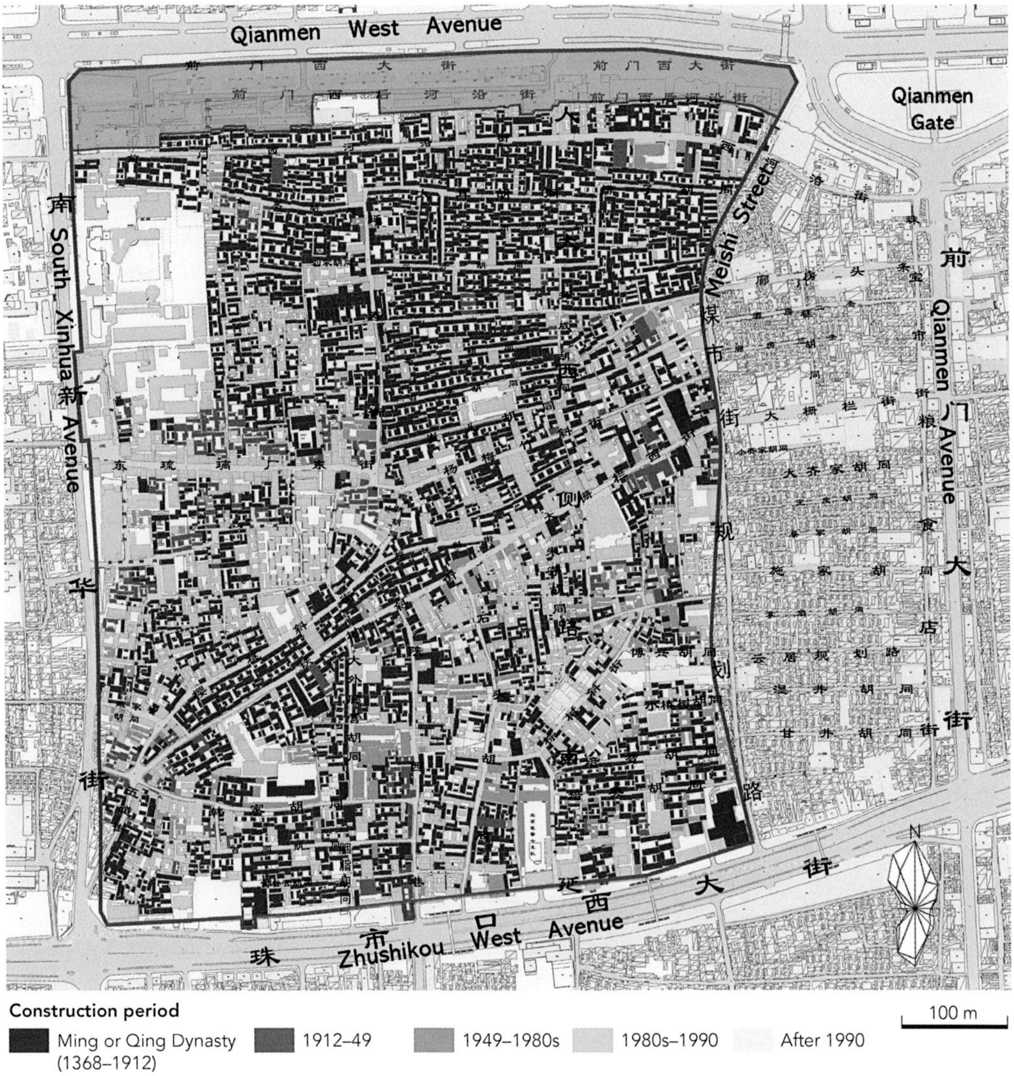

MAP 9.1 **Buildings, by Construction Period, in the Dashilar Area of Beijing**

Source: "Dashilar Regeneration Plan" [in Chinese], Beijing Dashilar Investment Company (BDIC) website (accessed March 12, 2019), http://www.dashilar.org.cn/; World Bank translation. ©Beijing Dashilar Investment Company (BDIC). Reproduced, with permission, from BDIC; further permission required for reuse.

historical, and cultural entity.[14] At the design and implementation levels, a phased and incremental approach was adopted that began with small-scale pilots for public space and infrastructure upgrading as well as renovation of selected public buildings and traditional courtyards. These pilots were then scaled up to additional streets, clusters of lanes and buildings, and ultimately the entire area.

The Dashilar regeneration model was in contrast with the common demolition-resettlement-reconstruction model and was the first urban regeneration program in China to engage a wide range of stakeholders and allow for the participation and empowerment of local communities. The model avoided callously uprooting local communities and imposing a wholly different development in the area. At the same time, the model leveraged the curation of art and design in urban spaces to revitalize the old neighborhoods and communities. In contrast to large-scale redevelopment driven by a single entity, the Dashilar model employed a process in which multiple stakeholders, including local businesses and residents, joined hands with public and private resources and worked together to revitalize Dashilar. The common goal was a place where newcomers could live in harmony with original residents, creative businesses could thrive among local shops, and eventually a new hybrid community could sustainably emerge with a renewed prosperity.

Staged Approach

Another important feature of the Dashilar regeneration model was its staged approach, which enabled the collaborative dynamics and negotiation of different stakeholders, sustainable organic growth, and better socioeconomic development results. The stages, as described below, were planned based on two years of thorough preparation, including research of global best practices in urban regeneration, market demand analysis, business upgrading strategies, and staging strategies, as well as baseline surveys of the architectural, infrastructural, cultural, historical, and socioeconomic aspects.

- *Stage 1: Pilot regeneration of Yangmeizhu Lane.* At the beginning of the regeneration process, the local government took the lead in building the trust and understanding of local residents, businesses, and other participants. Based on a systematic plan, the initial goals were to improve the quality of life for residents. Infrastructure and public-space upgrading were implemented to improve the services and environment of the neighborhood. At this stage, architectural conservation and renovation as well as standards for introducing and integrating new businesses were piloted for future practice. The Dashilar Platform—a hub of resources—set a firm foundation for the involvement of future partners.
- *Stage 2: Community participatory development.* As the pilot regeneration demonstrated successful results, the model was scaled up. Through collaboration with local residents and businesses, different innovation methods were established according to local needs. Community empowerment and codesign were introduced.
- *Stage 3: Comprehensive development (planned).* With community participation and the establishment of a multistakeholder platform, the regeneration continues to scale up in a sustainable manner. A series of tailored guidelines were developed to allow different stakeholders to drive the continued regeneration. The local government will continue its oversight and management roles to serve the community and will lead future planning.

Dashilar Pilot Program

The Dashilar Pilot Program was initiated in 2013 to bring design and planning practitioners together with residents and catalyze interventions to upgrade and revitalize the decaying neighborhood. Since 2011, the municipal government of Beijing has successfully worked with three ministries to organize the annual Beijing Design Week (BJDW), in which the Dashilar initiative has been a key and active participant. Leveraging the BJDW activities, the Dashilar Pilot Program called for local and international proposals for pilot projects that could be implemented in urban spaces. The themes of the program exemplified multidisciplinary solutions to regenerating traditional neighborhoods: conservation and renovation of traditional buildings, improvement of public spaces, revitalization of local economy, and rejuvenation of local culture.[15]

Unlike most other design competitions, the Dashilar Pilot Program pioneered some unique features:[16]

- The annual open call for proposals focused on real problems in Dashilar.
- All successful proposals were to be practical, providing implementation details.
- The selected proposals would be implemented in Dashilar through a seed fund.
- Consensus for the selected pilot projects had to be built among relevant businesses or residents, and a codesign process was encouraged.
- The program was updated every year based on the latest needs and implementation progress.
- The annual program followed a process to ensure incremental improvements in Dashilar. (Steps in the process included the call for proposals, proposal submission, proposal improvement through community engagement, proposal selection, public exhibition, and implementation.)

The program transformed one-off curation to long-term support for meaningful neighborhood regeneration. Since 2013, all the BJDW themes in Dashilar have centered around the progress of urban regeneration in Dashilar, and more than half of the exhibitions were initiated by the Dashilar Platform (photo 9.1). Each year, approximately 20–30 pilot projects—all mid-term or long-term projects—have been selected and implemented through the program. These projects have demonstrated a new approach of bottom-up neighborhood regeneration in China.

Placemaking and Heritage Conservation of Yangmeizhu Lane

The pilot regeneration and placemaking of Yangmeizhu Lane were the core of Stage 1. Yangmeizhu Lane was selected as a pilot of the Dashilar regeneration plan because (a) it is located in the heart of Dashilar; (b) it connects the Dashilar Commercial Street and the Liulichang Cultural Area; (c) it is mixed, with commercial and residential uses; and (d) it has dilapidated heritage buildings that could be conserved and adaptively reused. Stakeholders thus identified the lane as very representative of the Dashilar area, and lessons learned from such a pilot can be scaled up in the larger area. The pilot project included Yangmeizhu Lane, Yingtao Lane, and Yingtao East Lane, a total of 750 meters.[17] The pilot regeneration scope covered an area of 8.8 hectares around the lane (map 9.2).

PHOTO 9.1 **Banner for Beijing BJDW on Yangmeizhu Lane, 2017**

Source: ©Beijing Dashilar Investment Company (BDIC). Reproduced, with permission, from BDIC; further permission required for reuse.

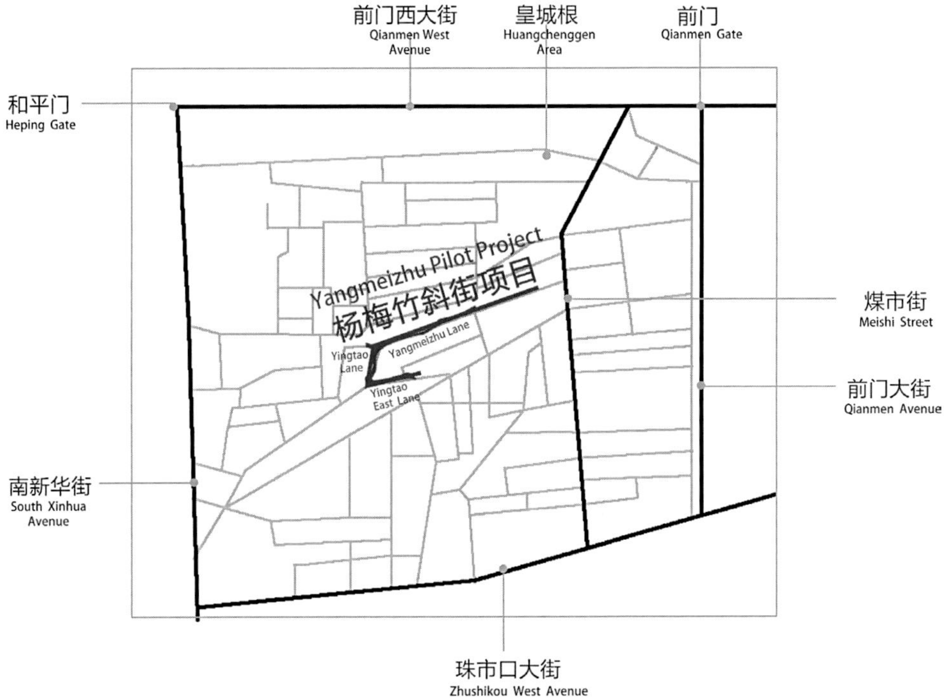

MAP 9.2 **Area of the Yangmeizhu Lane Pilot Project, Beijing**

Source: View Unlimited et al. 2012; World Bank translation. ©View Unlimited Landscape Architecture Studio (View Unlimited). Reproduced, with permission, from View Unlimited; further permission required for reuse.

View Unlimited Landscape Architecture Studio was commissioned to design the streetscape for the Yangmeizhu Pilot (figure 9.1). The design firm, together with several other designers, proposed a comprehensive design scheme that aimed to improve traffic management, walkability, vegetation and landscape, basic infrastructure, façades, pavements, street lighting, public furniture, facilities for older persons and people with disabilities, the signage system, and public art. Moreover, the project involved the internationally renowned Hara Design Institute in the visual design, including signage, lighting, websites, graphics, exhibitions, and so on.

To differentiate buildings based on cultural heritage values and current conditions, the architectural conservation and renovation adopted a three-grade strategy:

- *Grade 1: Designated cultural heritage sites* are to be conserved under strict procedures and guidelines under the cultural heritage administration.
- *Grade 2: Important historic buildings* are to be partially conserved and renovated based on authenticity.
- *Grade 3: Other old buildings* are to be renovated for diverse purposes, following design guidelines in harmony with traditional scale, styles, and materials.

Economic Revitalization Plan

The economic revitalization plan for the Dashilar area was based on thorough market analyses. The analyses identified the criteria for businesses entering

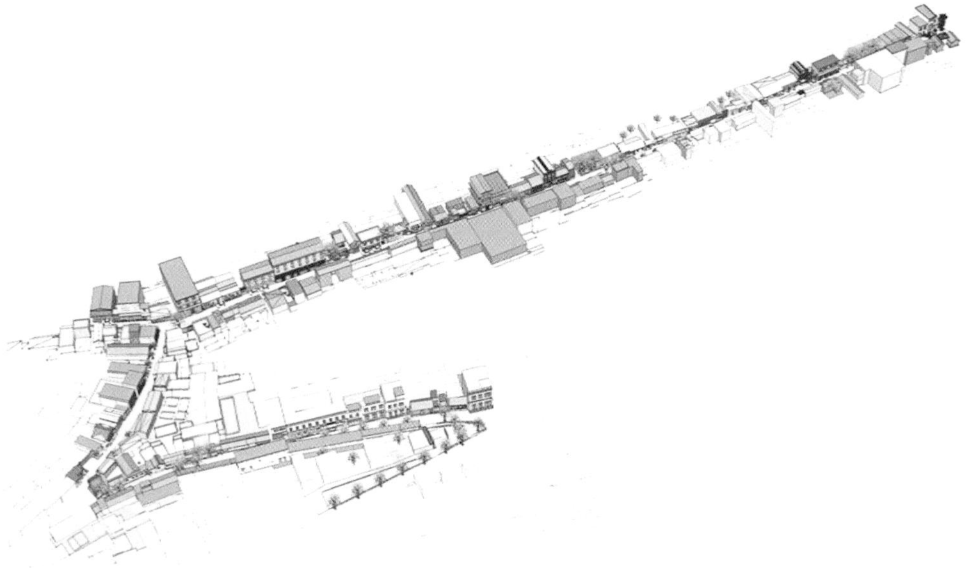

FIGURE 9.1 **Proposed Streetscape Design for Yangmeizhu Lane in the Dashilar Area, Beijing**

Source: View Unlimited et al. 2012; World Bank translation. ©View Unlimited Landscape Architecture Studio (View Unlimited). Reproduced, with permission, from View Unlimited; further permission required for reuse.

this area: those that can survive in decaying neighborhoods, respect the Old City culture and traditional architecture, not rely on heavy traffic flow or a large number of consumers in mature commercial centers, and have potential to attract future businesses in the Dashilar area. A "CPCP" method (representing culture, place, customers, and product or program) for selecting businesses was used, as follows:

- *"Culture"* means social responsibility rooted in the Old City culture.
- *"Place"* means suitability for location in traditional neighborhoods.
- *"Customers"* means ability to attract sufficient customers.
- *"Product or program"* means provision of products, services, and operating programs independent from existing commercial centers.

The CPCP analyses were adopted for any new business introduced into Dashilar to ensure sustainability, preserve the unique local culture, and maximize its cultural and economic impacts.[18]

Innovative approaches to attract suitable businesses were explored. The CPCP analyses identified a shared characteristic of suitable businesses: new-type enterprises that are culture-driven or design-oriented and sometimes representing emerging lifestyles. Such entrepreneurs often have cross-disciplinary backgrounds, which do not come easily through conventional business invitation channels. The first Beijing BJDW in 2011 provided a gateway to identify potential business partners that would match the value and culture of the Dashilar area. This experiment offered a new approach in economically revitalizing old neighborhoods—using design to attract broad interests beyond the conventional retail and restaurant networks and inspire diverse partners that potentially lead to setting up a business in the area.

Phase 3: Implementation

Infrastructure and Streetscape Upgrades

In 2012, innovative, incremental infrastructure upgrading began on Yangmeizhu Lane. In the original, narrow hutong space, the upgrading was incremental. Sewer and drainage systems were upgraded based on existing drains. The technical review process was tailored to enable the placement of a gas system in the narrow lanes, thus making Yangmeizhu the first lane of its width to have gas supply in Beijing. Electricity and telecommunication infrastructures were also upgraded to provide better services and environment.

At the same time, the lane's public spaces were significantly improved through the use of tailored and culturally sensitive designs to upgrade the pavement, façades, street furniture, and services. The Hara Design Institute guided the process of public-space improvement and visual design. The pavement was uniquely designed with gray bricks—integrating traditional materials, memories, and modern aesthetics (photo 9.2). The interfaces of pavement with each individual courtyard and house were tailored to maximize the attractiveness of the public space in the lane. Illegal signage was removed to preserve a more authentic hutong environment. Selected façades and architectural details were repaired and restored to enhance the cultural scene and visual harmony of

PHOTO 9.2 **Renovated Yangmeizhu Lane, Featuring Tailored Pavement and Signage Design, Beijing**

Source: ©Beijing Dashilar Investment Company (BDIC). Reproduced, with permission, from BDIC; further permission required for reuse.

the lane. Historical and urbanscape elements were integrated, including street lamps, garbage bins, public benches, plants, signage, sculptures, and night lights. The designs were intended to subtly preserve the architectural style while weaving history, memories, and culture into the landscape and reviving the authentic hutong culture in Yangmeizhu Lane.

Heritage Conservation

Among the 160 street-facing buildings on Yangmeizhu Lane, 95 percent of the owners reached an agreement with the project and participated in the conservation and renovation program. Among these buildings, 15 were classified under Grade 1 (designated cultural heritage sites), and 25 were classified under Grade 2 (important historic buildings) (figure 9.2). The remaining 75 percent were renovated with architectural and cultural elements from the Dashilar area as Grade 3 (other old buildings). A total of 56 illegal buildings were removed. The conservation and renovation schemes successfully preserved historical elements and integrated them with a contemporary appearance.[19]

Institutional Arrangements

A partnership between the government, the private sector, and the local community was created (figure 9.3). The regeneration was led by the Beijing Municipal Government and the Xicheng District Government. The Xicheng District Government strove to innovate in new schemes, such as

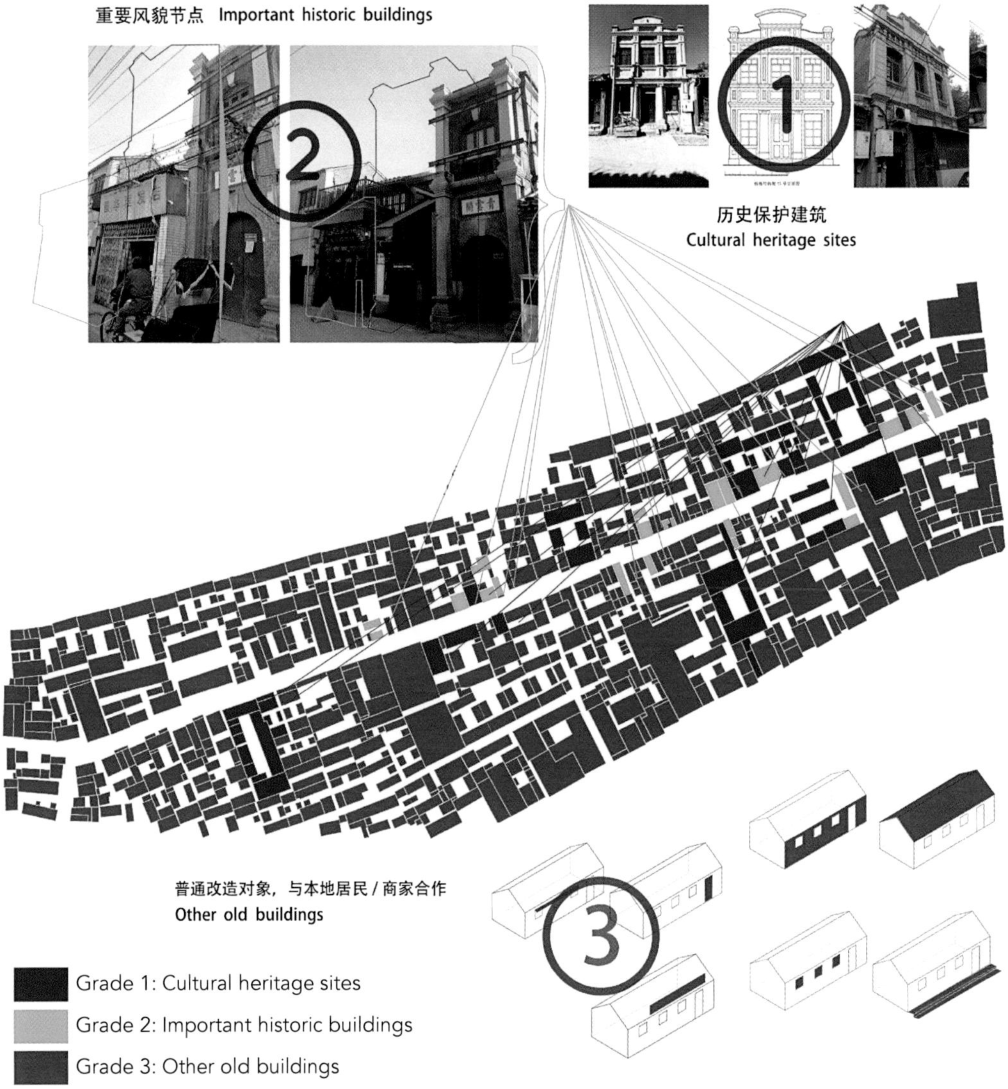

FIGURE 9.2 **Three-Grade Strategy for Cultural Heritage Conservation and Building Renovation on Yangmeizhu Lane, Dashilar Area, Beijing**

Source: ©Beijing Dashilar Investment Company (BDIC). Reproduced, with permission, from BDIC; further permission required for reuse.

establishing the Dashilar Regeneration Steering Committee, which coordinated different government agencies, as well as the state-owned Beijing Dashilar Investment Company (BDIC) as the implementation entity that led the regeneration process. With guidance from the government, the institutional arrangement incorporated active private sector participation along with flexibility for more stakeholders and innovative initiatives to come together and sustain the conservation strategy and long-term revitalization.

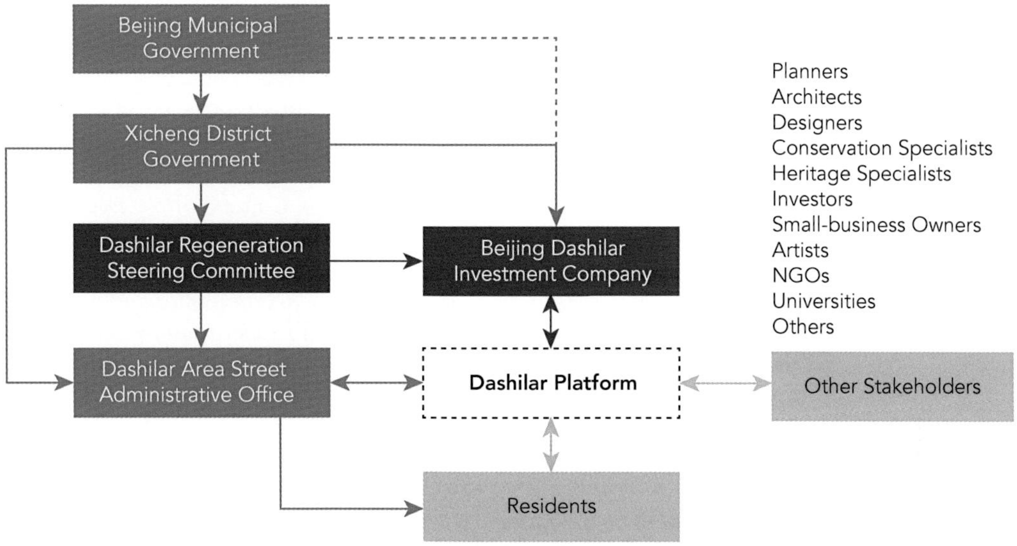

FIGURE 9.3 **Institutional Arrangement of the Dashilar Platform**

Source: ©World Bank. Further permission required for reuse.
Note: NGOs = nongovernmental organizations. The dotted line indicates the flexibility of the Dashilar Platform that interacts with other stakeholders. The blue colors indicate the Chinese government sector, while other colors represent different stakeholders.

During the planning phase, the BDIC initiated a multistakeholder Dashilar Platform to connect the BDIC with private sector players, multidisciplinary professionals, the residents and local business owners, and the local administrative office. The platform created a space for the authorities and state-owned enterprises (SOEs) to interact and build trust with stakeholders; it also mitigated tensions between the authorities, residents, and businesses and thus reduced issues that were common in other redevelopment projects. The innovative platform brought together diverse stakeholders such as entrepreneurs, residents, city planners, architects, designers, artists, nongovernmental organizations (NGOs), and academicians. The open platform strengthened the dynamic network and attracted multidimensional resources that contributed to the new regeneration model.[20]

Relocation

The Dashilar regeneration was one of the first urban regeneration projects in China that adopted voluntary relocation principles. Residents were offered options to either stay or relocate. Those who decided to relocate were offered monetary compensation or the choice of housing of larger sizes and with better infrastructure. Those who were compensated with new apartments were offered a choice between three different locations in Beijing—two at the south Fourth Ring Road and one at the north Fifth Ring Road, all equipped with services and convenient metro access. Additionally, Xicheng District worked with Daxing District (where the residents were relocated to) to establish a complete scheme to guarantee educational and health care services.

The remaining residents and businesses were offered different ways to collaborate with the regeneration program, such as either participating in housing renovation schemes and local business (separating the operational rights from housing ownership) or moving to a different, upgraded house in the same area to release clustered spaces. In such ways, they became active members in the regeneration process and business upgrading.

Under the voluntary relocation scheme of Stage 1, a total of 740 households (or 1,850 people) moved out, while 960 households (or 2,011 people) decided to stay. For the entire Dashilar area from 2011 to 2018, a total of 1,711 households (or 3,861 people) in 460 courtyards, together with 70 companies and organizations, were relocated voluntarily, releasing 75,920 square meters of space for new activities.[21]

Community Empowerment

Under Phase 2 of community participatory development in Dashilar, systematic community engagement and empowerment programs were organized to build community social capital in a self-sustainable manner. The Dashilar Community Development Initiative, founded by two professors of Tsinghua University and supported by the local administrative office, has led community empowerment in Dashilar for five years. The empowerment process and community initiatives complemented the improvement and use of public spaces in Dashilar to make the limited spaces better serve the communities.[22]

Based on socioeconomic surveys, the Tsinghua program designed a long-term process to identify, establish, develop, and scale up community-initiated organizations. Seed funds were provided to selected community organizations. Systematic training, hands-on advisory support, and experience sharing have been provided frequently. So far, nearly 40 formal training workshops have been provided to communities, based on different stages of community development over the period. The community empowerment program also uses social media and online platforms to provide training and share information (Liang 2017).

Phase 4: Management

The overall pilot investment was led by the municipal government, aiming for a balance of costs and benefits across the city and over the long term. As of 2018, a total of RMB 1.27 billion (US$191 million) has been invested in the Yangmeizhu pilot program, including nearly 90 percent on relocation compensation;[23] 5 percent (RMB 60 million, or US$9 million) on infrastructure, public-space, and architectural renovation; 2 percent on design, curation, and business development; and 3 percent on analytical work, management, and operations.[24] Because it was a demonstration project, most of the capital investment came from the government budget or the government's sectoral policy subsidies. The government invested in pilot projects in the early stages, with the expectation that future investments would be market-driven, through private sector funding and different collaborative models. These pilots continued to expand their influence beyond their boundaries.

To facilitate adaptive reuse, a public-private partnership was established to incentivize new businesses to conserve and renovate buildings. A total of RMB 30 million (US$4.5 million) was invested by the government through the BDIC to renovate selected assets. Most of the buildings were renovated by businesses themselves, with a cumulative private sector investment of approximately RMB 80 million (US$12.1 million).[25] This mechanism is continuing in a sustainable manner.

The operations and management of assets vary based on the ownership.[26] The municipal and environmental infrastructures are managed and maintained by the local administrative office, budgeted by different municipal utilities. For the public spaces and the BDIC-owned assets in Yangmeizhu Lane, an SOE is involved to pilot asset management in traditional neighborhoods. The steering committee is responsible for renovating publicly owned buildings and reviewing and approving renovation projects of privately owned assets without changing building structures. The municipal and district-level urban planning bureaus are responsible for reviewing and approving renovation proposals with structural changes to ensure compliance with the planning of the regeneration initiative.

Phase 5: Impact Evaluation

Social and Environmental Impacts

The regeneration has significantly enhanced quality of life and safety in Dashilar (photo 9.3). Access to basic services such as water, sanitation, and gas has significantly improved. About 90 percent of houses along Yangmeizhu Lane were conserved, repaired, or renovated. The environmental upgrading,

PHOTO 9.3 **Streetscape of Yangmeizhu Lane, Beijing, after Renovation**

Source: ©Beijing Dashilar Investment Company (BDIC). Further permission required for reuse.

demolition of illegal structures, asset management, and increasing popularity transformed Dashilar from an area with high safety risks to one of the "most beautiful lanes in Beijing" (Li 2018).

A recent survey showed that most residents of Yangmeizhu Lane felt positive about the improved environment, increased cultural and community activities, and friendliness of the entire area (Hou and Guo 2018; Li 2018). Furthermore, "big data" analysis of people's facial expressions in Yangmeizhu Lane showed that during BJDW or other cultural events, visitors were on average 18 percent happier than on usual days, and that the average level of happiness on Yangmeizhu Lane was double the happiness on an adjacent street.[27]

Rich results have been achieved through community empowerment. More than 20 community-initiated organizations have been established and empowered through the community development program (Liang 2017). The community organizations' missions vary and include improving community spaces through gardening; serving and supporting the local elderly; enhancing environmental awareness and promoting solid waste sorting; conserving intangible heritage; supporting start-ups; and promoting the culture and history of Dashilar. There are also a range of community interest groups on cooking, dancing, singing, reading, handicrafts, sports, photography, and others that organize events, performances, and exhibitions. For example, several eldercare organizations across the Dashilar area provide convenience services to elders, organize activities and excursions, and accompany single elders over the weekend. More than 20 residents organized a hutong tour guide team to introduce the cultural heritage, rich history, and ongoing changes in Dashilar to visitors (Liang 2017).

Economic Impacts

The local economy has significantly improved because of the regeneration efforts. Since the initiative launched, the variety of businesses in Yangmeizhu Lane has increased from a preponderance of small grocery and local service shops to a combination of shops that serve daily needs and new-type enterprises spanning a range of business categories. The regeneration nearly doubled the number of businesses in the area. New jobs were thus created for both local residents and newcomers. Total sales revenues from Yangmeizhu Lane were less than RMB 1 million (US$151,000) before regeneration; by 2018, they had increased to RMB 85 million (US$12.9 million).[28] The average asset value has more than doubled. The rent of shops tripled from RMB 2–2.5 per square meter per day before regeneration to RMB 6–7 per square meter per day in 2018.[29]

The popularity of Dashilar has significantly grown since the launch of the regeneration and branding of the area. Today, the Dashilar area attracts many more people than the redeveloped Xianyukou area east to Qianmen Avenue. In terms of visitors, Dashilar has become one of the most popular destinations in Beijing during BJDW based on big-data analysis.[30] Visitors to Yangmeizhu Lane stay for an average of 45 minutes, nearly six times longer than normal walking speed without stopping. Among visitors to Dashilar in 2016, 60 percent were from Beijing, and most visitors expressed interests in culture, design, cities, lifestyles, art, and so forth.[31] The regeneration transformed the area's public image from a decaying area to an emerging, creative, culturally unique neighborhood. A branding strategy has been adopted since the beginning to improve the value of the area, and the cultural brand of the area is widely recognized today.

With public-private investments and the resulting success in the regeneration of the area, the effects of some levels of gentrification is taking place in Dashilar. The demography in Dashilar went through several rounds of major socioeconomic changes in the past decades, which resulted in a concentration of older persons, people with disabilities, and low-income population in the area. Without regeneration interventions and insertion of new resources, the urban environment and local economy would have continued to deteriorate. There was also a need to ensure that this regeneration process was gradual and inclusive. The regeneration program, especially the "Re-Up Dashilar–Livable Yangmeizhu" initiative launched in 2017, directly targeted this issue through pension programs, eldercare facilities, community activities, a community development seed-fund program, and others. Community participation has been part of the regeneration process to incorporate local needs and bridge the local residents and newcomers.[32]

As Dashilar was regenerated hand-in-hand with BJDW, its brand value and influence continued to grow, attracting new interests and businesses into the area. Increasing numbers of enterprises, organizations, and individuals participated in conservation and adaptive reuse of cultural resources, community engagement, and economic revitalization. Since 2012, through pop-up shops, workshops, exhibitions, and events, short-term participants have become long-term business owners. So far, more than 80 new businesses have entered Dashilar, including publishing companies, bookstores, art galleries, design studios, boutique shops, craft workshops, cafés, themed restaurants, and others. They settled into the hutong life and slowly integrated with the local community. These businesses also revitalized and benefited more than 100 existing local businesses. New and old businesses coexist and have gradually strengthened the cultural identity of Dashilar and continued to attract more people.[33]

Demonstration Impacts

The Dashilar regeneration model demonstrated a multistakeholder, incremental, organic, and participatory approach in the regeneration of historic neighborhoods in China. The model innovatively addressed complex, multifaceted problems in historic neighborhoods in cities across China. Successful approaches incorporated by the model include the institutional arrangements; the phased approach; tailored infrastructure upgrading; detailed public-space design; market analyses and business entrance criteria; curation of BJDW in urban spaces; Dashilar pilot programs; voluntary relocation; private sector incentives; graded conservation and renovation; and community engagement.

Lessons learned from the Dashilar regeneration model have influenced similar projects in Beijing and across China. The model contributed to the latest program to upgrade public space in Beijing. Between 2015 and 2017, historic neighborhoods such as the Baita Temple, Shichahai, Tianqiao, Shijia Lane, and Shimo Chang joined Beijing BJDW one after another, learning lessons from the Dashilar model to regenerate decaying areas and build place-based brands. Other cities such as Shenzhen, Huangshan, Qingdao, and Tianjin have also begun to learn from Dashilar's experience and are planning to pilot similar approaches to urban regeneration.

The impacts also include the strengthening of partnerships with communities and the private sector. Between 2011 and 2018, the Dashilar Platform has interacted with approximately 10,000 officials of government departments, urban planners, architects, designers, artists, academicians, NGOs, historians, business owners, media, and investment companies across more than 10 countries.

DASHILAR POCKET SPACES

Phase 1: Context

Throughout China's history, most traditional neighborhoods such as Dashilar in Beijing never had designated, formal, or large public spaces other than the hutongs. Over the past 600 years, spaces such as guildhalls, temples, and small markets were scattered through the area, playing an important role in clustering social interactions, services, and community building (Lin 2013). Meanwhile, street corners were important daily gathering places for local residents. This tradition of limited public spaces and their poor condition means that, today, old neighborhoods can no longer meet modern standards and the changing demands of local residents, thus requiring improvements. The previous section focused on the regeneration of Yangmeizhu Lane; this section discusses improvements of other types of pocket spaces collectively.

Historically, temples and guildhalls were important, ubiquitous public spaces. In the Dashilar area during the Ming and Qing Dynasties, there were approximately 23 temples and 36 guildhalls in every square kilometer, meaning a temple in every 200 meters.[34] Temples used to play a critical role in community life in China. Beyond religious functions, they also served as open spaces and spaces for public assembly, which were otherwise highly restricted in the imperial capital. Temples, one of the few types of places open to everyone, served as multipurpose centers of public life in cities, where performances, markets, charity events, public speeches, complaints, religious celebrations, publishing events, and entertainment activities took place (Naquin 2000). Guildhalls, on the other hand, offered public services and high-quality gathering spaces, serving as either guesthouses or restaurants for people of similar origin or as gathering places for people with similar businesses. Most temples and guildhalls have disappeared in the past 100 years. The remaining ones have been conserved, but most are no longer freely open to the public.

Today, spontaneous, everyday spaces around the traditional lanes have emerged in old neighborhoods. People's daily needs have shaped public spaces in Beijing's old neighborhoods. These needs and mundane scenes have thrived in the corners around the lanes in the Old City and have formed the most common public spaces: the front window of a small local shop, an active street corner, the entrance to a restaurant, the shade under a tree, or the waiting area at the bus station. These spaces build important connections among local residents, fill the gap of scarce formal public spaces, and create the most authentic daily life in the Old City.

The siheyuans have become a special type of public space in traditional neighborhoods. The enclosed courtyards were formerly private spaces, open only to the owners' families, their guests, and servants. Because of historical changes since the 1950s, the ownership of most courtyards turned public, and the homes were divided and sublet to multiple families. Thus, these open courtyard spaces surrounded by houses became, in their own right, important public spaces that were shared by different families and neighbors. Today, however, most of these courtyards have been filled up with various informal, incremental structures to serve each family's needs, leaving only a narrow space for passing through and limiting quality spaces for gathering (Liu 2011).

Other unique public spaces that are an integral part of traditional neighborhoods include places where neighbors could meet, such as markets and public toilets. In traditional neighborhoods of Beijing, each neighborhood used to have its own open market with daily supplies of seasonal vegetables and fruits. Every family went to these markets for groceries, and thus they became places for social interaction. Furthermore, the old, narrow lanes of Beijing's Old City meant that installation of modern sanitation infrastructure inside individual homes was difficult, and therefore most residents in the traditional neighborhoods relied on public toilets—even until today. Most of these public toilets in the traditional lanes had no partitions because of the limited space, uniquely making them natural chatting rooms among neighbors.

Phases 2 and 3: Planning, Design and Implementation

The improvement of small public spaces in the Dashilar area went through two phases: The first phase, during 2012–16, was part of the Dashilar Pilot Program (discussed in the earlier section), with a focus on a series of "microupgrading" projects in the area to improve the urban landscape and public spaces. The second phase, from 2016 to the present, followed the launch of the new Beijing Master Plan (2016–35) as part of the municipal government's citywide support in improving urban public spaces and pilot projects in the Old City center (Beijing DRC 2017).

During the first phase (2012–16), a "nodal approach" was adopted to catalyze organic regeneration through targeted interventions—a series of small-scale public-space renovations—at selected urban nodes in the Dashilar area (map 9.3). This addressed local communities' pressing needs and responded to the municipal and district governments' plan to improve the urban environment in Dashilar. The program also found that key nodes identified by the residents and local businesses as well as through spatial, social interaction, and traffic-flow analyses coincided with the locations of important temples that existed today or in history. The findings showed that the historical spatial structure has generally remained intact and that this history could inform public-space analyses and design in the next steps.[35]

Critical to improving the local quality of life, public-space interventions in traditional neighborhoods were the most important topic in the Dashilar Pilot Program and under the latest citywide public-space improvement programs.

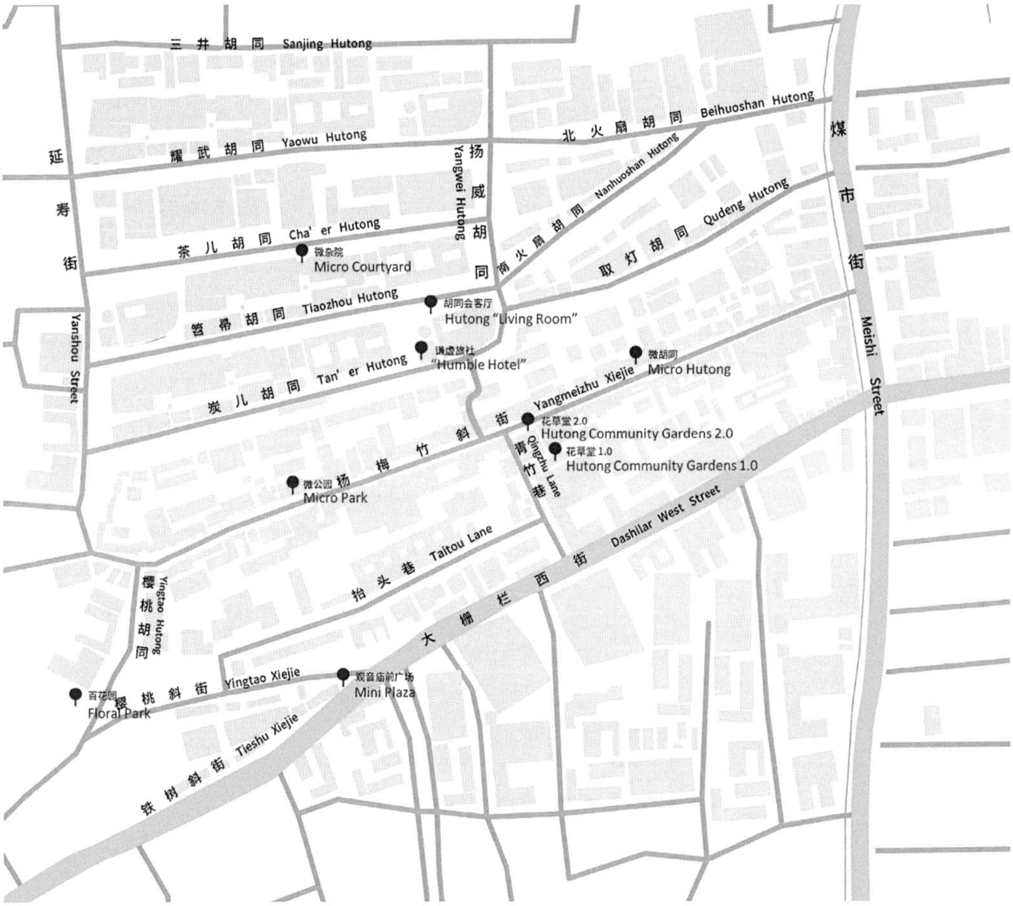

MAP 9.3 **Map of Key Renovated Pocket Spaces near Yangmeizhu Lane**

Source: ©Beijing Dashilar Investment Company (BDIC). World Bank translation. Reproduced, with permission, from BDIC; further permission required for reuse.

Numerous innovative interventions emerged as pilot projects were designed and implemented in the neighborhoods through an interactive, dynamic process. These interventions included improvements to street corners, shared spaces in the courtyards, miniparks, markets, green spaces, and façades. Between 2013 and 2017, 106 proposals related to public spaces were selected, and nearly one-third of them (about 30) were implemented in Dashilar. This section describes four representative pilot projects.[36]

Microcourtyard

The award-winning microcourtyard project piloted adaptive reuse and transformation of traditional courtyard spaces for surrounding residents, especially children and the older persons. The project exemplified the success of revitalizing deteriorated courtyard spaces and enabling the coexistence of old and new. This project was developed from one of the proposals under the Dashilar Pilot Program, focused on enhancing and revitalizing public spaces and community lives in courtyard spaces. The project courtyard is in Cha'er Lane next to a primary school. Before the intervention, the courtyard was dilapidated and overcrowded—a typical da-za-yuan (big-messy-courtyard)—encroaching on the limited open space.

ZAO/standardarchitecture tackled the complex challenges through innovative, culturally respectful, and socially inclusive design. The project won the Aga Khan Award for Architecture in 2016. The design preserved an old tree, respected the memory of incremental and unregistered structures in the courtyard as a layer of history, and innovatively created a multifunctional community art center space and an open terrace based on the footprint of these structures (photo 9.4). The project also renovated and repurposed a traditional house into a children's library and multifunctional art room. The design sought harmony with the surrounding buildings and traditional environment, using gray bricks, wood, and concrete for the buildings and yard pavement (AKDN 2019).

Hutong Community Gardens

The Hutong Community Gardens project piloted the use of gardening to improve overcrowded spaces and strengthen social ties between neighbors. The first garden transformed a narrow, deteriorated passageway into a pleasant green space (photo 9.5). The 66-meter zigzagged passageway—only 1–4 meters wide, formed over the years through incremental expansion of buildings—is shared by five surrounding households (20 residents) (Xie, Zhang, and Wang 2017). Through community engagement, the designer, together with input from historians, landscape architects, anthropologists, and artists, initiated cocreating a community garden along the passageway based on the residents' shared interests in gardening.

The green of passageways was subsequently scaled up to the broader Dashilar area. The scaling-up pioneered a community participatory approach

a. Before project **b. After project**

PHOTO 9.4 **Adaptive Reuse of Microcourtyard in Dashilar Area of Beijing**

Source: ©ZAO/standardarchitecture. Reproduced, with permission, from ZAO/standardarchitecture; further permission required for reuse.

PHOTO 9.5 **Design of a Hutong Community Garden along a Narrow Passageway on Yangmeizhu Lane, Dashilar Area, Beijing**

Source: ©View Unlimited Landscape Architecture Studio (View Unlimited). Reproduced, with permission, from View Unlimited; further permission required for reuse.

to city-level policy for creating urban green spaces. The government-led urban green space program, which started in 2017, focused on providing standard public gardens within a short period. Based on the deep-rooted gardening tradition among hutong residents, the pilot project established guidelines with residents to regulate their spontaneous gardening, offered training and advice on gardening, organized "sowing ceremonies," and presented a "Best Gardener Award" (Xie 2018). This initiative received positive feedback from the government and complemented the government-led policies while preserving the authenticity and spontaneity of community-driven gardening in hutongs (photo 9.6).

Hutong Micropark

The hutong micropark project piloted the insertion of multipurpose green spaces in narrow lanes. The pilot micropark is located in the west segment of Yangmeizhu Lane. In 2014, the project leveraged some existing plants, negotiated the use of temporary parking spaces, and transformed the small space to a park of 50 square meters. Although the available usable space was very small, the micropark was able to accomodate tables, chairs, flowers, shades, green pavement, a snack kiosk, and decorations (photo 9.7).

The park transformed a generic part of the lane into a popular place for residents and visitors to rest and have some snacks. The design also created a business opportunity for the kiosk owner. Following the success of the first micropark, another one was designed and built in front of a renovated house, serving as a "living room" for residents and visitors.

PHOTO 9.6 **Hutong Community Garden on Yangmeizhu Lane, Dashilar Area, Beijing**

Source: ©View Unlimited Landscape Architecture Studio (View Unlimited). Reproduced, with permission, from View Unlimited; further permission required for reuse.

a. During a weekend **b. On a weekday**

PHOTO 9.7 **Hutong Micropark, Beijing**

Source: ©Beijing Dashilar Investment Company (BDIC). Reproduced, with permission, from BDIC; further permission required for reuse.

Floral Park and Small Markets

The Floral Park was a key public-space project led by the district government under the latest Beijing Master Plan. The creation of this park was part of the top-down, citywide initiative to increase public spaces that started in 2017. Dashilar is a large neighborhood but had limited public spaces and no sizable parks. Under the government's latest goal of creating accessible parks within a 500-meter radius of walking distance of every resident in Beijing, the project demolished the Tiantao Market in the center of the Dashilar area and built the Floral Park of 1,850 square meters on the site, creating a precious green open space in the heart of the dense old neighborhood (Beijing DRC 2017).

Although small, the park was carefully designed, incorporating an accessible walking path; a shaded corridor; an exercise field; a pavilion; and a variety of trees, bushes, flowers, and grass (photo 9.8). Meanwhile, considering the needs of residents after demolition of the market, a series of small vegetable and fruit markets were built in the area. Though these simple markets cannot replace the former large Tiantao Market, this project is an example of balancing the trade-offs between the need for public spaces and the need for community amenities, such as grocery markets in overcrowded old city neighborhoods.

Phase 4: Management

Different stakeholders are involved during the operations and maintenance phase, including the district government, business owners, the asset management company, community organizations, and community members. For example, the district government and its Landscape and Greening Bureau is

a. Walking path b. Mini plaza

PHOTO 9.8 **Floral Park in the Dashilar Area, Beijing**

Source: ©CitylinX. Reproduced, with permission, from CitylinX; further permission required for reuse.

responsible for the operations and maintenance of the Floral Park, and the City Management Bureau manages the small markets. Business owners manage their affiliated public spaces, such as the microparks, to attract more customers while allowing residents and visitors to use such spaces without consuming their products, hence guaranteeing that the pocket spaces benefit the general public. A local resident, together with community organizations that use the spaces, manages the renovated microcourtyard. Community members maintain their own pocket gardens and collectively manage community gardens in the shared spaces.

Phase 5: Impact Evaluation

The small-scale public-space projects created a series of accessible, convenient, beautiful, multifunctional, and human-centered pocket spaces in the narrow, dense hutong area (photo 9.9). These projects addressed the complex challenge of the lack of public spaces in traditional neighborhoods and provided scarce public spaces with environmental benefits and social interactions for surrounding residents who live in overcrowded conditions. Through community participation, residents were engaged and empowered in the place-making process.

The pilot projects offered valuable lessons that pioneered an incremental, participatory approach based on tactical improvements in traditional urban neighborhoods, which was very new in the context of China and useful in the current high-level agenda of upgrading public spaces. These lessons inlcude:

- *The projects respected and adapted to the existing urban spatial features.* The creation of public spaces and the preservation of the authentic sense of place and culture were based on the use of existing spatial patterns and

PHOTO 9.9 **Multifunctional Community Art Center in the Dashilar Area, Beijing**

Source: ©CitylinX. Reproduced, with permission, from CitylinX; further permission required for reuse.

PHOTO 9.10 **Renovated Microcourtyard in the Dashilar Area, Beijing**

Source: ©ZAO/standardarchitecture. Reproduced, with permission, from ZAO/standardarchitecture; further permission required for reuse.

constraints in the hutong area. These tactical improvements incorporated global and domestic best practices but did not replicate any existing models in China (photo 9.10).

- *The projects enabled participation and benefited local communities.* The program adopted a codesigning, cobuilding approach with local communities. This approach allowed the projects to better address community needs and also built ownership and pride among residents to later use and take care of the spaces. The process also brought different neighbors together in designing and using the spaces, thus strengthening social networks. These are foundations for longer-term, sustainable urban regeneration.
- *The projects piloted spatial solutions to address complicated ownership issues in traditional neighborhoods.* With a mixture of state-owned, shared, and

privately owned assets that were further complicated with subdivisions, the pilot projects created a middle ground and a mitigating space through short-term and mid-term spatial solutions when coping with complicated property rights issues.

- *The projects combined bottom-up and top-down approaches in public-space improvements.* Besides the top-down approach, which is the predominant practice in China, the series of innovative bottom-up pilot projects were guided by the city master plan and were implemented alongside Beijing's latest public-space programs. The two approaches complemented each other to deliver better results and offered valuable lessons to improve the extensive ongoing top-down projects.
- *The projects engaged and incentivized business owners in placemaking.* The pilot projects purposely engaged business owners in the codesign and co-operating process to create multifunctional spaces that can increase economic opportunities for surrounding businesses. The improved cultural identity and spaces in the area also built a foundation for economic revitalization.

NOTES

1. Population and GRDP data from Beijing Municipal Bureau of Statistics, *Beijing Statistical Yearbook* (Beijing: China Statistics Press, 1978–2018).
2. Land area and use data from *Beijing Statistical Yearbooks 1978–2018.*
3. Ancient Chinese city planning was based on the Kao Gong Ji, or the Book of Artificers, a Confucius classic written around the end of the Spring and Autumn period (approximately 771–476 BC), which stated, "When the builder constructs the capital, the city should be a four-sided square shape, nine *li* [an ancient measurement unit] on each side with three gates each. In the city there are nine longitudinal and nine latitudinal streets, each of nine carriages wide. . . ."
4. The Beijing area served as the location of capital cities of the Yan, Liao, Jin, Yuan, Ming, and Qing dynasties.
5. "National Significant Cultural Heritage Protection Sites in Beijing," NCHA (National Cultural Heritage Administration) website: http://gl.sach.gov.cn/sachhome/service/national-key-units.html.
6. The *New Urban Agenda* was adopted at the United Nations Conference on Housing and Sustainable Urban Development (Habitat III) in Quito, Ecuador, on October 20, 2016. For more information, see "The New Urban Agenda," Habitat III (website): http://habitat3.org/the-new-urban-agenda/.
7. These are subsequent policies following the new-type urbanization plan and the 13th Five Year Plan, that are aligned with the same high-level principles and provided more sectoral details and specifics, but not directly part of the National New-Type Urbanization Plan or the 13th Five Year Plan.
8. Modern Beijing has launched seven master plans since 1949—in 1954, 1958, 1973, 1983, 1993, 2005, and 2017. Since the 1980s, the plans have increasingly emphasized development of the tertiary sector, efficiency of transport, service delivery, environmental quality, and historic conservation in Beijing.
9. The Qing Dynasty was the last imperial dynasty of China.
10. Public spaces affiliated with construction projects are common in Beijing. The review process by the planning commission focuses on compliance with plans and the architectural design. Landscape design is often considered secondary and is submitted to the Beijing Landscape and Greening Bureau for documentation.

11. The control plans in China are the most detailed in city planning systems, which regulate the land use, floor-area ratio, building heights, green-space ratio, scale, and requirements of infrastructure and services as well as land boundaries for infrastructure, green spaces, historic protection areas, and water bodies.
12. Discussion of 21st-century development is based on the authors' project experience in the Dashilar area and on an interview with Xing Zhao, senior urban planner at the Beijing Municipal Institute of City Planning & Design.
13. Heritage buildings in Dashilar include 2 national-level, 10 municipal-level, and 8 district-level cultural heritage sites; 185 historic buildings; 64 protected courtyards; and 158 significant remains ("Dashilar Regeneration Plan" [in Chinese], Beijing Dashilar Investment Company [website], accessed March 12, 2019: http://www.dashilar.org.cn/).
14. The Dashilar Regeneration Plan was directed by the Conservation Plan of 25 Historic Areas in Beijing Old City (2002) and the Beijing Central City Detailed Control Plan (2008). This plan also referred to the Conservation, Upgrading, and Revitalization Plan for Qianmen and Dashilar Area in Beijing (2005), which was approved by the Municipal Planning Commission in 2005 but was not implemented.
15. "Subvenue: Dashilar Historic and Cultural District," Beijing BJDW (website), accessed April 14, 2019: http://www.bjdw.org/bjdws/FHC/FHC201802.html.
16. "Dashilar Pilot Program" [in Chinese], Beijing Dashilar Investment Company (BDIC) (website), accessed March 12, 2019: http://dashilar.beijing99.cn/A/A2_B2.html.
17. Because Yangmeizhu was the main lane among the pilot lanes, the pilot project was referred to as the Yangmeizhu Lane Pilot.
18. "Dashilar Pilot Program," BDIC website.
19. Grade classifications of buildings on Yangmeizhu Lane are from Beijing Dashilar Investment Company (BDIC) records.
20. "Dashilar Regeneration Program" [in Chinese], Beijing Dashilar Investment Company (BDIC) (website), accessed March 12, 2019: http://www.dashilar.org.cn/.
21. Beijing Dashilar Investment Company (website), accessed March 12, 2019: http://www.dashilar.org.cn/.
22. Tsinghua University Community Revitalization Research Center (CRRC), Dashilar Community Development Initiative (website): http://thucrrc.org/zlfx/zjzl/dsl/.
23. Housing upgrading and relocation are under another government-led scheme.
24. "Dashilar Regeneration Program," BDIC website.
25. "Dashilar Regeneration Program," BDIC website.
26. All the urban land in China is owned by the state. Buildings can be privately owned, with lease of land ranging from 40 years to 70 years.
27. UrbanXYZ (Urban XYZ Science and Technology Co. Ltd.). 2019. "Platform for Human-Centric Observations in Dashilar" [In Chinese] (website), accessed May 17, 2019: http://www.urbanxyz.com/.
28. Sales revenue data from "Dashilar Regeneration Program," BDIC website. Tax revenue data cannot be disaggregated for the lane.
29. Based on BDIC records of the Dashilar regeneration program.
30. The BDIC collaborated with UrbanXYZ Science and Technology Co. to observe and quantify the regeneration results in recent years. Equipment such as Wi-Fi, cameras, infrared sensors, and a magnetic induction coil were used to collect data related to the area. The data were dynamically visualized through technologies such as DataV and Talking Data to present aggregated profiles of visitors such as by gender, age, origins, shopping interests, and so forth.
31. "Platform for Human-Centric Observations in Dashilar," UrbanXYZ website.
32. "Dashilar Regeneration Program," BDIC website.
33. "Dashilar Regeneration Program," BDIC website.
34. "Dashilar Regeneration Program," BDIC website.
35. "Dashilar Regeneration Program," BDIC website.
36. "Dashilar Pilot Program" [in Chinese], Beijing Dashilar Investment Company (BDIC) (website), accessed March 12, 2019: http://dashilar.beijing99.cn/A/A2_B2.html.

REFERENCES

AKDN (Aga Khan Development Network). 2019. "Hutong Children's Library & Art Centre." 2014–2016 Award Recipients (web page), Aga Khan Award for Architecture, AKDN, Geneva (accessed March 28, 2019), https://www.akdn.org/architecture/project/hutong-childrens-library-art-centre.

Beijing DRC (Beijing Development and Reform Commission). 2017. "Strengthening the Renovation of Urban Public Space." Press release, December 22 (accessed March 3, 2019), http://www.beijing.gov.cn/zhengce/jiedu/34/1856673/1427720/index.html.

Bian, Lanchun. 2016. "Unity and Diversity: Public Space Evolution of Beijing Urban Regeneration." *World Architecture* 4: 14–17.

BLGB (Beijing Landscape and Greening Bureau). 2019. "Beijing Municipality Plans to Build 31 Urban Parks This Year." Press release, January 24 (accessed February 3, 2019), http://www.bjyl.gov.cn/ztxx/mtjj/mtbd/201901/t20190124_214078.shtml.

Chen, Jun. 2004. "Beijing Urban Public Spaces: Deconstruction and Reconstruction." *Beijing Planning Review* 4: 27–29.

CPC Central Committee (Central Committee of the Communist Party of China) and State Council. 2016. "Guidelines on Enhancing Urban Planning, Development, and Management." Guidelines document, *Xinhua News*, February 6. http://www.xinhuanet.com//politics/2016-02/21/c_1118109546.htm.

Gaubatz, Piper. 2008. "New Public Space in Urban China: Fewer Walls, More Malls in Beijing, Shanghai, and Xining." *China Perspectives* 4 (76): 72–83.

Hou, Xiaolei, and Wei Guo. 2018. "Community Micro-Regeneration: Approaches to the Design Intervention of Old City Public Space of Beijing." *Landscape Architecture* 4: 41–47.

Li, Huanyu. 2018. "Ten Most Beautiful Streets and Lanes Were Selected in Beijing." *Beijing Evening News*, via *Xinhuanet Beijing Channel*, November 28 (accessed April 14, 2019), http://www.bj.xinhuanet.com/bjyw/2018-11/28/c_1123779421.htm.

Lian, Yan, Jiani Li, and Li Yin. 2016. "Planning and Management of Beijing Urban Public Space." *Beijing Planning Review* 1: 130–33.

Liang, Xiaoyue. 2017. "Collectively Build a Warm Community Home: Sharing the Case of Dashilar." Presentation at the Second National Forum on Community Development and Community Building, Shanghai, June 5.

Lin, Zheng. 2013. "From Forbidden Gardens to Public Parks: Creation of Public Spaces in Beijing in the Early Republic of China." *Cultural Studies* 15 (3): 119–32.

Liu, Lizao. 2011. "Study of the Evolution of Ownership of Courtyards in the Old City of Beijing." *Beijing Planning Review* 4: 21–24.

MoHURD (Ministry of Housing and Urban-Rural Development). 2017. "Guidelines on Ecological Rehabilitation and Urban Regeneration in Cities (2017)." *Jian Gui* (March) 59.

Naquin, Susan. 2000. *Peking: Temples and City Life, 1400–1900.* Berkeley: University of California Press.

PGBM (People's Government of Beijing Municipality). 2017. "Beijing Municipal Master Plan (2016–2035)." Planning document, September 29 (accessed April 14, 2019), http://www.beijing.gov.cn/gongkai/guihua/2841/6640/1700220/1532470/index.html.

View Unlimited Landscape Architecture Studio, Hara Design Institute, Weixin Huang, Approach Architecture Studio, and 8GG Design. 2012. "Design for Environmental Rehabilitation and Façade Renovation of Yangmeizhu Lane at the Dashilar Area Beijing." Unpublished design report, View Unlimited Landscape Architecture Studio, Beijing.

Wang, Jingwen, Qizhi Mao, and Anrong Dang. 2007. "Syntax Paraphrase for Social Dimension of Residential Public Space: The Case Study of Social Communication Pattern in Beijing Traditional Hutong Space." Huazhong Architecture 25 (11): 166–69.

Xie, Xiaoying. 2018. "Yangmeizhu Xiejie Environmental Renovation Plan and Mixed-Courtyard Public Space Design, Beijing." *Landscape Architecture* 4: 66–69.

Xie, Xiaoying, Yuan Zhang, and Xin Wang. 2017. "Integrating Resources: Design for Livability." *Urban and Rural Development* 22: 48–51.

Xinhua News. 2014. "National New-Type Urbanization Plan 2014-2020." [In Chinese.] *Xinhua News,* March 16 (accessed April 15, 2019), http://www.gov.cn/zhengce/2014-03/16/content_2640075.htm.

Zhang, Jinqi. 2008. *One Hundred Years of Dashilar Chongqing*. Chongqing: Chongqing Press.

CHAPTER 10

COLOMBO, SRI LANKA: ENHANCING URBAN RESILIENCE AND LIVABILITY BY LEVERAGING NATURAL AND ECOLOGICAL ASSETS

Nishanthi Marian Priyanka Perera and Charmini Kodituwakku

KEY TAKEAWAYS

- The Colombo Metropolitan Region is undergoing rapid urbanization and economic transformation. Meanwhile, the lack of systematic urban planning leaves the city vulnerable to flooding: eco-sensitive areas and valuable wetlands in the city (worth annually up to SL Rs 12 billion (US$66 million) to the Colombo Metropolitan Region, including flood protection) have significantly decreased, and a substantial proportion of urbanization is occurring on low-lying land. The Beddagana Wetland Park and Crow Island Beach Park demonstrate the efforts to regain small pockets of biodiversity and waterfronts in the heart of the city for the enjoyment of communities, even while urban expansion continues at a rapid pace.
- The Beddagana Wetland Park was an undervalued ecological asset of the local government that has been transformed into a high-quality space for citizens' recreational and educational activities. In the park, various awareness programs have reached out to about 2,000 students and 160,000 visitors between 2015 and 2018. The park has contributed to reducing the impact of flooding by absorbing runoff and preserving more than 200 species within an urban setting.

- The Crow Island Beach Park is a rehabilitated waterfront focused on providing a more accessible, inclusive, and safe area for residents and visitors. It has contributed to the improved use of a previously underutilized beach, now visited by about 400 people each weekday and about 2,000 people each day over weekends.

CITY DYNAMICS

Context and Background

The Colombo Metropolitan Region (CMR) is the center of the administrative functions and economic activities in Sri Lanka.[1] According to the country's 2012 census, the population of the CMR was nearly 5.9 million, and it accounted for 28.7 percent of the total population (DCSSL 2012). Further, the country's total 2012 urban population was 18.2 percent,[2] of which about 61.3 percent was concentrated in the CMR. Colombo District also had the highest population density: 3,438 persons per square kilometer.

The CMR covers 3,694 square kilometers, or nearly 6 percent of Sri Lanka's entire land area, making it a densely populated area. According to the Western Region Megapolis Plan, the population within the CMR is expected to increase to around 8.78 million by 2030 (DCSSL 2012; MMWD 2016).

The CMR's high productivity (45 percent of gross domestic product [GDP]) makes it one of Sri Lanka's most valuable growth engines (World Bank 2012). Further, the CMR is the international gateway to Sri Lanka and houses most of the country's manufacturing facilities and services. It accounts for 80 percent of all industrial establishments, 53 percent of industrial employment, and 31 percent of total employment in the country (MoF 2018; Weerakoon 2013).

Since the end of the civil war in 2009, new prospects for economic growth have been dramatically restructuring Colombo's urban landscape. Successive governments are working to brand Colombo as "a world-class city" (Van Dort 2016). In 2017, the Economist Intelligence Unit's (EIU) annual Global Liveability Report selected the city of Colombo as one of the five most improved cities during the past five years in terms of quality of life, crediting it with relative improvement especially after the end of the civil war with an increase of 2.5 percent in its EIU livability score (EIU 2017).

However, the transformations have triggered complex urban challenges, including housing disparities across the city. Based on the 2011 survey of Colombo carried out by the country's Urban Development Authority (UDA), an estimated 68,812 households were living in 1,499 underserved settlements, accounting for more than half the city's population (UDA 2011). These underserved settlements generally lack services and infrastructure for individual households. The substandard living conditions in these settlements have become a pressing concern in Colombo, and the government has initiated relocation programs for people who live there (MHC 2016; Rathnayake 2014).

The lack of systematic urban planning and infrastructure development enforcement has left Colombo vulnerable to flooding. Floods are mainly caused by changing land use, clogged drains and canal systems, and increasing runoff due to construction activities. About 20 percent of CMR land is a floodplain, which makes stormwater management a crucial issue. In particular, several main cities within the CMR, including Colombo and the capital, Sri Jayawardenapura Kotte, are built on and around wetlands. Colombo is a flat city with the highest points at just 18 meters above sea level. Historically, the Dutch had accounted for this low-lying, water-based topography by building canals in Colombo; British planners, however, preferred a grid layout and removed the main part of the canal system (Konau 2016). From 2008 onward, floods have regularly been recorded in Colombo and nearby districts. Severe floods in 2010 and 2016 inundated most parts of the CMR, with significant damage to housing and infrastructure. The 2016 flooding severely affected both the Colombo and Gampaha Districts (MNPEA and MDM 2016). Colombo (Colombo District) and Katana (Gampaha District) emerge as the two most vulnerable to sea-level rise (MoE 2010).

Public Spaces in Colombo

The urban form of Colombo has changed dramatically over the centuries. Colombo has had a prominent affiliation with green spaces before economic growth and urbanization of the CMR started to deplete these green spaces. Historically, the area where the city of Colombo is now located comprised different types of natural landscapes, including forests, wetlands, rivers, arable lands, pastures, and paddy fields (Konau 2016). Since Colombo became the capital of Sri Lanka under British rule, public spaces in the city have been mainly shaped by the British. In the first prominent plan for the development of the city in 1921, the main concept was to make the city of Colombo "the garden city of the East." One of the most important creations in city planning during that period was a vast extension of invaluable urban green spaces, such as Victoria Park (currently known as Viaharamahadevi Park), Galle Face Green, Hyde Park, and Campbell Park Grounds. However, some of the newly created green spaces—including racecourses, golf links, and cricket grounds—were and still are limited to private groups only (Dayaratne 2010; Konau 2016).

Starting in the late 1970s, the government began to focus on improving policies related to public spaces to meet increased demands associated with rapid urbanization, rising income levels, changing lifestyles, and concerns about healthy living.[3] However, Colombo has lost significant amounts of green space. Natural greenery is abundant in the city landscape, but these are relics of earlier eras rather than being planned or maintained. The beautiful tree-lined streets around Thummula, for example, are a reminder of the grand plan for the garden city but are fast disappearing because of lateral expansions from unplanned developments (Dayaratne 2010), lack of protection enforcement, and lack of a tree planting program.

The city lost 1.37 square kilometers of green space annually between 2001 and 2011, more than triple the rate of 0.46 square kilometers between 1980 and 1988 (figure 10.1). Green space decreased by a total of 6 percent from 2008 to 2015 (Li and Pussella 2017). These natural areas have been mostly converted into urban settlements, administration buildings, and industrial parks. As such, there is an urgent need for a comprehensive green space plan for the city and its suburbs to convert Colombo into a green city with comfortable living standards (Li and Pussella 2017).

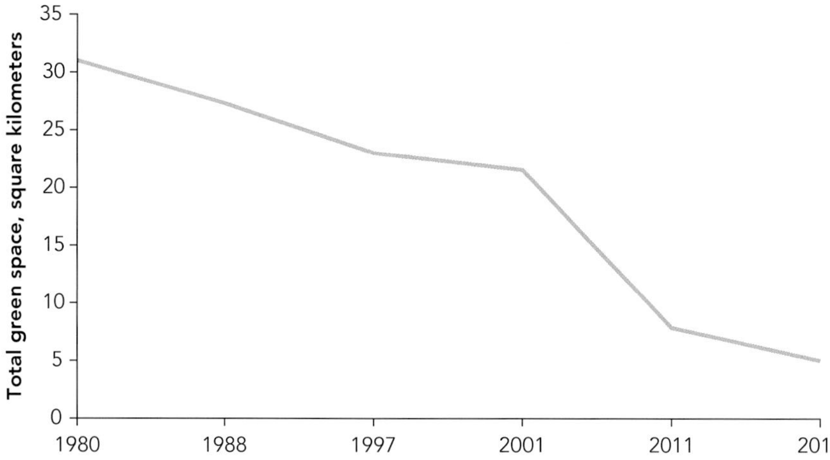

FIGURE 10.1 **Reduction of Green Space in Colombo, Sri Lanka, 1980–2015**

Source: Li and Pussella 2017.
Note: "Green space" is identified from Landsat Thematic Mapper (TM) and Enhanced Thematic Mapper (ETM+) satellite images. The changes in green space were analyzed using the Normalized Difference Vegetation Index (NDVI) values for different years.

More importantly, ecologically sensitive areas and wetlands have been threatened by the conversion of land into other urban uses. These ecological areas, located in the immediate surroundings of the urban core, have decreased by 80 percent since 1986. Similarly, wetlands in the peripheral areas have decreased, and the decrease exhibited a high correlation with urban density such as building density and population density (Amarawickrama, Singhapathirana, and Rajapaksha 2015).

To protect the remaining wealth of ecological green spaces in the area, some green spaces and ecologically sensitive areas have been declared as protected areas under conservation laws[4] or designated as Environmental Protection Areas[5] under the National Environmental Act. The Forest Ordinance has declared several forested areas as Reserved Forests. Only parts of these protected areas are accessible to the public for recreation and leisure. It is imperative that these areas continue to be protected, with strict implementation of the respective laws to ensure sustainable development in the region.

More recently, the government has put efforts into both refurbishing existing public spaces and creating new ones. During Sri Lanka's 26-year civil war, Colombo's public spaces were closed and became inaccessible, blocked off by high perimeter walls (Dayaratne 2010). Following the end of the war in 2009, the government focused on making Sri Lanka the "Wonder of Asia," and undertook numerous activities to improve Colombo's aesthetic value. These included many public-space improvement projects, such as removing the high perimeter walls, establishing new parks and open spaces, refurbishing selected colonial buildings, and improving the walkability of selected roads. Based on this approach, several open green spaces were built for passive and active recreational activities. For instance, the Viharamahadevi Park was revitalized by removing the existing walls and fences around the green spaces so that people can better access the park (Efroymson and Fernando 2013).

BEDDAGANA WETLAND PARK

Phase 1: Context

The Beddagana Wetland Park (BWP) was planned to maintain and preserve the wetland for flood retention and to conserve its biodiversity while providing a green space for the urban community for recreation and education. Because of high land demand and high land values in the surrounding area, the area was under tremendous development pressures by private developers and encroachment by squatters. Given the constant risk of flooding, the UDA wanted to conserve a flood retention area closer to official city limits to support environmental, social, and economic benefits to the communities.

The BWP is located in the Sri Jayawardenapura Kotte[6] Municipal Council area (SJKMC) adjacent to the Nippon Mawatha road, Baddegana Road, and Diyawanna Lake (also known as the Parliament Lake). It lies about 8 kilometers east of the commercial capital of Colombo, and the new Parliament Complex of Sri Lanka is also near this wetland (photo 10.1). The Diyawanna Lake and its environs, including the marsh and canal system, have been identified as a flood retention area by the Sri Lanka Land Reclamation and Development Corporation (SLLRDC), and most of the low-lying marshy land including the BWP is owned by the UDA. The BWP is also part of the Sri Jayawardenapura Kotte Sanctuary declared by the Department of Wildlife Conservation (DWC) in 1985 to preserve the area's biological wealth.

Access to the wetland was, from the beginning, unplanned with no formal paths. As such, it was often used as an informal picnic site and for consumption of liquor by the public. Dumping of garbage and subsequent degradation was observed in several locations. Part of the wetland was filled with dredged material from the Diyawanna Lake when the Parliament Complex was built. This filled area was used as a playground by the local community and also for

PHOTO 10.1 **Aerial View of Beddagana Wetland Park, Colombo, Sri Lanka**

Source: ©World Bank. Further permission required for reuse.

car races that damaged the ecological well-being of the wetland. Nippon Road, through which the wetlands are accessed, is also an area endowed with cultural heritage. Unfortunately, unregulated and unauthorized development has taken a heavy toll on the ramparts. They are fast disappearing from sight as people build on them with no regard for their cultural and historical value (UDA 2008, 2018).

These drivers of change, combined with large-scale flooding, prompted the UDA to protect the area through urban drainage and flooding infrastructure investments under the World Bank-funded Metro Colombo Urban Development Project (MCUDP). The project aimed to create a biodiversity park including passive recreational facilities, eco-recreation areas, and walking trails. The park opened to the public in 2016 and now provides recreational

BOX 10.1 THE SITE SELECTION PROCESS FOR BEDDAGANA WETLAND PARK

The site for Beddagana Wetland Park (BWP) was selected based on priorities for the improvement, management, and maintenance of Urban Development Authority (UDA)-owned flood detention areas around Diyawanna Lake, especially to mitigate the negative impacts from accelerated development.

In 2006, the UDA prepared the "Proposed Master Plan for the Wetlands around Parliament Lake," and 10 projects including the BWP were identified for implementation. This area falls within the wetland protection zone of the Sri Jayawardenapura Kotte Municipal Council (SJKMC) Development Plan prepared by the UDA. Development of this land is not permitted for any construction works other than the uses mentioned in the guidelines (predominantly for nature-based recreation and ecotourism) for the Western Province Wetlands Zoning and Relevant Regulations (UDA 2018).

The UDA identified the Beddagana wetland to be developed as a Biodiversity Park and Bird Sanctuary in association with the Ministry of Environment. In February 2010, the official inauguration ceremony for this activity was launched under the Ministry's Green Circle Project (UDA 2008).[a] The Sri Lanka Land Reclamation and Development Corporation (SLLRDC) was commissioned to carry out the canal clearance, but the work was not completed because of heavy floods in 2010 and political changes in the country. The UDA put forward the proposal to develop this 18-hectare wetland under the World Bank–funded Metro Colombo Urban Development Project (MCUDP) in 2012.

The environmental screening report of the MCUDP project for Beddagana identified serious environmental, ecological, and social impacts associated with the neglected and underdeveloped wetland (GoSL MCUDP 2014). These impacts included encroachments and unauthorized filling; dumping of garbage; lack of facilities for environmentalists, students, the public, and tourists to enjoy the scenic beauty and learn about wetland structure, function, and biodiversity; threats to biodiversity; visual pollution; and flooding.

(box continues next page)

space and educational opportunities to communities, including an information center, boardwalks with open decks, bird watching blinds, resting places, a bird watching tower, and a nature trail (box 10.1).

Phases 2 and 3: Planning, Design, and Implementation

One of the most significant challenges for designing the site was to recognize, coordinate, and integrate the various requests from a wide range of institutions responsible for managing the urban environment. The UDA and DWC were agencies that had some claim to the land, while the Department of Archeology had jurisdiction over the area's archeological heritage.

BOX 10.1 THE SITE SELECTION PROCESS FOR BEDDAGANA WETLAND PARK *(Continued)*

Importantly, the site's topology had untapped potential to improve the city's environmental conditions and to conserve its rich urban biodiversity. Despite an increase in the pace of urban development, the SJKMC area still contains reservoirs, swamps, marshy lands, and paddy fields. These local freshwater marshlands not only provide open spaces, the wetlands and Parliament Lake, but also act as retention areas for the heavy rainfalls during the southwest monsoon from May to August. In Ethul Kotte ward, for example, where Beddagana is located, approximately one-third (32 percent) of the area is covered by these marshy lands (Wijayapala 2003). The area surrounding the Beddagana wetland is low lying and is affected by frequent flooding. The Metro Colombo Wetland Management Strategy developed under the MCUDP also highlights the importance of protecting the BWP for its biological richness (GoSL MCUDP 2016).

The site also reflects an emerging urban typology, including both planned and unplanned new neighborhoods that are part of the growing Colombo Metropolitan Region (CMR) urban landscape. The SJKMC, the Colombo Municipal Council, and the Dehiwala Mt. Lavinia Municipal Council together form the most urbanized part of the CMR's core area. With the declaration of Sri Jayawardenapura Kotte as the capital city in 1982, population growth trends have increased, and the city began to experience an influx of people from Colombo and elsewhere because of the availability of land and infrastructure and good accessibility to the city. The neighborhoods surrounding the BWP today make up a diverse urban form. A small number of planned urban neighborhoods have emerged in recent decades through the efforts of government agencies. A combination of underserved settlements and new neighborhoods of expensive private housing have also emerged in the buffer area of this green space. A commercial entertainment area known as Diyatha Unyana has also been developed in the area.

a. The Green Circle Project is an initiative promoted by the Ministry of Environment to increase the green cover.

Given the multiple land uses in the area, the UDA undertook an institutional mapping exercise, which led to the development of specific design guidelines that would ensure preservation of the special characteristics of the wetland and the associated environment. In addition, the institutional mapping exercise helped identify all the project stakeholders to enable dialogue and ensure collective ownership for the sustainability of the proposed activities.

The BWP concept was to create a wetland nature park with eco-friendly, nature-based recreational activities while preserving the character of the site and the existing wetland environment. The UDA prepared a landscape master plan for the site based on Western Province Wetland Zoning Guidelines for a wetland protected zone (figure 10.2). The main objective of this plan was not to overdevelop the wetland but to provide proper access to students and the public for recreational and educational purposes. The master plan divided the wetland strategically into four zones to minimize the impact to the ecosystems when undertaking construction activities. The following interventions were to be implemented in each of these zones:

- *Zone 1:* Wader scrape and a shallow peripheral canal
- *Zone 2:* Car park, dry-weather playground, canal, nature trail, footpath, forest patch, reed pond, and two bird blinds
- *Zone 3:* Information center, main entrance bridge, and two side bridges
- *Zone 4:* Boardwalk, open-timber deck, resting place, bird watching tower, improvements to existing Bund Road, and visual barrier planting.

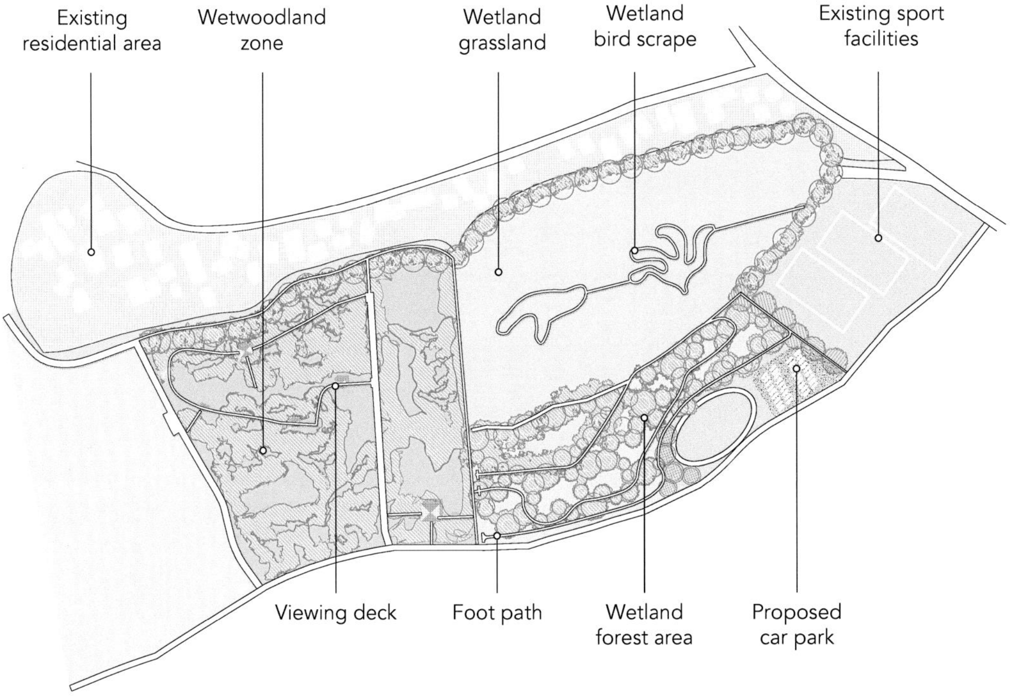

FIGURE 10.2 **Landscape Master Plan of Beddagana Wetland Park, Colombo, Sri Lanka**

Source: ©World Bank. Further permission required for reuse.

Subsequent approval for the plan was obtained by the relevant authorities such as the DWC, Central Environmental Authority (CEA), SJKMC, and SLLRDC. The UDA also held participatory stakeholder group meetings with community and nongovernmental organization (NGO) representatives from the area (such as the Sri Lanka Nippon Educational and Cultural Center and the Diyawanna Walkers Club). These discussions helped stakeholders to create a common understanding about planned activities and learn how citizens viewed the project and its attendant risks, impacts, opportunities, and mitigation measures.

The UDA undertook the planning, architectural design, landscape design, and engineering design for the park, while a contractor (Central Engineering Consultancy Bureau) carried out the ground-level construction activities. The guidelines laid down in the Environmental Management Plan (EMP) for the BWP were prepared with special focus on environmentally sensitive construction, especially when building the wader scrapes; on minimal use of machinery; and on sound site management (GoSL MCUDP 2014). The overall project supervision was undertaken by the UDA, while canal dredging, drainage, and excavation were supervised by the SLLRDC. Given the sensitivity of the site, a monitoring committee comprising the UDA's lead landscape architect, environmental specialists from the MCUDP, representatives from the DWC, and independent wetland experts paid regular supervision visits to the site, discussed issues, and provided technical assistance to the contractor. Further technical advice was obtained from the Wildfowl and Wetlands Trust Consulting Ltd. in the United Kingdom.

The design, development, and management of the BWP leveraged local community participation. Before the development of the park, locals regarded the Beddagana wetland area as informal public space and used it at will for various recreational and even illegal activities. At the early design stage, UDA officials worked closely with neighborhood communities through structured consultations to discuss the inital proposal and invite community feedback. These consultations ensured benefits to the community through changes to the park design, such as the designation of a separate space for a community park and play area with unrestricted access, creation of community livelihood opportunities, and so forth. The UDA also worked closely with NGOs such as the Field Ornithology Group of Sri Lanka (FOGSL), to improve the designs of the wetland park, using its expertise and knowledge of creating spaces conducive for birdwatching.

Access to the BWP Site

During construction, one of the initial interventions was to improve site accessibility. The narrow Nippon Road originally provided the only vehicle access to the BWP. Because the road is under SJKMC jurisdiction, the UDA carried out the road widening work and rehabilitation in collaboration with SJKMC, and the improved accessibility allowed construction vehicles to access the site. Construction materials were delivered only at designated times to minimize inconvenience to the public, especially joggers. Signage was placed at appropriate locations to inform the community. As part of the rehabilitation, a section of the Nippon Road bordering the BWP was subsequently upgraded into a proper jogging track and cycling path.

Access to the park is also designed for the benefit of pedestrians and the protection of ecosystems. The surrounding community in Sri Jayawardenapura Kotte can access the park using the network of small neighborhood roads such as Rampart Road and Beddagana Road. The placement of speed bumps along the park access road ensures that vehicles travel at slower speeds, minimizing damage to fauna. Visitor parking with designated spaces is located 150–200 meters from the park entrance. Porous tiles were used for parking area to allow rainwater to drain into the ground. Measures were also adopted to regulate vehicle traffic: material transport to the site is restricted to off-peak hours and selected times when the faunal species are inactive.

Recreational and Environmental Space Planning

The BWP's recreational space was carefully designed to enrich the habitat for the fauna and flora. The Beddagana wetland consists of a few natural water ponds and marshy areas with seasonally flooded grasslands and scattered pockets of scrubs. Three main habitat types are present across the park: water bodies, herb-dominated marshlands, and woodlands (figure 10.3). The wetland is a feeding and breeding ground for both birds and butterflies and is a popular stopover for a significant variety of migrating birds. As indicated earlier, the landscape of the park was zoned in four areas to allow different levels of physical and visual access and to minimize disturbance to wildlife. Considering the site's abundance of bird species, bird lookout points were constructed as educational and passive recreational spaces for visitors to enjoy.

Construction activities were scheduled during dry periods to reduce runoff flows that cause siltation and decrease water quality. Construction debris, spoil material, and dredged material were temporarily stored and covered on high ground away from flow paths before being permanently removed to preidentified locations. In addition, work was carried out to restore the habitats in the open space next to the wetlands, especially adjoining the Nippon Road.

The habitat was enriched for the wetland faunal population by improving the conditions of the wader scrapes, reed pond, and so forth. The waders were constructed according to specified size, shape, and contours. These interventions were carried out with a UDA landscape architect once a detailed planting plan was developed. Enrichment of the forest patch habitat was also strictly managed: tree locations, pit preparation, soil preparation, selection of species for planting, and so forth were determined by the area's environmental suitability, conservation or botanical interests, and other concerns. Part of the wetland area that had been filled many years ago and was being used by people for walking was replanted with native trees to create a mini jungle effect. A butterfly garden was also established by planting appropriate feeding and nectarine plant species.

Boardwalks within the Park

The boardwalks for park users were carefully designed, considering habitat structures and the flooding scenarios. The wetland is subject to periodic

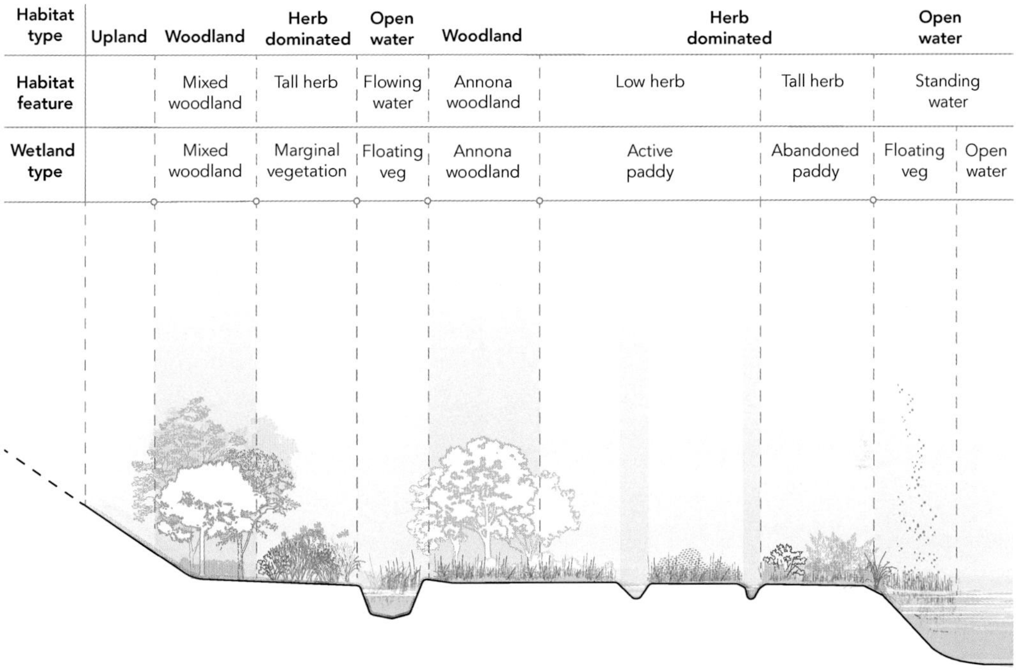

Habitat type
Upland
Woodland
Herb dominated
Open water
Woodland
Herb dominated
Open water
Habitat feature
Mixed woodland
Tall herb
Flowing water
Annona woodland
Low herb
Tall herb
Standing water
Wetland type
Mixed woodland
Marginal vegetation
Floating veg
Annona woodland
Active paddy
Abandoned paddy
Floating veg
Open water

FIGURE 10.3 **Stratification of Vegetation in a Wetland**

Source: ©World Bank. Further permission required for reuse.

flooding (three- to five-year return period) during monsoon rain seasons of up to 0.3–0.9 meters in depth, with inundation lasting for three to seven days. All the embankments for trails, proposed visitor centers, and structures for bird watching were designed considering these historical flood records and levels and without obstructing the existing drainage paths or flow regimes. Overall, the design considerations took care not to reduce the present flood retention and detention capacities of the wetland.

The network of boardwalks through diverse floral habitats provide the nature enthusiast with a rare opportunity to experience the biodiversity and natural beauty of the wetland (photo 10.2). The trail was designed with the assistance of UDA's landscape architect and environmental specialists. Design considerations for the trail layout included (a) harmony with existing vegetation; (b) where possible, horizontal alignment of the walkway to weave around existing trees, preserve large-diameter trees, and bring visitors into contact with key habitat features on the trail; and (c) vertical alignment of the walkway to maintain as much canopy cover as possible.

Phase 4: Management

Cost and Land Ownership

Most of the land within the site is owned by the UDA or required the UDA's authorization for land-use changes or modifications, because the site comes within the purview of the Sri Jayawardenapura Kotte Development Plan

a. b.

PHOTO 10.2 **Boardwalks in Beddagana Wetland Park, Colombo, Sri Lanka**

Source: ©World Bank. Further permission required for reuse.

developed by the UDA. Overall authority over the waterways is with the SLLRDC, specifically the canals associated with Diyawanna Lake. The UDA had to obtain clearances from the DWC, the CEA, and the Department of Archaeology for any land-use change or modification needed to reclaim land, because of the area's environmental sensitivity and proximity to historical sites. The Ceylon Electricity Board and Sri Lanka Telecom own the utilities within the site, and the SJKMC has primary authority over the byroads that have access to the site (Samarakoon and Nawaratne 2012).

Development of the BWP was fully funded under a US$1.2 million (SL Rs 175 million, in 2010 U.S. dollars) loan from the International Bank for Reconstruction and Development (IBRD) as a part of the "Metro Colombo—Towards a Flood Resilient Urban Environment" project trust fund, related to flood and drainage management.

Uses and Revenue Sources

The park officially opened to the public in 2015 and is open for visitors daily from 6:00 a.m. to 5:30 p.m. except on special holidays or under unavoidable circumstances such as floods. The main BWP user groups, according to its Management Plan, include the following:

- *Schoolchildren:* wetland, wildlife, and history education
- *Researchers:* nature, culture, history, and educational resources
- *Artists:* documentary and wildlife painting

- *Families and children:* relaxation and fun
- *Photographers:* wildlife and wedding photography
- *Commercial users:* wildlife- and environment-related film shoots.

The park does obtain some revenue from ticketing as well as fees from weddings and selected commercial shoots. To enter the park, visitors must obtain a ticket. Prices vary for locals and foreign tourists. The income generated from entrance fees from 2015 to 2018 was more than SL Rs 15.7 billion.

Daily Management Activities

Overall monitoring, technical supervision, and guidance for BWP management is conducted by the UDA's Environment and Landscape Division, which deploys a park manager, ticketing officer, and security staff for the daily management activities. A BWP management plan has been prepared with the mission to protect the urban wetland, promote understanding and research on its ecosystem, and facilitate ecotourism for both local residents and overseas tourists (UDA 2017).

A steering committee consisting of representatives of the UDA, SLLRDC, DWC, CEA, SJKMC, Sri Lanka Tourism Development Authority (SLTDA), Nippon Friendship Federation, and FOGSL has been established to guide the management interventions. The committee also includes two wetland scientists. The committee meets with local stakeholders periodically and with others as necessary, and it reports to the National Wetland Steering Committee. As a result of community-responsive design and operation, the park receives support from the local community, which the BWP management reciprocates with free excursions and awareness sessions for the locals.

Regulations for park maintenance have been developed and incorporated into the management plan. The habitat management work at the park is divided into three aspects: water, vegetation, and wildlife. Weeds and overgrown and invasive plant species are removed, while enrichment planting will be done with native plants to increase species diversity and attract wildlife. For example, nectar plants and larval food plants are planted for butterflies and reed plants along water edges for dragonfly habitation. Controlled cattle grazing is being promoted to maintain the wader feeding habitats. Water quality monitoring and keeping the canal network clean is undertaken by the SLLRDC. FOGSL recently undertook a fish survey of the wetland, and there has been a proposal to establish a database of the information collected.

The daily cleaning and maintenance of the BWP, the jogging track, the playground, and the Nippon Road has been contracted to a private party by the UDA for a monthly fee. The parking lot, toilet complex, and the kiosk are also leased out to a private party for operation and maintenance. This income is allocated into the BWP's special maintenance fund. Periodic maintenance is undertaken with the support of volunteer groups such as FOGSL, the Nature Team (University of Moratuwa), the Young Zoologist Association, or various private companies. Garbage collection is undertaken by the SJKMC.

Educational Programming

The UDA initiated several promotional activities to increase the community's and schoolchildren's knowledge about the BWP, in collaboration with the CEA's Environmental Pioneer Program in the schools and NGOs such as FOGSL. Programs targeting adults, youth, and children were conducted to spark their interests in bird watching and habitat restoration. Within BWP, information boards and leaflets explain the multiple benefits of the area and describe some of the key species present. Brochures and other educational materials available on-site explained the importance of biodiversity and species composition. Tags to identify species are placed in the environment closer to walkways to pique park users' interest and improve their knowledge of species. The BWP's management committee continuously supports research programs to improve long-term monitoring and new management techniques.

The BWP's administration has held discussions with the SLTDA about developing the park's tourism experience, given the urban and central location of the wetland. Sanitary facilities were provided near the entrance to the information center and near a picnic area. The area is provided with benches, bird hides, and name boards for educational purposes. Educational materials displayed at the information center on wetland biodiversity allow users, both young and old, to understand the value of the wetland ecosystems and their contribution toward human well-being in the CMR.

Overcoming Sustainability Challenges

Preserving the wetland ecosystem requires more sophisticated management expertise and capacity for park maintenance, especially for managing water quantity and quality, preventing spread of invasive species, and so forth. An event that demonstrated the need for proper expertise and management was experienced in October 2016, when the pond area surrounding the bird tower became completely dry from the lack of rain. It was found that water was seeping into wider Diyawanna Lake from several locations in the pond, and measures were taken to rehabilitate these locations. More recently, the spread of the invasive aquatic fern *Salvinia molesta* was discovered and innovative measures were required to mitigate this threat, as the use of boats in this area of the marsh was not an option. The invasive "pond apple" (*Annona glabra*) has also been identified in the park, which required specialized management.

Other wetland park management challenges, some of which have been addressed, include the following:

- *Lack of secure boundaries and surveillance*, mainly in the sections of the park bordering private property. This has led to safety and security concerns for visitors. The park management is looking into options such as installation of surveillance cameras and boundary walls at appropriate locations. The number of security personal was recently increased from four to six.
- *Insufficient park revenue* to meet the management costs, especially habitat maintenance activities. Collaboration with the private sector is being considered. It is anticipated that the development of Kotte Rampart Park will provide enhanced recreational and fund-generating opportunities. The two parks will operate as a single venue, with Nippon Road acting as the park connector.
- *Lack of connectivity, visibility from the main road* limits user access to the park. The UDA intends to develop additional park connectors from the BWP to

Kotte Rampart Park as well as to Diyatha Uyana (in English, "water park"), which is adjacent to the Battaramulla main road.

- *Complaints about misbehavior* of some young adults. Codes of conduct will be displayed at the park entrance indicating the vision and mission of the park.
- *Unregulated release of solid and liquid waste disposal from adjoining settlements* threatens the ecological balance and increases the environmental pollution loads released to the park. The management, with financial assistance from a FOGSL-funded project, recently installed a barrier to capture solid waste before it enters Diyawanna Lake.

Phase 5: Impact Evaluation

The development of the BWP demonstrates how environmental and social challenges can be tackled simultaneously to provide for a recreational space that is at once educational, protective of nature, and sustainable (figure 10.4).

Environmental Impact

An in-depth economic analysis in 2010 revealed that wetland benefits include flood protection, city temperature regulation, carbon storage, and wastewater treatment. These benefits are annually worth SL Rs 10–12 billion (US$ 66 million) to the CMR (Rozenberg 2015). Based on this understanding, the BWP wetlands have been preserved, which was an important component in the Ramsar accreditation of Colombo as a wetland city in October 2018.[7]

The BWP wetlands are rich in biodiversity and home to about 53 species of birds, 20 species of butterflies, 18 species of dragonflies, 13 species of fish, 3 species of reptiles, 5 species of mammals (including the globally threatened fishing cat), and 141 species of plants (GoSL MCUDP 2015). It is also one of the three known sites that the *Aganope heptaphylla*, a critically endangered woody climbing plant species native to Sri Lanka, is present. Preserving this land is further expected to function as a sponge for absorbing rainwater, thereby improving resilience to flooding (GOSL MCUDP 2012). The designed park also consists of microhabitats such as ponds, streams, scrubs, grasslands, small forest areas, and marshlands. The environmental impacts of the park need to be continuously monitored.

Social Impact

The park has attracted diverse groups of people for recreational activities. There are two main categories of visitors: The first are schoolchildren who come to learn about nature as a part of their annual excursion or under the CEA Environmental Pioneer program. The second are young adults between the ages of 18 and 25. In general, large crowds enter especially during the school holidays, and there is also a high demand from schools to include the BWP in their students' excursion activities. A user survey was conducted during the weekend of March 9–10, 2019, when the park was visited by 301 people on Saturday and 354 people on Sunday. Of these visitors, 85 percent were young couples, and the rest were all female or mixed groups (also below 30 years of age) or families. Most visitors had learned about the park through the internet. When questioned, visitors said they preferred the BWP because of its atmosphere and landscapes, where they can relax.

a. Before the BWP project, 2009

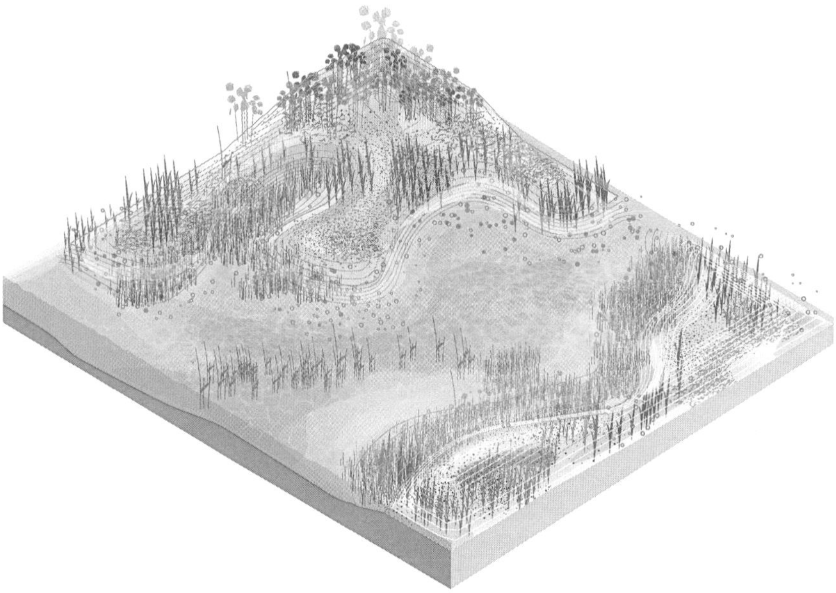

b. After the BWP project, 2016

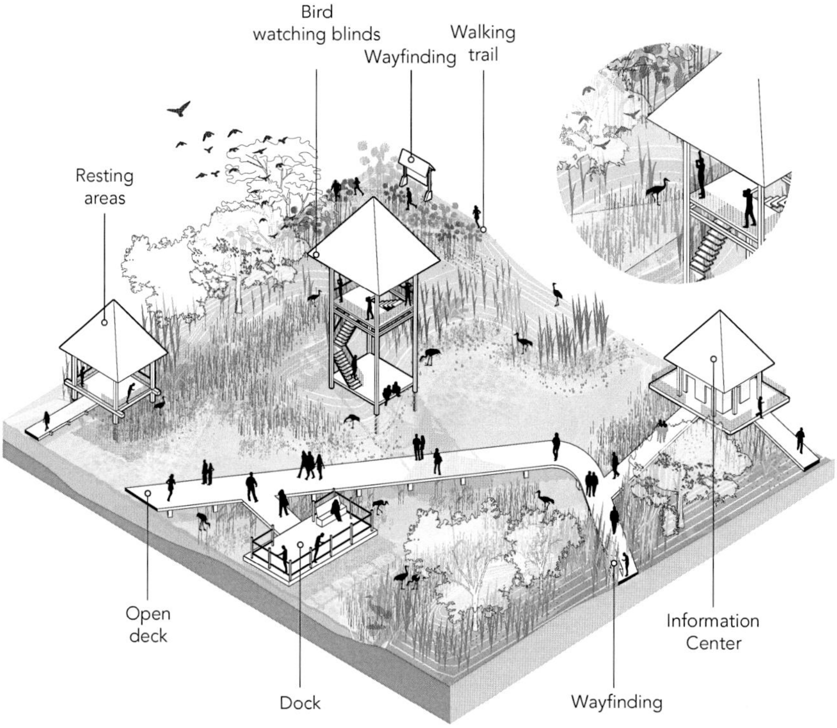

FIGURE 10.4 **Landscapes before and after Completion of the BWP Project, Colombo, Sri Lanka**

Source: ©World Bank. Further permission required for reuse.
Note: BWP = Beddagana Wetland Park.

The park promotes education and ecotourism, through various awareness programs. For instance, from June 2015 to the end of 2018, the BWP held 40 school awareness programs—reaching out to about 2,000 students and 164,203 paid park visitors, 96 percent being local. The BWP has become a training ground for bird watching and nature photographers. School Environmental Clubs, scouts, and private companies have partnered with park management to carry out various miniprojects, such as tree planting. The CEA Environmental Pioneer program uses the BWP as an important study site for its activities.

CROW ISLAND BEACH PARK

Phase 1: Context

The Crow Island Beach Park (CIBP) has been transformed from an abandoned area into a family-friendly, recreational beach park under the World Bank-funded MCUDP, following a request from the community. The objectives of the project were to enhance waterfront areas by preserving natural scenic beauty and to functionally upgrade the ancillary facilities for users.

The CIBP lies on the coastal boundary of Mattakkuliya, a highly residential area on the northern border of the Colombo Municipal Council (CMC). The 7.8-hectare beach stretch is 3.19 kilometers north of Colombo Harbor, and its northern section borders the mouth of Kelani River (photo 10.3). Most of the land is flat, including a sandy beach and a small lagoon at the southern corner with associated mangrove vegetation. The beach has a high aesthetic natural quality, along with numerous birds and plant species.

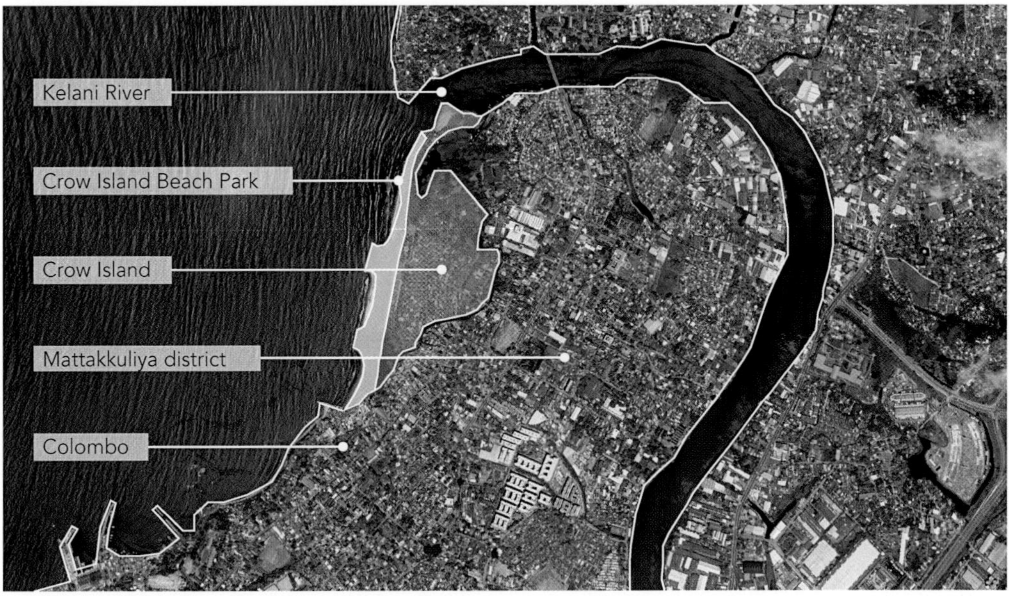

PHOTO 10.3 **Aerial View of Crow Island Beach Park, Colombo, Sri Lanka**

Source: ©World Bank. Further permission required for reuse.

However, the beach area was previously a neglected mangrove forest with a history of criminal activity and extensive pollution. By the beginning of this century, the beach had acquired a notorious reputation as a place for crime and other illegal activities. Because of a lack of formal management, there were squatters in the surrounding urban landscape, especially on the northern border of the park. Sea erosion is also an ongoing major problem at Crow Island, given that most of the land is only 2 meters above sea level. Frequent storms, high waves, and currents also affect the area.

After the December 2004 Indian Ocean earthquake and tsunami, the residential community got together to form the Crow Island Beach Park Management Society (CIBPMS).[8] In 2006, the CIBPMS with the assistance of the Coast Conservation Department (CCD), started improving the beach area with simple interventions such as developing small playgrounds, planting trees, and cleaning. The CCD also built further coastal defense structures. Nevertheless, the pressures of unregulated settlement, haphazard waste disposal, and the absence of continuous funding mechanisms or manpower hampered the sustainability of park management (CIBPMS 2006). Although the first efforts helped to make the beach more attractive—offering fresh air and seaside recreation in a congested environment—the lack of safety measures and facilities worried many visitors, and many gave up visiting the beach. Hence, the area continued to be perceived as a neglected seminatural urban park. During the civil war, access to some areas of the beach was limited because of security concerns associated with Colombo Port. These security measures were revoked in 2010 after the war ended.

To establish a formal development and management mechanism to transform the park into a safe public space for recreation, the CIBPMS and the CCD sought assistance from the Ministry of Defense and Urban Development (MDUD). The MDUD then decided to develop the CIBP, considering local needs, as a potential public space for safe recreational uses. Development of the beach park was agreed to by all stakeholders—including the CMC, which owned the site and saw potential environmental, recreational, and economic benefits. In 2014, the CMC kicked off the implementation process with financial assistance from the World Bank-funded MCUDP (US$2.1 million, SL Rs 380 million) (CIBPMS 2015).

Phase 2: Planning and Design

The CIBP project was designed through flexible and participatory planning processes. The CMC, with assistance from the MCUDP Project Management Unit, held the responsibility for developing the park in consultation with other stakeholders such as the CCD, UDA, SLLRDC, Department of Police, and CIBPMS as well as residents from neighboring villages (Peris Watta and Bokkuwaththa). During the development process, some of the footpaths previously used by the community were intentionally left untouched until feedback from residents was received on how to design them. Site visits, forums, briefing sessions, surveys, and interviews were conducted to understand and incorporate public opinion. The CIBPMS actively participated in the overall process as a representative of citizens.

The overall design concept was strategic in that it aimed to preserve the area's ecological value and character, as well as provide recreational green

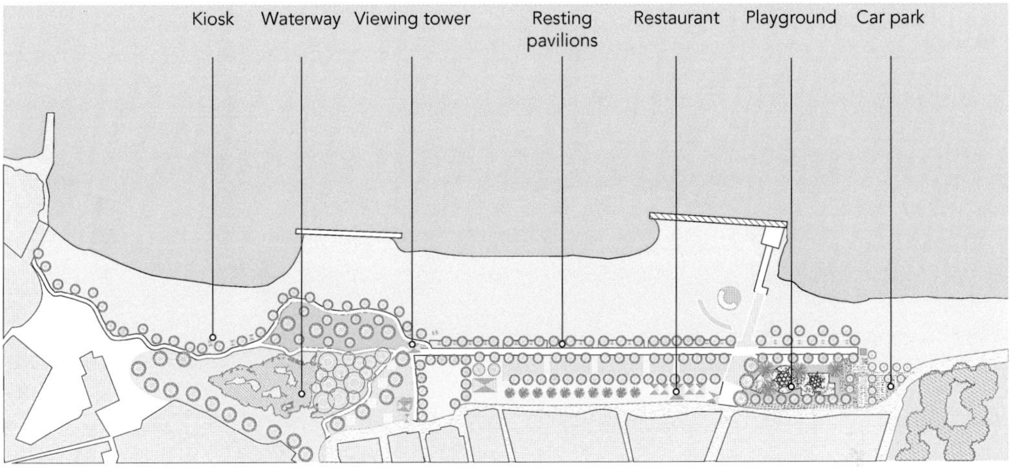

FIGURE 10.5 **Layout of Crow Island Beach Park, Colombo, Sri Lanka**

Source: ©World Bank. Further permission required for reuse.

space to benefit local communities. The layout of the park was jointly designed by CMC and UDA staff (figure 10.5). Several alternative designs were considered and discussed. A final design was selected based on the use of available land space on-site and conservation of vegetation.

Basic features developed as part of the eco-recreational areas include the mangrove forest area, a viewing deck, a bird watching tower, and pond area. Recreational facilities for the public include amenities such as restaurants and resting pavilions, kiosks, viewing decks, picnic tables, and an open-air theater. The children's park was developed with facilities such as a rock-climbing area, a log-climbing area, and an underground maze (a "rat run tunnel"). Government policy at the time stipulated that all recreational public spaces be maintained as open public spaces without fences. As such, the CIBP was designed without any fencing around the property, thus ensuring greater accessibility for the public.

Access to the Site

The park was designed to include a circuit pathway connecting the neighborhoods that were previously disconnected because of the Vetweik Canal on the southern border. The park is accessible by the Mattakkuliya main road and Crow Island Road. The 500-meter pathway connecting Point 7th Avenue and Beach Road is an ideal recreational space for joggers and pedestrians. The park community center, picnic area, picnic huts, restaurant, and kiosks around the CIBP have all been built to provide facilities for the communities accessing these public spaces.

The entrances to the park were also designed to prioritize pedestrian movement. Fences to control noise were removed because they obstructed connectivity between surrounding neighborhoods. Bollards at entrances prevent vehicles from coming into the park. The pavements are differentiated for separate cycling and jogging tracks to avoid interfering with pedestrian areas (photo 10.4).

PHOTO 10.4 **Paved Trail and Kiosks, Crow Island Beach Park, Colombo, Sri Lanka**

Source: ©World Bank. Further permission required for reuse.

Recreational Space Planning

The existing mangrove forest and waterways have been converted into ecological and recreational spaces. Built-up areas are separated from the conservation zones that provide refuge areas for flora and fauna to feed and breed. An existing canal was restored to increase water flow and to reduce pollution. The mangroves were restored by reestablishing the hydrological connectivity with the sea, intercepting sewer discharges, and removing garbage, along with controlled dredging of an associated saline pond. The timber deck placed at the edge of the coast provides a good viewpoint of the Colombo harbor and ships entering and leaving.

The new trails provided the community with increased opportunities for safe walking and other physical activities, which many local residents engage in every morning (photo 10.5). A police post was established to provide security and safety on the site.

Phase 3: Implementation

During the construction phase of the project, anticipated ecological and social impacts were carefully managed. For instance, heavy vehicle movement was regulated on the main road to avoid damage to the road and traffic congestion. Dust, noise, and air pollution were mitigated by spraying water and using dust and noise screens. To improve the water quality in the project site, the waterlogged mangrove forest area had to be dredged and the Vystwyke Canal cleared. This work was outsourced to avoid delays in implementation of the project. Throughout the design and construction process, stakeholders and designers met and exchanged views on the design solutions.

PHOTO 10.5 **Walking Path, Crow Island Beach Park, Colombo, Sri Lanka**

Source: ©World Bank. Further permission required for reuse.

Before implementation of the project, people who informally occupied the site for livelihoods or who lived on-site were consulted through various formal and informal channels. Resettlement compensation packages were offered through negotiations. This process was assisted by the MCUDP Project Management Unit as well as the clergy in the area. A dairy farmer, one of several informal users occupying the site, received compensation, and his settlement package included the sale of cattle and provision of a kiosk at the site once the park was developed; the farmer was satisfied with the settlement (GoSL MCUDP 2014). Six fisher families were compensated with alternative housing, which was also satisfactory to them. About 15 vendors who had been selling fast food at the site were awarded leases for kiosks within the park premises as compensation. The kiosks were planned to provide livelihood opportunities and to provide park users with easily accessible food, drinks, and games. A forum for local residents was also held at the community center in Crow Island, and their feedback was incorporated throughout the design process.

Phase 4: Management

The land occupied by the park is owned by the CMC. Permission to develop the land is granted by the CCD, as the area lies within the "coastal zone" under CCD jurisdiction. (The CCD mandate is to manage and conserve the coastal resources in Sri Lanka.) The development guidelines to the site were provided by the UDA, because this area is included in the Colombo Metropolitan Development Zone as designated by the UDA. The maintenance of the Vystwyke Canal comes under the jurisdiction of the SLLRDC.

Since the CIBP opened to the public in 2016, the park's safety has been the responsibility of the local government. Ensuring park safety was also done with the assistance of civil society. Two CMC officials are present at the site to supervise the park operation and undertake regular maintenance, while the security and cleaning of the park is outsourced. Because the park is open 24 hours with no secured boundary walls, 20 security personnel from the Civil Security Department are deployed by the CMC to provide security. Other than the permanent police post, three security checkpoints are located within the park boundaries that adjoin neighboring settlements. Mattakuliya mobile police also assist in keeping law and order, while three lifeguards from the police are also available, especially during the holiday season when large crowds gather.

As for maintenance, the park management currently works in accordance with daily and monthly maintenance plans. The CIBPMS also volunteers in monthly cleanup sessions and has initiated activities such as tree planting, supplying water through a well, and establishing a plant nursery with its own finances.

However, managing park facilities has recently become a key concern of the CIBPMS. Many park structures are coming apart just three years after the park's construction. The local government is responsible for ensuring that the CIBP remains in good order and is safe for the community. Solid waste management and mosquito control are two main issues that need to be addressed on an ongoing basis. To address these concerns, the CIBPMS called for additional funding to cover its management. This is in addition to monthly revenues of less than SL Rs 300,000 (US$1,650) generated from 16 kiosk leases, a car park, and a restaurant.

Phase 5: Evaluation

Environmental Impact

The CIBP project has contributed to the preservation and enhancement of the city's natural ecological assets. For instance, the mangroves have been restored by reestablishing the hydrological link with the sea, intercepting sewer discharges, and removing garbage from and controlling dredging of the saline pond. Moreover, although the area lacked sufficient green coverage and had only minimal roadside vegetation (Konau 2016), trees and grass have now been planted along the beach park. This can help improve the air quality and mitigate pollution from heavy traffic in the north of the city.

Social Impact

The project had transformed a deteriorated community space to a well-designed, people-centered recreational park with improved facilities such as kiosks and restaurants. The primary users are from the surrounding local communities, but the park is also becoming popular with local and foreign tourists.

The CIBP is free to access and open 24 hours a day. It is visited by more than 2,000 visitors per day during weekends and holidays, primarily enjoying this open space on weekends and especially during the evening hours. Mainly family groups are observed relaxing and enjoying the beachfront, playing, walking, or sitting and socializing. Discussions with the CIBPMS reveals that the residents were supportive of improved connectivity and the removal of fencing that obstructed access and views. Benches were placed at the entrance under trees, allowing people to rest. The open area has also been designed to allow parents to let the kids play while still being able to watch them, creating a better perception of safety in the park area.

In a March 2019 survey of CIBP users, about 80 percent of respondents said they had learned about the park by word of mouth before visiting the park.[9] All respondents had visited the park six months to one year preceding the survey. Respondents also highlighted that going to the park over the weekend has become one of their routine activities, because other nearby parks lacked facilities for children; did not have adequate green open spaces to relax; or lacked provisions for sitting, walking, and other activities. About 70 percent of the survey respondents live 3 kilometers or more from the park. Respondents agreed that CIBP was the only decent city park with open green spaces and facilities for children that was also accessible from their homes (in neighborhoods such as Mutuval and Wattala). On weekdays the park is visited by preschool and school groups as well as people in the area who use it for exercise (walking and jogging). This is a remarkable improvement, given that a 2011 survey found that there had been almost no visitors from outside of the area and that only a few residents visited the area for personal or recreational purposes because of its security risk (Konau 2016).

The provision of a safe, enjoyable waterfront park has helped improve the physical health of users from the community. Jogging and biking paths and

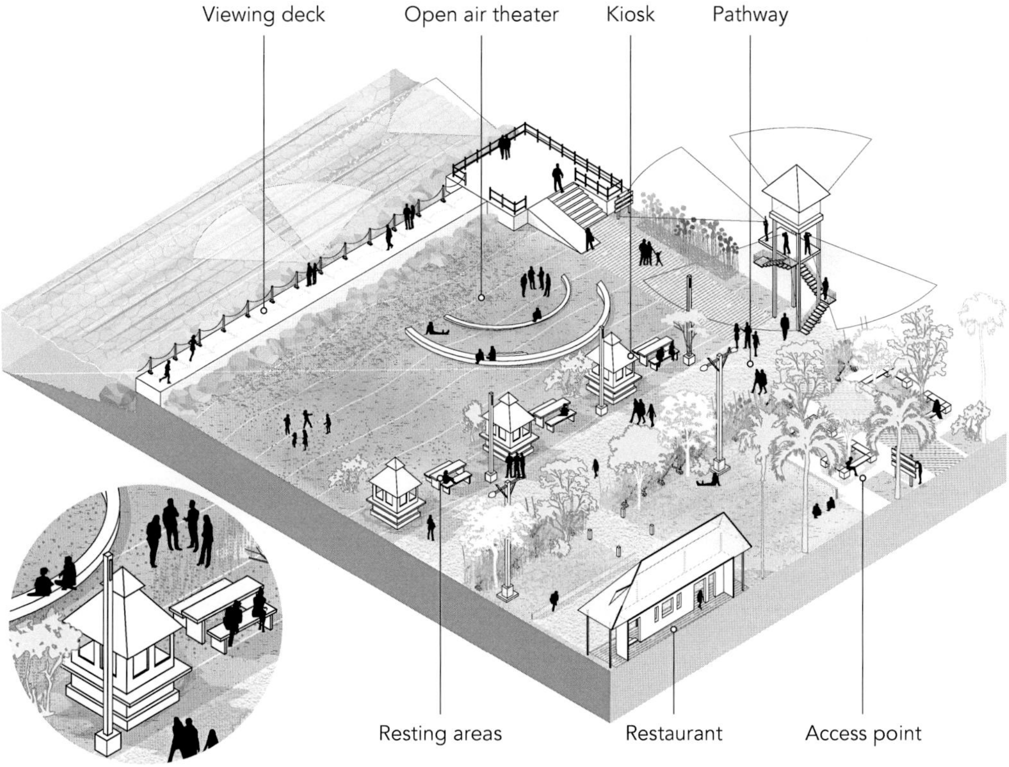

FIGURE 10.6 **How People Use Crow Island Beach Park, Colombo, Sri Lanka**

Source: ©World Bank. Further permission required for reuse.

the playgrounds encourage healthy lifestyles (figure 10.6). Survey respondents commonly observed that many local residents engage in physical activities in the park each morning. Around 400 people use the park daily for exercise between 5:30 a.m. and 9:00 a.m. (Konau 2016).

NOTES

1. The CMR consists of three districts: Gampaha, and Kalutara. Together they make up the Western Province of Sri Lanka (UDA 1998).
2. Areas coming under all municipal councils (MCs) and urban councils (UCs) are currently considered part of the urban sector in Sri Lanka. Before 1987, town councils were also included in the definition of urban areas. With the setting up of provincial councils in 1987, these town councils were absorbed into Pradeshiya Sabhas, which have since fallen into the rural sector. Although some areas were recently upgraded to UCs or MCs, many towns lost their urban status. This has led to underestimation of the degree of urbanization, and comparison became difficult over the years (DCSSL 2012).
3. In 1978, the government initiated the Colombo Master Plan, which covered the entire CMR encompassing three administrative districts: Colombo, Gampaha, and part of Kalutara. The UDA recommended a minimum standard of 1.4 hectares of land per 1,000 persons to be allocated for public outdoor recreation space (PORS). In 1985, the UDA initiated the "City of Colombo Development Plan," which introduced the zoning system to Colombo and planning regulations (UDA 2018).
4. For instance, the Bellanvila-Attidiya, Muthurajawela, and Sri Jayawardenapura Kotte Sanctuaries, as well as Horagolla National Park are declared protected areas under Sri Lanka's Fauna and Flora Protection Ordinance.
5. These areas include the Muthurajawela buffer zone, the Thalangama wetland, the Walauwatta Wathurana wetland, and the Bolgoda estuary.
6. Sri Jayawardenapura Kotte has historical importance as the last Kingdom of Sri Lanka. It was also declared as the Administrative Capital of the country in 1982.
7. The Ramsar Convention on Wetlands of International Importance is the oldest of the modern global intergovernmental environmental agreements, adopted in the Iranian city of Ramsar in 1971. Recognizing the importance of cities and urban wetlands, the Convention has recently introduced a Wetland City accreditation scheme. This voluntary scheme provides an opportunity for cities that value their natural or human-made wetlands to gain international recognition and positive publicity for their efforts. During the 13th session of the Conference of the Parties to the Ramsar Convention (COP13) in 2018, the Convention recognized 18 cities, including Colombo, that have taken exceptional steps to safeguard their urban wetlands. These pioneer cities will serve as examples and inspire deliberate actions for other cities toward sustainable urbanization. For more information, see https://www.ramsar.org/activity/wetland-city-accreditation.
8. Residents involved in formation of the CIBPMS especially came from the government employees who had quarters in the area. The CIBPMS is a nonprofit organization that is registered with the CEA (6/6/17/01/98) and the Colombo Divisional Secretariat (DS00095) and has 330 members who volunteer in the cleaning and maintenance of the park.
9. The survey was conducted during a weekend, March 9–10, 2019. The total number of survey respondents was 30.

REFERENCES

Amarawickrama, S., P. Singhapathirana, and N. Rajapaksha. 2015. "Defining Urban Sprawl in the Sri Lankan Context: With Special Reference to the Colombo Metropolitan Region." *Journal of Asian and African Studies* 50 (5): 1–25.

CIBPMS (Crow Island Beach Park Management Society). 2006. "CIBPMS 2006 Annual Report." CIBPMS, Colombo.

———. 2015. "CIBPMS 2015 Annual Report." Crow Island Beach Park Management Society (CIBPMS), Colombo.

Dayaratne, Ranjith. 2010. "Moderating Urbanization and Managing Growth: How Can Colombo Prevent the Emerging Chaos?" UNU-WIDER Working Paper No. 064, United Nations University World Institute for Development Economics Research (UNU-WIDER), Helsinki, Finland.

DCSSL (Department of Census and Statistics Sri Lanka). 2012. "Census of Population and Housing 2012: Final Report." [In Sinhala.] DCSSL, Colombo.

Efroymson, Debra, and Udan Fernando. 2013. "Public Space and Quality of Life: A Case Study of Mount Lavinia Beach." Unpublished paper, Colombo.

EIU (Economist Intelligence Unit). 2017. "Global Liveability Report 2017." Annual urban quality-of-life ranking report, EIU, London.

GoSL MCUDP (Government of Sri Lanka Metro Colombo Urban Development Project). 2012. "Social Screening and Impact Assessment for Sub-Projects: Beddagana Bio-Diversity Park and Bird Sanctuary with Rampart Nature Park." Report, MCUPD Project Management Unit, Ministry of Defense and Urban Development, Colombo.

———. 2014. "Environmental Management Plan: Beddagana Biodiversity Park." Planning document, MCUPD Project Management Unit, Ministry of Defense and Urban Development, Colombo.

———. 2015. "Wetland Management Strategy Technical Report 02: Ecological Status." Consultancy Services for the Preparation of Management Strategy for Wetlands and Carrying out an Assessment of Water Quality in the Inland Waterways and Lakes within Metro Colombo Area, MCUDP, Government of Sri Lanka, Colombo.

———. 2016. "Final Metro Colombo Wetland Management Strategy." Consultancy Services for the Preparation of Management Strategy for Wetlands and Carrying out an Assessment of Water Quality in the Inland Waterways and Lakes within Metro Colombo Area, MCUDP, Government of Sri Lanka, Colombo.

Konau, S. K. 2016. "Urban Green Spaces: Bridging Cultural, Ecological and Political Planning Gaps to Make the City of Colombo a Leading 'Greener-City.'" Doctoral thesis, University of Essex, U.K.

Li, L., and P. G. R. N. I. Pussella. 2017. "Is Colombo City, Sri Lanka Secured for Urban Green Space Standards?" *Applied Ecology and Environmental Research* 15 (3): 1789–99.

MHC (Ministry of Housing and Construction) 2016. "Housing and Sustainable Urban Development in Sri Lanka: National Report for the Third United Nations Conference on Human Settlements—Habitat III." MHC, Government of Sri Lanka, Battaramulla.

MMWD (Ministry of Megapolis and Western Development). 2016. "The Megapolis Western Region Master Plan 2030 Sri Lanka: From Island to Continent." Western Region Megapolis Planning Project document, MMWD, Government of Sri Lanka, Battaramulla.

MNPEA and MDM (Ministry of National Policies and Economic Affairs and Ministry of Disaster Management). 2016. *Sri Lanka Post-Disaster Needs Assessment: Floods and Landslides.* Colombo: MDM.

MoE (Ministry of Environment). 2010. "Sector Vulnerability Profile: Urban Development, Human Settlements and Economic Infrastructure." Supplementary document to "National Climate Change Adaptation Strategy for Sri Lanka, 2011 to 2016," strategy booklet, Climate Change Secretariat, MoE, Colombo.

MoF (Ministry of Finance). 2018. "Framework Development and Infrastructure Financing to Support Public Private Partnerships: Environmental Assessment & Management Framework (EAMF)." Framework project document, MoF and National Agency for Public Private Partnership, Government of Sri Lanka, Colombo.

Rathnayake, Ishara. 2014. "Urban Poverty in Sri Lanka—2013." Briefing paper No. 14, Centre for Poverty Analysis, Colombo, Sri Lanka.

Rozenberg, J. 2015. "Long-Term Strategic Planning for a Resilient Metro Colombo: An Economic Case for Wetland Conservation and Management." Paper presented at the American Geophysical Union (AGU) Fall Meeting 2015, December 14–18, San Francisco.

Samarakoon, Indika, and P. Nawaratne. 2012. "Institutional Mapping of Beddegana Wetland Park and Kotte Rampart Nature Park." Report, Urban Development Authority, Ministry of Housing and Urban Development, Battaramulla.

UDA (Urban Development Authority). 1998. "Colombo Metropolitan Regional Structural Plan: Volume 1 Synthesis." Planning document, UDA, Ministry of Housing and Urban Development, Battaramulla.

———. 2008. "Biodiversity Park and Bird Sanctuary at Beddagana." Report, Ministry of Urban Development and Sacred Area Development, Sri Jayawardenapura Kotte, Sri Lanka.

———. 2011. "Public Outdoor Recreation Space Planning as an Integral Part of Landscape Master Plans for Urban Areas in Sri Lanka." Planning document, Environment and Landscape Division, UDA, Battaramulla.

———. 2017. "Management Plan of Beddagana Wetland Park, Sri Jayawardanapura Kotte." Planning document, Environment and Landscape Division, UDA, Battaramulla.

———. 2018. "City of Colombo Development Plan (Compiled Edition)." Planning document, UDA and Ministry of Megapolis and Western Management, Government of Sri Lanka, Battaramulla.

Van Dort, Leoma T. 2016. "Neoliberalism and Social Justice in the City: An Examination of Postwar Urban Development in Colombo, Sri Lanka." Master's thesis, St. Cloud State University, St. Cloud, MN.

Weerakoon, K. G. P. K. 2013. "Overview of Urbanization in Geodemographic Approach; Colombo Urban Area, Sri Lanka." *European Academic Research* 1 (9): 2819–31.

Wijayapala, S. L. F. 2003. "City Profile: Sri Jayawardenapura Kotte Municipal Council." Report for the United Nations Human Settlements Programme (UN-Habitat) Sustainable Cities Programme, Sustainable Sri Lankan Cities Programme (SSLCP), executed by Ministry of Housing and Plantation Infrastructure, Colombo.

World Bank. 2012. *Turning Sri Lanka's Urban Vision in to Policy and Action*. Colombo: World Bank.

CHAPTER 11

KARACHI, PAKISTAN: RECLAIMING SAFE AND INCLUSIVE URBAN SPACES THROUGH CITIZEN MOBILIZATION

Farhan Anwar

KEY TAKEAWAYS

- Although Karachi has long been the economic and cultural center of Pakistan, public spaces in the city have lost their vibrancy and support less social activity than in the past because of deprivation and safety issues. The three case studies in Karachi illustrate how declining social trust can be repaired by reclaiming public spaces through citizen mobilization.
- Eduljee Dinshaw Road and Pakistan Chowk, once neglected and deprived spaces in a historic downtown area, have been transformed to enjoyable open spaces where citizens can use without concerns about safety and cleanliness. These projects, which were initiated and funded by philanthropic sources, resulted in public spaces that now accommodate a variety of social activities, attracting people with various backgrounds across the city.
- The I AM KARACHI movement is a civic campaign aimed at inspiring cultural rejuvenation and creativity by engaging people in dialogue and encouraging social interaction in public spaces. The movement also included the renovation of sport facilities that benefited more than 5,000 young people in underserved neighborhoods and the redesign of approximately 450 feet of deteriorated walls along sidewalks across

six neighborhoods that have been victims of violence, by engaging more than 200 local artists and designers.

- These cases demonstrate how civil society and the private sector can be effective lead actors in public space transformation and interventions, by mobilizing funding and resources and organizing public support.

CITY DYNAMICS

Context and Background

Karachi has long been the economic and cultural center of Pakistan. Founded as the port of Sindh Province 200 years ago, the city accounts for around 15 percent of national gross domestic product (GDP). Karachi had a population of 16 million people in 2017, accounting for one-fifth of Pakistan's urban population.[1] Massive migration into the city over the recent decades has diversified its ethnic composition, which has led to changes in political and cultural backgrounds (World Bank 2018).

Karachi is one of the least livable cities in the world according to the Global Liveability Index (EIU 2017). Severe gaps in urban infrastructure and basic services are mostly filled by informal service providers. More than 50 percent of Karachi's population lives in informal settlements with limited access to water and public sewerage networks. The entire system of public transport is informal, and only 40 percent of solid waste is properly collected (World Bank 2018). While Karachi has experienced urban sprawl over the last decades, infrastructure investments have been uncoordinated and have yet to catch up with demand. Segregation and social exclusion are also critical challenges that call for immediate action.

Public Spaces in Karachi

Karachi has a history of vibrant and activated public spaces, including streets, markets, and squares. The Saddar area, the heart of Karachi since the creation of Pakistan in 1947, had been the most vibrant, visited, and multicultural public-space precinct in the city. Karachi was transformed from a small fishing village into a dynamic city with beautified streets and modern buildings, and its port had grown into one of the grandest harbors in India. Saddar was also known for its vibrant nightlife of dance clubs, bars, cafés, and restaurants. In 1947, the city ranked as one of the cleanest and healthiest cities in India (Rustomji 1952).

However, Karachi has gradually lost its charm since the 1970s. Public activities, such as drinking and partying, were increasingly prohibited for religious and political reasons. This led to a drastic decrease in cultural spaces, and Saddar experienced urban blight on an exceptional scale. About 80 percent of Saddar's cultural spaces disappeared between 1965 and 1995 (figure 11.1). The precinct's transport scenario also changed: tram service was discontinued because of claims that it caused traffic hazards at stops on roads. Public transport was replaced by informal sector activities such as minibuses, which in turn resulted in traffic chaos and congestion. Pedestrian spaces were encroached upon by cars and buses.

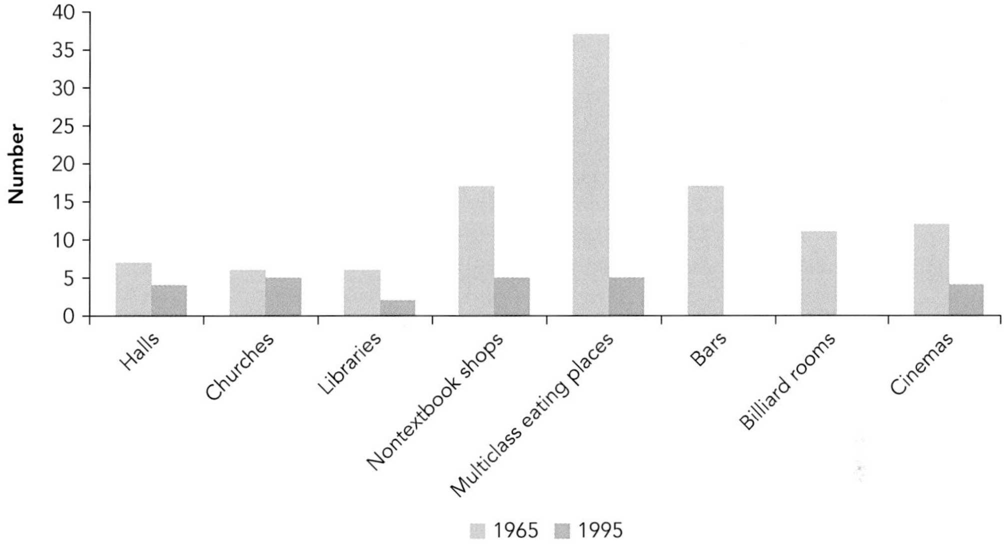

FIGURE 11.1 **Decline in Cultural Spaces in Karachi, Pakistan, 1965–95**

Source: Data from Hasan 2010.
Note: No 1995 data are shown for bars and billiard rooms because they disappeared entirely.

Moreover, building bylaws were changed to permit the development of high- and medium-rise buildings. This led to the demolition of a large number of old historic buildings and changed the architectural character and authenticity of the inner city. This rapid densification and vertical growth were accelerated by the intervention of commercial interests and the availability of funds for construction (Hasan 2010).

Consequently, the creation and upkeep of public spaces in Karachi have been deprived of political support. Open green spaces as a share of total urban footprint declined from 4.6 percent in 2001 to 3.7 percent in 2013 (World Bank 2018). This is closely related to a lack of policies focused on providing and maintaining public spaces. While earlier master plans for Karachi mentioned development of public recreational spaces, the latest Karachi Strategic Development Plan 2020 did not expand on the city's plans for public space (CDGK 2007). For example, the plan's section on "Regenerating the Inner City" does not adequately lay out how the renewal of public spaces, access to those spaces, and public activities could help restore the urban center's architectural heritage and cultural diversity. Some open green areas are included in the 2020 plan only as part of residential neighborhood zoning. Moreover, different types of public spaces—architectural heritage sites, public markets, streets, and others—are simplified and managed under a single regulation, "Amenity Plots," in Karachi.[2] This single policy has been inadequate in providing public-space facilities, such as benches, shades, streetlights, wayfinders, and toilets.

The government's limited capacity for public-space management has contributed to a decrease in the quantity and quality of public spaces in Karachi (Azam and Burke 2018). Improving and providing pedestrian access has also been neglected, and over time this failed to fulfill the recreational and social needs of the populace. In 2018, the city government finally launched an "Adopt a Footpath" initiative to improve walkability and livability in the city. Notably, the initiative promotes an integrated approach among different land agencies and also allows private sector investment in cleaning and installing facilities for safety on pedestrian networks (*Express Tribune* 2018).

In Karachi, public spaces can facilitate positive social interactions within communities and are critical for promoting social inclusion. However, most roads in Karachi lack basic safety features or are not maintained regularly, which hampers accessibility and mobility, particularly for women, the elderly, and people with disabilities. Degraded public spaces and limited access to basic facilities are also a factor limiting youth engagement in and across communities. According to the United Nations Development Programme (UNDP), 90 percent of youths in Pakistan have never accessed sport facilities, which puts youths at a high risk of being intolerant to others (UNDP 2017). Unsafe public spaces, in addition to increasing exposure to crime and violence, also constrain women's and girls' opportunities to participate in public life and employment (UNDP 2017).

EDULJEE DINSHAW ROAD

Phase 1: Context

The Eduljee Dinshaw Road (EDR) once was one of the most neglected roads in Karachi (photo 11.1). The approximately 1-kilometer road serves two prestigious, century-old architectural landmarks: the Karachi Port Trust Building and the Imperial Custom House. After the decline of Karachi's vibrant street culture in the 1970s, the EDR became an unfriendly space for pedestrians. It was misused as a dumping area, was overrun by parking lots and warehouses, and was frequented by drug peddlers. Pedestrians trying to enter the new Custom House also encountered disorganized and filthy areas as well as barriers on the

PHOTO 11.1 **Aerial View of Eduljee Dinshaw Road, Karachi, Pakistan**

Source: ©World Bank. Further permission required for reuse.

street, which made accessibility an issue. During the rainy season, overflows of sewage and rainwater filled the street. The road's entrances were congested and messy owing to heavy truck traffic, apartment buildings and warehouses, and truck stands.

An effort to revive the street culture on the EDR was launched by a group of concerned citizens and supported by government officials, including Tariq Huda (the customs collector at the time) and the governor of Sindh Province. The citizens and other stakeholders formed the Eduljee Dinshaw Road Project Trust (EDRPT), which included government officials and technical experts.[3] The commissioner of Karachi City instructed city offices to provide all possible support to the project. The Customs House then partnered with a team of leading city planners and designers, to reclaim and rejuvenate the EDR.

Phase 2: Planning and Design

The EDR project—inaugurated by the former Sindh governor, Ishratul Ibad Khan, on November 11, 2014—had three main objectives (Anwar 2015):

- To create best-practice neighborhood development in which all stakeholders are in close coordination
- To reduce congestion and create public-friendly spaces by improving road connectivity and walkability
- To turn the street into a fun place and a social hub to visit and meet people.

The EDR design was divided into two phases: the first for rapidly visible results and the second for longer-term improvements that required more planning and effort. The rapid-results phase included seven components: vehicle lane narrowing; cobblestone treatments; tree lining; parking lot wall renovation; street lighting; street furniture (benches, seating, and waste bins); and water bodies (such as fountains). The phase for longer-term impacts included preservation of the Imperial Custom House, creation of a Custom House Museum, creation of bistros, upgrading of Mandir Temple, introduction of specially designed kiosks, and parking lot organization for truckers (Zuby 2015).

Beyond the design of each component along the street, the main challenge was also in the integration and revival of the neighborhood immediately around the EDR. For instance, a cement parking lot wall and dilapidated apartment buildings along the street made the street look dark and unfavorable. To solve this issue, the design scheme looked beyond installing new street furniture with a proposal to redesign the entire parking lot wall with classical details, mixed with trees, hedges, and green walls to be consistent with the classical façade of the Imperial Custom House. The apartment blocks were also repainted to be in line with the classical image of the EDR and parking lot wall. The road was paved with cobblestones, and the façades of the Imperial Custom House and the Port Trust Building were cleaned up. Finally, the entire road was pedestrianized with street lighting and chained bollards in the center (figure 11.2).

Special attention was given to the installation of street furniture to promote usability and vibrancy. The paving was also designed for pedestrian walkability. Street furniture included seats, which were arranged around

a. Plan overview

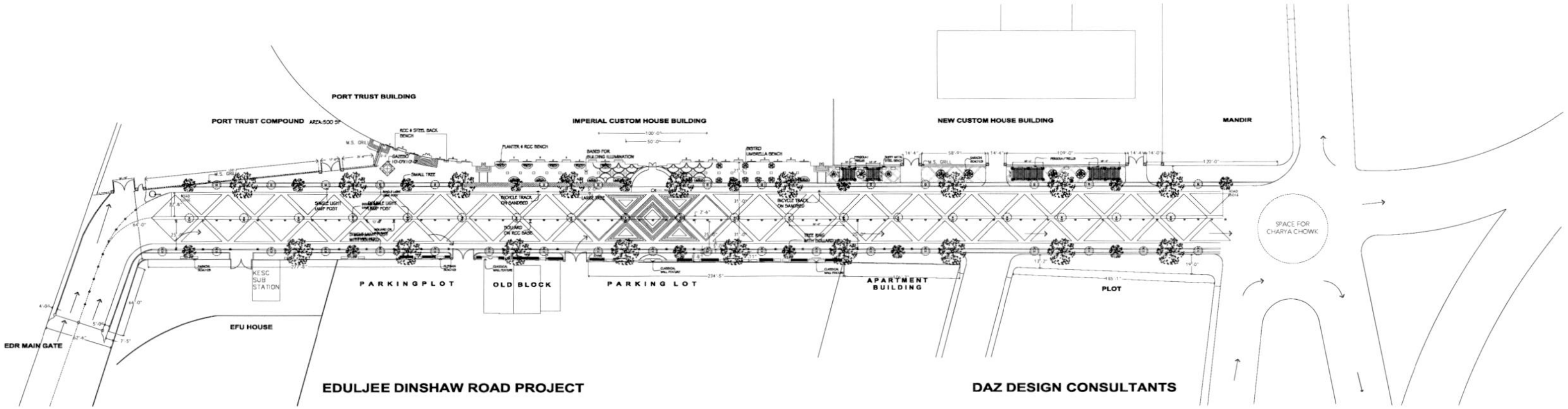

FIGURE 11.2 **Master Plan of Eduljee Dinshaw Road Project, Karachi, Pakistan**

(figure continues next page)

b. Street-level elevation

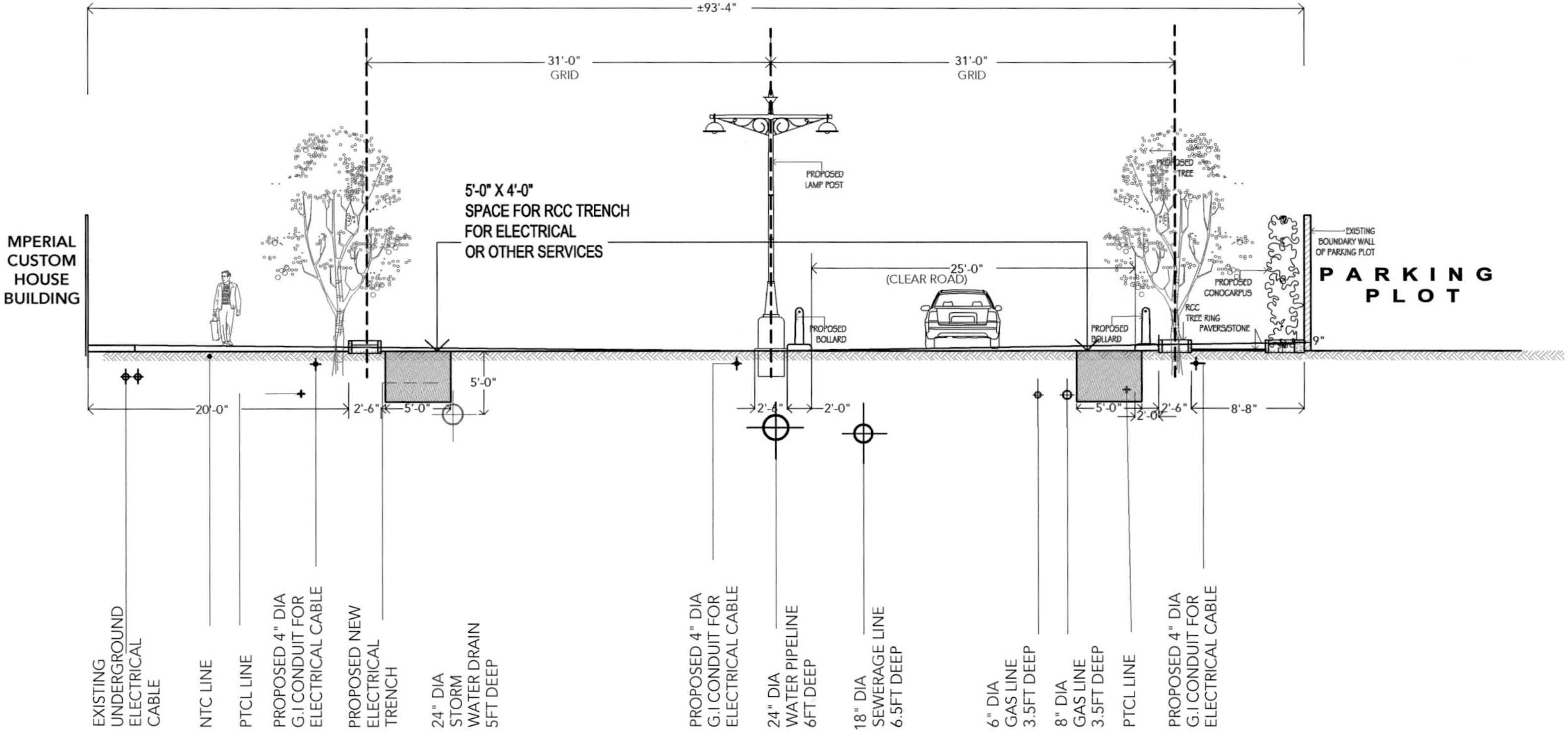

FIGURE 11.2 **Master Plan of Eduljee Dinshaw Road Project, Karachi, Pakistan (*Continued*)**

Source: ©Danish Azar Zuby. Reproduced, with permission, from Danish Azar Zuby; further permission required for reuse.

planters, and benches. All other street furniture—including street lighting, main gates, and classic details on the parking lot walls—were designed by the project team to reflect the local historical background as part of EDR's overall design concept.

Phase 3: Implementation

The success of the EDR project stems from the core EDRPT team's conscious effort to make the process participatory and sustainable. The EDRPT supervised the design and construction process, and the team endeavored to take on board all the stakeholders to make key decisions. One of the aims was to ensure that EDR could receive the needed political and financial support, so that it wouldn't need to rely heavily on the public sector for its funding and implementation.

The proposed design scheme was finalized in several meetings. A fund-raising scheme raised the amount required for project completion, mostly from the private sector. A slogan, "Give Back to the City," was used as part of the campaign to realize the project. The project took about a year to complete, costing about PRs 50 million (US$500,000).[4]

Given the project's focus on sustainability and reviving the entire neighborhood, the first step of implementation was to fix the overflowing sewerage lines (photo 11.2, panel a). The road was upgraded with slopes and improved drainage systems to avoid flooding after rain. Manhole covers were also designed to match the EDR aesthetic. Pavement works also needed to be completed quickly because the EDR served as an important service road for citizens. The work was challenging for the EDRPT. For example, during the EDR project implementation, there was no space to store removed tarmac because the work was carried out in a very constrained space. Existing underground infrastructure, including the water pipes and telephone and gas lines, had to be managed because they were connected to the office buildings and apartments at the end of the road. To limit interruptions to building access and services, the strategies included night shifts and prioritizing the completion of key components such as pedestrian walkways.

During the implementation stage, many design components were revisited to address newly found challenges. For example, while the team was working on cleaning the façades of the Imperial Customs House, it realized that all the doors and windows needed to be repaired to improve accessibility. Several old, unused arched doors of the building were cleaned and made functional again (photo 11.2, panel b). An effort was also made to design and install the main gates at the EDR so as to provide the Port Trust Building with a separate access point for traffic.

Renovation of private shop fronts opposite the restored Custom House was the most difficult part of the EDR project to implement. Shop owners were of the view that the EDRPT should pay for cleanup as well as improvements. Although a unified design for shop fronts was provided, shop owners refused to share the upgrade costs (photo 11.2, panels c and d). The issue was eventually resolved by funding this renovation under the EDR funds (Zuby 2015).

Other interventions that sought to improve the surrounding neighborhood areas included reviving the neighborhood's Hindu temple, Jhule Lal Mandir, to restore its historic appearance; relocating and renovating the

a. Before: Main road's informal parking lot and dumping area
b. After: Walkable pedestrian street
c. Before: Private shop entrances and apartments
d. After: Cleaned and redesigned exteriors

PHOTO 11.2 **Views of Components before and after EDR Project Implementation, Karachi, Pakistan**

Source: ©Danish Azar Zuby. Reproduced, with permission, from Danish Azar Zuby; further permission required for reuse.
Note: EDR = Eduljee Dinshaw Road.

Custom House Museum; improving the triangular space between the Port Trust Building and Mandir Temple with the introduction of a fountain for visitors and installation of statues depicting Pakistani heroes; and creating performing areas for local artists.

Phase 4: Management

The EDRPT also manages ongoing activities along with the EDR projects. A maintenance committee supported by dedicated staff has been established to oversee maintenance works on-site. Most of the required funds are generated through donations from local stakeholders such as government offices and local businesses. The Custom House has assumed responsibility for maintaining the upgraded pedestrianized street and related services.

As a public space, the EDR also serves as an active space for outdoor events, such as "Qawwali" musical events, that attract large audiences. The EDRPT oversees the registration of social events and recruited event management companies to support coordinating the details of registered events.

Phase 5: Impact Evaluation

Through citizen action, the street that was once an unpleasant space, often flooded with sewage and trash and overrun by parked vehicles, is now an active public space and enjoyed by people. The transformation is depicted in the "before" and "after" comparisons that illustrate how this street has been dramatically converted into a pleasant, pedestrian-friendly space without garbage dumping, uncontrolled parking, or dirty shop fronts. This change made the EDR safer and enabled families to come out and enjoy the EDR even after dark (photo 11.3).

Another measure of the EDR project's success is the number of culturally significant or major events that were organized on the road, attracting visitors from both the city and elsewhere. For example, this was the location where the finals of the cricket match of the Pakistan Super League was screened. The success of the outdoor screening event, which attracted crowds, subsequently led to an online poll, seeking feedback from citizens about what other content should be aired for the public.

The EDR has become a venue for national commemoration as well. For the 70th anniversary of the independence of Pakistan in 2017, the EDR displayed many artworks to celebrate the rich biodiversity of Pakistan's landscape. The Italian artist Maurizio Boscheri painted 70 flora and fauna species of Pakistan and presented the works as a gift from the Italian people to Pakistan and its people. The artwork was placed on the EDR, signifying the importance of the space and levels of citizen visitation that it draws. On the 69th Independence Day of Pakistan, Chronicles of Khan, a musical group, performed on the EDR among the performers for the Azadi Rocks Festival, where leading singers of the country participated. And a candlelight vigil was recently held in remembrance of a famous singer, Amjad Sabri.

PHOTO 11.3 **Pedestrian-Friendly Space at Night on Eduljee Dinshaw Road, Karachi, Pakistan**

Source: ©Danish Azar Zuby. Used, with permission, from Danish Azar Zuby; further permission required for reuse.

PAKISTAN CHOWK INITIATIVE

Phase 1: Context

Pakistan Chowk is located within a historic educational area that is also the location of one of Karachi's busiest taxi stations (known as the Purana Tonga Stand). The Pakistan Law House, a bookseller and publisher that had become a hub for discussing academic and political issues, is also located in the area. Many restaurants and shops near the square serve communities and tourists as well as students from nearby institutions. The square hosted various cultural activities, and in the 1980s a marble monument was established in the square with trees. Pakistan Chowk has remained a significant heritage site, bringing together people from various cultural and religious backgrounds for public debate and discussion.

As the condition of the historic downtown in Karachi deteriorated over time, Pakistan Chowk also lost its sense of place. From the early 1990s, the monument in the square has been defaced by political slogans, and the Chowk turned into the largest public dumping place in the neighborhood. While the amount of waste increased, there were no proper disposal facilities. Increasing inequality between social classes in Karachi also led to the restriction of culture and arts, and growing security issues in the Chowk limited public uses over a few decades in the name of public safety (Khalid 2017).

To address this chaos, a group of civic society activists led by Marvi Mazhar formed the Pakistan Chowk Initiative (PCI) in 2016 to lead community mobilization and the rejuvenation of the historic neighborhood of Saddar, which faced urban blight. The PCI identified 33 public squares as pilot projects for improvement and subsequently successfully lobbied for political support from Sharmila Farouqi, a parliamentarian and member of the Pakistan People's Party (PPP). As one of the first initiatives, she offered personal donations for the restoration of Pakistan Chowk in Aram Bagh Quarter. The intent was to reclaim this significant public space and to give it back to the community.

Phase 2: Planning and Design

The designs for the Chowk were developed by a German design consulting firm, Zoohaus. The Goethe Institute in Karachi had initially connected Zoohaus and the PCI to design a public installation at Pakistan Chowk as part of a joint research project titled "Urbanities—Art and Public Spaces in Pakistan."[5] The design concept aimed to revitalize the Chowk as an urban cultural hub by applying simple placemaking approaches. This included installing benches, art sculptures, and trees as well as repaving and cleaning up the square (figure 11.3).

The PCI consulted and engaged stakeholders for the restoration of Pakistan Chowk, including local architects,[6] government officials, and civil society representatives. Members of the Pakistan Chowk business and trading community, including the Garakha Welfare Trust and the Tajir (trader) Community of Old Town, were involved in the design process through Muhalla Saazi (community dialogue). Later, the District Municipal Corporation (South) was brought on board.

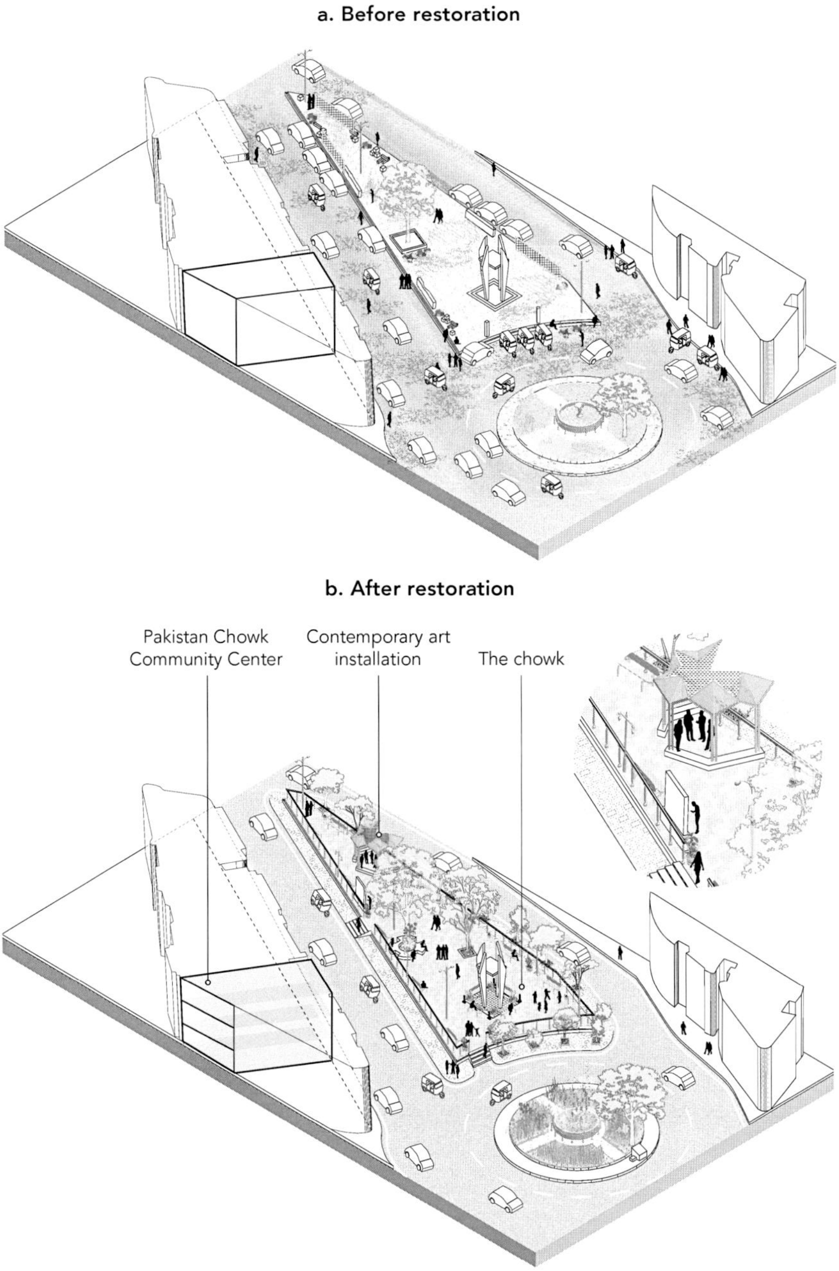

FIGURE 11.3 **Pakistan Chowk Restoration Project, Karachi, Pakistan**

Source: ©World Bank. Further permission required for reuse.

Phase 3: Implementation

The cost for restoration of Pakistan Chowk was estimated at PRs 8 million (about US$8,000), which was funded partly by a personal donation[7] and partly by the Goethe Institute. At the 2016 Goethe Institute conference in Munich, the Institute donated approximately US$3,000 to the PCI, which was used to set up the Pakistan Chowk Community Center (PCCC). The restoration project was headed by the Marvi Mazhar and Associates architecture firm as a pro bono venture. It took nine months to complete the restoration of Pakistan Chowk (December 2016 to August 2017).[8]

The Chowk renovations included the installation of 32 benches, each named after a prominent resident of Karachi, such as Abdul Sattar Edhi, Sabeen Mahmud, and Parveen Rehman, who advocated for and worked toward more inclusive civic engagement in the city. Trees were planted, and massive cleaning of the area was carried out. The project team installed lampposts, dustbins, a history board, and a contemporary art installation in collaboration with the German design team, Zoohaus, and in doing all of this transformed a garbage dump into an urban cultural hub.[9]

Meanwhile, community mobilization began to take place. Called Muhalla Sazi (community building), this community movement sought to ensure community participation for the project and promoted demand-based activities. The local community then began to use this space and participated in events such as art fairs and events focused on music and reading. An Earth Day celebration and Mulaqat Over Chai (meeting over tea) also took place at the Chowk. On the weekends, artists began to use the Chowk as a space to paint and sketch.

The number of public-space activities signaled the importance of having a more permanent presence in the area. The PCCC, established to meet this demand, was housed on the first floor of the historic Sultani Mahal Building, just 30 feet away from Pakistan Chowk. The PCI established the PCCC to make available different forms of arts, culture, and literature activities to all members of the Old Town community. Moreover, the PCCC is a space that the residents can take ownership of, experiment with, and use. These activities were seen as also helping to improve social cohesion with the communities living in the historic downtown. The Chowk has become an open space that facilitates events such as art fairs and musical celebrations, while the PCCC complemented the open space by serving as an enclosed space for more intimate gatherings.[10]

Phase 4: Management

The PCI maintains the Pakistan Chowk and curates cultural programing at the PCCC along with community members and artists. After the PCCC opened, the I AM KARACHI (IAK) movement donated approximately US$5,000 for PCCC operations. The IAK Pakistan Chowk Cultural Initiative, active from October 2017 to January 2018, sponsored activities such as art classes, arts fairs, and reading and storytelling sessions in which a total of 742 people participated—405 male and 337 female. Presently, the PCCC works on a nonprofit model, sustained through the personal funds of Marvi Mazhar and donations from civil society.[11]

Although this model currently works well, people have raised concerns that public spaces in Karachi will face critical challenges going forward, including how they can be sustainability managed, particularly if there is no long-term commitment by the public and private sectors to help manage these spaces. This project has demonstrated that participatory community design is an important process that should be incorporated as part of public-space rehabilitation.[12] There are also strong views that design of public spaces as places for social cohesion in Karachi should be prioritized, and it will be important for the local government to engage with such ideas and be a partner to enhance the longevity and sustainability of public spaces in Karachi.

Phase 5: Impact Evaluation

The PCI has successfully contributed to the enhancement of a part of the historic downtown. The "before" and "after" comparisons show how the Chowk has been cleaned up and transformed for public use. New seating arrangements invite people, and historical assets such as the monument and a mature tree have been preserved as part of the public-space improvement works (photo 11.4).

a. Before: Pakistan Chowk monument, 2014

b. After: Pakistan Chowk monument, 2017

c. Before: Chowk area without seating

d. After: New paving and benches for visitors

PHOTO 11.4 **Views of Pakistan Chowk Components before and after the PCI, Karachi, Pakistan**

Source: ©World Bank. Further permission required for reuse.
Note: PCI = Pakistan Chowk Initiative.

The rejuvenated space has been used for numerous community activities that help improve social cohesion. For example, the PCCC regularly organizes events that engage the local community and foster networking as well as participation by other civil society groups and stakeholders. For example, an "open mic" event is held regularly where people share experiences, problems, and ideas. A "Talking Circle" event creates a space where people come together and talk about issues that affect their immediate environment and provides a platform to initiate community action.

A major outcome of the project is that the events organized in the Chowk and at the PCCC have attracted people from all over the city, from different backgrounds and walks of life. The public space has reportedly been able to bring together people from different socioeconomic and age groups around common community activities.[13] At the time of this writing, an estimated total of 65 events have been organized by the PCCC, all within the span of eight months, with an average participation rate of about 120 people for outdoor events and 30 people for indoor events.[14]

I AM KARACHI MOVEMENT

Phase 1: Context

The I AM KARACHI (IAK) movement began as a civic campaign in 2011. It has transformed from a donor-funded initiative by the U.S. Agency for International Development (USAID) into an independent nongovernmental organization (NGO) focused on the reclamation of public spaces in Karachi. It started as a response to the growing violence in public places and the resulting loss of life in the city. Because of detrimental social and cultural shifts, public spaces in Karachi have declined in quality, in number, and in accessibility. IAK aims to spur cultural rejuvenation, creativity, and expression by getting people to engage in dialogue and interact in public spaces. Most importantly, IAK's main focus is on youth engagement, because the young are the group most vulnerable to crime and violence in Karachi.

IAK has been working on reclaiming the vibrant culture and lost avenues of exchange of ideas, art, music, theater, cinema, and sports that Karachi was famous for, while also creating safe public spaces. Increasing violence based on ethnic, political, and religious differences has caused people to segregate themselves for protection. IAK believes that revived public spaces can provide neutral ground where people can gather and start the healing process.[15]

Phases 2 and 3: Planning, Design, and Implementation

IAK's public-space initiative is built on several pillars, including its Walls of Peace and IAK SPORT projects.

Walls of Peace

An initial flagship pilot project was the creation of "IAK Walls of Peace" to spread messages of peace and harmony across the city. In Karachi, public façades and walls are often filled with aggressive, politically charged graffiti that negatively affects the urban environment. IAK's initiative sought to replace the graffiti with art and messages celebrating Karachi's heritage and cultural and ethnic diversity. By 2017, IAK had painted 800 walls, extending approximately 457 feet, focusing on six neighborhoods that have been victims of urban violence.

The IAK Walls of Peace project was designed and implemented through nine steps (IAK 2017):

1. Walls were identified and shortlisted after site visits.
2. The walls were measured and documented in their current conditions.
3. A design concept was chosen depending on local contexts.
4. Non-objection criteria were attained for the selected sites.
5. Research on visual criteria was conducted to create specific designs.
6. Designs were collected through design competitions, attracting local and international artists, and then selected and approved by IAK and shared with artisans for implementation.
7. The walls were prepared by plastering and cementing them to create clean, flat surfaces for painting.
8. Artisans began work at the sites to implement the designs on the walls. The walls were varnished after completion.
9. Surveys were carried out throughout to collect public feedback.

Among the numerous IAK Walls of Peace sites that have been successfully implemented, the work at the H. J. Rustomjee Bagh private residential complex, housing 20 apartments, is an example that best represents IAK's values. The site is near many schools in the area and is a neighborhood with students, parents, and teachers with diverse ethnic backgrounds.

Seventy-six walls in this area were selected for the project, with the objective of using wall art to promote diversity and inclusion. On these walls, IAK composed a "storybook" propagating themes of hope, pride, ownership, and diversity. The entire wall can be read as an enchanting story that includes fun anecdotes, hidden places, and the rich and complex history of Karachi. Heritage sites, religious institutions, and food culture specific to a variety of ethnicities were also beautifully depicted by the paintings and artwork on these walls. Local painter Gulraiz Khan and calligrapher Zia-Ur-Rehman Khan were hired to work on the designs and text (IAK 2017).

IAK SPORT

IAK also initiated an IAK SPORT program that revived 14 sports fields in Karachi. Accessibility to sport facilities can be a game changer for youth, especially in underprivileged areas. IAK SPORT relies on funding through private sector and philanthropic support. The cost to restore all the sports venues was estimated to be around PRs 730,000 per academy, disbursed in an in-kind support format. In addition, PRs 20,000 was to be set aside as staff support for each academy. IAK SPORT has developed a mobile boxing ring and is engaging youth in underprivileged areas like Lyari, where communities have affinities toward sports activities but are not well served with any facilities (IAK 2017).

Phase 4: Management

Managing the facilities that IAK has helped create has been critically challenging. Even though IAK had planned out a budget for the maintenance for all the completed Walls of Peace, it has been difficult to maintain the facilities and scale up to other neighborhoods across the city with limited funding and support from the local government. IAK indicated that, in the long run, wide-scale and sustainable change requires much more government support and facilitation.

On the positive side, it is not costly to sustain the quality of the renovated walls once they are implemented. Some of the walls painted five years ago remain intact with little or no additional intervention from IAK. Also, the funding and volunteer support from communities and the private sector has been most encouraging.

Phase 5: Impact Evaluation

The IAK Walls of Peace campaign has been an instant success story because of its innovative nature, high visibility, and inclusiveness. It brought together citizens from a variety of backgrounds to participate, including university students, local communities, artists (more than 270 so far), and designers. In time, organizations other than IAK took up Walls of Peace. Many local artists who participated in the project expressed that it has created behavioral changes in communities by transforming the walls' depressed look to a delightful, beautiful, and modern depiction of cultural heritage that people can be proud of (Qamar 2016).

IAK SPORT has had an impact on five sports activities: cricket, football, hockey, badminton, and tennis. A total of 14 IAK SPORT facilities are located across 10 neighborhoods that have been revived, including Malir, Lyari, Old Golimar, Korangi, Mauripur, and Shireen Jinnah Colony. These are generally poorer neighborhoods with few amenities. The initiative has directly benefited more than 5,000 people, including 1,500 women. Combined, the IAK SPORT and Walls of Peace projects have demonstrated the great potential in providing social benefits through the revitalization of public spaces in Karachi.

NOTES

1. Data from "Block Wise Provisional Summary Results of 6th Population & Housing Census-2017 [as on January 03, 2018]," Population Census, Pakistan Bureau of Statistics (accessed May 15, 2018), http://www.pbs.gov.pk/content/block-wise-provisional-summary-results-6th-population-housing-census-2017-january-03-2018.
2. An "amenity plot" refers to a plot allocated exclusively for amenity uses as defined in chapter 19 of *The Karachi Building & Town Planning Regulations* (Khan 2002). Specific amenity uses include government uses (19-2.2.1); health and welfare uses (19-2.2.4); religious uses (19-2.2.5); parks and playgrounds (19-2.2.7); burial grounds (19-2.2.8); transportation right of way (19-2.2.9); parking (19-2.2.10); and recreational areas (19-2.2.12).

3. Members of the EDRPT included the commissioner of Karachi City, Shoaib Siddique; architect Shahid Abdulla; former Citizens-Police Liaison Committee cochairman Jameel Yusuf; and financial adviser Meraj Zuberi.
4. Interview with Danish Azar Zuby, by Farhan Anwar, on design details of the EDR project, April 5, 2018.
5. "Urbanities—Art and Public Spaces in Pakistan" was a joint project of the Goethe Institute Pakistan and the Lahore Biennale Foundation, in collaboration with Vasl Artists' Collective, Annemarie-Schimmel-Haus, and Marvi Mazhar & Associates.
6. These included renowned city architects such as Arif Bilgaumi, Zain Mustafa, Maryam Ifthikhar, and Ali Reza Dossal.
7. The donation was from Sharmila Farouqui.
8. Interview with Marvi Mazhar, by Farhan Anwar, on details of the Pakistan Chowk Initiative project process, March 19, 2018.
9. Interview with Marvi Mazhar, March 19, 2018.
10. Interview with Sabahat Zehra, by Farhan Anwar, on the establishment of the Pakistan Chowk Community Center, November 20, 2017.
11. Interview with Marvi Mazhar, March 19, 2018.
12. Interview with Marvi Mazhar, March 19, 2018.
13. Interview with Sabahat Zehra, November 20, 2017.
14. Interview with Marvi Mazhar, March 19, 2018.
15. Interview with IAK Executive Director Ambareen Kazim Thompson, by Farhan Anwar, on the background of the I AM KARACHI Movement, November 27, 2017.

REFERENCES

Anwar, Farhan. 2015. "A Vision to Reclaim the Streets of Karachi." *Express Tribune*, August 24.

Azam, Muhammad, and Farkhunda Burke. 2018. "Green Spaces and Governance." *Dawn*, April 22.

CDGK (City District Government Karachi). 2007. "Karachi Strategic Development Plan 2020." Planning document, Master Plan Group of Offices, CDGK, Karachi, Pakistan.

EIU (Economist Intelligence Unit). 2017. "Global Liveability Report 2017." Annual Urban Quality-of-Life Ranking Report, EIU, London.

Express Tribune. 2018. "Karachi's City Administration Launches 'Adopt a Footpath Initiative,'" November 2.

Hasan, Arif. 2010. "The Growth of a Metropolis, Karachi." In *Karachi: Megacity of Our Times*, edited by Hamida Khuhro and Anwer Mooraj, 171–96. Oxford: Oxford University Press.

IAK (I AM KARACHI). 2017. "I AM KARACHI Walls of Peace." Digital book, Vasl Artists' Collective Publication Series, Karachi. https://issuu.com/vaslartistscollective/docs/walls_of_peace_digital_book-issuu.

Khalid, Awais. 2017. "The Pakistan Chowk Initiative." *Youlin Magazine*, August 28.

Khan, Mahfooz Yar. 2002. *The Karachi Building & Town Planning Regulations*. Karachi: Asia Law House.

Qamar, Saadia. 2016. "'Walls of Peace': Painting of 457-Foot-Long Wall Complete." *Express Tribune*, October 16.

Rustomji, Behram Sohrab H. J. 1952. *Karachi, 1839–1947: A Short History of the Foundation and Growth of Karachi*. Karachi: Excelsior Electric Printing Works.

UNDP (United Nations Development Programme). 2017. *Pakistan National Human Development Report: Unleashing the Potential of a Young Pakistan*. Islamabad, Pakistan: UNDP.

World Bank. 2018. *Transforming Karachi into a Livable and Competitive Megacity: A City Diagnostic and Transformation Strategy*. Directions in Development Series. Washington, DC: World Bank.

Zuby, Danish Azar. 2015. "The Design and Making of EDULJEE DINSHAW ROAD." Unpublished paper, Karachi.

CHAPTER 12

LIMA, PERU: TRANSFORMING FRAGMENTED AREAS INTO INCLUSIVE PUBLIC SPACES THROUGH LOCAL GOVERNANCE

Sofía García Núñez

KEY TAKEAWAYS

- Public spaces in Lima are scarce and inequitably distributed for several reasons: the city's fragmented governance has led to inadequate provision of services in low-income districts, and maintaining green spaces is expensive in a city built on desert where it rarely rains. A history of sociospatial segregation and violence has also resulted in public spaces becoming fenced, overly regulated, and isolated from people.
- In this context, the local government of San Isidro, Lima's wealthiest district, started a public space initiative, "+Ciudad," to make the district inclusive and provide quality plazas, parks, and street space for the enjoyment of all citizens. Plaza 31, Las Begonias Street, and Parque Ecológico showed that inclusive public spaces can benefit not only a specific neighborhood but also the entire city, physically and socially connecting people and spaces.

- Plaza 31 has been transformed from a set of underused parking lots to a popular gathering place that serves San Isidro and its immediate lower-income neighbor district, Surquillo. Las Begonias, a streetscape intervention, helped reassert San Isidro financial district as a city destination for local residents and more than 800,000 daily commuters and visitors. The Parque Ecológico site had been used for storage spaces and municipal offices that interrupted access along the city's 9-kilometer coastline. A vision to transform the site into places for urban farming, local markets, and spaces for respite is being planned and implemented.

CITY DYNAMICS

Context and Background

In Peru, one of the most capital-centric countries in the world, sits Lima, a city of 10 million people that extends for 1,500 square miles, concentrates 32 percent of the country's population, and accounts for 45 percent of the national gross domestic product (GDP; Berube et al. 2015). Since the mid-1950s, Lima began to experience an unprecedented stream of migration. Informal and precarious settlements rapidly expanded on Lima's periphery, facilitated by a general laissez-faire in the government, lack of housing policy, and weak law enforcement (Driant 1991). The rapid and unplanned urbanization has increased not only the disparities between the capital city and the rest of the country but also the inequalities within Lima. Most families in Lima live in substandard houses; rarely pay property taxes; and have inadequate waste collection, public spaces, security, and public transport (Lima Cómo Vamos 2018).

Lima's governance and institutional structure is marked by deep fragmentation and challenging institutional coordination. It has a metropolitan government with one elected mayor. However, the city is also composed of 43 local districts, each with an elected local mayor, municipal tax collection, and a significant degree of autonomy from the metropolitan municipality. Moreover, within the 3,000 square kilometers of territory commonly known as Lima sits El Callao, an independent province and one of the 25 regions of Peru. Its territory of 132 square kilometers comprises seven local districts with the same institutional characteristics and functions as those in Lima. In total, then, one metropolitan municipality, one regional government, one provincial municipality, and 50 local governments represent, govern, and manage this vast metropolitan capital city. This chapter, when referring to Lima, will refer to Metropolitan Lima and El Callao.

In addition, people, polling companies, and researchers have unofficially divided the city into five interdistrict groups that share characteristics: Lima Center, Lima North, Lima South, Lima East, and Callao. The population distribution is widely differentiated among these zones: although 1.9 million people live throughout the 16 districts of Lima Center, one single district of Lima East—San Juan de Lurigancho—concentrates 1.1 million people (Vega Centeno 2017).

This fragmented form of governance is detrimental to how citizens perceive their communities and the duties that local governments have toward them. As urban sociologist Pablo Vega Centeno indicates, the atomization of local governments in Lima has accentuated the concept of "neighbors" to the detriment of "citizens." Local governments are pressured by their constituents to meet their demands and pay less attention to those who are transient (Vega Centeno 2017). The problem is that, in a large urban agglomeration like Lima, many *nonresident* inhabitants—also referred to as "floating population"—do "live" or remain in territories away from their home areas longer than the actual residents (Vega Centeno 2017). As will be seen later, this misperception of citizenry hugely affects the management of public spaces.

Public Spaces in Lima

Public Space as a Luxury Good

Public spaces are scarce and unequally distributed in Lima. Given that Lima is a city built on a desert and that it rarely rains, maintaining green areas is expensive; therefore, gardens and parks are predominant in central wealthy districts of Lima that can afford to water them.[1] Although 38.7 percent of the population in Lima Center lives less than a block away from a park, only 17.8 percent does so in Lima South.

These disparities are reflected in surveys of citizen satisfaction with public spaces in their districts. In the 2018 Lima Cómo Vamos survey, 47.8 percent of the population in Lima Center was satisfied with the provision of public spaces in their neighborhoods, but only 9.4 percent felt the same in Lima South (Lima Cómo Vamos 2018). Interestingly, when the same question was formulated regarding satisfaction with public spaces in the *city*, as opposed to the *neighborhood*, the data were inverted: in Lima Center, satisfaction dropped to 34.1 percent, while in Lima South, satisfaction grew to 23.7 percent. This reveals the importance of improving public spaces at a metropolitan level and the role of the city in improving the quality of life of neighbors who live in poor districts.

Municipalities tend to overlook the importance of quality public spaces under their limited financial and technical capacities, in part because of the urgency of other challenges. Nearly half of the recently cited survey respondents indicated they are unsatisfied with the way authorities manage and take care of public spaces. However, only 5.2 percent of respondents considered the poor quality or insufficient quantity of public spaces to be an urgent matter in Lima (Lima Cómo Vamos 2018). Respondents considered insecurity and violence, poor public transport, and insufficient solid waste collection to be much more important issues.

This survey also suggests that citizens may be underestimating the importance to city livability of investing in good public spaces. For instance, in 2017, commuters in Lima spent on average more than two hours per day in transportation, and 61.8 percent of commuters did so on foot, not because the city is walkable but because there are no other adequate public transport modes (CAF 2017). In this regard, as global experience suggests, investing in pedestrian-friendly sidewalks, crosswalks, and other public spaces can significantly improve safety and mobility for pedestrians and commuters.

Class, Growth, and Terrorism: A Brief History of Detachment from Public Spaces

Until the 1950s, Lima was a capital city that maintained the class and power structures from colonial times. From its independence from colonial Spain up to the first half of the 20th century, the Peruvian ruling class (primarily of European origin) limited the city's ability to change and safeguarded elite power over the indigenous and working class (Ludeña 2002). At the beginning of the century, important public spaces were envisioned and built primarily for the mobility, enjoyment, and recreation of the ruling class. Such spaces included the Plaza San Martín, the city parks Parque de la Exposición and Parque de la Reserva, and the big avenues with promenades like Arequipa and Salaverry (Vega Centeno 2013).

From the second half of the 20th century onward, two particular processes contributed to the detachment of citizens from public spaces: the first related to the way the city grew, and the second to the sociopolitical upheaval of the 1980s. Two urbanization processes shaped public spaces in Lima: formal developments in suburban areas and the informal process of urbanization (Fernández-Maldonado 2007; Vega Centeno 2017). In the Metropolitan Development Plan for Lima-Callao 1967–1980, clearly influenced by the modernist era, the streets and avenues that connect Lima Center to suburban developments were conceived as road networks where sidewalks were kept to a minimum rather than designed as public spaces (Vega Centeno 2017). In the new "formal" city, parks were designed for recreational purposes for those who lived in the neighborhoods, with several use restrictions and closely monitored by local municipalities (Vega Centeno 2017).

Meanwhile, large areas of land were reserved on the periphery for the "parques zonales" (zonal parks) to serve the informal expansion of the city. Today there are eight of these large, open recreational spaces—some as big as 66 hectares—in Lima North, Lima South, and Lima East. Although these parks are necessary and very much used by the population, they were not designed to integrate organically into the urban grid. Instead they have a dividing peripheral wall, which prevents them from functioning as collective public spaces that are freely accessible to all citizens (Vega Centeno 2006). Moreover, the Municipality of Lima renamed the parks as "zonal clubs" and doubled the entrance ticket price. The "zonal club" denomination has been harshly criticized by experts in Lima. One researcher indicates that it "distorts the meaning of these spaces, disrupts their role as a public facility, and reduces them to be 'exclusive' and paid recreation centers" (Facho 2018).

Later on, in the 1980s, Lima withdrew from the creation of accessible public spaces, mainly for security reasons. The country suffered its deepest economic crisis and was hit by brutal attacks from terrorist groups such as Shining Path and the Túpac Amaru Revolutionary Movement. These groups were active in Lima through the mid-1980s, exploding car bombs, kidnapping citizens, and causing panic throughout the capital. The population responded by raising walls between houses' setbacks and sidewalks, putting concrete blocks in residential areas to thwart vehicle attacks, and adding control gates to restrict nonresidents' access to their streets (figure 12.1). Parks and public spaces in general were less and less used. Now that terrorist groups have

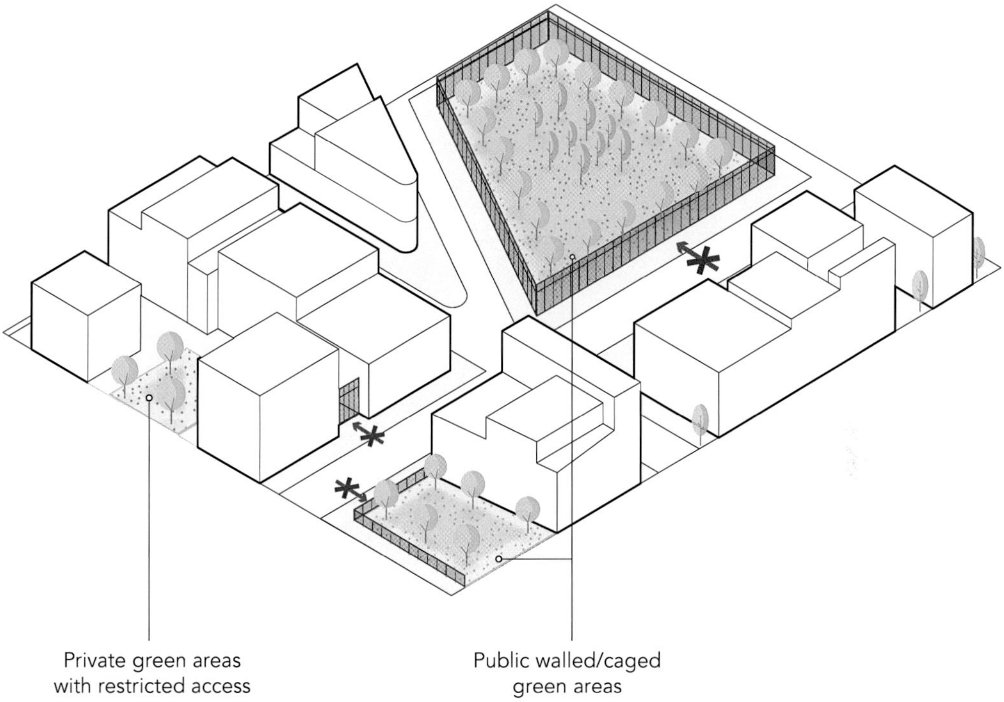

FIGURE 12.1 **Lima, Peru: A Caged City**

Source: ©World Bank. Further permission required for reuse.

pacified, insecurity has persisted in the capital city. An estimated 3,000 barriers blocked access to streets, and close to 400,000 people lived in these "fortified neighborhoods" (Plöger 2006). In 2010, it was estimated that more than 90 percent of these gates had been built illegally, without municipal authorization (Radio Capital 2015).

Fortification of public spaces is planned and financed by neighbors in response to the insecurity in their districts, fundamentally based on the fear of "others" who are not part of the neighborhood (Vega Centeno 2017). In 2016, 40 percent of citizens in Lima thought that when neighbors agreed among themselves, they had the right to install gates and restrict access to strangers (Vega Centeno 2017). In upper-class districts like San Isidro and Miraflores, citizens have protested on several occasions that they were prevented from using district parks as nonresidents on account of their race (Liza 2015).

Perversely, in a city governed by atomized local governments, locality can bring much discrimination. Local residents fortify and subscribe to the view that authorities must attend only to the needs of district residents, not to the needs of a city as a whole. As a result, the disconnection between citizens and their right to public spaces has also diminished their potential to reclaim them and has put pressure on authorities to defend public space from different forms of discrimination and privatization that limit free access to them.

"+Ciudad": A Public Space Recovery Policy by San Isidro Municipality

Context of the (Mis)conception of Public Spaces in San Isidro

San Isidro is one of oldest and most privileged neighborhoods in Lima. It was originally planned as a low-density residential area with big, single-family house plots; a private golf club; and tranquil streets. However, because of its central location, strategic connection to the rest of the city, and high environmental quality, San Isidro underwent a process of urban densification. Through the construction of tall residential towers on the perimeter of the golf club and along main avenues, the district started to change its urban character and land use. As banks and businesses moved their headquarters from downtown Lima to San Isidro, the district also became the city's major financial quarter. San Isidro has become an aging district and has lost part of its younger population because of the lack of affordable housing supply, which has been limited by zoning and extremely high land values.[2]

As the district's land uses and demographics changed, the local government struggled with serving conflicting interests of stakeholders. On the one hand, San Isidro comprises around 58,100 residents who are mostly old and rich people. The residents prioritized privacy, low-density buildings, more road space for cars and public parking, and a highly restrictive use of public spaces. On the other hand, a much larger population of around 800,000 people who do not live in the district commute daily to San Isidro, especially in the areas around the financial center for work and other activities. They comprise mainly young adults who are 18–45 years old (San Isidro Municipality 2016). The good service delivery—such as security, waste collection, and park maintenance—that residents regularly receive is mainly funded by property taxes on the district's commercial and financial activity, which in turn has attracted a more diversified population to San Isidro (San Isidro Municipality 2015).

However, over time, the municipal government's planning decisions started to become responsive only to the demands of residents, and this had contributed to the different forms of "privatization" of public spaces. The municipality expanded parking lots and planned overly regulated parks with little or no sitting for users. As a result, public spaces in the district were filled with cars, inactive parks that were devoid of visitors, and residential areas that lacked a vibrant mix of uses. The result was that younger people started to avoid the district.

2015: The Start of Urban and Political Transformation

In October 2014, the local government, under the leadership of San Isidro Mayor Manuel Velarde, launched a new initiative to reverse these trends: the "+Ciudad" program, which focused on leveraging abandoned public spaces to create a continuous corridor of safe streets and vibrant public spaces throughout the district.

What made this initiative remarkable in Lima was its wealthiest district's efforts to turn into an inclusive district for the benefit of the city. It should be noted that San Isidro represents only 0.58 percent of the population of Lima, occupies around 1 percent of the built environment, and had an executed budget in 2016 of US$14,604 per capita, whereas the average for Lima was US$1,962 per capita (CEPLAN 2017). To share this affluence with all citizens beyond the district's residents, the program's strategy was twofold: First, it would foster the recovery of public spaces that residents perceived as dangerous, which had driven them instead to private spaces such as clubs or houses for recreational use. Second, it would create quality public spaces for visitors and commuters. +Ciudad represented a paradigm shift toward the use of public space to catalyze a greater process of community creation.[3]

The +Ciudad program was planned at different urban scales (neighborhood, district, and metropolis) using evidence-based approaches. In 2015, for the first time in the San Isidro district, a comprehensive study on the quality of parks and streets was made, including the affluence of users and pedestrians.[4] This research helped to identify the projects to be carried out under the program and to inform the specific interventions and methods of implementation. Although there is no complete inventory of every intervention made at every scale under the umbrella of +Ciudad, according to available data from the municipality, the program recovered approximately 95,000 square meters and 183,000 square meters of public land in 2015 and 2017, respectively, with a total investment of US$6.4 million.[5]

+Ciudad was a multisectoral program that recovered and revitalized public space through a mixture of physical interventions, redefinition of traditional civic culture, and activities focused on social integration. The program created an intersectoral management platform within the municipality that oversaw the efficient use of resources directed toward the objective of creating a humane city (San Isidro Municipality 2018c). This platform was initiated and led by the Urban Planning Office (OPU), which was in charge of the project, in close cooperation with other units such as the Sustainability Office, Public Works Office, Cultural Office, Human Development Office, and Risk Management Office. According to the mayor, this approach to enhancing local governance and the recovery of public spaces also required a budget reform: "We had to cut the current expenditure and redirect that budget to public investment." At the same time, "we had to work with different units to align their budgets toward the execution of different components of one same project."[6]

The +Ciudad program has been successful in transforming public spaces and improving the quality of life for San Isidro residents and Lima citizens. In September 2018, the Municipality of San Isidro received an international award from the Iberoamerican Union of Municipalities for its actions to recover public spaces in favor of a more humane city. It was possible for local interventions in San Isidro to improve the quality of life in greater Lima because of San Isidro's central location, its main role as the financial center of the city, and its high budget capacity in contrast to the rest of Lima.

This chapter focuses on three particular projects of +Ciudad: Plaza 31, Las Begonias, and Parque Ecológico (photo 12.1). They were selected not only because of their importance to the success of +Ciudad but also because they sought to overcome different problems within the district, had different implementation processes, and are good examples of how +Ciudad operates at different urban scales (neighborhood, district, and metropolitan). The Municipality

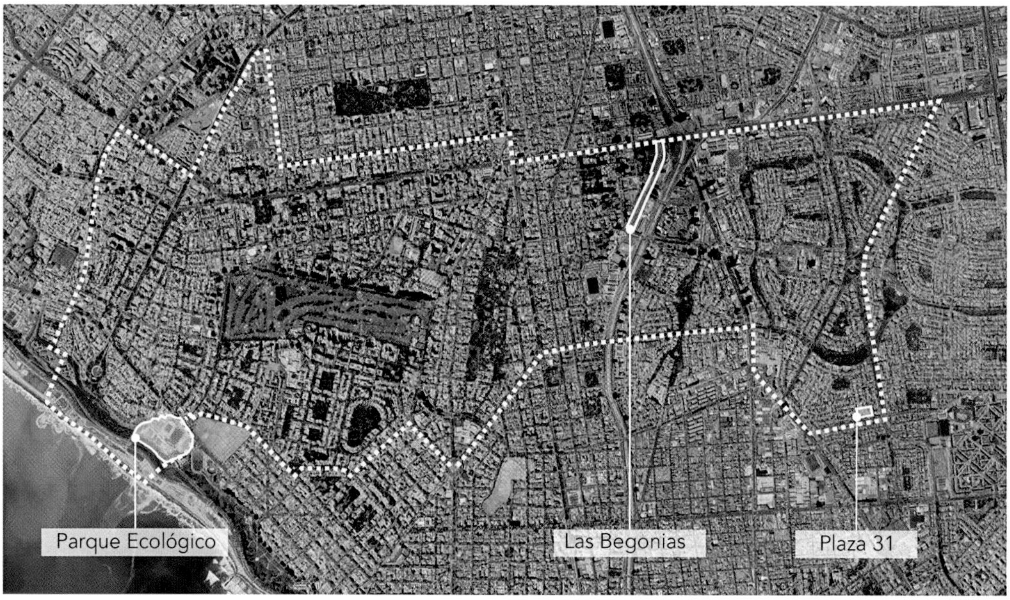

PHOTO 12.1 **Sites of Three Selected +Ciudad Projects in Aerial View of San Isidro District, Lima, Peru**

Source: ©World Bank. Further permission required for reuse.

of San Isidro leads the implementation of +Ciudad, and the three projects discussed were completely financed with public resources. The investment levels varied widely according to the scale of each project, ranging from US$244,000 for a neighborhood project like Plaza 31 to US$1.9 million for Las Begonias and US$3.4 million for a project of metropolitan scale like Parque Ecológico. All three projects were or are being executed by private companies selected through public tender.

PLAZA 31

Phase 1: Context

Plaza 31 is located in the southeastern area of San Isidro, on what previously was known as Calle 31 (31st Street). This area is adjacent to Surquillo, a low-income district with the highest population density in Lima, inadequate green and public spaces, and serious security problems (photo 12.2). For many years, this area had been abandoned by the different municipal administrations, and in response residents made little use of public space.

Before the intervention of +Ciudad, Calle 31 was a parking lot, used by many as a private parking space to keep old cars parked for weeks or months. There was 1,000 square meters of space exclusively dedicated to cars and an additional 1,000 square meters of road that served as access to the parking lot (figure 12.2, panel a). The area was deteriorated, with many closed businesses and abandoned buildings.[7]

PHOTO 12.2 **Site of Plaza 31, Near the Border between San Isidro and Surquillo Districts, Lima, Peru**

Source: ©World Bank. Further permission required for reuse.

Phases 2 and 3: Planning, Design, and Implementation

Plaza 31 project was a neighborhood-scale intervention that aimed to transform 2,000 square meters of parking lot and roads into a plaza for pedestrian use only. It was a rapidly implemented, three-month project that cost approximately S/. 807,000 (US$244,000). Today, the renovated plaza has green spaces, more than 30 newly planted trees, free wireless internet access, and benches and resting places accessible to people with disabilities. The city government also considered the presence of safe public spaces and conversion of a parking lot into an active, vibrant plaza to be a feasible solution to address citizens' security concerns (figure 12.2, panel b).[8] Some of the removed parking lots as well as parking spaces for bicycles were reinstalled on the two edges of the square.

The entire planning and design process of Plaza 31 was managed by the Urban Planning Office (OPU) of San Isidro Municipality. The OPU's urban design team was responsible for the architectural and design aspects of the projects, and an urban planning team focused on zoning, land use, and urban norms in general. These two teams were joined by a third group of experts in community participation. The urban diagnosis made by OPU was complemented and validated by residents organized in neighborhood associations; the residents also reviewed and approved the urban design guidelines that would inform the materialization of the design.

At a technical level, in addition to physical beautification of the plaza, which was appreciated by citizens, the city government made land-use changes to catalyze the development of new neighborhood commercial uses that would attract more diverse activities and visitors. The municipality's Human Development Office also opened the district's second municipal gym in Plaza 31, which has significantly complemented the functionality of the plaza and increased its impact.

a. Calle 31, before its conversion to Plaza 31

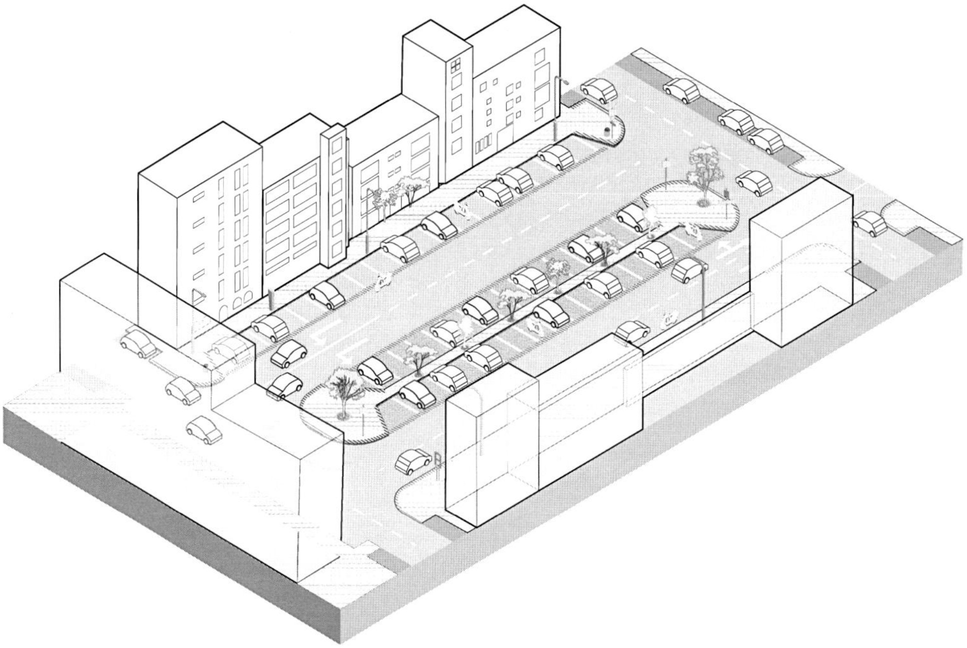

b. Completed Plaza 31 project

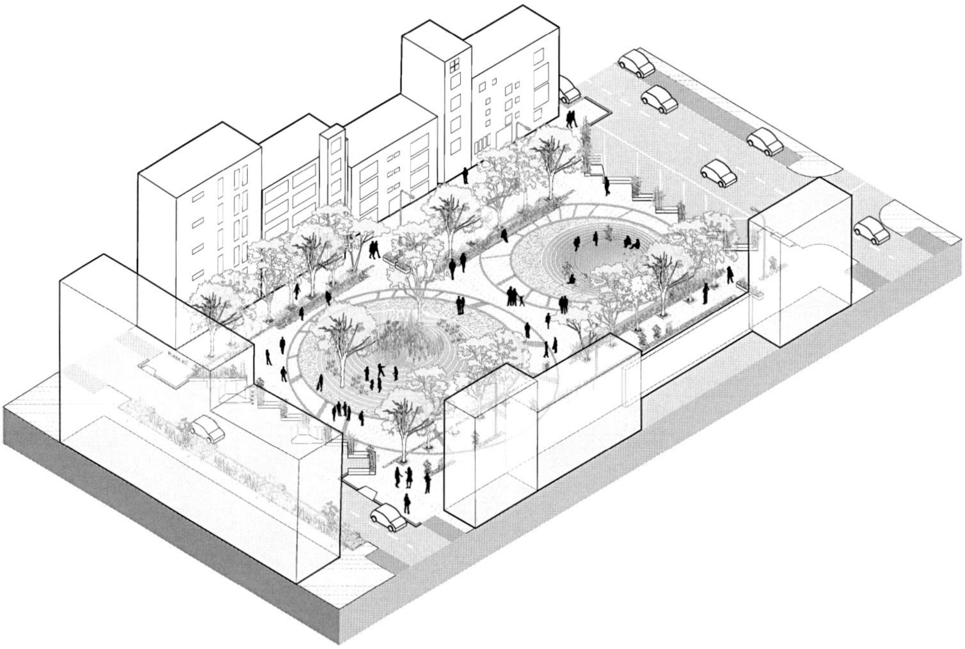

FIGURE 12.2 **"Before" and "After" Views of Plaza 31, San Isidro District, Lima, Peru**

Source: ©World Bank. Further permission required for reuse.

The OPU had to address some residents' fear of visitors from neighboring districts. This concern was bluntly expressed in various meetings, and the municipality was firm in indicating "that public space should be for people and that you cannot restrict the use to anyone because she or he does not belong to the district."[9] To implement the project, the municipality sought the support of the neighborhood association. The municipality understood that the neighborhood association was keen to attract public investment—because the area had been abandoned and forgotten by several administrations—and persuaded the association that the project would improve the urban quality of the area. This helped convince other residents, which led to the project's successful implementation.

Phase 4: Management

The Plaza 31 project site is public land, and therefore no resettlement or compensation to private owners was needed during the implementation or management. The OPU is in charge of managing facilities and spaces and surveying users. Rather, the main challenges to the project were dealing with residents who saw a threat to the status quo and entrenched local political interests. In an interview, San Isidro Mayor Velarde said, "There was fear [of] change, and as well there were some particular interests that operated inside the municipality that had blocked for many years important reforms."[10] According to the mayor, San Isidro had been controlled almost entirely by a group of residents who had long dominated the neighborhood councils and who maintained decision-making processes in a closed and opaque environment. Although these residents were legitimately chosen to be representatives of the different councils, voter turnout was extremely low, sometimes not reaching 10 percent of the total voting population. And although neighborhood council elections were held every year, residents were not fully aware of them or did not see elections as important or relevant for the district's future.

One of the main changes made by the municipality was to invite other residents to public hearings. This engaged more diverse groups of people, younger than the "official" groups of residents, most of whom had never participated in municipal affairs. For a long time, the affairs of the municipality were not conducted in the name of public interest. However, "+Ciudad somehow acted beyond the physical interventions; it achieved including in the agenda the importance of public space," said Anderson García, an OPU citizen participation specialist.[11] Although there were some objections to +Ciudad projects being implemented, the program also gained many supporters who had never raised their voices before to defend the program.

Phase 5: Impact Evaluation

The Plaza 31 project was successful in transforming a parking lot into a public plaza that welcomed people to stay. The transformation of Plaza 31 has led to a fourfold to fivefold increase in the number of people who use the plaza for resting, eating lunch, meeting friends, reading, strolling, and so forth. Specifically, before the intervention, the public space was used by a maximum of 49 people per hour (midday), but after the project, the pedestrian use of the plaza was 150–249 people per hour at midday (San Isidro Municipality 2018b). In a municipal report, 36 percent of users indicated that they used the public space five times a week. All respondents (100 percent) rated the project positively (57 percent as very good, and 43 percent as good). While 41 percent of respondents didn't want any changes to the plaza, 15 percent wished for more comfortable seats and resting infrastructure (Maguiña 2018). A separate evaluation that observed user behavior on Plaza 31 revealed that on warm summer days, people used the space less for recreation and more for transit.[12] The postulated reason for this pattern of usage was that trees were still too young to provide adequate shade and comfort.

The user evaluation also showed that half of the Plaza 31 users are residents of San Isidro, and the other half are not (Maguiña 2018). This reflects the vision and intention of +Ciudad that local governance and projects can improve the quality of life of Lima as a whole. As well, 93 percent of respondents said the Plaza 31 rehabilitation made them feel part of San Isidro, and 86 percent of respondents said the municipality should do this type of intervention in other places of the district (Maguiña 2018).

LAS BEGONIAS

Phase 1: Context

The five-block street, Las Begonias, is one of the most transited areas in San Isidro and only one block away from the high-traffic Bus Rapid Transit (BRT) stations that serve the district. Located in the heart of the financial center of San Isidro (and Lima), it concentrates people from the entire city. Both sides of the street have commercial use, which offers an opportunity to create an attractive, pedestrian-friendly street (photo 12.3).

PHOTO 12.3 **Aerial View of Las Begonias in the San Isidro Financial District, Lima, Peru**

Source: ©World Bank. Further permission required for reuse.

However, before +Ciudad's Las Begonias project, the street had many deficiencies that impeded pedestrian access and the full enjoyment of public space. The road favored vehicles with three lanes of road space, and the sidewalks were insufficient for the pedestrian density of the area. The west side of the street had the potential of offering a good walkable experience, given the granularity and density of shops along the street. In addition, there was room to increase space for pedestrians by transforming 54 diagonal parking spaces that were mostly used by a few financial center employees from 7 a.m. to 7 p.m. each day. The east side of the street was dominated by "dead walls," entrances to department store parking lots, and railings between the sidewalk and the street.

Phases 2 and 3: Planning, Design, and Implementation

In this context, the design proposal was to create an attractive street, not dominated by parking and vehicular circulation, where people would want to be and stay, with quality urban furniture and seating and play areas. According to Velarde, "This project wanted to give a message of inclusiveness: create quality public spaces that can positively impact the life of those 800,000 commuters that come daily to San Isidro and add much value to the district."[13]

A study revealed that 96 percent of Las Begonias users weren't residents of San Isidro, and 63 percent of users worked in the area and probably spent more time in San Isidro than where they live (Maguiña 2018). The result of the study was interpreted by the municipal government as a duty that the district had toward the rest of the city: it was a district-level project that welcomed commuters from the entire city, as part of the San Isidro community.

Public-Private Urban Planning and Design Synergy

The design of Las Begonias was led by the municipality's OPU. However, unlike other projects in the district, there was close collaboration with Urbanova, the main real estate developer in San Isidro for this project. Urbanova shared many of the municipality's concerns about the car-oriented urban forms in the financial center and the impact they had had on the area's declining streets and urban quality. Urbanova executives expressed their conviction that if the municipality wanted to make San Isidro an attractive place for real estate investments in the long term, it had to invest in improving public spaces.[14]

Urbanova hired Sasaki, an American architecture and urban design firm, to develop a master plan for the financial district. The plan aimed to "create a new urban center in Lima, Peru: a premier metropolitan and regional destination for business, leisure, and culture. By establishing a strong district identity, diverse urban experience, and cohesive framework for growth, the master plan sets a new benchmark for development in Lima" (Sasaki 2015). The vision for the financial district considered a phased implementation strategy "aimed at enhancing value over time" (Sasaki 2015). One stage of the strategy was rehabilitating and remodeling the five-block street Las Begonias and turning it into an attractive boulevard.

The Municipality of San Isidro agreed to work collaboratively with Urbanova to redesign the street and begin the transformation of the financial district. The OPU outlined its objectives for Las Begonias, which were transformed into a set of guidelines that Sasaki would have to follow in its design. The guidelines included specifications on the minimum size of sidewalks, the durability of the pavers, the type of bike infrastructure, the distance between cars and pedestrians, and so on. Urbanova also committed to reduce as much as possible the car entrances onto Las Begonias from their new buildings. Moreover, the company commissioned an analysis of the shadows cast by buildings onto the street, which informed the building plans. Both public and private stakeholders started an interactive urban design process that led to the final design of the street. The planning studies were entirely funded by Urbanova, and the execution of the project was entirely funded by the municipality.

This type of synergy toward a common and shared objective was unprecedented and unseen in the planning and execution of many urban planning and design schemes in San Isidro and Lima. Urbanova's executives also expressed that this inclusive public-private process was constructive and that stakeholders learned from one another about much more than just the urban design solution. Interestingly, stakeholder participation and interest were varied. Two retail stores that occupy more than 50 percent of one side of Las Begonias were invited to participate in the design, but they showed less interest, stopped attending consultation meetings, and dropped out early on. A possible reason was because Urbanova possessed wide-ranging investments in the San Isidro real estate business; and by contrast, the other two retail companies had no other real estate investments in the district.

Micro-, Intermediate, and Macrointerventions

Awareness campaign. Before the macrointervention was executed in 2018, micro- and intermediate interventions that focused on placemaking and tactical urbanism approaches were carried out to prepare the street and engage the users for the project. The first microintervention was an awareness campaign, "14 m^2 of Life." Its objective was twofold: First, it planned to create awareness about the great amount of public space occupied by a single vehicle on the street: 14 square meters is the normative size of a parking space in Peru (photo 12.4). Second, it was designed to highlight that despite citizens' acclimation to the monofunctionality of a parking space (serving only to park a car), many more pedestrian-friendly activities could occupy these 14 square meters.

For two weeks, from 10 a.m. to 6 p.m., two parking spaces were dedicated exclusively to different activities such as pottery, urban farming, and yoga classes. DJs and artists were invited to occupy the 14 square meters and play music or paint for one whole day. Seats and benches allowed people to sit and watch a small magic show, a cooking class, or a musician playing a violin. Pedestrians were asked about what they would do in 14 square meters of space, and some of these suggested activities were implemented in the space (Espejo 2016).

Placemaking and tactical urbanism approaches. After the "14 m^2 of Life" campaign, the municipality designed and implemented an intermediate intervention focused around placemaking and urban tactical urbanism to prepare

PHOTO 12.4 **Parking Spaces on Las Begonias before Intervention, 2016**

Source: ©San Isidro Municipality. Reproduced, with permission, from San Isidro Municipality; further permission required for reuse.

the street for the final execution of the project. The 54 on-street parking spaces were closed, and temporary grass benches occupied the new liberated space while potted plants were installed along the edge of the street and in the newly recovered area. The OPU was in charge of the design of the temporary furniture (photo 12.5).

Permanent transformation. Las Begonias was chosen as a good street for a macro-scale permanent transformative intervention not only because of its strategic location, high pedestrian use, and metropolitan impact potential but also because, being a local street, its management depends almost entirely on the local municipality.

When it comes to local roads, local governments have a fairly large amount of independence to change them. However, changes in road intersections, for example, need to be discussed with the metropolitan municipality. In this case, the Municipality of San Isidro had to negotiate approval from the Metropolitan Municipality of Lima to build the elevated street crossings. For a time, the local and metro governments disagreed on the design of these proposed pedestrian crossings, and the negotiation period impeded timely completion of the work. Given that in Lima there was little or no experience of raised intersection and pedestrian crossings along a whole street, there was uncertainty that this could work. In the end, the differences were resolved, and the work was completed three months after the expected date.

PHOTO 12.5 **Intermediate Intervention, Las Begonias, 2017**

Source: ©San Isidro Municipality. Reproduced, with permission, from San Isidro Municipality; further permission required for reuse.

In all, the final intervention (photo 12.6) took nine months to complete and cost around S/. 6.3 million (US$1.9 million).[15]

Phase 4: Management

In the case of Las Begonias, the micro- and intermediate interventions were smoothly carried out by the local government with the support of Urbanova. For the intermediate intervention, the OPU had designed the temporary furniture, while Urbanova took on maintenance of the grass benches and flowers on the five-block street.

However, for the permanent macrointervention, the process was more complicated. During the design of Las Begonias, the municipality realized that parts of the sidewalks on both sides of the street were privately owned and that by law the municipality cannot invest public money in private property. Fortunately, all of the retail space on one side of the street (with the diagonal on-street parking) was owned by a single entity: Urbanova. Negotiation with a single stakeholder reduced the construction delay risks of the project. Urbanova executed the project on the part of the sidewalk belonging to it, following the same design and plans that the municipality was using for the whole street. Unfortunately, the big retail stores on the other side of Las Begonias were not as agreeable, and the sidewalk there could not be renovated entirely. Today, that small, private section of the sidewalk has a different pattern and materials than the rest of the street.

PHOTO 12.6 **Final Macrointervention, Las Begonias, 2018**

Source: ©San Isidro Municipality. Reproduced, with permission, from San Isidro Municipality; further permission required for reuse.

Another barrier to +Ciudad's implementation of Las Begonias was the resistance by some residents to the proposed reduction of parking space for pedestrian use. In San Isidro, 73 percent of households own a car, compared with 18 percent in Lima (Lima Cómo Vamos 2018). San Isidro residents were more likely to think that parking is a right and not a privilege and that if you want it, you have to pay for it. To challenge this perception, the communications team implemented several campaigns that reaffirmed the right of people to public space. As part of +Ciudad, more than 200 activities or microinterventions were deployed throughout the four years of Mayor Velarde's term in office. These included concerts, magic shows for kids, and movie screenings in the parks.

Slowly, by using active public spaces more, people became more aware of their importance and realized that parks were not just decorative but rather to be used. In that sense, the objective was to empower citizens to value and defend public spaces and therefore understand that cars cannot have a greater priority than human beings over this space. The slogan for +Ciudad was "Ciudad para las personas," meaning "a city made for people." This message was continuously repeated in communication campaigns, microinterventions, and *El Olivar,* the municipal newspaper distributed monthly to households (San Isidro Municipality 2018a).

Another fear that the San Isidro Municipality had to counter was that benches installed in newly recovered public spaces were going to bring strangers and therefore insecurity to the area. The government saw this as a manifestation of the poor use of public spaces that had dominated the district in the past, feeding on a fear of strangers. However, "this was also part of a racist and classist speech that the municipality would not tolerate in the district," recalls Velarde. "We were not going to change our objectives or interventions because of unfounded arguments that were built on fear, racism, and distrust."[16] For this, there was an effort to persuade residents that, contrary to their views, active public spaces with people using benches and spending time on the street actually offered a form of passive surveillance that would increase the security of the area. Author and urban activist Jane Jacobs's famous discourse about "eyes on the street" was one of the OPU's strategies to communicate about projects (Jacobs 1961).

Phase 5: Impact Evaluation

Given that the macroproject Las Begonias has only recently been inaugurated, this section focuses on the municipality's evaluation of the intermediate intervention. Before the intervention, use of the street was concentrated in the first block, mainly as a crossing point to get to the BRT station. Since the intervention, the number of pedestrians has become more evenly distributed along the road, as people started to use parts of the street that they previously avoided (San Isidro Municipality 2018b).

Before the intervention, there was no place for pedestrians to rest and to sit. However, when the on-street parking was closed and benches were installed, these spaces were used more frequently. In a survey conducted during the day, it was found that as many as 30 people used the new temporary furniture within a span of 15 minutes (San Isidro Municipality 2018b). Based on the total of people surveyed, about 43 percent indicated they had used the new public space, and 57 percent said they had not used it. Twenty percent mentioned that the benches were uncomfortable. Interestingly, 15 percent said they had never used the space because they did not know whether public use was free, and 5 percent thought the redesigned spaces belonged to the shops behind them. These responses revealed how unaccustomed people were to having public space with furniture available for free use. Even when benches were installed in areas that were evidently public—such as the area between the road and the sidewalk—people assumed that these new and beautiful grass benches were for private uses (Maguiña 2018).

When asked about uses for the newly created public space once the intermediate intervention was over, respondents suggested that there should be tables that people could use to have lunch. At noon, more than 6,000 people use the street per hour, and 60 percent of the people who used the temporary furniture used it at lunchtime. This shows that citizens want free public spaces to have lunch and also that the district and the city in general enormously lack these types of spaces. The population in Lima has become used to paying for the use of comfortable space (such as entering a food court and needing to buy something in order to use a table), and too many times people have been told to not eat in parks. +Ciudad wanted to radically transform this understanding of public spaces, and people were surprised by projects like these.

PARQUE ECOLÓGICO

Phase 1: Context

At the beginning of the 20th century, when Lima started to grow west toward the Pacific Ocean, districts developed facing inland, leaving the space bordering the ocean cliff empty and deteriorated. Lima's coastline is not exactly next to the ocean; the city is situated on top of an 80-meter cliff that separates the upper part of the city from the coast.

In the case of San Isidro, a small part of the coastline was used for a park and a sea sidewalk (called Malecón Bernales). However, a big portion of the prime coastline (20,000 square meters) historically has been used by the municipality for mechanics' workshops, storage space, machinery repair, municipal offices, and so forth. This represented a misuse of valuable public space for the district and interrupted Lima's connectivity along its coastline. The districts of Chorrillos, Barranco, and Miraflores (south of San Isidro) are connected by a coastal sidewalk that connects some of the coastal districts of Lima—although it could be greatly improved. The public works facility in San Isidro acted as an impermeable barrier, interrupting this 9-kilometer promenade.

Phases 2 and 3: Planning, Design, and Implementation

The objective of this macro-scale project was to "eliminate the barriers of the city and connect it to the ocean"[17] through the creation of a 2-hectare park with a clear ecological function—a "Parque Ecológico" (photo 12.7).

PHOTO 12.7 **Aerial View of Proposed Parque Ecológico Location and Environs, San Isidro District, Lima, Peru**

Source: ©World Bank with information from San Isidro Municipality 2017. Permission required for reuse.

The park design has several specific objectives (San Isidro Municipality 2017):

- *Pedestrian connection to the city:* The project aims to connect the city horizontally, connecting San Isidro to other districts that border the ocean and that have a promenade along the coast. The proposed pedestrian connections with Miraflores District through the new network of sidewalks and through a new bridge ("Puente de la Amistad" or "Friendship Bridge") are soon to be built. Today, a road leading to the ocean divides the cliff in two and therefore separates Miraflores from San Isidro. Therefore, the projected bridge will stitch both sides of the cliff together, and the pedestrian connectivity of the new park will contribute to it.
- *Connection with the sea:* The project also aims to connect the district vertically with the Pacific Ocean. The idea is to transform the traditional way in which districts in Lima grew—facing inland—and capture the value from being located next to the ocean waterfront (photo 12.8). A closer identification of the citizens with the ocean and a higher appreciation of its urban value will contribute to the appropriation of the lower part of the cliff—called Costa Verde—that has been recklessly managed in the past 10 years and has been irresponsibly converted into an urban highway.

PHOTO 12.8 **Illustration of Seaside View from Proposed Parque Ecológico, 2018**

Source: San Isidro Municipality 2017. ©San Isidro Municipality. Reproduced, with permission, from San Isidro Municipality; further permission required for reuse.

- *Revitalization of public facilities:* One of San Isidro's most valuable assets is its public market, known as "Mercado de Precursores." Next to the proposed rejuvenation of the public space, the market hosts vendors who have established their livelihoods there for more than 30 years and are greatly valued by residents of the area and communities that the market serves. The Parque Ecológico aims to improve and revitalize the existing market while preserving its vibrancy and tradition.
- *Public space and urban farming:* Among the main components of the project is to create awareness of the importance of using green areas within the framework of food sustainability. The new Parque Ecológico will use 585 square meters of its green space for urban farming (photo 12.9). When finished, this space will also be used to teach adults and children how to plant crops at home and about the importance of urban agriculture for food security, environmental sustainability, and healthy nutrition.
- *Cultural hub and small-scale commerce:* One of the main pillars of this new park is to create a multiuse destination that is flexible enough for a diverse programming of the space with performing arts, concerts, and so forth. To this end, the project will design a multipurpose, multiuse plaza and open gardens where these activities can all be accommodated. As well, the park will have a small commercial space of 476 square meters for restaurants and cafés. These will be built reusing the buildings that had previously housed municipal offices.

PHOTO 12.9 **Illustration of Urban Agriculture for Proposed Parque Ecológico, 2018**

Source: San Isidro Municipality 2017. ©San Isidro Municipality. Reproduced, with permission, from San Isidro Municipality; further permission required for reuse.

One of the biggest challenges was to reorganize the collection of offices and workshops used for construction, repair, and maintenance of machinery parts that were owned by the municipality and were occupying this valuable land. Many of these municipal assets are too old to move and were sold or donated to scrap yards to be recycled. The rest of the machinery and the public works offices were moved to a plot just behind the new park where the citizen security office used to operate. In addition, the citizen security office was relocated to another site of the district that is publicly owned and was built for this purpose some months before.

There was a big concern among residents that giving too much space for commercial use inside the park would attract too many people beyond the capacity of the area. The municipality did not agree on eliminating all the commercial space planned for restaurants and cafés, but it did agree to reduce it to 476 square meters.

Impact and Outlook

No evaluation information is yet available for the Parque Ecológico, given that the project is still being implemented. However, this +Ciudad project has already begun a major change toward the revaluation of public space in the city. The boldness of its interventions in San Isidro—one of Lima's most conservative districts—has set a precedent for inclusive urban governance. But the project's sustainability is in question given the weak institutional capacity and government continuity. This is because the political term for mayors in Peru is only four years, and they cannot be reelected to consecutive terms. The continuity of leadership is often a critical factor in sustaining successful urban policies.

It is also important to think about possibilities for scaling up innovative programs like +Ciudad at the city level. Although the program was considered a success, this was because of San Isidro's income per capita, availability of a land cadaster, and capacity for tax collection, which differ enormously from other districts in Lima that have less access to own-source revenues and funding. San Isidro's in-house capacity for planning and design, and for execution of public works in a relatively short time, is an exceptional situation in Lima.

This said, innovative financing methods—including land-based financing and federal and private sector contributions—can be explored to bring better infrastructure and public spaces to the rest of Lima. +Ciudad does not need to be replicated exactly; it can be reinvented according to the needs, possibilities, and sociocultural nuances of each district. The importance of the program is less about a detailed vision than about the broad pillars that sustain it.

NOTES

1. The amount of water spent watering parks is a problem. Although the government recommends using treated wastewater instead of potable water, it does not prohibit the use of the latter to water green areas. In January 2017, the national newspaper *El Comercio* reported that in just one month, municipalities had used 1.1 million cubic meters of potable water to water green spaces (Paz Campuzano 2017).

2. Interview with Solángel Fernández, by Sofía García Núñez, on an overview of San Isidro, November 29, 2018.
3. Interview with Manuel Velarde, by Sofía García Núñez, on an overview of +Ciudad, November 25, 2018.
4. Llama Urban Design identified the affluence of people in each sidewalk, plaza, and park of the district and also evaluated the spaces using six categories: capacity, flexibility of uses and activities, accessibility and inclusivity, attractive characteristics, environmental quality, and perception of security (Laurie 2015).
5. Exchange rate used: US$1 = S/. 3.30.
6. Interview with Manuel Velarde, November 25, 2018.
7. Interview with Solángel Fernández, November 29, 2018
8. Interview with Manuel Velarde, November 25, 2018.
9. Interview with Anderson García, by Sofía García Núñez, on placemaking for +Ciudad, November 29, 2018.
10. Interview with Manuel Velarde, November 25, 2018.
11. Interview with Anderson García, November 29, 2018.
12. Interview with Anderson García, November 29, 2018.
13. Interview with Manuel Velarde, November 25, 2018.
14. Interview with Urbanova executives, by Sofía García Núñez, on the Las Begonias project, December 30, 2018.
15. Las Begonias cost data are from the "Obras" dashboard data set of Datos Abiertos, the open data portal of the Municipality of San Isidro, Lima, Peru: http://datosabiertos.msi.gob.pe/dashboards/9230/obras/.
16. Interview with Manuel Velarde, November 25, 2018.
17. Interview with Manuel Velarde, November 25, 2018.

REFERENCES

Berube, Alan, Jesus Leal Trujillo, Tao Ran, and Joseph Parilla. 2015. "Global Metro Monitor 2014: An Uncertain Recovery." Report of the Metropolitan Policy Program, The Brookings Institution, Washington, DC.

CAF (Development Bank of Latin America). 2017. "Crecimiento urbano y acceso a oportunidades: un desafío para América Latina." Economy and Development Report, CAF, Caracas, República Bolivariana de Venezuela.

CEPLAN (National Center for Strategic Planning). 2017. "Perú: Información Departamental, Provincial y Distrital de Población que Requiere Atención Adicional y Devengado Per Capita." Statistical publication (accessed April 10, 2019), https://www.ceplan.gob.pe/wp-content/uploads/2017/08/Matriz-de-indicadores-nacionales-a-Julio-de-2017.pdf.

Driant, Jean-Claude. 1991. *Las barriadas de Lima: Historia e interpretación.* Lima: Institut français d'études andines (IFEA)–Centro de Estudios y Promoción des Desarrollo (DESCO).

Espejo, Karen. 2016. "San Isidro: '14 m2 de Vida' en áreas de parqueo." *Publimetro,* August 15. https://publimetro.pe/actualidad/noticia-san-isidro-14-m2-vida-areas-parqueo-49235.

Facho, Aldo. 2018. "Discriminación Urbana." *Urbanistas.lat Red Latinoamericana* (blog), June 18. http://urbanistas.lat/discriminacion-urbana/.

Fernández-Maldonado, Ana María. 2007. "Fifty Years of Barriadas in Lima: Revisiting Turner and De Soto." Paper presented at the European Network for Housing Research (ENHR) International Conference, "Sustainable Urban Areas," Rotterdam, Netherlands, June 25–28.

Jacobs, Jane. 1961. *The Death and Life of Great American Cities.* New York: Random House.

Laurie, Angus. 2015. "San Isidro Análisis y Diagnóstico Urbano." Unpublished paper, Municipality of San Isidro, Lima, Peru.

Lima Cómo Vamos. 2018. "VIII Informe de Percepción sobre Calidad de Vida en Lima y Callao." Survey report, Lima Cómo Vamos Observatorio Ciudadano, Lima, Peru.

Liza, Víctor. 2015. "Racismo en San Isidro: Acusan a alcalde de convertir El Olivar en 'parque zonal de los conos'." *Lamula.pe* (blog), December 22. https://redaccion.lamula.pe/2015/12/22/racismo-en-san-isidro-acusan-a-alcalde-de-convertir-el-olivar-en-parque-zonal-de-los-conos/victorliza/.

Ludeña, Wiley. 2002. "Lima: poder, centro y centralidad. Del centro nativo al centro neoliberal." *EURE Santiago* 28 (83): 45–65.

Maguiña, María Eugenia. 2018. "Servicio de consultoría para la elaboración de reporte de impacto del Programa +Ciudad 3rd Report." Internal document, Municipality of San Isidro, Lima, Peru.

Paz Campuzano, Óscar. 2017. "Lima y Callao gastaron S/. 7,3 mlls en agua potable para regar." *El Comercio,* March 6.

Plöger, Jörg. 2006. "La formación de enclaves residenciales en Lima en el contexto de la inseguridad." *Revista Ur[b]es* 3 (3): 135–64.

Radio Capital. 2015. "¡Alarmante! 92% de rejas en Lima no están autorizadas," May 17. https://capital.pe/actualidad/alarmante-92-de-rejas-en-lima-no-estan-autorizadas-noticia-797979.

San Isidro Municipality. 2015. "Plan Urbano Distrital del distrito de San Isidro 2012–2022 y su actualización." Internal document, San Isidro Municipality, Lima, Peru.

———. 2016. "Compendio Estadístico 2016." Annual statistical report, San Isidro Municipality, Lima, Peru.

———. 2017. "Creación del Parque Ecológico de San Isidro en el Sector 2 Memoria descriptiva de arquitectura." Internal document, San Isidro Municipality, Lima, Peru.

———. 2018a. "Ciudad para las personas: Suplemento especial." *El Olivar*, November. https://es.calameo.com/books/004210439ec675ab384d7.

———. 2018b. "Postulación al Premio a las Buenas Prácticas en Gestión Pública 2018: Recuperación de espacios públicos para las personas en el distrito de San Isidro." Nomination document, San Isidro Municipality, Lima, Peru.

———. 2018c. "San Isidro: Construyendo una Ciudad para las Personas." Brochure, San Isidro Municipality, Lima, Peru.

Sasaki. 2015. "Las Begonias Financial District Master Plan." Online project summary, Sasaki, Watertown, MA. http://www.sasaki.com/project/398/las-begonias-financial-district-master-plan/.

Vega Centeno, Pablo. 2006. "Lima: Espacio público y ciudad sostenible." Palestra portal of public affairs, Pontifical Catholic University of Peru (PUCP), http://repositorio.pucp.edu.pe/index/bitstream/handle/123456789/11907/lima_espacio_publico_Vega_Centeno.pdf.

———. 2013. "¿Dónde somos limeños? Explorando los espacios públicos de la ciudad." In *Lima, Siglo XX: Cultura, socialización y cambio*, 123–44. Lima, Peru: Fondo Editorial de la Pontificia Universidad Católica del Peru.

———. 2017. "La desigualdad invisible: el uso cotidiano de los espacios públicos en la Lima del siglo XXI." *Territorios* 36: 23–46.

CHAPTER 13

BROOKLYN, NEW YORK: CREATING AN INNOVATION DISTRICT THROUGH PLACEMAKING, AND PUBLIC AND PRIVATE INVESTMENTS

Vivian Liao, Manuel Mansylla, and Tucker Reed

KEY TAKEAWAYS

- In Brooklyn, the city's Tech Triangle Strategic Plan leveraged public spaces to connect existing urban forms that were fragmented by bridges, expressways, and industrial sites, and to create conducive spaces for entrepreneurs and artists.
- From 2012 (when the plan was initiated) to 2015, the number of innovation firms and employees increased by 22 percent and 45 percent, respectively. Forty-five percent of surveyed innovation firms in the area responded that they chose to be in Brooklyn because of the neighborhood character and amenities that Brooklyn offered.
- Selected public spaces in the DUMBO (Down Under the Manhattan Bridge Overpass) area and the Brooklyn Cultural District were re-created at different scales for different purposes, including pocket parks, squares, an archway under a bridge, streetscapes, and cultural buildings. These spaces collectively helped rebrand the neighborhoods as attractive destinations for firms, residents, and visitors.

- Private sector and local community engagement was key to the successful implementation of the plan. The city's public-space-related policies and efforts have spurred more than US$1 billion of private investments and dramatically increased property values in Downtown Brooklyn.

CITY DYNAMICS

Context and Background

If Brooklyn were an independent metropolis, its 2.6 million residents would make it the fourth most populous city in the United States, only behind the other boroughs of New York City combined, Los Angeles, and Chicago. Downtown Brooklyn is the central business district of the borough. It has been a magnet for commerce since the early 19th century when the "Road to Jamaica" led pedestrians inland from the landing where Robert Fulton's steamships ferried passengers back and forth between Brooklyn and Manhattan, and the waterfront industrial economy fueled Brooklyn's growth for two centuries.

In the 1970s and 1980s, the decline of the industrial economy took a toll, and Downtown Brooklyn became a victim of neglect and disinvestment, its landscape littered with the mistakes of urban renewal. Massive infrastructure like the Brooklyn-Queens Expressway (BQE) and the Brooklyn and Manhattan Bridges created barriers between neighborhoods and interstitial, underused spaces, while major arteries like Flatbush Avenue, Flushing Avenue, and Adams Street allowed cars to dominate, contributing to a lack of ground-floor activity and pedestrian vibrancy that was difficult to overcome.

Renewed private sector interest in the 1990s, however, crystallized in the development of MetroTech Center, a 5.7 million-square-foot office park that repositioned the area as less expensive than Manhattan yet comparably attractive to potential commercial tenants (BNY, DBP, and DUMBO BID 2015). Collectively, the area's building blocks—rich transportation infrastructure, academic and cultural institutions, the seat of local government in Brooklyn's Civic Center, and a diverse stock of buildings that could support future job growth—provided a foundation of local resources from which to build.

Today, Downtown Brooklyn has become one of the country's most competitive cities, benefiting from

- A residential development boom, with nearly 11,000 apartments in development and more than 14,000 completed since 2003 (DBP 2018);
- A college town, home to 11 institutions and more than 60,000 students (BNY, DBP, and DUMBO BID, 2015); and
- Shopping, entertainment, and cultural destinations that welcome more than 30 million annual visitors, encouraging the development of more than 2,600 hotel rooms (DBP 2018).

This unprecedented growth is the result of years of planning, advocacy, and smart public-private partnerships, all of which positioned the area for the organic growth of an innovation district starting around 2012, known as the Brooklyn Tech Triangle.

A Regional Approach: Brooklyn Tech Triangle

Traditionally, Downtown Brooklyn had been home to back-office operations for New York City's FIRE (finance, insurance, and real estate) industries, as well as the seat of local government, the court system, and the legal sector that supports them. However, its infrastructure had aged, and its occupancy had been trending downward, with a vacancy rate of around 10 percent on its 17 million square feet of office space, leaving over 1.5 million square feet of available office space to experiment with to attract new industries and jobs to the area (BNY, DBP, and DUMBO BID 2015). Moreover, anecdotal feedback from local companies revealed a generally poor perception of Downtown Brooklyn as "unsafe," outdated, and "too far away" from the communities on the waterfront.

Meanwhile, two other regional neighbors—DUMBO (Down Under the Manhattan Bridge Overpass) and the Brooklyn Navy Yard—had enjoyed attracting innovation economy firms. Specifically, in DUMBO, public-space interventions and innovative placemaking had helped its waterfront neighborhood begin to attract a sizable cluster of digital media, advertising, and tech companies. Innovation firms were drawn to the area's historic loft buildings, cobblestone streets, and existing community of artists and artisans.

In this context, a new narrative was needed to reposition Downtown Brooklyn's commercial assets. It had to be one that honored the area's rich history and authenticity, and one that did not offend the existing land owners and tenant base—the backbone of the local economy. Benefiting from DUMBO and the Brooklyn Navy Yard's earlier success and diverse assets, a vision began to present itself of a central business district comprising three complementary anchors: (a) front-office headquarters in Downtown Brooklyn, (b) a virtual design and advertising suite in DUMBO, and (c) the factories and distribution hub to make and ship products at the Brooklyn Navy Yard (map 13.1).

Perhaps most importantly, this new hub would be integrated into the larger community of existing companies and creative uses. These companies would situate in existing buildings in the urban fabric, not in walled-off office parks only accessible by automobile in the traditional mode of tech campuses. This integration would encourage growth to spill over not only in terms of supporting local retail through increased buying power, but also potentially by creating jobs and internship opportunities for the area's 60,000 college and graduate students. Thus the clustering effect of like-minded companies in one area had already led organically to create the conditions from which to build an innovation district (BNY, DBP, and DUMBO BID 2015).

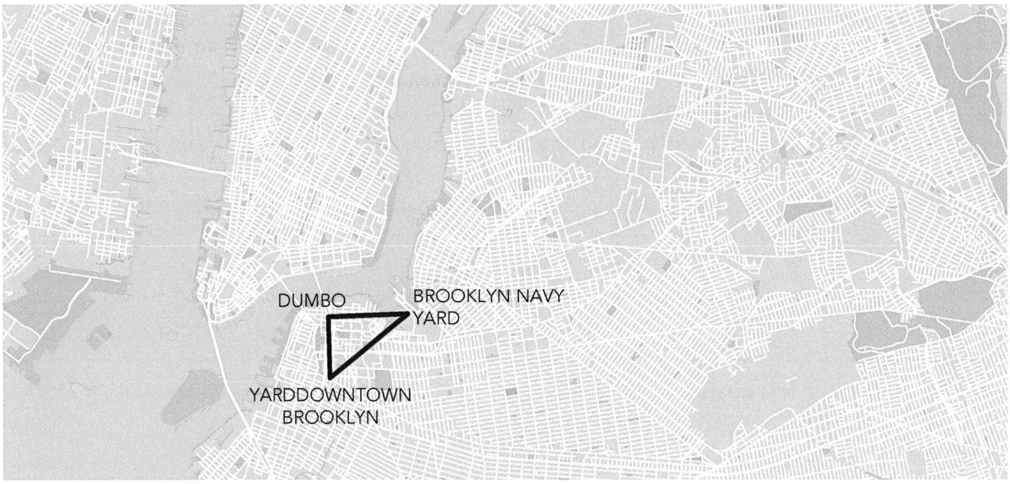

MAP 13.1 **Location of the Brooklyn Tech Triangle, New York City**

Source: ©World Bank. Further permission required for reuse.

A Sizable Tech Ecosystem

To realize this vision, leaders of the area's local development corporations—the Brooklyn Navy Yard Development Corporation, the Downtown Brooklyn Partnership, and the DUMBO Improvement District—banded together to quantify the movement afoot and hired a consultancy firm, Urbanomics, in 2012 to prepare a study of the local knowledge economy in the three connected neighborhoods.[1] A summary of key findings revealed that Tech Triangle innovation firms were growing rapidly and that 523 innovation firms were already operating there. These businesses employed close to 10,000 people directly, supported 23,000 additional jobs, occupied 1.7 million square feet of real estate, and had a total economic impact on Brooklyn's gross domestic product (GDP) of more than US$3 billion (Urbanomics 2012).

These firms could have been located in many locations across the world because of the digital nature of their business but chose to be in Brooklyn because of the area's unique talent pool, quality of life, and global brand. They indicated their belief that the local tech industry was already having a significant impact on the Brooklyn economy. Twenty percent of all tech firms surveyed had been started in the previous 16 months, and 48 percent expected to at least double in employment size in the next three years. For the first time in a generation, there seemed to be an industry base that was choosing to be in Brooklyn, dictated not out of proximity to a customer base, or from economic necessity due to cheaper real estate, but because they were founded there or were attracted there by the quality of life that Brooklyn had to offer. In fact, after rent and proximity to transit, when asked to identify the three most important factors in their real estate selection, firms ranked neighborhood character and amenities as their next most important considerations (figure 13.1).

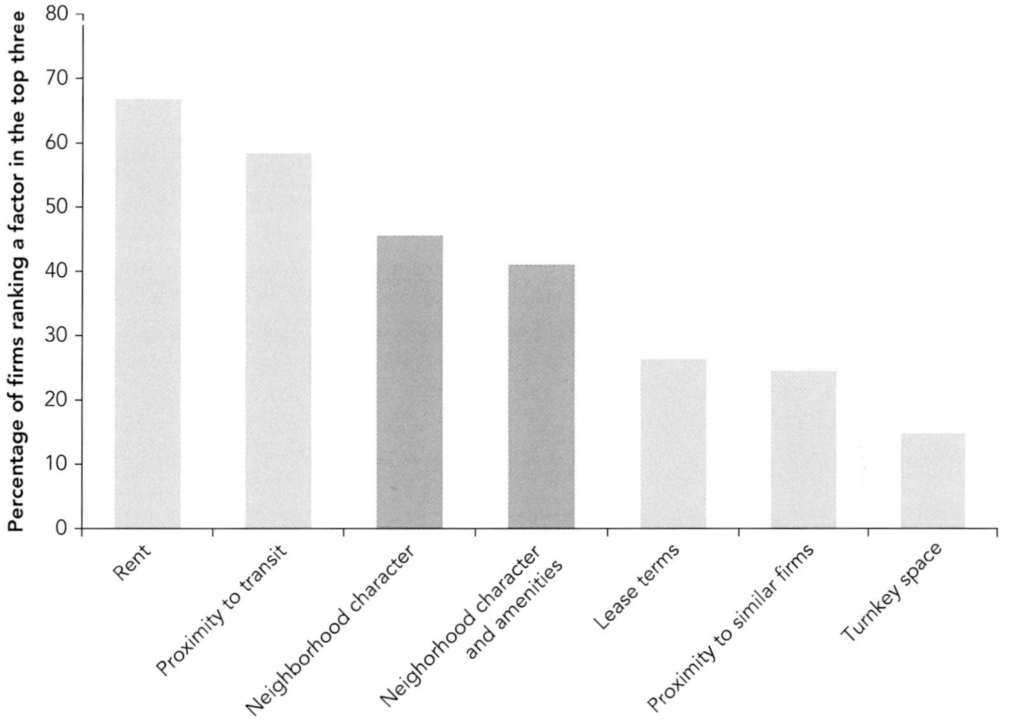

FIGURE 13.1 **Neighborhood Character and Amenities Ranked as Top Factors in Real Estate Selection, Brooklyn Firms, 2012**

Source: World Bank, based on Urbanomics 2012.
Note: Figure represents 185 survey responses from innovation firms (in the technology, creative, or arts fields) either operating in the Brooklyn Tech Triangle or considering moving there. The firms were asked to select the three most important factors in their decision to locate in the Tech Triangle.

This growth, while building on many smart economic development decisions that had set the stage for it over the past decade, was largely organic up to this point. The survey also confirmed, even from a cursory glance, that these firms would face a number of challenges in continuing to expand at such a rapid clip:

- *Limited availability of suitable real estate* to keep pace with future space demands
- *Transportation challenges*, both within the Tech Triangle and to connect with other parts of Brooklyn and Queens, where much of this innovation economy workforce was increasingly living
- *Need to lay the necessary infrastructure* in the forms of open space, retail amenities, housing options, and information technology (IT) bandwidth that creates the neighborhood character these companies thrive on
- *Need to connect local Brooklynites to the jobs* these sectors were creating. Many companies described labor recruitment to be a constraint to growth, because they were creating more jobs than they could find suitable applicants to fill.

These challenges would require the support of the public sector, and the coalition recognized the need for public-private partnerships to step in and bridge the gap. To secure the resources necessary would require a holistic blueprint, with buy-in from myriad local stakeholders who would charter a smart course forward and respect the area's history and culture while also laying out a vision for the future. These efforts got a boost from Jerry Hultin, then president of Polytechnic University,[2] with strong political and financial support from then City Council Speaker Christine Quinn, who announced a "Nine Point Job Creation Strategy" highlighting the opportunity for "creating a Brooklyn Tech Triangle by connecting potential tech office space in Downtown Brooklyn to the nearby tech hubs of DUMBO and the Brooklyn Navy Yard" (NYC Council 2011). Furthermore, with the City Council's support in legitimizing the effort, the coalition was able to turn to partners in the Michael Bloomberg and Andrew Cuomo mayoral and gubernatorial administrations, respectively, for additional resources. These included further study funding from both the New York City Department of Small Business Services and the Empire State Development Corporation. Grants from New York University (NYU) and the Brooklyn Community Foundation rounded out the study support.

The term "Brooklyn Tech Triangle" soon began to take on a life of its own. The real estate brokerage industry started using it to reposition local real estate assets to potential investors. The news media recognized an easily packaged real estate trend and began to write about the area prolifically, with more than 200 press stories between 2012 and 2015 that referenced "Brooklyn Tech Triangle."[3] The power of this free media reach was instrumental in turning the idea into a brand, and the echo chamber in many ways legitimized the vision put forward simply by turning the term into common parlance.

Regional Master Planning

The Tech Triangle partners issued a public Request for Proposals in July 2012 and eventually designated a consortium led by architecture and urban design firm WXY to develop a master plan that would translate the initial vision for the innovation district into an action-oriented blueprint for the continued growth of the area. It also would address physical constraints related to placemaking, transportation, infrastructure, and land use (WXY 2013).

Following a year-long process that included meetings with more than 200 stakeholders—including 90 focus group participants, guidance from an advisory committee of 27 government offices and agencies, and a task force of 36 local companies and organizations—the Brooklyn Tech Triangle Strategic Plan that emerged in 2013 outlined five key challenges, with a corresponding array of recommendations to address them. This includes:

- *Space for Tech to Grow.* Activate underutilized commercial spaces and create incentives to refurbish spaces for the innovation economy;
- *A New Tech Ecosystem.* Create an innovation training hub to address emerging job opportunities;
- *Connections across the Tech Triangle.* Expand bus routes and create new bike lanes on key corridors;

- *Dynamic Places for Tech.* Reimagine selected spaces as activity areas for events, food, and interaction, along with improved lighting, parks, and streets; and
- *Tech Triangle Interface.* Expand public WiFi throughout the district and give start-ups the chance to pilot their products locally in the Tech Triangle.

Implementation of the more than 60 concrete recommendations falling under these five themes was undertaken collaboratively, where each of the Tech Triangle partner organizations agreed to move its individual priorities forward while promoting and marketing any success under the Brooklyn Tech Triangle brand. In 2015, a new economic impact analysis to assess the midterm impacts of the Tech Triangle projects found the number of innovation firms in the area had exceeded previous projections—growing to more than 1,350 innovation companies, a 22 percent increase.[4] Employment in the Tech Triangle was also on track to exceed expectations, with the number of innovation employees then reaching more than 17,300—a 45 percent increase between 2012 and 2015 (BNY, DBP, and DUMBO BID 2015).[5]

But although job creation and economic growth were on track with previous projections, at the time of the 2015 update, the Tech Triangle partners foresaw a potential space crisis that threatened to halt momentum. Office space in the region had increased by just 1.2 percent in three years, a small fraction of what had been called for in the initial strategic plan, while vacancy rates had plummeted. As such, the coalition used the release of the update to sound the alarm and call for more space to be created to accommodate future growth.

Four years later, the market has largely responded. Since 2015, approximately 3.4 million square feet of new office and manufacturing space has been created across the Tech Triangle. This includes the Pioneer Building in Downtown Brooklyn, an old storage facility that was converted into 230,000 square feet of Class A office space now anchored by podcast company Gimlet Media; Dock 72, a 675,000-square-foot ground-up development at the Brooklyn Navy Yard with WeWork as the anchor tenant; and a former tobacco warehouse in DUMBO that has been transformed into a 300,000-square-foot creative office and retail hub known as Empire Stores (photo 13.1).

The result of these efforts has led to a spike in office rents. For instance, the average commercial rent per square foot in Downtown Brooklyn and DUMBO is now approximately US$48, versus US$36 in 2012, when the Tech Triangle efforts began—an increase of 33 percent.[6]

Public Spaces Anchored in the Brooklyn Tech Triangle

Several public-space components were integrated into the key strategies of the Strategic Plan 2013, including (a) better "Connections Across the Tech Triangle" for improved transit access across the region, and (b) creation of "Dynamic Places for Tech" to enhance physical spaces—from interior office environments to outdoor public plazas to interstitial connections. Since the initial plan's release, transit improvements have come in the form of better bus service (specifically, expanded routes to link the Brooklyn Navy Yard to

PHOTO 13.1 **Façade of Empire Stores Office and Retail Hub, DUMBO Area of Brooklyn Tech Triangle**

Source: ©World Bank. Further permission required for reuse.
Note: DUMBO = Down Under the Manhattan Bridge Overpass.

area transit hubs); bike connections through the city's bike-share program; and solutions to infrastructure constraints such as the presence of the BQE, which could have significant impact on the culture and appeal of a location. As such, placemaking is a critical component of both the Tech Triangle's organic evolution—what originally helped to attract the innovation economy here—and its future continued success.

Since then, various interventions ranging from tactical to comprehensive ones identified in the plan have been implemented. Some of the tactical interventions include better lighting and activation at MetroTech Commons and the US$11 million rehabilitation of the bluestone paving in Columbus Park surrounding Borough Hall in 2015.

The most visible public-space initiative coming out of the Tech Triangle Strategic Plan is the Brooklyn Strand, a community-based effort to connect nearly 50 acres of disconnected parks and plazas, stretching from Borough Hall to Brooklyn Bridge Park, to each other and the waterfront. A master planning effort led by the Downtown Brooklyn Partnership and WXY resulted in the Brooklyn Strand Community Vision Plan in 2016, which included recommendations to transform the quality of public space, better connect people in surrounding neighborhoods, and make the waterfront more accessible (WXY 2016).

After years of incremental progress, the plan got a major boost in October 2018, when the state designated Downtown Brooklyn a winner of the third round of its Downtown Revitalization Initiative (map 13.2), which includes a US$10 million investment toward several proposed Brooklyn Strand projects (NYS 2018). They include reconfiguration of the BQE interchange ramps along Tillary Street to remove physical barriers and improve connectivity to Commodore Barry Park; improvement of the pedestrian experience along Park Avenue, a wide street that runs underneath the elevated BQE; and reconnection of Downtown Brooklyn and surrounding neighborhoods to the waterfront and each other through sidewalk widening, fence removal, enhanced bike lanes, and other interventions. Underpinning these initiatives is the recognition that inclusive growth can be aided by using more cohesive design strategies and improving connections between parks and the communities they serve.

Indeed, public space and placemaking efforts are, in some ways, the most tangible indicators of the progress—and still untapped potential—of the Brooklyn Tech Triangle as an innovation district. A closeup analysis of such efforts in the DUMBO neighborhood is illustrative.

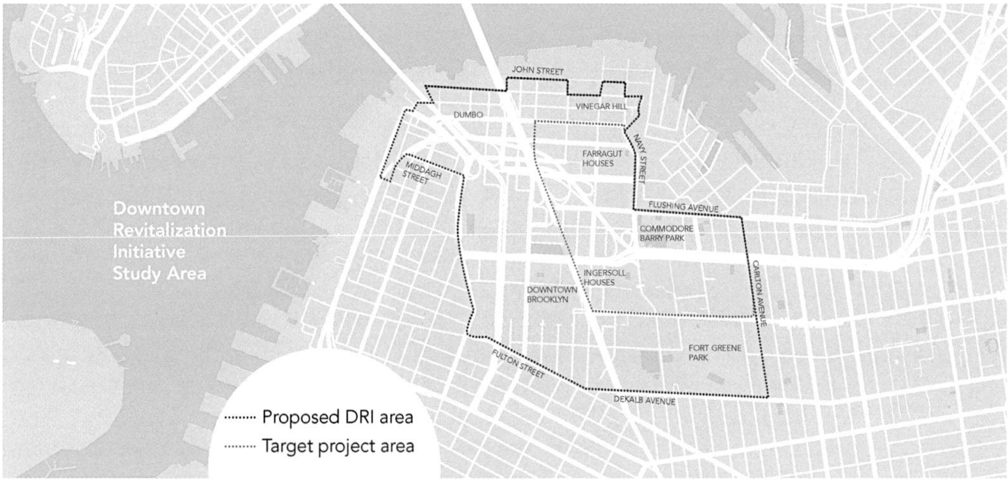

MAP 13.2 **Study Area of Brooklyn Downtown Revitalization Initiative**

Source: ©Totem, based on Downtown Brooklyn Partnership (http://www.downtownbrooklyn.com/) and DUMBO Improvement District (https://dumbo.is/) websites. Reproduced, with permission, from Totem; further permission required for reuse.
Note: DRI = Downtown Revitalization Initiative.

PUBLIC SPACES OF DOWN UNDER THE MANHATTAN BRIDGE OVERPASS (DUMBO)

Phase 1: Context

As highlighted earlier, DUMBO has become so popular with new-economy companies that it functions in many ways as an incubator, with dozens of social events such as Flea Food under the Archway and Digital DUMBO; many coworking spaces and traditional incubators that ensure access to the neighborhood for freelancers and companies of all sizes, including StudioMates, DUMBO Startup Lab, The Green Desk, and the NYU Tandon School of Engineering Incubator; and the Independent Filmmaker Project (IFP) "Made in New York" Media Center, featuring classrooms for the New York–based education company General Assembly. This "clustering" effect has helped to facilitate the growth of the larger innovation district around DUMBO, while major public-space developments like Brooklyn Bridge Park have also transformed the area into a world-class waterfront destination.

Phase 2: Planning and Design

This transformation from forgotten enclave to a cauldron of economic activity did not happen by accident; it is the culmination of hundreds of millions of dollars of pioneering private investment and reactive public policy decisions related to land use and public infrastructure. Key to organizing these efforts was the decision by local property owners in 2005 to institute an additional property tax and pool the resources to create the DUMBO Improvement District—a business improvement district (BID) tasked with the further revitalization of the neighborhood.

One of the first actions undertaken by the nascent DUMBO BID was to audit the neighborhood's public-space infrastructure. New York City and New York State were in the midst of a massive US$350 million investment in a public-space waterfront reclamation project that would become known as Brooklyn Bridge Park, but little attention had been paid to the interior of the neighborhood (Bonislawski 2017). This inventory quickly revealed a vast amount of physical space occupied by the New York City Department of Transportation (DOT) in and around the entrances of the Brooklyn and Manhattan Bridges as well as underused parking and roadbed areas that could be considered for enhanced public access and use.

Recognizing the new demands placed on the neighborhood's infrastructure by the changing demographics of the community, the BID saw opportunity to create public spaces in these forgotten nooks and crannies of the neighborhood that could act as place-based amenities and further investment attraction tools. With the BID's advocacy, the Archway was returned to the public under the NYC Plaza Program.[7]

Phase 3: Implementation

Pearl Street Triangle

The first space that the BID focused on was an underused parking lot adjacent to the Anchorage of the Manhattan Bridge on Pearl Street (map 13.3).

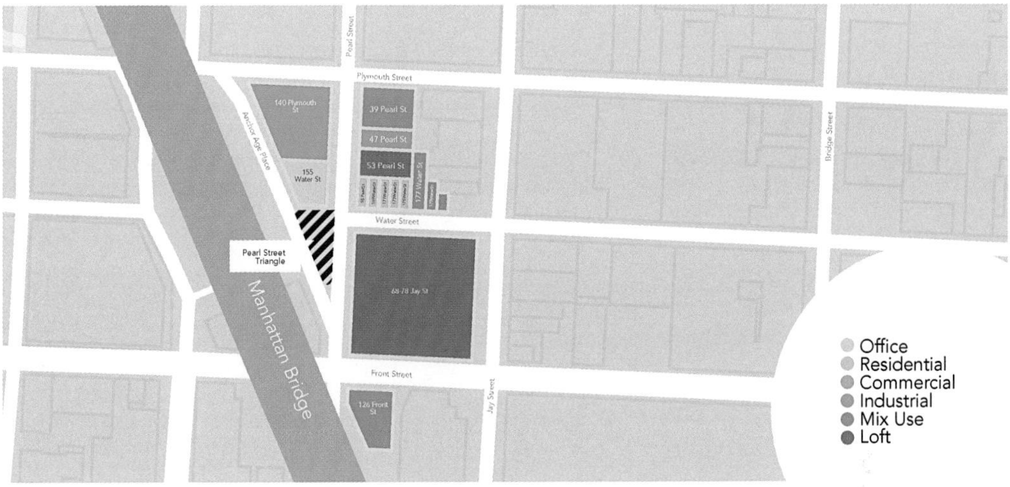

MAP 13.3 **Pearl Street Triangle Site and Environs, Brooklyn, New York City**

Source: ©World Bank. Further permission required for reuse.

The triangular-shaped space served as a parking lot for 14 cars, was not welcoming to pedestrians, and lacked activity at a street scale despite a preponderance of retail and office lobbies with frontage facing the parking lot. The lack of human activity served as a deterrent to significant investment in the buildings directly adjacent to the space and further presented a public safety issue because limited foot traffic next to the imposing bridge infrastructure combined to create an uninviting environment that in its worst form could conceal crime owing to lack of clear sight lines, lighting, and "eyes on the street" (Jacobs 1961).

Working with DOT, which has jurisdiction over the city's streets, the BID developed a proposal for replacing the parking spaces with a pedestrian plaza. The initial design developed out of a relationship with the Pratt Institute, a local architecture and planning school based in nearby Clinton Hill. The school committed a class of graduate student architects to study DUMBO's public infrastructure and to develop concepts with the BID for placemaking opportunities, culminating in a presentation to the neighborhood Community Board.

The reclamation of the space for more active public use would go on to become an experiment in community building. The staff of the DUMBO BID enlisted the support of local architecture firms whose employees volunteered their time to physically paint the floor of the plaza, install planters, and plant trees and flowers. Adjacent retail businesses that faced the plaza donated handcrafted furniture to adorn the space, and a local gallery loaned an iconic piece of public art.

In 2007, the Pearl Street Triangle successfully opened to the public, featuring approximately 4,000 square feet of space with seating, public art, landscaping, and features such as salvaged granite blocks from the local bridges (photo 13.2). The impact of this public improvement was felt almost immediately—not only in the qualitative opinions of neighborhood residents, workers, and visitors who used the space but also in quantitative data like

PHOTO 13.2 **Pearl Street Triangle, Brooklyn, after DUMBO BID Intervention**

Source: ©Totem. Reproduced, with permission, from Totem; further permission required for reuse.
Note: BID = business improvement district. DUMBO = Down Under the Manhattan Bridge Overpass.

property values and rent levels, and policy outcomes like zoning changes and additional city investment to restore and preserve the neighborhood's historic cobblestone street and landmark significant buildings. The plaza's development was successful in that it became a template for other communities and inspired the creation of DOT's NYC Plaza Program to create neighborhood plazas to transform underused streets into active public spaces.[8]

Other Public-Space Improvements

Building on this success, DOT and the DUMBO BID undertook additional placemaking projects in the neighborhoods, including reopening of the Archway of the Manhattan Bridge in 2008 and creation of Old Fulton Plaza in 2011.

For decades, the Archway served as a storage area for bridge repair materials but acted as a wall separating the north and south sides of DUMBO (photo 13.3, panel a). The area to the south, between the Manhattan and Brooklyn Bridges, was the early home of reinvestment in DUMBO as private residences, office space, and retail flourished. But the area to the north failed to attract the same level of market attention. Working with renowned firm Marvel Architects, DOT repurposed existing steel storage structures as an armature for uplighting and benches while also restoring the historic cobblestone paving that was uncovered beneath the modern asphalt. Today, the space is an anchor point in the neighborhood for a wide variety of events, such as sporting events, concerts, and markets (photo 13.3, panel b).

Old Fulton Street—a thoroughfare that serves as a main entrance to Brooklyn Bridge Park and the tourist attraction at Fulton Ferry Landing, as well as a commuter hub for the East River Ferry System—lacked logical space

a. Archway while closed b. Archway after reopening

PHOTO 13.3 **Archway of the Manhattan Bridge, Brooklyn, before and after 2008 Reopening**

Source: ©Totem and DUMBO Business Improvement District (BID). Reproduced, with permission, from Totem and DUMBO BID; further permission required for reuse.

for leisure and rest. DOT worked to replace a car lane and extend the sidewalk to create new public space. The design incorporates repurposed stone from the anchorages of the surrounding bridges that act as buffers to separate the plaza from car traffic; shading elements like planters, trees, and umbrellas; and movable tables and chairs (photo 13.4). This dynamic plaza can now accommodate the scores of tourists who frequent the Brooklyn waterfront and the historic Brooklyn pizza restaurants that abut the plaza.

The placemaking efforts at the Pearl Street Triangle and the Manhattan Bridge Archway became a major bridge between the east and west ends of DUMBO and literally paved the way for enhanced public and private investment in the neighborhood. Since 2008, when the Archway opened, the city has committed more than US$45 million to make the plaza improvements at Pearl Street permanent and rehabilitate the historic Belgian Block streets throughout the district (Cuba 2018).

Phase 4: Management

Today, the public spaces mentioned above are managed by the DUMBO BID, a public-private partnership that collects an assessment from the commercial properties within the district, defined by its boundaries (map 13.4). In New York City, the BID tax is collected by the New York City Department of Finance and then shared with individual BIDs across the city, which use these funds to provide supplemental services like street cleaning, public safety, landscaping, holiday lighting and marketing, and small-business support.

The DUMBO BID was established in 2005 with a budget of US$375,000, which has grown to an operating fiscal year 2017 budget of more than US$925,000, in part to keep up with the increased demands on the organization to operate and maintain more public spaces (DUMBO BID 2019). None of the BID plazas was classified as parkland, so did not receive financial support from the city. DOT, which does own the land, had no mechanism

PHOTO 13.4 **Old Fulton Plaza, Brooklyn, after Intervention, 2011**

Source: ©DUMBO Business Improvement District (BID). Reproduced, with permission, from DUMBO BID; further permission required for reuse.

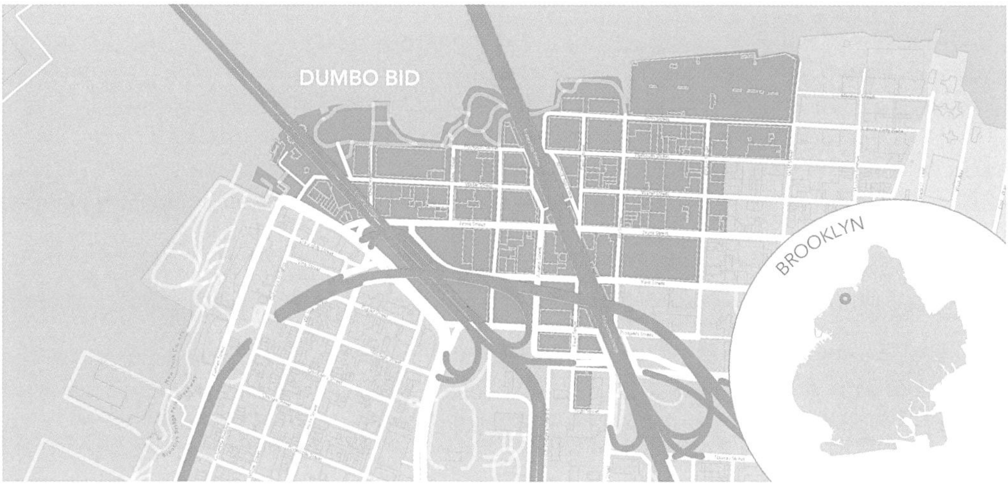

MAP 13.4 **DUMBO BID Boundary, Brooklyn, New York City**

Source: ©World Bank. Further permission required for reuse.
Note: BID = business improvement district. DUMBO = Down Under the Manhattan Bridge Overpass.

or resources to maintain these spaces, either. As a result, the city turns to BIDs or, where BIDs do not exist, to other community-based organizations to care for these public spaces. Successful urban design interventions are often dependent on public-private partnerships like BIDs to administer, manage, and maintain the spaces.

In return for taking on this responsibility, BIDs exercise considerable control over their programming, and everything from event permission to commercial activations like concessions must receive the approval of BID management in one form or another. The BID uses this leverage to extract donations or charge fees for commercial uses in the public space, which help to underwrite the upkeep and maintenance of the spaces. Beyond these concession fees, the DUMBO public spaces have become sought-after locations because of their proximity to the iconic architecture of the bridges and the historic character of the neighborhood. As such, the area has become a go-to destination for film and magazine shoots, with producers and camera crews regularly paying the BID for use of the sites.

In terms of maintenance responsibilities, at minimum each plaza is swept and cleared of garbage by BID staff daily. They will work with landscapers and arborists to maintain or replace plants, trees, and flowers, and with specialty contractors to keep the area's street furniture and lighting in good working order or install lighting installations for holidays or special events.

Phase 5: Impact Evaluation

The development of DUMBO's public spaces demonstrates how the intentional and inclusive creation of public space can produce myriad economic development benefits—from investment attraction and property value increases to pedestrian activity and public policy outcomes like advocacy for additional neighborhood infrastructure and land-use changes.

Property Value

An analysis of properties adjacent to the Pearl Street Triangle and Manhattan Bridge Archway public plazas illustrates how placemaking efforts can increase property values. Out of the 15 properties adjacent to the public spaces, 4 are industrial, 6 are residential (comprising 1–16 units), 2 are mixed-use, 2 are commercial lofts (serving as offices), and 1 is a traditional office building.

To examine the impact on property values of the new public space, this analysis focuses on a value per square foot basis. Because Pearl Street Plaza opened in 2007, the analysis focuses on three property value snapshots: 2006 (before opening); 2012 (5 years after opening); and 2018 (11 years after opening) (Roldos 2018). Considering these time frames, the properties developed after 2014 have been disregarded because the ongoing impact of the plaza's creation has likely been fully absorbed into market pricing today.[9]

From 2006 to 2018, all of the properties adjacent to the Pearl Street Plaza increased their property value (figure 13.2). The property with overall greatest value spread within the 12-year analysis time frame was 55 Pearl Street, a multiuse property with a staggering 2,703 percent value change. And the significant increases overall were not limited to a specific asset class: the average percentage increase of adjacent industrial properties was 347 percent per square foot, adjacent residential properties saw an average increase of 382 percent, and mixed-use properties benefited from the largest jumps in property value—an average of 1,379 percent. By comparison, during this same time period, the average residential real estate property values in DUMBO

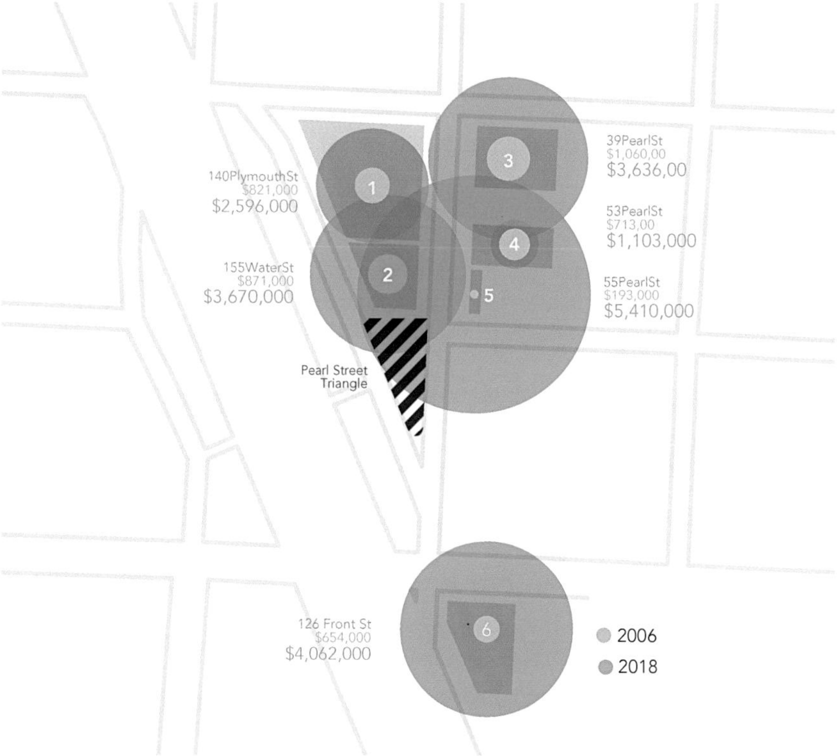

FIGURE 13.2 **Sample Changes in Property Value, Pearl Street Triangle, Brooklyn, 2006–18**

Source: ©World Bank. Further permission required for reuse.

and Downtown Brooklyn–wide jumped by 123 percent, and grew citywide by approximately 84 percent.[10]

Pedestrian Activity

Subway passenger ridership at the York Street F train station, which primarily serves the DUMBO neighborhood, increased by 72.4 percent from 2011 to 2016 (figure 13.3). At the same time, ridership increased by 75.7 percent at the nearby High Street Subway station.[11]

General foot traffic in the area also increased, according to data collected by DOT on one of DUMBO's most heavily trafficked pedestrian corridors—along Washington Street between Front Street and Water Street, two blocks away from the Manhattan Bridge Anchorage and Pearl Street Plaza. The earliest data available are from 2007, and the most recent survey was conducted in 2017.[12]

DUMBO saw a significant increase in foot traffic between 2007 and 2017 after the public-space improvements were added to the neighborhood. At all times of day and during weekdays and weekends alike, pedestrian activity in the neighborhood increased significantly. A 60 percent increase in morning weekday activity is a good indicator of increased economic activity likely tied

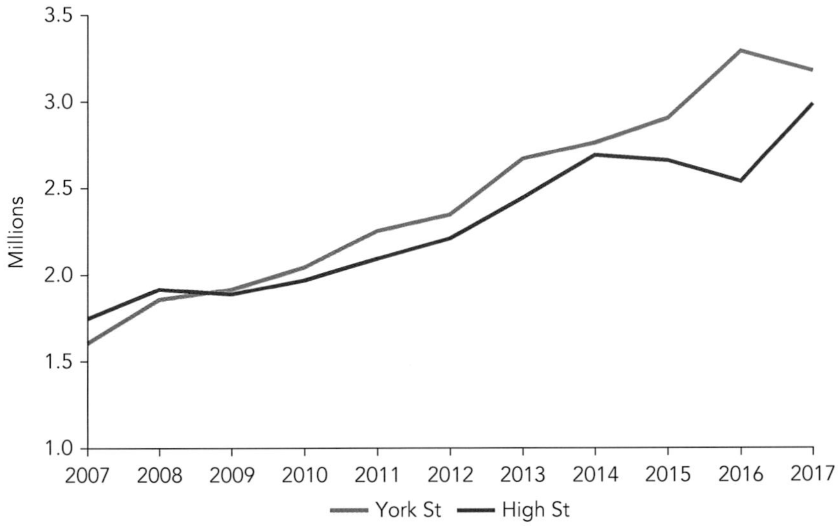

FIGURE 13.3 **Growth in Subway Ridership, DUMBO Area, Brooklyn, 2007–17**

Source: World Bank illustration based on Metropolitan Transportation Authority (MTA) "Annual Subway Ridership" data, http://www.mta.info/. ©World Bank. Further permission required for reuse.

to job and housing growth. But close to a 200 percent increase in nighttime and weekend activity is a clear indication that DUMBO has become a more desirable destination for leisure activity.[13]

Cultural Events

This pedestrian flow increase may be attributable to DUMBO's popularity as a tourist attraction, but it is also undoubtedly tied to the significant number of events produced in the area's public spaces. The BID hosts year-round events marketed on its website and other channels that attract locals, tourists, and residents from other boroughs. In 2018, they included more than 90 public events—from the World Cup finals in the Archway to community concerts and block parties, welcoming approximately 30,000 attendees (DUMBO BID 2019).

The public spaces in DUMBO have also been reborn as de facto open art galleries. The gray walls and pillars of massive infrastructure are used as a blank canvas for DUMBO Walls murals.[14] Every first Thursday, new video arts are featured on the Manhattan Bridge. The old St. Ann's Warehouse is also repurposed as an international theater. Notably, the Archway is recorded as one of the top performance venues in the neighborhood, including Live at the Archway, a weekly pop-up gallery and community art project (DUMBO BID 2019).

Public Policy

Perhaps the greatest impact of the DUMBO placemaking interventions was their influence on public policy, especially related to landmarking, zoning, and land use. In 2007, the NYC Landmarks Preservation Commission (LPC) designated many blocks of DUMBO as a "landmark district," which protected approximately 91 buildings that, according to the LPC's designation report, "reflect important trends in the development of industrial architecture in the United States during the nineteenth and twentieth centuries, and embody an important era of Brooklyn and New York City history. The most radical innovation in DUMBO's industrial architecture occurred at the beginning of the twentieth century, when buildings constructed entirely of reinforced concrete began to appear. These factories, erected by the Gair Company and other firms, were among the earliest large-scale reinforced-concrete factory buildings to be erected in the United States" (NYC LPC 2007). The Gair buildings described in a part of the LPC report about the Archway and the Pearl Street Triangle have become the de facto heart of DUMBO from which many of the preserved historic buildings emanate.

In July 2009, two years after the creation of the Pearl Street Triangle and following the designation of the landmark district, which preserved the historic character of the neighborhood, the city felt comfortable moving forward with a rezoning of the neighborhood to facilitate additional investment in the area and help the marketplace realize the latent desire for new development.

The enclave surrounding the Pearl Street Triangle was rezoned from light industrial M1 and M3 districts to mixed commercial/residential M1-4/R7A and M1-4/R8A districts to allow for more flexibility of use. The rezoning considered the preservation of the neighborhood's character through contextual language and scale.[15] All buildings surrounding the Pearl Street Plaza are under R8 zoning, which allows more density, therefore perpetuating the need for even more public space (map 13.5).

The rezoning of the east side of DUMBO in 2009 mimicked the uses and density that various previous rezoning applications had brought to the west side of the neighborhood throughout the late 1990s and 2000s. Importantly, however, for the first time in DUMBO, the action provided zoning incentives for the creation of affordable housing in new construction in the form of density bonuses for the inclusion of affordable housing in market-rate developments.

Two years after the public-space improvements at the Archway and Pearl Street Triangle were opened to the public, the city undertook a rezoning of about half of the neighborhood to accommodate the growth that renewed interest in the neighborhood presented. The placemaking interventions knit together the pedestrian corridors of the community, attracted new retail and visitors to the area, and inspired a closer focus from the municipal government on the development potential and tax revenue gains that could be unlocked through modest land-use and preservation changes.

BROOKLYN CULTURAL DISTRICT

Phase 1: Context

The idea of a cultural district in Brooklyn dates back to the 1970s, when Harvey Lichtenstein served as president of the Brooklyn Academy of Music (BAM), a world-class institution in the heart of Fort Greene with prime transit access but surrounded at the time by empty lots. Nonetheless, he believed the area could be transformed into a thriving hub for the arts that would help spur its revitalization. Despite this vision and brave moves over the decades by other

a. DUMBO before rezoning, 2009

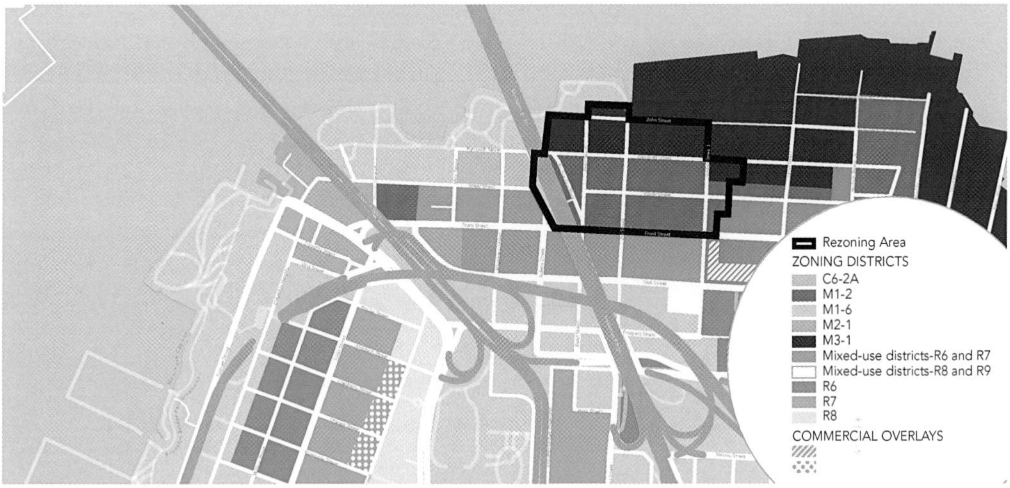

b. DUMBO after rezoning, 2009

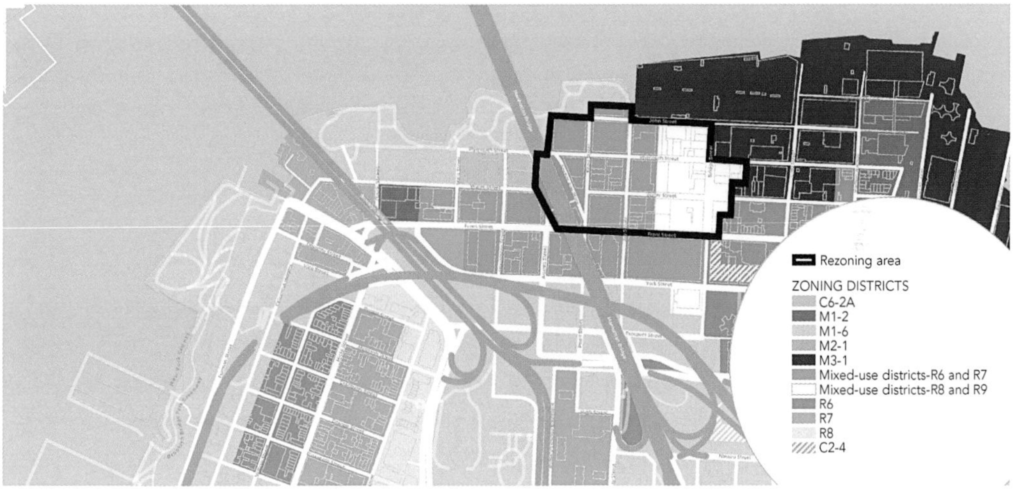

MAP 13.5 **Rezoning of DUMBO Area, Brooklyn, New York**

Source: ©NYC Department of Planning. Reproduced, with permission, from NYC Department of Planning; further permission required for reuse.
Note: DUMBO = Down Under the Manhattan Bridge Overpass.

world-class institutions like Mark Morris Dance Group (MMDG) and the Museum of Contemporary African Diasporan Arts (MoCADA) to locate in the district, the area lacked a cohesive identity and struggled to attract private investment.

Phase 2: Planning and Design

The design concept for the Brooklyn Cultural District got a major boost with the rezoning of Downtown Brooklyn in 2004. With the Cultural District contemplated as part of the plans to add density and facilitate a more mixed-use urban environment, the Bloomberg administration also announced a cumulative investment of more than US$100 million to create four world-class cultural venues, marquee public spaces, and state-of-the-art streetscape improvements for the area (NYCEDC 2012). The venues included new performance and art spaces for nonprofit institutions including BAM, BRIC, Theatre for a New Audience (TFANA), and UrbanGlass, as well as a 16,000-square-foot public plaza to provide open space for local residents, artists, and visitors.

The decision was interpreted at the time as a risky proposition in an unproven neighborhood as well as potentially wasteful spending in a neighborhood in desperate need of tangible economic development. However, coupled with a subsequent multiagency, public-private effort to create a full-scale sports and entertainment arena nearby, now known as Barclays Center, the Bloomberg administration's decision would quickly demonstrate an explicit value proposition that investment in culture can pay significant dividends in the form of tax revenue, new housing, and space for job creation.

Several comprehensive improvements planned for the Brooklyn Cultural District—now Downtown Brooklyn's premier cultural hub, centered around a cluster of cultural venues on the eastern end—include the rehabilitation of BAM Park, a 10,000-square-foot triangular-shaped public space across the street from BAM that had long been shuttered because of irregular subsurface conditions. The project is expected to be completed in late 2019, while implementation of a streetscape plan meant to knit together the area's distinct spaces continues apace.

Phase 3: Implementation

Since the 2004 announcement of the cultural plans, development of much of the Brooklyn Cultural District has been completed, including

- *The 40,000-square-foot BAM Fisher Building*, which opened in 2012, featuring flexible performance, rehearsal, and classroom space;
- *The new home for BRIC and UrbanGlass*, which opened in 2013 featuring flexible performance space, art galleries, television studios, and a state-of-the-art glass workshop (photo 13.5); and
- *The 27,500-square-foot Polonsky Shakespeare Center*, managed by TFANA, which started hosting performances in 2014 and also includes an outdoor Arts Plaza that was developed by the New York City Economic Development Corporation (photo 13.6).

Recently completed projects include the 15,000-square-foot public plaza at the base of a private rental development, which opened in 2017 (photo 13.7), and the 17,500-square-foot home for The Center for Fiction (a literary organization whose growing collection originated in 1820 with the former Mercantile Library of New York), which opened next door to MMDG this year.

Partners and Community Engagement

In the summer of 2015, with the area at an inflection point, new buildings rising, and residents flocking to the neighborhood, the time seemed right for cultural stakeholders to begin to knit together the public and private investments and proactively position the area as a leading arts destination in New York City and beyond.

PHOTO 13.5 **Home of BRIC and UrbanGlass, Brooklyn Cultural District**

Source: ©Totem. Reproduced, with permission, from Totem; further permission required for reuse.

PHOTO 13.6 **Polonsky Shakespeare Center, Brooklyn Cultural District**

Source: ©Theatre for a New Audience (TFANA). Reproduced, with permission, from TFANA; further permission required for reuse.

Over the course of a year, a collaborative effort spearheaded by the Downtown Brooklyn Partnership (DBP) and Downtown Brooklyn Arts Alliance (DBAA)—an advocacy organization made up of more than 50 cultural groups—convened more than 100 stakeholders including residents, cultural organizations, government agencies, local business, real estate, and

PHOTO 13.7 **The Plaza at 300 Ashland, Brooklyn Cultural District**

Source: ©Two Trees. Reproduced, with permission, from Two Trees; further permission required for reuse.

other not-for-profit entities in a series of planning sessions to create an operational framework to guide the district's future growth.

Part of that process would include the eventual expansion of what had been the narrowly defined geographical "BAM Cultural District" (surrounding the concentration of cultural venues in Fort Greene) to a broader notion of a "Brooklyn Cultural District" that encompasses all of Downtown Brooklyn, DUMBO, and the Brooklyn Navy Yard and includes diverse cultural groups representing nearly every artistic discipline.

The resulting plan, released in July 2016 as "Culture Forward," encompassed four areas of focus, generally around promoting opportunities for artists and arts groups; animating the district's public spaces; better marketing the area as a hub for creativity; and providing the appropriate resources and governance to ensure the district's long-term success (AEA, DBAA, and DBP 2016).

Opportunities for Artists

The first major objective in Culture Forward was to address the ongoing challenge of the rising cost of living and working in Brooklyn by maximizing opportunities for artists to access affordable housing and other resources that could facilitate their livelihoods.

Although concrete initiatives to develop affordable artist workspaces in the neighborhood have not borne much fruit, largely for lack of funding or creative public programs that can help subsidize rents, other ways of promoting existing resources available to artists have met with more success. Organizations like The Actors Fund regularly hold affordable housing workshops to educate participants on how to navigate the complicated public lottery system, while the DBAA hosts professional development opportunities for its members, addressing targeted topics of interest such as social media marketing and how to file for a special event alcohol permit.

Another initiative aimed at developing a talent pipeline of future arts leaders resulted in the creation of the Downtown Brooklyn Arts Management Fellowship, a paid six-month opportunity for a cohort of young people to gain experience and skills for careers in arts management. Started in 2018 with funding from the Theatre Subdistrict Council and New York Community Trust, fellows rotate through assignments at partner organizations: BRIC, MMDG, MoCADA, and TFANA. The eventual goal is to increase the diversity of staff in these cultural organizations and create a route into arts management without unpaid internships or master's degrees. Early metrics show the program's potential: among the first cohort of seven fellows, six have gone on to gain full-time employment in the arts (two of them at institutions in the Brooklyn Cultural District), with the seventh pursuing further graduate studies in the arts. A cohort of four fellows recently wrapped up the program's second cycle.

Animating Public Space and Marketing the District

The next two objectives of Culture Forward are interconnected in that they both sought to elevate the identity of the Brooklyn Cultural District, whether through public-space interventions or marketing. On the public-space side, the opportunity centered around an effort to stitch together the district's diverse assets, create a unique sense of place, and animate the area through public art and performances. An effort led by the DBP and architectural and urban design firm WXY led to the creation of a new Streetscape Plan for the Cultural District, the culmination of multiple planning efforts over the previous two decades.

The plan sought to unify the Cultural District streetscape—then comprising six different pavement types, nonstandard and unkempt tree pits, and nine distinct lighting fixtures—into a cohesive plan that features dark stone sidewalks embedded with lights along with new seating and streetscape elements.

Since the plan was approved, the streetscape plan has been implemented in four new developments across the district, with construction under way in three more developments (figure 13.4).

However, placemaking is not about good design or the physical environment alone. Spaces must be programmed and activated to ensure their success and integration among the community. When done well, public space can serve as a platform for telling stories about the place itself as well as its inhabitants.

Initiatives outlined in Culture Forward to stage regular performances in public spaces and create a districtwide arts festival have been largely driven by the DBP and culminated in the first Downtown Brooklyn Arts Festival in September 2018. The three-day festival included dozens of free events at venues throughout the district and in a new marquee public space created as part of a private development known as The Plaza at 300 Ashland.

On the digital marketing front, some progress has been made to create a centralized source for promoting events in the district. The DBP website (http://www.downtownbrooklyn.com) lists events hosted by Downtown

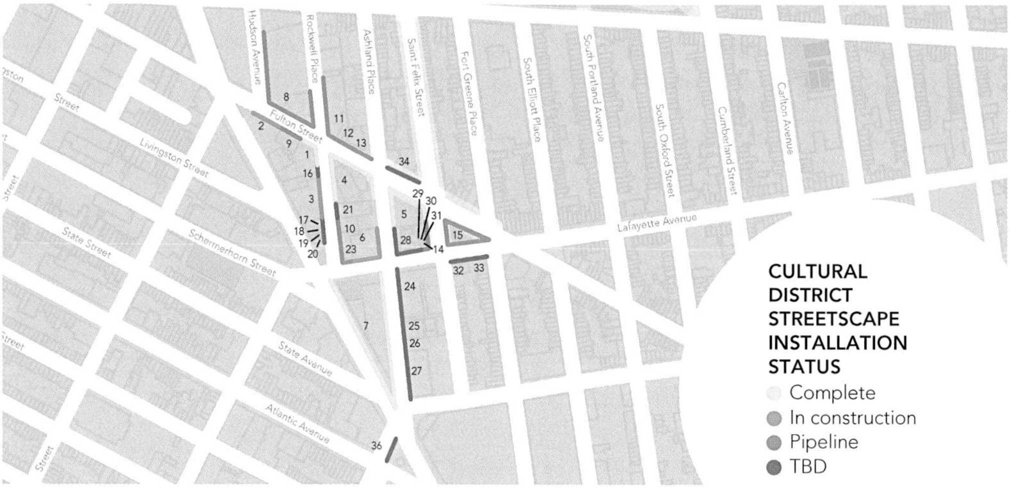

FIGURE 13.4 **Brooklyn Cultural District Streetscape Installation Status, April 2019**

Source: ©Totem. Reproduced, with permission, from Totem; further permission required for reuse. TBD = to be determined.

Brooklyn cultural groups, and better citywide collaboration to promote cultural events was mentioned as a priority in the CreateNYC initiative, the city's first comprehensive cultural plan, released in July 2017.

Phase 4: Management

Culture Forward also recognized that the stakeholders would need to continue their close collaboration, not only to execute the initiatives outlined in the report but also to generate the resources needed to manage their long-term success. It was agreed during the planning process that those duties would largely fall to the DBP and DBAA as the two organizations best poised to oversee implementation. For the DBP's part, this aligned with a simultaneous effort to expand the footprint of one of its existing BIDs—the MetroTech BID—to cover implementation, maintenance, operations, and programming of the several-block radius now encompassing nine cultural venues and new private mixed-use developments.

The proposed expansion of the MetroTech BID resulted from a two-year effort to create a new BID that was intended to encompass the newly created Brooklyn Cultural District (map 13.6). This area was on the receiving end of hundreds of millions of dollars of public and private investment, and stakeholders wanted to ensure these newly created assets were maintained to the highest of standards, especially considering the tremendous influx of new residents, visitors, and workers who would take advantage of the completed developments.

Several issues caused the concept of a new, stand-alone BID to be abandoned. After months of productive discussions with area stakeholders and the NYC Department of Small Business Services, a steering committee was established to explore the potential of instead enlarging the current MetroTech BID to cover several of the previously targeted locations. The committee endorsed this course of action, which was further approved by

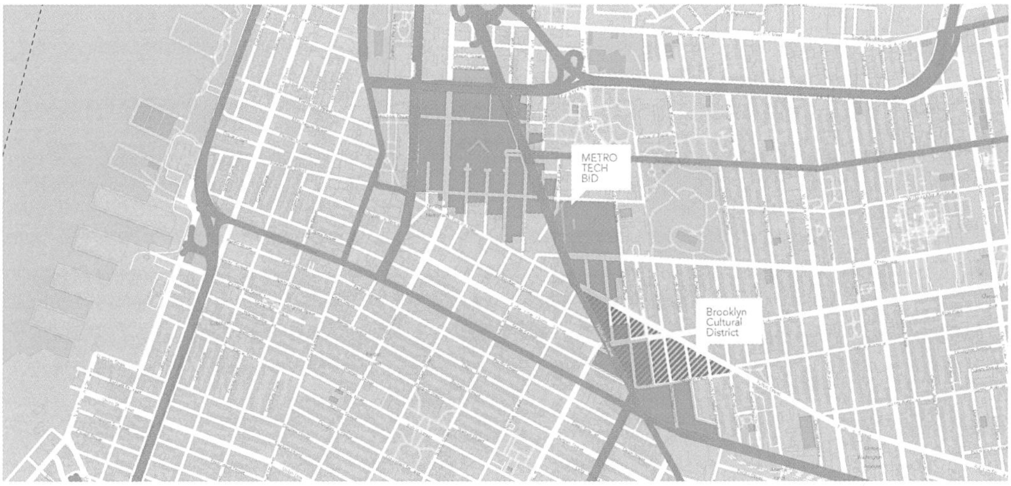

MAP 13.6 **Boundary of MetroTech BID and Brooklyn Cultural District**

Source: ©Totem. Reproduced, with permission, from Totem; further permission required for reuse.
Note: BID = business development district.

the current MetroTech BID Executive Committee and full board of directors. The reasoning was fourfold:

- *The expansion area and the rest of the MetroTech BID had a similar property mix:* large commercial and residential buildings and an abundance of small and larger retailers.
- *The expansion area was to be primarily residential, and the MetroTech BID allows for a residential assessment.* This was vital because allowing a residential assessment spreads the BID costs more evenly across all area stakeholders and beneficiaries; without it, certain property owners would pay disproportionally high assessments.
- *Local stakeholders desired stronger links between this area and the rest of Downtown Brooklyn,* because the area had historically been detached from the commercial core.
- *Enlargement would leverage economies of scale and efficiencies* with the rest of the MetroTech BID, including administration, contracts, and purchasing.

The expansion area, approved by the City Council in January 2016, operates as a subdistrict of the current MetroTech BID, with its own budget funded by assessments on properties within its boundaries. This was important to both the current MetroTech BID and local stakeholders in the expansion area because it will create a self-sustained funding source dedicated to the needs of this specific area to ensure it remains an inviting place to live, work, and visit.

On the part of the DBAA, through the funds it receives on a sliding-scale basis from its 51 members, the organization was positioned to more effectively advocate for its members, an effort that has manifested itself largely in two concrete ways: First, administratively, the organization was granted in 2019 its 501(c)(3) nonprofit tax exemption status, which will allow it not only to serve as a fiscal sponsor and make grants to its members but also to focus proactively on fundraising for its own long-term sustainability and programming. Immediate plans on this latter front include taking on coordination of the Downtown Brooklyn Arts Management Fellowship Program, which in 2020 will undergo a transition year to recalibrate so that it can bring on a greater number of fellows who benefit organizations of varying sizes and missions.

Second—and perhaps more importantly from an advocacy standpoint—the DBAA's role has evolved to promote a rooted neighborhood story of how the arts contributes to Brooklyn, based on local needs. This promotion could take the form of direct advocacy for capital investment in the arts in underserved neighborhoods to better leverage the private investment flowing into the district.

Phase 5: Impact Evaluation

The Brooklyn Cultural District project has spurred private investments in the neighborhood. Since 2007, 11 major real estate development projects have been

BOX 13.1 VOLUNTARY INCLUSIONARY HOUSING: NEW YORK CITY'S AFFORDABLE HOUSING PROGRAM

In 1987, the city created a Voluntary Inclusionary Housing program in high-density R10 and R10-equivalent commercial districts, whereby new developments could increase their maximum floor area ratio (FAR) by providing affordable housing for low-income families (defined as 80 percent of area median income and below). Each square foot of affordable housing receives 1.25–3.5 square feet of bonus floor area, depending on whether the affordable housing is provided on-site or off-site; whether it is added through new construction, rehabilitation, or preservation; and whether or not it receives public funding. As of February 2017, according to the NYC Department of City Planning (DCP), the program has created nearly 4,000 units of permanently affordable housing.

The program was extended to other medium- and high-density areas rezoned for new housing opportunities between 2005 and 2013. These "Inclusionary Housing Designated Areas" were established in R6- through R10-zoned districts in the outer boroughs, where the "base" FAR allowed if the development does not participate in the Inclusionary Housing program is generally lower than the standard FAR for the district, and the maximum FAR available with the bonus is higher than the standard FAR. As the program description states, "In general, developments within a Designated Area can increase permitted FAR by 33 percent if an amount of floor area equivalent to 20 percent of the building's floor area, excluding ground-floor non-residential floor area, is provided for affordable housing. Affordable housing created through the program must remain affordable in perpetuity for households at or below 80 percent of Area Median income (AMI)."

And in 2016, DCP launched a "Mandatory Inclusionary Housing" (MIH) program that requires that 25–30 percent of new housing created through

(box continues next page)

undertaken in the several-block stretch from Fulton Street to Barclays Center. In total, they represent more than US$1 billion of new investment in the neighborhood and have contributed more than 2,000 new apartments and close to 350,000 square feet of new office space. Perhaps most importantly, these developments contributed almost 550 units of affordable housing—a significant portion of the approximately 2,500 units of affordable housing in Downtown Brooklyn today—as well as close to 200,000 square feet of new retail space that has helped infuse the area with new tenants like bars, restaurants, and coffee shops while also creating dozens of new jobs for the local community (DBP 2018).

On the other hand, investment attraction to the area at this scale has the inevitable unintended consequences related to gentrification and displacement of the artistic community that these measures were designed to support and serve—with ready-made solutions for preserving the character of neighborhoods few and far between. To address this issue, New York City does have a long and established precedent to encourage affordable housing development through zoning incentives (box 13.1).

BOX 13.1 VOLUNTARY INCLUSIONARY HOUSING: NEW YORK CITY'S AFFORDABLE HOUSING PROGRAM *(Continued)*

zoning actions be set aside as permanently affordable for neighborhood residents. MIH is a key component of Mayor Bill de Blasio's housing plan, with a goal to build or protect 300,000 units of affordable housing by 2026. To date, the program has already financed more than 120,000 homes since its inception in 2014.

At the federal level, the Low-Income Housing Tax Credit (LIHTC) is the most prolific tool available to developers for creating affordable housing for low-income Americans. These tax credits are distributed by the federal government to developers through state government intermediaries, and developers can then sell them to investors to raise money for their affordable housing projects.

Nothing in this process prohibits developers from setting aside an affordable housing preference for artists. However, at the municipal level, public policy intended to encourage inclusion can have the unintended consequence of making it impossible to set aside housing specifically for a special class of people like artists without violating the law. The New York City Human Rights Law prohibits discrimination on the basis of occupation in housing accommodations. This means that in New York City, artist housing preference is not allowable because it might be interpreted as discrimination on the basis of occupation. So, the esoteric web of government tax policy and antidiscrimination laws combine to make it incredibly difficult for the market to deliver affordable artist housing, even where there is a desire to do so.

Sources: "Inclusionary Housing," Zoning Tools, NYC Department of City Planning (website), accessed June 8, 2019: https://www1.nyc.gov/site/planning/zoning/districts-tools/inclusionary-housing.page; "Housing New York," NYC Housing Plan, City of New York (website), accessed June 8, 2019: https://www1.nyc.gov/site/housing/index.page.

Despite all these challenges, a handful of housing opportunities targeted to artists can be found—including one in the Brooklyn Tech Triangle at 160 Schermerhorn Street, where a New York City–based nonprofit called The Actors Fund partnered with a local developer to provide 100 studio apartments for eligible individuals from the local community. Although the units are not exclusive to artists, The Actors Fund worked with partners to market them to artist communities and offer services that help them navigate the complicated application process. For instance, one of the most challenging aspects of providing affordable housing to artists is a basic one, as one artist put it (Arnow 2018): "Documenting a consistent income level while working in a career filled with unknowns and inconsistencies." This is important, because applicants must self-report annual income to remain in compliance with tax credits and other affordable housing programs, and developers are required to certify incomes to ensure that they have not exceeded the set thresholds. Thus, the affordable housing application system favors individuals with a regular income stream from one employer, which is not the case for most artists (Arnow 2018).

Exacerbating these affordability challenges is a growth trend poised to continue as nearly half a dozen new projects are currently under construction or in the planning pipeline that will contribute nearly 2 million square feet of additional new development.

However, this growth is something to celebrate as well. It provides an excellent example of how targeted public investment can create vast returns in the form of private investment in new housing, office, and retail space that generates hundreds of millions of dollars in tax revenue for the city.

Going forward, the challenge will be to ensure that the investment in and contribution of the arts and culture in Brooklyn is adequately conveyed to the broader community in order to sustain the Brooklyn Cultural District for the long term. A 2014 economic impact analysis conducted by the Downtown Brooklyn Partnership found that impact to be US$310 million in economic activity, drawing more than 4.5 million annual visitors to the area (DBP 2014). The popularity of the Brooklyn Cultural District would be a welcome achievement for any city hoping to follow its blueprint.

NOTES

1. Urbanomics studied the economic impact, growth trends, employment, and space needs of innovation firms that were in the Brooklyn Tech Triangle or considering moving there. They began with a survey of firms over a two-week period in March 2012. The survey yielded a response rate of just over 25 percent and included 185 viable responses.
2. Polytechnic University was a long-time driver of innovation in Brooklyn that had recently merged with New York University to create NYU-POLY, NYU's engineering school, today known as NYU Tandon School of Engineering.
3. Media coverage was identified using the LexisNexis Data Query Tool: https://customertestdata.risk.lexisnexis.com/.
4. Data for the 2015 Strategic Plan Update used New York State Department of Labor Zip Code Business Pattern data, which included more-updated numbers of innovation firms than were available at the time of the 2012 Economic Impact Study. Thus, the percentage increase is calculated based on 1,107 firms in 2012.

5. Data for the 2015 Strategic Plan Update used New York State Department of Labor Zip Code Business Pattern data, which included more-updated numbers of innovation firms than were available at the time of the 2012 Economic Impact Study. Thus, the percentage increase is calculated based on 11,967 in 2012.
6. "A Look Ahead: Brooklyn Tech Triangle." Brooklyn Tech Triangle (website), accessed November 30, 2017: http://brooklyntechtriangle.com/.
7. "NYC Plaza Program," New York City Department of Transportation (website), accessed January 30, 2019: https://www1.nyc.gov/html/dot/html/pedestrians/nyc-plaza-program.shtml.
8. "NYC Plaza Program," NYC DOT website.
9. "Property Related Data," New York City Department of Finance data set, NYC Open Data Portal, accessed January 30, 2019: https://www1.nyc.gov/site/finance/about/open-portal.page.
10. Property value data compiled from various data sets using the CoStar commercial database: https://www.costar.com.
11. "Annual Subway Ridership," Metropolitan Transportation Authority (MTA) (website), accessed March 1, 2019: http://web.mta.info/nyct/facts/ridership/ridership_sub_annual.htm.
12. "Annual Subway Ridership," MTA website.
13. "Pedestrians," Data Feeds, New York City Department of Transportation (NYCDOT) (website), accessed March 1, 2019: http://www.nyc.gov/html/dot/html/about/datafeeds.shtml#Pedestrians.
14. For more about the DUMBO Walls project, begun in 2012, see "DUMBO Walls," DUMBO (website), accessed June 8, 2019: https://dumbo.is/dumbo-walls.
15. M1-4 use allows a maximum commercial and manufacturing floor area ratio (FAR) of 2.0 (FAR being the ratio between a building's total usable floor area and the total area of the lot on which the building stands). On the residential side, R7A Inclusionary Zoning allows a base residential FAR of 3.45 and a maximum residential FAR of 4.6 (80 feet), and R8A Inclusionary Zoning allows a base residential FAR of 5.4 and a maximum residential FAR of 7.2 (120 feet).

REFERENCES

AEA, DBAA, and DBP (AEA Consulting, Downtown Brooklyn Arts Alliance, and Downtown Brooklyn Partnership). 2016. "Culture Forward." Booklet, AEA, DBAA, and DBP, Brooklyn, NY.

Arnow, Daniel. 2018. "Affordable Housing for Artists in New York City: What Are the Challenges?" *Multiple Cities* (blog), April 16. https://www.multiplecities.org/home/2018/4/16/affordable-housing-for-artists-in-new-york-city-what-are-the-challenges.

BNY, DBP, and DUMBO BID (Brooklyn Navy Yard, Downtown Brooklyn Partnership, and DUMBO Improvement District). 2015. "A Look Ahead: Brooklyn Tech Triangle, 2015 Update." Report, BNY, DBP, and DUMBO BID, Brooklyn, NY.

Bonislawski, Adam. 2017. "Brooklyn Bridge Park Is Turning Everything It Touches to Gold." *New York Post*, February 16.

Cuba, Julianne. 2018. "Between a Block and a Hard Place: Plan to Revamp Dumbo Plaza and Nearby Belgian-Block Streets Draws Mixed Reactions." *Brooklyn Paper*, August 17.

DBP (Downtown Brooklyn Partnership). 2014. "Brooklyn Cultural District's $310 Million Impact." Article, DBP website, November 14. http://downtownbrooklyn.com/about.

———. 2018. "Downtown Brooklyn: Development Matrix, Q3 2018." Development data summary, Downtown Brooklyn Partnership, Brooklyn, NY.

DUMBO BID (Down Under the Manhattan Bridge Overpass [DUMBO] Improvement District). 2019. "Annual Report, DUMBO Improvement District, 2018–2019." DUMBO BID, Brooklyn, NY.

Jacobs, Jane. 1961. *The Death and Life of Great American Cities*. New York: Random House.

NYC Council (New York City Council). 2011. "Speaker Quinn Outlines Nine Point Job Creation Strategy." Press release, October 18.

NYCEDC (New York City Economic Development Corporation). 2012. "Mayor Bloomberg Announces Three Major Milestones in the Revitalization of the Downtown Brooklyn Cultural District." Press release, November 28.

NYC LPC (New York City Landmarks Preservation Commission). 2007. "DUMBO Historic District Designation Report." NYC LPC, New York.

NYS (New York State). 2018. "Governor Cuomo Announces Downtown Brooklyn as $10 Million New York City Region Winner of Third-Round Downtown Revitalization Initiative." Press release, October 2.

Roldos, Miguel. 2018. "The Impact of Public Plazas on DUMBO Real Estate Value." Research paper, May 7.

Urbanomics. 2012. "The Brooklyn Tech Triangle: Economic Impacts of the Tech and Creative Sectors." Report for the Brooklyn Tech Triangle, Urbanomics, Brooklyn, NY.

WXY. 2013. "Brooklyn Tech Triangle: Strategic Plan 2013." Plan report prepared for the Brooklyn Navy Yard Development Corporation, Downtown Brooklyn Partnership, and DUMBO Improvement District, WXY, Brooklyn, NY.

———. 2016. "Brooklyn Strand: Urban Design Action Plan." Presentation, WXY, Brooklyn, NY.

CHAPTER 14

SEOUL, REPUBLIC OF KOREA: REJUVENATING NEIGHBORHOODS BY CREATIVELY REPURPOSING URBAN INFRASTRUCTURE AND BUILDINGS

Seong Soo Kim, Kil Yong Lee, Jiyoung Lim, and Taehoon Ha

KEY TAKEAWAYS

- Seoul is the economic and cultural center of the Republic of Korea, but its historic city core has experienced dilapidation over the years. The three case studies—Gyeongui Line Forest Park, Gusandong Library, and Yonsei-Ro—exemplify Seoul's recent efforts to rejuvenate neighborhood areas by recovering green and cultural spaces for communities.
- The creative reuse of abandoned railway infrastructure land to become the Gyeongui Line Forest Park has led to several outcomes: connecting adjacent communities and residential areas that were previously physically separated or disconnected; improving vibrancy; attracting younger visitors; introducing more greenery to the city, which helped mitigate heat island effects by lowering surface temperatures; and improving property values along the park area, which increased by 6.7 percent within a year of project completion—twice the average increase of other neighborhoods in Seoul.
- The repurposing of a cluster of old residential buildings into the Gusandong Library not only helped preserve the local identity but also improved services to an underserved local community, especially for older persons,

young adults, and children. The municipality also leveraged the private sector to operate and manage the library.

- The transformation of Yonsei-Ro, a main street in a commercial neighborhood, into a more pedestrian-friendly design has led to improved walkability, mobility, and pedestrian safety in the area. One year after project completion, the number of visitors to the street and adjacent areas increased by 28.9 percent. Public-space users' satisfaction rate also drastically increased, by 40 percent. The project was part of a citywide transit-oriented development strategy and has been associated with the reduction of traffic accidents by 54.5 percent along the street as well as reduction in traffic congestion.

CITY DYNAMICS

Context and Background

Seoul has been the economic and cultural center and the capital city of the Republic of Korea for about 600 years. Its population increased from 2 million in the 1950s to 10 million in 2010 and has stabilized since then. The urban footprint of Seoul has more than doubled, from 288 square kilometers in 1963 to its current 606 square kilometers in 2010. This urbanization process has been highly correlated with the city's economic growth, which has increased by about 36 percent between 2000 and 2010.

In 2010, Seoul's gross regional domestic product (GRDP) reached ₩247 trillion (US$247 billion) (Kim 2015). Notably, the capital metropolitan region of the Republic of Korea (comprising Seoul, Gyeonggi-do Province, and Incheon) accounts for a dominant share of the Korean economy, representing 49 percent of its population, 49.6 percent of all jobs, and 48.7 percent of Korea's GDP in 2009 (OECD 2012).

However, Seoul has seen a degradation of its historic downtown areas and a declining sense of place in recent years. The decline in the old downtown has negatively affected its resident population, businesses, and quality of buildings. The population in the old downtown decreased by 22 percent between 2003 and 2016, twice the city's overall rate of population decline (11 percent). The number of businesses shrank by 13 percent between 2003 and 2010, and the downtown's deteriorated physical condition has resulted in the high number of fires—17 per 10,000 persons per year—which is three times higher than the city average.[1]

The urban fabric of Seoul has dramatically changed as well. The basic urban unit of Seoul originated from the hanok, the traditional Korean-style house. This historical building archetype, however, has almost disappeared from effects of war and urbanization. The last surviving such buildings can only be found in some areas of Gangbuk, the district north of the Han River. This trend can be exemplified by the newly developed district of Gangnam. Influenced by the modern urban planning style of Western cities, the district has completely transformed into large urban blocks, and the street network has consequently changed from being pedestrian-centered to being vehicle-centered with wider roads.

To address these challenges, the city government has made substantial efforts over recent decades to regenerate the downtown area. In the 1980s, regeneration focused mostly on smaller-scale projects such as renovating individual buildings and widening streets. This phase was followed by residential redevelopment and transit-oriented development (TOD) in the 1990s. The city halted urban degradation by preserving the historical assets of the downtown area through the Seoul Downtown Management Master Plan in 2000. This plan was successful in improving some physical conditions in the downtown area, but it had a limited effect in transforming the city in an integrated way (Amirtahmasebi et al. 2016).

Public Spaces in Seoul

Seoul has successfully increased the number of public spaces in the city through a virtuous cycle of economic urban growth that is coupled with public service provision to attract more people. Over the past five decades, the total park area in Seoul has increased more than sixfold, from 25.5 square kilometers in 1945 to 169.8 square kilometers in 2010.[2] Seoul also has a variety of cultural facilities and amenities such as public libraries, museums, galleries, and culture centers, and their number has also increased since the 1990s.

The creation of public spaces has kept pace with rapid urban growth, largely because of the country's well-developed legal and political system. In Korea, the provision of different typologies of public spaces are specified as urban infrastructure in the Presidential Decree in Article 2 of The National Land Planning and Utilization Act (NLPUA). The provision of public spaces is thus a requirement and controlled under legislation, including the Museums Promotion Law and Urban Park Act (Lee et al. 2012) (table 14.1).

However, since the 2000s, improving accessibility to high-quality public spaces has become a main challenge. In Seoul, many of the total open green areas are inaccessible, such as mountain areas.[3] This geographical characteristic of the city underscores the need for more urban parks that people can easily access and enjoy. Moreover, privately owned public spaces (POPS) have had

TABLE 14.1 **Acts Related to Urban Public-Space Supply and Management in the Republic of Korea**

Type of public space		Related acts and installation standards
Traffic facilities	Road Pedestrian street Bike lane	Urban planning facilities regulations, Road Act, traffic laws, pedestrian walkway guidelines, Bicycle Act
Space facilities	Urban park Green areas Plaza	Urban planning facilities regulations, Urban Park Act
Public, cultural, and athletic facilities	Cultural facilities (theaters, libraries, museums)	Urban planning facilities regulations, Public Performance Act, Public Library Law, Museum and Art Museum Promotion Law
	Athletic facilities	Urban planning facilities regulations, Sports Facilities Act
	Government office	Urban planning facilities regulations
Disaster-prevention facilities	River	Urban planning facilities regulations, River Act, Small River Maintenance Act

Source: Korea Research Institute for Human Settlements (KRIHS).

limited success in terms of providing more accessible public spaces. In 2016, of the 1,587 POPS across the city, 17 percent were limiting public access by illegally installing fences, hosting private facilities, and advertising. This practice hampers walkability, especially in dense areas where POPS play a critical role in providing rest areas to citizens (Kim 2016). Spatial disparities in accessibility to nearby public facilities among municipalities were also observed. Some districts have less than one cultural facility per 100,000 persons, even though Seoul has the highest number of cultural facilities across Korea.

To reverse these trends, the Ministry of Land, Infrastructure and Transport (MOLIT) has shifted its policies and priorities from the development of new towns to the restoration of existing cities with better provision of public services. MOLIT has initiated the Making Livable City Project[4] and passed a Special Act on Promotion and Support for Urban Regeneration to foster diverse types of neighborhood upgrading projects. The Seoul Metropolitan Government (SMG) also promoted human-centered designs for public spaces and streetscapes, with a focus on people who are socially vulnerable, including children, older persons, and informal sector workers.

GYEONGUI LINE FOREST PARK

Phase 1: Context

Gyeongui-seon is a former railway line connecting the southern and northern parts of the Korean peninsula. This infrastructure was in existence since 1904 and started as a temporary military railway during the Japanese occupation before becoming part of an international railway connecting Seoul to Manchuria and Europe in 1911. Unfortunately, this railway became disconnected between the Democratic People's Republic of Korea and the Republic of Korea when the Korean War broke out in 1950.[5] Currently, the Gyeongui-seon functions as a connector between Incheon International Airport, Seoul, and new towns in the northwest of the Republic of Korea.

In 1996, the SMG requested that the Korea Rail Network Authority (KRNA) move Gyeongui-seon underground because the land it occupied disrupted regional growth and caused environmental degradation to nearby neighborhoods. In 1997, the KRNA announced the construction of an underground double-track line to replace the Gyeongui-seon line above. Subsequently, the city government spearheaded the proposal that a park be implemented over the land that has been freed from the train tracks. The proposal faced resistance because there was also a strong demand to expand roads on the site instead. Despite these controversies, MOLIT was able to approve the development of the linear park as proposed by the city government (figure 14.1).

The Gyeongui Line Forest Park (GLFP) was thus planned as a linear park and station complex along the 6.3-kilometer section of the freed-up railway site. This project aimed to enrich local culture by preserving the history and the memory of the Gyeongui railway, and promote inclusive communities by improving the urban green space. The GLFP connects several neighborhoods with different characteristics, across seven zones (map 14.1): Yeonnam-dong (Zone 1), Waugyo (Zone 2), Sinsu-dong (Zone 3), Daeheungdong (Zone 4), Yeomni-dong (Zone 5), Saechang Gogae (Zone 6), and Wonhyoro (Zone 7).

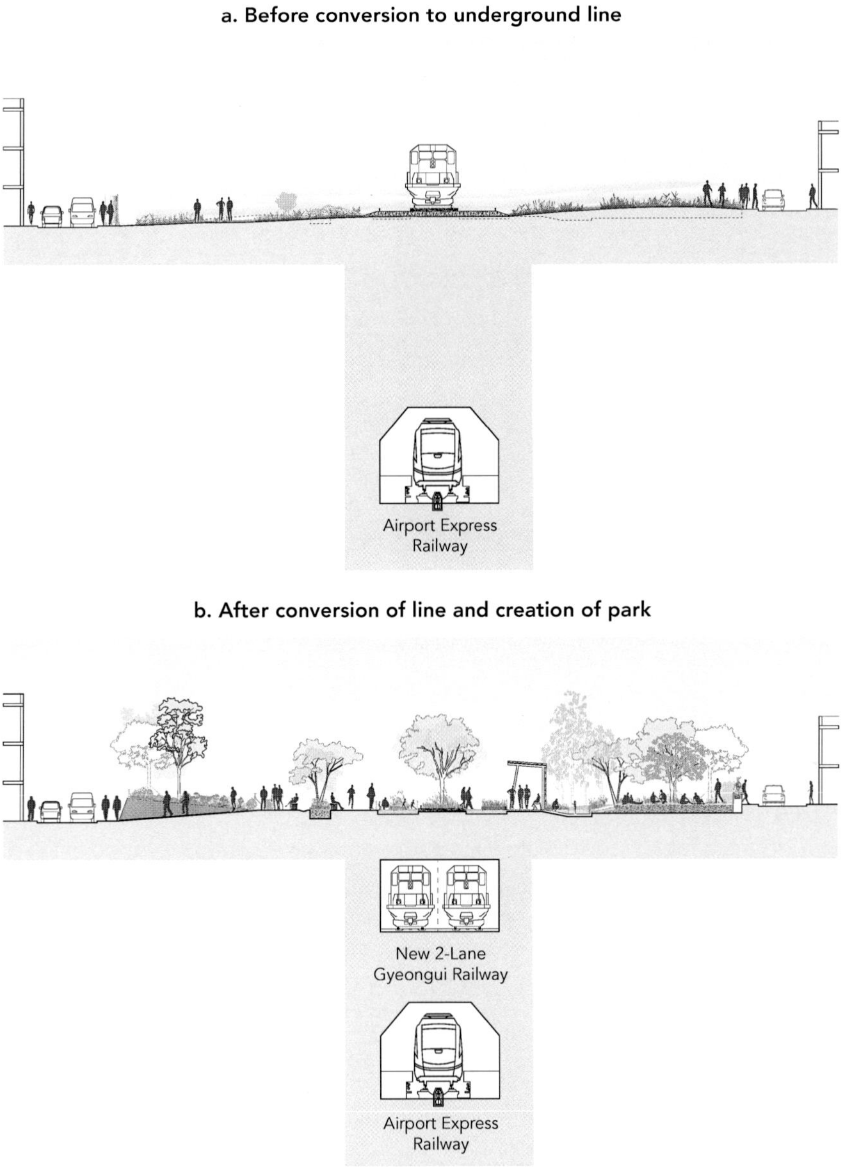

FIGURE 14.1 **Section of Gyeongui-seon before and after Conversion Project**

Source: ©World Bank. Further permission required for reuse.

Phase 2: Planning and Design

Participatory and Flexible Planning

The GLFP was designed through a participatory planning process. Forums, briefing sessions, surveys, and interviews were conducted to hear public opinions. As a result, the final design called for an accessible and porous park with minimal facilities, so as to provide communities with flexible free spaces to use as they want. In other words, the main design strategy was an "unfinished park." Trees were intentionally planted sparsely, leaving physical space to be filled by citizens in the future (figure 14.2). Moreover, the linear park

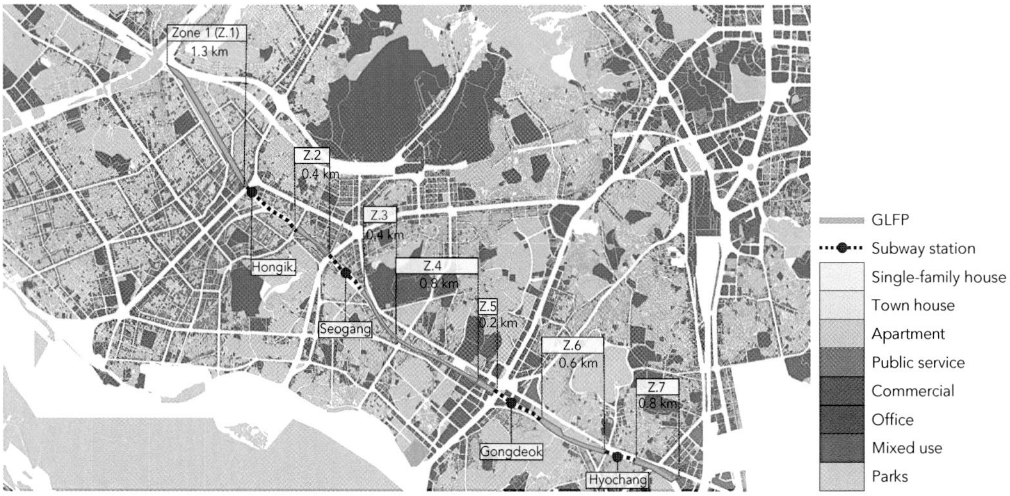

MAP 14.1 **Land Uses in GLFP Zones and Surrounding Areas, Seoul**

Source: ©Korea Research Institute for Human Settlements (KRIHS). Reproduced, with permission, from KRIHS; further permission required for reuse.
Note: GLFP = Gyeongui Line Forest Park.

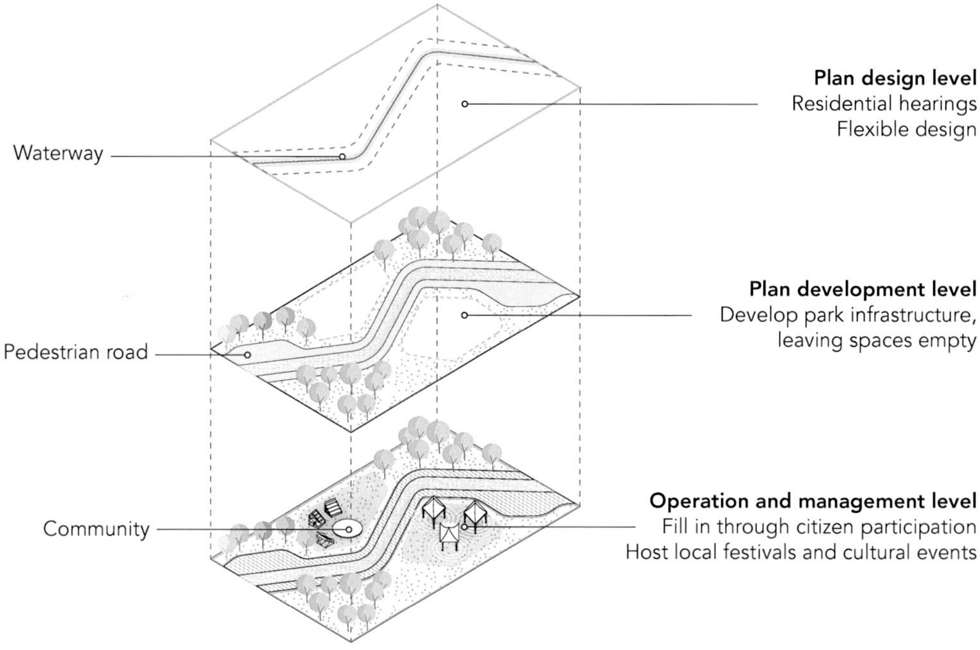

FIGURE 14.2 **Levels of Citizen Participation in GLFP Design Process**

Source: ©World Bank. Further permission required for reuse.
Note: GLFP = Gyeongui Line Forest Park.

PHOTO 14.1 **Diverse Design Concepts for Different GLFP Zones, Seoul**

Source: ©Hyung Ho Lee. Reproduced, with permission, from Hyung Ho Lee; further permission required for reuse.
Note: GLFP = Gyeongui Line Forest Park.

implemented differentiated designs for various zones and neighborhoods. These features were manifested in the design of waterways, squares, picnic areas, and bookstores using old rails (photo 14.1).

Urban Forests and Waterways

The railway lines, measuring over 15 meters in width, were transformed to an ecological park with green and blue spaces. A tree-lined street and urban forests were planned along the linear site. Waterways, such as streams and ponds, were restored in some zones (photo 14.2, panel a). For example, in Yeonnam-dong section (Zone 1), an old stream has been restored as a 1-meter-wide waterway using leachate water from the subway (photo 14.2, panel b). It is connected to the Hongjecheon, an existing nearby stream.

Restructuring of Walls and Entrances for Openness and Privacy

The layout of the park features a zigzag-shaped pathway to better connect neighborhoods on both sides of the park. These neighborhoods were

a. A pond in GLFP　　b. A stream along tree-lined streets

PHOTO 14.2 **Waterway in Yeonnam-dong Section, Gyeongui Line Forest Park, Seoul**

Source: License-free image from http://m.blog.naver.com/you1620.
Note: GLFP = Gyeongui Line Forest Park.

previously separated by the railroad and noise-control fences. The access points are interconnected with the adjacent street blocks to provide easy access to residents and visitors (figure 14.3; photo 14.3, panel a). The adjacent streets are also paved with road-calming material to limit the speed of vehicles to prioritize pedestrian safety and ease of movement (photo 14.3, panel b).

Although the GLFP has been designed as a free space for the public, efforts were also made to address the privacy of residents in the area. During the initial phase of the project, the surrounding building conditions were surveyed to determine the physical characteristics (such as façade width, building height, and topography) as well as the types of existing uses at the ground floor. The design of the GLFP then responded to these existing conditions. For example, if the ground floor of a building was for residential use, low-rise walls were designed to provide privacy to residents' units while maintaining visual connection to the park.

Phase 3: Implementation

Before the implementation of the project, a series of discussions about land ownership was conducted among public entities. Because the KRNA owns the land, the SMG is required to pay an "occupation fee" to KRNA to

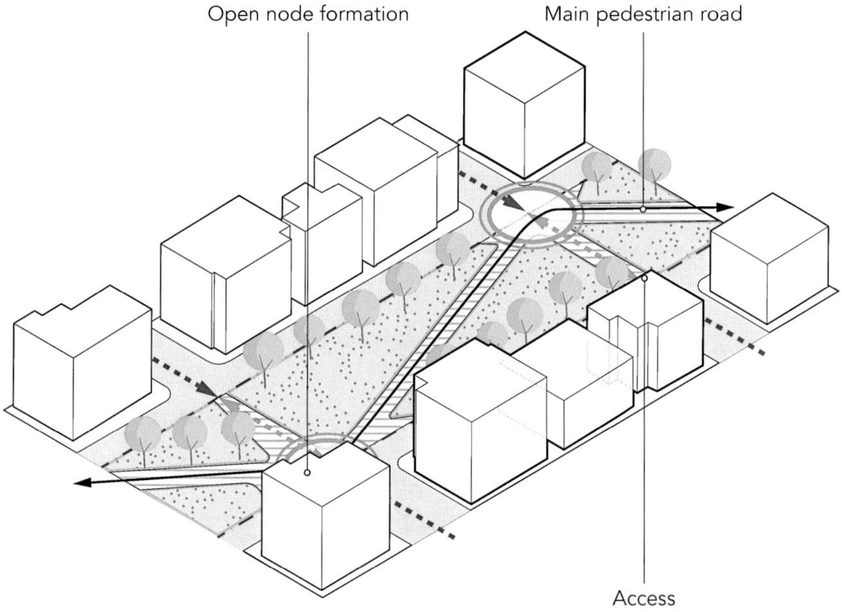

FIGURE 14.3 **Plan for Connecting Pedestrians with Surroundings in GLFP, Seoul**

Source: ©World Bank. Further permission required for reuse.
Note: GLFP = Gyeongui Line Forest Park.

a. Connection between park and residential areas **b. Differentiated paving designs for vehicle flow**

PHOTO 14.3 **Openness in Yeonnam-dong Section (Zone 1) of GLFP, Seoul**

Source: ©Hyung Ho Lee. Reproduced, with permission, from Hyung Ho Lee; further permission required for reuse.
Note: GLFP = Gyeongui Line Forest Park.

develop the park on the site, as with most other development projects of this nature.

The SMG and KRNA, however, agreed on an alternative solution: in 2010, both agencies signed a memorandum of understanding (MOU) that guaranteed the SMG the right to use the site free of charge for 50 years in

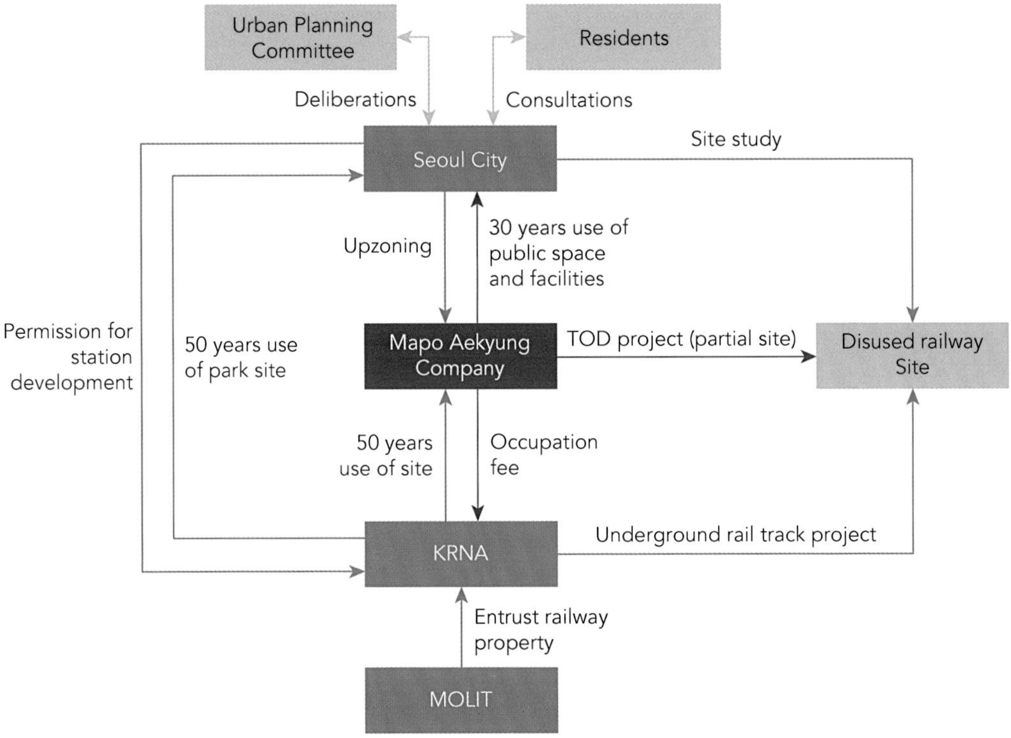

FIGURE 14.4 **Stakeholders of Gyeongui-seon Line Forest Park Project, Seoul**

Source: ©World Bank, based on Park et al. 2016. Further permission required for reuse.
Note: KRNA = Korea Rail Network Authority. MOLIT = Ministry of Land, Infrastructure and Transport. TOD = transit-oriented development.

exchange for authorizing KRNA's TOD projects near the GLFP project site (figure 14.4).

The agreement enabled the SMG to start the implementation in 2011 and to successfully complete the park in 2016. The SMG funded the entire cost of GLFP implementation (₩45 billion, or US$45 million), which was completed in three stages:

- *Stage 1:* The project was piloted in Zone 4 and completed within a year, in 2012.
- *Stage 2:* The designs for the second stage were revised to reflect lessons learned from the first stage, and three zones (Zones 1, 5, and 6) were completed in 2015.
- *Stage 3:* The remaining three zones (Zones 2, 3, and 7) were completed and opened in 2016.

As part of the GLFP implementation, the KRNA leveraged the development of four station complexes to serve and rejuvenate the surrounding neighborhoods. This was possible because the GLFP site was directly connected to several multimodal stations that had the potential to provide more open spaces and public facilities (photo 14.4).

PHOTO 14.4 **Connection between GLFP and Entrance to Hongik Subway Station, Seoul**

Source: ©Hyung Ho Lee. Reproduced, with permission, from Hyung Ho Lee; further permission required for reuse.
Note: GLFP = Gyeongui Line Forest Park.

These projects were implemented through public-private partnerships led by the KRNA. The necessary licenses and permits, including to change land uses, had been obtained from the SMG through the MOU in exchange for the SMG's use of the land. For example, the KRNA established a special purpose vehicle (SPV), Mapo Aekyung, to develop a 17-story building complex at Hongik subway station, one of the busiest multimodal stations in Seoul. The agreement made for this development required that, in return for upzoning its building complex, the SPV is required to (a) pay the KRNA, the owner of the land and railway facilities, occupation fees for the use of the site for 30 years; and (b) create public spaces on the site to provide walkable urban space connected with the GLFP (figure 14.4).

Phase 4: Management

The SMG oversees the management of the GLFP, but it has been a challenging task, especially because of the park's popularity and its large area. The park's daily maintenance costs and facilities are funded through the city government's budget, totaling approximately ₩4.6 billion (US$4.6 million) annually. In addition to funding the maintenance, the SMG had to manage many conflicts and tensions between a wide range of stakeholders across different neighborhoods. For example, in some residential neighborhoods adjacent to the park, residents have complained about privacy, noise, and garbage problems to the city government. Also, when the park is overcrowded, there have been instances of various user groups such as pet walkers, bicyclists, and music performers quarrelling over the limited park spaces.[6]

To better address these management issues, a nonprofit "Friends of GLFP" was formed in 2015, made up of local experts, volunteers, and residents.[7] The nonprofit supports park maintenance, event programming, and conflict resolution between stakeholders. It is organized into four regional groups, representing different neighborhoods to address local needs and to estimate operating costs for each neighborhood. A total of about ₩7 million (US$7,000), funded by the city government in 2018, was allocated to sustain the nonprofit and to organize activities such as events and the establishment of park use regulations to resolve the conflicts between residents and visitors.

In addition to the city's investments in infrastructure such as the installation of garbage cans, the Friends of GLFP carried out a public campaign to reduce garbage and littering in the park. The campaign saw some success when surrounding shops and residents voluntarily joined, and a forum for residents was also held at the community center in Yeonnam-dong to establish the "Gyeongui Line Forest Park Use Regulations." This resulted also in the installation of informational banners and signs to maintain the clean environment of the park and surrounding areas.

Phase 5: Impact Evaluation

Boost to Retail Activities and Property Values

The neighborhoods around the newly opened GLFP saw an increase in the number of businesses, mostly new restaurants and retail stores. For instance, the Waugyo section (Zone 2), formerly a deteriorated commercial area, benefited significantly in terms of business generated: The number of businesses in the Waugyo section increased by 101.3 percent in 2017 over 2015, before the park was constructed. The average monthly sales per shop in the retail sector rose by 151.3 percent in the same area. This is a remarkable increase relative to the sales in nearby commercial areas such as Shinchon (16.8 percent) and the Ewha Women's University area (9.7 percent) in the same period (SMG 2018).

In the areas surrounding the GLFP, property values rose by 6.7 percent between 2016 and 2017, which is the highest recorded rate of increase among the 25 districts in Seoul (twice the rate in Seongbuk District, at 3.4 percent). Real estate experts attributed the rise of property values in this area to the creation of the GLFP. Particularly, the appraised prices of 28 land plots out of 68 around the Yeonnam-dong section rose by 20 percent after the project (SMG 2018).

Environmental Impact

Although the GLFP's full environmental benefits have yet to be quantified, it has been anticipated that the creation of a park in dense urban areas can contribute to the improvement of microclimate—mitigating urban heat islands and increasing flood resilience through the large increase in permeable land area and inclusion of lush greenery such as trees, lawn, and flowers (photo 14.5).

PHOTO 14.5 **Environmental Features in the Yeonnam-dong Section of the GLFP, Seoul**

Source: ©Hyung Ho Lee. Reproduced, with permission, from Hyung Ho Lee; further permission required for reuse.
Note: GLFP = Gyeongui Line Forest Park.

A study found that after the GLFP was implemented, surface temperatures were lower along the park area than in the surrounding urban built-up areas (Kim, Yi, and Lee 2019).

Social Inclusion

The GLFP project is viewed as a successful transformation of a disused state-owned railway infrastructure into a public space that caters to people and adds to the vibrancy of the surrounding neighborhoods. Groups of people use the park for a variety of everyday uses, such as performances, pop-up markets, and picnics (photo 14.6). The linear park is also being used for nonmotorized transport (NMT) urban mobility, because it connects different zones in Seoul.

A user survey found that area residents are highly satisfied with the park, and its most appreciated features are (a) better accessibility and pathways connecting to other neighborhoods and surrounding areas; (b) removal of fences and walls that had previously obstructed views of the park; and (c) the overall revitalization of the surrounding areas (Yun 2017). Visitors who are not area residents were most satisfied with the large, scenic open space offered by the GLFP as a destination for after-work and weekend recreation.

PHOTO 14.6 **Variety of Activities at Gyeongui Line Forest Park, Seoul**

Source: ©Hyung Ho Lee. Reproduced, with permission, from Hyung Ho Lee; further permission required for reuse.

GUSANDONG LIBRARY VILLAGE

Phase 1: Context

The Gusandong neighborhood is a highly residential area with 11 elementary, middle, and high schools (map 14.2). However, despite being a residential area that is home to many families with school-age children, the neighborhood had no libraries or cultural facilities in the vicinity. The lack of public facilities led more than 2,000 residents to sign a petition on May 11, 2006, to build a library. In response, the Eunpyeong District Office took on the task of creating a new library facility and decided to start planning for and assembling land and property in Gusandong for the project.

In contrast to other top-down development projects, the Gusandong Library Village project actively solicited the opinions of residents during its planning, design, and implementation. Unsurprisingly, the parents of schoolchildren became active and involved with the project. Notably, the library was named as a "ma-eul" ("village") to highlight the library's unique characteristics in addressing local needs to promote social capital in the neighborhood. The project sought to provide a wide range of

MAP 14.2 **Land Use around Gusandong Library Village, Seoul**

Source: ©Korea Research Institute for Human Settlements (KRIHS). Reproduced, with permission, from KRIHS; further permission required for reuse.

services for all ages and groups while also preserving the local context by using existing buildings and streets to form the structure of the new library (figure 14.5).

Phase 2: Design

The Gusandong Library Village was conceptually innovative and architecturally novel, because it sought to repurpose a series of existing residential buildings into a collection of spaces for education, communication, and entertainment instead of demolishing them for new construction. After conducting basic planning research, the Eunpyeong District Office sought several design proposals for its implementation. To evaluate the development and design options, a committee was formed, consisting of seven judges selected from members of the resident participation committee, the District Office construction committee, and the Seoul public architect association. The final design selected for the library was Design Group OZ's proposal, which centered around three core design principles:

- Preserving memories of the neighborhood;
- Building community-centered space; and
- Repurposing existing residential buildings and rooms as reading spaces, and road networks as corridors and bookshelves.

First, the project used numerous streets and residential buildings built from the 1970s to the 1990s, including three existing houses and one dead-end road. The project team decided to preserve these buildings to house

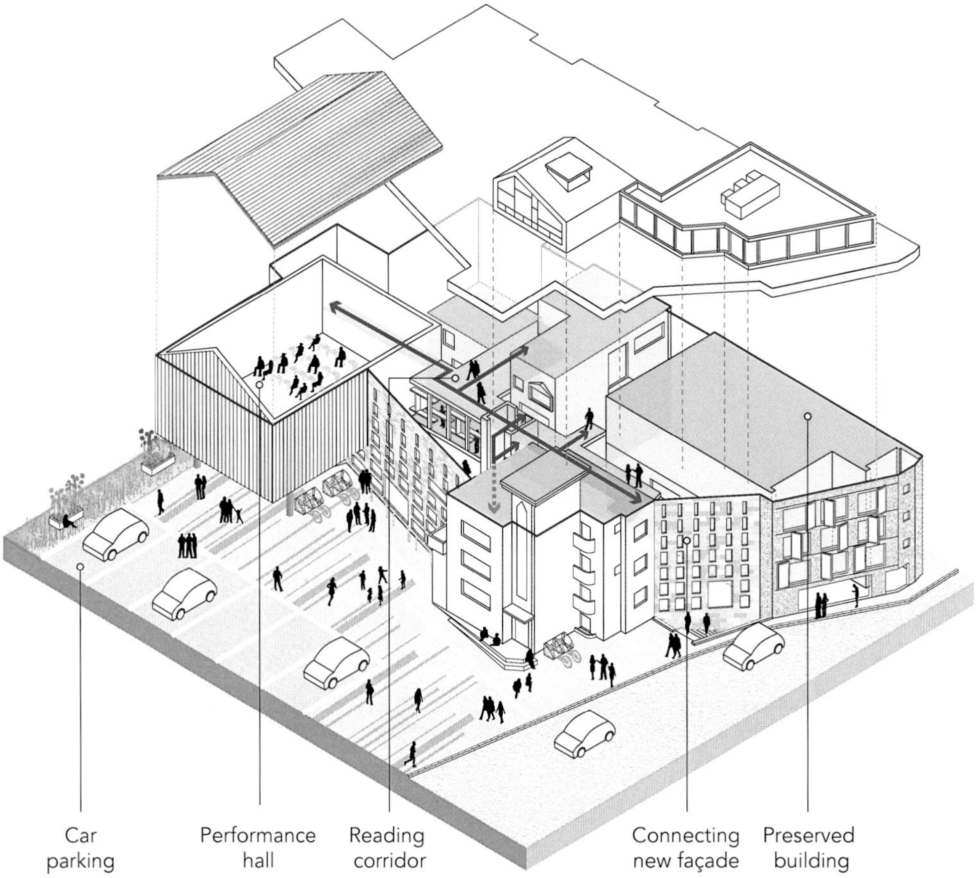

FIGURE 14.5 **Gusandong Library Village, Seoul: An Inclusive Structure for Diverse Activities and Users**

Source: ©World Bank. Further permission required for reuse.

key spaces and designed new structures to connect those spaces. This approach not only saved cost and time but also organically incorporated the new library into the local context. The resulting library structure was an interesting one: it incorporated five existing buildings into one new building that functions as a façade (figure 14.6). As a result, the exterior façades of the old residential buildings were transformed into the interior walls of the new library.

Second, given the site's location within a dense residential neighborhood, it was important to offer a variety of open spaces where residents could gather to study, communicate, and enjoy activities. Residents actively participated in assigning spaces for dynamic programs to reflect their needs, and the District Office also advised the design team on applicable programs based on best practices.

Finally, the existing building structure and roads were repurposed as rooms and corridors of the library. In all, 55 rooms of existing residential buildings were redesigned as spaces for various activities such as music recording, cartoon collecting, discussions, and club activities that meet the

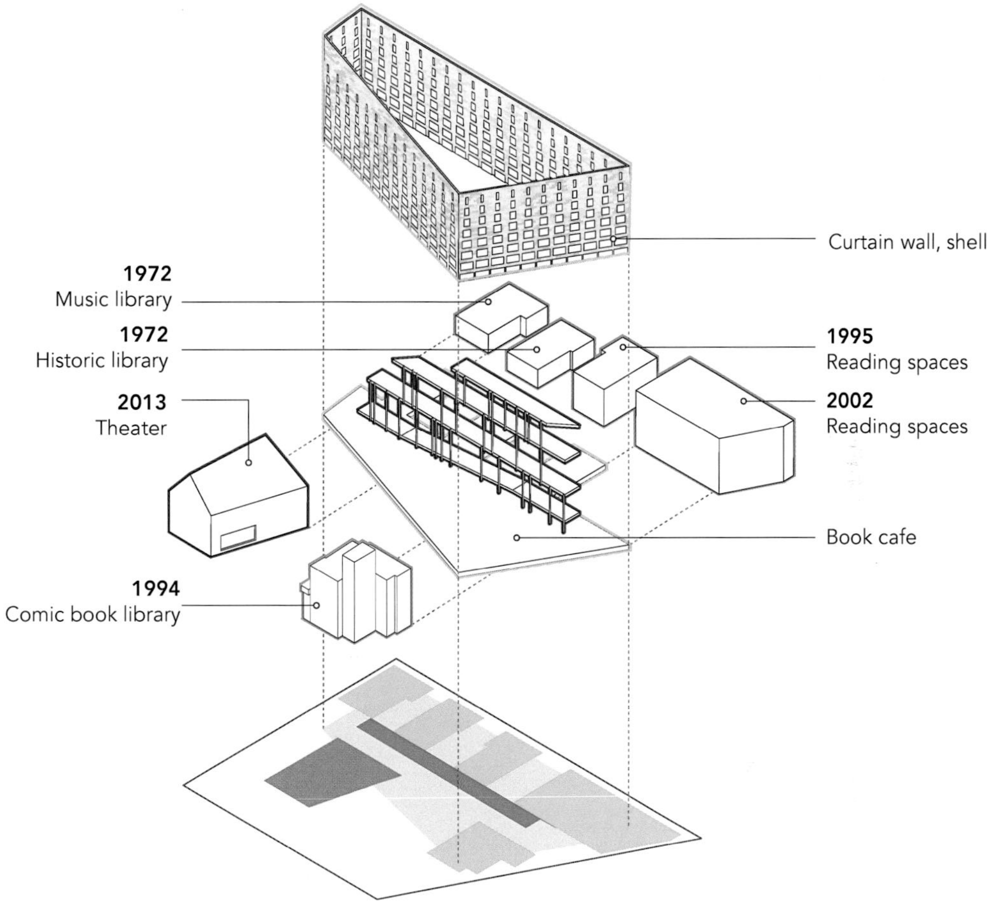

FIGURE 14.6 **Final Design Plan for Gusandong Library Village, Seoul**

Source: ©World Bank. Further permission required for reuse.

Note: Light blue designates existing residential buildings; other colors designate new structures. Years indicate the construction year of existing buildings.

residents' needs (photo 14.7, panel a). The road space has been converted into an interior connector to other library rooms and a reading space along with bookshelves and chairs (photo 14.7, panel b).

Phase 3: Implementation

Budget Secured through Participatory Budgeting

The construction of the library was challenging because of a budget deficit at the beginning. Five years after the petition was submitted, the project was resumed in 2011 with the city government's introduction of the participatory budgeting system, enabling citizens to participate in the budgeting process. The budget of ₩1.9 billion (US$1.9 million) was initially secured, but it was still insufficient to implement the project. After a discussion between residents and the district government, the district council decided

a. Main lobby connected to rooms of old residential buildings

b. Road transformed into a library corridor

PHOTO 14.7 **Interior of the Gusandong Library Village, Seoul**

Source: ©Hyung Ho Lee. Reproduced, with permission, from Hyung Ho Lee; further permission required for reuse.

to secure additional funding of ₩3.5 billion (US$3.5 million) from both the central and the district governments. In the end, the total budget increased to ₩6.5 billion (US$6.5 million), including ₩1 billion from the central government, ₩3.5 billion from the city government, and ₩2 billion from the district (Gu) government.[8]

Challenges Resolved through Active Citizen Participation

Given that the construction site was in a densely populated area, the implementation timeline was accelerated to minimize public inconvenience and complaints during the construction period. However, meeting the planned timeline became challenging after the design and construction plans went through a number of variations. For example, the gross floor area of the building was doubled from 1,215 to 2,946 square meters, and the total cost also increased proportionally. This was mainly because structural defects were found in some of the old buildings, which necessitated additional ground reinforcement work and construction of new structures (Lim, Kim, and Kim 2017).

Through active engagement by residents, the construction of the library was completed within two years after the sufficient budget was secured and was opened in 2015. At weekly consultation meetings with residents, neighborhood parents voluntarily contributed to various activities such as conducting surveys. The designers also regularly communicated with residents and tried to reflect their opinions in modifications during the implementation stage. This process helped the designers to address the needs of the community and to propose appropriate design solutions quickly.

Phase 4: Management

In 2015, the Eunpyeong District Office recruited the Eunpyeong Library Village Cooperative as a professional operator from the private sector. The cooperative was formed to promote the "Libraries for All Citizens" program organized by motivated citizens, including women who staffed the libraries and people working for community revitalization. The program began as a small reading group and an organizer of library events titled "Libraries on Every Corner." To meet the growing demand from citizens, the cooperative's mission shifted into more proactive citizen action, such as submitting proposals to develop new libraries and improve the efficiency of operation and maintenance for libraries. The cooperative was officially registered as a nonprofit organization in 2013 and designated as an operator of Gusandong Library Village in 2015, with three-year contract extensions allowed.

In addition to maintaining the facilities of Gusandong Library Village, the cooperative conducts research on library-related policies and develops plans for cultural events to promote the use of the library as a "multifunctional community center" (Kim 2017). Events organized by the cooperative included lecture series, music festivals, writing classes, artistic and independent film screenings, farmers markets, and volunteer programs in collaboration with 17 schools nearby.[9]

Phase 5: Evaluation

Improved Neighborhood Services and Social Cohesion

The Gusandong Library Village is targeted at youths (even with a section dedicated to comic books) and has been positioned as a "sarangbang," which is a community space for the neighborhood. According to a 2016 satisfaction survey, youths accounted for more than 60 percent of the library's total users.

The project also helped to improve services and revitalize the neighborhood. Of the total users, 87 percent were residents who walked to the library, and more than half visited the library at least twice a week. The survey also found that users highly appreciated the library's building design and internal spaces, which encouraged all ages and groups to freely meet and communicate with each other—a departure from the traditional designs of Korean libraries (Lim, Kim, and Kim 2017).

Innovative and Collaborative Model for Public Architecture

In recognition of these achievements, the library received the Korea Public Architecture Award and the Seoul City Architecture Award in 2016. Judges from the Korea Public Architecture Award acknowledged Gusandong Library Village as an innovative model of public architecture that has been built through excellent collaboration among residents, designers, and the local government. Judges from the Seoul City Architecture Award commented that the library is a successful model that could be replicated for future public projects in Korea (MOLIT 2016). Since its implementation, the innovative concept adopted by the project has influenced public library projects in other regions, such as the Wolgok Dream Picture Library project and a youth library in the Seongbukgu District in Seoul.

YONSEI-RO

Phase 1: Context

Yonsei-ro is a street located in the western part of Seoul's old downtown, located close to mountains and that traverses several neighborhoods that were once vibrant but have since declined. The neighborhood is accessible to public transportation and universities. As such, the land around Yonsei-ro is predominantly commercial in nature. These areas include the Sinchon Commercial Area and the Ewha Commercial Area, where restaurants and fashion-related companies targeting young people are located (map 14.3). These areas used to be vibrant meeting places for youths in the 2000s, but neglect and poor management resulted in poor walkability and accessibility. Narrow roads are encroached upon by street vendors, are plagued by traffic congestion (with vehicle speeds averaging about 10 kilometers per hour all day), and lack pedestrian-friendly spaces.

Beginning in the late 2000s, improving pedestrian safety and walkability became an important policy agenda in Korea, and relevant policy initiatives were put in place and piloted in cities. Yonsei-ro in Seoul was selected as a pilot project. In 2006, the MOLIT announced the "First Public Transport Master Plan" and sought to explore and establish transit malls to reduce traffic demand and improve walkability in congested urban areas.[10] In 2011, MOLIT proposed the expansion of transit mall projects through the "Second Public Transport Master Plan."

In line with these national initiatives, the SMG announced a new vision of "Pedestrian-Friendly City Seoul" in 2012 and made efforts to reorganize the public transportation system, giving priority to pedestrians and public

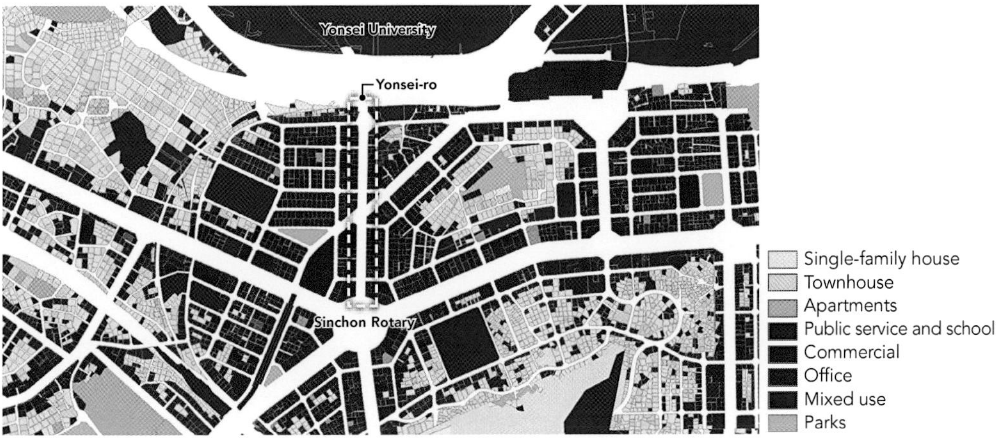

MAP 14.3 **Land Uses Surrounding Yonsei-ro, Old Downtown Seoul**

Source: ©Korea Research Institute for Human Settlements (KRIHS). Reproduced, with permission, from KRIHS; further permission required for reuse.

transportation over motorized vehicles. The city also established the "Seoul Transit Mall Comprehensive Plan" in 2012, and candidate sites for transformative transit mall projects across the city were selected based on a set of criteria, including their land use, accessibility to public transportation, and number of public transportation users. Yonsei-ro—which extended 550 meters, from Shinchon Rotary to the entrance of Yonsei University—was selected as the first pilot transit mall project in Seoul, out of 10 candidate sites.

Phase 2: Design

Walkability Improvement

To improve pedestrian walkability, various targeted design techniques were applied (figure 14.7). Sidewalks were widened significantly because they were too narrow for pedestrians. Previously, sidewalks were 3–4 meters wide, but only 1–2 meters were available for pedestrian use because of the presence of informal street vendors and large electricity distribution boxes.

Because the reclamation of street space for more sidewalk space was limited, a site study of traffic and pedestrian flows was conducted to determine an optimal design that could accommodate all types of street users, like pedestrians, buses, and street vendors. A main finding of the study was that pedestrians tended to crowd at certain specific points, such as pedestrian crossings and subway entrances, and that these areas could be better designed (Kim and Lee 2014).

Based on these findings, the SMG took a design approach that varied the width of sidewalks based on the patterns of pedestrian flows—for instance, widening sidewalks to a maximum of 8 meters around the crowded spots. In addition, barriers along sidewalks were removed to make way for pedestrian use. This included the removal of 40 large electricity distribution boxes, with the cooperation of the Korea Electric Power Corporation (KEPCO). Street kiosks' structures were also standardized and placed in designated areas.

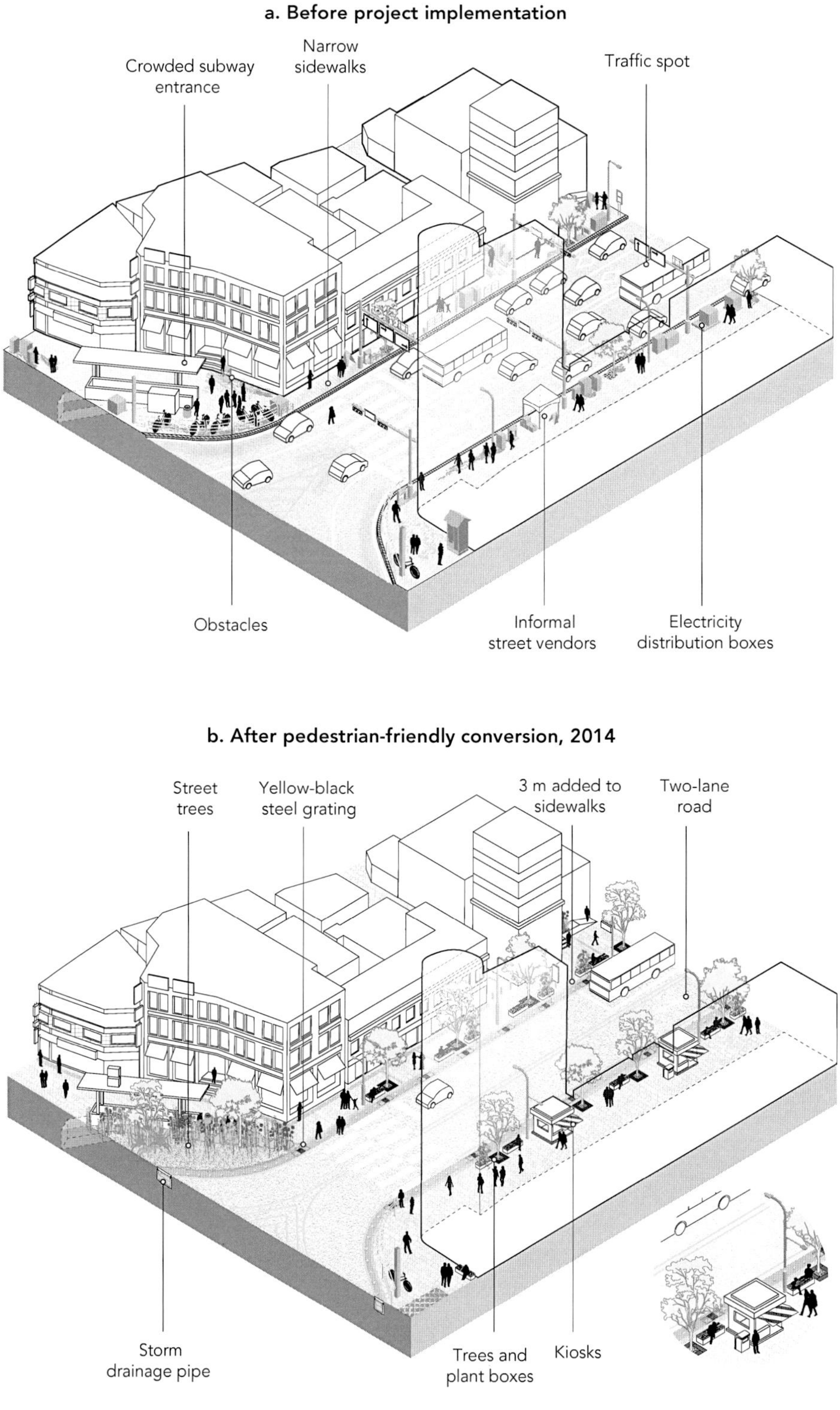

FIGURE 14.7 **Walkability and Mobility Improvements on Yonsei-ro, Old Downtown Seoul**

Source: ©World Bank. Further permission required for reuse.

Other design plans included the following:

- Construction of chicanes and speed bumps to moderate traffic speeds and improve pedestrian safety;
- Removal of level differences between the sidewalks and the roads, and the installation of street trees and plant boxes to separate pedestrians from the road;
- Designation of Yonsei-ro as "Zone 30" for pedestrian safety[11]; and
- Installation of underground stormwater drainage pipe along the street in place of the existing open gutters, as well as infiltration trenches in numerous locations.

Transport Planning

Yonsei-ro was a traffic-congested area with average vehicle speed of 10 kilometers per hour, which is slower than the rest of downtown Seoul. The SMG's traffic survey of Yonsei-ro revealed that the main cause of the congestion was the presence of heavy bypass traffic between the north and south of the city through Yonsei-ro in both directions. This resulted in very low traffic volume of about only 1,500 vehicles per hour (Kim and Lee 2014).

In anticipation of additional traffic congestion that could potentially result from the prioritization of pedestrian space along Yonsei-ro, the SMG in 2012–13 preemptively piloted a car-free zone on the project site in many different ways. These pilots showed that pedestrianizing Yonsei-ro slowed down traffic flows in the surrounding areas, worsening congestion in some cases. The city then piloted additional treatments to smooth traffic flow, including (a) creating an intersection at a congested area; (b) installing more crosswalks in front of the main gate of Yonsei University to link bus lanes and sidewalks; and (c) changing side streets to one-way lanes. These efforts enabled the transformation of Yonsei-ro into a transit mall without creating traffic congestion, and in some areas, traffic flows were even partially improved when the transit mall was implemented in 2013.

Phase 3: Implementation

The challenges faced during the implementation phase largely concerned the need to manage conflicts among various stakeholders. A steering committee was organized to engage all stakeholders, including the SMG, Seodaemun District Office, Seoul Metropolitan Police Agency, KEPCO, residents, merchants, civic groups, Yonsei University, and Hyundai Department Store (figure 14.8).

The committee held public hearings and resident briefing sessions and sought, through the use of objective data, to persuade stakeholders to accept alternative design solutions. For instance, shop owners were concerned about a decrease in revenues and worsened traffic congestion during construction and after project completion. To abate these concerns, the committee conducted background research showing that the proposed designs would have negligible impact on shop owners' revenues, because more than 80 percent of vehicles using Yonsei-ro were not shopping in or enjoying the adjacent neighborhoods but were rather passing through the area (Kim and Lee 2014).

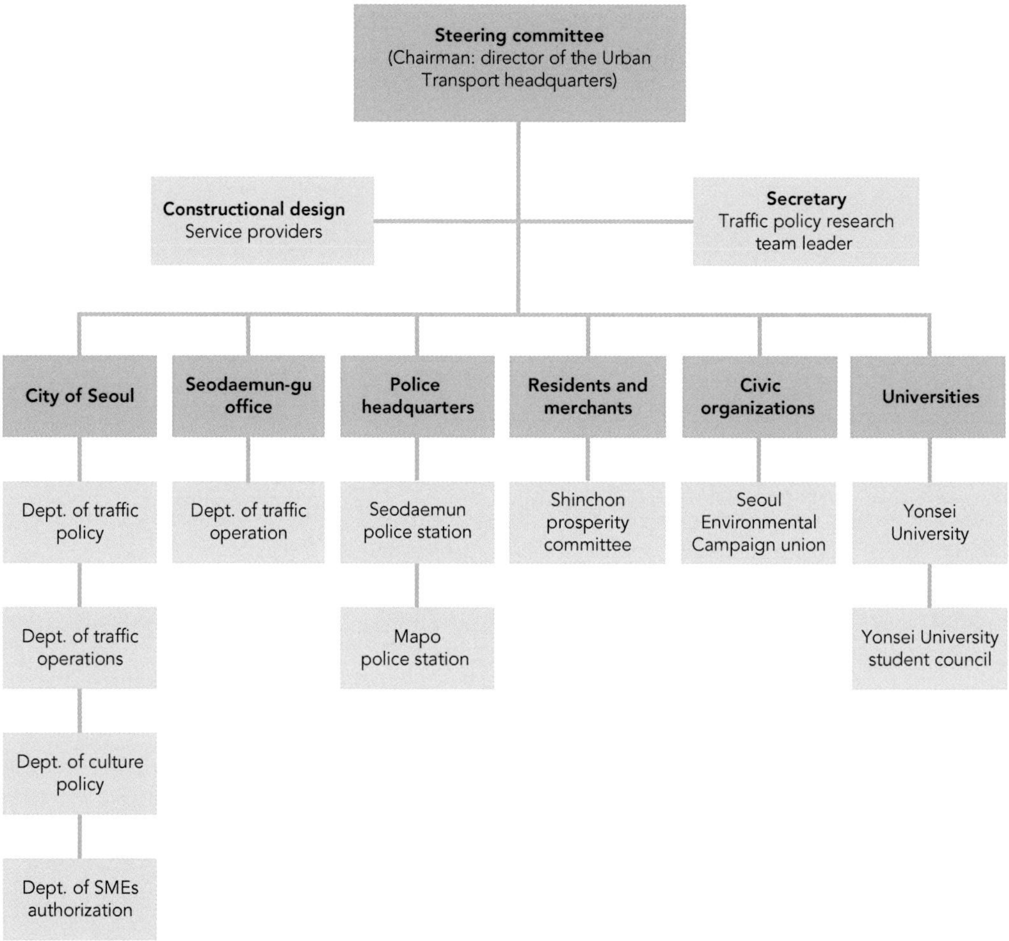

FIGURE 14.8 **Steering Committee for Yonsei-ro Project, Seoul**

Source: World Bank, with input from Korea Research Institute for Human Settlements (KRIHS).
Note: SMEs = small and medium enterprises.

The SMG and committee's responsiveness to administrative and legal issues was a key factor that led to the efficient project implementation, enabling the SMG to complete the project within a year. It was a remarkable record compared to similar projects that had taken several years to be implemented, because of unresolved conflicts among stakeholders. The total project cost was about ₩7.6 billion (US$7.6 million), of which 83 percent was borne by the SMG and 17 percent by the central government. In addition, the costs to move electricity boxes were borne by KEPCO.

Phase 4: Management

Yonsei-ro is managed by the Seodaemun District Office. To maintain a clean and walkable street, various departments within the district office, such as the construction unit, community revitalization unit, and facility management

a. Upgraded kiosk design with street painting

b. Kiosk at night

PHOTO 14.8 **Standardized Kiosks on Yonsei-ro, Seoul**

Source: ©Hyung Ho Lee. Reproduced, with permission, from Hyung Ho Lee; further permission required for reuse.

unit, were required to coordinate and work together. In recognizing the importance to the streetscape maintenance of formalizing and upgrading street kiosks, the community revitalization unit and facility management unit jointly provided consulting services to street vendors and monitored the kiosks' conditions. For instance, in 2016 the community revitalization unit collaborated with young artists to paint the shutters of kiosks so that a total of 25 kiosks on the street become public art when they are closed in the mornings (photo 14.8, panel a). The facility unit also keeps track of illegal dumping or misuses of street facilities to keep Yonsei-ro clean and organized (photo 14.8, panel b).[12]

The registration of public performances is under the purview of the district government, with a view toward managing the use of the open spaces and addressing complaints. Any performance can be registered at the government site. Among the rules, events can only be held before 9 p.m. to mitigate noise complaints from residents, and restrictions are in place for events with commercial purposes so that people can enjoy the "public atmosphere."

Phase 5: Impact Evaluation

A Successful Pilot Project, Aligned with City Visions

Yonsei-ro is considered to be the first implemented transit mall in Seoul. The SMG previously planned transit mall projects and pedestrian-only districts at other sites, but they were not implemented because of conflicting views between stakeholders and insufficient support for the proposed projects. The Yonsei-ro project overcame these challenges by effectively managing stakeholder conflicts through active communication, enabling the stakeholders to reach common ground in a short time.

The success of Yonsei-ro enabled the city to scale up the approach to other neighborhoods. More ambitiously, the city plans to completely convert the district into a pedestrian-only district in the long run. The plans are aligned with Seoul's longer-term vision of prioritizing pedestrians and public transport to create a sustainable urban environment.

Improved Walkability, Safety, and Vibrancy

The overall streetscapes of the neighborhood have been significantly improved. Sidewalks have been widened, cleaned, and connected with subway stations, squares, and shopping malls. A main feature includes the conversion of previously narrow sidewalks fronting the entrances to Sinchon subway station into Yonsei-ro's main square. The main square provides ample safe, walkable urban spaces for pedestrian use (photo 14.9). In addition, as a result of the street transformation, the number of traffic accidents on Yonsei-ro were reduced by 54.5 percent between 2013 and 2014 (SMG 2014).

The improved walking environment has also revitalized the street. The number of visitors in Sinchon increased by 28.9 percent in 2014, and total sales volume was 4.2 percent higher than in 2013 (SMG 2014). Yonsei-ro has also became a popular destination for youths and is a hotspot for artists and cultural activities. Through temporary road closures, Yonsei-ro turns into a pedestrian-only street from Fridays to Sundays, when the variety of events on the street include music festivals, concerts, and art exhibitions. On weekdays, newly created squares along the street become stages for performances such as dancing and busking.

This transformation has been highly successful. A 2014 survey found that the satisfaction rate of pedestrians on the street dramatically increased to 78.5 percent from 18.3 percent in the previous year. However, merchants' perceptions toward Yonsei-ro are somewhat more polarized: even though their

PHOTO 14.9 **Street View of Yonsei-ro, Seoul, at Night**

Source: ©Hyung Ho Lee. Reproduced, with permission, from Hyung Ho Lee; further permission required for reuse.

satisfaction rates increased from 34 percent to 41 percent, dissatisfaction rates also doubled from 20 percent to 45 percent in the same period (SMG 2014). This is primarily because banning private vehicles inconvenienced the merchants in terms of commuting.

NOTES

1. Population and other data from the Statistical Database, Korean Statistical Information Service (KOSIS) (website), accessed May 30, 2018: http://kosis.kr/eng/.
2. "Parks and Green Spaces," Seoul Research Data Service (website), accessed June 10, 2018: http://data.si.re.kr/node/356.
3. "Natural Park" areas made up 38.8 percent of the total park areas in 2010. Natural parks are mostly located in areas isolated from urban centers, such as mountains and forests, according to the Korean statistical categorization. Population and other data are drawn from the Statistical Database, Korean Statistical Information Service (KOSIS) (website), accessed May 30, 2018: http://kosis.kr/eng/.
4. The Making Livable City Project was initiated by the Ministry of Land, Transport and Maritime Affairs from 2007 to 2009 with a budget of ₩14 billion. The project goal was to improve the quality of life by improving the public environment and promoting township projects in local cities, such as improvement in urban walking environments, river management, creation of small parks, and fostering of historic culture (Lee et al. 2012).
5. After the 2000 summit between the Democratic People's Republic of Korea and the Republic of Korea, both sides agreed to reconnect the Gyeongui line, and from that year, the linking construction began between Munsan in the South and Gaesong in the North. In 2007, a freight train connecting Munsan Station in the South and Panmun Station in the North started operation. However, operations have been suspended from time to time because of the fluctuating relationship between the Democratic People's Republic of Korea and the Republic of Korea.
6. Interview with Woojin Hong and Inseon Jeong, representatives of SMG's management of the GLFP, April 16, 2019.
7. The group's name has been changed to the Gyeongui Line Forest Committee.
8. This amount excludes the cost of purchasing land and buildings, because the district government had purchased them after the residents' submission of the petition. The additional budget included the funding from the "Support Program for Children Library" of the Ministry of Culture, Sports and Tourism.
9. For more information, see the Gusandong Library Village website: http://www.gsvlib.or.kr.
10. A transit mall refers to a street that prohibits or restricts private vehicle traffic and permits public transport, bicycles, and pedestrians only. Since the 1960s and 1970s, in Europe and North America, transit malls have been introduced and operated mainly in cities where automobile traffic is concentrated to promote walking and public transport. For case studies of transit malls in the United States, see SFCTA (2013).
11. In Zone 30, only pedestrians, high-capacity vehicles (with 16 or more passengers), emergency vehicles, and bicycles are permitted to enter. All vehicles, including buses, should travel at speeds of less than 30 kilometers per hour.
12. "Actions for Revitalization of Street Shops and Physical Environments" [in Korean], Seodaemun District Office (website), accessed May 30, 2018: http://www.sdm.go.kr/admininfo/public/realnametarget.do?mode=view&sdmBoardConfSeq=288&sdmBoardSeq=212328.

REFERENCES

Amirtahmasebi, Rana, Mariana Orloff, Sameh Wahba, and Andrew Altman. 2016. *Regenerating Urban Land: A Practitioner's Guide to Leveraging Private Investment.* Urban Development Series. Washington, DC: World Bank.

Kim, Gwang-nyeon. 2016. "Severely Privatized Use of Privately Owned Public Spaces in Seoul." *Gukto-Ilbo,* October 11 (accessed May 30, 2018), http://www.ikld.kr/news/articleView.html?idxno=62887.

Kim, Jinmyeong. 2017. "A New Library that Is Owned by Its People." *Naeil Newspaper,* October 11, (accessed May 30, 2015), http://www.naeil.com/news_view/?id_art=252727.

Kim, Kijung, Changhyo Yi, and Seungil Lee. 2019. "Impact of Urban Characteristics on Cooling Energy Consumption before and after Construction of an Urban Park: The Case of Gyeongui Line Forest in Seoul." *Energy and Buildings* 191: 42–51.

Kim, Sang-shin, and Su-jin Lee. 2014. "Walking and Enjoying a Street of Dreams: An Instruction of SinChon Transitmall Construction." *Journal of the Korean Society of Civil Engineers* 62 (2): 34–45.

Kim, Tae-hwan. 2015. "National Urban Policy in Korea: Toward a Smart and Inclusive Growth." Report, Korea Research Institute for Human Settlements (KRIHS), Anyang.

Lee, Eun-yeop, Jeong-gon Kim, Jooho Yim, and Seong-woong Heo. 2012. "A Study on the Improvements of Institutions for Investigating and Creating Urban Public Spaces." Report, Presidential Commission on Architecture Policy, Seoul.

Lim, Yoo Kyung, Soo Bin Kim, and Ji Hyun Kim. 2017. "Co-creating Public Libraries: Gusandong Library Village." Report, National Public Building Center, Architecture & Urban Research Institute, Sejong City.

MOLIT (Ministry of Land, Infrastructure and Transport). 2016. "Gusan Library in Eunpyeong-Gu Awarded Grand Prize for Public Architecture." Press release, October 15 (accessed July 25, 2018), http://molit.go.kr/front/boardView.jsp?.

OECD (Organisation for Economic Co-operation and Development). 2012. *OECD Urban Policy Reviews: Korea.* Paris: OECD.

Park, So Yong, Wang-Geun Lee, Sang-Yeon Lim, Jung-eun Park, So-Yang Jung, You-Sun Jung, and Sung-Je Kim. 2016. "Enhancing Public Sector Cooperation for Regeneration of Vacant or Underutilized Urban Public Property." Research report, Korea Research Institute for Human Settlements (KRIHS), Anyang.

SFCTA (San Francisco County Transportation Authority). 2013. "Transit Mall Case Studies." Reference document for *Urban Street Design Guide.* New York: National Association of City Transportation Officials (NACTO) and Island Press. https://nacto.org/docs/usdg/transit_mall_case_studies_sanfran.pdf.

SMG (Seoul Metropolitan Government). 2014. "Six Months of Transit Mall: Fewer Accidents, More Bus Users." Press release, July 28, Seoul Information Communication Plaza (accessed April 30, 2019), http://opengov.seoul.go.kr/press/2190191?tr_code=open.

———. 2018. "2017 Housing Survey in Seoul." Statistical report, July 19 (accessed June 15 2019), http://opengov.seoul.go.kr/data/15699129.

Yun, Da-wun. 2017. "Study on the Change of Adjoining Building and Its Outdoor Space at Gyeongui Line Forest." Master's thesis, Seoul National University.

CHAPTER 15

SINGAPORE: ENHANCING URBAN HEALTH AND VIBRANCY BY LEVERAGING STREETS, PARK CONNECTORS, AND MARKETPLACES

Ken Lee, Mina Zhan, Elyssa Kaur Ludher, Thinesh Kumar Paramasilvam, and Viknesh Gnanasagaran

KEY TAKEAWAYS

- Singapore has undertaken successful efforts to improve livability and vibrancy in a high-density urban setting. The city-state's careful planning and integration of open and green spaces in neighborhoods are studied through three cases: the Park Connector Network, Orchard Road, and Hawker Centers.
- The Park Connector Network (PCN) has creatively transformed underutilized or vacant spaces along roads, overpasses, and drainage reserves into bridging public spaces that link scattered parks. It also provides ecological corridors to attract endemic biodiversity and ensure a conducive environment for both park users and wildlife.
- Orchard Road, a well-designed green and vibrant commercial street, is one of Singapore's most visited free-access attractions. The successful development of Orchard Road was achieved, in part, through the government's efforts to incentivize private sector stakeholders to enhance the overall

streetscape, including by implementing human-scale designs and emphasizing pedestrian-focused elements in a high-intensity, dense urban context.

- Hawker centers, originally developed to accommodate unlicensed food vendors who ply their trade on Singapore's streets, have evolved into inclusive, community-centric spaces for selling clean, affordable, and culturally diverse foods. Although early hawker centers were stand-alone, functional developments, the more recently built hawker centers are more sensitively and carefully designed. Many incorporate universal design elements to meet the needs of the elderly and people with disabilities. A number of them are co-located with a range of other community-centric amenities and facilities.
- Key factors in the success of public-space projects are their integration with long-term neighborhood- and city-level strategies, and the coordinated interagency approach to their implementation. These projects have been continuously improved over several decades to ensure that they remain relevant and effective in meeting the needs and enhancing the quality of life of Singapore's population.

CITY DYNAMICS

Context and Background

Singapore has a land area of 719 square kilometers, a population of just over 5.8 million people, and a population density of almost 7,800 persons per square kilometer. As an island nation with no hinterland, Singapore faces significant land constraints. It is also both a city and a country, and there is a need to accommodate the needs of a nation state within a relatively limited land mass: apart from the urban infrastructural needs of housing, transport, and commerce, it also has to allocate land for uses such as seaports and airports, military training grounds, water catchments, and industrial parks—all of which are not typically expected or planned for in a city.

Singapore gained self-governance from Great Britain in 1959. At the time, much of the country's population of about 1.7 million resided in overcrowded, ethnically segregated districts in the city's Central Area. The Central Area also had poor transport connectivity with other parts of Singapore: there was no urban rail system, and the privately owned network of commuter buses was badly run and unreliable. Singapore was neither livable nor sustainable: there were slums, traffic congestion, disease, water shortages, and periodic flooding.

The government acted quickly to resolve many of these pressing problems. It established the Housing and Development Board (HDB) and built thousands of affordable new homes; developed infrastructure to provide clean water to households, industries, and other sectors; cleaned up Singapore's waterways and waterbodies; acquired and redeveloped districts affected by urban blight; embarked on an ambitious landscaping program across the island; and built new roads and highways.

Sixty years on, Singapore's population has tripled, but it is one of the greenest and most livable cities in the world despite its high population density. This is the result of decades of long-term-focused, carefully coordinated urban planning and development. The country's development efforts involved dozens of specialized government agencies adopting a sensitive approach to managing its scarce land resources. Although economic growth has been a critical priority shaping how Singapore manages and uses its land, development has not taken place haphazardly. As far as possible, Singapore's planners have balanced economic growth imperatives with the need to safeguard and enhance livability outcomes. This has manifested itself in several ways, including the establishment of well-planned and attractive public spaces.

Planning Act. Singapore's Concept Plan and Master Plan (both further described below) are statutory land-use plans prescribing the allowable use of each land parcel in Singapore. These plans have legal effect under the Planning Act, meaning that they cannot be arbitrarily amended or revised without proper legal procedure. The Planning Act also prescribes how an individual or corporate body can develop and use any given land parcel. Appropriate approvals must be obtained from the planning authority and other technical agencies before any development can be constructed. At the same time, the Act provides flexibility for prescribed uses to be reviewed and amended upon application from agencies, developers, and land owners; this allows some degree of deviation from established planning parameters but only if there is a demonstrable need. This integrated and formalized planning and development framework guides the finalization and implementation of plans at the national and local scales.

Concept Plan. At the national level, long-term urban policies and infrastructure investment needs are integrated through a common national Concept Plan, which sets out broad land uses over a time horizon of 40–50 years. Updated every 10 years, it determines the overall spatial structure of the country, indicating broad land-use allocations in consideration of long-term population needs and economic growth projections.

Master Plan. The Master Plan translates the Concept Plan in greater detail. This detailed plan prescribes how Singapore's land parcels can be developed to (a) accommodate existing and future needs in sectors such as commerce, industry, housing, and the community; and (b) provide open space and greenery, public amenities, transportation networks, and other forms of infrastructure. The Master Plan has a 15- to 20-year horizon to guide Singapore's development over the medium term and is reviewed every four to five years to respond more nimbly to changes in land-use needs.

In 2019, the government embarked on a review of the Master Plan. The review focused on several key land-use and planning themes, including the creation of livable and inclusive communities. To achieve this, the government will develop new residential precincts that provide a variety of community-centric amenities and vibrant public spaces. It also plans to continue long-standing efforts to conserve the country's natural heritage and expand the islandwide network of parks, sports facilities, and green spaces.

Another theme of the Master Plan is the rejuvenation of "familiar places": districts in Singapore with a strong sense of local identity and familiarity to residents. The government is intending to implement urban planning and design interventions to safeguard and enhance the distinctive qualities of these districts, including through the improvement of existing public spaces and streetscapes.

As with previous reviews, the 2019 review of the Master Plan was undertaken in consultation with government agencies, civil society groups, professional institutes, and private sector experts, among other stakeholders. The plans were also exhibited to the public at the Urban Redevelopment Authority's (URA) headquarters in downtown Singapore, with visitors encouraged to give their feedback and comments. This wide-ranging and meaningful consultation process was intended to ensure that the government's land-use plans incorporate the views of different groups in society and result in outcomes that will meet the needs and interests of the community at large.

At the local level, the URA also maintains detailed plans for selected areas which translate the relatively broader planning vision of the Master Plan in even further detail. These plans are typically applied to areas of significant planning importance, such as the retail corridor of Orchard Road and new Central Business District (CBD) of Marina Bay. Through these plans, the URA imposes specific planning and urban design guidelines covering features such as building height, building form, building edge, pedestrian networks, and vehicular access requirements. These plans enable the URA to take a finer-grained approach to determining the overall physical quality of these districts.

Greening Singapore

Visitors to Singapore are often struck by the amount of greenery and landscaping throughout the city. Indeed, parks, gardens, and greenery are key features in Singapore's urban fabric and central to its development story.

Singapore's early leaders had a vision to develop Singapore into a "Garden City" and embarked on decades of sustained focus and commitment to green the country—seeing this as a necessary move to stave off urban blight and pollution even as Singapore pursued economic growth and industrialization in the decades immediately following its founding as an independent city-state. Singapore also perceived value in the development of lushly landscaped public spaces as a means to spur the growth of the tourism industry as well as enhance the country's attractiveness to foreign investors (photo 15.1). The Garden City Action Committee (GCAC) was thus set up in 1973 to drive this effort by fostering pervasive greenery and establishing a network of green spaces comprising parks, gardens, and nature reserves.

Decades of effective greening efforts have resulted in several positive outcomes for Singapore's population. Today, almost 10 percent of Singapore's land is made up of parks and nature reserves. More than 80 percent of households are within a ten-minute walk of a park. An extensive network of

PHOTO 15.1 **Mass Rapid Transit (MRT) Train Passing through a Lush, Green Area of Singapore**

Source: Jason Goh. License-free image from Pixelbay.

landscaped park connectors extends for more than 200 kilometers, and some 1,000 hectares of bodies of water are open for recreational activity. There are also more than 20 hydraulic engineering and water management projects under the "Active, Beautiful and Clean Waters" program, which have transformed utilitarian concrete drainage canals into attractively landscaped, publicly accessible streams (MND and MEWR 2015).

In many parts of the country, urban design and planning interventions such as the Landscaping for Urban Spaces and High-Rises (LUSH) program have transformed the cityscape in a unique and striking way. Under the LUSH scheme, developers are granted building incentives to integrate landscaping at the ground level, on building rooftops, and in intermediate parts of new developments. Many buildings feature extensive green walls and landscaped façades, roof gardens, and outdoor planters, providing a visual counterpoint to the high-rise, dense urban environment.

These and other efforts to promote urban green cover and landscaping have enabled Singapore's residents to live in a high-quality environment with pervasive greenery. Beyond nature reserves in and around areas such as the Central Catchment Area and Bukit Timah (a planning area and residential estate in the westernmost part of the Central Region), there are extensive park spaces in the heart of the CBD (such as Gardens by the Bay), smaller green spaces in interim spaces between high-rise developments (such as Tanjong Pagar Park), and neighborhood "pocket parks" with fitness and playground equipment for recreation. In many public housing estates, residents are even encouraged to use such spaces for community gardening and small-scale farming.

ORCHARD ROAD

Phase 1: Context

Orchard Road, one of Asia's most famous shopping streets, is often compared with New York's Fifth Avenue and Paris's Avenue des Champs-Élysées. Stretching over 2.6 kilometers, the street extends from Tanglin Road, an upmarket residential area in the west, to Bras Basah Road, which connects to the CBD toward the east (photo 15.2).

Orchard Road started life in the 1830s as a central artery servicing nutmeg and pepper plantations in the vicinity. Over the following decade, as an unknown crop disease triggered a decline in crop yields and agricultural activity in the area, Orchard Road took on a more residential character, with bungalows and shophouses being built on plots formerly used for farming (Abraham 2003).

By the early 1900s, shops and businesses began opening along Orchard Road to serve residents, heralding the start of the area's commercialization. In 1917, the Singapore Cold Storage Company opened a store to distribute food supplies, and the Orchard Road Market provided fresh produce for residents (Cheah 2003). In 1958, the landmark department store C. K. Tang opened on Orchard Road. The district's image as a retail street continued to develop in the 1970s and 1980s, when many more shopping centers were built. With the opening of other commercial developments such as hotels and entertainment centers, Orchard Road established itself as a major shopping, entertainment, and hotel district in Singapore.

Orchard Road was a busy thoroughfare even in the early days of horse-drawn carriages and *jinrikisha* (rickshaws) and was one of the first streets in Singapore to be macadamized in 1912 (Cheah 2003). Motorized traffic replaced these outmoded forms of transport in the following decades, but Orchard Road took on

PHOTO 15.2 **View of Orchard Road, Singapore, from the Junction of Paterson and Scotts Roads**

Source: Jason Goh. License-free image from Pixelbay.

an increasingly pedestrian-oriented character in the 1970s when Stamford Canal, built in the 1960s to alleviate flooding in the area, was covered up to expand public gathering and pedestrian spaces along the street (CLC 2015).

Sidewalks were first built as part of a 1976 state-implemented project to promote pedestrian walkways along Orchard Road. These and other subsequent street improvement projects provided both sides of Orchard Road with the wide pedestrian malls that have become one of the area's most visible characteristics. The pedestrian-oriented character of Orchard Road was reinforced in 1987 with the opening of three underground Mass Rapid Transit (MRT) stations, which significantly improved public transport access to and within the Orchard Road district, burnishing its position as Singapore's preeminent retail corridor.

By the end of the century, Orchard Road had developed a distinct commercial identity encompassing a variety of uses along the street. Retail and commercial developments such as Centrepoint Shopping Centre and Tang Plaza catered to local and overseas shoppers, hotels like the Mandarin Orchard and Hilton Singapore met the needs of tourists and visitors, and recreational complexes like the nightlife-oriented Peranakan Place and Orchard Cinema enhanced Orchard Road's appeal as a premier entertainment area. Mixed-use developments integrating residential uses such as Lucky Plaza and office uses such as Ngee Ann City added diversity and urban texture to the area, as they drew a resident population and office workers to the retail-oriented district (map 15.1).

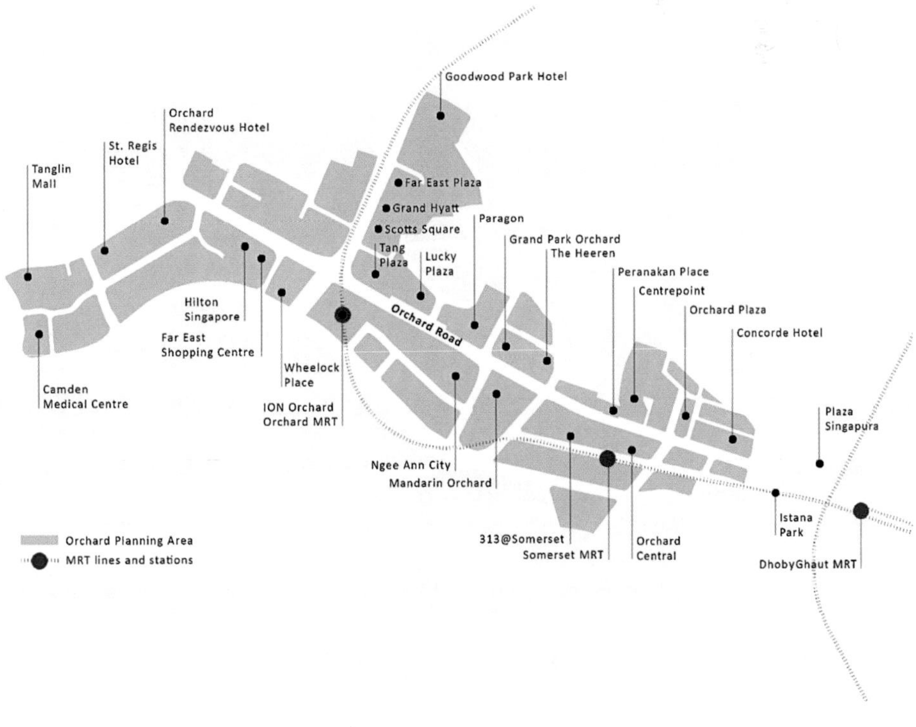

MAP 15.1 **Key Destinations along Orchard Road, Singapore**

Source: ©Centre for Liveable Cities (CLC). Reproduced, with permission, from CLC; further permission required for reuse.

Note: MRT = Mass Rapid Transit.

From the 1960s to the 1980s, Orchard Road's appeal to overseas visitors as a leading retail destination with a wide offering of shopping experiences and attractive prices and merchandise rose in tandem with the growth of Singapore's tourism industry. However, in the early 1980s, Orchard Road's growth was affected by a slump in the tourism industry. In its November 1984 report, the Ministry of Trade and Industry's (MTI) Tourism Task Force assessed that Singapore, in its quest to build a modern metropolis, was losing its "oriental mystique and charm," of which old buildings, traditional activities, and bustling roadside activities were key elements. A strong Singapore dollar and rising cost of living also meant that Singapore was no longer the inexpensive shopping paradise it once was to foreign visitors (CLC 2015).

The tourism industry experienced greater fluctuation and uncertainty in subsequent decades. Global events such as the 1997 Asian financial crisis, the September 11 attacks in the United States, and the outbreak of severe acute respiratory syndrome (SARS) in Asia jolted Singapore's economy, adversely affecting visitor arrivals and tourism revenue over a number of years (Meng, Siriwardana, and Pham 2013). As Singapore's neighboring countries rapidly developed, local retail was also affected by increasing competition from other regional hubs like Kuala Lumpur, Bangkok, and Shanghai (NAS 2004).

Domestically, new malls and commercial centers had proliferated in Singapore's suburban areas since the late 1990s. These new centers were built as part of the decentralization strategy of the 1991 Concept Plan. The plan called for the creation of regional, subregional, fringe, and town centers across Singapore to relieve congestion in the CBD and to bring cultural, recreational, shopping, and entertainment facilities, as well as employment opportunities, closer to residents in newly built housing estates. As a result, although Singapore saw an increase in the amount of retail space islandwide, the bulk of it was located in suburban developments such as Tampines Mall (1995) and Causeway Point (1998)—new shopping complexes popularly known as "Heartland malls"—in the new towns of Tampines and Woodlands, respectively. These two shopping centers alone accounted for more than 100,000 square meters of retail space in Singapore.

At the local level, the government encountered significant challenges in implementing spatial plans to enhance Orchard Road's appeal as a shopping attraction. Historically, Orchard Road had not been planned or conceived as a coherent shopping and entertainment street; rather, the area had grown relatively organically to accommodate a wide range of retail profiles and spatial typologies. Consequently, the area lacked elements such as visual harmony in the design of retail frontages, which can be seen in many major shopping streets in more established retail capitals in Europe. This was not an easy problem to address because much of Orchard Road was already built up, with limited vacant land available for major planning interventions. It was therefore necessary to adopt incremental, creative, and collaborative efforts with development owners to rejuvenate Orchard Road.

Phase 2: Planning and Design

Over a decade starting from the late 1990s, the government implemented several incremental design- and planning-based interventions to improve Orchard Road. These involved efforts such as streetscape improvements and a reshaping of features such as building façades (figure 15.1).

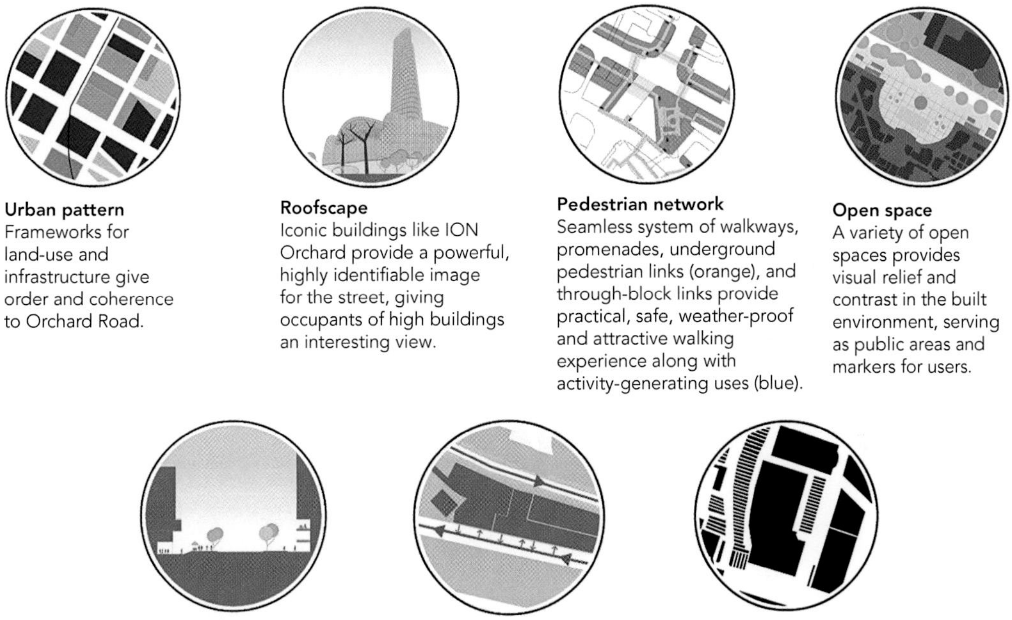

Urban pattern
Frameworks for land-use and infrastructure give order and coherence to Orchard Road.
Roofscape
Iconic buildings like ION Orchard provide a powerful, highly identifiable image for the street, giving occupants of high buildings an interesting view.
Pedestrian network
Seamless system of walkways, promenades, underground pedestrian links (orange), and through-block links provide practical, safe, weather-proof and attractive walking experience along with activity-generating uses (blue).
Open space
A variety of open spaces provides visual relief and contrast in the built environment, serving as public areas and markers for users.
Streetscape
Building edges, scale landscape, and street activities add to the experience at street level and give Orchard Road its unique character.
Vehicular access
Location of vehicular access points along secondary service roads minimizes pedestrian-vehicular conflict and ensures the smooth flow of pedestrians (orange) and traffic (brown).
Building form
Variations in height and volume give Orchard Road character and visual interest while responding to the surrounding context.

FIGURE 15.1 **Integrated Design Components for Orchard Road Improvements, Singapore**

Source: ©Centre for Liveable Cities (CLC). Reproduced, with permission, from CLC; further permission required for reuse.

Tourism and Economic Strategies

Orchard Road has been designated a shopping street in Singapore's land-use master plans since 1958. The improvement of Orchard Road has been coupled with tourism and economic strategies at the city level. A major response to the slump of the tourism industry in the 1980s was a S$1 billion Tourism Product Development Plan—Singapore's first master plan to direct its tourism landscape development over the next decade (STB 2014). Another major thrust to the development of Orchard Road came with the "Tourism 21—Vision of a Tourism Capital" plan in 1997, which sought to capitalize on the rising tourism potential within the Asia-Pacific market in the 1990s by focusing on experiential "software" such as the provision of quality services and programs (CLC 2015; box 15.1). These plans, complemented by other development plans, helped to steer and support the implementation of the broad vision and strategies set out in the tourism plans.

In the late 1990s, zoning revisions resulted in the creation of 55 "local planning areas" across Singapore. Fifty-five Development Guide Plans (DGPs)—one for each local planning area—were consolidated to form Master Plan 1998. The DGP for the Orchard Road Planning Area designated it as a primary commercial and residential belt within Singapore's Central Area (a planning term used to denote Singapore's city center) that included areas such as the Downtown Core. The plan acknowledged Orchard Road's success as the result of a good

BOX 15.1 TOURISM 21—VISION OF A TOURISM CAPITAL

A major thrust to the development of Orchard Road came via the 1997 "Tourism 21—Vision of a Tourism Capital" framework, produced by four committees set up in 1995 to facilitate the development of a comprehensive plan to boost Singapore's tourism industry.

Unlike the earlier tourism plan that emphasized "hardware" improvements, Tourism 21 emphasized "software"—specifically, the provision of quality services and programs for tourists (CLC 2015). Along with 11 other popular tourist areas such as Chinatown, Singapore River, and Little India, Orchard Road was identified as a district where existing offerings could be enhanced and repackaged into a variety of tourism products. The plan also proposed ideas to reposition and develop a retail belt extending from Orchard Road to Marina Bay (in the heart of the Downtown Core) as a "Mall of Singapore."

The Tourism 21 plan further recommended "tapping the commercial experience of the private sector" and forming "mutually beneficial partnerships" by creating and supporting stakeholder and trade associations to help oversee future retail development in Singapore. This resulted in the formation of the Orchard Road Committee, a representative body comprising major shopping centers along Orchard Road. This committee evolved into the Orchard Road Business Association (ORBA), a place management organization that works with the Singapore Tourism Board (STB) on collaborative efforts to promote Orchard Road. More than 120 members comprising building owners, retailers, and other stakeholders voluntarily contribute membership fees to ORBA to support events and marketing activities designed to enhance the district's visitor experience and attractiveness.

To foster a pro-business culture and create a conducive operating environment for the tourism industry, the Tourism 21 plan proposed financial incentives in the form of a Tourism Development Assistance Scheme to help local tourism-related companies upgrade their products and services.

In the late 1990s and early 2000s, Singapore's tourism industry faced increased competition from other regional cities. Global shocks such as the severe acute respiratory syndrome (SARS) outbreak further dampened sentiments in the tourism industry. In a bid to revitalize the sector, the Ministry of Trade and Industry (MTI, which oversees the STB) launched the Tourism 2015 plan in

(box continues next page)

mix of office, shops, and hotel uses but highlighted the need for new developments to reinforce existing commercial uses along the street and address the lack of residential population along Orchard Road. The DGP also identified various issues facing pedestrians in the area, setting the ground for a slew of subsequent interventions.

Following the DGP, the URA also introduced a Landmark and Gateway Plan, under which strategically located vacant land parcels, such as those above the underground Orchard MRT station and Somerset MRT station,

BOX 15.1 TOURISM 21—VISION OF A TOURISM CAPITAL *(Continued)*

January 2005 to promote tourism growth over the next 10 years. The MTI established a fund amounting to S$2 billion to support initiatives in a number of areas, including infrastructure development, capability development for tourism and retail sector workers, the organization of signature events, and development of unique tourist-oriented products.

As for the development of Orchard Road, various government agencies complemented the broad tourism promotion strategy by announcing a series of initiatives to spruce up the street, including a planned S$40 million investment to expand Orchard Road's public infrastructure. These initiatives included efforts to improve pedestrian walkways and create "urban green rooms" for events. As part of this proposal, three distinct themed zones were created at Orchard Road, each with enhanced road and pedestrian mall lighting that highlighted the district's mature trees and foliage to create attractive night streetscapes. This initiative was driven by an STB-led taskforce comprising agencies such as the URA, the Land Transport Authority (LTA), and the National Parks Board (NParks).

The government's plans to enhance Orchard Road's appeal, including its attractiveness to tourists and Singaporeans, continue to take shape. In recent years, agencies have focused on making Orchard Road a "lifestyle destination," with innovative retail concepts, attractions, entertainment, and events. In 2019, an interagency review of the district's development resulted in a comprehensive approach to split the area into the four subzones of Tanglin, Orchard, Somerset, and Dhoby Ghaut, each with customized strategies to enhance their respective identities. These include positioning Tanglin as an arts- and culture-focused area, Somerset as a center of youth culture, and Dhoby Ghaut as a family-friendly destination.

The 2019 Master Plan further showcased many of these plans, including efforts to improve connectivity across buildings and activate vacant land parcels across the district as locations for pop-up events such as concerts and markets. The Master Plan also highlighted efforts to "Bring Back the Orchard," which would entail the provision of new infrastructure to enhance green spaces throughout the precinct.

Sources: STB 2005, 2014; STPB 1997; URA 2001, 2007.

were identified as potential focal points that could be developed in a way that would make the city center more distinctive and memorable (URA 2001). By redeveloping these vacant parcels, new mixed-use developments incorporating innovative retail concepts and public space began to take shape along Orchard Road. In the case of the vacant site above the Orchard MRT station, planning authorities relaxed existing urban planning rules (for example, on building height), allowing for the development of a 218-meter-high retail and residential development, ION Orchard.

Urban Design Strategies

The URA has introduced a series of urban design guidelines since the early 2000s to guide the physical development of buildings fronting Orchard Road. Over the years, these guidelines have been reviewed, updated, and expanded, taking into account feedback from architects and stakeholders, to remain relevant and pro-business. The guidelines help to shape the visitor experience along the street by providing guidance to developers and property owners on matters such as allowable uses, building forms, pedestrian networks, and vehicular access arrangements.

Shaping Building Setbacks and Edges. Urban Design Plans and Guidelines for Orchard Road were first published in 2002 following a joint STB and URA exhibition to gather public and stakeholder feedback on proposals to enhance Orchard Road (URA 2013b). Key focus areas of the guidelines were façade articulation and urban verandas. The guidelines pushed for changes in building façades to create better physical and visual connections between the street and building activities (figure 15.2) and recommended the use of transparent materials to make shopfront displays more visible and attractive (URA 2005c). Urban verandas, intended as publicly accessible, unenclosed extensions of buildings, were also encouraged.

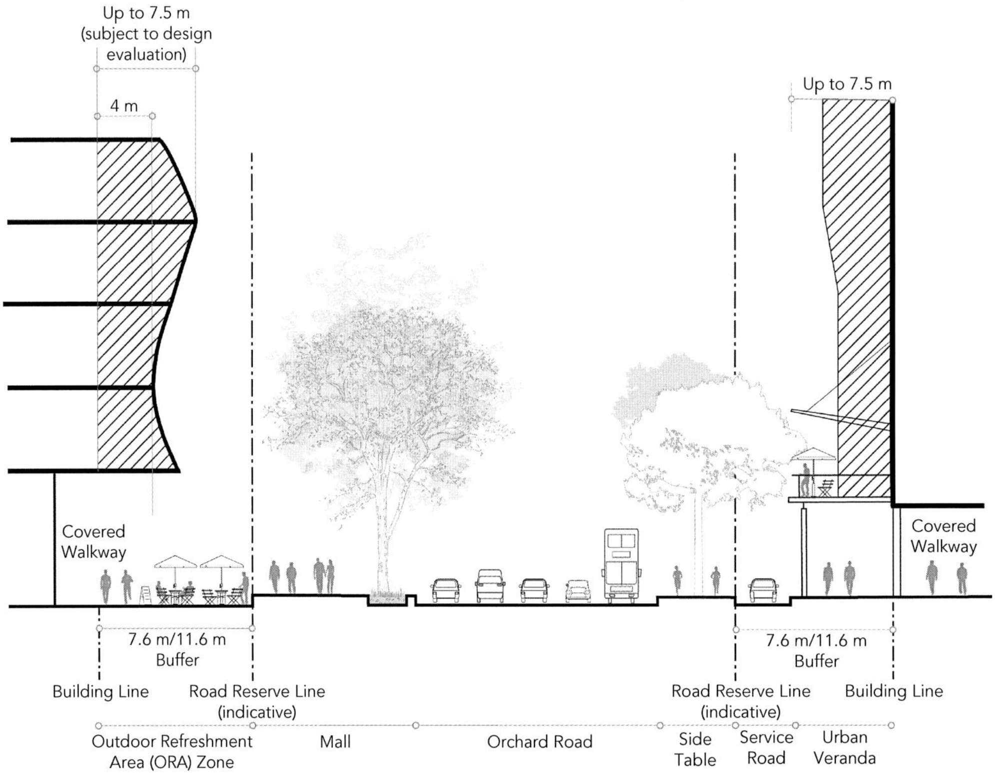

FIGURE 15.2 **Possible Urban Veranda and Façade Articulation Incentives in Orchard Road, Singapore**

Source: ©World Bank, based on Urban Redevelopment Authority (URA). Further permission required for reuse.

The URA extended an incentive to building owners by allowing them to build floor area above the permissible development intensity for such extensions. This prompted many of them to overhaul their properties. For example, Wisma Atria, a commercial development on Orchard Road, announced a S$31 million makeover in the early 2010s to create greater frontage visibility for retailers as well as improved accessibility (Sng 2015).

The guidelines and associated incentives worked well: in the 2000s, "nearly every building fronting the street underwent a façade transformation in return for additional income-producing space," transforming old, familiar retail spaces into new destinations (Anderson et al. 2012). These guidelines shaped and articulated building setbacks along Orchard Road in a way that safeguarded the contiguity of the pedestrian mall and maintained a sense of openness to the street. While ensuring some degree of uniformity at the street block level, the URA's framework of urban design guidelines was flexible enough to accommodate a variety of façade configurations, enabling the creation of diverse visual and spatial experiences along the street.

Reducing Pedestrian-Vehicular Conflict. In the early days, multiple vehicular entrances and driveways to individual buildings along Orchard Road affected the pedestrian experience because there was no continuous promenade. Planning guidelines introduced in the 1980s required new developments to locate vehicular entrances at the rear of buildings. But gaps still remained because these requirements were not imposed on existing developments (Cheah 2003). To address this issue, the DGP 1994 recommended the creation of comprehensive rear service lanes for new developments along the street (URA 2001). This approach was expanded in 2000, when the URA implemented a plan to remove front-facing vehicular access points to several buildings and establish a rear service-road system (CLC and SI 2016).

Gradually, the number of pedestrian-vehicular intersections along Orchard Road was reduced as new development and redevelopment proposals complied with the new guidelines. For example, when the owners of the Mandarin Orchard submitted a redevelopment proposal to the URA in 2009, planners required the hotel to relocate its vehicular drop-off points fronting Orchard Road to the site's western boundary along Orchard Link. Additionally, the hotel lobby was relocated to the upper floors to accommodate more retail uses at the ground level, which would open to Orchard Road (Anderson et al. 2012).

The effect of this was to enhance the porosity of the development and add texture to the promenade through the provision of different shopfronts and window displays. As they were applied from one plot to the next, the building frontage guidelines enhanced the Orchard Road promenade and further improved pedestrians' experience of the area (photo 15.3).

Creating a Comprehensive Pedestrian Network and Active Streetscape. The URA used specific urban design guidelines to provide seamless pedestrian connectivity between MRT stations and key developments. Working closely with building owners and developers, the URA spearheaded plans for the development of a comprehensive pedestrian network at the basement level as well as at the ground or second levels in Orchard Road and other parts of the Central Area. To promote all-weather connectivity, a Central Area Underground Master Plan was drawn up to map existing and

PHOTO 15.3 **Covered Walkways and Urban Verandas at the Ground and Second Floors of Mandarin Gallery in Orchard Road, Singapore**

Source: ©Ken Lee. Used with the permission of Ken Lee; further permission required for reuse.

proposed underground pedestrian links, and private sector stakeholders were incentivized to contribute toward their implementation. In some cases, the URA imposed requirements on developers to incorporate features such as knock-out panels in the walls of MRT stations to provide seamless links between stations and future developments, or through-block links at ground level to create internally permeable street blocks.

To ensure that the pedestrian realm remained vibrant throughout the day, the URA encouraged developers to locate activity-generating uses such as retail, food and beverage outlets, and recreational uses along key pedestrian thoroughfares. The URA exempted these pedestrian thoroughfares from GFA computation, and developers were required to abide by various planning conditions, such as ensuring that these thoroughfares be kept free of obstructions (for example, structural installations) that could hinder pedestrian flow and remain open to the public at all times.

Given that most buildings along Orchard Road were built before mandatory accessibility requirements were introduced in 1990, the Building and Construction Authority (BCA) worked closely with building owners to improve barrier-free access to their premises. This was done through the provision of monetary grants to defray upgrading and construction costs. As a result, about 90 percent of buildings along the Orchard Road shopping belt are currently universally accessible, up from only 41 percent in 2006 (Keung 2018).

These and other interventions helped create pedestrian connections that integrate the diverse uses on Orchard Road in a coherent way. For example, a new through-block connection at 313@Somerset, a commercial development, serves as a busy pedestrian thoroughfare that not only provides direct access from Orchard Road to the Somerset MRT station but also features various uses that imbue it with a lively, street-like character.

Promoting Roadside and Vertical Greenery. Lush greenery at multiple levels, within both the public realm and private developments, has contributed significantly to the spatial quality of Orchard Road and serves as an important visual signpost of the area's historical incarnation as plantation land. Public spaces along the pedestrian malls were defined by an avenue of *pterocarpus indicus* (commonly known as "angsana" trees), first planted in the 1970s as part of the Garden City Movement that aimed to transform Singapore into a clean and green city (CLC and SI 2016).

In subsequent years, the URA and NParks used numerous guidelines and policies to encourage developers and building owners to provide landscaped areas in their developments. Many of these have been incorporated into the LUSH framework (figure 15.3). Under the LUSH program, the Landscape

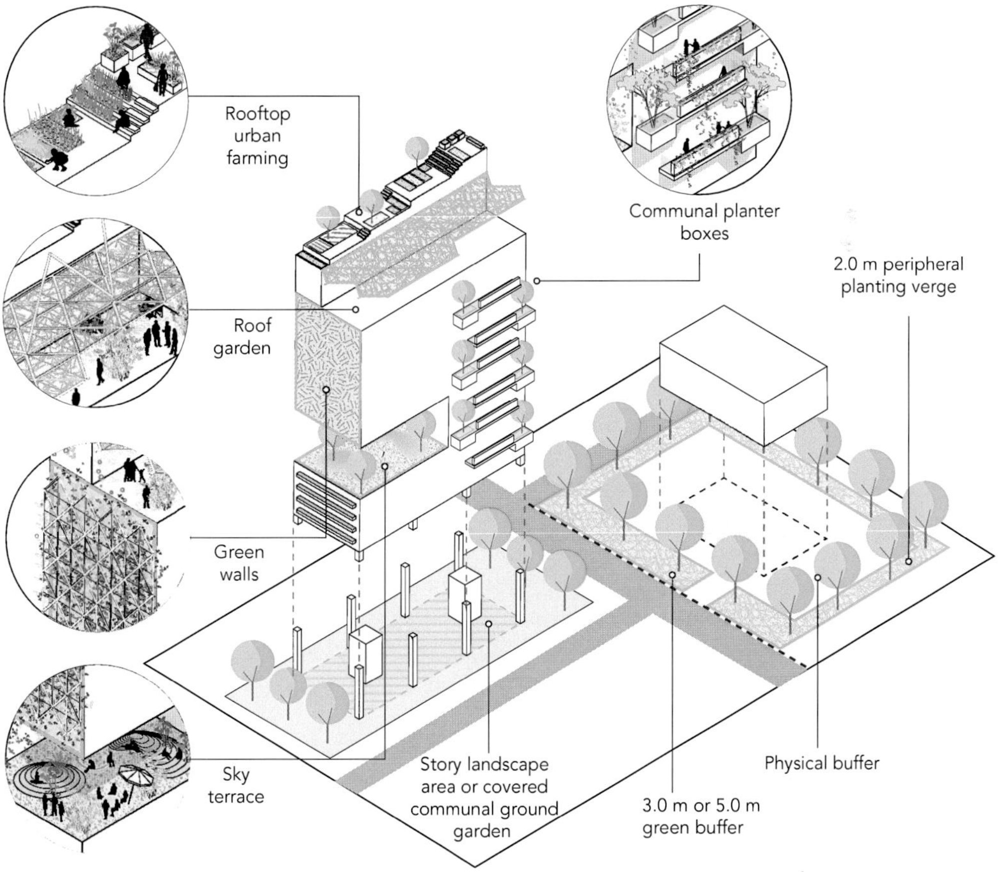

FIGURE 15.3 **Possible Types of Landscape Replacement Areas under the LUSH program, Singapore**

Source: ©World Bank, based on Urban Redevelopment Authority (URA). Further permission required for reuse.
Note: LUSH = Landscaping for Urban Spaces and High Rises; m = meters.

Replacement Area Guidelines for selected strategic development areas in Singapore require developers to replace greenery in the form of landscape areas within the new development project. The total area of landscaped space, which could be provided at ground level, rooftops, or mid-level sky terraces, has to be minimally equivalent to the development site area. In addition, there are also other guidelines on GFA exemptions for communal sky terraces, and GFA incentives for rooftop outdoor refreshment areas to encourage developers to convert their existing roofs into roof gardens or green roofs (URA 2014).

The LUSH program today is complemented by the NParks's Skyrise Greenery Incentive Scheme (SGIS), whereby developers can tap public funds to pay for 50 percent of the cost of installing rooftop and vertical greenery. These initiatives have been adopted by the developers and owners of many developments in Orchard Road, including 313@Somerset and Orchard Central, which feature extensive vertical and rooftop green spaces (NParks 2017).

Looking beyond the Site

As part of the government's 2019 plans for the future development of Orchard Road, agencies highlighted an intention to improve the connectivity of the district's main promenade with surrounding areas. For example, there are plans to enhance the diversity of visitors' experience of the precinct by encouraging them to explore historic side streets such as Emerald Hill and Killiney Road, which connect the main shopping district to surrounding residential enclaves. There are also plans to implement urban design interventions to provide seamless connectivity between Orchard Road and other parts of Singapore through having more mixed-use transit-oriented developments (TODs) sited above the future Orchard MRT interchange station, incorporating the Thomson-East Coast Line (URA 2019a).

Phase 3: Implementation

Agencies are aware that the success of urban planning and design strategies requires the active participation of developers and landowners, particularly in the densely textured, mixed-use context of the Orchard Road precinct. In order to achieve this, agencies have used a combination of incentives and regulations to both encourage and require private sector stakeholders to adopt spatial changes to meet various planning, economic, and social objectives for Orchard Road.

Government Land Sales to Spur Rejuvenation: Clear Guidelines to Ensure Win-Win Outcomes

One of the important ways in which the government has worked closely with the private sector to enhance the Orchard Road precinct is through the sale of state-owned land parcels for new commercial and mixed-use developments. The Government Land Sales (GLS) program, established in 1967, enabled the construction of several landmark developments along

Orchard Road in the 1970s and 1980s, including the Centrepoint, Le Méridien Singapore, and Orchard Plaza.[1] In latter decades, the GLS program proved to be a successful tool in catalyzing the rejuvenation of Orchard Road, especially when the precinct appeared to be ceding its position as Singapore's preeminent retail attraction to newer developments in other areas.

In the mid-2000s, for example, the URA decided to release three new parcels of state land for commercial development to bring new energy and excitement to the area (CLC 2017). These parcels had been kept in reserve for almost 20 years after the MRT stations along Orchard Road opened in 1987, to manage the supply of new commercial space in the area and prevent a glut. By this time, the government assessed that the release of these prime parcels would be a timely move to kick-start a new phase in Orchard Road's development and bolster its prospects as an important retail corridor in the heart of Singapore. Indeed, these parcels have been developed into some of the most popular retail destinations along Orchard Road today.

The URA, as sales agent for the state, sold these land parcels to the private sector for development, with specific guidelines and conditions to ensure that the future developments would respond well to their immediate context and contribute to the success of Orchard Road as a destination. The sales conditions included requirements on the provision of public spaces and pedestrian connections, activity-generating uses, the location of vehicular and emergency access points, and various streetscape improvements. This land sales and development approach allowed the public sector to play a significant role in influencing the forms and functions of new private developments on Orchard Road.

For example, one of the three GLS sites was at the junction of Orchard Road and Paterson Road, occupying a central location ideal for a development that could serve as a visual gateway to the district. In offering the site for sale, the URA sought to realize the potential for the future project to be a landmark development for the district. It decided to relax the prevailing height controls for the site, enabling the construction of ION Orchard, a 218-meter-high complex comprising a retail podium with direct connection to the Orchard MRT station at the basement level and a 56-story residential tower overhead. Today, ION Orchard, on the southeastern corner of the Orchard-Paterson junction, is a striking contemporary visual counterpoint to the 33-story Tang Plaza hotel tower directly across Orchard Road, which was built in 1982 with a traditional Chinese hard hill roof.

The URA also required the development to incorporate cultural and civic uses: ION Orchard houses spaces for events and public activities and an observation deck offering a panoramic view of the surrounding cityscape. In addition, the URA imposed requirements to improve pedestrian connectivity between ION Orchard and other parts of Orchard Road. For example, the developer was required to build a public concourse contiguous with the preexisting MRT concourse at the basement level. Planning conditions such as this helped create new underground connections between ION Orchard and surrounding buildings like Wisma Atria and Wheelock Place. A public space was also created along the pedestrian mall at the ground level, adding a new civic space to Orchard Road (URA 2005b).

Design Quality

To ensure exceptional urban and architectural design quality, selected strategic projects and key development precincts in Singapore have to go through a Design Advisory Panel (DAP) chaired by the URA. The DAP usually comprises members from the architectural industry along with representatives from other related fields. Under this DAP model, the overall design and layout of all key development proposals at Orchard Road are guided by the panel as part of the formal development control process.

The DAP evaluates each proposal in two stages. In the first stage, the panel considers broad urban design elements, including features related to building form, massing, pedestrian connectivity, vehicular circulation, view corridors, and landscaping. Projects that satisfy the DAP's criteria are then granted provisional permission by the URA, meaning that developers can commence some initial construction work on the development. In the second stage, the DAP reviews more specific elements such as architectural design features, building layout, building materials and finishes, and external lighting plans. Proposals that meet the DAP's review standards at this stage are then granted final planning permission by the URA (URA 2005c).

Incentivizing the Private Sector

The government also introduced incentives to promote place management efforts at Orchard Road. For example, the URA introduced an "Art Incentive Scheme for New Developments in Central Area" from 2005 to 2012, through which developers could obtain additional buildable floor area above the stipulated development intensity for their sites by providing public art installations in their developments. To qualify for the scheme, the art works must be evaluated and endorsed by a Public Art Appraisal Committee convened by the URA and the National Heritage Board (the public agency that manages Singapore's art and history museums), and developers must ensure that the works are accessible for free public viewing (URA 2005a).

The STB also initiated schemes to offset the costs that private sector stakeholders may incur in contributing to the rejuvenation of Orchard Road. For example, the STB supported companies in obtaining tax allowances for establishing flagship concept stores along the shopping street. Developers purchasing selected GLS sites at Orchard Road could also enjoy a remission on the amount paid in Goods and Services Taxes (GST, which is levied on the purchase of commercial real estate, including vacant land parcels), subject to various conditions. Such schemes have created win-win propositions between the private and public sectors, contributing significantly to the rejuvenation of Orchard Road in recent years.

Phase 4: Management

Providing Planning Flexibility to Encourage Redevelopment

To encourage rejuvenation through innovative and high-quality development projects that would enhance Orchard Road as the premier shopping street, the Orchard Road Development Commission (ORDEC) was in place from 2005 to 2015 to evaluate whether major additions and alterations (A&As) or redevelopment proposals, which deviate from the prevailing planning parameters, could be regarded as special innovative projects of high quality that merit the deviations.

The commission, chaired by the CEO of URA with members from other relevant government agencies, was empowered to propose incentives and allow variations in planning requirements to support innovative development ideas. It encouraged the development of projects with unique design concepts, those that enhanced the public realm with benefits to the community, and those that featured innovative business concepts and provided economic development benefits. Based on ORDEC's recommendations of the value brought about by redevelopment, URA supported these redevelopment proposals by granting them various development incentives; for example, projects were allowed to deviate from existing planning parameters such as plot ratios, permissible uses, and building height restrictions (URA 2013a).

More recently, URA introduced the Strategic Development Incentive (SDI) scheme in March 2019 as an expansion of the ORDEC scheme. The SDI scheme applies to strategic developments islandwide and aims to encourage the redevelopment of older buildings in strategic areas into new bold and innovative developments that will positively transform the surrounding urban environment.

Addressing Challenges

Orchard Road currently faces new challenges. The emergence of e-commerce and evolving consumer preferences are rapidly reshaping the brick-and-mortar-centric retail landscape (Koh 2018). As the Singapore government continues to pursue a policy of discouraging private motor vehicle use, there has been extensive discussion on how to further improve the pedestrian experience and rethink Orchard Road's position as a public space (MTI 2017).

Efforts have been made to address these concerns. In September 2017, a committee led by the ministers in charge of urban development, transportation, and industry was formed to drive efforts for the rejuvenation of Orchard Road (MTI 2017). In the near term, there are plans to refresh Orchard Road's streetscapes by activating other vacant parcels of state land in the area. New pedestrian crossings in the form of 30-second scramble walks were tested at selected junctions during late 2017 and early 2018 to improve pedestrian connectivity across Orchard Road (Koh 2018). New retail offerings were also planned to enhance the street's attractiveness as an integrated lifestyle and leisure precinct (STB 2017). These include Design Orchard—a retail-cum-incubation space for Singaporean brands and designers to test and promote their products—which opened in January 2019.

Safeguarding and enhancing Orchard Road's appeal in the face of new challenges is a continuous process, and one that will require close collaboration between agencies, development owners, businesses, and other stakeholders in the precinct.

Place Management

Beyond the physical characteristics of a place, there has been increasing recognition of the need to enhance human vitality, buzz, and identity through a collaborative multistakeholder management process. This process requires the commitment of area stakeholders to improve the management of a precinct, on the basis of a shared understanding that an improved precinct can reap tangible benefits for businesses and property owners.

PHOTO 15.4 **Pop-Up Event at Orchard Road, Singapore**

Source: ©Ken Lee. Used with the permission of Ken Lee; further permission required for reuse.

At Orchard Road, the STB has been working with ORBA to drive place management initiatives to enhance Orchard Road's image as a premier shopping and lifestyle destination. With ORBA acting as the overall place manager, local business owners and other stakeholders have been encouraged to contribute actively through business development, promotion, and marketing activities.

Place management efforts were earlier initiated as part of the STB's tourism promotion drive. But many of these early projects have come to positively affect not only the lives of visitors but also of Singaporeans (Hee 2017). One such initiative is the annual Orchard Road Christmas Light-Up, launched in 1984, which has become a popular event with both tourists and locals.

More recently, pop-up events planned by the STB, ORBA, and other stakeholders have injected vibrancy to Orchard Road (photo 15.4). These include promotional festivals held during the "Great Singapore Sale" each year—when retailers work together on a schedule of events held in public areas and within shopping centers to showcase their products—as well as Fashion Steps Out, when a long stretch of Orchard Road is closed to traffic and converted into an outdoor fashion catwalk.

These events generate excitement and anticipation among shoppers, creating more opportunities to draw visitors and enhance business activity on Orchard Road (Cheah 2003). Similar to place management efforts in other parts of Singapore, public agencies and businesses work together on these initiatives, pooling their expertise and resources.

Phase 5: Impact Evaluation

Orchard Road emerged as Singapore's key retail corridor in the 1970s and 1980s, displacing former commercial hubs centered on areas in the Downtown Core such as Raffles Place and High Street. Over the years, the precinct has come to play a central role in the development of Singapore's tourism industry and in the country's positioning of itself as a cosmopolitan, open, and friendly destination for regional and international visitors. At the same time, Orchard Road is a familiar, well-loved gathering and recreational spot for generations of Singaporeans from different backgrounds.

In recent years, Orchard Road has faced intense competition from e-commerce and newer commercial precincts in suburban locations and other parts of the Central Area. Indeed, tourism figures suggest that it is ceding ground to other retail attractions. In 2003, nearly 4.6 million visitors—representing 76 percent of all tourist arrivals—visited Orchard Road; by 2016, its share of visitors had fallen to roughly 50 percent (STB 2016). Tourism aside, Orchard Road remains an appealing location for Singaporeans: beyond shopping, a plethora of events draws thousands each month, and well-planned, attractively designed public spaces encourage many to visit, mingle, and socialize.

Retail rental figures suggest that Orchard Road has managed to retain its position as Singapore's preeminent retail draw. Despite the highly competitive retail environment, businesses appear willing to pay an increasingly higher premium to locate themselves in Orchard Road. In the first quarter of 2019, the median rental rate for retail space in the Orchard Planning Area was about S$107 per square meter, or 84 percent higher than the median rental rate for retail space in other parts of the Central Area. In the first quarter of 2014, five years prior, Orchard Road rentals outstripped those in other parts of the Central Area by a more modest 63 percent (URA 2019b). Beyond the retail sector, the value of residential property in and around Orchard Road remains robust. For example, in April 2018, the URA sold a residential site on nearby Cuscaden Road for almost S$2,400 per square foot, setting a new record for the price of GLS land.

The government's planning and design measures at Orchard Road have yielded many positive outcomes for businesses and landowners. More importantly, these interventions have created tangible improvements to the public realm, most notably to the central promenade, and through the provision of extensive spaces for leisure and enjoyment, ensuring that Orchard Road remains appealing to visitors and Singaporeans alike.

PARK CONNECTOR NETWORK

Phase 1: Context

When the Park Connector Network (PCN) was being conceptualized, the intention was to achieve a matrix of green connectors weaving through urban spaces and linking up Singapore's parks, gardens, and nature reserves, thereby increasing residents' accessibility to nature and greenery. This involved the curation of regional walking and cycling loops connecting major green spaces as well as interregional connections. Each cycling loop would adopt the character of the region and the parks that it connects, thereby offering users a varied recreational experience across Singapore.

The PCN would also serve as a network of green ecological pathways. Fast-growing, native trees and shrubs were intentionally planted to attract endemic biodiversity such as native birds and butterflies along the PCN. This would encourage Singaporeans to appreciate nature at their doorstep, thus fostering the environmental stewardship that underlies NParks's "City in a Garden" vision.

Phase 2: Planning and Design

One of the key planning and development principles of the PCN was to optimize unused narrow, linear land strips by converting them into landscaped recreational corridors. These were typically spaces that had been set aside for future uses, such as widening of roads (road reserves) and drains (drainage reserves). Even unused land next to a park has been considered and redesigned as a cycling bridge in the PCN (photo 15.5).

The other key principle was to provide a dedicated, recreational experience that was easy to maintain, with sufficient track width and good thermal comfort provided by shade canopy trees. PCN tracks would either be in asphalt or concrete for hardiness and fuss-free maintenance. Other supporting infrastructure, such as lighting, toilets, shelters, dedicated bicycle crossings, and wayfinding signage were also necessary for the safety and convenience of PCN users as well as to build up the PCN identity (photo 15.6).

In terms of spatial needs, studies ascertained that a 4-meter-wide track was sufficient, and this gave rise to two main typologies for the entire PCN:

- *Along roads:* Under this typology, the 6-meter roadside PCN comprises a split track of 4 meters in width (2.5 meters for cycling and 1.5 meters for footpath) and a 2-meter-wide planting strip on one side of the track (figure 15.4, panel a).
- *Along waterways:* When the PCN runs alongside a waterway, the land take will be 6 meters wide, measured from the edge of the outer drain wall. These 6 meters will comprise a split track of 4 meters in width (2.5 meters for cycling and 1.5 meters for footpath) and a 2-meter-wide planting strip next to the canal (figure 15.4, panel b). The latter will soften the canal edge and provide the option of a meandering track to break the monotony of long stretches of the drains. The availability of space provides the flexibility to design the planting verge on either side of the track.

The PCN can also use or visually "borrow" greenery from adjoining developments to enhance the recreational experience and better create a sense of spaciousness. For example, such borrowed greenery is found in park connectors adjoining porous public housing developments or waterfront developments (photo 15.7).

Phases 3 and 4: Implementation and Management

From Piloting to Long-Term Implementation

The PCN is an innovative idea for a small, land-constrained island state like Singapore. It creates an islandwide green recreational network that is easily accessible for a majority of residents. After rounds of interagency discussions, the Garden City Action Committee (GCAC) officially endorsed the PCN initiative on December 4, 1991. The Kallang Park Connector, which links Bishan-Ang Mo Kio Park to Kallang Riverside Park, was implemented as a pilot project. Mr. S. Dhanabalan, then Minister for National Development, opened the first completed park connector along Kallang

a. Before: Unused land near a park **b. After: Cycling bridge**

PHOTO 15.5 **Urban Voids Redesigned as Dedicated and Recreational Public Spaces in the PCN, Singapore**

Source: ©National Parks Board (NParks). Reproduced, with permission, from NParks; further permission required for reuse.
Note: PCN = Park Connector Network.

a. Before: Unused drainage reserve **b. After: Attractive cycling path**

PHOTO 15.6 **Re-Created Pedestrian Networks in the PCN, Singapore**

Source: ©National Parks Board (NParks). Reproduced, with permission, from NParks; further permission required for reuse.
Note: PCN = Park Connector Network.

River in August 1992. This was followed in quick succession by the Ulu Pandan Park Connector, which was completed in December 1994.

The popularity of these pilot PCNs gave rise to the first PCN program, which was approved in 1994 to implement 36 kilometers of park connectors (14 stretches) between 1995 and 1999—kick-starting an almost three-decades-long effort. This marked an important milestone in the journey of the PCN as the implementation of park-to-park recreational green links became a mainstay in the master planning of the city.

First-generation park connectors were basic tree-lined trails, simply furnished with benches and bins. In terms of implementation, the biggest challenge was (and still is) finding enough space in a heavily built-up environment with competing development needs. With pavements, covered linkways, drains, utility service pipes, and roadside greenery squeezed into the narrow spaces beside roads, it is often difficult to imagine where the additional 6 meters of

a. Roadside

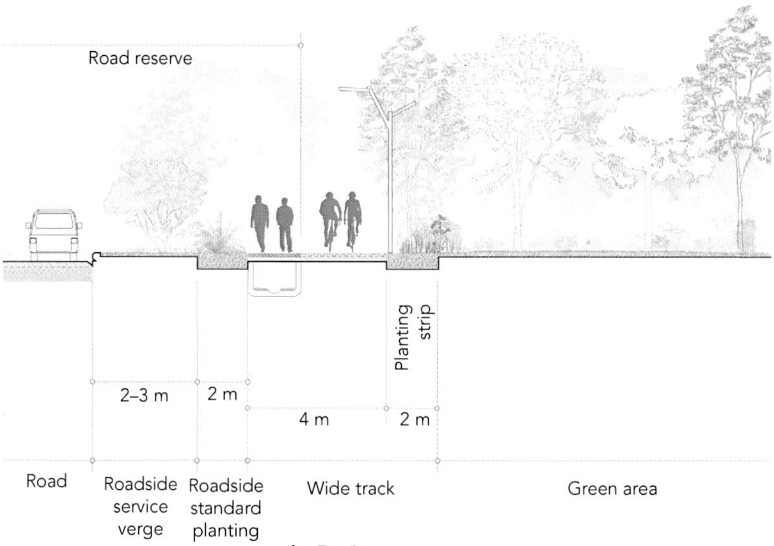

b. Drainage reserve

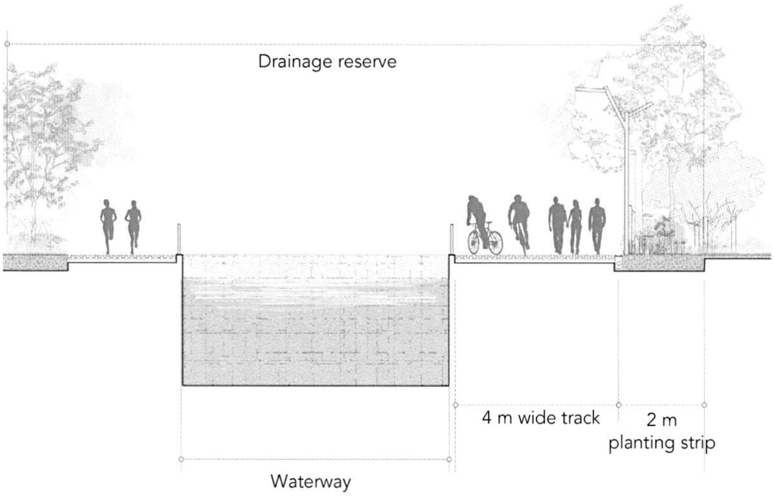

FIGURE 15.4 **Typical Spatial Design Typologies for the PCN, Singapore**

Source: ©World Bank, based on National Parks Board (NParks). Further permission required for reuse.
Note: PCN = Park Connector Network; m = meters.

PHOTO 15.7 **"Borrowing" of Greenery from PCN-Adjacent Bedok Neighborhood, Singapore**

Source: ©National Parks Board (NParks). Reproduced, with permission, from NParks; further permission required for reuse.
Note: PCN = Park Connector Network.

width for the park connector would come from. Close cooperation with other government agencies and private landowners was necessary to ensure that the right spaces were safeguarded in the larger interest of public recreation. In this respect, having design considerations and clear typologies ready up front were useful during stakeholder discussions and negotiations. Where connections were not ideal, management solutions were implemented, such as barriers to slow down cyclists or signs asking them to dismount and push their bikes.

Transforming Lifestyles with the PCN Experience

To date, Singapore has achieved an islandwide network comprising seven regional loops of 20–40 kilometers each, linking not only parks but also transport nodes and residential, commercial, and even industrial districts. Office workers can now enjoy a refreshing commute to work through a green corridor while getting their daily dose of exercise. The Western Adventure loop was completed in 2009, followed by the Northern Explorer Loop and the North-Eastern Riverine Loop in quick succession in 2010 and 2011, respectively.

To date, 320 kilometers of park connectors have been completed, and Singapore aims to achieve 400 kilometers by 2030. In addition, the LTA has started implementing intratown and intertown cycling paths to complement

NParks's PCN, enhancing connectivity across the island. This seamless and integrated cycling network has brought immense benefit to the community and brings Singapore one step closer to being a car-light city.

Round Island Route: The Green Cycling Highway

Together with the growth of the PCN, cycling as a form of recreation or commuting has gained mainstream popularity among Singaporeans. There was a need to facilitate a smooth cycling experience for longer rides. This gave rise to the Round Island Route (RIR). Conceptualized by the URA and NParks, the RIR is planned to be a 150-kilometer continuous green cycling highway looping around mainland Singapore (map 15.2). It intended to offer a unique experience by bringing users through diverse natural and urban landscapes, including nature reserves, beaches, wetlands, farmland, residential heartlands, business parks, and downtown districts.

Phase 5: Impact Evaluation

As more park connectors were built to meet the needs of the growing population, it was necessary to understand the PCN's impact on the community at large. Research has shown that contact with green spaces has been associated with benefits to mental health, particularly reduced levels of stress (Van den Berg et al. 2010), and that physical activity in green spaces improved mood

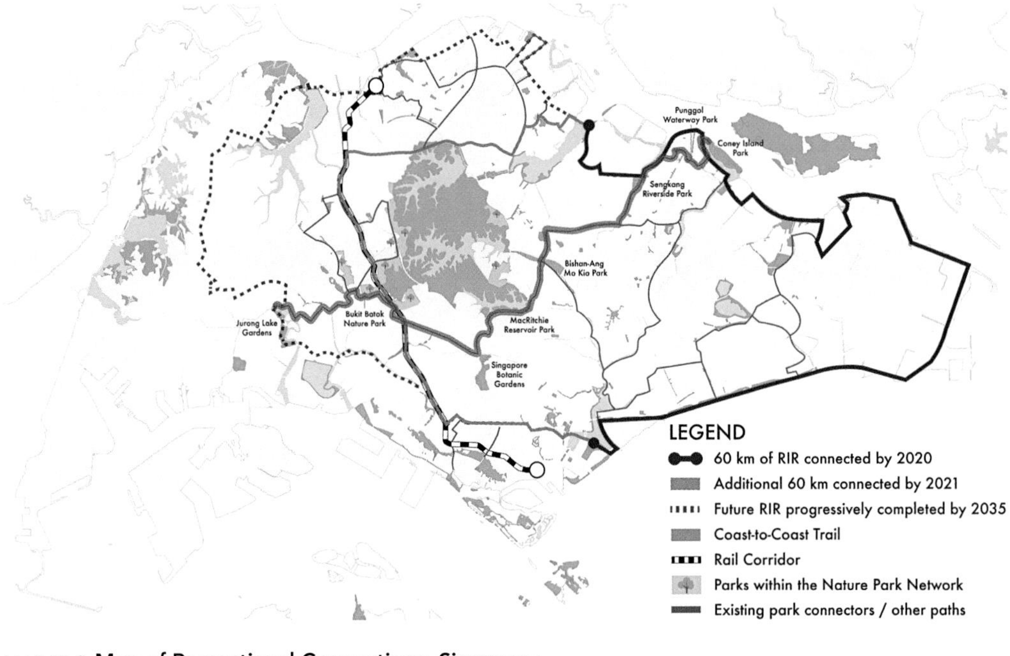

MAP 15.2 **Map of Recreational Connections, Singapore**

Source: ©National Parks Board (NParks). Reproduced, with permission, from NParks; further permission required for reuse.
Note: PCN = Park Connector Network.

and a sense of "belonging" within a work community, which in turn translates to increased workplace productivity (Barton and Pretty 2010).

NParks's Park Usage and Satisfaction Survey 2016 found that 88 percent of respondents visited parks and park connectors at least once in the preceding 12 months (NParks 2016). This was an increase of 16 percent from the previous survey conducted in 2014. In the same 2016 survey, 50 percent of respondents felt that park connectors were getting busier. This implied that with the steady expansion of the network, the use of parks and the PCN had significantly increased.

The survey findings also helped NParks to better understand PCN utilization patterns and was useful in refining the planning process for future park connectors to continue to enhance the PCN experience. NParks is also exploring "family-friendly PCN loops" of around 5–10 kilometers that are easy for both young and old to complete in approximately an hour. Such loops will promote the use of nature-based recreation for a healthy lifestyle, family bonding, and outdoor learning. Singapore also aims to offer refreshing experiences on the PCN such as the Coast-to-Coast Trail, which brings people to different scenic and interesting places across the island.

From providing simple green links between parks to recreational commuting infused with native flora and fauna, NParks's PCN journey continues to evolve. The larger intention is to connect Singaporeans from different walks of life, foster cohesion, and build social resilience through a network of pervasive greenery, with the PCN as its backbone. NParks envisions the PCN as offering a new dimension of recreational opportunities in close proximity to residential areas that are themselves venues for lifestyle, social, and community activities. NParks continues to innovate and provide new experiences for the public in shaping Singapore into a biophilic "City in a Garden"—a green oasis comprising an interconnected network of verdant streetscapes, gardens, parks, nature reserves, and vertical greenery.

HAWKER CENTERS

Phase 1: Context

Access to local food features greatly in Singaporean culture and everyday life. Food markets—more commonly referred to as hawker centers in Singapore—are purpose-built, naturally ventilated complexes of stalls that sell cooked food at affordable prices. With strict regulation and upgrading over time, these food nodes have evolved to become clean, accessible social spaces frequented by people from all walks of life. Hawker centers were originally built to resettle and organize street vendors and hawkers so as to better manage public health and sanitation issues associated with hawking food on the streets. They have since become a mainstay in the urban landscape, offering a variety of cooked fare at affordable prices islandwide while preserving Singapore's unique food heritage. Over time, hawker centers have become integral to Singapore's way of life and serve as "community dining rooms" where Singaporeans from different races, religions, and diverse backgrounds come together to share meals.

A hawker center was a solution to manage the streets of Singapore, which were once rife with itinerant hawkers and street peddlers. Hawking was an important means of livelihood for many, especially immigrants, because it required little capital and could generate a good income. In the 1930s, some 6,000 licensed itinerant hawkers and 4,000 unlicensed hawkers were estimated to have roamed the streets, selling affordable cooked food and local produce (Thulaja 2016). By 1966, the number had grown to 40,000 licensed and unlicensed hawkers (Tan, Jean, and Tan 2009).

The government could not, however, ignore the urban problems that arose as the number of street hawkers increased. The Hawkers Inquiry Commission Report recommended that hawkers be removed from the streets because the activities of hawkers conflicted with the goals of development, for they were competing directly with the modern sector for land usage. In addition, hawkers usually did not have a proper water supply and posed risks to public health (Hawkers Inquiry Commission 1950).

After independence, the government stepped up to address these urban challenges. From the 1960s to 1980s, hawkers islandwide were registered, licensed, and relocated from main streets to side lanes and eventually to purpose-built hawker centers. Enforcement against illegal hawking was tightened.

Authorities also had to be cognizant of the benefits and services offered by the street hawkers. In 1970, Health Minister Chua Sian Chin said the government recognized that hawkers served a need in society. Hawkers kept food prices low, moderating the cost of living for ordinary people, and created jobs (*Singapore Herald* 1970). The government was thus reluctant to remove hawkers completely (Lim 2013).

In 1970, an ambitious five-year plan was announced to clear all hawkers off the streets into purpose-built "hawker centers" (*Straits Times* 1970). To encourage resettlement, hawkers would be given an indoor stall at a subsidized rental. The earlier licensing exercise was useful in identifying bona fide hawkers to be relocated into permanent facilities (Tan, Jean, and Tan 2009). Hawker centers were built into new townships, as part of each town's commercial center. According to guidelines, a hawker center was to be built for every 4,000–6,000 households. This ensured that hawkers would be located near a ready client base, ensuring greater likelihood of business sustainability.

Since then, hawker centers have emerged as crucial social spaces in the Singaporean urban landscape by ensuring access to affordable, diverse food options alongside the inclusiveness of access to these affordable cooked food options—making them a food paradise for all, a celebration of Singapore's multicultural identity, and a unique social leveler. By 2018, there were 114 wet markets (selling produce) and hawker centers managed by the National Environment Agency (NEA), with plans to build 13 more hawker centers (map 15.3).

The following sections will share how the program was implemented through policy, monitoring, and enforcement; cover the design of hawker centers to adhere to their social objective as a public space; and describe the considerable positive impacts hawker centers have had on Singapore residents.

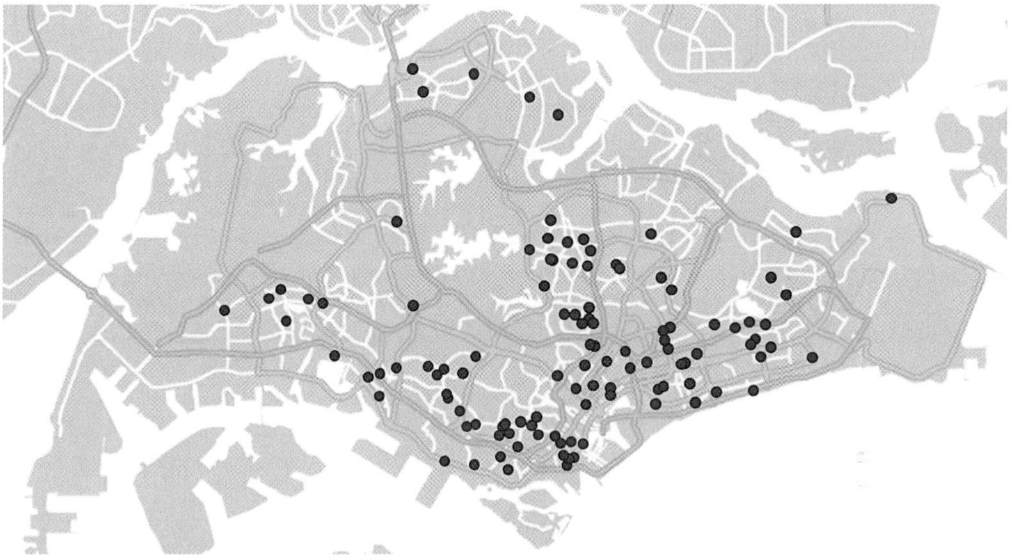

MAP 15.3 **Locations of 114 Hawker Centers in Singapore, July 2018**

Source: Centre for Liveable Cities (CLC) with data and base layer from National Environment Agency (NEA) and Singapore Land Authority (SLA), respectively. ©CLC. Reproduced, with permission, from CLC; further permission required for reuse.

Phase 2: Planning and Design

The 1971 Concept Plan advocated shifting the population away from the city center, leading to plans that were drawn up to design and build self-contained housing estates, each with its own commercial, institutional, and recreational facilities. Each new estate, depending on population size, typically had a town center and a few neighborhood centers featuring many shop units and a hawker center, often with an adjoining wet market to serve the residents in the town.

Hawker centers are designed to be inclusive spaces for all and reflect the ethnic and cultural makeup of Singapore through their diverse food options. They serve flavors from the Malay, Indian, and Chinese ethnic groups as well as cuisines from other ethnicities. With Singaporeans spending an average of 37 percent of their food budgets on hawker fare, these hawker centers have become convenient primary sources of food (Tan 2015). This is particularly significant for lower-income groups, underlining the need to keep hawker food prices affordable. Recently built hawker centers, such as in Our Tampines Hub and Kampung Admiralty, are also co-located with community centers, recreation facilities, and government service offices for residents' ease. The co-location also allows for maximizing uses of limited land.

The planning and design of hawker centers involve several considerations, as discussed below.

Access and Layout

Early hawker centers were located in town centers and neighborhood centers within housing estates, close to residents' homes in order to meet their shopping and dining needs. Today, new hawker centers may be built in neighborhood centers, but they are planned to be accessible from multiple sides to connect with various transport nodes, community facilities, and housing areas (BCA 2016). Where feasible, pedestrian links to key amenities are also built in. For example, Pasir Ris Central Hawker Centre has pedestrian links to adjacent buildings, ramp connections to surrounding parkland and facilities, and bicycle path connections (Kung 2018).

Where possible, hawker centers are located on ground floors; otherwise, escalators and lifts are provided to allow easy access. They are generally designed to be on a single level without steps or split levels. Where necessary, a gradual ramp or slope of a suitable gradient is permitted to mitigate differences. Floor finishes are firm, slip-resistant, and durable (BCA 2016).

Food and service counters, seating areas, and toilets are designed for patrons to maneuver easily. Hawker centers were thus planned with a clear and ergonomic layout and with unobstructed access routes to facilitate easy and independent access throughout (BCA 2016). Some common layouts that can be found in hawker centers include the central layout, grid layout, linear or axial layout, and free-form layout (figure 15.5).

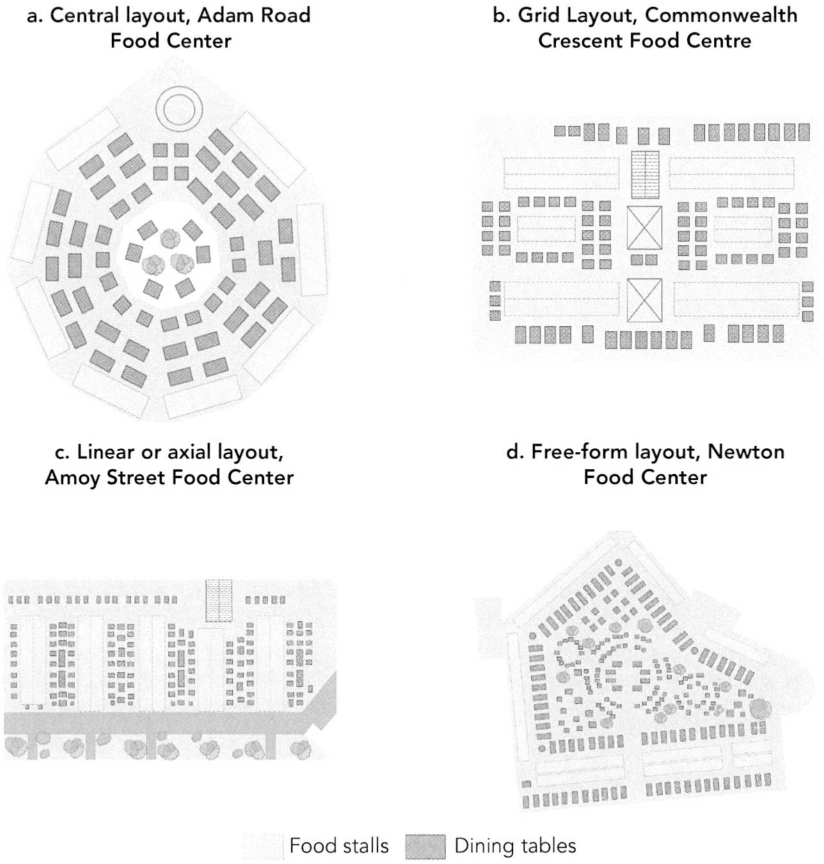

FIGURE 15.5 **Site-Specific Layouts and Universal Designs for All: External Structures and Internal Flow of Hawker Centers, Singapore**

Source: ©Centre for Liveable Cities (CLC), with information from the National Environment Agency (NEA). Reproduced, with permission, from CLC; further permission required for reuse.

Ventilation

Good ventilation and comfortable microclimate are important considering Singapore's hot and humid conditions. Designers learned from experience in implementing and upgrading the existing hawker centers. Greater air movement is facilitated through exhaust flue systems in cooked-food stalls and fans sited in the refreshment area. The exhaust flue system extracts hot air from stalls and discharges it outside the hawker center, reducing heat buildup within the center while the fans enhance the natural ventilation.

More recently, computer simulations have been used for designing new hawker centers to improve ventilation. Fans are controlled by a central timer that operates only during opening hours to conserve energy. For example, Pasir Ris Central Hawker Centre uses a combination of (a) a customized metal façade panel High-Volume Low-Speed (HVLS) with openings and aerofoil louvers, and (b) double-volume high ceilings to maximize airflow. In recent years, HVLS fans have been added to further improve airflow circulation efficiency (Kung 2018).

Tables and Seats

Because hawker centers are social nodes, design guidelines also include varied, flexible arrangements of tables and seats for patrons with different needs and abilities, like families with young children, the elderly, and wheelchair users (BCA 2016). For fixed seating, at least 1 of every 10 tables (or part thereof) is provided for use by persons with disabilities, or at least 2 tables, whichever is greater. At least 5 percent of overall seating should be family-friendly, which may consist of a table or seat mix of regular and child-friendly heights.

Over time, many of these design elements were also updated to continuously ensure that hawker centers are inclusive spaces for all. For example, many new hawker centers feature Braille and tactile information on staircase handrails to guide the visually impaired. Family-friendly features—like a family room with nursing and diaper-changing facilities, and parking spaces for wheelchairs and prams—are also common sights. To date, four new hawker centers have been awarded the BCA's Universal Design Awards since 2016 (NEA 2017; photo 15.8).

a. Bukit Panjang Hawker Centre **b. Yishun Park Hawker Centre**

PHOTO 15.8 **Award-Winning Hawker Center Designs within Walking Distance from Residential Communities, Singapore**

Source: ©Ken Lee. Reproduced, with permission, from Ken Lee; further permission required for reuse.

Phase 3: Implementation

In 1971, the government approved a sum of S$15 million for the building of markets and hawker centers (Loh and Wong 1987). The HDB was directed to construct hawker centers with the dual objectives of resettling street hawkers as well as to provide amenities for the new towns. In 1976, a further S$21.4 million was approved for the construction of markets and hawker centers (Loh and Wong 1987). The last of these hawker centers was built in 1985, resettling the remaining licensed hawkers.

Each hawker center comprised a market section and a cooked food section. The centers were provided with essential amenities such as proper sewage connections, piped water and electricity, and bulk bin centers for the disposal of refuse. The cooked food stalls were also compartmentalized and lined with glazed tiles. Fixed tables and stools for customers became a common feature in all hawker centers. Ceiling fans and toilet facilities were also available for the comfort and convenience of the patrons (Tan, Jean, and Tan 2009).

Beyond the residential estates, the Jurong Town Corporation (JTC) was tasked with developing industrial estates, and hawker centers were also built there. Some of the street hawkers were resettled into hawker centers built within the industrial estates.

By the late 1990s, many of the hawker centers were at least 20 years old and in poor physical condition. Because these centers provided essential amenities to residents, they had to be upgraded to match the rejuvenation that was taking place in the housing estates where they were located. The Hawker Centres Upgrading Programme (HUP) was launched in 2001 at a cost of S$420 million. The program, which spanned more than 10 years, improved the conditions and facilities of all hawker centers in Singapore (Leong 2001).

In 2011, after a hiatus of 26 years, the government responded to the public's requests for more hawker centers and announced the building of 10 new ones, focusing on the Housing and Development Board (HDB) towns facing an underprovision of eating options. A further 10 were announced in 2015. In all, 20 new hawker centers will be built by 2027, of which 7 have been completed. To better optimize land and public assets, and to better manage them by providing multiple uses and community services, some of the new hawker centers are also co-located with other public facilities such as community centers, police posts, polyclinics, and sports facilities.

Centrally locating hawker centers in townships and urban spaces was also crucial to the success of resettlement. It ensured that displaced hawkers could continue their businesses with a ready supply of customers from neighboring housing and provided central "marketplaces" that serve as landmarks and meeting spaces today.

Phase 4: Management

After the construction of hawker centers, a set of regulations was put into place to uphold basic sanitation levels. An Environmental Public Health Act was introduced in January 1969 to incorporate public health practices into the licensing and control of hawkers and food establishments. In the 1970s, 140 hawker inspectors from the Ministry of the Environment carried out spot checks for sanitation; hawkers had a six-month grace period to get used to new health regulations (*New Nation* 1973). Under the law, all stallholders selling food and hawker centers were required to prominently display food prices. Surprise checks to ensure that hawkers displayed food prices on their signboards were also common. Offenders were liable to a maximum fine of S$150 in the first instance and to a further fine of up to S$50 for each day the offense continued after conviction (*New Nation* 1977).

Despite legislation and strict enforcement, many hawkers continued with unhygienic practices, raising concerns about public health and the sanitation of cooked food (*Straits Times* 1985). Thus, in the 1970s and 1980s, the Ministry of the Environment organized a series of public health campaigns to promote good food hygiene practices (Lim 2013). This doubled as a soft tool to encourage better practices among hawkers while also educating the public, because legislation and strict enforcement alone had not been effective in getting the hawkers to adopt better food handling practices. In 1987, a Points Demerits System was introduced as a systematic method of imposing penalties on hawkers who did not meet public health standards. Potential or new hawkers were also required to obtain a Food Hygiene Certification before they could register (Lim 2013). This was later revamped, and currently the Singapore Food Agency requires hawkers to complete the Basic Food Hygiene Course conducted by the Workforce Development Agency's accredited training providers.

In 1998, a grading system was put in place to complement the Points Demerit System. The grading system used a simplified method to indicate the cleanliness of each stall. Every food stall must be graded once a year, and stalls are required to display these grades (Lim 2013). This system incentivizes hawkers to improve cleanliness levels because it makes the public aware of the cleanliness levels of each stall. Singapore's Health Promotion Board also introduced the Healthier Dining Programme to encourage consumers to choose whole grain, "Low GI (low glycemic index)," and lower-calorie meal options (Gan 2017). It is hoped that 4 in 10 hawker stalls will have at least one healthier dish by mid-2019.

In 2003, authorities consolidated the hawker center development, management, and policy functions under the NEA. With this consolidation, the HDB transferred the management functions of the HDB hawker centers to the NEA on April 1, 2004. The ownership of the HDB hawker centers and markets continues to reside with the HDB.

Phase 5: Impact Evaluation

Public Health

Even as hawkers had access to potable water and other amenities, food cleanliness and safety at the stalls were challenges. As noted earlier, a Points Demerit System was introduced in 1987 to penalize hawkers who violated public health laws. Repeat offenders were liable to have their licenses suspended or revoked (NLB 2010). However, this did not help the public to make well-informed choices. Its replacement in 1997 with a grading system specifically helped to (a) ensure that the public could discern stall hygiene, and (b) encourage stalls to raise their hygiene standards. Stalls were scored based on overall hygiene, cleanliness, and housekeeping standards to receive a grade. Grade A indicated a score of 85 percent or higher, and grade D, the lowest, indicated a score of below 40 (NLB 2010). Grades were reviewed annually by NEA inspectors. All stalls had to display the grades prominently. This program was largely successful: in 2006, 77 percent of licensees were graded either A or B; this rose to 99 percent by December 31, 2018.[2]

With almost all licensees being graded A or B, the grading system has, however, become less useful in helping consumers to distinguish good performers. In June 2018, the NEA introduced a new Food Hygiene Recognition Scheme for licensed food retail establishments. This scheme recognizes retail food establishments that have consistently upheld high hygiene standards over the years.

Furthermore, since June 2012, the latest grades, suspension records, and accumulated demerit points of licensed food premises have been published on the NEA website. This allows patrons to make informed choices and has spurred operators and food handlers to maintain good hygiene practices throughout the year.

Food Affordability

Hawker centers and wet markets were built by the government between the 1960s and 1980s with the main objective of resettling hawkers from the streets. They also provided eating and marketing amenities for residents in new towns.

The role of hawker centers has evolved over the years into an important social one. A key aim of hawker centers is to provide affordable food for all. This has been largely successful, and hawker centers remain an important source of reasonably priced food. Food remains a significant portion of household expenditure, constituting an average of 20 percent of household expenditure (DOS 2014). One in three Singaporean residents eat out more than they eat at home. When eating out, 81 percent say hawker food is their meal of choice (Weber Shandwick 2015).

The NEA's existing tender policies help to moderate rentals of stalls, ensuring that food prices are kept low. Prices are also kept affordable by building new centers to increase the supply of hawker stalls, ensuring that stalls are personally operated (without the practice of subletting), and abolishing the concept of reserve rent. The removal of reserve rent allows bidders to take up stalls at rental rates below the assessed market rent, thus keeping stall rentals down (Balakrishnan 2015).

To further assist hawkers to keep their costs low, NEA launched a Productive Hawker Centres program in 2017 to help hawkers improve their productivity. Under the program, the NEA cofunds the operating costs of stallholders when the centers adopt productivity formats such as centralized dishwashing and automated tray return systems. The NEA also launched a Hawkers' Productivity Grant whereby the government cofunds the hawkers' purchase of kitchen automation equipment. These initiatives aim to help hawkers cope with manpower constraints, manage costs, and keep food prices low for consumers.

Cultural Value

Hawker centers are integral to the Singaporean way of life. Today, 114 hawker centers serve as "community dining rooms" where people from diverse backgrounds gather and share the experience of dining over breakfast, lunch, and dinner (photo 15.9). Hawker centers are placed not only in residential townships but also in popular recreational areas to provide affordable food options.

In August 2018, Singapore announced its plans to nominate Singapore's hawker culture for inscription onto the United Nations Educational, Scientific and Cultural Organization's (UNESCO) Representative List of the Intangible Cultural Heritage of Humanity. Singapore's hawker culture—constituting the hawker centers, the wide variety of food they offer, and their role as vibrant community spaces—is an important part of the country's intangible cultural heritage. The selection of hawker culture was made after a series of public engagement efforts involving Singaporeans from all walks of life. Across the sessions, hawker culture was consistently highlighted as an intangible cultural heritage that best represents Singapore's multicultural heritage, with hawker centers viewed as important community spaces. The findings from the focus group discussions were similar to other studies conducted in the past. For instance, a survey conducted by the NEA in 2016 found that close to 85 percent of respondents felt that hawker centers played an important role

PHOTO 15.9 **Diners at Maxwell Food Centre, Singapore**

Source: ©Ken Lee. Reproduced, with permission, from Ken Lee; further permission required for reuse.

in community bonding. The same survey revealed that 90 percent of respondents strongly agreed that hawker centers are an integral part of Singapore's identity. More importantly, hawkers and their repertoire of skills are central in keeping hawker culture sustainable.

Through this and other efforts, it is hoped that there will be an increased awareness, recognition, and appreciation of hawker culture as well as encouragement of the active transmission of hawker trade from one generation to the next. These efforts will ensure that hawker centers continue to be vital public spaces for Singaporeans for generations to come.

NOTES

1. The Singapore government launched the Government Land Sales (GLS) program in 1967 to sell state-owned land parcels to private developers for residential, commercial, industrial, and other developments. GLS sites are sold through an open tender process, to the highest bidder. The government prescribes what each site can be developed for and the allowable development intensity (both parameters being reflected in the Master Plan); often, specific planning and urban design guidelines are stated up front in the conditions of tender. Thanks to the clarity, fairness, and transparency of the tender process, the GLS program has emerged as one of the most successful examples of a public-private partnership in Singapore that safeguards the interests of both the government and businesses in the realization of urban infrastructure projects.
2. Each food establishment will be graded annually based on its food hygiene and food safety standards before its license expires. The Food Establishment Inspection Checklist for the list of criteria to assess the grading of hawkers consists of 13 key areas, including premises, storage, food processing equipment, food handling and staff facilities, product identification, and dispatch and transport. Food establishments cannot be awarded grade A if major nonconformities are found (SFA 2012).

REFERENCES

Abraham, Alex. 2003. *Awestruck on Orchard Road: A Collection of Short Stories.* Aminjikarai, Chennai: EastWest Books.

Anderson, Colin, Fumihiko Maki, Kenneth Frampton, Debbie Ball, and D. P. Architects. 2012. *Evolution of a Retail Streetscape: DP Architects on Orchard Road.* Singapore: Images Publishing Group.

Balakrishnan, Vivian. 2015. "Rental Costs a 'Small Fraction' of Running a Hawker Stall: Vivian Balakrishnan." Channel NewsAsia, July 27.

Barton, Jo, and Jules Pretty. 2010. "What Is the Best Dose of Nature and Green Exercise for Improving Mental Health? A Multi-Study Analysis." *Environmental Science & Technology* 44 (10): 3947–55. doi:10.1021/es903183r.

BCA (Building and Construction Authority). 2016. *Universal Design Guide for Public Places.* Singapore: BCA.

Cheah, Gilbert. 2003. *Remaking of Orchard Road: Street of Singapore.* Singapore: Singapore Tourism Board.

CLC and SI (Centre for Liveable Cities and The Seoul Institute). 2016. *Walkable and Bikeable Cities: Lessons from Seoul and Singapore.* Singapore: CLC.

———. 2017. *Urban Systems Studies: Working with Markets: Harnessing Market Forces and Private Sector for Development.* Urban Systems Studies Series. Singapore: Centre for Liveable Cities.

CLC (Centre for Liveable Cities). 2015. *Urban Systems Studies: Planning for Tourism: Creating a Vibrant Singapore.* Urban Systems Studies Series. Singapore: CLC.

DOS (Department of Statistics Singapore). 2014. "Report on the Household Expenditure Survey 2012/13." Statistical report, DOS, Ministry of Trade and Industry, Republic of Singapore.

Gan, Kim Yong. 2017. "Measures to Restrict Distribution of Food and Beverage Products with High Glycemic Index." Response by Gan Kim Yong, Minister of Health, October 2. Parliamentary Debates Singapore: Official Report Contents 94 (51): 19–20.

Hawkers Inquiry Commission. 1950. *Report of the Hawkers Inquiry Commission, 1950.* Colony of Singapore: Government Printing Office.

Hee, Limin. 2017. *Constructing Singapore Public Space.* Singapore: Springer Singapore.

Keung, John. 2018. "No More Barriers: Promoting Universal Design in Singapore." Urban Solutions (Issue 6, Active Mobility): 36–41.

Koh, Michael. 2018. "Reimagining Orchard Road: Putting People on the Street." *Urban Solutions* (Issue 12, Inclusive Urban Regeneration): 44–53.

Kung, Jane. 2018. "Dining in a Park in a… Hawker Centre?" News and Insights, CPG Corp., April. https://www.cpgcorp.com.sg/news-insights/dining-in-a-park-in-a-hawker-centre.

Leong, Phei Phei. 2001. "All Hawker Centres to Be Upgraded." *Today*, February 19.

Lim, Tin Seng. 2013. "Hawkers: From Public Nuisance to National Icons." *BiblioAsia* 9 (3): 10–17.

Loh, A. T., and K. M. Wong. 1987. "Long Term Policy on Markets and Food Centres." Ministry of the Environment and Water Resources, Singapore.

Meng, Xianming, Mahinda Siriwardana, and Tien Pham. 2013. "A CGE Assessment of Singapore's Tourism Policies." *Tourism Management* 34: 25–36.

MND and MEWR (Ministry of National Development and Ministry of the Environment and Water Resources). 2015. *Our Home, Our Environment, Our Future: Sustainable Singapore Blueprint 2015.* Singapore: MND and MEWR.

MTI (Ministry of Trade and Industry). 2017. "Speech by Minister S. Iswaran at the Tourism Industry Conference 2017." Singapore Tourism Board, April 13.

NAS (National Archives of Singapore). 2004. "Speech by Dr. Vivian Balakrishnan, Acting Minister for Community Development, Youth and Sports and Senior Minister of State for Trade and Industry." The Association of Shopping Centres (TASC) Shopping Centre Conference on "Managing Shopping Centres," Raffles City Convention Centre, Singapore, November 24.

NEA (National Environment Agency). 2017. "Together for a Sustainable Future: Annual & Sustainability Report 2016/2017." NEA, Singapore.

New Nation. 1973. "Cleanliness Lesson for Hawkers." *New Nation*, September 13.

———. 1977. "Checks on Price Tags." *New Nation*, July 23.

NLB (National Library Board). 2010. "Hawker Centres." Singapore Infopedia, National Library Board, Singapore.

NParks (National Parks Board). 2016. "Park Usage and Satisfaction Survey." Internal report, NParks, Singapore.

———. 2017. "Discovering Greenery in the Sky." *MyGreenSpace* 1 (32). Quarterly newsletter, National Parks Board (NParks), Singapore.

SFA (Singapore Food Agency). 2012. "Food Establishment Inspection Checklist." Regulatory document, SFA, April 1 (accessed April 30, 2019).

Singapore Herald. 1970. "All Hawkers Off Streets – in This Govt Plan." *Singapore Herald*, August 5.

Sng, Lydia. 2015. *The Evolution of Singapore Real Estate: Journey to the Past and Future: 1940–2015.* Singapore: Knight Frank Pte Ltd.

STB (Singapore Tourism Board). 2005. "Singapore Sets Out to Triple Tourism Receipts to S$30 billion by 2015." Press release, January 11.

———. 2014. "Annual Report 2013/14." Singapore Tourism Board.

———. 2016. "Annual Report on Tourism Statistics." Statistical report, Singapore Tourism Board.

———. 2017. "Design Orchard to Cultivate Singapore Designers." Press release, October 30.

STPB (Singapore Tourist Promotion Board). 1997. "Tourism 21—Vision of a Tourism Capital." Planning document, STPB, Singapore.

Straits Times. 1966. "The 'Small' Man Who Has Become a Big Problem." *The Straits Times*, January 20.

———. 1970. "Hawkers Off the Street by 1975." *The Straits Times*, August 5.

———. 1985. "Hawker Centres or Shocker Centres?" *The Straits Times*, October 6.

Tan, Shin Bin. 2015. "Keeping Char Kway Teow Cheap—At What Price?" Case study, Lee Kuan Yew School of Public Policy, National University of Singapore.

Tan, Yong Soon, Lee Tung Jean, and Karen Tan. 2009. *Clean, Green and Blue: Singapore's Journey towards Environmental and Water Sustainability*. Singapore: Institute of Southeast Asian Studies.

Thulaja, Naidu Ratnala. 2016. "Travelling Hawkers." National Library Board Singapore Infopedia (accessed January 8, 2019), http://eresources.nlb.gov.sg/infopedia/articles/SIP_47_2004-12-27.html.

Tung, Ai Jui. 2016. "Hawker Centres." National Library Board Singapore Infopedia (accessed June 11, 2019), http://eresources.nlb.gov.sg/infopedia/articles/SIP_1637_2010-01-31.html?s=Hawker%20Centres.

URA (Urban Redevelopment Authority). 2001. "Making Orchard Road More Happening!" *Skyline* (March–April): 6–10.

———. 2005a. "Art Incentive Scheme for New Developments in Central Area." Circular to Professional Institutes, Circular No. URA/PB/2005/23-CUDD, Urban Redevelopment Authority, Singapore.

———. 2005b. "Sale of Site for Commercial Development on Land Parcel at Orchard Road /Paterson Road (Orchard Turn): Technical Conditions of Tender." Document, Urban Redevelopment Authority, Singapore.

———. 2005c. "Urban Design (UD) Plans and Guidelines for Orchard Planning Area: (A) Revision to Façade Articulation Guidelines (B) Guidelines for Party Wall Developments." Circular to Professional Institutes, Circular No. URA/PB/2005/07-CUDD, Urban Development Authority, Singapore.

———. 2007. "Revving Up Orchard Road." *Skyline* (November–December): 14–16.

———. 2013a. "Orchard Road Development Commission (ORDEC)." Circular to Professional Institutes, Circular No. URA/PB/2013/06-CUDG, Urban Development Authority, Singapore.

———. 2013b. "Urban Design (UD) Plans and Guidelines for Developments Within Orchard Planning Area." Circular to Professional Institutes, Circular URA/PB/2013/15-CUDG, Urban Redevelopment Authority, Singapore.

———. 2014. "Landscaping for Urban Spaces and High-Rises (LUSH) 2.0 Programme: Landscape Replacement Policy for Strategic Areas." Circular to Professional Institutes, Circular No. URA/PB/2014/12-CUDG, Urban Redevelopment Authority, Singapore.

———. 2019a. "Plans to Enhance Orchard Road as a Lifestyle Destination Unveiled." Press release, January 30, Urban Development Authority, Singapore.

———. 2019b. "Real Estate Information System." Retrieved from https://spring.ura.gov.sg/lad/ore/login/findOutMore.cfm.

Van den Berg, Agnes, Jolanda Maas, Robert A. Verheij, and Peter Groenewegen. 2010. "Green Space as a Buffer between Stressful Life Events and Health." *Social Science & Medicine* 70 (8): 1203–10.

Weber Shandwick. 2015. "Asia Pacific Food Forward Trends Report II." Weber Shandwick, Singapore.

CHAPTER 16

TBILISI, GEORGIA: PRESERVING HISTORIC PUBLIC SPACES IN A RAPIDLY CHANGING CITY

Irakli Zhvania

KEY TAKEAWAYS

- Although land-use planning and urban development policies in Tbilisi have strengthened over the past decade, much of the city's public and green spaces has been replaced by private development from past zoning amendments. In this context, two representative public-space cases in Tbilisi show different ways of preserving public spaces, one through the efforts of the local government to rejuvenate a historical area, and the other driven by citizen activism to protect a historic park.
- New Tiflis is a streetscape rehabilitation project in major historic parts of Tbilisi on the both sides of the Mtkvari River. The renovated streets brought back vibrancy and connected different historical areas, attracting both tourists and local residents. This also led to the overall increase in property value in the area.

- The Vake Park case study reiterates the importance of citizen engagement, and the high value that communities put on places. The gradual privatization of a public park led to a citizen protest and movement to protect the historical landmark. The movement also included raising the awareness of the importance of the park for public activities, by holding citizen-organized events such as concerts and art exhibitions. A proposed private development within the park gave way to the parks' preservation and rehabilitation.

CITY DYNAMICS

Context and Background

Tbilisi is the capital and the largest city of Georgia. The city is home to 1.2 million inhabitants, about one-third of the country's total population, and it is the economic and cultural center of Georgia, generating around 50 percent of its gross domestic product (GDP) (GeoStat 2016). Being located on the crossroads between the East and the West, Tbilisi has been a subject of interest for different powers throughout history.[1] It also became a melting pot of different cultural influences, which are expressed in its architecture. For instance, Soviet modernism and post-Soviet developments can be found across the city, memorializing the very different past of the newly emerged free market in independent Georgia. More recently, Tbilisi has become a popular destination for international tourism. As with other transitional economies, the Tbilisi government pursued laissez-faire approaches and prioritized the private sector through the easing of regulations and through political decisions.

Tbilisi's urban policies have been largely affected by the Soviet Union. During 70 years of Soviet rule, Tbilisi had three urban "master plans" that were elaborated in state planning agencies.[2] These top-down master plans prescribed a future for the city, including planned infrastructure and urban services. The private sector was cut out of all urban development. In the 1990s, the economic and governing structures of the planned Soviet economy collapsed, leaving the city without basic services and management schemes. The informal sector began to take over and serve the urban population's needs in transportation, commerce, and other areas. Regulatory oversight collapsed, and this allowed illegal construction, acquisition of land, and makeshift infrastructure schemes to reach a scale that significantly altered the city. During this period, the privatization of infrastructure, buildings, and land was a step toward a free market. The emerging private business sector began to acquire and manage properties and services previously owned by the state. But this process was not well managed, leading to chaotic, unplanned development.

From 2003 onward, as economic development accelerated and post-Soviet political institutions were established, different attempts to strengthen urban management have been undertaken with various results. A land-use plan based on German practices and models, developed in 2009, helped improve the accountability of policies and developments in the city.

Public Spaces in Tbilisi

In general, according to the city's land-use plan, green spaces are mostly defined as recreational zones.[3] These smaller green areas or playgrounds between residential buildings or within blocks tend to be included in residential or public-commercial zones. Sidewalks, plazas, or squares are included in transport zones. These zoning policies have been modified several times to accommodate private developments (Zhvania 2015). The lack of public finances to maintain municipality-owned public spaces has led to the privatization of open and green spaces. Large land plots of formerly state-owned enterprises have been subdivided into multiple land plots with higher building densities. In this context, private owners of these plots were not interested or incentivized to create public spaces on privately owned land, especially when such zoning regulations and requirements do not exist.

Deregulation of economic policies in Georgia since 2006 has significantly changed the creation and preservation of public spaces in the city. Green spaces in Tbilisi have been declining, a trend mainly associated with unplanned construction and inadequate management. To protect parks and green spaces, citizens and activists have resorted to organizing civic movements, such as Green Feast and Guerrilla Gardeners. Guerrilla Gardeners is a popular civic movement that advocates action for activities such as tree planting, caretaking of urban green areas, and raising awareness about these areas. The organization also participates in consultations with municipal officials and conducts advocacy to make the city greener.

Streetscapes have also been encroached upon by new stakeholders. Traditionally, ground-floor areas were mostly reserved for residential uses, were raised around 1–1.2 meters from the street level to provide comfort to residents, and were mainly accessed through building entrances by elevators. However, with the proliferation of new commercial uses such as shops, galleries, and offices, the elevated access to these ground-floor spaces created new problems for the public and pedestrians. Commercial property owners added stairs to the façades of buildings to secure direct access from the street, taking away already limited public spaces for these ad hoc structures. This effect was especially severe when a former apartment property was subdivided into several commercial spaces, whereby multiple stairs along a single street would create barriers to pedestrian movement. In the 1990s and early 2000s, such additions were mostly illegal, but after the mid-2000s, permits were granted to support small businesses, at the expense of public space (Zhvania 2015).

Managing cars and parking lots within sidewalk spaces has been challenging as well. Because of the increase in private cars and insufficient parking lots, vehicles often occupy sidewalks and push pedestrians out onto the driveways, increasing the danger of traffic accidents. To solve this problem, the municipality and property owners decided to officially draw parking lanes within selected sidewalks. However, even with these demarcated lots, vehicles would still need to drive onto the unmarked parts of sidewalks to access or leave these parking lots. This similarly resulted in the displacement of pedestrians from sidewalk spaces (photo 16.1).

PHOTO 16.1 **Cars Parked on Sidewalks in Tbilisi, Georgia**

Source: ©Irakli Zhvania. Used with the permission of Irakli Zhvania; further permission required for reuse.

NEW TIFLIS

Phase 1: Context

The New Tiflis project aims to rehabilitate major historic parts of Tbilisi on both sides of the Mtkvari River to make these areas more attractive for tourism and economic development, and to improve the urban environment for local residents. It is also a follow-on initiative after a previous project started in 2011 on Aghmashenebeli Avenue, the main avenue on the left bank of the Mtkvari River (TDF 2014). Aghmashenebeli Avenue was developed in the 19th century, when the area was populated by German settlers. Back then, the avenue was not part of the city, but when the city subsequently expanded, Alexanderdorf settlement, with its collection of classical buildings, became part of the city (photo 16.2).[4]

The 2011 project also partially rehabilitated the right (southwestern) riverbank—the medieval downtown with the highest concentration of businesses and the most cultural and tourist-oriented attractions (map 16.1). While this first project was implemented in a very short period of three to four months, the work was criticized for its poor quality (*Netgazeti* 2011). The New Tiflis project is a renewed initiative by the municipal administration that started its design activities in 2015.

PHOTO 16.2 **Aghmashenebeli Avenue before and after 2016 New Tiflis Project, Tbilisi, Georgia**

Source: ©Tbilisi Development Fund (TDF). Reproduced, with permission, from TDF; further permission required for reuse.

Phases 2 and 3: Planning, Design, and Implementation

The design and implementation process of New Tiflis had been led by the Tbilisi Development Fund. The fund, established by the city government of Tbilisi Municipality in 2010, aims to rehabilitate the historic parts of Tbilisi to rejuvenate the city and create value. The rehabilitation work focused mainly on areas that connect to tourist routes. These investments were complemented by the restoration of heritage buildings to enhance the attractiveness of historic areas and places.

MAP 16.1 **New Tiflis Project Intervention Area, Tbilisi, Georgia**

Source: "New Tiflis Project in 2016" [in Georgian], Tbilisi Development Fund (TDF) website, accessed March 15, 2019: http://www.tdf.ge. ©TDF. Reproduced, with permission of TDF; further permission required for reuse.
Note: Blue shading designates areas rehabilitated before 2015. Green shading represents the areas rehabilitated under the New Tiflis project after 2015 and connecting both sides of the Mtkvari River.

The design phase started in 2015, when private urban planning and architectural companies developed detailed urban development and design concepts for Aghmashenebeli Avenue and its adjacent streets (figure 16.1). During the seven months of renovation work in 2016, 52 buildings were rehabilitated, 42 of which were listed as monuments of cultural heritage. The underground infrastructure was completely rehabilitated, including sewerage, stormwater drainage, gas supply, water supply, electricity, and other associated infrastructure. Two small public parks were rehabilitated, and 2,500 plants and 26 trees were planted to enhance landscaping and shade. A 400-meter stretch of Aghmashenebeli Avenue was also pedestrianized.[5] During the construction, the project site from Marjanishvili Square to Saarbrucken Square was closed to traffic. Starting in 2016, GEL 35 million[6] from the municipal budget was allocated and used to fund the project.[7]

The following phase of New Tiflis was launched in 2018 and is set for completion at the end of 2019. Funding of GEL 60 million was allocated for the restoration of 19 buildings (including 13 listed monuments), the construction of underground parking for 150 cars, and the replacement of underground infrastructure. This phase would include the demolition of old buildings and construction of new ones.[8] This time, the rehabilitation takes place on

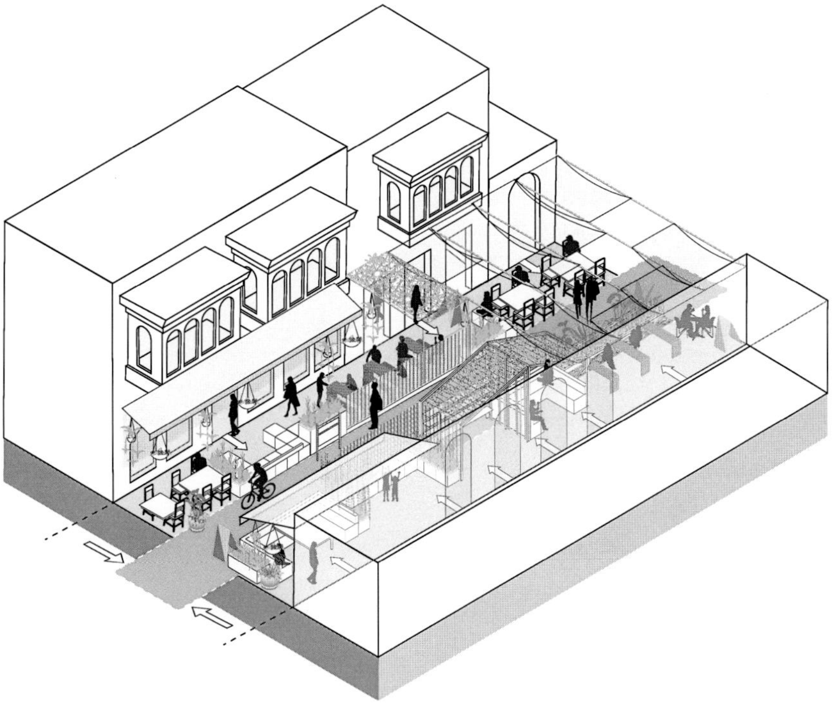

FIGURE 16.1 **Streetscape of Aghmashenebeli Avenue, Tbilisi, Georgia**

Source: ©World Bank. Further permission required for reuse.

the right (southwestern) bank of the Mtkvari River and will connect to the pedestrianized part of Aghmashenebeli Avenue via an existing bridge. Parks on both sides of the river will be connected via a pedestrian tunnel under the bridge. Another 400 meters of the street would also be pedestrianized to connect two existing parks: "9th April Park" and a small park on Orbeliani Square.[9] It is envisaged that the pedestrianized and rehabilitated areas on both sides would also be connected.

Phase 4: Management

The Tbilisi Development Fund is responsible for funding the maintenance of public spaces (fixing the pavement, maintaining the lighting, and taking care of street furniture). Within the liability period, any needed repairs to newly upgraded public spaces would be carried out by the construction companies without additional costs to the municipality. After the liability period ends, the Tbilisi Development Fund would be responsible for maintenance and recently added a new position to oversee these efforts with a deputy director for management and monitoring of rehabilitated areas. Municipal or private companies that provide urban services in the city are responsible for the maintenance of other related citywide services, such as waste management, street lighting, water, and others, although some maintenance responsibilities would still need to be negotiated among government stakeholders.

The most difficult part of the project management phase for the Tbilisi Development Fund was the negotiation of agreements with 200 owners on the scope of renovation works within their properties. Some rehabilitated dwellings in historic neighborhoods have multiple owners or condominium members. The threshold for agreement was very high: if just one owner opposed the renovation, then the agreements would not be signed, and work could not begin. Often, one owner or member would not agree to the proposed renovation and their reasons vary: a lack of interest, unwillingness to live next to a construction site for an extended period, or a desire to negotiate for more benefits (such as improvements to other assets on private property, for example). Another big challenge was the removal of improvised or illegal additions within courtyards, such as extended terraces, bathrooms, or storage. Although the rehabilitation was intended to restore the building to an original state, some owners did not want to lose their additions.[10]

Phase 5: Impact Evaluation

After its completion, the newly rehabilitated portion of Aghmashenebeli Avenue became very popular, drawing visitors and Tbilisi residents to the avenue. The pedestrianized street has hosted Christmas markets on the grounds of a former church; later, cinema shows, exhibitions, and other events were also held. The attractiveness of the area has also dramatically increased property values (figure 16.2). For instance, in 2015, the price per square meter of residential properties along the avenue ranged between US$700 and US$1,500. After the rehabilitation, in 2017, average prices increased from

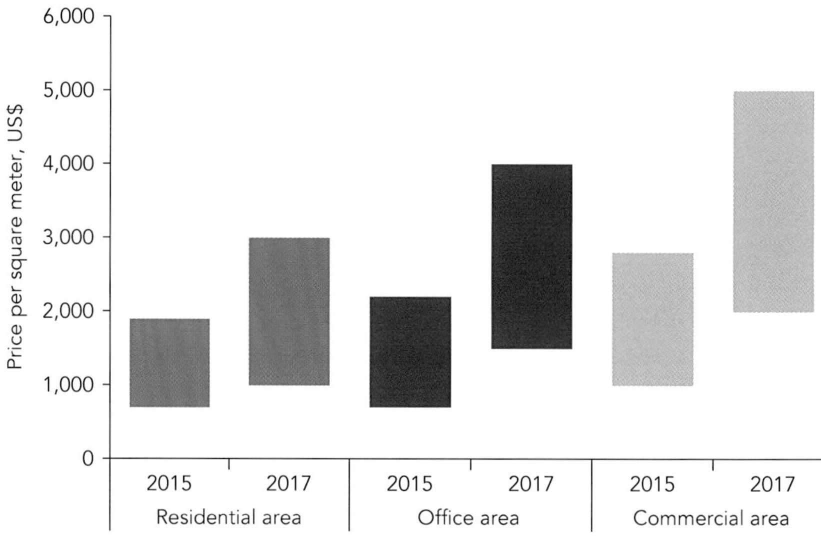

FIGURE 16.2 **The Range of Property Values in New Tiflis Rehabilitation Area, Tbilisi, Georgia, 2015 and 2017**

Source: World Bank, from Tbilisi Development Fund 2018 data.

US$1,500 to US$2,500 per square meter. Consequently, own-source revenues from payments and taxes from commercial companies operating in the rehabilitated areas such as shops, hotels, restaurants increased dramatically.

As with many other pedestrian streets in Tbilisi, cafés and restaurants soon started to extend seating and tables onto Aghmashenebeli Avenue. From both sides of the streets in the historic district, private businesses occupied half or even two-thirds of the street to accommodate more guests. This private encroachment onto public spaces created difficulties for pedestrian movement on busy days, and would benefit from proper regulations on public-space use (photo 16.3).

An unintended consequence of the rehabilitation of public spaces is the onset of gentrification. Some small grocery shops serving locals have started to disappear because they couldn't afford higher rents after the renovation. Businesses and higher-income individuals are buying up apartments to run hotels or Airbnb rentals, leading to a change in the social environment.[11] To mitigate the gentrification process and to retain the mixed-use character of the place, various policy instruments were considered for implementation, such as the introduction of vertical zoning in selected areas, to facilitate

PHOTO 16.3 **Outside Seating on Erekle II Street in Historic Downtown, Tbilisi, Georgia**

Source: ©Irakli Zhvania. Used with the permission of Irakli Zhvania; further permission required for reuse.

mixed-use buildings with the ground floors for commercial uses and upper floors for mostly residential uses. Even so, many existing residents and beneficiaries may ultimately decide to monetize their real estate or to relocate elsewhere for better housing.

VAKE PARK

Phase 1: Context

Vake Park is the largest urban park in Tbilisi. It is located in Vake neighborhood, at the foothills of a green ridge with Turtle Lake on the plateau uphill. Vake Park is connected to the lake by cable car, hiking trails, and a road. Surrounding the lake are a pedestrian trail, sports fields, rental boat facilities, outdoor training equipment, and cafés. The natural landscape surrounding Vake Park and Turtle Lake creates an enchanting recreational zone for Tbilisi's residents.

The park was built in 1946 and represents an example of Soviet landscape architecture of its time. The layout of the park is organized by a main axis with stairs: On the north end, the main entrance to the park is located on Chavchavadze Avenue. On the south end, a water cascade comes down from the World War II monument on the hill slope. In the center of the axis is a fountain where pedestrian boulevards converge in a radial pattern (photo 16.4). On the east side, the park borders the Vake residential neighborhood, and on the west side is where the Mikheil Meskhi Stadium is located. Vake Park is also a listed monument of the city's cultural heritage.

The 1990s in Tbilisi gave way to an economic depression and at times were also plagued with weak institutions. During this period, many plots of land in Vake Park became privatized because of poor enforcement and protection of the park, especially the land parcels along Chavchavadze Avenue on the northern side, and along Mishveladze Street on the eastern side. These private plots are now the sites of the Ukrainian embassy, the Iranian embassy, residential townhouses and high-rise buildings, the Georgian Football Federation, and three restaurants.

One of the privatized land plots sits in the middle of the park, where the Budapest Restaurant was once located. It was a two-story building and state-owned enterprise, which became dilapidated and was later demolished. In 1997, former employees of the restaurant formed a company and privatized the building and the plot of land. The property was subsequently sold to another company in 2007. In 2013, it was bought by Tiflis Development Fund, which then initiated the construction of the Budapest Hotel on the site (Tsintsabadze 2018).

According to the land-use plan, the plot was zoned as recreational Zone 2. Regulations adopted by the city council in 2009 did not allow construction there, but a 2011 amendment included the hotel as a permitted use for this zone. In 2013, an exemption from the rule was explicitly allowed and a decree granting the construction of the hotel in recreational Zone 2 was issued. The decree allowed the construction to exceed by 2.5 times the previous legal floor area ratio (Tsintsabadze 2018). As proposed, the Budapest Hotel had seven floors, and its construction demolished trees and greenery to clear the

PHOTO 16.4 **Overview of Vake Park from the North End, Tbilisi, Georgia**

Source: ©Irakli Zhvania. Used with the permission of Irakli Zhvania; further permission required for reuse.

way for a parking lot. According to the plan, the hotel grounds were to be fenced off and made inaccessible to park users.

Phases 2 and 3: Planning, Design, and Implementation

The privatization of parts of the historic public spaces in Vake Park had concerned citizens for more than a decade. Significant parts of the park were gradually privatized starting in 2002, and in 2012 only about two-thirds of the park remained publicly accessible (map 16.2).

A citizens' movement to protect Vake Park started in September 2013, when the municipality announced the rehabilitation of Vake Park. During a casual visit to the park, a citizen activist noticed construction activity all around the park and recorded it with a mobile phone. The video spread on social networks and caused great interest among concerned citizens (Tsintsabadze 2018).

Through information gathered via the internet, it was learned that construction of the Budapest Hotel would proceed without engaging the public in the decision-making process and without any meaningful public participation. This led to a big protest in Vake Park. Activists and their supporters began to mobilize to discuss strategies for defending the park.

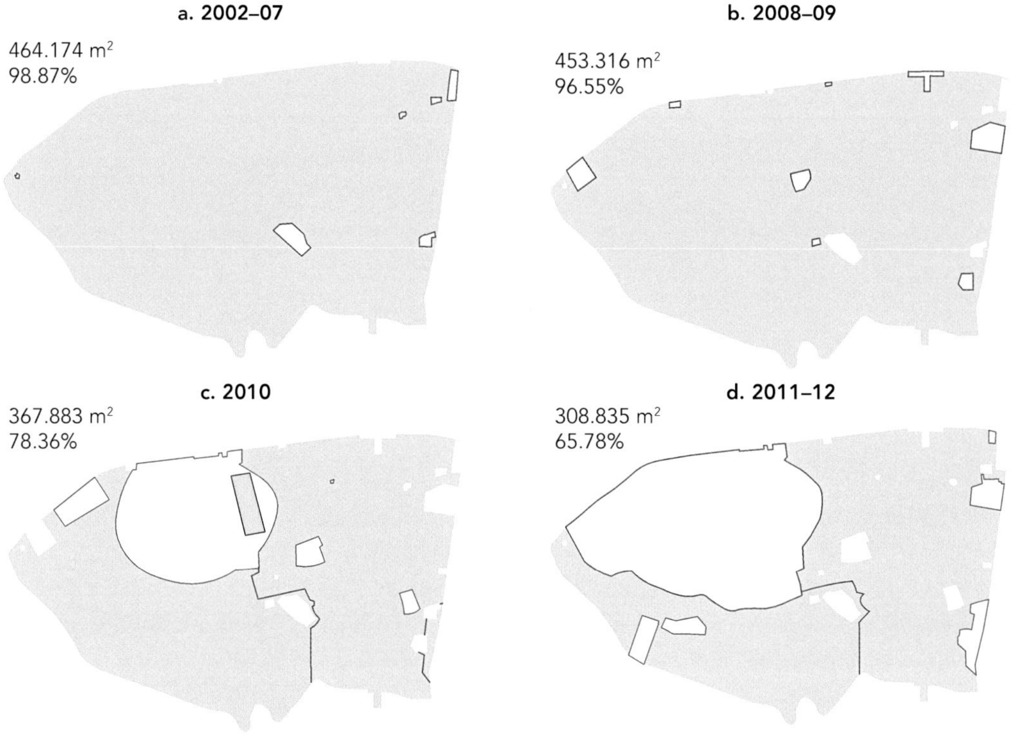

MAP 16.2 **Expansion of Privatized Area in Vake Park, Tbilisi, Georgia, 2002–12**

Source: ©World Bank, based on Tsintsabadze n.d.
Note: Green areas designate the publicly owned and accessible areas; white areas have been privatized. Percentages in each panel refer to the share of publicly accessible area. m^2 = square meters.

Information gathered by activists through publicly available sources was spread through social networks. The media got involved and started to interview protesters. In December, 2013, a meeting with citizens and activists at the city council was agreed to, but it ended without any results. Activists signed a petition and held the first protest meeting in front of the council building and regularly gathered in the park to block construction works. Meanwhile, the investor funding the hotel expressed willingness to meet with protesters, but this meeting did not yield any meaningful consensus either.

In December, 2013, around 100 activists held a protest gathering at the Tbilisi City Hall demanding that the council

- Revoke the construction permit;
- Prohibit any construction in the park;
- Agree on a land swap with the hotel investor; and
- Fill the excavation and plant trees.

The organizers circulated a petition that was signed by 6,000 people. After negotiations failed, activists decided that a more radical public protest was needed. A secret group called Guerrilla Gardeners was created on social media to collect and solicit ideas for action. Many individual activists also joined the movement and discussed various options to save the park (Tsintsabadze 2018).[12]

The Guerrilla Gardeners conferred online and set rules for making decisions. Ideas that didn't need much discussion were announced in the group and were voted on online. More important issues were discussed during gatherings, and decisions were made through majority vote. Attention was given to the communication with the media. Activists from different professional fields were invited by the media to speak about different topics that they cared about. When meeting with municipal officials or journalists, the group was represented by members who were lawyers, planners, or architects, as well as by many other civic activist groups.

In an online meeting, the Guerrilla Gardeners decided to set a permanent tent in Vake Park in December, 2013. In January 2014, more tents were added, and activists occupied the site 24/7. Other supporters helped and supplied protesters with food, warm drinks, and firewood. Activists set up a text message system to notify all supporters about all emergency situations, and the texts were posted on social networks. To prevent construction machinery from entering the site, they barricaded the only road leading there through the park.

From January 2014 to January 2016, around 50 different protest gatherings were held in Vake Park and at municipality and city council buildings. These gatherings lasted for three years. During this period, different events were held to show public appreciation for the park and the park's significance as a public green space. Photo and art exhibitions, flea markets, music and sports events, and film screenings were held. Many posters, stencils, and other examples of street art were created. Through a variety of donations and organizations, funds were raised for art materials, illumination, tools, and saplings (photo 16.5). As a result, the protest gained a lot of attention from the media.

Activists acknowledged the need for, and the importance of, a judicial due process, and a strategy for this was also planned. In 2014, three different cases from independent groups of citizens and an environmental group, Green Alternative submitted three appeals to the Tbilisi City Court, demanding annulment of the hotel construction permit. The case was reviewed by the city court in November while protests in the park continued.

In March 2016, the court accepted the appeal and announced that the construction permit was annulled. The investor went to the Court of Appeals, which then reversed the decision of the City Court in 2018. Although this decision was in favor of the investor, the construction permit had already expired in 2016. Activists interpreted the appellate decision as a way to avoid conflict with the investor and leave the final word either to the Supreme Court or City Hall if the investor tried to get a new construction permit. Protesters could go to the Supreme Court, but this would involve a long bureaucratic battle and leave the issues unsolved, and there was the possibility that the investor would win and apply for a new construction permit.

a. Music event at Tbilisi City Hall

b. Art installation at Vake Park

PHOTO 16.5 **Event-Centered Protests to Defend Vake Park, Tbilisi, Georgia**

Source: ©Guerrilla Gardeners. Used with the permission of Guerrilla Gardeners; further permission required for reuse.

After the decision of the Court of Appeals, the mayor of Tbilisi, Kakha Kaladze, said he would, if possible, not allow construction of the hotel in Vake Park. In January 2019, after a short negotiation between the investor and City Hall, an agreement was reached to either swap the land or compensate the investor.

Phases 4 and 5: Management and Impact Evaluation

The lack of engagement with the public led to public outcry when Vake Park was slowly encroached upon by private developments. Through the actions of Guerrilla Gardeners, ground-up activism that gathered citizens' opinions and communicated with stakeholders helped protect the park from further privatization of public space.

The park is currently managed by the municipality, and awareness of its cultural value to communities, the importance of green public spaces, and the need for citizen engagement have been engrained into future plans for the park. By the end of 2018, the municipality decided to rehabilitate Vake Park, and it invited members of Guerrilla Gardeners to participate in discussions on how to proceed with the design and rehabilitation process. As of March 2019, discussions about how to properly organize the project were still ongoing in Tbilisi City Hall.

NOTES

1. The Roman and Byzantine empires, Persians, Mongols, Arabs, Seljuk Turks, the Russian Empire, and Soviets dominated or invaded the city, sometimes bringing devastation or putting an end to its flourishing periods.
2. Interview with Irakli Zhvania (architect and urban planner and designer), by Hyunji Lee, on "Urban Planning and Public Space over Time in Tbilisi," November 20, 2018.
3. Definitions of different zones for city land uses derive from The National Law on Spatial Arrangement and Urban Development Principles, Governmental Decree No. 59 on Use of Settlement Territories, and Main Statutes on Development Regulation ("Tbilisi Zoning Map," Tblisi City Hall [website], accessed March 20, 2019, http://maps.tbilisi.gov.ge/#/C=44.7807474-41.7138468@Z=14).
4. The primary architectural style of the street façades is classicism or eclecticism with a few exceptions of art nouveau; behind the street buildings are typical Tbilisi-style courtyards with gallery-type balconies.
5. "New Tiflis Project in 2016" [in Georgian], Tbilisi Development Fund (TDF) website, accessed March 15, 2019: http://www.tdf.ge.
6. GEL = Georgian lari. It is difficult to convert this amount to U.S. dollars because of currency fluctuations since 2015. At the current exchange rate, GEL 35 million = US$13.2 million.
7. "New Tiflis Project in 2016," TDF website.
8. "New Tiflis Project in 2016," TDF website.
9. The "9 April Park" is named after the tragic date of April 9, 1989, when Soviet soldiers attacked a peaceful demonstration in Tbilisi and massacred 21 people.
10. Interview with Irakli Zhvania (architect and urban planner and designer), by 1st Channel of Georgian Public Broadcaster C Studio on "Concept of the Aghmashenebeli Avenue Development and the Project New Tiflis," September 29, 2016.
11. After the privatization in 1992, around 95 percent of the housing stock could be purchased by residents. Therefore, the discussion of gentrification should consider that residents are not forced to leave. Rather, they leave of their own accord, often to sell their property for a good price and move to better housing conditions (Zhvania 2015).
12. Information on Guerrilla Gardeners also comes from an interview with group leader Nata Peradze, by Irakli Zhvania, March 20, 2019.

REFERENCES

GeoStat (National Statistics Office of Georgia). 2016. "2014 General Population Census." Annual census report, GeoStat, Tbilisi.

Netgazeti. 2011. "Aghmashenebli Avenue Regeneration in 2011." [In Georgian.] *Netgazeti*, November 17 (accessed March 20, 2019), http://netgazeti.ge/culture/11493/.

TDF (Tbilisi Development Fund). 2014. "New Tiflis Project in 2016." [In Georgian.] Press release, November 8 (accessed March 15, 2019), http://www.tdf.ge/index.php/2014-11-08-14-20-31.

Tsintsabadze, Anano. 2018. *Case of Vake Park: Studying the Example of Civic Activism*. [In Georgian.] report, Tbilisi: Center for Training and Consultancy.

———. n.d. "The History of a Disputable Land Plot." [In Georgian.] *Vake Park* (blog), https://vakisparki.wordpress.com/%E1%83%98%E1%83%A1%E1%83%A2%E1%83%9D%E1%83%A0%E1%83%98%E1%83%90/ .

Zhvania, Irakli. 2015. "Transformation of the Historic District through Residential Developments in Tbilisi." In *From Private to Public: Transformation of Social Spaces in the South Caucasus*, edited by Hans Gutbrod, 120–50. Tbilisi: Heinrich Böll Stiftung South Caucasus.

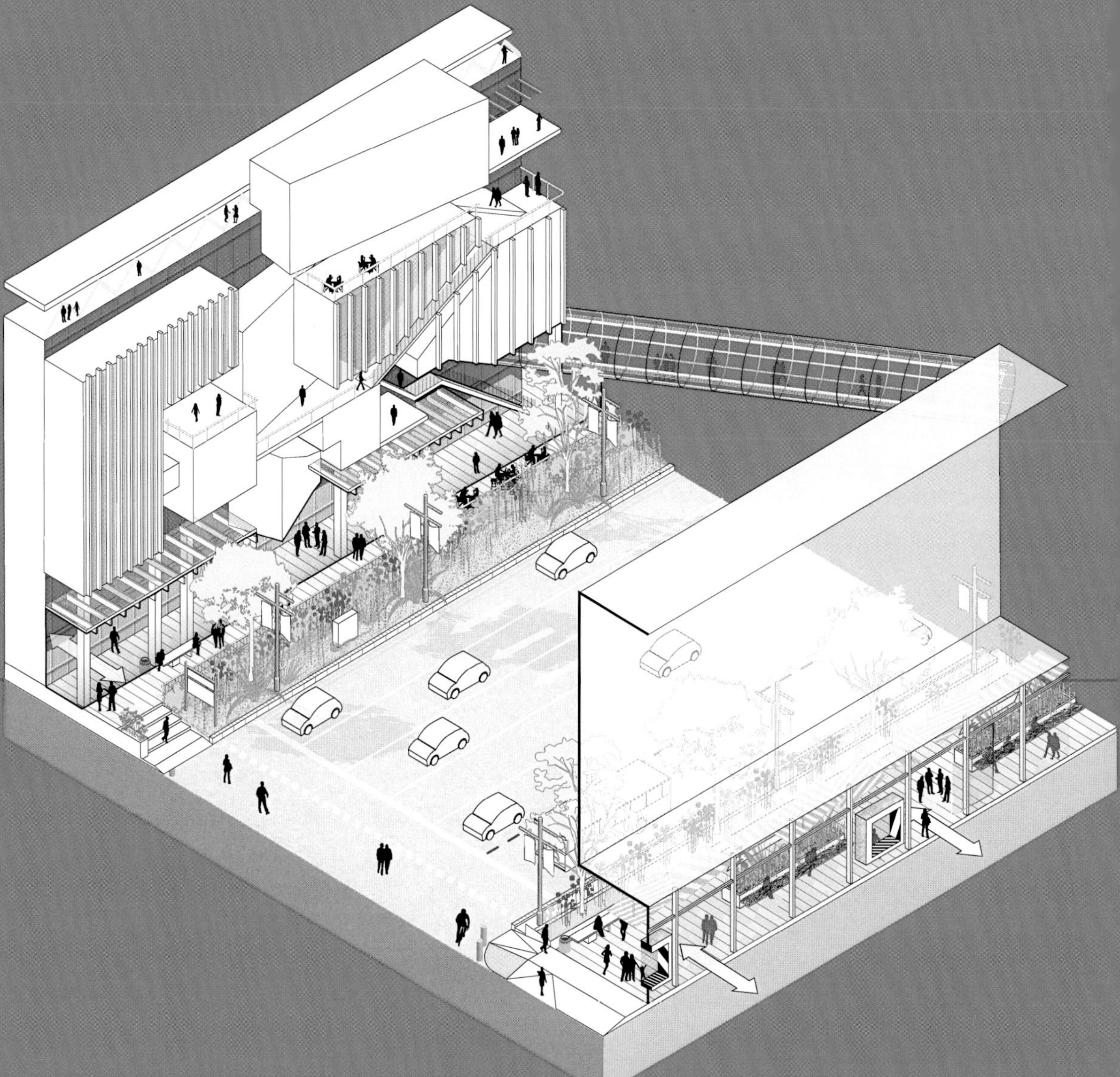

APPENDICES

APPENDIX A

DEFINITIONS OF SPATIAL TERMS

URBAN EXTENT

Classifying urban form based on built-up areas and land uses is a traditional way of understanding cities. The definition of "urban" has been at the center of discussions for decades, given its significant impact on city-related analytics and policies. Urban areas are defined in different ways across countries. Most definitions of urban fall into three broad categories: densely populated areas, built-up areas, or economic functional areas, as follows:

- *Definition by population density:* The United Nations Department of Economic and Social Affairs' (UN DESA) *World Urbanization Prospects* is a comprehensive reference that measures urbanization by population density (UN DESA 2018). Although this approach offers globally available data, its key weakness is that population data are bounded to administrative boundaries that are set differently across countries. For example, Germany considers 150 persons per square kilometer as the urban threshold, whereas China's standard is 1,500 persons per square kilometer. Moreover, the lowest level of administrative units determines its resolution, meaning the available resolution is generally coarse. More recently, sophisticated ways of combining population data and satellite imagery have emerged, such as WorldPop and the Gridded Population of the World, version 4 (GPWv4).[1]

- *Definition by extent of built-up areas:* The European Space Agency's (ESA) Earth Observation for Sustainable Development (EO4SD) Urban service analyzes urban expansion based on satellite images of the physical extent of built-up areas. No further analysis based on morphology or functional areas was applied, but the data still provide a solid basis for such analysis. In this book, depending on data availability, EO4SD analyzed two points in time to compare urban expansion and growth of the physical extent of built-up areas. The United Nations Human Settlements Programme's (UN-Habitat) citywide assessments also applied the use of urban footprints to examine urban expansion over time.
- *Definition by economic functional areas:* The World Bank's *World Development Report 2009* identified urban settlements above a certain threshold of population size and density within a certain commuting time using a measure known as an agglomeration index (World Bank 2009). The Organisation for Economic Co-operation and Development (OECD) launched a similar approach consisting of three steps: identifying urban cores that are contiguous or highly interconnected densely populated areas; grouping these areas into functional areas; and defining the "hinterland" of functional areas as a commuting shed. The OECD takes population minimum size thresholds between 50,000 or 100,000 people across different countries and takes population minimum density thresholds as 1,000 or 1,500 people per square kilometer, to define urban (OECD 2012).

Notably, the second definition—the extent of built-up areas, which is based on mapping impermeable areas by using satellite imagery—has increasingly been utilized because of its comparability and simplicity (Mason 2017). The United Nations Sustainable Development Goal (SDG) Indicator 11.7.1[2] and most of the citywide assessment tools also rely on this built-up area definition.

The typologies of land uses also have been globally standardized by remote sensing techniques. For instance, the land use and land cover (LULC) classification used for the pan-European Urban Atlas is widely used by analysts, but it does not account for the wide variation in specific land use and zoning definitions and designations across cities.[3] The standardized land-use typologies derived from remote sensing are beneficial for basic comparative analytics, as well as for offering a complementary way of understanding land uses in low- and middle-income countries that lack proper zoning policies and data.

PROXIMITY TO PUBLIC SPACES

Physical proximity has been widely discussed as a key proxy to measure the quality and inclusivity of public services. Because public space is an essential public service, numerous organizations and researchers have tried to provide reliable indicators to measure proximity to public spaces.

There are two common indicators for spatial proximity to public spaces: (a) the share of urban areas within walkable distance from public spaces, and (b) the share of population living within walkable distance from public spaces. The first indicator is simpler, focusing on spatial disparity; the latter takes into account the population density and the spaces' inclusivity for people. Although there are a wide range of ways to define "proximity," a five-minute walking distance (400 meters) is considered a reasonable proximate catchment area of public-space networks (AIRI 2003; EPA 2015; Natural England 2010; UN-Habitat 2016; WHO 2016).

There are, however, some country-specific guidelines. According to Natural England's "Accessible Natural Greenspace Standard for England," different sizes of public spaces need different standards for proximity (Natural England 2010). This standard suggests that all citizens should live

- Within 300 meters linear distance of a public space of around 2 hectares in size;
- Within 2 kilometers of a public space of around 20 hectares in size;
- Within 5 kilometers of a public space of around 100 hectares in size; and
- Within 10 kilometers of a public space of around 500 hectares in size.

In addition, there should be at least one statutory local nature reserve per 1,000 population (Natural England 2010).

The World Health Organization (WHO) also recommends designing green area networks so that all residents live within a 15-minute walk of an open space, and the U.S. Environmental Protection Agency (EPA) and the Food and Agriculture Organization of the United Nations (FAO) also refer to WHO's guidelines (WHO 2016).

Various other indicators of physical proximity to public spaces have been suggested by multiple organizations, as follows:

- The European Commission's European Common Indicators (ECI) project proposes to use the percentage of citizens living within 300 meters from a public open area of at least 0.5 hectares in size as an indicator of physical proximity to public spaces (AIRI 2003).
- The EPA evaluates the percentage of residential population within 500 meters walking distance of a park entrance at a census block level (EPA 2015).
- Along with other international indicators, UN-Habitat's City Prosperity Index (CPI) considers the percentage of citizens living within 400 meters of a public open area (UN-Habitat 2016).
- UN-Habitat's safety, inclusivity, accessibility, and distribution (SIAD) tool[4] proposes that the percentage of total urban areas falling within the 400-meter catchment area be aligned with SDG Indicator 11.7.1.

However, numerous academic studies have revealed a clear gap between *physical* proximity and *perceived* proximity. Particularly in low-income neighborhoods, the mismatch between physical and perceived accessibility is greater than in higher-income neighborhoods. This is because streetscapes in disadvantaged areas are in poor condition, which negatively affects people's willingness to walk to them (Macintyre, MacDonald, and Ellaway 2008).

NOTES

1. The WorldPop project, initiated in October 2013, combined the AfriPop, AsiaPop, and AmeriPop population mapping projects to provide a global open-access archive of spatial demographic data sets. For more information, see the WorldPop website: https://www.worldpop.org/. The GPWv4 models the distribution of human population (counts and densities) on a continuous global raster surface. It is produced by the Socioeconomic Data and Applications Center (SEDAC) of the National Aeronautics and Space Administration's (NASA) Earth Observing System Data and Information System (EOSDIS) and hosted by the Center for International Earth Science Information Network (CIESIN) at Columbia University. For more information, see the GPWv4 website: https://sedac.ciesin.columbia.edu/data/collection/gpw-v4.
2. SDG 11 (Sustainable Cities and Communities), Indicator 11.7.1, refers to the "average share of the built-up area of cities that is open space for public use for all, by sex, age and persons with disabilities" ("Sustainable Development Goal 11," UN Sustainable Development Goals Knowledge Platform, accessed July 17, 2019, https://sustainabledevelopment.un.org/sdg11.
3. The Urban Atlas provides pan-European comparable LULC data for Functional Urban Areas (FUAs) of more than 100,000 inhabitants. The Atlas is a joint initiative of the European Commission Directorate-General for Regional and Urban Policy and the Directorate-General for Enterprise and Industry in the frame of the EU Copernicus program, with the support of the European Space Agency and the European Environment Agency. For more information, see the Urban Atlas website: https://land.copernicus.eu/local/urban-atlas.
4. The SIAD framework scores each dimension on a scale of 0 percent (worst) to 100 percent (best). Each dimension comprises numerous citywide and site-specific indicators. City case studies that apply the SIAD assessment are detailed in chapter 6.

REFERENCES

AIRI (Ambiente Italia Research Institute). 2003. "European Common Indicators: Towards a Local Sustainability Profile." Final Project Report, Development, Refinement, Management and Evaluation of European Common Indicators Project (ECI) Grant Agreement: Subv. 00/294518, AIRI, Milan.

EPA (U.S. Environmental Protection Agency). 2015. "Percent of Residential Population within 500m of a Park Entrance." *EnviroAtlas* fact sheet, August (accessed June 5, 2019), https://enviroatlas.epa.gov/enviroatlas/DataFactSheets/pdf/ESC/PercentofResidentialPopulationWithin500mofaParkEntrance.pdf.

Macintyre, S., L. MacDonald, and A. Ellaway. 2008. "Lack of Agreement between Measured and Self-Reported Distance from Public Green Parks in Glasgow, Scotland." *International Journal of Behavioral Nutrition and Physical Activity* 5: 26–33.

Mason, David. 2017. "Bright Lights, Big Cities? Review of Research and Findings on Global Urban Expansion." Background paper for *World Resources Report: Towards a More Equal City*, World Resources Institute, Washington, DC.

Natural England. 2010. "'Nature Nearby': Accessible Natural Greenspace Guidance." Guidance document, Natural England, Sheffield, U.K.

OECD (Organisation for Economic Co-operation and Development). 2012. *Redefining "Urban": A New Way to Measure Metropolitan Areas.* Paris: OECD.

UN DESA (United Nations Department of Economic and Social Affairs). 2018. *World Urbanization Prospects: The 2018 Revision.* New York: UN DESA.

UN-Habitat (United Nations Human Settlements Programme). 2016. "Measurement of City Prosperity: Methodology and Metadata." Methodology for the City Prosperity Index (CPI), UN-Habitat, Nairobi.

WHO (World Health Organization). 2016. "Urban Green Spaces and Health: A Review of Evidence." Report for the European Environment and Health Process, WHO Regional Office for Europe, Copenhagen.

World Bank. 2009. *World Development Report 2009: Reshaping Economic Geography.* Washington, DC: World Bank.

APPENDIX B

METADATA FOR EO4SD-URBAN PUBLIC SPACE ASSESSMENT

OVERVIEW

This appendix presents the main elements of the Earth Observation for Sustainable Development–Urban (EO4SD-Urban) service:[1] identification of public spaces based on remote sensing, open data, and ancillary data sets.

The strength of the EO4SD-Urban service is that it supports rapid, efficient assessments for cities that lack the data and capacities to meet urgent needs, by using remote sensing and spatial analysis methodologies. It also provides data at various regional scales, ranging from detailed block-level information with geographic information system (GIS) layers to neighborhood- and city-level indicators. However, its drawback is that this service is not suitable for measuring public-space quality components and user activities.

DATA

The EO4SD-Urban service uses numerous complementary data sets (table B.1), consisting of the following:

- *High-resolution optical EO data:* The high-resolution (HR) earth observation (EO) data are acquired for historical and current mapping of urban land use and land cover (LULC), urban extent, and imperviousness within the peri-urban area. Data are accessible and downloadable free of charge.

TABLE B.1 **EO4SD-Urban Data Sources**

Category	Coverage area	Accessibility	Satellite	Time points	Details (resolution)	Use
Very high resolution (VHR) optical EO data	Core urban area	Commercial EO data providers (for example, European Space Imaging)	Quickbird	One scene in 2017, two scenes in 2006	MS (2.4 meters), PAN (0.6 meters)	Detailed urban use such as public space, buildings, roads, and so on
			Pleiades	One scene in 2017	MS (2.8 meters), PAN (0.5 meters)	
High-resolution (HR) optical EO data	Peri-urban area	Public	Landsat 5	Two scenes in 2006	MS (30 and 120 meters)	Historical mapping of land use
			Sentinel 2	One scene in 2017	MS (10, 20, and 60 meters)	Current land use and land cover
			Landsat 8	280 scenes in 2017	MS (30 meters), PAN (15 meters)	Current land use and land cover
Ancillary data	All	—	Digital elevation model (DEM)	—	30 meters	Terrain height
		Public	OpenStreetMap (OSM)	2017	—	Identify road networks and public spaces
		Provided by user	Local administrative units	—	—	Set a boundary and analysis unit
		Public	Global population grids (GPWv4, WorldPop)	2015	1,000 meters and 100 meters	Population estimates
		Public	Population census	2010	Ward level	Population estimates

Note: — = not available. EO4SD = Earth Observation for Sustainable Development–Urban. EO = earth observation. GPWv4 = Gridded Population of the World, version 4. MS = multisectoral data. PAN = panchromatic data.

- *Very high resolution optical EO data:* The very high resolution (VHR) EO data are acquired for detailed mapping within the core urban area. Data are acquired and purchased through commercial EO data providers such as Airbus Defence & Space, European Space Imaging, and others.[2]
- *Open data and ancillary data sets*
  - OpenStreetMap: Thematic vector data available through the OpenStreetMap (OSM) portal are mainly related to road networks and

places of interest.[3] OSM data are further refined and updated by visual interpretation for creating a full, consistent road network as a solid basis before producing mapping products.

- Digital elevation model: The digital elevation model (DEM) used for orthoimage production[4] is based on the standard 1 arcsec SRTM DEM (SRTM = Shuttle Radar Topography Mission), providing a ground spatial resolution of 30 meters × 30 meters. The SRTM data meet the absolute horizontal and vertical accuracies of 20 meters (circular error at 90 percent confidence) and 16 meters (linear error at 90 percent confidence).
- Local administrative units: Data for local administrative units (wards of the core city) are from open sources or provided by users.

METHODOLOGY

Different methodologies were applied to three types of public spaces identified by the EO4SD-Urban service: open and green areas, streets, and public facilities (UN-Habitat 2013).

Open and Green Areas

The geographical scope of open and green areas (OGAs) draws mainly upon existing categories of the Copernicus Urban Atlas definition: "artificial non-agricultural vegetated areas" (green urban area) and "public or commercial area with associated land" (sports and leisure facilities).[5] In addition, OGAs are further detected using a semiautomated identification method. More precisely, a binary raster OGA layer is created, which consists of pixels and/or classes that are extracted from multispectral VHR scenes following designed OGA identification algorithms. Postprocessing steps are then applied to this layer, such as eliminating the pixel groups under the minimum mapping unit (MMU) and merging various result layers from each single VHR scene. The raster layer can be converted into a vector format, and a smoothing algorithm can be applied before delivery to users.

The identified set of OGA polygons are then classified by a rule-based classification method into public-space typology based on six selected criteria (figure B.1):

1. *Distance to road:* A "distance to road" filter is applied to identify public-space polygons that are more than 100 meters away from the nearest road. These areas are categorized as inaccessible potential public spaces to exclude the more-isolated areas that people cannot reach or use.
2. *Adjacency to water:* If a polygon is adjacent to a water body that is larger than 10 hectares, it is classified as waterfront. The size condition was set to avoid the classification of small polygons next to small ponds as waterfronts.
3. *Compactness or linearity:* The compactness or linearity of a polygon is measured to differentiate linear areas from other public spaces. Linearly shaped

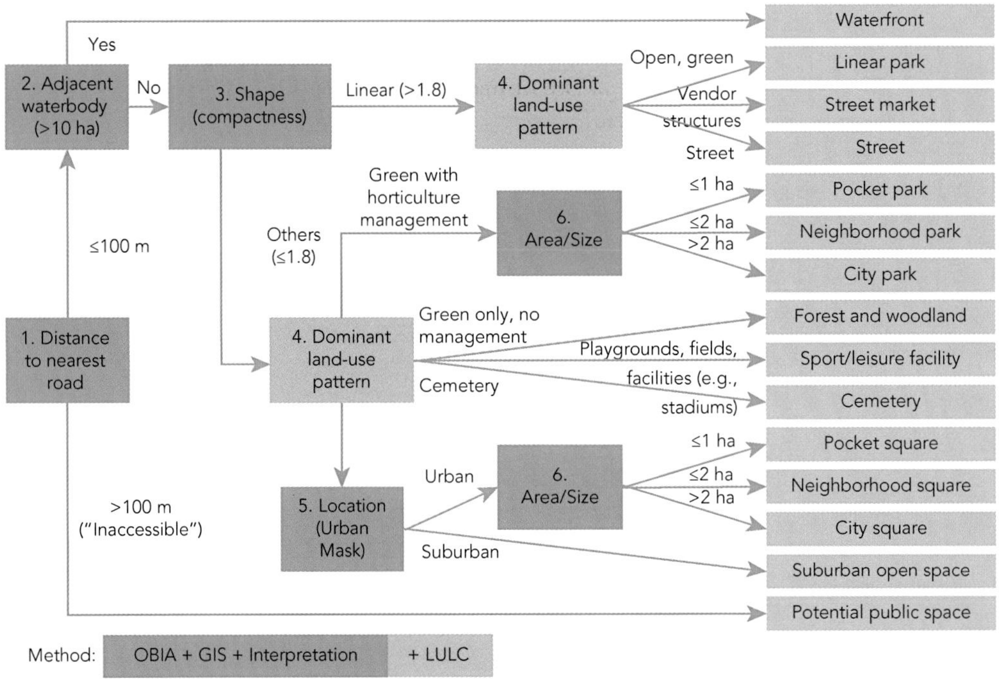

FIGURE B.1 **Rule Set for Classifying Public Spaces**

Source: ©World Bank. Further permission required for reuse.
Note: GIS = geographic information system. ha = hectares. LULC = land use and land cover. m = meters. OBIA = object-based image analysis.

areas have the potential to function as "connectors" between destinations. A public space is classified as "linear park" when a polygon has over 1.8 aspect ratio.

4. *Land patterns:* Land-use patterns of the remaining public spaces are examined to ascertain whether they possess high vegetation, high built-up and open areas, or horticultural management. These characteristics are used to determine whether the area in question is a well-managed park, an urban forest, or a plaza.

5. *Location:* The location of a public space is also differentiated between urban and suburban areas, based on the level of road intersection density, with the assumption that urban areas exhibit higher densities of road intersections (UN-Habitat 2013).

6. *Size:* Public spaces are then differentiated by their size. Polygons larger than 2 hectares are classified as "city level," and polygons of 1–2 hectares are classified as "neighborhood level." Polygons smaller than 1 hectare are defined as "pocket level."[6]

Notably, because of this complex machine-learning approach, as well as varying geographic contexts across cities, many identified areas may fall under "unclassifiable areas" if their characteristics cannot be captured through the aforementioned criteria. In such cases, it would be necessary to review whether there is a need to calibrate classification thresholds to fit the local context. This underscores the importance of engaging local partners to provide local context to the methodology. Any modifications of thresholds should be well documented to support subsequent comparative analyses across cities in different regions. The final OGA classification is summarized in table B.2.

TABLE B.2 **Nomenclature of Open and Green Area (OGA) Classification**

Level 1		Level 2		
Code	**Name**	**Code**	**Name**	**Remarks**
10	Square and open	11	Central city square	Apparent squares or large crossings with visible "public" function
		12	Neighborhood city square	
		13	Pocket city square	
		14	Suburban square	
		15	Other open space	
20	Market	21	Market (open sky)	Including large streets with concentration of stalls
30	Street	31	Street	Roads surrounded predominantly by urban residential and nonresidential fabric (excluded: capacity roads, highways, overpasses, underpasses, and road links)
40	Waterfront	41	Beach	Excluding mangrove forests, industrial areas, and port areas except berthing places for "public" river transport
		42	Waterfront park	
		43	Berthing and boardwalk	
50	Greenery	51	City park	Horticultural management is visible or very likely from land cover composition
		52	Neighborhood park	
		53	Pocket park	
		54	Linear park	
		55	Linear green	Other elongated green
		56	Trees, suburban forest or woodland	Forest and trees within city outline; no horticultural management apparent
		57	Other green	Other unsorted green (residual class)
		59	Airport green	
60	Cemetery	61	Cemetery	
70	Recreation, sport, and leisure facilities	71	Recreational facilities	Green sport areas, including buildings and associated land, playgrounds, amusement parks, golf courses, and so on
		72	Leisure and amusement parks	
		73	Stadiums and sport facilities	
		74	Sport fields	
90	Inaccessible OGA	n.a.	n.a.	n.a.

Note: n.a. = not applicable.

Streets

Streets are identified by geoprocessing operations in the GIS environment based on the road network layer and EO4SD-Urban LULC layer. The road network layer either comes directly from OSM or could be further adapted by visual interpretation (addition of missing segments, reclassification of segments, or removal of surplus segments) before geoprocessing. The included streets are living streets with a potential for being "public spaces" and "spaces for economic activities." As such, the following attributes are considered in the geoprocessing workflow:

- Roads are split into segments between junctions (crossings).
- Segments outside the urban area (based on the LULC mask) are rejected.
- Segments of first-level capacity roads (highways and motorways) are rejected.
- Segments of second-level capacity roads may be optionally rejected using additional interpretation assuming
    - Visible presence of heavy traffic on wide (multilane) roads; or
    - Mostly recruiting from primary and secondary roads.
- Remaining segments are filtered out depending on the level of being surrounded by residential and nonresidential urban fabric blocks from the LULC layer.

This workflow can be adjusted according to local contexts and user definitions. Transport connectivity nodes are generated by network analysis at the junctions of aggregated capacity segments.

Public Facilities

Public facilities are identified using places of interest (POIs), buildings, and land use as classified in the OSM data sets, in addition to the sports and leisure facilities identified from OGA layers. Table B.3 lists the subsets under

TABLE B.3 **OpenStreetMap (OSM) Categories of Public Buildings**

OSM buildings (osm_buildings)	OSM land use (osm_landuse)	OSM POIs (osm_pois)
"basilica," "clinic," "college," "hospital," "church," "mosque," "public," "school," "university," "cathedral"	"cemetery," "park," "recreation_ground," "forest," "grass"	"cinema," "college," "courthouse," "department_store," "hospital," "library," "mall," "museum," "monument," "memorial," "park," "picnic_site," "playground," "post_office," "public_building," "school," "supermarket," "sports_centre," "swimming_pool," "stadium," "theatre," "theme_park," "university," "viewpoint," "zoo," "town_hall"

Source: OpenStreetMap, https://www.openstreetmap.org/.
Note: POIs = places of interest.

applicable OSM categories. However, these facilities are generally excluded from the set of analyses introduced in this book, because they are often incomplete, and it is hard to estimate the exact size of each facility.

ACCURACY ASSESSMENT AND VALIDATION

Accuracy Assessment

Accuracy assessments of OGA layers were completed for Dhaka, Bangladesh; Karachi, Pakistan; Ramadi and Fallujah, Iran; and Bamako, Mali. Considering the complexity of the EO4SD-Urban OGA product, the accuracy of the EO4SD-Urban products is checked using standard protocol, which defines three components:

- *The sampling design,* which determines the spatial location of the reference data
- *The response design,* which describes how the reference data are obtained
- *The analysis design,* which defines the accuracy estimates.

Sampling design, the first step, is either a one-stage or two-stage stratified random sampling, depending on the product. Two-stage sampling involves the LULC standard product with several classes, while one-stage sampling is used for specialized optional products such as OGA. The number of samples is allocated and subsequently randomly distributed to the strata. The final sample size for each class can be considered to be as close as possible to the proportion of the area covered by each stratum, considering that the target was to determine the overall accuracy of the entire map (Olofsson et al. 2013). Clustering effects and consequent spatial autocorrelation are avoided by maintaining a minimum distance between the sample points (by default, set at 150 meters). The total sample size per stratum is determined by the expected standard error and the estimated error rates, based on the formula assuming a simple random sampling without considering further stratification (Olofsson et al. 2013).

Response design is based on a pseudo ground-truthing process using independent interpretation of EO imagery. Reference information can be extracted for each sample point by visual interpretation for all mapped classes using the VHR data used in the production process. The size of the area to be observed is related to the MMU of the map product. The reference information of each sampling point is then compared with the mapping results, and the numbers of correctly and incorrectly classified observations are recorded for each class.

Analysis design applies an error (confusion) matrix representing means to derive quantitative errors of a categorical map. Class-wise errors of omission and commission and their 95 percent confidence level intervals are denoted.

Validation

Ground truthing (on-site observation) needs to be optionally conducted for selected specialized products in cooperation with task teams, if applicable.

This enables cities to supplement missing components from remote sensing, such as facilities, user surveys, or ownership surveys.

Ground truthing was piloted for a case-study city, Dhaka, in this volume; a total of 224 points have been selected as the public spaces to visit for ground truthing through random sampling methodology. A task team visited the listed sites and interpreted the types of public spaces: (a) square; (b) vacant or abandoned open space; (c) market; (d) waterfront; (e) park; (f) trees or forest; (g) other greens such as shrubs or grass; (h) cemetery; and (i) recreation, sport, and leisure facilities. After checking the types of the sites, the team can further evaluate the quality of the sites, as applicable, such as existence of facilities and the number or groups of users. Finally, once the data are properly collected, they are analyzed to reach the accuracy assessment result.

NOTES

1. The European Space Agency's (ESA) EO4SD-Urban Service analyzes urban expansion based on satellite images of the physical extent of built-up areas. For more information, see the EO4SD-Urban website: http://www.eo4sd-urban.info/.
2. Under the EO4SD-Urban project, the VHR EO data had to be purchased under sole-license agreements between the Munich-based geospatial information firm, GAF AG, and the EO data providers. If the EO data had to be distributed to other stakeholders, then further licenses for multiple users would have to be purchased.
3. See the OpenStreetMap portal at https://www.openstreetmap.org/.
4. An orthophoto, orthophotograph, or orthoimage is an aerial photograph or satellite imagery that is geometrically corrected (or "orthorectified") such that the scale is uniform. Unlike an uncorrected aerial photograph, for example, an orthophoto can be used to measure true distances because it is an accurate representation of the Earth's surface, having been adjusted for topographic relief, lens distortion, and camera tilt.
5. The Copernicus Urban Atlas provides pan-European comparable LULC data for Functional Urban Areas (FUAs). It is a joint initiative of the European Commission Directorate-General for Regional and Urban Policy and the Directorate-General for Enterprise and Industry in the frame of the European Union's (EU) Copernicus program, with the support of the European Space Agency and the European Environment Agency. For more information, see the Urban Atlas website: https://land.copernicus.eu/local/urban-atlas.
6. The different size thresholds for pocket, neighborhood, and city scales are drawn from the "Urban Design Compendium" (Llewelyn-Davies Ltd. 2007) and also consider technical feasibility. For instance, through remote sensing technology, too-small parcels (for example, 0.04 hectares) are not likely to be identified clearly. This classification can be different from local understanding, and UN-Habitat defines pocket-, neighborhood-, and city-level public spaces as follows: smaller than 0.04 hectares, 0.04–0.4 hectares, and 0.4–10 hectares, respectively.

REFERENCES

Llewelyn-Davies Ltd. 2007. "Urban Design Compendium. 2nd ed." Urban design project development guide for the English Partnerships and the Housing Corporation, London.

Olofsson, P., G. M. Foody, S. V. Stehman, and C. E. Woodcock. 2013. "Making Better Use of Accuracy Data in Land Change Studies: Estimating Accuracy and Area and Quantifying Uncertainty Using Stratified Estimation." *Remote Sensing of Environment* 129: 122–31.

UN-Habitat (United Nations Human Settlements Programme). 2013. *Streets as Public Spaces and Drivers of Urban Prosperity*. Nairobi, Kenya: UN-Habitat.

———. 2015. *Global Public Space Toolkit: From Global Principles to Local Policies and Practice*. Nairobi, Kenya: UN-Habitat.

APPENDIX C

METADATA FOR UN-HABITAT'S PUBLIC-SPACE MEASUREMENT

DATA ON SHARE AND USE OF PUBLIC SPACES

City Open-Space and Street Databases

- *The City Prosperity Initiative (CPI)* of the United Nations Human Settlements Programme (UN-Habitat) is both a metric and a policy dialogue that offers decision makers the conditions to formulate adequate policies based on good data, information, and knowledge (UN-Habitat 2018). The CPI data are organized in the following dimensions: productivity, infrastructure development, quality of life, equity and social inclusion, environmental sustainability, and urban governance.
- *The Atlas of Urban Expansion* is an online mapped data set initiated in 2012 by UN-Habitat, New York University, and the Lincoln Institute of Land Policy.[1] This database is one of the most reliable public-space data sources recently developed, offering public-space data for over 200 cities across the world.
- *UN-Habitat's Citywide Public Space Inventory and Assessment database* includes the results of the survey of public spaces.[2] The data have been collected through the free, open-source KoBoToolbox suite of tools, which is available via either a web platform or a mobile-based application.[3] This is a participatory tool that allows communities to map their public spaces, using a structured questionnaire, and take part in the analysis as well as to propose strategies on how to improve their public spaces at a city scale.

Notably, these data sets have been collected differently and can improve evaluation by ensuring that the limitations of one type of data are balanced by the strengths of another. This will help to increase the validity and reliability of the results from the use of these data sources together.

Local Knowledge

Local knowledge—such as from local governments, community leaders, opinion shapers, nongovernmental organizations (NGOs) working on the ground, and others—is a key source of data, particularly regarding the location and use of open public spaces. In many cities, open public spaces often get converted to other uses such as commercial services, often making them hard to track based on old, outdated city databases and satellite imagery.

Local knowledge is also particularly important for identifying open public spaces, which can aid primary data collection and help create a good understanding of disaggregation elements such as safety, usability, provisions for different groups (such as by gender and age), walkability of streets, and so on.

Open-Source Data Sets

Diverse open-source databases exist at the global and regional levels and provide relevant information ranging from simple metrics (such as presence of streets and their hierarchy) to the presence and use of various public spaces. Some of the key data sets usable for computation of UN-Habitat's public-space measurement include

- *OpenStreetMap (OSM):* A global database containing information on streets and their hierarchies;[4]
- *Landsat and Sentinel satellite missions:* Satellite images downloadable from the U.S. Geological Survey (USGS) website and the Copernicus Open Access Hub;[5] and
- *Google Earth:* A searchable resource that represents the earth's surface in 3-D based on satellite imagery, which is used as a baseline for initial identification and digitization of open public spaces to estimate street widths as well as to verify the completeness of street data from OSM.

METHODOLOGY

Measuring the Share of Open Public Spaces for SDG Indicator 11.7.1

As noted in appendix A, the computation for United Nations Sustainable Development Goal (SDG) Indicator 11.7.1 relies on the "average share of the built-up area of cities that is open space for public use for all, by sex, age and persons with disabilities."[6]

The method to estimate the area of public space has been globally piloted in more than 400 cities and follows a series of methodological developments from the past seven years.[7] The finalized methodology is a five-step process:

1. Spatial analysis to delimit the built-up area of the city
2. Estimation of the total open public space

3. Estimation of the total land area allocated to the streets (LAS)
4. Local data collection to compute the amount of land allocated to open public spaces through a consultative process (UN-Habitat 2015)
5. Disaggregation of data to "city-proper" level (in cases where the urban extent is larger than the area of the city proper).

The final computation of the indicator—the percentage of a city's built-up area that is open space in public use—is performed using the following formula:

$$\left(\frac{\textit{total surface of open space} + \textit{total surface of LAS}}{\textit{total surface of built-up area of the urban agglomeration}} \right) \times 100$$

Safety, Inclusivity, Accessibility, and Distribution (SIAD) Assessment

As discussed in chapter 6, the SIAD tool is a two-step analysis and visualization tool that allows cities to compare their progress in provision of public space and toward development of citywide public-space strategies. It contains nonspatial and spatial measuring tools. The nonspatial tool is a Microsoft Excel-programmed spreadsheet containing the three main objectives (safety, inclusivity, and accessibility) and a set of indicators that are measured and weighted. The second part of the SIAD tool includes a spatial analysis of open-space distribution. This analysis can be performed using any geographic information system (GIS) analysis software that supports multicriteria analysis. The concept of multicriteria analysis is to form a criteria tree that consists of the indicators used as the input data for evaluation.

The 18 SIAD indicators are assessed based on each criterion's concept of what is acceptable and unacceptable.[8] The indicator values also call for interpretation and standardization because all indicators' values come with different dimensions (for example, the proportion of land allocated to open public space in a city, the percentage share of land that is within a 10-minute walk, or public space per capita). Then the scores are weighted to draw a representative SIAD score at the city level (table C.1).

TABLE C.1 **Indicators and Criteria for SIAD Assessment of Citywide Public Spaces, by SIAD Dimension**

SIAD dimension	Indicator	Unit	Benchmark (min–max)		Standardization[a]	Weight within dimension	Weight of each indicator
Safety (S)	Share of public spaces that have had acts of crime or robbery	percent	0	100	2	1/4	0.0625
	Share of public spaces with antisocial behavior	percent	0	100	2	1/4	0.0625
	Share of public spaces where accidents occurred	percent	0	100	2	1/4	0.0625
	Share of public spaces with working streetlights	percent	0	100	1	1/4	0.0625

table continues on next page

TABLE C.1 **Indicators and Criteria for SIAD Assessment of Citywide Public Spaces, by SIAD Dimension (*continued*)**

SIAD dimension	Indicator	Unit	Benchmark (min–max)		Standard-ization[a]	Weight within dimension	Weight of each indicator
Inclusivity (I)	Share of public spaces with facilities that promote usability	percent	0	100	1	1/7	0.0357
	Share of public space with sound (noise levels) below 70 decibels	percent	0	100	1	1/7	0.0357
	Share of public space with multifunctional and plurifunctional activities	percent	0	100	1	1/7	0.0357
	Share of public spaces that are children-friendly	percent	0	100	1	1/7	0.0357
	Share of public spaces that are youth-friendly	percent	0	100	1	1/7	0.0357
	Share of public spaces that are senior-friendly	percent	0	100	1	1/7	0.0357
	Share of public spaces that are persons with disability-friendly	percent	0	100	1	1/7	0.0357
Accessibility (A)	Share of public spaces with unrestricted access	percent	0	100	1	1/3	0.0833
	Share of public spaces with wheelchair access	percent	0	100	1	1/3	0.0833
	Share of public space with no user-specific streets	percent	0	100	2	1/3	0.0833
Distribution (D)	Share of land within 400 meters (5-minute walk) to a public space	percent	0	100	1	1/4	0.0625
	Public space per capita	m^2/hab	15 m^2/hab		3	1/4	0.0625
	Share of built-up area that is open public space	percent	12.5		3	1/4	0.0625
	Green area per capita	m^2/hab	9 m^2/hab		3	1/4	0.0625

Note: m^2/hab = square meters per inhabitant.

a. The measured indicators are standardized in three types: In Class 1, no standardization process is required; in Class 2, the measured scores need to be reserved; and in Class 3, the measured indicators are recalculated as a percentile of the benchmarks (for example, 15 m^2/hab for public space per capita).

NOTES

1. For more information, see the Atlas of Urban Expansion website: http://www.atlasofurbanexpansion.org/.
2. The official database has not been launched as of August 2019.
3. For more information, see the KoBoToolbox website: https://www.kobotoolbox.org/.
4. For more information, see the OpenStreetMap portal: http://www.openstreetmap.org.

5. For information about the Landsat satellite images, see the USGS Landsat website: https://landsat.usgs.gov/. The Copernicus Open Access Hub is accessible at https://scihub.copernicus.eu/dhus/#/home.
6. "Sustainable Development Goal 11," UN Sustainable Development Goals Knowledge Platform (accessed July 17, 2019), https://sustainabledevelopment.un.org/sdg11.
7. For more information, see UN-Habitat's training module: https://unhabitat.org/wp-content/uploads/2019/02/Indicator-11.7.1-Training-Module_Public-spaces_Jan_2019.pdf.
8. The SIAD framework scores each dimension on a scale of 0 percent (worst) to 100 percent (best). Each dimension comprises numerous citywide and site-specific indicators, totaling 18 indicators in the overall SIAD analysis.

REFERENCES

UN-Habitat (United Nations Human Settlements Programme). 2015. *Global Public Space Toolkit: From Global Principles to Local Policies and Practice*. Nairobi, Kenya: UN-Habitat.

———. 2018. "Metadata on SDGs Indicator 11.7.1." Definitions, methodology, rationale, and data sources for SDG Indicator 11.7.1, UN-Habitat, Nairobi, Kenya (accessed June 5, 2019), https://unhabitat.org/wp-content/uploads/2019/04/Metadata-on-SDG-Indicator-11.7.1.pdf.

Environmental Benefits Statement

The World Bank Group is committed to reducing its environmental footprint. In support of this commitment, we leverage electronic publishing options and print-on-demand technology, which is located in regional hubs worldwide. Together, these initiatives enable print runs to be lowered and shipping distances decreased, resulting in reduced paper consumption, chemical use, greenhouse gas emissions, and waste.

We follow the recommended standards for paper use set by the Green Press Initiative. The majority of our books are printed on Forest Stewardship Council (FSC)–certified paper, with nearly all containing 50–100 percent recycled content. The recycled fiber in our book paper is either unbleached or bleached using totally chlorine-free (TCF), processed chlorine–free (PCF), or enhanced elemental chlorine–free (EECF) processes.

More information about the Bank's environmental philosophy can be found at http://www.worldbank.org/corporateresponsibility.

green press INITIATIVE